The Trial of the Germans

The Trial of the
GERMANS

*An account of the twenty-two defendants
before the International Military Tribunal
at Nuremberg*

Eugene Davidson

UNIVERSITY OF MISSOURI PRESS
Columbia and London

Copyright © 1966 by Eugene Davidson
First published by Macmillan in 1966.
First University of Missouri Press paperback edition, 1997.
University of Missouri Press, Columbia, Missouri 65201
Printed and bound in the United States of America
All rights reserved
5   4   3   2   1   01   00   99   98   97

Library of Congress Cataloging-in-Publication Data

The Trial of the Germans : an account of the twenty-two defendants
    before the International Military Tribunal at Nuremberg / by
    Eugene Davidson.
        p.   cm.
    Originally published: New York : Macmillan, 1966
    Includes bibliographical references and index.
    ISBN 0-8262-1139-9 (pbk. : alk. paper)
        1. Nuremberg Trial of Major German War Criminals, Nuremberg,
    Germany, 1945–1946.   2. War crime trials—Germany.   3. World War,
    1939–1945—Atrocities.   4. War crimes.   5. World War, 1939–1945—
    Germany.   I. Davidson, Eugene, 1902–   .
    D804.G42T75   1997
    341.6'90268—dc21
                                                                97-21795
                                                                CIP

⊗ ™   This paper meets the requirements of the
American National Standard for Permanence of Paper
for Printed Library Materials, Z39.48, 1984.

Cover Designer: Kristie Lee
Typesetter: BOOKCOMP
Printer and Binder: Thomson-Shore, Inc.
Typefaces: Electra; Galliard; Gill Sans

TO THE MEN AND WOMEN
OF THE 20TH OF JULY

Contents

Acknowledgments

A considerable number of people have helped me to write this book. I am deeply indebted to two foundations, the Lilly Endowment, Inc., and one other, which, following the wishes of its founder, prefers to remain anonymous, for grants that permitted me to spend the better part of seven years to do the research and writing. In addition, a generous supporter of the Foundation for Foreign Affairs has provided the photographs used in this book as well as many indispensable volumes from the section of its library dealing with the National Socialist period.

The staff of the Institut fuer Zeitgeschichte in Munich has been most helpful, and I wish to thank especially Anton Hoch and Franziska Violet for their unfailing assistance. I am also indebted to the staffs of the Wiener Library in London and of the American Document Center in Berlin, where Ernst Muranka, who knows its thousands of documents as well as good collectors know the contents of their private libraries, not only found material I was looking for but called my attention to many things that might easily have been missed. I am also obligated to Fraeulein Truchsess of the Amtsgericht in Munich and to the staffs of the Staatsarchiv in Nuremberg and Munich, the Bundesarchiv in Koblenz, the Rijksinstituut voor Oorlogsdocumentatie in Amsterdam, the law section of the Library of Congress and the National Archives in Washington, and the Law Library of Northwestern University in Chicago.

The defense lawyers have been unfailingly cooperative in answering questions. I should like to express my appreciation of the help of the late Martin Horn, of Otto Kranzbuehler, Walter Siemers, Kurt Kauffmann, Alfred Thoma, Friedrich Bergold, Alfred Seidl, Hans Laternser, Hanns Marx, Robert Servatius, Egon Kubuschok, Hermann Jahrreiss, Alfred Schilf, Viktor von der Lippe, and the family of Gustav Steinbauer, who allowed me to read an unpublished manuscript Dr. Steinbauer had written about his defense of Seyss-Inquart. I should like to thank, too, the President of the Tribunal, Lord

Justice Lawrence, now Lord Oaksey, for his kindness in discussing the case. The three defendants I was able to talk to, Admiral Doenitz, Hjalmar Schacht, and Franz von Papen, willingly answered questions about the issues of the trial and their participation in it. To Luise Jodl I am especially grateful for placing at my disposal personal papers left by her husband and for much information both on General Jodl and on the German High Command. I should also like to thank General Warlimont for letting me read the documents in his possession relating to the Commissar and Commando Orders.

It is a pleasure to express my indebtedness to Professors Robert H. Ferrell and Fritz T. Epstein, both of the University of Indiana; they have read every chapter and invariably have made criticisms and suggestions that have considerably improved the text. I wish, too, to thank the director of the Rijks-instituut voor Oorlogsdocumentatie in Amsterdam, Dr. L. de Jong, who read the chapter on Seyss-Inquart, and the executive director of the Foundation for Foreign Affairs, David S. Collier, for his loyal support of the entire project. Finally I am greatly indebted to my bilingual secretary, Elisabeth Halasz, who not only typed and retyped the manuscript but has checked many of the translations, and to Jean Smith of The Macmillan Company, who did the copy editing with great dispatch and competence.

Foundation for Foreign Affairs
Chicago, June, 1966

The Trial of the Germans

1

In the Palace of Justice

On the night of October 15–16, 1946, the strokes of the bell tolling the hours in Nuremberg were being heard for the last time by eleven men lying in their cells in the Palace of Justice, the vast prison of the city that had been the center of the Nazi ceremonies celebrating the power and glory of the Party and its Fuehrer. Few lights burned in the city. The reddish high-pitched house where Albrecht Duerer had lived and hundreds like it were open to the skies. The prison, a scattering of half-destroyed houses, the bell tower of the cathedral, and the mounds of rust-colored rubble alongside broken walls were all that remained of the city that on January 7, 1945, in a half-hour air attack had been left in ruins. In Nuremberg as in the rest of Germany the threadbare people who had survived the war cared very little what was in store for the men who in the space of twelve years had helped to make the German Reich the master of Europe and to destroy it.

For one man, a general condemned to die, and for his wife, the bell (so they had said to one another) would be their last communication. The letters had been written, the farewells said. All they could share was the tolling now that his hour had struck, as it had struck for millions of soldiers who had marched under the orders he had signed. Only the thread of sound brought the echoes of the old city to life. The Nazi jackboots, the blaring bands of the Party days of the thousand-year Reich, the hoarse voice of the Fuehrer, the shouts of jubilee of the masses who had lined the streets every September in the city that was the capital of National Socialism had long been overlaid by the tumult of the bombs and the battles and after them the busy traffic of the American occupation.

The Great German Reich had been battered to fragments. What was left

1

of it was being governed by foreign powers, and the men responsible for the enormities that had accompanied its rise were being or had been tried, or would be tried in the course of the next few years if they were alive and to be found. Their trials were intended not only to bring the guilty to justice but to make clear to Germans and their conquerors as well how a great *Kulturvolk* whose science, music, scholarship, philosophy, and literature had been in the forefront of mankind's creative achievements had come to its moral and political collapse. In addition, the trials, especially as the Americans saw them, were to be a projection of the new world order that would justify the universal suffering brought about by the crime—the crime of war committed by the men who had led the Germans. To punish those guilty of the murder of millions of combatants and noncombatants, to evidence the continuing collaboration of the victorious Allies, to establish once and for all in a court of law the personal responsibility of political and military leaders for the crimes of aggressive warfare and of a totalitarian Fascist state against its own people and those of foreign countries—that is what American officials in Washington and London and Nuremberg told their allies, as well as the Germans and neutrals, the Allies had been fighting for. The crimes of the Nazi leadership were in fact indisputable; the record was so overwhelming that the prosecution found its chief difficulty to be mastering the tons of documents that came to Nuremberg in truckloads. The documents as well as the preconceptions of the Allies dealt with real crimes and imaginary ones, with crimes common to both sides and crimes only Germans had committed. Which Germans were guilty of them was clear from the beginning in some cases and was never to be satisfactorily decided in others. The case of General Alfred Jodl, for whom the bell was tolling, was one of the latter, as were the cases of the admirals and some of the others who were tried with him.

The idea of punishing war criminals, at least those who had fought unsuccessfully, was by no means new in history. Samuel killed King Agag, hewed him to pieces before the Lord; the anger of Samuel was sharpened and justified by a sense of righteousness of his cause. Joshua, the Old Testament records, when the Hebrews invaded the land of Canaan, slew "both man and woman, young and old and ox and sheep and ass with the sword . . . the young man and the virgin, the suckling also and the man with gray hairs." Vercingetorix was put to the sword. And in the Middle Ages the crusaders at Béziers killed the entire population of 20,000 "by reason of God's wrath wonderfully kindled against it." A long procession of defeated kings and generals marched to execution in the victory parade of conquerors. In the more humane climate of the nineteenth century, when Napoleon surrendered to the British after his defeat at Waterloo, he was not tried but merely was made harmless by removal to the rock of Saint Helena, although he had been universally denounced as the enemy of the peace of Europe.

At the end of World War I a list of 4,900 war criminals, including the Kaiser, Hindenburg, Ludendorff, and Bethmann Hollweg, was eventually brought down to a baker's dozen by the refusal of the Dutch to surrender the Kaiser, by the reappearance of old cleavages of interest among the victorious powers, and by German resistance to the Allies' demand to surrender the alleged violators of the customs and usages of war to foreign powers. This, the Germans said, was illegal under German law. They also pointed out that turning over Germans to Allied courts would only fan the unrest that flared up all over Germany in the postwar years. Nine trials took place before the German Supreme Court in Leipzig two and a half years after the end of the war. Of the 901 men tried, 888 were acquitted or the charges were summarily dismissed for want of sufficient proof. Only thirteen cases ended in convictions, and these carried relatively short terms of imprisonment. A German major was sentenced to two years in jail for the killing of French prisoners of war. One man was sentenced to ten months' imprisonment, another to six months for mistreatment of British captives. Two defendants were sentenced to four years for having taken part in the sinking of a hospital ship, the *Llandovery Castle*, and then of having fired on the lifeboats. This they had been ordered to do because the captain of their submarine had believed the *Llandovery Castle* to be carrying munitions under the cover of its red cross, had found that it was not, and had wanted to destroy the witnesses to his crime.[1]

The differences among the Allies after World War I were wide despite the unanimous conviction they held of the Germans' responsibility for the war and for innumerable atrocities, and despite the clause in the Versailles Treaty stating that their purpose was to try the Kaiser "for supreme offenses against international morality and the authority of treaties," along with those who had violated the laws and customs of war. The Special Commission of fifteen, appointed on January 25, 1919, consisting of two members from the chief Allied and associated powers (Great Britain, France, the United States, Italy, and Japan) and one each from the smaller powers, had split. The American and the Japanese representatives opposed an international tribunal with "a criminal jurisdiction for which there was no precedent, precept, practice or procedure." [2]

The Americans went further. They declared that the German military and political leaders and the alleged violators of the customs and usages of war could not be guilty of crimes under international law, since no international penal statutes existed on such violations. The British, who during the war had strongly favored trying the Kaiser as well as those guilty of violations of the rules of war, especially when the violations had to do with the use of submarines, professed themselves surprised to find the names of Hindenburg, Ludendorff, and Bethmann Hollweg on the list of the French and Belgians, which at this point had been brought down to 896 names.[3]

Lloyd George, who in the heat of an election campaign had declared that his intention was to hang the Kaiser, said that no self-respecting state would accept the trial of a military leader by other powers and that when he had first discussed the matter with Clemenceau he had thought of trying only those guilty of crimes against women and children—acts of such nature that the Germans too would accept them as crimes. Although the Allied Supreme Council had agreed on December 4, 1918, that William II and his principal accomplices should be tried for war guilt, for violations of neutrality, and for war crimes, its members never, despite Lloyd George's political speeches, demanded a death penalty. It was thought that exile would serve the political and legal purposes. After the election, Lloyd George, with an eye to restoring the balance and comity to the Continent that made for the security of Great Britain, had wanted the participation of German judges in any trials, but in this he was vigorously opposed by Clemenceau, who missed no opportunity to show the Germans that they were a defeated people whose leaders were to be judged by Allied tribunals only. Nitti, the Italian Prime Minister, representing a country that at the beginning of the war had been allied to Germany and now again was wary of France, supported the German counterproposal to hold trials before a German court with Allied representatives present as observers.

No one wanted the trial of the Kaiser held in his own country. The Belgians explained that as representatives of a country governed under a constitutional monarchy they could scarcely favor trying a former king and emperor. The French said that public feeling ran too high in France for the Kaiser to be tried there. And Wilson would not consider having the trials held in the United States.[4] The Dutch refusal to surrender the Kaiser saved the Allies any further embarrassment as to where or how a trial would take place.[*] And news that the Germans were preparing a list of Allied nationals who had allegedly committed atrocities may have had an effect on the Allied decision to let the Germans try their own cases.

Many of the Allied policies of World War II were set by the failures of the policies of World War I. This time, President Franklin D. Roosevelt said, no stab-in-the-back legend would spread among the German people, and he demanded unconditional surrender. This time it would be brought home to the Germans that war, aggressive war, is a crime, that they had been not only the victims of but also the participants in a criminal regime, a criminal conspiracy planted in the Prussian-German soil of militarism, and that the uprooting of such evil growths must be thorough. No disagreement marred the Allied plans for this purpose. The Germans were to be ruled under a strict Allied military occupation; heavy industry was to be destroyed or dismantled and the remaining factories were to turn out small articles that could have only peaceful uses. The entire adult population was to be screened for its National Socialist and militaristic sentiments.

* Professor Simon, jurist at the Dutch University of Utrecht, pointed out that the political adversaries of the Kaiser would be both judge and prosecution in the case, that an impartial judgment without prejudice was unlikely, and that "the development of a new law cannot start with an injustice" (Hans-Heinrich Jeschek, *Die Verantwortlichkeit der Staatsorgane nach dem Voelkerstrafrecht* [Bonn: Ludwig Roehrscheid Verlag, 1952], p. 63).

The trial of the relatively few major offenders—the individuals whose crimes had not been limited to one country but were on such a scale that only an international court could deal with them—now taking place in Nuremberg was to be only the first of a series. But it turned out to be the only one held before American, British, Russian, and French judges. Although the twelve later trials held in Nuremberg were called international, they were purely American, and a proceeding like that of the *Peleus* trial (see Doenitz, Chapt. 10) was international only in the sense that it was conducted under a British military court of five British and two Greek judges. The trials of the major Japanese war criminals were held before an international tribunal established by the Supreme Commander for the Allied Powers, General MacArthur, who issued the order appointing the nine members who had been nominated by the nations that had gone to war with the Japanese.[5]

WHO WAS GUILTY?

Although no war can be fought in the twentieth century without the psychological offensives that reduce issues to black and white, the Allied propagandists in World War II had an easy assignment. By 1942 the nations outside the countries occupied by the Germans knew without question that atrocities on an enormous scale were being perpetrated against Jews, prisoners of war, and civilian populations. Eyewitnesses, including Germans, had escaped or had managed to tell what they had experienced to visiting neutrals. The underground movements in Poland, Russia, France, and the Low Countries sent a stream of information and circumstantial accounts to London and Washington and Moscow. The *Israelitisches Wochenblatt*, published in Switzerland, regularly carried news that reached it through the underground of the deportations and killings.[6]

When the war ended, most of the men responsible for these crimes answered to the governments of those countries where the crimes had been committed. The United Nations War Crimes Commission had been established on October 7, 1942, to draw up lists of such criminals who would be tried in due course. Fifteen nations were represented, including the United States and Great Britain but not the Soviet Union, which in this as in other matters preferred to pursue its own course. These lists did not include the names of the so-called major war criminals. In the autumn of 1943 the United States Secretary of State, Cordell Hull, journeyed to the Soviet Union, where he and Molotov and Eden signed the Moscow Declaration of November 1, promising the trial of war criminals but naming no one. It declared:

> Those German officers and men and members of the Nazi party . . . who have been responsible for . . . atrocities, massacres and executions will be sent back to the countries in which their abominable deeds were done in

order that they may be judged and punished according to the laws of these liberated countries. The above declaration is without prejudice to the case of the major war criminals whose offenses have no particular geographical localization and who will be punished by the joint decision of the governments of the allies.[7]

Even before the United States entered the war, President Roosevelt and Winston Churchill together had warned the Germans that they would be held accountable for war crimes. In a statement on October 25, 1941, Churchill declared, "Retribution for these crimes must henceforward take its place among the major purposes of this war." These warnings were often repeated in the course of the war by all the warring nations. In March, 1943, the United States Senate and House of Representatives in a concurrent resolution declared unanimously: "The dictates of humanity and honorable conduct in war demand that the inexcusable slaughter and mistreatment shall cease . . . and that those guilty of these criminal acts shall be held accountable and punished." [8] The Allied foreign ministers, as well as Stalin, Churchill, Roosevelt, and indeed any attentive reader of the press, had no doubt whatever as to who the perpetrators of these crimes were. The chief criminals were the leaders of the Nazi Party and State, the High Command of the Army and Navy, the diplomats, the industrialists, the bankers, the judges, and the bureaucrats. At the war's end the Americans were holding for trial some 300 "major" criminals. The Russian judge I. T. Nikitchenko thought the list in his country might run to 500, but the chief "major" criminals were easy to identify. Soviet Foreign Minister Molotov wrote on October 14, 1942, "The whole of mankind knows the names and bloody crimes of the leaders of the criminal Hitlerite clique: Hitler, Goering, Hess, Goebbels, Himmler, Ribbentrop, Rosenberg." [9] Such members of the Roosevelt Administration as Secretaries Stimson and Stettinius and Attorney General Biddle wrote a memorandum to the President for the Yalta Conference on January 1, 1945, saying, "The names of the chief German leaders are well known and the proof of their guilt will not offer great difficulties." [10]

When Stalin appeared at Potsdam with a list of those to be tried as major war criminals, no objections were made to any of the names by the British or the Americans. On the Russian list were names equally well known among the Western Allies—Goering, Hess, Ribbentrop, Keitel, Doenitz, Kaltenbrunner, Frick, Streicher, Krupp, Schacht, Papen, Hans Frank—and this lineup was promptly accepted at the August 1 meeting of the Big Three at Potsdam.[11] Looking at the list, President Truman expressed a mild objection, remarking that while he liked none of the German industrialists, he thought that naming some individually might cause others to think they could escape. Stalin, however, said that those listed were only examples. Krupp was there, he said, to show the general reason for trying German industrialists, and if the Americans or British preferred to name another he would have no objection.[12] This view was stated more strongly by the chief American prosecutor at

Nuremberg, Mr. Justice Robert H. Jackson, who said, "It has at all times been the position of the United States that the great industrialists of Germany were guilty of crimes charged in this indictment quite as much as its politicians, diplomats and soldiers." [13]

The German people themselves were never to be formally indicted. The French prosecution, alone among the four victorious powers, made no distinction between the Nazis and the rest of the nation. The Americans were careful to draw a line between the general population and those on trial. Thomas J. Dodd, in his opening statement, said, "As every German Cabinet minister or high official knew, behind the laws and decrees of the *Reichsgesetzblatt* was not the agreement of the people or their representatives but the terror of the concentration camps and the police state." [14]

Mr. Justice Jackson declared in his opening speech, "We have no purpose to incriminate the whole German people. We know that the Nazi Party was not put into power by a majority of the German vote," but by an alliance of extreme Nazis, German reactionaries, and the most aggressive of militarists.[15]

In effect, despite the disclaimers, the indictments were inevitably directed against the German people. When one defense lawyer heard the testimony of the razing in 1943 of the Warsaw ghetto, where 65,000 Jews were killed in what was called a military action although the police and SS troops involved lost only sixteen men, he spoke of the indelible besmirching of the German name—a reaction expressed by a number of the defendants during the course of the trial. "A thousand years shall pass," said the former Governor General of Poland, Hans Frank, "and this guilt of Germany will not be erased." Robert Ley, who hanged himself before the trial started, said much the same thing in a farewell note. Others talked as though they had been awakened from a fantastic dream in which they had somehow played a part. Now they found themselves in a prosaic non-Nazi world where murders of innocent people had to be accounted for, and they stared at the pictures of atrocities in disbelief and horror. They confessed and squirmed and alternately blamed themselves and even more readily the men and creeds they had served. Some swore they had known nothing of these events; they had carried out their duties in a state where by order of the Fuehrer every area was sealed off from matters outside its limits. But outside the courts of law, Catholics and Protestants met in solemn sessions to confess their responsibility for what had happened. Collective guilt, though always rejected, clung to millions of Germans despite the philosophical and historical demonstrations that it could scarcely exist.[16]

THE MASS MURDERS

The story that unfolded in the course of this trial and of the later ones shook the complacency of a Western culture that had overestimated the depth of its civilized qualities. It was the story of the planned mass murder of populations of children, old people, men and women; of Jews, Gypsies, and Slavs; of prisoners of war; of soldiers and civilians killed not in the heat of combat but in convoys or actions over a period of years as a policy, a duty to the race. Witnesses and detailed documents told of a return to slavery and organized plunder on an enormous scale; of institutions such as hospitals and courts of law designed to assuage human pain and injustices that had been warped to the purpose of inflicting them. A total of 80,000 technicians of slaughter had been involved in the extermination process, it was calculated, but to make their operations possible in the wide reaches of the empire of the Great German Reich, a well-trained bureaucracy and a superb army had been required too, as well as the cooperation, willing and unwilling, of millions of people in Germany and the occupied territories.

The picture of the tragedy would never be complete. Sections of it appeared in trials throughout Europe and later in Israel, where the tattooed numerals of Auschwitz were worn as badges of honor. What was heard and recorded in the trials shocked the mid-twentieth-century war generation accustomed to the statistics of mass killing. Attitudes toward race and toward the charismatic leader can never be the same as they were before the Nazis demonstrated their destructive power. To be sure, the 80,000 people who served the apparatus of extermination were not the only hangmen, nor were the Germans alone guilty. The first Nuremberg trial brought up the faked accusation that the Germans had murdered thousands of Polish prisoners of war at Katyn. These shootings, as the Poles told Roosevelt and Churchill, were done by the Russians. Nor did German concentration camps and forced labor deal only with Jews and foreigners; there were 500,000 "Aryan" Germans among the early inmates of the camps.

What had distinguished the Nazi State from other totalitarian systems was the efficiency of its inversion of every value. Not only was God to be killed, but with him religion, the family, and old notions of justice. Law was merely something that reflected the intuition of the race. The extermination process was as rationalized as the production of war goods; it was self-justifying, an end in itself. The victim was born into it; once placed in an undesirable category, he could not escape. After the prisoners had been reduced to the status of creatures who were intended to lose their sense of identity with other human beings, death followed. One concentration-camp man called his dog Mensch (human being) and would turn him loose on the prisoners, shouting, "Mensch, go after the dogs!" This was not the aberration of a single SS man; it was an expression of a complicated party line. The efficiency of the process of extermination—its careful records, the turning of science and technology to pseudoresearch and inflicting of horrors—was unique. The SS men involved in the killings kept talking of their hard task and the incomprehension of many of their own countrymen who did not like to have to take part in them. The commandant of the concentration camp at Auschwitz, Rudolf Hoess, who supervised the execution of a million and a half prisoners, took to poetry to describe what he had experienced. "In the Spring of 1942," he wrote, "many blossoming people walked under the blossoming fruit trees of the farmstead, most of them went with no premonition to their deaths." His blossoming fruit trees were next to the gas chambers.[17]

The camps were brutal in a surrealistic fashion. In one operation, two Gypsy children were sewn together to create Siamese twins. The witness reporting this work of SS Dr. Fritz Mengele, who succeeded in escaping from Germany after the war, said their hands were badly infected where the veins had been resected. Children in the death camps helped spread the ashes of the cremated victims on the roads. Women slept twelve to a shelf, so tightly packed that they had to lie head to feet, and when one turned the others had to turn too. Experiments on methods of castration were carried out on Greek boys. The tattoos, which have been described so often, were actually sought because they meant that life would be spared for at least a time. The numbers of the original inmates who came and perished went so high that the later arrivals had to have their numbers prefixed with the letters A and B. When Hungarian Jews arrived at Auschwitz in 1944, other prisoners told them to get tattoos as soon as possible, because a number meant being registered, becoming part of the camp work force. The work force would eventually be liquidated too, but there was an interval between the arrival of the registered prisoners and their being gassed. Those who came to the camp too weak to work after the exhausting marches and transports were herded immediately to the death house. They had no records; they came and went anonymously. Other means of identification were used under other circumstances. An SS man who saw a man swallow something before he entered the gas chamber marked his chest with chalk. After the gassing, bodies thus marked were cut open so that diamonds or other articles of value might be recovered.

Accounts that filtered out of Germany and the occupied countries, documents found in the walls of half-destroyed buildings, archives saved from burning, personal records like those of Hans Frank, who turned over the 38 volumes of his diary to the Allies because he said he acknowledged his guilt and wanted the truth to be known, served to fill out what the Allied troops had seen as they captured the concentration camps. The starvation of the prisoners at Dachau was so advanced that hundreds died after the liberation despite the medical aid and careful feeding American doctors immediately provided. Before they died, some of the prisoners asked to be allowed to see a soldier or wanted a piece of a uniform to hold in their hands.

THE CHIEF CRIME

The phrasing of the indictment for these crimes did not long delay the Allied jurists. Discussions leading to the London Agreement of August 8, 1945, establishing the court and outlining its jurisdiction, disclosed only one serious difference of opinion.* Some wrangling developed over the phrasing of the clause on aggressive warfare eventually adopted.

Long before atom bombs exploded over the New Mexico desert and Japan, statesmen and publicists—mainly from countries whose borders had been extended by World War I and from the United States—had argued the necessity of outlawing war, of regarding an attack on any nation as an assault on the international community, and punishing perpetrators, just as lawbreakers are punished by domestic society.

Opponents of this collective-security policy maintained that it threatened to make every local conflict into a major war involving the Great Powers; that it tended to preserve the *status quo*, however unjust or unstable it might be; that throughout history war, however reprehensible and primitive its means, had been the sole and last resort for establishing new power relations; and that in any event a decision to declare war was an act of state—a political expedient, not a personal act, rooted in custom and international law. War might prove only which was the stronger power, but it remained the final means of decision in international disputes that reached an incandescent extreme where the issues could not be negotiated. But for the proponents of collective security the only just war was the war of defense against an aggressor. In their opinion, the mechanization of war, with its attacks on civilian centers, had dehumanized armed conflict to the extent that wars were now mainly contests between machines, proving only which were the most ruthless and efficient.† Wars, they said, had become no more than wholesale slaughter with automatic weapons.

* The London Agreement, said the chief American prosecutor, Robert Jackson, in his report to the President, represented "the solemn judgment of 23 governments representing some 900 million people" (Robert H. Jackson, *Report to the International Conference on Military Trials, London, 1945*, Department of State Publication 3080 [Washington: US Government Printing Office, 1945], p. 8. Hereinafter referred to as *Jackson Report*). Actually, two Russians, General I. T. Nikitchenko and A. N. Trainin; two Frenchmen, Robert Falco and André Gros; Sir David Maxwell-Fyfe, on behalf of Great Britain; and Robert Jackson, with a number of advisers, drew up the agreement.

† The idea of the "just war"—the war raged on behalf of the civilized community—was an old one (see Jeschek, *op. cit.*). Rome regarded any war in which she was engaged as just, for Rome was the center of the law and its source. The concept of the "just war" of the Middle Ages as a war fought against a state that had damaged the interest of Christendom had been stated by Augustine in the fourth century and by Thomas Aquinas almost 900 years later. It was further developed by European writers representing a Christian culture where natural law was all-embracing. Men of law and of philosophy wrote in this spirit: Francisco de Vitoria declared that the victor became the judge of the guilty, as well as the stronger prince imposing his will; Francisco Suárez regarded the just war as an expedition of punishment against a wrong; the Italian Alberico Gentili thought it possible that the issue of justice might be unclear, in which event a third state might be neutral, but a just war was one conducted against a state that had injured the laws of God and men. To Hugo Grotius, often called the father of international law, the victorious state acted on behalf of the international community when it punished the wrongdoers, providing that neither the prince nor his followers had been themselves involved in the wrongs committed.

The counterschool in which the later *Realpolitiker* flourished dealt with not the morality

In the years during and after World War II the battle between the proponents and opponents of collective security continued, but with far less vigor. The concept of the aggressor had become firmly established in the language of statesmen and their constituents, even if the definition continued to elude

---

but the facts of power. Thomas Hobbes declared a ruler to be bound by no rules but his own. Machiavelli instructed his master in the rules of the ruthless struggle of political life and in how to survive and be successful. Montesquieu, reflecting the amenities of a milder political climate than that of the Italian city-state, thought a ruler had the right to destroy a society composed of citizens but not of men; that is, he could destroy the form of an enemy state but not its people. Rousseau too believed a war to be a conflict between states, not between individuals. The argument continued into the nineteenth and twentieth centuries, when with the complete secularization of juridical principles the national states sought support of their citizens as well as of neutrals by declaring that they were fighting for a world order established under treaties and agreements of international law if not under the will of God. The dicta of popes and princes were replaced by treaties and references to the conscience of mankind, but war—when it was successful at least—remained an expedition of punishment against the enemy.

The increasing difficulty of remaining neutral in any major conflict was the result of not only technological and economic changes but the theories being expounded about involvement. The eighteenth-century Swiss jurist Emmerich von Vattel wrote in his *Droit des Gens:* "If therefore there was anywhere an unquiet nation, always ready to damage others and to cross them, to bring to them domestic troubles, there is no doubt that everyone would have the right to join together to restrain it, to punish it and even to put it forever out of the possibility of doing damage." If the rights of the matter seemed to be in dispute, then both sides would be regarded as legal participants in a struggle, and the prince who went to war in good faith was to be free of punishment. In the nineteenth century Bismarck sounded like a provincial Prussian when he opposed any trial of Napoleon III, who had declared war on Prussia, saying that the victor was in no situation to judge the vanquished with a moral codex in his hand. The punishment of princes and of people for offenses against moral laws, he wrote, had to be left to the god of battle.

The various Hague and Geneva Conventions aimed at minor improvements in the lot of the embattled nations (safeguarding the wounded and sick and prisoners of war) and at reducing horrors. But the warring nations, which had to find as much support as possible for what they did, continued to act, they said, on behalf of humanity. The European powers in the confident days of the early nineteenth century had intervened in the Greek-Turkish war, they said, because of the atrocities committed. In 1863 the Great Powers protested against the inhuman treatment accorded the Polish uprising. Protests from other powers rained in on the Turks for mistreatment of Christians and on the Csarist Russian Government for its mistreatment of Jews. The United States intervention in Cuba against Spain was undertaken because of alleged Spanish misdeeds committed against Cuban patriots. During World War I the *Edinburgh Review* called the invasion of Belgium not an act of war but a criminal act, and the reparations Germany paid afterward were said to be for damages for the perpetration of an illegal war. Article 231 of the Versailles Treaty stated, "The Allied and Associated Governments affirm, and Germany accepts, the responsibility of Germany and her allies for causing all the loss and damage to which the Allied and Associated Governments and their nationals have been subjected as a consequence of the war imposed upon them by the aggression of Germany and her allies." Still, the notion that the war was criminal was not upheld by the Allied Special Commission, which said, "The premeditation of a war of aggression . . . is conduct which the public conscience reproves and which history will condemn, but a war of aggression may not be considered as an act directly contrary to positive law." The attack on Belgium and Luxembourg had been a violation of international law, "but the Commission is nevertheless agreed that no criminal charge may be made against the responsible authorities or individuals; the future should provide such penal sanctions." The damages to Belgium were to be paid by Germany as a consequence of her breach of the guarantee treaty of 1839.

them. Influential Americans, both Republicans and Democrats, swinging sharply from isolationism, declared that World War II would not have come about had the United States joined the League of Nations and repeatedly stated their determination in the course of the war to make sure that this same blunder would not occur again.

Mr. Justice Jackson, a man of urgent idealism and not without political ambitions, came to the trial in the firm belief that aggressive war was a crime; that the idea of neutrality had been outmoded by the Kellogg-Briand Pact of August 27, 1928, outlawing war; and that individuals who acted in behalf of their governments were to be held responsible for what had previously been acts of state. For him the outlawing of war was the cornerstone of the new world order. Even the crimes against the Jews were to be linked to a conspiracy to wage aggressive warfare. Otherwise, Mr. Justice Jackson feared, the perpetrators could not properly be brought before the court. The Kellogg-Briand Pact, he said, had started a new era in which the criminal responsibility of statesmen who deliberately resorted to war in violations of treaties must be made clear. He declared at London, in the course of the meetings that prepared the indictments and procedures for the trial:

> The Lend Lease program, the exchange of bases for destroyers, and much of American policy was based squarely on the proposition that a war of aggression is outlawed. The thing that led us to take sides in this war was that we regarded Germany's resort to war as illegal from its outset, as an illegitimate attack on the international peace and order. And throughout the efforts to extend aid to the peoples that were under attack, the justification was made by the Secretary of State, by the Secretary of War, Mr. Stimson, by myself as Attorney General, that this war was illegal from the outset and hence we were not doing an illegal thing in extending aid to peoples who were unjustly and unlawfully attacked. . . . We want this group of nations to stand up and say, as we have said to our people, as President Roosevelt said to the people, as members of the Cabinet said to the people, that launching a war of aggression is a crime and that no political or economic situation can justify it. If that is wrong, then we have been wrong in a good many things in the United States which helped the countries under attack before we entered the war.

Since the German war was illegal in its inception, he continued, so the United States was justified in abandoning the rules of neutrality, and ". . . when it came to dealing with war criminals the position of the President was clearly stated to the American people—the launching of a war of aggression was a crime." [18] Germany, he pointed out, had not attacked the United States, and American intervention was justified because the war itself was illegal.

The French expert in international law who was present at the London Conference, Professor André Gros, and the Russians remained unconvinced that individuals could be tried for committing war. Gros, taking the traditional view of responsibility for acts of state, declared, "We do not consider as a criminal violation a war of aggression. If we declare war a criminal act of an individual we are going further than the actual law." The principle, he thought, might become law in the years to come, "but as it now stands we do not believe these conclusions to be right." In the meeting of July 23, during the discussions on charging crimes under international law, he said that what the conferees were doing in declaring certain acts, like aggression, criminal was "a creation by four people who are just four individuals—defined by those four people as criminal violations of international law. These acts have been known for years before and have not been declared criminal violations of international law. It is *ex post facto* legislation." [19] Representing a power that had for the first time been admitted to membership in the Big Three at this London meeting, Gros was cautious if scholarly. Two days later, on July 25, he said that the American draft attempted to cover too much, and on the matter of reprisals was trying to "dispose of the whole question . . . existing for the last 500 years: and you cannot wipe it out in just one word." [20]

The Russians (with their own experience of having been declared aggressors in the Finnish war of 1940–41 by the League of Nations no doubt in mind) sided with Gros. General Nikitchenko said he did not think aggression could be included in the charges. He pointed out that "although when people speak of it they know what they mean, they cannot define it." As discussion dragged on, he added that if the debate were to continue, the criminals would die of old age.

The Soviet position on aggression was also presented by Nikitchenko's colleague at the London Conference, Professor A. N. Trainin.[21] A member of the Moscow Institute of Law, Trainin had written a book in 1944 on the Nazi war guilt, which he linked to an industrial-economic order characteristic of Germany before Hitler took power as well as after. Trainin quoted Molotov's speech of January 6, 1942, which declared this war to be not a customary one but a bandit war with the aim of exterminating peace-loving peoples. Tracing German history in this light, Trainin detected what he called the "bandit" features of German imperialism in the reign of William II and in the behavior of Prussia in 1870–71. "*Pacta sunt servanda*" (treaties must be observed), he quoted. He continued, saying that aggression was the most dangerous among international crimes, but the concept did not of course apply to wars of liberation. The rank and file of the Fascist troops had been cruel, thick-witted, and greedy. The higher-ups were the genuinely guilty ones: the heads of government, the industrial and financial leaders, the masters of the economy. These German leaders would be tried by the "political verdict of the victorious democratic states." The entire political and military history of Prussian Germany had moved along the road to crime. "It is a criminal court which is approaching, stern and inflexible . . . against the brigand machinery of the Hitlerite tyranny saturated with vile Prussianism." *

Trainin's book had been read and carefully studied by most of those present at the London Conference. Sir William Jowett, the Lord Chancellor in the Labour Government, called in the delegates to the Conference on August 2, 1945, and declared himself anxious "to finalize" what they were doing. He suggested that the indictment follow the text of Trainin's book, calling aggression "a crime against peace" instead of a crime of war, as proposed by the Americans.

The Russians made few concessions to the Americans, nor were they as respectful to the member of the United States Supreme Court as were the representatives of the other powers. Mr. Justice Jackson, chafing at the long argumentation and apparently under the impression he was making a threat, declared that the United States would withdraw from the trial and leave the prisoners to the other powers. After one of these outbursts at the meeting of July 25, Nikitchenko merely restated the Soviet position: "Is it supposed then to condemn aggression or initiation of war in general or to condemn specifically aggressions started by the Nazis in this war? If the attempt is to have a general definition that would not be agreeable." When Mr. Justice Jackson talked on the subject of the power of the President of the United States (who, he pointed out, had no authority to convict anybody) and went on to say that no political executions took place in the United States, Nikitchenko remarked, "Perhaps I am mistaken but I understood our purpose was not to discuss the philosophy of law but try and work out an agreement . . . the carrying on of justice in the naming of the war criminals." [22] Eventually the Russian

---

* George A. Finch, in the *American Journal of International Law* (cited in *Trials of War Criminals Before the Nuremberg Military Tribunals Under Control Council Law No. 10. October 1946–April 1949* [Washington: US Government Printing Office, 1946–49], I. G. Farben, Vol. VIII, p. 875 [hereinafter referred to as *TWC*]), pointed out how closely at times Mr. Justice Jackson followed the text of Trainin's book. Trainin had written, "In meting out punishment to the Axis war criminals, Russia would not permit herself to be restricted by traditional legalisms." The reason that no international law existed, he said, was that the powers of the world had wanted a united, criminal front against the Soviet Union. "This is by no means accidental. Its roots can be traced to the general character of international relations during the period of imperialism" (A. N. Trainin, *Hitlerite Responsibility under Criminal Law*, A. Y. Vishinsky, ed., Andrew Rothstein, trans. [London: Hutchinson & Co., Ltd., 1945], p. 7).

Mr. Justice Jackson, in his report to the President of June 6, 1945, wrote, "We must not permit it [the state of law] to become complicated or obscured by legalisms developed in the age of imperialism for the purpose of making war respectable" (*Jackson Report*, p. 51). Trainin's view that the coming trial should establish the guilt not only of the military and civilian chiefs of the Nazi State but also of the large industrialists was also adopted in the Allied Control Law No. 10, governing the military occupation of Germany, as well as in the list of those to be prosecuted in the first and subsequent trials. (*Cf.* Quincy Wright, *American Journal of International Law*, Vol. 41, pp. 41 ff.)

Russian influence was evident too in an American memorandum of April 30, 1945, drawn up for the San Francisco meeting of the United Nations. It repeatedly refers to "Hitlerite organization," "Hitlerite leaders"—terms characteristic of Soviet usage but otherwise extremely rare.

delegates produced a redraft of the clause on aggression that solved the matter very simply. It was far narrower than what Mr. Justice Jackson had hoped for. It declared the crime to be "Aggression or domination over other nations carried out by the European Axis in violation of international laws and treaties." *

This was a useful and workable formula from the Soviet point of view, for, when the indictment was drawn up, Estonia, Latvia, and Lithuania were stated in it to be part of Soviet territory. On October 6, Mr. Justice Jackson wrote a formal reservation in a letter to the other chief prosecutors: "This language is proposed by Russia and is accepted to avoid the delay which would be occasioned by insistence on an alteration in the text." [23] Nothing in the indictment, he declared austerely, was a recognition by the United States of Russian sovereignty over these countries.

THE ACCUSED ORGANIZATIONS

The London Conference named as defendants twenty-four men and six organizations. The idea of indicting organizations was also mainly American. Mr. Justice Jackson argued that the individual members of one of these criminal groups would be tried in due course on their own account but that the adop-

* No Italian was tried by Allied military courts, not because Italians had not made war (Italy had attacked France toward the close of the campaign in the west, and later Albania and Greece, and had joined in the war against Russia) but because Italy had changed governments and sides in the war. Politically it would have been undesirable, if not legally impossible, to try Italians before courts of their later allies. Another consideration may have been the kind of war the Italians had fought, which left the Allied nations with a sense of security in regard to future Italian military power. The Germans and Japanese had been first-class soldiers, and wars of aggression committed by them had to be met not only with equal or superior armed forces but with superior ideas, in order to prevent the likelihood of future wars of aggression on their part. The Italians could be dealt with in more casual fashion, as though in fact they had never gone to war and the crime of aggression stopped at their borders. This was one of the many Italian victories after Italy broke with their German allies—victories won by political legerdemain.

If Italians could not be tried for waging war, the Allies, as the trial would disclose, could obviously not be guilty of the crime. For example: The Russians could not be tried for entering the war against Japan, which had a nonaggression pact with Russia and had been trying to persuade Moscow to act as an intermediary with the United States to obtain peace. The invasion by American forces of the North African possessions of France (to prevent, as President Roosevelt had said, the occupation of this strategic area by the Germans) and the occupation of Iceland and Greenland by American troops could not be compared with the German invasion of Norway and Denmark. The trials were not trials of the Allies or of the Italians or of the Finns, although the Finns had crossed the borders of the Soviet Union with the Germans. Only two years before this attack on the USSR, they themselves had been attacked. Earlier, the Soviet invasion of Finland had caused the Russians to be cast out of the League of Nations, a development that had no appreciable effect on the Russo-Finnish war but might have been used by the British and the French to justify going to the aid of Finland had not the unexpected peace forced a change in their plans. Now, if either of these embattled powers of 1940 had been in the dock, it would have been the Finns, not the Russians.

tion of the Anglo-American concept of the conspiracy of a group would help clarify the legal situation, save time, and avoid holding innumerable trials to prove the same point.

This proposal ran into no great difficulties and was accepted, although the idea of a conspiracy was foreign to both French and Russian law. The Russians, criticizing the indictment of the Nazi organizations as a mere complication, pointed out that the groups had been disbanded, that their crimes had been thoroughly established, and that, while the Soviet Union like France had laws directed against agencies or organizations dangerous to the state, the Russian prosecution preferred to try individuals.*

General Nikitchenko said that the Gestapo and SS had already been declared criminal by authorities higher than the Tribunal. "The fact of their criminality has definitely been established. We cannot imagine . . . the Tribunal might possibly bring out a verdict that any one of these organizations was not criminal when it has already been labelled so by the governments." [24] But the point made no great difference to the Russians, and Nikitchenko more than once pointed out to Mr. Justice Jackson that the Soviet Union, although at first opposing the prosecution of organizations, had generously changed its mind and accepted the American proposal. The memorandum sent to President Roosevelt for his use at Yalta, signed by Stimson, Stettinius, and Biddle, had proposed that the chief German leaders be tried along with the organizations in which they had been employed: the SA, the SS, the Gestapo. Putting these leaders to death without a trial, said the memorandum, would violate "the most fundamental principles of justice common to all the United Nations."

The Nazi organizations had been necessary for carrying out the criminal purposes of the regime, the prosecution argued. In the SA, it said, the mass organization of the Party had first been concentrated; in the SS the Party had been carried into the armed forces; and in the High Command and the General Staff the conspiracy against the peace of the world had its origins. The organizations indicted, like the individuals, varied widely in what they

---

* The decision was to arouse lively protest. Eminent American jurists, among others, spoke up against the idea of collective guilt. Mr. Justice Jackson argued for the guilt of the organizations before the Tribunal, and cited the laws in the United States against the Ku Klux Klan. The British prosecutor referred to British laws against the Thugs in India in the nineteenth century. A clear precedent, he said, was that of the pirate ship. It was enough to have been a member of the crew to be brought to justice; even the cook was presumed to have participated in crimes committed by the more active pirates, and cooks could be and had been hanged along with the rest of the crew. But pirates, the defense pointed out, were tried under the national law of the power that captured them, not under international law, and this tribunal was an international one. The other precedents cited for collective punishment were also of antique character. If a community in the Middle Ages had assisted fugitives to escape from the justice of the king, the inhabitants might be punished collectively. Or if a town had defended itself to a point where victorious attackers considered their losses disproportionate to the justice of their cause, the defenders might be put to the sword.

had done. The SA had dwindled in importance after the murder of scores of its leaders, including its commander, Ernst Roehm, in 1934. Even so, among the indicted groups were political leaders of the Party and State, called in the indictment the Reichsregierung, and all the SS, the SD, and SA.* The SD was the security service that had started as the intelligence arm of the Party and had developed until its network of terror spread over Europe and the occupied territories. The Gestapo had been established by Hermann Goering as a secret police to ferret out enemies of the State, and before long it could order the arrest of anyone without a court proceeding.

WHAT KIND OF TRIAL?

On the question of the kind of trial that would be held, opinions had conflicted in the course of the years. Secretary of State Hull had thought that the German leaders should be given short shrift—tried, as he said, by a drumhead court-martial. This view was shared by a number of prominent British, including Winston Churchill, who said he wanted the top Nazi criminals taken out some morning and shot without preliminaries. This was also the opinion of the American Secretary of the Treasury, Henry Morgenthau. The Chief Justice of the United States Supreme Court said he could understand that a spontaneous act of this kind might take place, but he had serious doubts about a trial with the attributes of law and justice which, under the circumstances, would inevitably be more a political than a legal proceeding. Curiously, Mr. Justice Jackson had once held this view. *Life* magazine quoted a speech he had made warning against the use of the judicial process for nonjudicial ends, in which he had attacked cynics who saw no reason why courts like other agencies should not be used as weapons. "If we want to shoot Germans," he wrote, "as a matter of policy, let it be done as such, but don't hide the deed behind a court. If you are determined to execute a man in any case, there is no occasion for a trial; the world yields no respect to courts that are merely organized to convict." [25] What had changed Mr. Justice

* The prosecution had not been able to master the complicated machinery of the Nazi police apparatus. The Main Office of Reich Security, headed by Heinrich Himmler, had under it the Sipo, the Security police, the Gestapo, and the SD, as well as other important subdivisions, like Eichmann's Bureau IV A, 4b. More than a hundred of these offices of the RSHA (Reichssicherheitshauptamt) existed, including one devoted to forging foreign banknotes. These offices, the higher SS, and police officials were directly under Himmler. The SD was largely manned by professional hatchet men who did their jobs methodically, whether in actions against partisans or in executing prisoners of war who were turned over to them. One of its tasks was reporting on the morale of the civilian population, and these summaries were remarkably objective, with little attempt to paint a rosier picture than was warranted. In this vein the SD reported in occupied France in 1944 near Lyons that it had closed down an orphanage: forty-one children between the ages of three and thirteen, it solemnly declared, had been taken into custody and no articles of value had been found.

Jackson's mind is not clear. Perhaps his appointment as chief American prosecutor, and the opportunity to present the case for a new legal world order offered by the judicial exposure of the Nazi criminals, was decisive for him. Or perhaps his political ambitions were decisive.

A British *aide-mémoire* to Judge Samuel Rosenman, President Roosevelt's friend and representative during the preliminary negotiations leading to the trials, said that a long trial would arouse unfavorable public reaction and would furthermore look like a "put-up job." Both the Russians and the President of the United States, however, wanted a full-dress trial, although for very different reasons. Roosevelt and many of his advisers, such as Stimson, Stettinius, and Biddle, saw the court as a symbol of a new international order. For the Russians the question of guilt had already been decided; it need only be reenacted, made plain before the world. The trial would confirm decisions already taken. Before the trial started, the Russian judge, Nikitchenko, said, "We are dealing here with the chief war criminals who have already been convicted and whose conviction has already been announced by both the Moscow and Crimea declarations and by the heads of the governments." The tribunal therefore, he thought, had only to carry out the just punishment immediately. Nor was there any necessity, he said, "to create a sort of fiction that the judge is a disinterested person who has no legal knowledge of what has happened before . . . [that] would lead only to unnecessary delays." [26]

THE CHARTER OF THE INTERNATIONAL MILITARY TRIBUNAL

The London Agreement of August 8, 1945, was drawn up in accordance with its far-reaching purposes by the United States, Great Britain, the Soviet Union, and France. These four nations acted on behalf of the United Nations —that is, for the twenty-six countries that had gone to war with Germany. The agreement declared that the signatories, after consulting with the Allied Control Council for Germany, would establish the International Military Tribunal for the trial of war criminals whose offenses had no particular location. It was signed by Robert Falco for France, Sir William Allen Jowett for Great Britain, I. N. Nikitchenko for the Soviet Union, and Robert H. Jackson for the United States. Thus the chief American prosecutor and the Attorney General of Great Britain joined with the Russian member of the tribunal and the French alternate member to establish the court.

The charter of the tribunal, which was part of the London Agreement, provided that the competence of the tribunal could be challenged neither by the prosecution nor by the defense; that its decisions would be made by majority vote, the deciding vote in the event of a tie to be cast by the President of the Court. This office the Russians had at first wanted rotated, but they accepted the proposal to make a renowned and practiced jurist, the British member of the tribunal, Lord Justice Geoffrey Lawrence, President of the Court.

During the meetings in London, Nikitchenko and Trainin held stubbornly to making the seat of the trials Berlin, where the records would be kept and the decisions made, although they were willing to let the first trial be in Nuremberg, where 1,200 prisoners could be jailed. No building large enough to house that many prisoners remained undestroyed in Berlin.

The Russians did not join in the visit to inspect the Palace of Justice at Nuremberg, although Nikitchenko at first had accepted Jackson's invitation to go there with representatives of the other powers. At a dinner in the Savoy Hotel in London he unexpectedly told him that he and Trainin would not go. Jackson offered to change the date to suit their convenience, but Nikitchenko said that no date would be suitable. Obviously, the instructions from Moscow were against such undue fraternization. The Russians were already starting what was before long to called the "cold war" in Berlin, Poland, and the Balkans and did not feel called upon to make social occasions of the preparations for the trial.

The court, according to the charter, could try any citizen of the enemy nations; the indictments need not be limited to Germans, and among the accused were two Austrians. It had the task of trying and punishing those persons who, acting in the interests of the former European Axis countries, had planned to wage, or had waged, aggressive war, and those who had committed war crimes or crimes against humanity. Four categories of crimes were described in detail:

1. Crimes Against Peace [there were two of these]: namely, (a) planning, preparation, initiation, or waging of a war of aggression, or a war in violation of international treaties, agreements, or assurances, or (b) participation in a Common Plan or Conspiracy for the accomplishment of any of the foregoing.

2. War Crimes: namely, violations of the laws and customs of war, [including] murder, ill-treatment or deportation to slave labor . . . of [the] civilian population . . . in occupied territory, murder or ill-treatment of prisoners of war, or persons on the seas, killing of hostages, plunder, . . . wanton destruction of cities, towns, or villages, or devastation not justified by military necessity.

3. Crimes Against Humanity: namely, murder, extermination, enslavement, deportation, and other inhuman acts committed against any civilian population, before or during the war, or persecutions on political, racial, or religious grounds . . . in connection with any crime within the jurisdiction of the tribunal, whether or not in violation of domestic law of the country where perpetrated.

Thus crimes committed in Germany were included despite the Nazi laws of the period. The fact that a defendant had acted under an order of his government or of a superior was not to free him from responsibility for having carried it out, although superior orders could be considered in mitigation of punishment if the tribunal decided that such would be in the interest of justice. In this provision the charter of the tribunal took care of what was certain to be a chief defense of many of the accused. A clause expressly prohibiting the carrying out of inhuman or illegal orders had prudently been inserted in the military manuals of the British and American armies only a year before. Up to that time the accepted doctrine of both armies had been that a soldier must obey the orders of his superiors whether he liked them or not. With the trials coming up, the regulations were changed to provide that no order that offended a soldier's conscience need be carried out.* (Curiously, the German Army had a similarly phrased order. The German soldier in World War I and even under the Nazis was told in his book of military law that he was not to carry out orders he knew to be illegal.†)

---

* In the *British Manual of Military Law* (London: Command of the Army Council, 1929), Chapter XIV, "The Laws and Usages of War on Land," read: "It is important, however, to note that members of the armed forces who commit such violations of the recognized rules of warfare as are ordered by their government, or by their commanders are not war criminals and cannot therefore be punished by the enemy. He may punish the officials or commanders responsible for such orders if they fall into his hands, but otherwise he may only resort to the other means of obtaining redress which are dealt with in this chapter."

This was changed in April, 1944, to read: "The question, however, is governed by the major principle, that members of the armed forces are bound to obey lawful orders only and that they cannot therefore escape liability if, in obedience to a command, they commit acts which both violate unchallenged rules of warfare and outrage the general sentiments of humanity."

The American orders, *Basic Field Manual Rules of Land Warfare*, had read: "Individuals of the armed forces will not be punished for these offenses in case they are committed under the orders or sanction of their government or commanders. The commanders ordering the commission of such acts, or under whose authorities they are committed by the troops may be punished by the belligerent into whose hands they may fall."

This was changed on November 15, 1944, to read: "Individuals and organizations who violate the accepted laws and customs of war may be punished therefor. However the fact that the acts complained of were done pursuant to order of a superior or government sanction may be taken into consideration in determining culpability, either by way of defense or in mitigation of punishment. The person giving such orders may also be punished."

† Rittau, ed., *Militaerstrafgesetzbuch, in der Fassung vom 10 Oktober 1940—mit Einfuehrungsgesetz und Kriegsstrafrechtsordnung*, (Berlin: Walter de Gruyter Verlag, 1943). "*Militaerische Verbrechen und Vergehen*," par. 47, p. 99:

"1) If carrying out an order in the course of duty should violate a law, only the superior who gives the order is responsible. However, the subordinate who obeys it is punishable as a participant:
   a. if he goes beyond the given order or
   b. when he knows that the superior's order would have the aim of leading to a military or other crime or violation."

See also *Trial of the Major War Criminals before the International Military Tribunal. Nuremberg, 14 November 1945–10 October 1946*, Vol. II (Nuremberg: 1947–49), p. 150 (hereinafter referred to as N II, N III, N IV, etc).; *Reichsgesetzblatt 1926*, No. 37, p. 278, Art. 47, cited by *Jackson Report*.

THE COURT AND THE PRISON

The tribunal was made up of four members and four alternates—that is, two judges from each of the Allied powers.* During the proceedings they appeared dressed in their judicial robes, with the exception of the Russians, who wore military uniforms. The courtroom, holding some 600 people, was on the second floor of the Palace of Justice. The defendants were brought in by way of an elevator which opened into the courtroom. They came into the court one by one past a series of checkpoints, each of which telephoned word of each prisoner's arrival to the next. They were housed in separate cells, before each of which a guard was stationed night and day. They were not allowed to talk with one another during their twenty-minute exercise periods or in the showers, but those who were on speaking terms could exchange opinions in the dock during recesses. No military insignia could be worn, nor was German military rank recognized by the Allies, for otherwise it would have been necessary to follow the Geneva Convention on the treatment of prisoners of war, who, under it, could not be held in solitary confinement. For those in need of clothing (a number of the accused had only the clothes in which they had been arrested), a suit was made by a Nuremberg tailor; it could be worn only during the hours of the trial and had to be taken off promptly on the prisoner's return to his cell.

* Lord Justice Geoffrey Lawrence for the United Kingdom of Great Britain and North Ireland was President of the Court; his alternate was Sir William Norman Birkett; former Attorney General Francis Biddle for the United States and Judge John J. Parker of North Carolina, alternate; Professor Donnedieu de Vabres for the French Republic and M. le Conseiller R. Falco, alternate; Major General (of Jurisprudence) I. Nikitchenko for the USSR and Lieutenant Colonel A. F. Volchkov, alternate.

For the United States prosecution Mr. Justice Robert H. Jackson was Chief of Counsel. Executive Trial Counsel were Colonel Robert G. Storey and Thomas J. Dodd. Associate Trial Counsel were Sidney S. Alderman, Brigadier General Telford Taylor, Colonel John Harlan Amen, and Ralph G. Albrecht. In addition there were sixteen American Assistant Trial Counsel, including the German-born Dr. Robert M. Kempner.

The British Chief Prosecutor was His Majesty's Attorney General, Sir Hartley Shawcross, K.C., M.P. The Deputy Chief Prosecutor was the Rt. Honorable Sir David Maxwell-Fyfe, P.C., K.C., M.P., who had been the Attorney General under the Churchill government. The leading counsel was G. D. Roberts, K.C., O.B.E.; in addition there were four junior counsel.

The Russians' Chief Prosecutor was General R. A. Rudenko. The Deputy Chief Prosecutor was Colonel Y. V. Pokrovsky; the Assistant Prosecutors included two state counselors of justice of the second class, L. R. Shenin and M. Y. Raginsky, a state counselor of the third class, N. D. Zorya, and four others.

The French had two Chief Prosecutors, François de Menthon and Auguste Champetier de Ribes; two Deputy Chief Prosecutors; three Assistant Prosecutors who were chiefs of section; and five plain Assistant Prosecutors.

THE INDICTMENT

In the eyes of the victorious nations two groups of defendants were the targets of the trial. One was the German General Staff, the object of attack not only by the Allies but by "liberal" German critics long before Hitler. The American prosecution called it the perennial source of evil from which the Nazis, or any other temporarily ruling political organization, took orders. Because the General Staff obviously had had to be supported with the tools of war, Mr. Justice Jackson, following the formula of the Potsdam Conference, ordered one of his assistants to find two or more industrialists to indict. To fail to find the High Command guilty, said the chief American prosecutor, would be worse than freeing the entire group of defendants.[27] Jackson's view of the iniquity of the General Staff was widely held. It was shared by eminent figures in England and France, as well as by former United States Undersecretary of State Sumner Welles, by former Secretary of War Henry L. Stimson, and by Presidents Roosevelt and Truman.*

The indictment called the Nazi Party the "Central Core of the common plan or Conspiracy." The conspirators had planned, it said, "to abrogate . . . the Treaty of Versailles and its restrictions upon the military armament and activity of Germany; to acquire the territories lost by Germany as the result of the World War of 1914–18 . . . to acquire . . . *Lebensraum* . . . at the expense of neighboring and other countries . . ." and to this end had used "fraud, deceit, threats, intimidation, fifth-column activities, and propaganda."

* Telford Taylor during the trial of the Krupp defendants said, "The Third Reich dictatorship was based on this unholy trinity of Nazism, Militarism, and Economic Imperialism." And in the Flick case he repeated that on the shoulders of industrialists like Krupp and Thyssen and Flick, of military men like Beck, Fritsch, and Rundstedt, Hitler had ridden to power and from power to conquest. But Beck had planned the arrest of Hitler in 1938, and Fritsch was cashiered after the faked charges of his homosexuality had been entirely disproved. He was never fully rehabilitated by Hitler; he went to the Polish front in the autumn of 1939, where on a patrol in the course of the fighting he sought and met a soldier's death. Beck made two unsuccessful attempts to kill himself when the July 20 plot failed and was mercifully given the *coup de grâce* he asked for by a sergeant. Mr. Taylor was indulging in judicial or political rhetoric (August von Knieriem, *The Nuremberg Trials* [Chicago: Henry Regnery Company, 1959], p. 502).

Taylor's comment was an echo of what Trainin had written in his book on the criminal responsibility of the Hitlerians. Trainin had said: "We know the Nazis had a social base— the German trusts, financial and economic. . . . The fifteen big trusts including I.G. Farben and Krupp . . . these are the masters for whom the Nazi State works. . . . From the point of view of penal justice the members of the Nazi association of international malefactors are the following: Hitler and his ministers, the commanders of the German Army—Goering, Hess, Goebbels, Himmler, Ribbentrop, Rosenberg, and the other members of the Hitler clique—are the organizers and the authors of grave crimes against the bases of the international community and human morality, while the directors of the financial and economic trusts that sustained this clique are the organizers of and accomplices in the same crimes." (A. N. Trainin, *La Responsibilité pénale des Hitlériens* [Paris: La Press Française et Etrangère, 1945], pp. 154–160.)

Their doctrines included the view that persons of German blood were superior, a master race, that the Germans themselves should be ruled under the *Fuehrerprinzip*, that war was a noble and necessary activity of Germans, and that the leadership of the Nazi Party "was entitled to shape the structure, policies, and practices of the German state."

Under the rule of the Party, 5,700,000 Jews had disappeared, so the indictment charged, out of the 9,600,000 who had formerly lived in the countries that had come under Nazi domination. "The Nazi conspirators . . . extended a system of terror against opponents . . . or suspected opponents of the regime . . . [they] destroyed the free trade unions . . . by promoting beliefs and practices incompatible with Christian teaching, sought to subvert the influence of the churches over the people and in particular over the youth of Germany . . . pursued a program of persecution of priests, clergy, and members of monastic orders." They reshaped the educational system of Germany to prepare youth psychologically for war. They deprived labor of its rights, and with "the industrialists among them, embarked upon a huge re-armament program. . . . They led Germany to enter upon a course of secret re-armament from 1933 to March 1935 . . . to leave the International Disarmament Conference and the League of Nations." Their plan was to reoccupy and fortify the Rhineland, in violation of the Treaty of Versailles and other treaties, and to acquire military strength and political bargaining power against other nations. The occupation of the Rhineland in March, 1936, had opened the way for the major aggressive steps to follow: the invasion of Austria in 1938 and then of Czechoslovakia. After that came the formulation of the plan to attack Poland, the expansion of the war into a general war of aggression, the planning and execution of attacks on Denmark, Norway, Belgium, the Netherlands, Luxembourg, Yugoslavia, and Greece. Then "on June 22, 1941, the Nazi conspirators deceitfully denounced the Non-Aggression Pact" that had been made with Russia on August 23, 1939, "and without any declaration of war invaded Soviet territory thereby beginning a War of Aggression against the U.S.S.R."

The German conspirators had collaborated with Italy and Japan to wage aggressive war against the United States and had made a ten-year military-economic alliance with those countries in Berlin on September 27, 1940, which had strengthened the limited pact made on November 25, 1936. They had exhorted Japan to seek "a new order of things." The indictment continued: "Taking advantage of the wars of aggression then being waged by the Nazi conspirators, Japan commenced an attack on December 7, 1941, against the United States . . . and against the British Commonwealth of Nations, French Indo-China and the Netherlands."

The Nazi conspirators also conspired to wage war "in ruthless and complete disregard" of the laws of humanity and laws and customs of war. Thus "the defendants with divers other persons," the indictment said, "are guilty of a common plan or conspiracy for the accomplishment of Crimes Against Peace;

of a conspiracy to commit Crimes Against Humanity in the course of the preparation for war and in the course of the prosecution of war; and of a conspiracy to commit War Crimes not only against the armed forces of their enemies but also against non-belligerent civilian populations." [28]

This remarkable document succeeded in so confusing the real issues of the trial as they emerged in the course of the postwar years that they never were entirely untangled. While accusing the Germans of having invaded Poland as part of a conspiracy, the prosecution and the tribunal ignored what had made the invasion a safe operation—namely, the nonaggression pact Hitler had made with the Soviet Union in August, 1939, and the secret document that had accompanied it, under the terms of which the Red Army invaded Poland a few weeks later and took up prearranged positions. At the same time, the Russo-German nonaggression pact was cited in the indictment as the treaty the Germans had violated when they invaded the USSR in June, 1941. Violations of the Treaty of Versailles—a document that since 1919 had been increasingly under fire by leading statesmen and historians in the Allied countries as well as in Germany—and the occupation of the Rhineland were put on the same level as the killing of millions of defenseless noncombatants.*

The passages on the Nazi attacks on churches and minds of youth and the promotion of "beliefs and practices incompatible with Christian teaching" might have caused the trace of a smile on the faces of the Soviet representatives, who for the purpose of the trial were as indignant as any of their Western colleagues at such malpractices.

It was not new for Western statesmen and observers to see in the Russians a devotion to Christian principles, which when glimpsed strengthened hopes of Moscow's cooperation. Roosevelt had said that Stalin's character showed evidence of his early theological training, and many British and American clergymen declared that in one form or another freedom of religion existed in the Soviet Union or that Communism was closely related to Christianity—especially primitive Christianity, which had also faced a hostile world with comradeship and the sharing of a meager stock of the world's goods.

THE TWENTY-FOUR

The chief defendant among the twenty-four originally named in the indictment was former Reichsmarschall Hermann Goering, whose designation in 1939 by the Fuehrer as his successor remained in force until near the end of the war, when Hitler accused him of high treason and ordered his arrest. Next

* At London Mr. Justice Jackson had said, "We propose to punish acts which have been regarded as criminal since the time of Cain and have been so written in every civilized code." Thereupon he, and later the indictment, simply listed the violations of pledges, such as the invasion of the demilitarized Rhineland by the German Army in 1936, the invasion of Czechoslovakia and Poland, the wiping out of whole populations, and the use of slave labor (*Jackson Report*, p. 50).

in importance was Joachim von Ribbentrop, Foreign Minister of the Reich during most of the years Hitler was Chancellor. Ribbentrop was unanimously considered one of the vainest and most incompetent of the men around the Fuehrer.

There followed a cross section of the *Prominente:* Hans Frank, who had been Governor General of Poland. Alfred Rosenberg, the turgid theoretician of the Party, had been appointed to administer the Eastern Territories but never succeeded in doing so. Also listed were the two chief officers of the OKW (Oberkommando der Wehrmacht, the High Command of the Armed Forces), Field Marshal Wilhelm Keitel and General Alfred Jodl; the ranking admirals of the German Navy, Erich Raeder and Karl Doenitz; the secretary of the Party chancellery, who had not been captured (and seems to have permanently disappeared), Martin Bormann; the head of the RSHA (Reichssicherheitshauptamt, the Reich Central Security Office) and the closest to the dead Heinrich Himmler the Allies were able to lay their hands on, Ernst Kaltenbrunner; the chief of the Labor Front of the Reich, Robert Ley; the devoted Austrian Nazi who had become civil administrator of the Netherlands, Artur Seyss-Inquart; the head of the German youth movement, who had published some of the most undistinguished poetry ever to appear in Germany, Baldur von Schirach; the most notorious among the anti-Semitic journalists and spellbinders, Julius Streicher; and a former German Chancellor and a Foreign Minister who had served under Hitler after he overcame their conservative parties and principles, Franz von Papen and Constantin von Neurath.

Fritz Sauckel, who had been in charge of the forced labor of more than six million men and women, was also indicted. Sauckel had brought convoys of foreign workers to Germany from all the countries of Europe, and with him in the dock would be the man who had made use of them, Albert Speer, an architect by profession, who with this mixed force of slave labor and German workers achieved such prodigies of production that, despite the bombings, Germany's manufacture of war materials, airplanes, tanks, guns, and everything essential to keep the nation fighting had gone up steadily until the end of the war.

Speer had succeeded the builder of the West Wall and the Autobahnen, Fritz Todt, after the latter's death in an airplane accident. As Minister of Arms and Munitions, Speer had become the head of all German war production which before him had been under the direction of his codefendant Hermann Goering, whose many assignments and offices greatly exceeded his capacity to cope with them. It was Speer who had suggested to Hitler the appointment of a nonparochial Gauleiter—the Fuehrer named Sauckel—as head of the Labor Front. Interested solely in efficiency, Speer had conducted his ministry with such disregard for the National Socialist sentiments of the men he employed that Himmler and Bormann declared his Armament Ministry to be a center of anti-Nazi activity.[29]

Rudolf Hess was another individual to stand trial, although his British jailers had thought him insane. Hess had been the Fuehrer's deputy, the third man in the Reich, designated after Goering to succeed Hitler until he had flown to Britain in 1941 in a wild effort to stop a war which he was certain could only bring disaster to both England and Germany. In England he had shown unmistakable delusional symptoms and had twice tried to commit suicide. He had been diagnosed as pyschotic by the English doctors who had examined him as carefully as the British intelligence-service men had during his confinement. But Hess remained a key figure among the Nazi great, one of the "Aryan" fanatics, and doggedly throughout his delusions stayed pro-English and anti-Communist. The Russians were particularly suspicious of him because of his 1941 flight. Stalin asked Clement Attlee at Potsdam why Hess was fed and treated so well in England. Attlee replied soothingly that Stalin had no cause to be troubled, and Ernest Bevin promised that Hess would be duly produced at the forthcoming trial, as indeed he was; he was flown over just before it started.

One of the men both the Russians and the Americans had immediately agreed upon to indict was Hjalmar Schacht, banker and world-renowned prestidigitator of German finances, who had originated the plan that rescued the German mark from its worthlessness in 1923 and then a decade later, conjured up the loans and complicated financing that made German rearmament possible. Mr. Justice Jackson said that either he was a great war criminal or he was nothing, and Nikitchenko, heartily agreeing, said that such men were greater criminals than the minor people who carried out the murders and who were directly guilty of ill treatment and similar crimes.[30]

Hans Fritzsche, who had been chief of German broadcasting, was indicted, representing one of the branches of the activities of his former chief, the late Minister of Propaganda, Joseph Goebbels. Goebbels' sphere was also represented by Walther Funk, who had been director of the German press before he took over Schacht's job as Minister of Economics and became responsible for exploitation of German and foreign labor and resources. Another defendant, Wilhelm Frick, had been Reichsminister of the Interior, Governor General of Lower Styria and Upper Carinthia in Austria and of Alsace-Lorraine and Norway, and then Reichsprotektor of Bohemia and Moravia, following the killing of Reinhard Heydrich.[31]

Gustav Krupp was regarded by all the Allied Powers as one of the most important of the war criminals. Krupp, who had headed the chief armaments firm of Germany and of Europe, had been a member of the Reich Economic Council and President of the Reich Association of German Industry. After an early period of hostility to Hitler, he became one of the Fuehrer's most devoted supporters among German industrialists. Born Gustav von Bohlen und Halbach, he had added his wife's family name when he married Berta von Krupp.

The entire prosecution was united on the desirability of trying a member of the Krupp family, and they argued long and learnedly on behalf of their governments for an indictment. The Americans were anxious to try Gustav, although he was in a hospital. If he could not be present in the court, Mr. Justice Jackson argued, he could be tried *in absentia*. In any event the symbolism of trying a Krupp was all-important. If Gustav could not under the circumstances be tried, then his son Alfried should be substituted, according to Justice Jackson, because "the United States . . . submits that no greater disservice to the future peace of the world could be done than to excuse the entire Krupp family from this trial." [32]

The American prosecutor had to admit under questioning of the court that Gustav could not be tried *in absentia* before an American court, but he was joined in his plea by the British prosecutor Sir Hartley Shawcross, who also believed it would be better to try Gustav but if this were not permitted agreed that Alfried might be willing to take the place of his father and thus occasion no delay in the proceedings.

The French prosecutor did not think that the elderly Krupp could be tried until he had regained his health, but the French too regarded the trial of Alfried with favor since they agreed that it was imperative to try a Krupp. The Russians were ready to try father or son or both. A medical panel chosen by the tribunal reported that the seventy-eight-year-old Gustav, suffering from senility, could not stand trial: he could not understand the nature of the proceedings. The court decided that the indictment should remain pending against him so that he could be tried in the future should he recover. This he never did, but Alfried was tried by a later American court, found guilty of divers crimes, including the use of forced labor, and sentenced to twelve years' imprisonment. He served seven years and was then released. His property which had been ordered confiscated was returned to him.

OUTSIDE THE PALACE OF JUSTICE

Some of the most eligible candidates for trial and punishment would not appear at Nuremberg. Hitler and Goebbels were dead, Bormann had disappeared but would be tried *in absentia*, and Himmler had bitten into a cyanide crystal during an examination by a British doctor and died within a few moments. The Allied net was wide, and it caught thousands of large and small fry, although some of them, like Eichmann, successfully mixed with the millions of war prisoners, took jobs on farms, disappeared into the anonymity and misery of the German cities, or got off to foreign parts.

Streicher, the Jew-baiter, grew a beard but was recognized and taken prisoner by an American lieutenant who was himself a Jew. Oswald Pohl, who had lived disguised as a gardener, was run down by British authorities after months of searching. The British, fearing he would try to commit suicide, worked the successful trick of having a German policeman tell him he was wanted for questioning at the local police station on suspicion of having stolen a bicycle. The ruse worked; Pohl was relieved of the two vials of poison he carried and turned over to the British authorities. Pohl, a notorious organizer of SS slave labor in the concentration camps, was to be a key witness against Funk and was himself tried by a later court.

But dozens among the party *Bonzen* (bigwigs) committed suicide—some with their entire families. Others successfully escaped detection, living for years under assumed names in Germany or abroad. Sometimes they were identified when their names came up in the course of later trials, and they were belatedly arrested and tried on their own account. Some escaped to Egypt or South America and were never found or, if found, were never extradited and brought to trial in Germany. A few countries, including Argentina, granted them "political asylum," a strange category in cases such as that of former SS doctor Mengele, who was accused not of holding undesirable political views but of the murder of thousands of concentration-camp inmates.

After 1945 every trial of Nazi war criminals resulted in indictments and the eliciting of evidence for new trials. Witnesses sometimes revealed in the course of their testimony that they or another had been more than an onlooker to an incident. Each trial set off a chain of trials of other defendants. In the trial of the major war criminals it was dangerous for even the innocent to testify. In the years immediately after the war Germans had no rights other than those bestowed by the victorious powers, and if testimony of a witness sounded dubious or unfriendly to the prosecution, it was an easy matter to order his arrest. Some of the witnesses joined the defendants in the cells of the Palace of Justice although they had come to Nuremberg as free men. One of the defending lawyers, Professor Metzger, who represented Neurath, was suddenly arrested in Nuremberg and spent six weeks in a cell in the same jail as his client without learning the charges against him.[33] A former chief of *Abteilung Fremde Heere West*, Colonel Sottmann, telegraphed his willingness to be a witness to testify to the British preparations for landing in Norway and was promptly arrested.[34]

The guilty were picked up too. During later trials men who had been living quiet, well-camouflaged lives as lawyers, businessmen, doctors, or otherwise harmless citizens were identified as having played a part in the murders as prison officials, prosecutors, guards, judges, generals, or "scientific" researchers.

Between the autumn of 1945 and March, 1948, about 1,000 cases involving some 3,500 persons were tried in many countries on the Continent before Allied courts, although the United Nations War Crimes Commission had compiled a list of 36,800 names of men who were either to be held as material witnesses or against whom it was considered likely a case could be made.[35] These figures do not include the cases of those tried before German courts, which were of two kinds; the denazification proceedings that took place in the first years of the occupation and led to thousands of convictions and sentences of imprisonment; * and the later trials that came as a result of criminal charges brought after denazification courts had finished their work. The later trials, those of people accused of crimes committed during the Nazi period, were to occupy German courts to the present writing and beyond. To assist the prosecution of persons whose misdeeds came to light in the future, the Bundesrepublik established a bureau in Ludwigsburg in 1958 to collect and sift evidence.

In the United States courts in Nuremberg in the period from July, 1945, until July, 1949, 199 people were tried, of whom 38 were acquitted, 36 sentenced to death (18 of whom were executed), 23 to life imprisonment, and 102 to shorter terms. (American courts in Dachau sentenced 420 to death.) In the event all prison sentences were cut down, men sentenced to life usually were free within seven years. But these figures reveal little of what went on.

The American trials at Nuremberg were for defendants by occupational categories—for those who had been directors in big businesses or who had served in the diplomatic service as well as in the SD, for generals as well as members of the extermination squads. In the early years of the occupation it was as great a crime under Control Council Law No. 10 to have committed aggressive warfare or to have been head of a factory employing 3,000 people as to have been a member of the Gestapo, and the judgments of the American courts were bewildering—in some cases they conflicted with one another. The court that tried the so-called Krupp case quoted in its judgment forty pages from the prosecution's brief. In one case a judge denounced the proceedings as "unfair." In another, the court admitted that it had made an error in convicting a defendant and declared that it was pleased to rectify its error. Men guilty of crimes, as well as defendants who merely fitted into categories regarded as unsavory—"big industry," "munition makers," "officer caste," diplomats—all appear in figures cited.

Soviet Russia held trials while the cases before the international court at Nuremberg were being heard. Some German generals were sentenced to prison terms or were executed. Others, members of the Free Germany movement that had been formed among German officers captured during the war—among them Field Marshal Paulus, who appeared as a prosecution witness at Nuremberg—were held in a kind of honorable arrest, from which many, however, would not return. The Soviet Union, like Rome, regarded any war in which it was engaged as a just war and those who had fought against it as criminals.

* The three men freed in the trial of the major war criminals—Schacht, Papen, and Fritzsche—were sentenced to prison terms for the part they had played in the Nazi State by subsequent German denazification courts functioning in the *Laender* of the American Zone under the law enacted "for the liberation from National Socialism and Militarism," in which four classes of persons were defined: major offenders, offenders, lesser offenders, and followers. All three were found guilty as major offenders.

But its decisions as to who should be tried were made with due regard to the criminals' possible usefulness to the Soviet Union in the postwar years.*

Hans Fritzsche, Admiral Raeder, and Raeder's wife were captured by Russian troops and sent to Moscow to be interrogated.† Both Fritzsche and Raeder were treated well enough by the Russians and were returned to Nuremberg for trial, but the admiral's wife was in jail for years—part of the time in a prison outside Berlin—and repeated attempts to bring her to Nuremberg as a witness for her husband were unsuccessful. She had been charged with no crime.

Russia was not alone in *Sippenhaftung,* the arrest of members of the family of war criminals. The Western Allies jailed wives of the major war criminals, but this was done only sporadically, and the imprisonment did not last long. Frau Goering and her young daughter were in prison for some months, as were the wives of Baldur von Schirach and Walter Funk, but wives of the other defendants were never arrested. The decisions apparently were made *ad hoc* and as a result of rumors as much as by weightier evidence. Any seizable family property in the form of bank accounts or art collections was uniformly confiscated without regard to the family's guilt or innocence on the assumption that it belonged to or had come from the husbands.

THE PROSECUTION AND THE DEFENSE

A large staff labored for the Allies on preparations for the trials. Of the 100,000 captured documents screened, 10,000 were selected for use. The Americans alone had more than 600 people at work in Nuremberg, and about the same number were employed by the other Allied Powers. The German lawyers were chosen from a list drawn up by the Allied authorities, but the defendants could ask to be represented by a lawyer not on the Allied list who then had to be approved. Some of the German counsel, including the former head of the German bar, had been Party members, but others had been anti-Nazis—as one would say in the course of the trial—who had lost everything because of the Nazis and the war.

* The combined figures for all cases tried both in Allied and German courts up to 1963 were as follows according to official German sources (*The Bulletin,* Bonn, January 7, 1964): In the American zone 1,814 people were sentenced, of whom 450 were given the death penalty. In the British-occupied area, where trials were held only for crimes against the laws and usages of war, 1,085 were sentenced, 240 to death. In the French zone, of 2,107 persons sentenced, 104 received the death penalty. Of those sentenced to death more than half were executed (*cf.* also Viscount Maugham, *UNO and War Crimes* [London: John Murray, 1951], p. 21).

German authorities estimate that more than 10,000 persons have been sentenced by the Soviet Union to either imprisonment or death.

German courts since the end of the war have arraigned 12,846 persons, of whom 5,426 were convicted and 4,027 acquitted.

† It was rumored later that Raeder and his wife had taken poison but were found by a Russian officer, who called in medical help. Raeder's lawyer, Walter Siemers, who knew the admiral well, does not corroborate the story.

The German defense was conducted under handicaps of monumental proportions. In theory the German counsel had the same task as the prosecution in dealing with the mass of documentary material assembled, but the Germans had no access to the material and could not find out what was in it. The documents were in the charge of the Allies, and although the court repeatedly ordered the prosecution to make the captured material available to the defense, when the German lawyers tried to get hold of it they were told they first had to say what they wanted. There were no indexes and no ways of knowing the contents of particular documents, so they could scarcely know what to ask for. In addition, Allied files were closed to them. They had no access to British and French plans to invade Norway, nor could they question witnesses on the attempts by the British and French to persuade the Russians to join the Western Alliance. The defendants could make no preparation for their cases until they knew the charges, so until the indictments were served on October 18 on Fritzsche and Raeder, who were in Russian hands in Berlin, and on October 19 on the others, neither the defendants nor their lawyers knew the specific charges.

The lawyers then had a month to prepare their cases, for pleas had to be entered by November 20. The law under which the defendants were to be tried was mainly Anglo-American with some Continental inclusions to make the procedures more flexible. Such Anglo-American practices as agreement by stipulation that both sides accept certain trial procedures in the interest of efficiency were strange to the Germans. The concept of a contest between the prosecution and the defense with the judge as impartial arbiter does not exist in Continental law, and the German lawyers had no experience in rough-and-tumble cross-examination, nor any clear idea of what was expected of them when they were told to take over a witness.

In Continental theory, if not wholly in practice, the presiding judge, as well as the state's attorney and the defense lawyers, as officers of the court have the same purpose: getting at the truth of the matter at issue before the tribunal. If the prosecution discovers something to the advantage of the defendant, its duty is to bring it to the attention of the court. The defending attorneys, while there to bring out and emphasize evidence to aid their client, are equally under obligation to set the facts straight. The presiding judge, the president of the court, is the most active person in a German trial. He questions witnesses, conducts at the same time the direct and cross-examinaton of the defendants and the witnesses, and is far removed from the dispassionate referee of the Anglo-American courts who is supposed to hold the balance even between defense and prosecution.

THE TRIBUNAL AND THE DEFENSE

The President of the Nuremberg tribunal, Lord Justice Lawrence, conducted the trial with imperturbable courtesy and patience, remarkably maintaining both during the more than nine months of heated and protracted argument about the guilt or innocence of the enemies of the states he and his colleagues represented. Despite his well-schooled efforts to be impartial, the President and the Court, as a whole, could not but have had a different standard for the Germans and the Allies. When Soviet prosecutor Andrei Vyshinsky, who had been in charge of the Russian purge trials, came to Nuremberg, he sat with the prosecution. During the trial a banquet given in his honor was attended by all the judges and the prosecution.[36] There were other anomalies. On hearing of the death of Harlan F. Stone, Chief Justice of the United States Supreme Court, Lord Justice Lawrence expressed the sympathy of the tri= bunal and asked Mr. Justice Jackson to say a few words for the occasion.

Lord Justice Lawrence was often sharp with the defense. But he also patiently explained why they could not be treated in precisely the same fashion as the prosecution, which could and did surprise the defense with documents and witnesses.* The difference of treatment of the prosecution and the defense was explained as the result of technical difficulties in having to translate the mass of documents and in transporting witnesses—who had to be brought to Nuremberg by the Allies since the Germans had no facilities for communication or travel other than those provided by the occupation authorities. But the difference, in fact, was that the Allies were able to bring in evidence for which the defense could make no preparation. Moreover, the prosecution, because of the need for military security in an enemy country, had full advance knowledge of who the defense witnesses were, as well as the power of retaliation over those witnesses whose testimony they judged suspicious or unfriendly. Any official publication of any member state of the United Nations was automatically admitted by the court as evidence, and few questions that might conceivably be embarrassing or disturbing to the powers sitting on the bench were permitted.

The Soviet Chief Prosecutor, General Rudenko, could cross-examine Hans Fritzsche on "the German aggression against Poland," but Fritzsche could go into no details on a matter known to everyone in the court—that the attack had been made certain and its success assured by the signing of the nonaggression pact between Hitler and Stalin, with its secret clauses that divided Poland between the Soviet Union and Germany. When the evidence for this secret treaty appeared, it came in the form of an affidavit of the former legal adviser of the German Foreign Office, Friedrich Gaus, who had gone to Moscow with Ribbentrop to help draw up the document which the Russian prosecutor at Nuremberg said he had never heard of.

Any argument based on the Versailles Treaty and its influence on German politics and decisions was impermissible. The Russian treatment of German prisoners of war and the use of German forced labor could not be described,

---

* The defense lawyers had to explain the relevance of both before they could be admitted. Of the nineteen witnesses Jodl's lawyer asked to call, he was allowed four (N VIII, pp. 182, 590–92).

nor could Paulus be questioned on the subject, although he could have testified on what had happened to the survivors of the Sixth Army, only some 5,000 of whom eventually returned to Germany out of the 123,000 who had surrendered at Stalingrad.[37] The bombing of German cities, such as Dresden (where some 150,000 people were killed, almost all noncombatants, for Dresden was full of refugees), could play no role in the issues under debate, although the German air attacks on Warsaw, Belgrade, Rotterdam, and other population centers were brought up many times and the bombing of Rotterdam was part of the indictment. The millions of German men, women, and children who had been driven from their homes in Poland, Hungary, Czechoslovakia, Rumania, and Bulgaria, where their families had been settled for centuries, could not be mentioned, nor could the alleged atrocities committed against German troops by any of the Allied nations.

The British handbook of irregular warfare, instructing the Commandos to act like gangsters not soldiers, could not be brought into the trial, although Jodl's lawyer, Franz Exner, pleaded that the British orders affected the German reprisals against the Commandos and that the British Government had officially defended this kind of warfare as acceptable.* The President of the Court merely said that the tribunal could take the matter into consideration.[38] Tu quoque was permitted as a defense only in one instance, with regard to the German Navy and the defense of Admirals Doenitz and Raeder, whose lawyers argued that they had conducted submarine warfare under the same rules as the Allies, and in its verdict the court accepted this defense as justified. The court quoted the testimony of British and American officers, most importantly of Admiral Chester Nimitz, who in an affidavit declared that American submarines from the first day of the war against Japan had orders to sink any Japanese ship in the Pacific without warning. The British Admiralty also conceded that British submarines had orders to sink any ship on sight in the Skagerrak.

THE RECORD

The trials, with their truckloads of documents (those of the SS alone filled six freight cars), with the searching out of witnesses from the wreckage of the Great German Reich, from the former concentration camps, from the prisoner-of-war stockades of neutral and Allied countries, were to bring to light—despite the contradictions in the testimony of the accused and the misconceptions of the prosecution—the bone and flesh of the Nazi State, as well as the bizarre case histories of those who had served it. The records were so detailed and in such quantity that all the prosecution and defense lawyers together could scarcely master them. Mr. Justice Jackson, reporting to President Truman after the trial, said that there were more than five

* Copies of the handbook had been found on captured British Commandos.

million pages in the typewritten record. In the twelve subsequent American trials at Nuremberg, some 2,000 printed pages of the records of each trial were published, and an additional 20,000 pages on each trial remained unpublished.

Since the Allies had charge of printing the records and the proceedings, the choice of material to be published was sometimes one-sided—for example, the index of the forty-two volumes of the trial of the major war criminals contains no mention of Russian aggression or of other matters unfavorable to any of the Allies. Nevertheless, the gross historical record is to be found in the pages, if sometimes indirectly, as when it is noted that the interrogatories prepared by the German lawyers were answered by Germans awaiting trials or sentences mainly in American and British internment camps. Only two such interrogatories were answered from Russian camps and none from the French—in part, no doubt, because conditions in those camps could not always bear the scrutiny of foreign observers. When Goering, who was understandably critical of the Allied conduct of the trials, said that a Russian interrogatory accurately reported his testimony, he did so because in this case it was a matter of no consequence to either side. In general, the answers to Russian interrogations and the affidavits and witnesses from Soviet sources, including testimony of German officers from Russian prisoner-of-war camps, had a distressing sameness of vocabulary: "the Hitlerite aggressors," "the Fascist criminals," "the peaceloving Soviet Union."

THE DEFENSE LAWYERS

The defense, in addition to the difficulty of getting at the Allies' collection of documents in Nuremberg, lacked an equal opportunity for getting books of documents useful to their cases from abroad. *Stars and Stripes* and occasional issues of other Allied papers were to be had, but it was impossible for them to obtain a copy of a book which dealt with the events preceding the German attack on Russia by former Foreign Minister of Rumania and Ambassador to the Soviet Union Grigore Gafencu. The Gafencu book was on sale in every Swiss bookstore, but the defense could not get a copy of it or of the final war report of the American Chief of Staff, General George C. Marshall, which had been published in Allied newspapers. Marshall wrote that American investigators had been unable to find a concerted plan between the Japanese and the German Governments or General Staffs—a fact relevant to any charge of conspiracy to wage war.

The Germans had, in fact, been as surprised by Pearl Harbor as everyone else, although they had urged the Japanese to attack Singapore, as well as the British and Dutch possessions in the South Pacific. Neither before the start of hostilities nor later had joint war plans been worked out between the two countries.

The Germans could learn of such Allied evidence by chance conversations or through the German newspapers licensed by the Allies and published in Germany. They had no foreign currency and could not travel except by Allied permission even within Germany. Since no publications from outside Germany were available, the Germans continued to live in much the same intellectual desert as under Hitler. Sometimes they were able to establish friendly relations with Allied soldiers or civilians at Nuremberg, and Dr. Siemers, the lawyer for Admiral Raeder, obtained from one of these a photocopy of the secret treaty between Russia and Germany that corroborated the testimony of Friedrich Gaus.

In general, the Germans worked, almost wholly dependent on the Allies, in a dimly lighted room confronted by thousands of documents of which they had no advance knowledge. The defense lawyers were treated with a mixture of tolerance and goodwill, as pariah Germans. Their rations, like those of the prisoners, were much better than those of ordinary Germans, who were going hungry on 1,200 and less calories a day outside the walls of the Palace of Justice.

The American guards at the prison hustled the lawyers as they searched them and sent them on their way through the controls. On occasion the guards brought them before Allied superiors on charges of having behaved with inadequate respect to Allied authority. One lawyer, who before a lunch break had been arguing a point on behalf of his client, kept the impatient court waiting for a half hour after it reconvened. When he turned up, he apologetically related that the American guards for some unexplained reason had refused to let him come back into the courthouse. There were far fewer cups and serving trays than the number of people who ate in the lunchroom assigned to the defense counsel. In the early days of the trial the accused met for conferences with their lawyers in a single room under surveillance of American MPs. Throughout the trial the defense counsel complained that copies of documents submitted by the prosecution were not given them, although in at least one case a considerable number of copies had been made available by the prosecution to newspapers.

The defense lawyers were attacked in the German press, and at the end of the trial the Bar Association of Cologne threatened an investigation of their backgrounds. This proposal was officially denounced by the court, which did its best to protect the attorneys against such attacks and in the end praised them all on behalf of the legal profession for having performed an onerous and dutiful task. Rarely, some of them met socially with members of the prosecution, and on one occasion Maxwell-Fyfe, the British prosecutor, penned a note of congratulations to a German lawyer, Alfred Seidl, for a spirited speech on behalf of his client, Rudolf Hess.

The stain of collective guilt was on the lawyers, too. The court spoke in different tones to them than to the prosecution. They were told to move along with their cases, to pay attention, to stop talking about irrelevant matters like the Versailles Treaty or Allied misbehavior, and the usually gentle and urbane voice of the President of the Court could crack over their heads when, as sometimes happened, they talked at cross purposes. And yet nothing could conceal from the lawyers, the spectators, or even the defendants that the trial was being conducted, in comparison with the summary procedures of the Third Reich, with decorum and considerable fairness.

IN PURSUIT OF THE OPEN QUESTIONS

The trial of these Germans was a collective trial, but it is through the life stories of each individual that many hidden springs of the National Socialist State may be detected. The twenty-two men and the six organizations which were tried were deliberately chosen because they could be identified as the foremost representatives of the men and groups who had brought Hitler to power and kept him there against the aroused wrath and armed forces of almost the entire world.* Even if the trial was imperfect and the representatives of the Soviet Union charged the Germans with crimes the Russians had committed, the trial had to be held in some form. A catharsis of the pent-up emotions of millions of people had to be provided and a record of what had taken place duly preserved for whatever use later generations would make of it. The record would not completely document the infamy in the twentieth century, but it would reveal one vast concentration of evil that could be exorcised.

The trial raised many questions that are raised again in the pages that follow. The responsibilities of the individuals indicted, of the German people, of Prussian militarism, of big business, and of the German national character were clearer at the end of the trial than they were at the beginning. They are clearer now than they were during the trial. The Third Reich was not the first or the last of the totalitarian regimes that have appeared in the last fifty years. It is, however, the most completely documented, and in this contribution to history the trial also played its role.

NOTES

1. *History of the United Nations War Crimes Commission*, compiled by the United Nations War Crimes Commission (London: H. M. Stationery Office, 1948), pp. 46–51. Hereinafter referred to as *History of UNWCC*.

2. Hans-Heinrich Jeschek, *Die Verantwortlichkeit der Staatsorgane nach dem Voelkerstrafrecht* (Bonn: Ludwig Roehrscheid Verlag, 1952), p. 55.

3. *Ibid.*, p. 48. See also Eric Gabus, *La criminalité de la guerre*, Dissertation (Geneva: Université de Genève, Editions Générales, 1953). J. Daniel, *Le*

* The original twenty-four included Krupp; Ley, who committed suicide; and Bormann, who was never found but was tried *in absentia*.

problème du châtiment des crimes de guerre d'après les enseignments de la deuxième guerre mondiale (Cairo: R. Schindler, 1946). Sheldon Glueck, *War Criminals: Their Prosecution and Punishment* (New York: Alfred A. Knopf, Inc., 1944).

4. J. W. Bruegel, "*Das Schicksal der Strafbestimmungen des Versailler Vertrages,*" in *Vierteljahrshefte fuer Zeitgeschichte*, Vol. VI, No. 3, 1958, pp. 263–70.

5. *Occupation of Japan*, Department of State Publication 2671 (Washington: US Government Printing Office). *Judgment of the International Tribunal for the Far East* (Tokyo, November, 1948).

6. *Nazi Conspiracy and Aggression* (hereinafter referred to as NCA), Supp. A, M-161 (Washington: US Government Printing Office, 1946–47), p. 1225.

7. *History of UNWCC*, pp. 107–8. Also *Documents on United States Foreign Relations 1943–1944* (Washington: US Government Printing Office, 1945), pp. 231–32.

8. Jeschek, *op. cit.*, p. 123.

9. Robert H. Jackson, *Report to the International Conference on Military Trials, London, 1945*, Department of State Publication 3080 (Washington: US Government Printing Office, 1949), p. 17. Hereinafter referred to as *Jackson Report*.

10. *Ibid.*, p. 5.

11. *Foreign Relations of the United States. The Conference of Berlin (the Potsdam Conference) 1945*, Vol. II (Washington: US Government Printing Office, 1960), pp. 984–85.

12. *Ibid.*, p. 572.

13. *Trial of the Major War Criminals before the International Military Tribunal, Nuremberg, 14 November 1945–10 October 1946*, Vol. I (Nuremberg, 1947–49), p. 137. Hereinafter referred to as N I, N II, etc.

14. N III, p. 403.

15. N II, pp. 102–3.

16. Karl Jaspers, "The Significance of the Nuremberg Trials for Germany and the World," in *Notre Dame Lawyer*, Vol. XXII, January, 1947.

17. Rudolf Hoess, *Kommandant in Auschwitz* (Stuttgart: Deutsche Verlags-Anstalt, 1958), p. 125.

18. *Jackson Report*, pp. 299, 383–84.

19. *Ibid.*, p. 335.

20. *Ibid.*, p. 381.

21. A. N. Trainin, *Hitlerite Responsibility under Criminal Law*, A. Y. Vishinsky, ed., Andrew Rothstein, trans. (London: Hutchinson & Co., Ltd., 1945).

22. *Jackson Report*, p. 115.

23. N I, p. 95.

24. *Jackson Report*, p. 107.

25. *Life*, May 28, 1945, p. 34.

26. *Jackson Report*, pp. 104–5.

27. *Keesing's Contemporary Archives*, Vol. V (London), August 25, 1945.

28. N I, pp. 30–41.

29. Erich Kordt, *Wahn und Wirklichkeit* (Stuttgart: Union deutsche Verlagsgesellschaft, 1948), p. 351.

30. *Jackson Report*, p. 254.

31. N XII, pp. 157–306. Also N XVIII, pp. 164–89.

32. N I, p. 138.

33. Viktor von der Lippe, *Nuernberger Tagebuchnotizen November 1945 bis Oktober 1946* (Frankfurt a.M.: Fritz Knapp, 1951), p. 193.

34. Luise Jodl, unpublished biography of General Alfred Jodl.

35. *History of UNWCC.*

36. Lippe, *op. cit.*

37. Heinz Schroeter, *Stalingrad*, Constantine Fitzgibbon, trans. (New York: Ballantine Books, 1958).

38. Jodl, *op. cit.*

2

The Core of the Conspiracy

JULIUS STREICHER

The defendants who sat in the dock were an oddly mixed collection of the leadership of the Hitler period. Only a handful of them had kept their unquestioning *Treue* to the Fuehrer or retained his confidence intact until the end of the war. Schacht had been retired from his job as president of the Reichbank before the invasion of Poland and had been sent to a concentration camp toward the end of the war. After the July 20, 1944, attempt on Hitler's life, he had been defended before a Nazi People's Court by the same lawyer who was defending him at Nuremberg. Speer, a greatly gifted technician and organizer, had been one of the few men courageous enough to tell Hitler the war was lost. When he became aware that Hitler was in fact ordering the destruction of Germany, he worked out a plan to kill the Fuehrer in his bunker. Franz von Papen's secretary had been shot in 1934 by the SS at the time of the Roehm murder. Papen had been arrested but had afterward served the Nazi State both in Austria and Turkey, although he was always mistrusted by the Party. Neurath had been relieved of his post as chief administrator of Czechoslovakia before the start of the war with Russia, because his loyalties were suspect and it was thought he dealt too lightly with the Czech resistance. Only a few months before Hitler took power, Neurath (he was then Foreign Minister in Papen's Cabinet) had told Hindenburg that the naming of Hitler to the post of Reich Chancellor would be a catastrophe for German foreign policy. But he and Papen had wanted to keep their positions in the forefront of German political life, to

39

prevent worse things from happening, they told themselves, and it was for this that they had made their unstable peace with Hitler.

Among the men who had remained faithful to the Fuehrer to the end and beyond was Julius Streicher. His convictions about the baseness and wickedness of the Jews matched those of Hitler; they went far beyond the anti-Jewish regulations imposed by the Nuremberg Laws. Streicher said at his trial that he had not been called on to help frame this statute and had felt neglected. His anti-Semitism was of the brass-knuckles kind. He had delighted in the destruction of the synagogues, the beatings, the smashing of people and storefronts, in every turn of the screw, up to the Final Solution in the pits and gas chambers. He had always wanted the Jews exterminated. Streicher was the core within the core of the Party. He stood for the one thing all the defendants had in common. Although the others did their best to keep their distance from him, all had believed, in some part, at least, in the endlessly repeated message he wrote as editor of Der Stuermer, which had as a subtitle "Nuremberg weekly for the fight for truth."

He was in his way the perfect anti-Semite. This term, which came into use only in the latter part of the nineteenth century, replaced the earlier, cruder "hater of the Jews." Streicher had the qualities of the fanatic who could readily combine the medieval belief in the accursed Jew who was the killer of God with the contemporary anticapitalist, anti-Communist, anti-marketplace jargon of the Nazis and their immediate predecessors, recruited as most of them were from the uprooted, disenchanted millions brooding over Germany's incomprehensible World War I defeat—people no longer with a fixed place in their society. Anti-Semitism was international. The books of learned foreigners like Count Gobineau and Ernest Renan—who in the nineteenth century declared race instead of economics or geography or politics to be the decisive factor in history, and the Nordics to be the most creative and illustrious of the planet's inhabitants—had been eagerly seized upon by German writers like Wilhelm Marr, who seems to have invented the term "anti-Semite," and the economist Eugen Duehring, who believed that the Jewish religion was a sign of the inferior race and monotheism a sign of the Jews' desire to rule other people.[1] Racists of many varieties flourished. The Social Darwinists held that above all the species must be maintained, the unfit should be sterilized, the stronger races had the right to stamp out the weaker.[2] There were men like Arthur Moeller van den Bruck, who merely believed the Germans to be a superior people and who, in a book published in 1923, invented the name Hitler borrowed—the "Third Reich"; and Hans F. K. Guenter, who conducted an investigation in Dresden that showed the streetcar motormen to have more Northern blood than the conductors.*

* After Hitler came to power, Hans F. K. Guenter became a professor at the University of Jena.

In the purer forms of this racial doctrine, by no means limited to Germany but developed there with all the trappings of pseudoscholarship, the Jews were not to be improved, since they were racially inferior, as were the black and yellow peoples. They were nomads, moving in to plunder the healthy-minded farmers and workers who were the "real" Germans, or the "real" French or British. Édouard Drunon, in *La France Juive*, said that Jews were not French but merely lived in France as guests. Their mission, he said, was to destroy the middle class. As representatives of the anonymous capitalists, the Jews, not the French, were guilty of France's decadence. Drunon's book had one of the largest sales (more than one million copies) among the best-sellers of nineteenth-century European publishing. The German orientalist Adolf Wahrmund also bore down on the theme of the nomad Jew. So did Houston Stewart Chamberlain, who wrote of the enormous cultural accomplishments of the "Aryans." (The term was borrowed from authentic linguistic researchers of the nineteenth century—Max Mueller and others—who used it to identify the Indo-Germanic family of languages. In this meaning it had no connection whatever with race, but was merely concerned with speech.)

The new racist doctrine (the word "race" came into English and German through French and until late in the nineteenth century the Germans spelled it in the French fashion; only later did it become Germanized to *Rasse*) considered the Jew a mutation, a different kind of creature, a humanoid subspecies, a parasite living off the creativeness of superior races, one who could not be saved or changed by baptism. The medieval hatred of the Jew became secularized. He was unchangeable, as respectable scholars like Fichte and Treitschke saw him. In France, Russia, the United States, and England, the anti-Semites distributed learned books, pamphlets, and magazines, some of which, in America, were pornographic. When these doctrines reached the popularizers, who combined smut with their anti-Semitism, the Streichers came into their own. In Germany one Hartwig Hundt-Radowsky, a pre-Streicher writer on the subject, proposed that male Jews be sold to the English and castrated and the women turned over to prostitution. This would cleanse the country of the vermin, the bacilli that must be destroyed. Such writers were particularly persuasive to a lunatic fringe in Germany in the post-World War I years, which found Germans like Streicher in a new environment that had characteristics of a no-man's-land.

Germany at the beginning of the twentieth century had lived more than any other European country by a fixed protocol. Everyone had his place in the society and knew its forms. A French observer reported that even the thickness of the crust of pastry was supposed to be adapted to the social milieu or sex of the consumer: crustier servings for men and for women of the lower classes, more delicate ones for the *bürgerliche* Hausfrau. In such a society the loss of landmarks could only be explained by the existence of devils—that is, by people or forces outside the society's culture. The Jews became the targets. In the United States, Henry Ford in the *Dearborn Independent* made Jews guilty of causing the loss of the horse-and-buggy age, and he charged them with Marxism and Darwinism and starting wars and being responsible for short skirts and lipstick.[3] Lothrop Stoddard wrote on *The Rising Tide of Color*, and his *Revolt Against Civilization* was translated into German under the title *Der Kulturumsturz, die Drohung der Untermenschen* (The Overthrow of Culture, the Threat of the Inferior Races).

In Germany after World War I almost everything was worthless. Despite all the sacrifices and the victories, the war was lost, faiths were lost, property and jobs were lost. The signal lights had disappeared. The liberal principles that had helped emancipate the Jew now became the means of his destruction, for the religious absolutes of the Middle Ages were gone, and in a society where moral judgments were relative or meaningless it seemed reasonable to say that what was right for the *Volk*, the race, was the sole guide to the judgment of right and wrong. Political parties became sects; they existed for every shade of dissent. In Bavaria alone there were fifty parties in 1920. In the disordered Germany of the early 1920's Streicher was not the psychopath he would have been in, let us say, 1912. In the Germany of the 1930's his obscene, inept scribblings were a grotesque, distorting mirror of what both the rank and file and the Party leaders believed. In Nuremberg—the city he administered as Gauleiter and Statthalter—the Party found its spiritual home.

Streicher preached the central ideology of the movement, the one article of belief they all agreed on: The Jew was the sole or main cause of the disaster that had befallen Germany. Streicher was far closer to the springs of Adolf Hitler's undiluted anti-Semitism than was the muddled theoretician Alfred Rosenberg. Streicher was one of the few men whom Hitler called *Du*.[4] He had the lowest intelligence of the twenty-one accused, with an IQ of 102, and in his long and faithful years of service to the cult of anti-Semitism he had been brought to trial in both Party and German criminal courts for many offenses—offenses that ran all the way from slander to sadism to rape. In 1933 he was in fact suspended from his office as Gauleiter for the many irregularities that occurred in his province of Franconia, and in 1940 he was finally dismissed. But he kept on with his newspaper and his writing (in addition to *Der Stuermer*, he owned the *Fraenkische Zeitung*), and he kept his membership in the Reichstag, to which he had been elected in 1933. A Party court decided that he should be thrown out of the Party, but Hitler never approved this verdict. Streicher remained a Nazi both officially and at heart until he was hanged.[5]

Julius Streicher, born on February 12, 1885, was one of nine children in the family of a schoolteacher in Swabia. In World War I he fought in the infantry and rose to the rank of lieutenant in the Bavarian army, where he was awarded the Iron Cross, both first and second class. After the war he returned to civilian life to teach in an elementary school.

At this time Hitler was making speeches in the beer halls.* Streicher not only was among the first to join the Party, but brought to it his own sizable band of anti-Semites. He had had a speckled political career, having belonged to one of many branches of the Socialist Party for a time and then moving over to the ranks of those who, like the members of the German Werkgemeinschaft, placed blame for the woes of the German workers on the Jewish exploiters, who became the symbol of capitalism. In 1920 he had founded his own party, based wholly on anti-Semitism, and in 1921 he presented its entire membership as a gift to Hitler and the National Socialists. In 1925 he was named Gauleiter. Seven years later, after the Nazi seizure of power, there was almost no limit, despite his enemies in Munich and Berlin, to his importance in Franconia.

Streicher was married twice, the first time, in 1913, to Kunigunde Roth, a brewer's daughter from Bamberg who bore him two sons. She died in 1943,

* In the early days of the Party meetings, the Jews were uniformly identified, as they were to be throughout the Nazi period, with the capitalist right and the Marxist left, as well as with the cabalistic anti-Christians equipped with secret books and rituals. The "serfdom of interest" was also a favorite topic for an audience looking for plain labels to cure their malaise. The range of anti-Semitism was fairly wide. Hitler himself was employed between 1919 and 1920 as a V-man, or agent of the Army, and he took part as an instructor in the "Enlightenment Courses" given at the Lechfeld barracks, designed against leftist ideas. Hitler's Army audience consisted mainly of returning prisoners of war about to be demobilized. He was never (as he and Roehm and many others reported) an officer of instruction in the Reichswehr. The Army continued to refer to him as Gefreiter—still the corporal of World War I—but he delivered lectures to soldiers and noncommissioned officers in the same general program as the university professors who gave courses to the officers. Hitler talked on a variety of subjects: the Brest-Litovsk Treaty, conditions of peace and reconstruction, social and economic slogans, and political questions. But no matter what he discussed, he always made his position clear on the Jews and their responsibility for the ills of Germany.

While Hitler was still in the Army (he was discharged on March 31, 1920), he made his first speeches in the beer halls. In fact, it was as a political agent of the Army that he first came to know the German Workers' Party, which became the National Socialist Workers' Party. Army reports were made on those meetings. The Bavarian Government, because of the unstable and dangerous situation in Munich after the collapse of the Raeterepublik, had moved to Bamberg, and since it was part of the Army's job in the absence of the civil government to keep track of political trends in the capital of the *Land*, observers were sent to the meetings where the Hitlers and the Streichers talked. It is interesting to note that the Army in its "Enlightenment Courses," possibly because of the tastes of the man put in charge, Captain Mayr, who was later to join the Social Democratic Party and to die in Buchenwald, made use of both Feder, whose only theme was the serfdom of interest, and Hitler, two of the favorite beer-hall speakers. The Army accounts of the meetings were all marked by a detectable bias in favor of the nationalist sentiments of the speakers. But they matter-of-factly describe how dissidents would sometimes shout out their objections. One such account tells how a man "who called Herr Hitler a monkey" was "quietly" told to leave, and how a man who yelled "Pfui" was hustled out and taken under police protection. From the use the Army made of Adolf Hitler, and from the tone of the reports concerning him and similar anti-Semitic spellbinders, it seems clear that the younger officers covering such meetings, as well as their superiors, believed in at least half the equation so popular in the beer halls—namely, that the Jews were not only the wheels of the leftist parties but of the threatening revolution as well (Ernst Deuerlein, "Dokumentation. Hitlers Eintritt in die Politik und die Reichswehr," in *Vierteljahrshefte fuer Zeitgeschichte*, Vol. VII, No. 2, 1959, pp. 177–227).

and early in 1945 Streicher married his secretary, Adele Tappe, so they could die together in Nuremberg, he told the court, in the last-ditch defense of the city.

Even in the 1920's the children in Streicher's classes in the elementary school where he taught were told to greet him with "Heil Hitler" when class began. He made such a nuisance of himself among his fellow teachers—accusing them of taking part in the anti-German republican attack on the minds of their pupils, and taking sick leave at a time when his health permitted him to join a rally of the Brownshirts in Munich—that charges were brought against him in 1928. An eighty-seven-page report by the school commission found him guilty of conduct unbecoming a teacher, and he was dismissed from his post. This biographical item he proudly added, after the Nazis came to power, to his sketch in the German *Who's Who*.[6]

Streicher's real teaching was done outside the classroom. When he first heard Hitler speak, he knew immediately that this was the leader to whom he could devote his energies and life. A man sitting next to him in the beer hall said that he could see a halo around Adolf Hitler's head, and with this Streicher was always to agree. But so erratic was the working of his mind that he managed to be in constant trouble, even after 1933, with influential members of the Party leadership—men who were ordinarily not overconcerned with peccadilloes of a Gauleiter as long as he remained unconditionally faithful to the Fuehrer and the creeds. Streicher, no matter how devoted to Hitler and to the faith of the Party, was so dishonest, so corrupt with his drive toward easy money and his sadism, that the Party leaders, for all their disposition to black-and-white judgments, had to take account of his criminality. He basked in the substantial comforts of a Gauleiter and favorite of the Fuehrer. He not only could drive when others had to walk during the war years, but used the precious gasoline to drive to the stores to get food for his dog. He was even unable to keep out of trouble with eminences like Goering, who were in a position to threaten his sybaritic life. When Goering became the father of Edda, Streicher was foolish enough to write that the Reichsmarschall was only indirectly the father of the child, who had really been conceived by means of artificial insemination. Goering was angered by the accusation, which, although later retracted by Streicher, remained a barrier between them. It was Goering who appointed the commission that scrutinized Streicher's personal life and business transactions and led to his partial retirement in 1940.

The letters written to *Der Stuermer* by admiring readers, and the columns of the paper, plainly reveal the role of the man who was for almost twenty years the master rabble-rouser of the Party. The files of *Der Stuermer* are full of letters that tell of malign experiences. One is from a mental hospital, where the writer had been sent, he confides, as a result of a Jewish conspiracy. Another man (this was in the 1920's) said that he was fed opium by the Jewish head of the asylum where he was a patient and that people made loud noises to keep him awake while other pretended to be ghosts as part of a plot to derange him. A dentist wrote to complain of a Jewish colleague whose gold plates, he said, disintegrated. One *Stuermer* subscriber wrote that a shirt he had bought in a Jewish-owned shop was not delivered. Another complained that his boss was philandering with a Jewish girl and that in effect the employees of the factory were paying for the immoral conduct of its owner. One of the favorite topics of writers of *Der Stuermer* involved the proof that Christ was not a Jew. A reader wrote to Streicher asking for help in proving this contention, which he said he had heard from friends and acquaintances among priests and religious families. The concern to Aryanize Christ was by no means limited to a few provincial readers. It was shared, among others, by Hitler and Himmler.

Young men wrote in to protest that girls they knew danced with Jews, or that a Jew was seen at a party in the field gray of the German Wehrmacht. Nothing was too small or preposterous for the subscribers of *Der Stuermer* or for its editor if it had to do with the guilt of the Jews for the woes of the world. When the *Hindenburg* exploded at Lakehurst, New Jersey, Streicher declared that this too was part of the Jewish plot. He and his readers were full of concern for German traditions. Even on the subject of women's fashions, issues of vice were raised. On the appearance of the *Bubikopf* (bobbed hair) in the 1920's, *Der Stuermer* said that it was a plot to destroy sound German mores and the even sounder German Hausfrau, and that it was invented by the Jewish Bolshevist conspiracy to break up German society. A subscriber wrote, "This is no matter of harmless style. It is a Jewish attack, an Oriental influence to make visible the Jewish victory over Christians. The *Bubikopf* is Bolshevism." [7] Another reader, indignant over the malicious rumor that Streicher had in his house a maid who wore the abominable haircut, wrote that he knew this to be another Jewish swindle and hoped that Streicher would deny it in order to give the lie to the spreaders of such libels.

The stories of alleged histories of ritual murder and of the luring of children to what would have been their doom had it not been for the resourcefulness of the child or adult who saw through the Jew's offer of candy, the stories of the girls saved from fates worse than death, which appeared in the articles and books issued by the paper, were matched by the experiences of the subscribers. One man told how a Party lad riding in a train saw a German girl offered a banana by a Jew sitting in the same compartment, and but for the fortunate presence of the Nazi (doubtless himself) she would inevitably have fallen victim to his wily approach.

Streicher carried a riding whip as he strode through his Gau, and his personal life was enlivened, as dozens of people testified during his many trials, by beatings that he liked to administer in the presence of witnesses. Once, he visited the Nuremberg jail where a young man was imprisoned for some minor offense, and, with two friends watching him, beat the youth with a whip. He felt relieved, he said, after that; he often needed to work off his tensions in this fashion. Another time, he was accused of rape, and he was over and over again sued for libel. The Party *Bonzen* found his mendacity and thievery too much; like his anti-Semitism they were gross. What he stole was meant to enrich him. This was different from the case of Goering's art collection, which went to the semiofficial Karinhall and then perhaps later might go to the Reich. The inquiry into his activities proved that he made a good deal of money by way of the transfer of Jewish properties in his Gau. A Jewish factory, house, or car that had to be "Aryanized" was normally sold at figures fixed by the State. While the Jewish owners rarely if ever got the amount the government agency said was the fair value of the property, the "Aryan" buyer was supposed to pay the official sum, and any difference between the selling price and the official price was to benefit the Reich. But Streicher and his friends were too experienced in the illegal byways of the Party and too firmly convinced of their rights to the perquisites due them to be taken in by this law. The corruption in Nuremberg was such that the Goering commission investigating Streicher was able to return 63,938.92 RM to the vaults of the Reich. On the average, 10 per cent of the official price was paid by friends of Streicher for the Jewish property they acquired, and in some of the exchanges thousands of marks could be made in a day. One man paid 100 RM for an automobile with a tax value of 1,850 RM, then made a gift of 100 RM to the SA. He thereupon gave the car to his brother, who ran a garage, because he himself already had a car. A Gauamtsleiter named Schoeller was able for 5,000 RM to get a piece of land valued at 50,000 RM. Another property, bought for 4,200 RM, was sold a week later for 48,000 RM.[8] One city councilor was given a Christmas present of 8,000 RM, and other smaller gifts as well, by a grateful constituent who had bought a piece of property advantageously. The councilor himself was expected to make a present to the Party organization, in this case the Bund Deutscher Maedel, but he never got around to doing that. Another official was given large sums —15,000 RM, 11,000 RM, and 12,000 RM at various times—and cars were put at his disposal for his friendly aid on behalf of a buyer. With the help of men like these, property could be exchanged among friends, and official city forms could be filled out and filed without question. Streicher bought a factory, the Mars Werke, for 5 per cent of its face value, paying 5,600 RM instead of the 112,500 RM at which it was valued. He did very well, as may be seen by the fact that he sold a villa he owned on Lake Constance to the Hungarian Consul in Munich for 240,000 RM, a transaction that was completed without the Consul's even bothering to take a look before he bought. Streicher testified at Nuremberg that he had never been paid for his services as Gauleiter. He obviously needed no salary of such relatively modest proportions.[9]

For all these elaborate dealings and for his personal vices, Streicher was reprimanded from time to time, and in 1940 he was finally deprived by Hitler of his Party post of Gauleiter. But eminences of the Party continued to visit him, and he continued to hold his editorial position and to engage in writing. First and foremost, he was a crusading anti-Semite, *the* anti-Semite of Germany, one of the old fighters of the movement. It was hard for the Fuehrer to think that any man with those qualifications would be capable of deep wrong to the world's foremost Aryan state.

Streicher set the crane in motion that started the demolition of the main synagogue in Nuremberg. He told the court that people had complained that it contrasted incongruously with the rest of the architecture of the old city, so he had ordered its destruction. But he had a good deal of help. Later, at the time of the modestly named *Kristallnacht*, it was the Nuremberg fire department that burned down the remaining synagogues, although a number of observers pointed out that the population as a whole disapproved of the wanton damage. At Nuremberg Streicher declared that he had shared this disapproval, although at the time he wrote editorials saying the Jews got what they deserved.

Streicher wrote at great length on the ritual murders committed by the Jews, and devoted a special number of *Der Stuermer* to the topic. The Jews, he told a mass meeting of the Anti-Jewish World League in 1935, were preparing for the greatest ritual murder of all time—a new war.[10] He demonstrated that the Jews were responsible for the depression, the unemployment, and the inflation in Germany; that Jews were white slavers; that 90 per cent of the prostitutes in Germany were brought to their profession by Jews; that Jews had taken over the businesses and best lands of the indulgent Germans; and that Jews who had swarmed in from the East had become millionaires in a short time. He quoted alleged Jewish sources which said it was legal and moral to violate a non-Jewish girl who was more than three years old. Jews believed, he declared, that Christ's mother was a whore, that Christ's real name was Ben Studa (whore's son).[11] They also believed, he wrote, that Christian money had no real owner, and that Jews had every right to take it away. In fact, according to Streicher, the Jews believed that all non-Jewish women were whores and that a marriage between a Jew and a Christian was really whoredom. He said too that Jews held it to be a great sin for a Jew to make a present to a Christian; he might help the poor and visit the sick but this would only be a cover for his sinister activities. The Jew was the eternal racial enemy, the Marxist, the Bolshevik, and the capitalist wire-puller. Streicher foamed against all this, and the slavery of interest as well.

Streicher's teachings were repeated, albeit in more refined form, by many of his betters. Any number of the respectable Germans testifying at Nuremberg or writing depositions—generals and diplomats and character witnesses—stated that the crude anti-Semitism of the Party fanatics was, of course, repugnant to them, but at the same time the Eastern Jews, who were different from the German Jews, had swarmed in from Poland after World War I and had done a land-office business during the German inflation and depression, to the enormous disadvantage not only of the German people but also of their own fellow Jews, the victims of the anti-Semitism the Eastern Jews unleashed. The writers of *Der Stuermer* and other anti-Semite publications invented stories that the more sophisticated of their countrymen thought funny or ridiculous. For example, there was the story of a Polish count who forced a neighbor's Jewish serfs to climb trees and call out "cuckoo," and would then shoot them and declare he had killed a cuckoo, not a Jew. And to appease his neighbor he would make him a present of ten of his own Jews. While the more normal Nazis balked at stories of shooting Jews out of trees, they shook their heads over the presence of Jews in Germany and said too many of them were there.

German action against the Jews was stimulated by Poland's anti-Semitic legislation. The Polish Government announced in 1938 that anyone holding a Polish passport who had lived outside Poland for five years would lose his citizenship. The Reich promptly moved to expel Polish Jews, and when the Poles refused to accept them, these exiles with no legal status of any kind would often move back and forth for weeks in a no-man's-land between the borders. It was the son of such a family who shot vom Rath in the Paris Embassy of the German Government on November 7, 1938, and this gave Goebbels the pretext for organizing the pogrom of the *Kristallnacht*.

Nothing Streicher wrote was far from the Fuehrer's own thinking. Hitler had written in *Mein Kampf*: "The blackhaired Jew-boy lurks for hours, his face set in a satanic leer, waiting for the blissfully ignorant girl whom he defiles with his blood." [12] For foreign consumption such statements were watered down. For example, when Frick addressed the foreign diplomats in Berlin in 1934, he used the same statistics as Streicher but explained how fairly and decently the Jews were being deprived of their jobs and means of living. Since foreigners were likely to be squeamish, he added that the United States too had its immigration laws designed to protect its racial integrity.

Against Streicher's violent attacks, the Jews, before Hitler's coming to power, took legal and extralegal measures designed to awaken the public conscience. They sued Streicher and often were awarded damages: sums of 200 RM and 300 RM. Sometimes Streicher was sentenced to jail, where he stayed for a few days before returning to his paper and his onslaughts. In the early 1920's individual Jews even invaded the beer halls where the Nazi speakers talked to audiences of up to 5,000. A rabbi rose to his feet after the notorious Jew-baiter Ruetz had spoken and, despite catcalls and boos, tried to answer Ruetz's charges that the Talmud enjoins the Jews when they go to war to fight in the rear lines so they can be first in the retreat. The rabbi was escorted to the door; his five friends were struck and pushed around before being expelled from the hall. Ruetz had declared that the Jews tried to prevent the dissemination of the Talmud. The rabbi replied that, on the contrary, many copies were available in the city library. Shouts and beatings were the only result.

In the 1920's and on into the late 1930's—well after the Nazis were entrenched in power—an attempt was made to counterattack the anti-Semite propaganda by organizations of Jewish veterans of World War I who had fought in the front lines for Germany, or, as they had then believed, for their country. One such group was made up of Zionists who favored emigration. Others, like the Renewal Movement of German Jews (Erneuerungsbewegung der juedischen Deutschen), wanted to take part somehow in the rebuilding of Germany, even under the National Socialists. The police records disclose orders to forbid speakers for such assimilationist groups from addressing Jewish audiences but permitting the Zionist speakers to appear before meetings.[13]

At this time Himmler, Goering, Bormann, and the rest were thinking in terms of a solution that would rid Germany of its Jews by emigration, forced and voluntary. Madagascar as a possible Jewish colony was first talked about in 1938.

The Jewish war veterans wrote letters of exhortation and protest to one another and to Nazi officials, saying they too wanted to participate in Germany's renewal. Following the Nazi cult of physical fitness, they called on the sons and daughters of their membership to come out for exercise. Sometimes they were even useful to the Government—for example, during the Olympic Games of 1936, when the Propaganda Ministry utilized the occasion to impress world opinion with German tolerance as well as the exemplary health and physique of its people. The members of the Makkabi and the Jewish Front Line Soldiers were permitted for a few weeks to use German athletic fields on certain days—at hours when they would not contaminate the Aryan population that played games there. As part of their counterattack they put out, in Nuremberg, a newspaper called first the *Anti-Stuermer*, and later *The Light*.

Streicher went on telling the Germans how the Jews were poisoning them, how Salvarsan, according to an eminent medical practitioner's article in *Der Stuermer*, was really a poison and had never cured anyone of syphilis. The doctor, Erwin Silber, was one of the innumerable so-called "Reform" doctors who flourished in Germany—men who opposed "school medicine" and relied on a therapy of herbs and diets. Silber said that the drug not only had cured no one but had caused brain damage. He had written a pamphlet on the subject, and the article about him in *Der Stuermer* declared that he too was a fuehrer and "we should follow his leadership."

Streicher published exciting stories for children, made speeches to them, and wrote plays for them. The children responded. One of them wrote to reveal that his aunt traded at Jewish stores, and another offered to supply a list of the customers who dealt with a Jewish firm. Streicher arranged puppet shows. In a gathering on Christmas Eve, he told his audience of children that the father of the Devil was the Jew. Then he asked them, "Who is the father of the Devil?" and the children chorused, "The Jew! The

Jew!" Deep as was his feeling for the little Germans he talked to, he had not a shred of sympathy for the children of the abominable race. When they were excluded step by step from the public life of Germany—from the theaters, the motion pictures, the schools—he wrote, "Yes, they are weeping now, but their tears will do them no good." Under his imprint, picture books for children were published showing drawings of blond German children jeering while Jewish children had to leave school, "Crying, weeping, fury and anger doesn't help. Away with the Jewish Brood," wrote the author.[14]

Some of Streicher's articles must have seemed badly timed to the Fuehrer. In January, 1938, the London *News Chronicle* reported that Hitler had banned *Der Stuermer* for a period because of an article advocating the death penalty for Jews who had relations with Aryan women. The law that provided for such a penalty was actually decreed after the war began.

Streicher had always been clear in his understanding of what Hitler meant and what needed to be done. In a speech in April, 1925, he said that it was time to destroy the Jews.[15] At the start of the war, in September, 1939, a letter in *Der Stuermer* urged that the Jewish people be exterminated root and branch. "The Jewish question," Streicher wrote in that same month, "won't find its solution by way of emotional reactions [*Affekt-Handlungen*] but through discipline and seeing into the future." Hitler, too, commented on the differences between emotional anti-Semitism and what he called "the anti-Semitism of reason." In a letter written as early as September, 1919, he had said that the anti-Semitism of reason had to follow a planned legal getting rid (*Beseitigung*) of the Jews—and no wonder, for the same letter declared that Jews were the cause of racial tuberculosis.[16] Neither Hitler nor Streicher was ever to change his mind, nor were their minds ever at odds on this issue so fundamental to their fixed ideas.

Der Stuermer had had a top circulation of between 600,000 and 800,000. During the war it averaged 150,000 to 200,000.[17] But its covert readership and its influence were extensive. It served the tastes and beliefs of a wider audience than just the subscribers, for Streicher delighted in tales of blood and murder and death, and so did his readers.

In May, 1939, three months before the pact with the Soviet Union was signed, *Der Stuermer* published an article that said, "There must be a punitive expedition against the Jews in Russia, a punitive expedition which will provide the same fate for them that every murderer and criminal must expect: death sentence and execution. The Jews in Russia must be killed. They must be utterly exterminated. Then the world will see that the end of the Jews is also the end of Bolshevism." [18] On October 31, 1939, Streicher told a German audience, "This is our mission at home, to approach these future decisions without hesitation, to do our duty and to remain strong. We know the enemy, we have called him by name for the last twenty years: he is the World Jew. And we know that the Jew must die." [19] Early in January, 1940, *Der Stuermer* declared editorially, "The time is near when a machine will go into motion which is going to prepare a grave for the world's criminal—Judah—from which there will be no resurrection." On July 4 the paper declared, "Pogroms were at all times demonstrations of the will of the people." A little later it said, "Jewry is criminality. The Jewish rabble will be exterminated like weeds and vermin."

Streicher found supporters and friends not only in Germany but in Anglo-Saxon and other countries as well. In May, 1935, he had written to the British Fascist Oswald Mosley, congratulating him on a speech. Mosley had replied to thank him and to say that as long as the Jews still governed people, the world would not be liberated. "Everywhere," he wrote, "the Jew is in power." Streicher's views were shared, as late as 1946, in the notes written by Jodl in Nuremberg after he was sentenced, in which the condemned general said that the Nazi program had not been all evil, that Hitler had aimed at ridding Germany of the shackles of the Versailles *Diktat*, of Marxism and the concept of the class struggle, and of the cultural and economic domination of the life of Germany by the Jews. To some degree this kind of apologia appeared in the testimony of all the defendants at Nuremberg, as well as in the stock of beliefs of any number of enlightened Germans, whether of the Army or politics or industry.

Streicher was charged on two counts in the indictment: having conspired to commit aggressive warfare and committing crimes against humanity. He made a poor appearance on the witness stand with his shaven bullethead and incoherent fulminations against his enemies who were all around him. He seemed both insane and criminal. He told the court that he had been beaten up by American Negro soldiers after his arrest. This testimony was struck from the record on Justice Jackson's motion. If the testimony had been permitted, the court would have had to conduct an investigation. Streicher's accusations were likely to be illusionary, but this one may have been true. He fought in open court with his lawyer, an able attorney by the name of Marx, over the manner in which Marx was conducting the case. Aside from the accusation of having plotted aggressive warfare, there was not much that Streicher could be defended against. Marx, questioning his client as carefully as possible, nevertheless was unable to avoid touching off paranoid reactions. Streicher was sharply reprimanded by the President of the Court and told he would be sent back to his cell if he did not behave himself. Mr. Justice Robert Jackson wanted him cited for contempt of court, but the president quietly told Marx to resume his questioning. Streicher made speeches again, but this time to a critical audience. "If it is proved that someone," he shouted wildly, "says that we are forcing Hitler into war, then I can certainly say that a man who knows that Hitler is being forced into war is a mass murderer." Nazi Germany, he declared, had permitted the same freedom of the press as the democratic countries. When asked why he had beaten up a man (he had done this in one of his sadistic onsets), he said that his victim had behaved in such a cowardly fashion that it became necessary to chastise him.[20]

He was capable of crude political gestures that comported with the Nazi view that a man who had committed even a serious transgression might still be saved if he were Aryan. He told the court how in his benevolence he had given an annual Christmas party in the 1930's in the Deutscher Hof in Nuremberg for men let out for the day from the nearby concentration camp at Dachau.[21] But there was really not much that could be dug up in his defense. The other dedicated anti-Semites of his stripe among his fellow prisoners were quiet now and even turned their backs on him. He had been the most conspicuous preacher of the crusade they had all joined, but now that the words were heard out of context they sounded like zombi shrieks— shrill, ranting, filled with hate—and the other defendants wanted nothing to do with them. Still, the position of the "correct" ones at Nuremberg and in the rest of Germany had somehow to be justified. For these people there was the other argument, shared by millions of reputable, well-meaning citizens, that while the excesses of the Streichers were of course deplorable, they themselves had never countenanced or participated in them. They told one another and the court at Nuremberg that there had been too many Jewish lawyers, doctors, and university professors, and too much Jewish influence in the cultural life of Germany—its theater, music, books, newspapers. Furthermore, the Jews from the East had made enormous sums from the German inflation. It was never explained by what black magic these Eastern Jews, speaking little or no German and themselves impoverished, managed these wonders against even the competition of their German coreligionists. There were too many rich Jews, too many Jewish bankers, too few Jewish farmers. (In one Nazi view, the city was corrupt, morally enervating. City people had no opportunity of breathing the fresh Volkish air that sustained farmers.) The Germans had wanted to get rid of the Jews by shipping them to Madagascar or some other remote place (although the argument here could become circular, for it was widely held that, if transported, the Jews would form a center of the conspiracy against Germany, and they should therefore not be allowed to emigrate to Palestine or Madagascar or anywhere else). No place on earth existed for Jews. Ghettos were centers of crime, but if Jews lived outside them it would be repulsive to the healthy racial sense of the Germans to have to see them in the trains, restaurants, and other public places.

This attitude was exemplified in the case of two SS men who in the course of the war against Poland had killed fifty unarmed Jews. In defense it was said that one of the SS men was especially sensitive on the Jewish question and had unfortunately been given a gun while he guarded the Jews, who were members of a working party. The chance coming together of the Jewish workers, the sensitive SS man, and the gun that was handed to him resulted in the shootings. There was an Army trial of this crime, conducted by German officers. The Army prosecution asked for death sentences, but the men were sentenced to nine years' and three years' imprisonment, respectively. Both, however, were pardoned as part of a general amnesty after a few months. The Army, in trying them at all, was following a tradition that had gone out of fashion. Hitler had ordered that no penalties be imposed on soldiers who attacked or killed Jews. The Army had managed to water down the effect of this invitation to mayhem and murder by declaring that the order applied only in cases when a soldier was not acting for his personal advantage.[22]

In the Reich the steps toward a violent solution of the Jewish problem were gradual. The mythical crimes, such as ritual murder (beloved of the early issues of Der Stuermer), and the tales of seduction, rape, thievery, and blood lust (ranging from the orthodox slaughter of animals to the alleged finding of a child's body from which the blood had been drained) were part of an anachronistic, lunatic folklore that went back to the medieval belief that the Devil was a Jew. But the legends of Jewish enrichment at the expense of honest and exploited Germans, of the Jewish capitalist in league with an international cabal of the Right or with the Jewish Communists came closer to the conspiratorial solutions that were part of the folklore of the twentieth century. Such legends took root especially among provincial, unsophisticated peoples, as may be seen in the anti-Catholic, anti-Negro, anti-yellow crusades of the late nineteenth and early twentieth centuries in the United States and other countries. The doctrines of race and of the innate desirable and undesirable characters of sections of mankind not only were widely accepted by the half-educated, but also preached by the learned. A Nobel Prize winner in physics, Professor Philipp Lenard, would one day speak up on behalf of a "German physics." The head of anthropology of the Kaiser Wilhelm Institut in Berlin appeared at a meeting with SS men to discuss what might be done to get rid of inferior races in the East. There was no lack of respectability for the race theory that won the hearts of millions of Germans. Racial animus raged through Germany, as it did in France, Eastern Europe, and parts of the American South and North. But in Germany it came to power through a sizable minority and bolstered by a theoretical structure. The racial doctrine in its most dogmatic and fanatical form Streicher made his own; he concentrated on the subhuman qualities of one "race," although Der Stuermer also took for granted the inferiority of the Negro. But once the black French regiments had left the Rhine, Negroes held little interest for Streicher. The Germans who later opposed the violent measures—and many of them did (the SD and other eyewitness reports are filled with examples of public resentment)—could do little about it. The German population reacted unfavorably to the boycott of Jewish stores led by Streicher in 1933, the burning of the synagogues, and the destruction of other Jewish property, as was remarked by Streicher, the SD, and foreign observers. But public opinion was of little importance; it was merely something to be manipulated. The German population as a whole did not know until after the war of the existence of extermination camps. This was a closely held secret, despite Allied broadcasts and handbills distributed by the Resistance, whose members operated at the risk of their lives. The Streichers who knew of them were enthusiastic.

Streicher's mind was filled with phantoms, and much of his life was lived second hand. He had a large collection of pornography.[23] A servant girl who worked for him was examined at his request for her virginity because she had previously worked for a Jew who had a Christian wife. In 1938 he asked the inmates of the concentration camp at Dachau whether ther wives were faithful and if they said "yes" asked them how they could know. He questioned children about their sex practices—for example, whether they masturbated. He told them that he himself had nightly wet dreams and once showed his chauffeur the semen to prove it.

The discipline committee of the public school system that reviewed Streicher's case in 1928 pointed out that he had been repeatedly punished for criminal slander; that in 1922 he had paid a fine of 2,000 RM on the complaint of members of the Jewish community; and that in 1923 he was fined 10 million RM for having said that a Jew had wanted to murder an anti-Semitic speaker (this was the year of the inflation, and 10 million RM was an insignificant sum). In May, 1924, when the currency had been revalued, he paid a 200-RM fine for slander, and in June he had to pay another 200 RM or go to jail for twenty days for the same offense. He paid 200 RM for saying that a Party member he disliked had taken food from a canteen during World War I, and he was fined 2,100 RM for having accused a man of adultery. In December, 1925, he was sentenced to two months in jail for having written that the mayor of Nuremberg, an old opponent named Luppe, did favors for relatives and for the Jews. The school discipline committee that examined the evidence against him sentenced Streicher to another 500-RM fine, but in extenuation pointed out that he had served twenty-four years in the school system and had a good war record. They censured the conduct of the mayor, who, they said, while on an official visit had gone into an old-clothes store and bought an overcoat, which they considered undignified behavior.

While Streicher headed the lunatic fringe of the Party, his betters were not far behind. One learned man, Staatsrat Professor Kurt Astel, professor for research on human heredity and race politics (*menschliche Erbforschung und Rassenpolitik*) at the University of Jena, answered the hypothetical question whether his daughter should be permitted to marry a man one of whose eight great-grandparents was a Jew. He would have to tell his daughter, he said, that she should not enter into such a marriage because she would then have Jewish relatives. In World War I, he said, he had met Jews who took pride in their ancestry. One man, for example, one-quarter Jew, had told him that while the other three-quarters of his ancestors and all of Astel's were climbing trees the Jews had a flourishing culture. Now, declared Astel, a German hero in the person of Adolf Hitler had appeared, and one cannot make a compromise with this problem. The country must be not only free of Jews but free of people with Jewish ancestry.[24]

The protests of patriotic Jews in the early days of the Nazi regime—for example, a letter written in 1934 by the former company commander of a Saxon regiment, a Jew, saying that the anti-Jewish demonstrations in Hamburg had unfortunately been seen by many foreigners at a time when the German Government was negotiating a commercial treaty with the English—were kept in the Streicher files, but they might as well have been thrown in the wastebasket. The former Jewish commander wrote that such actions harmed the German fatherland of the Jews and the Aryans as well. The Jews, he said, had suffered a great deal in silence, but he was writing this letter in the interest of Germany. Every German should try to prevent foreign misunderstanding of Germany, and the singing of such Nazi songs as one heard in Leipzig should, in the Reich's interest, be forbidden. He hoped that the Gauleitung would understand his concern for the German fatherland and signed the letter "With the German greeting!"—the closest to "Heil Hitler" he could possibly come. Another letter, written in 1933 by the Association of Jewish War Veterans, said they wanted to do their share in reshaping the German fatherland. This letter had been sent to *Der Stuermer* by a reader who was indignant over the arrogance of the Jews in presuming to want to help.*

The plans for sending the Jews to Madagascar or permitting *Mischlinge* to keep positions in industry, which Rudolf Hess approved of for a time, seem mild enough when compared with actual events. In November, 1938, a year in which Jews were still permitted to have *Sportsvereine*, their right to wear the uniforms of the German or Austrian armies was revoked. Some-

---

* The Army had similar documents (MA-31). One member of the organization, in a letter to President Hindenburg in March, 1934, said that many of the Jews in the Army had been rooted in Germany for decades and had done their duty as soldiers. What they wanted was to be honorably incorporated into the Nazi State, and this he considered to be important not only from the point of view of the Jews but for the Germans too. In World War I, he said, 100,000 Jews had served in the German Army. A letter from the "Aryan" wife of a Polish-born Jew said that two of her brothers had been killed in action fighting for Germany, that her four children were baptized Christians, and that her husband had been converted. She added that under the Nuremberg Laws the family would be cast out of the German community. The Ministry replied (Jan. 16, 1936) that it regretted it could not help, since it was a civil not a military case. Letters of appeal were also written to Hitler on behalf of Jewish notaries who had been wounded in World War I, many of them with high war decorations. Under the decree on professions they had to give up their practices, as did Jewish doctors and other professionals. Could they not serve Jewish clients, they asked, or be permitted to go on with their work if they had been in practice for many years? Some of them were still suffering from war injuries. Nothing came of these letters. But while Hindenburg was alive, Hitler had to deal far more carefully with Jewish war veterans than he would later.

times, for propagandistic or practical reasons, the policies evidenced a deceptive thaw, but they hardened inexorably in the direction of the Final Solution. In 1935 the Ministry of the Interior decided that in a factory owned by Jews the Reich flag could be hoisted if the majority of the workers were Aryans. With the Olympic Games coming up, the Ministry also announced that it did not want signs saying "Jews Not Wanted" to be seen in public places. Reports were reaching the Wilhelmstrasse that participation in the Olympic Games might be canceled by a number of countries in which the public reacted strongly against the Reich's treatment of Jews. That was the reason the Jewish organizations of war veterans were given permission to use sport fields. Hitler and the Foreign Office were determined, even at the price of making concessions to the Jews, to hold the games. The floodlights of propaganda to be turned on for the visitors from all over the world were so useful to the Nazis that they could permit a handful of Jews to play games together. Jews were also given the right to have their own youth hostels, but not more than twenty guests could be present at a time. The last signs of leniency were accorded the people who were accounted neither Jews nor Germans: a Fuehrer order of August 8, 1940, permitted the use of *Mischlinge* of the first grade (that is, those with two Jewish grandparents) in the Army as superior officers. But such men were always under suspicion—soldiers with the brand of Cain upon them. One of them, a submarine officer, when asked at Nuremberg by a prosecution lawyer if he had belonged to the Party, said in surprise, "I could not belong to the Party because of the Nuremberg Laws." He nevertheless had been awarded high decorations, owing to the friendly attitude of his immediate superior in the German Navy, which remained relatively free of the security forces' snooping after suspicious persons. But this submarine officer was an anomaly. The last words Hitler wrote in the bunker were a call to carry on the battle against the Jews.

Streicher was a restless prisoner at Nuremberg. Even before he was sentenced to be hanged he had nightmares and cried out in his sleep, disturbing the prisoners whose cells were near his. The court found him not guilty of having conspired to wage aggressive warfare, since he had taken no part in the plans for invasions and had not been a military, political, or diplomatic adviser to Hitler. No one had paid attention to anything he had said except on the one subject he had made his own. Streicher was the first among the *Bonzen* to preach publicly the extermination of the Jews, and when he heard that the death camps were in action he celebrated this as an achievement. He tore the veil from the respectable bourgeois anti-Semites, who shrank from him. Long before the Wannsee Conference, he told the Germans that the Jews had to be destroyed. In 1925 he warned his readers, "You must realize the Jews want our people to perish." If that was so—and Streicher and thousands of others were convinced it was—it followed that the Jews must be exterminated root and branch. He told a Nuremberg audience on April 3, 1925, "For thousands of years the Jews have been destroying peoples; make a beginning today [so] that we can destroy the Jew." [25] In 1937 he said, "The Jew always lives from the blood of other peoples, he needs such murders and such sacrifices. . . . The victory will be only entirely and finally achieved when the whole world is free of Jews." [26] In 1943, with the gas chambers working at full capacity, he wrote that Adolf Hitler was indeed freeing the world of its Jewish tormentors and that this "will be the greatest deed in the history of mankind." [27] And in *Der Stuermer*, January 6, 1944, he wrote, "Developments since the rise of National Socialism make it probable that the continent will be freed from its Jewish destroyers of people and exploiters forever, and the German example after the German victory in World War II will also serve to bring about the destruction of the Jewish world tormentors on other continents." [28]

Streicher never changed his mind. Nothing affected his private world. His last words when he mounted the steps to the gallows were "Heil Hitler."

NOTES

1. Alexander Bein, "*Der moderne Antisemitismus und seine Bedeutung fuer die Judenfrage*," in *Vierteljahrshefte fuer Zeitgeschichte*, Vol. VI, No. 4, 1958, pp. 340–60.

2. Hans Buchheim, Martin Broszat, Hans-Adolf Jacobsen, Helmut Krausnick, *Anatomie des SS-Staates*, Vol. II (Olten and Freiburg i. Br.: Walter-Verlag, 1965), p. 296.

3. John Dos Passos, "*Der Autokoenig. Zum Bilde von Henry Ford*," in *Sueddeutsche Zeitung*, May 5/6, 1962.

4. Otto Dietrich, *12 Jahre mit Hitler* (Munich: Isar Verlag, 1955), p. 172.

5. Count Lutz Schwerin von Krosigk, *Es geschah in Deutschland* (Tuebingen and Stuttgart: Rainer Wunderlich Verlag Hermann Leins, 1952), p. 265.

6. *Wer Ist's?* (Berlin: Degener Verlag, 1935), p. 1573.

7. *Der Stuermer*, January 19, 1927 (B.D.C.).

8. N XXVIII, 1757-PS, p. 103.

9. *Ibid.*, pp. 55-234.

10. N XXXVIII, 002-M, pp. 111–12.

11. *Juedische Selbstbekenntnisse* (Leipzig: Hammer Verlag, 1929).

12. Adolf Hitler, *Mein Kampf* (Munich: Zentralverlag der NSDAP, Franz Eher Nachf., 1941), Chap. XI, "*Volk und Rasse*," p. 357.

13. Hans Mommsen, "*Der nationalsozialistische Polizeistaat und die Judenverfolgung vor 1938*," in *Vierteljahrshefte fuer Zeitgeschichte*, Vol. X, No. 1, 1962, pp. 68–87.

14. Elvira Bauer, *Ein Bilderbuch fuer Gross und Klein* (Nuremberg: Stuermer-Verlag, 1936). Quoted in 32-M.

15. NCA VIII, 013-M, p. 11.

16. "Letter to Gemlich, September 16, 1919," in *Vierteljahrshefte fuer Zeitgeschichte*, Vol. VII, No. 2, 1959, pp. 203–5.

17. N XII, p. 342.

18. *Ibid.*, 811-D, p. 358.

19. NCA V, 2583-PS, p. 311.

20. N XII, pp. 338, 339, 368.

21. *Ibid.*, p. 334.

22. N XX, pp. 449–51, also N XXXV, 421-D, pp. 91–93.

23. Schwerin von Krosigk, *op. cit.*

24. *Judenfragen*, February 10, 1944 (B.D.C.).

25. N XXXVIII, 013-M, p. 122.

26. *Ibid.*, 004-M, pp. 112–13.

27. *Ibid.*, 136-M, pp. 187–89.

28. *Ibid.*, 150-M, p. 191.

3

The Number-Two Man

HERMANN WILHELM GOERING

In contrast to the disreputable Streicher and sitting on the same front bench with him at Nuremberg was the man who had been Reichsmarschall, the ranking military officer in the Third Reich—an art lover, a war hero with the highest German decoration of World War I (Pour le Mérite), but also a narcotics addict and plunderer on a monumental scale—Hermann Wilhelm Goering.

During the trial Goering appeared in a uniform (his pants were pressed every day by the prison tailor) that was much too large for him, for he weighed only 153 pounds, as against the 275 in the days of his high living. Since his cell had no mirror, he made use of the dark suit of his visiting attorney as a background to make the glass partition separating them into a looking glass that reflected the state of his hair.

Goering had always had an eye on the gallery. At the trial, with his eye on history, he played the role of the leader of the lost cause, the defeated but faithful paladin of the Fuehrer, true to the end to his liege lord. When the defendants took their midday meals together, he took it upon himself to organize them into some sort of agreement to present a patriotic and united front to the enemy.* When he did not like the testimony of one witness, he audibly called him a *Schwein* as the man left the stand and went by the prisoners' dock. He told his lawyer with gratification that Doenitz now realized that his appointment as the Fuehrer's successor was no more

* At first the prisoners took their midday meals together. Later they ate in groups of four, with the exception of Goering, who ate alone in his cell.

59

than a fluke—that only a misunderstanding had prevented the Fuehrer from carrying out his long-established commitment to Goering. In his opinion, either Himmler or Bormann had intercepted his letter to the Fuehrer explaining that the Reichsmarschall had believed he was carrying out Hitler's orders in offering to negotiate with the Allies on the Fuehrer's behalf. He could never accept the fact that Hitler had finally turned against him.

He told his lawyer triumphantly that he was now the acknowledged corporal of the defendants. But he could scarcely conceal what everyone in the courtroom heard—namely, that most of the defendants thought little more of him than they did of the other top-ranking Party leaders who had brought them all to the shadow of the gallows. Schacht testified that Goering, who had headed the Four-Year Plan for the German economy, was an ignoramus in economics. Other witnesses told of his colossal vanity, his drug addiction, his abnormal habits of behavior and dress. Schacht said he had been told that Goering had appeared at a tea dressed as a Roman gladiator with painted toenails showing in his sandals, rings on his fingers, and rouge on his cheeks.

During the trial Goering made no attempt, as did so many of his co-defendants, to place the blame on others or to hide behind the corpse of Hitler. On the contrary, he strove to emphasize the significance of his own role in the Reich. A witness who had served under him in the Luftwaffe, Field Marshal Erhard Milch, was asked when his conversation with Hitler had been reported to Goering, and Goering answered from his place in the dock, "Immediately." He also wanted to make it clear to the court that the information had come to him directly from the Fuehrer, not from Milch. He always exaggerated his importance.

In the course of the war Goering had gradually lost favor. His decline began in 1940, when the German Air Force failed to defeat the British Spitfires over London; it accelerated in 1941, when the Luftwaffe failed to repeat the decisive victories in Russia that had been won in the earlier campaigns; it plunged still lower after Goering had promised that he could supply the Sixth Army at Stalingrad; and it hit bottom as the enemy bombers poured destruction on German cities. After the fall of his prestige, Himmler, Bormann, Goebbels, and Speer became closer to Hitler and took over jobs Goering had once held. On April 23, 1945, a squad of SS men arrested him on orders of the Fuehrer, signed by Bormann; and on the following day they received orders to shoot the Reichsmarschall and his family if Berlin fell.

Goering could not admit in public that he had ever lost his influence with Hitler, although in private conversations he confessed that beginning in 1941 Hitler had cooled toward him. In 1944, he said, he was deathly sick from a tonsil infection, but Hitler, who had once been so solicitous, did not even inquire after his health. He declared that Hitler would doubtless have gotten rid of him but for the Reichsmarschall's wide influence with the German people. To shore up what remained of his collapsed world, he (like Eichmann) romanticized himself as the true hero of a historic cause. He declared at Nuremberg that he had indeed meant his oath of allegiance to the Fuehrer: "I identify my fate with yours for better or worse; I dedicate myself to you in good times and in bad, even unto death." Now he added: "I really meant it and still do."

He was much affected by what he thought was his success or failure with an audience. After he routed Mr. Justice Jackson in their verbal duel on the part he had played in making plans for war, he confided his satisfaction to one of his lawyers: "Jackson is not up to me."[1] But when the American journalists in a poll decided 32 to 0 that Goering would be executed and this news was communicated to him, he said he should have shot himself in August, 1945.[2] Even his eternal *Treue* to the Fuehrer was in part a tactic for the gallery. In conversations with his lawyers he admitted that it would have been better if Hitler had been killed in an automobile accident in 1938 and that the Fuehrer's suicide had been a betrayal of the German people, just as Hitler had called the suicide of the mayor of Leipzig—at the time the mayor and his family had died together as the American troops approached the city—"a cowardly flight from responsibility." [3]

Goering had suicide much on his mind. He came to his first prison with a vial of cyanide hidden in his navel, secured by an adhesive. It was found and confiscated. He had told his brother that he himself would determine how and when he died, and that was one of his few prophecies that came true. "What am I doing here anyway?" he once asked at Nuremberg in a mood of despair. He thought in such moments that perhaps Kaltenbrunner, the former SS chief, was right in saying that the court was a sham and that he too should reject its authority and deny everything. But the chance of making a last heroic appearance on a world stage was too alluring; he needed to remain even an unfrocked Reichsmarschall as long as he could.

Goering had been liked and admired by countless foreigners as well as by the Germans for an outward bonhommie that contrasted with the austerity of the vegetarian Hitler and the taut faces of so many of the dedicated *Bonzen* who were making a religion of their revolution. He appeared to be a good fellow given to hearty laughter and sumptuous living. The procession of foreign diplomats who visited him in his palace in Berlin and in Karinhall —Poles, British, Frenchmen, Americans, Italians, Japanese—found him an amiable and hospitable host. For both foreigners and Germans he was a wholesome, amusing, intelligent as well as corpulent figure, a flier with a brilliant war record and a man who aimed at political targets inside Germany in building up its economy and air force.* Shrewd anti-Nazi observers like André François-Poncet, Colonel Józef Beck, Lord Halifax, British Ambassador Nevile Henderson, and the Swedish Birger Dahlerus and Knut Bonde were convinced of his desire to avoid war. Henderson worked with him even

---

* Goering's bonhommie appealed greatly to the Germans, as is evidenced by the large stock of jokes in which he played a leading and comic part.

after the invasion of Poland, and Bonde until December, 1939, because they thought he was the one man of influence in the Reich who opposed the war and would do what he could for peace.

At the Nuremberg trial, Goering had a different reputation among his fellow prisoners and many of the witnesses, although a few of his old admirers came to his aid. Most of those who answered questions about him said that he was lazy, vain, arrogant, pretentious, and unsuccessful; that everything in his hands had fallen to pieces; that he had been superseded in almost all his active offices; that only fragments of the vast economic empire he had ruled and of his Luftwaffe had remained at the end, and then he was no longer in charge of either of them. The Allies had won complete air supremacy over Germany, and the foolish boast with which he had begun the war—that no Allied plane would drop a bomb on Berlin—became grotesque as the German centers were destroyed by the overwhelmingly superior numbers of Allied planes. "Call me Meyer," he had once said (neither the Berliners nor the rest of Germany ever forgot it), "if a single bomb is dropped on Berlin."

Cast out of the Party by Hitler as a traitor and condemned to death, and long before this, supplanted in the chain of command by Himmler and Goebbels and Speer, Goering at Nuremberg heard himself called incompetent by a procession of witnesses who testified that he was no more successful in the various jobs that he took over in the course of the Nazi rebuilding of the economy than he was in his contributions to the strategy and tactics of the war. Nevertheless, he had built the Luftwaffe from zero to the most powerful air force in the world. In his single-minded concentration on the development of German air power he had, when he wanted to, protected Jewish officers who were thrown out of their jobs in the Army. "A Jew is whoever I say is one in Germany," he had declared, and Field Marshal Milch, who testified for him at Nuremberg, was living evidence of this. Milch's legal father was of Jewish blood, but Milch was officially declared to be 100 per cent "Aryan" when it was decided that his biological father was a Christian and not the man his mother had married.

This was one of a number of cases where Goering had decided in favor of a man he needed or liked or because his vanity or sentiments were appealed to over the rigors of the anti-Jewish laws. But his *Gemuetlichkeit* could vanish quickly. It was Goering who called the Wannsee Conference, which planned the manner in which the Jews of Europe were to be destroyed, and who chose one of the most bloodthirsty killers in Germany, Reinhard Heydrich, to administer the Final Solution. The solution itself he doubtless accepted as reluctantly as he did the war. He wanted neither of them, but what could he do but accept them without question as the faithful paladin of the Fuehrer? He delighted in brandishing his authority, in appearing before the public in an array of specially designed uniforms, and in returning as soon as he could to the grandiose domesticity of Karinhall, where he got himself up in costumes suitable to romantic fantasies. In his country retreat he was the *grand seigneur*. He met Herbert Hoover in an armless doublet, wearing a shirt of red-brown raw silk and a neckerchief thrust through with a long pin ornamented with a green jewel.[4] He strutted in his varied wardrobe before the gaze of the Germans and of his tame lions. He brought together from all the occupied countries one of the greatest collections of art (as he boasted) in all Europe if not in the world. He entertained visiting diplomats in the theatrical architecture of Karinhall, where he had among other things a toy railroad on which he could drop a toy bomb from an airplane that was launched from a distant corner of the huge room.

Goering was a zoophile, as evidenced in his love not only for lions, which he kept in the house, but also for all four-legged or feathered creatures. As chief forester of Germany he took every precaution to see to it that game was humanely hunted. Traps of a cruel or unusual kind were forbidden, and a retriever had to accompany the hunter to bring in wounded birds. The hunting codes adopted had to be of the kind that appealed to his warm sentiments for animals. He abolished the hunt with horse and hounds. Germans and his foreign visitors had to hunt on foot. Neither falcons nor eagles (the symbol of the Third Reich) could be shot, nor could artificial light be used to attract animals at night. All this was proof of his keen sportsmanship—proof not only to himself but also to many of his English visitors who made no comment when he appeared carrying a spear and dressed like a sixteenth-century hunter; and they responded warmly to his kindness to animals and his firm stand against vivisection. "People who torture animals insult the feelings of the German people," he declared. Toward the German folk, too, he harbored sentiments of abiding charity. Even Germans who were criminals remained Germans, he said. When the talk turned to food supplies in a war winter, he said he was certain of only one thing—namely, that the Germans were not to go hungry, whatever happened to the people who had grown and harvested the crops.

Goering was born in 1893 in Rosenheim in Bavaria. The name, according to one of his biographers, comes from "Ger," meaning boundary, and "ing," a descendant.[5] Hermann was next to the youngest of five children, three sons and two daughters. Their father, Heinrich Ernst Goering, was a provincial judge in Germany and became a German colonial official when Bismarck appointed him Commissioner of Southwest Africa in 1885. Heinrich, in addition to his administrative duties, had the assignment of enlarging, as far as he could, the sphere of influence and the territories that Germany, coming late to the colonial table, had acquired. He performed his duties with considerable success, and young Hermann heard much from his father of the adventurous years when Southwest Africa was won for the Reich.

At the time Hermann was born his father was Consul General of Haiti, but his mother was living in Bavaria. Hermann was brought up in Berlin (his father had returned to the city after retiring from government service). The Goerings lived for a time with a rich friend, Hermann von Epenstein, nominally a Christian but of Jewish descent, who had met Heinrich Goering when they were both in Africa. Epenstein was Hermann's godfather, and according to one source, Goering's mother, Franziska, was his mistress. In any event Epenstein, an eccentric, self-important man, helped meet the expenses of Goering's education and left him considerable property, including the castle of Veldenstein, where he and the Goerings had lived together.[6]

Hermann attended the cadet schools in Karlsruhe and Gross-Lichterfelde as a member of the Royal Prussian Cadet Corps and served in World War I from the beginning. Hospitalized for an attack of rheumatism in 1914, he got back into action through the Air Force, in which he flew as an observer before he became a pilot. In 1915 he was wounded in the leg and thigh by a British flier. By 1917 he was leader of a group in pursuit squadron #3. The celebrated pilot Baron Manfred von Richthofen, whose successor he became, was leader of squadron #1. According to the account of a Dane, Captain Paulli Krause-Jensen, who flew against him for the French, Goering was one of the most redoubtable and chivalrous of pilots. Krause-Jensen reported that during a dogfight, when his machine gun had jammed and he had beat his fist against it in desperation, Goering saw what had happened and, instead of firing his own machine gun and finishing him off, had banked his plane and saluted him. From that time on, Krause-Jensen said he had an admiration for the Germans that had never left him.[7] Goering took over the command of the Richthofen Squadron after Richthofen's death and emerged from the war with the two main German military decorations—Pour le Mérite and the Iron Cross First Class. He refused to carry out the order to deliver his squadron's planes to the Americans at the time of the armistice and flew them instead from France to Duesseldorf.

After World War I Germany was incomprehensible to Goering. In 1918, a year after the Bolshevik revolution, Soldiers' Councils on the Soviet pattern were organized among the returning troops. One Communist speaker, a member of the city council of Nuremberg, told Goering's squadron that he had fought in the front line while the German officers had remained safely in the rear, but what he said was palpable nonsense. Air Force officers were combat fliers—Goering, for one, had downed twenty-five enemy planes—and the Air Force men knew it. The new Prussian Minister of War, General Walther Reinhardt, addressed a meeting after he had issued an order for officers to remove their shoulder insignia and to wear instead blue stripes on their sleeves. He came to the meeting wearing the stripes. Goering, a young officer of twenty-five, rose from his seat to rebuke him:

> Mr. Minister, I was convinced that you would be present here today. But I hoped to see a mourning band on your sleeve to express your deep regret for the wrong which you propose to do us. Instead, you are wearing the blue colours on your arm. Mr. Minister, you should have chosen red! . . . We

officers have done our duty for four long years on land, on sea and in the air. We have risked life and limb for our fatherland. Now we have come home —and what do they do with us? They spit on us and want to take from us what was our honor. And, I tell you, it is not the people that is responsible. The people were our comrades, every one of them, whatever might be his rank, for the four hard years of the War. It is not the people, but those who have inflamed it, who stabbed our splendid army in the back and have no other wish but to rule, so that they may enrich themselves at the people's expense. . . . But the day will come, I know it and I beg you to believe it, when these men will have shot their bolt and when we'll kick them out, out of our Germany. Make yourselves ready, be prepared for that day and work for it. For it will surely come!* 8

Goering had returned from the front with no idea of what to do and no job. But he was a well-known flier, and the Fokker company invited him to demonstrate their aircraft at an exhibit in Copenhagen. For some weeks he flew paying customers at a seaside hotel in Denmark, then moved on to Sweden, where he got a job first with a firm manufacturing parachutes and later with the Swedish airline. It was in Sweden that he met his first wife, Baroness Carin von Fock, a woman four years older than he and already married. The two fell in love immediately. Goering, with a passenger, had made a forced landing on her estate, which seemed to both of them the hand of fate. They were an incurably romantic pair, addicted to sudden impulses and a belief in happy endings. She soon started divorce proceedings against her husband, who made no objection, and she and Goering were married in Munich, where Goering had settled in 1921. They were greatly attached to each other. Although Carin was an invalid, she traveled devotedly and gladly with her husband during their exile after the attempted putsch of 1923. They were never separated if they could avoid it during the decade of their life together before her death, in 1931. Carin was not very intelligent. Her letters to her family are childish, filled with exclamation points and adoration of Hermann and, next to him, of the Fuehrer.

In 1921 Goering still had no clear idea of what he wanted to do. He was vaguely interested in political science, in which he took courses at the University of Munich. He attended nationalist political gatherings, and one day he heard Hitler speak. He sought out the Fuehrer-to-be and heard the very program he had himself been groping for spelled out by the man who could talk to him as persuasively as he did to the thousands of people in a beer hall. The Versailles Treaty had to be repudiated, the Jews and Communists and the Republicans had to be driven from power, a broad mass movement had to be created based on nationalism and socialism. Goering had said the same things to himself. Like thousands of returning soldiers, he had never

* The account appears in Goering's official biography, published in 1937. The book was written by Erich Gritzbach and edited by Goering himself. It is the kind of legendary story that filled National Socialist literature. A captain even in the Germany of 1919 was not likely to address a general in such terms.

been able to digest the defeat, and Hitler had a plan of action for undoing it. Hitler even gave him the opportunity of putting on a uniform again, for he made Goering head of the SA. A war hero decorated with a Pour le Mérite gave a cachet to the budding army of the Party. Goering said at Nuremberg that the Fuehrer had told him he had been looking for a young flier or submarine officer to whom he could give an important Party post. Ever since the end of the war, Goering and Hitler had separately been searching for a man who would complement their own talents, and both of them knew when they had found the ordained person.

Goering marched in the front lines with Streicher at the time of the attempted putsch, and at the Feldherrnhalle, when the police opened fire, he was shot in the leg. Because of his wound he escaped imprisonment. He was taken to a hospital in Munich and then was smuggled across the border to Austria, while Hitler and Hess and others went to the Landsberg prison. The Party was left to wither on the vine for a time. Carin joined her husband in Innsbruck, and they made their roundabout way back to Sweden. They lived cheaply at the hotels run by Party sympathizers in Austria and Italy, paying their way on the proceeds of the sale of the house Carin had bought in Munich.

It was at this time, apparently, that Goering became addicted to morphine, which he had been given because of his wounds. In 1925 he took his first cure in Sweden, where he came under psychiatric observation, but he was never to rid himself entirely of the habit. In 1927 he repeated the cure in Germany. He seems to have been free of the habit for some years, but he reverted to it under the stresses of the war. At Nuremberg he was still in need of the drug, but the prison authorities did not give it to him. He had a large supply of paracodeine tablets when he surrendered to the Americans, and he had flushed an even larger supply down the toilet before the Americans came, thinking it unbecoming to have so much on hand.[9]

With the 1927 amnesty Goering was able to return to Germany from Sweden, where he was making a modest living as an agent of a parachute firm but, because of his politics, in a less cordial atmosphere than he had experienced before. He and his wife settled down, this time in Berlin, and the following year he ran for and was elected to the Reichstag as one of the twelve National Socialist deputies. The Nazis polled only 3 per cent of the votes, but, owing to the proportional representation that helped produce the splinter parties that bedeviled the Weimar regime, Goering got in. He was chosen chief of the Party delegation. In 1932 he was elected to the Presidency of the Reichstag and promptly prepared the way for the dissolution of Parliament. He gave up the leadership of the SA and concentrated on Party affairs in the Reichstag and the country as a whole. Hitler took him seriously, for Goering had marched in the front rank of the uprising and was utterly devoted to the Fuehrer. Goering never competed with Hitler, never dreamed, as Roehm and Gregor Strasser for example did, of supplanting him. The two men were opposites and they complemented each other. For Goering, Hitler was the political genius who could move the masses with the true doctrine. For Hitler, Goering was a warrior of superior middle-class origins who could gain the respect of business people and former Army officers and was, above all, a man of unswerving fidelity.

In 1932 the National Socialist Party became the largest party in the Reichstag. Goering, as President of that body, used his office adroitly against Chancellor Franz von Papen. At a stormy session, Goering made common cause with the Communists in his maneuver not to recognize Papen, who was seeking in vain to get his eye so that he could announce the dissolution of the Reichstag, which Hindenburg, on his request, had ordered. A presidential decree of dissolution would have enabled Papen to continue in office under emergency powers. Goering turned instead to a woman Communist delegate who made a motion for a vote of no confidence in Papen—a vote that Goering knew would be adopted. When Hitler was called to the chancellorship by Hindenburg, to head what the President and Papen believed was to be a coalition cabinet, Goering was named Minister Without Portfolio. He and Wilhelm Frick were the only National Socialist ministers in the Government, but Hitler quickly consolidated his position. Goering soon succeeded Papen as Minister President of Prussia, an office Papen had insisted on retaining when he accepted the vice-chancellorship (at the time he had thought of this as a shrewd deal to keep Hitler in check under the coalition).

Goering collected jobs. In addition to Minister President, he was Minister of the Interior for Prussia and in this capacity had the Prussian state police under him. He founded a secret police—the Gestapo (Geheime Staatspolizei)—and the first concentration camps, where the enemies of the regime, brought in by his police, could be kept. At the time of the Reichstag fire he headed the roundup of members of the opposition parties, using the emergency as a pretext for getting rid first of the Communists, whom he immediately declared responsible for setting the blaze, and then of the equally hated Social Democrats. At Nuremberg he was accused of having set the fire himself, but the evidence for this is as flimsy as that which Goering used to try to convict the Bulgarian Communist Georgi Dimitrov and two of his countrymen, Simon Popov and Vasili Tanev, for their alleged part in causing the fire.* During his trial, Dimitrov was able to turn the

* Who set the Reichstag fire remains a mystery. A book by Fritz Tobias, *Der Reichstagsbrand*, has been published on the subject and learned articles have been written in scholarly journals, including Martin Broszat's *"Zum Streit um den Reichstagsbrand,"* in *Vierteljahrshefte fuer Zeitgeschichte* (Vol. VIII, No. 3, 1960), but the case is still unclear. Marinus van der Lubbe, a twenty-four-year-old Dutchman who had once belonged to the Communist Party and who said he wanted to do a deed against Nazism that would be noted by the world, was immediately arrested and charged with the crime. Van der Lubbe was certainly guilty. The only question is whether he was the only person involved or had assistance, either from outsiders or from members of the Nazi Party who had used him as a stooge. While his trial was taking place at Leipzig, a countertrial was held under the auspices of a committee composed of jurists from England, the United States, Sweden,

tables on Goering when Goering appeared in the witness box against him. Twelve years later Goering was to turn the tables on Mr. Justice Jackson in a similar way. Dimitrov used the trial and his undoubted innocence to turn Goering's bludgeoning accusations back on the prosecution. He asked Goering, who said he had known from the first that the Communists had set the fire, whether he bothered to look for anyone else who might be guilty. The exchange developed into name-calling, with Goering losing both his temper and the argument. It was all a curious preview of what a dozen years later was to happen at Nuremberg.

In this period Goering was the most important of the *Bonzen*, but he was not yet Hitler's official successor.[10] (At Nuremberg he said he had discussed the question with Hitler as early as 1934.) [11] The Fuehrer's crown prince at the time was probably Rudolph Hess, and it was only with the start of the war that Hitler publicly decreed Goering as his successor. Goering was always more indispensable to Hitler than Hess. Among those closest to Hitler, only Goering had sufficient credit with the armed forces to preside over the trial of Colonel General Freiherr Werner von Fritsch, even though Goering had been promoted at one stroke from his former captain's rank to general, a dazzling rise unprecedented in the German Army. The court that tried the former Commander in Chief of the German Army consisted in addition to Goering of Admiral Erich Raeder, General Walther von Brauchitsch, and two Army judges. It found Fritsch innocent of the faked charges of homosexuality, which had been brought against him as part of the running battle between the Gestapo, by this time under Himmler, and the Army. But its verdict did not result in Hitler's reinstating Fritsch, nor did it allay the rumors among those who mistrusted Goering that he had engineered the charges to get rid of Fritsch. Raeder and Brauchitsch considered Goering a conservative National Socialist, and both his rank and

---

Holland, France, and some other countries, and they found it probable that the Nazis were guilty. The Leipzig judges found the Bulgarians innocent (which enraged Hitler and Goering), but sentenced van der Lubbe to death.

Much was made at the Nuremberg trial of the underground tunnel leading from Goering's palace to the Reichstag and of Goering's boast that he had been responsible for the destruction of a building whose architecture, he said, he had deplored. But no convincing evidence has ever come to light that links him directly with the fire.

What is certain is that Goering, Hitler, and company knew how to make use of the event. The Communist delegates to the Reichstag were prevented from taking their seats. The Gestapo made wholesale arrests, and the atmosphere of nascent terror accounts in some part for the powers voted Hitler by the two-thirds majority he needed to take over both the full legislative and executive powers granted him in the Enabling Act (*Ermaechtigungsgesetz*). It is true that he would have obtained the two-thirds vote even if the Communists had been seated, but the fire and its aftermath played an essential part in softening the hitherto stubborn opposition. The *Ermaechtigungsgesetz* could only be passed with the votes of long-standing enemies of the Nazis, including the Center. The Center voted in favor of the act only under the strongest pressure. (Erich Matthias, "*Die Sitzung der Reichstagsfraktion des Zentrums am 23. Maerz 1933,*" in *Vierteljahrshefte fuer Zeitgeschichte*, Vol. IV, No. 3, 1956).

his grasp of the issues seemed to entitle him to act as President of the Court trying Fritsch. Many military men, including Raeder, disliked Goering but thought of him as a bona fide soldier and one who lacked the fanatical Party dogmatism the Army and Navy so mistrusted.

At the time of the Roehm putsch Goering again played an ambiguous part. With Hitler and Himmler, he was in charge of the SS and police action that resulted in the arrest and shooting of scores of former high SA officers as well as of men who, like General Kurt von Schleicher and Gregor Strasser, were accused of plotting to overthrow Hitler. At Nuremberg Goering was charged by Hans Gisevius, a former Gestapo man who had aided the American OSS during the war, with having been responsible for the killing of Schleicher by the police who had been sent to arrest the general. Gisevius' testimony, however, often seemed exaggerated to some observers, and the court did not find Goering responsible for the murders charged against him by Gisevius. Goering did order the police to burn the records of what had gone on during the purge, and he undoubtedly played one of the chief roles in the arrest and execution of those he and Hitler regarded as attempting revolution. Some of the police documents that have survived disclose that Schleicher was murdered, not killed with a weapon in his hands with which he threatened the police, as Goering explained at the time.[12] Whether or not Goering ordered Schleicher to be killed, he played a characteristic part during the action against the alleged revolters by following orders, no matter how brutal, and by believing in whatever plot Hitler believed in. At the same time he did protect Papen from being sent to a Gestapo prison or from suffering the same fate as Papen's secretary, who was shot down. Goering was not by nature a killer. The idea of murdering a former Chancellor and member of Hitler's government was certainly repugnant to him, but he would have had no compunctions against doing even that had Hitler ordered it.

Goering accepted the purge at face value. He had disliked Roehm, as he disliked Himmler, Heydrich, and Goebbels, all of whom were too rigid and dogmatic for his tastes, and he carried out the conflicting jobs of helping to organize the purge and of protecting Papen, whom the SS regarded as one of their major enemies.[13] Hitler thanked Goering for the part he played. The Fuehrer told the Reichstag two weeks after the "revolt" was put down: "Meanwhile Minister President Goering had previously received my instructions that in case of a purge, he was to take analogous measures at once in Berlin and in Prussia. With an iron fist he beat down the attack on the National Socialist state before it could develop." [14]

Goering took no pleasure in killing, but he could be as ruthless as anyone when in a rage or when his own notions of justice were flouted. He could order the death sentence—even of an officer he liked—when he thought the young man had shown contempt for his leadership. During the Russian campaign three young soldiers who stole some cans of meat were shot by an officer. Goering was incensed. He wanted the officer who had killed them executed, but the Fuehrer refused. Another time, some young Luftwaffe officers returning from a party were stopped by an Army officer who demanded their papers. They handed them over to him, but when they saw their trolley car coming along, the last one that would run until morning, they snatched them back and ran for it. They were arrested, charged with mutiny, and shot. Goering was enraged. He stormed at the Army general under whose command the trial and execution had taken place, but he went no further, for his authority ran only as far as the Fuehrer permitted and he could take no undue risks.[15] He accepted Fritsch's humiliation, although he knew him to be innocent. In the Fritsch case he was acting as the Fuehrer wanted him to. In the case of the young officers, he was following his own impulses, which were, more often than not, generous. The Army had far more confidence in him than in the other political advisers close to Hitler, but they mistrusted him too. He occupied a middle position, about as Nazi as Nazi General Walter von Reichenau, but far removed from the threat represented by the Roehms and the Himmlers, who wanted to take over or supplant the Army—Roehm with the SA, and Himmler with the SS.

Witnesses at Nuremberg declared that Goering had deliberately plotted the downfall of War Minister (Reichskriegsminister) Field Marshal Werner von Blomberg. They said he had induced the Fuehrer to be a witness to Blomberg's marriage with, as it turned out, a registered prostitute, as part of a plot to get Blomberg's job. The evidence, based mainly on Gisevius' testimony, is flimsy. Goering had told Hitler that the marriage would be regarded by stiff-necked Army generals as inappropriate—the lady, Fraeulein Erna Gruhn, was Blomberg's secretary. It is not clear how much more about her Goering knew at the time. The police records of her prostitution were turned over to him only later by the president of the Berlin police, Count Wolf von Helldorf. Goering immediately took them to Hitler, and Blomberg had to resign. The evidence that Goering had contrived these plots to get both Fritsch and Blomberg out of the way in order to realize his ambition to become Secretary of War rests on no more stable a foundation than the conjectures of people who, like Gisevius, did not like him.

Goering was charged at Nuremberg on four counts: he had plotted to wage aggressive warfare; he had waged it; he had committed war crimes; he had committed crimes against humanity. He was universally considered guilty from the outset and appeared on all the lists of war criminals. When he first surrendered to American General Stack in Bavaria, he was treated as a prisoner of war of high rank, retaining his marshal's baton and, together with his family, dining with the general. But that lasted only a very short time. The next day it was made clear to him that he was to be regarded not as a prisoner of war but as a war criminal. Goering was stripped of his Reichsmarschall's insignia as soon as he was brought from General Stack's headquarters to Kitzbuehel. From there he went to the collection camp, which was in a beer cellar in Augsburg, and then after a stay at Mondorf—Ashcan— was shipped to Nuremberg. Wherever he went he was an object of curiosity. Soldiers wanted his autograph, officers wanted to talk to him, and a rumor went around that he was beaten by his captors. If so, he never complained of it. He knew what lay in store for him. His only task, as he saw it, was to set an example to go down, now that the ship had sunk—but to go down as the former second in command who, since the captain had killed himself, was in full charge of what remained of the wreckage. Not much of what had been the pomp of the Nazi state had kept its gloss, so Goering held on to his *Treue* as something that could not be taken from him as readily as his Reichs- marschall's baton.

Goering made no secret at Nuremberg of having done all he could to rearm Germany, to retool the economy to this end, to make the Reich blockade-proof, and to build bombers and fighters as rapidly as possible and in as great numbers as the economy and personnel training programs per- mitted. The prosecution alleged that four-engined bombers were aggressive weapons, and one of Goering's witnesses testified that the Germans had very few of them. On taking the stand, Goering said that he would have been glad to have the four-engined bombers, that he had merely decided against them in favor of other types, and that the decision had nothing to do with aggression but concerned only the allocation of scarce resources. He proudly told the court that he gloried in the *Anschluss* and that he was the man mainly responsible for it. The records of all his telephone conversa- tions with Seyss-Inquart and the other Nazi officials in Vienna, as well as with Ribbentrop in London, were in the hands of the Allies in any case, but Goering, far from wanting to defend himself, magnified what he had accomplished in engineering the change of government that got rid of Kurt von Schuschnigg and put Seyss-Inquart in his place. Austria was ripe for the plucking, but Goering's instructions in the last hours of the republic were well timed and he held all the cards, for the little state, without foreign support and with not much internal cohesion left, was no longer viable.

Goering's lawyer, Otto Stahmer, had to defend him against charges that pointed to his complicity in a far greater crime than turning the rejoicing Austrians over to the Reich Government. The Nazi conspirators, Goering among them, were charged with the mass murder of 11,000 Polish soldiers in the Katyn forest. It was a charge the Russians insisted on including in the indictment, despite the reluctance of the Americans and British. Any number of people at Nuremberg knew that the evidence against the Ger- mans was dubious or worse, for the Poles had already made a careful investigation of the massacre. They had published a pamphlet on the sub- ject in London, and what they, as well as American and British intelligence officers, had discovered would be borne out in the future investigations that in due course would be conducted by an American congressional committee, as well as by historians. The Russians, not the Germans, had committed the crime in the Katyn forest, and many people in the courtroom, including no doubt the Russian prosecutors and judges, knew it. The Polish underground was convinced the Germans had not committed the murders. Eleven Polish senators and ten deputies of the government-in-exile sent their opinion to Mr. Justice Jackson before the start of the trial, telling him that it would be "inadvisable" to include Katyn among the charges against the Germans. In fact, according to a Polish source, one of the Russians the Poles accused of having taken part in the crime was acting as a prosecutor at Nuremberg.[16] The members of the American and British prosecution—and officials far higher than they—were caught in an embarrassing dilemma. Neither the Nuremberg court nor, before it convened, the leaders of the Western Allies could deal effectively with the charge against the Russians. President Roosevelt, when he heard the story from George Earle, Special Emissary for Balkan Affairs, told Earle he had been taken in by Goebbels' propaganda. And Churchill, forbidding General Wladyslaw Sikorski to investigate further, said, "If they [the Polish officers] are dead nothing you can do will bring them back." [17] When Earle persisted and wanted to publish an account of the tragic episode, Roosevelt expressly forbade it, and Earle, an expert on the Balkans, was shipped off to Samoa, where he remained until after Roosevelt's death. The Russians insisted that the Katyn massacre be made part of the Nuremberg charges, but they could make no case. The court did not allude to the massacre in its verdict. The Soviet prosecution brought three witnesses: the deputy mayor of Smolensk during the German occupation, who seemed to Dr. Stahmer to be reading the answers to the questions asked him by the Soviet prosecutor; a Russian doctor, whose testimony repeated what the official Soviet investigation had said; and a Bulgarian, who had served on the international committee the Germans had called together when the bodies were first discovered in the mass graves. The Bulgarian, Dr. Marko Markov, recanted his earlier findings that the Russians had committed the crime and now blamed the Germans. What he said at Nuremberg was most unconvincing, and the tribunal, aside from the Russian members, was unimpressed by him. Markov had a little earlier been brought before a Soviet court, and after he had formally repudiated his earlier views he was brought on to Nuremberg to testify. As a witness who would be returned to Bulgaria he was no more free to testify at Nuremberg than he was before the Soviet court in his own country.

The plain facts of the Katyn murders could not easily be covered up. Fifteen thousand Polish soldiers (including 8,300 officers) captured by the Russians had been missing since the spring of 1940. Letters from them to their families, which had formerly been written once a month, abruptly ceased in mid-April, 1940—more than a year before the German attack on Russia. The efforts of the Polish underground and then of the Polish General Wladyslaw Anders, who was released from a Soviet prison camp, and other officials to get information from the Soviet Union as to the whereabouts of the soldiers were unsuccessful. The missing men were badly needed to officer and man the new Polish Army that was to be recruited in Russia. In February, 1943, the German Communications Regiment 537 discovered the corpses of some 4,500 to 4,800 Polish officers. These officers had been evacuated from the former Soviet prisoner-of-war camp at Kozelsk to the Katyn forest, not far from Smolensk. The German Propaganda Ministry, which heard about the matter in April, 1943, made a great fanfare of the discovery, accusing the Russians, and asked the International Red Cross to send a team of doctors to investigate. Red Cross authorities felt they could not do this unless the Soviet Government also invited them. Then the Germans formed a group of practitioners of forensic medicine from twelve states, from among their allies and from neutral and occupied countries. Switzerland, Finland, Belgium, France, Denmark, Italy, and other countries were represented. For once, the Germans needed to provide no stage setting, and the commission was able to make its examinations and findings in complete freedom. The Poles sent to the scene a twelve-man medical team of their own, as well as members of the underground, and they, along with the International Commission, soon had no doubt as to who the perpetrators were. The executed men wore winter overcoats. The trees that had been planted over their graves, a microscopic analysis showed, had been placed there in 1940, not in the summer of 1941, when the Germans arrived on the scene. The physical state of the corpses, the decalcification of the skulls, the diaries and letters found on the bodies all confirmed that they died in April, 1940, and not later.

Otto Stahmer dealt with the charge, as did a number of the other German defense counsel, including Otto Kranzbuehler, who was representing Admiral Doenitz, and Hans Laternser, who was representing the German High Command. Against which defendant the charges were being made was vague. It was clear only that the German armed forces, the High Command, and the "Nazi conspirators" were implicated. The Soviet prosecutor directly charged one of the German witnesses with having done the deed, but this accusation fell through when the accused man, Colonel Friedrich Ahrens, could prove that he had not even been at the site when the crime was alleged by the Russians to have been committed. The Soviet prosecutors, as was their inveterate practice, put words into the mouths of their witnesses and were admonished by the court. But when Laternser tried to find out from the President of the Court just who was being made responsible for the committing of the crime of Katyn, Lord Justice Geoffrey Lawrence replied, "I do not propose to answer questions of that sort."

In the end no one was held responsible. The case was not cited in the verdict against Goering or any of the other defendants. From the Allied point of view it was by far the weakest point of the trial. Goering's lawyer had asked General Anders, commander of the Polish Army in the Soviet Union, for material in his possession that the Poles had collected. Anders was ready to comply, but as an Allied officer he needed the permission of his superiors, which he asked for but never obtained. Mr. Justice Jackson said later that he had never heard of General Anders' offer.

Goering had had nothing to do with the Katyn murders, and some of the other minor charges against him also were weak. The prosecution, in its search for conspiracies, was grappling with organizations that either had never existed or had played no important role in the Third Reich. Thus Goering was charged by Mr. Justice Jackson with being chairman of the Reich Defense Council, an organization that clearly sounded ominous to the prosecution and might have indeed aided and abetted rearmament and the wars the Reich fought—had it ever functioned. Goering testified that this first secret body, founded in 1933, was dissolved in 1938 without having met. The second publicly announced Defense Council, founded in 1938, played no important role, apparently because it was too unwieldy.[18] A meeting of November 18, 1938, consisted almost entirely of an address by Goering to a large audience on the aim to triple German armaments, to improve the transport system, and to help the financial situation of the Reich by seizing Jewish property. There was no discussion and no action was taken. The meeting was merely a sounding board for the plans of its chairman.[19] Goering testified that he did not even attend another large gathering of this body, and after a year it was converted into a ministerial council. The Defense Council had not much more significance, as far as Goering's guilt was concerned, than the organization Goering said he had invented on the spur of the moment to help Neurath save face. When Ribbentrop was appointed Foreign Minister, Goering proposed to Hitler that Neurath be named chairman of something he thought they should call the Secret Cabinet Council. This, he believed, would sound impressive and be widely thought to have important functions. Hitler objected that Neurath could scarcely be chairman of a nonexistent body, so Goering, as he told the court, whipped out a pencil and paper and wrote down the names of the members who would serve under Neurath's phantom chairmanship, naming himself last. Neurath was duly appointed, but the Secret Cabinet Council never met.

The real case against Goering—namely, that as second man in the Reich he bore a major share of responsibility for the murders and exterminations, as well as certain of the war crimes—was developed slowly. Mr. Justice Jackson's first question on cross-examining him was: "You are perhaps aware that you are the only living man who can expound to us the true purposes of the Nazi Party and the inner workings of its leadership?"

GOERING: "I am perfectly aware of that."

JACKSON: "You, from the very beginning, together with those who were associated with you, intended to overthrow and later did overthrow the Weimar Republic?"

GOERING: "That was, as far as I am concerned, my firm intention."

Those were questions that could have been given the same answers by any successful revolutionary leader.

Goering was not vulnerable as a revolutionary or as one who had done all he could to get rid of the shackles of Versailles. What he was criminally guilty of was murder, and the key document in this charge was the order he sent to Heydrich on July 31, 1941, which said:

> Complementing the task that was assigned to you on January 24, 1939, which dealt with carrying out by emigration and evacuation a solution of the Jewish problem as advantageous as possible, I hereby charge you with making all necessary preparations with regard to organizational and financial matters for bringing about a complete solution of the Jewish question in the German sphere of influence in Europe.
>
> Wherever other governmental agencies are involved they will cooperate with you.
>
> I request furthermore that you send me before long an over-all plan concerning the organizational, factual and material measures necessary for the accomplishment of the desired final solution of the Jewish question.[20]

That order set the extermination process in motion. Goering issued it under his authority as head of the Four-Year Plan and as the second man in the Reich, who issued directives under a wide ambience, for the Fuehrer did not have time for everything. The Wannsee Conference, attended by, among others, Adolf Eichmann, followed as a result, and it was this conference that worked out the blueprints for the mass slaughter. The protocol of the meeting begins as follows: "Chief of the Security Police and of the SD, SS Obergruppenfuehrer Heydrich, told at the outset of his being named commissioner of the final solution of the Jewish problem by the Reichsmarschall . . ." Goering, in his letter to Heydrich, had used the same word, "Endloesung," which, as events were to show, had but one meaning in the Nazi vocabulary—namely, extermination. At Nuremberg, Goering told Mr. Justice Jackson that "we had written total solution, not final solution." Jackson did not press him on the distinction. Actually, in the first paragraph of his letter to Heydrich, Goering had used the word "Gesamtloesung," which means "complete solution," and in the final paragraph he had used the word "Endloesung," or "final solution." It was the Endloesung that Heydrich, as he said, was working out at the Wannsee Conference on Goering's orders.

Mr. Justice Jackson read out the steps Goering had taken against the Jews: he had proclaimed the Nuremberg Laws; he had promulgated an act in 1936 making it a crime punishable by death to transfer property abroad; in April, 1938, under the Four-Year Plan, he had published the decree requiring the registration of Jewish property, the precursor to its complete confiscation; and then, as the vise tightened, he had published the decree that Jews might not own retail stores or offer goods or services for sale at markets, fairs, or exhibitions, or be leaders of enterprises. Goering remembered issuing all these decrees, and to the last question he answered, "Yes. Those are all part of the decrees for the elimination of Jewry from economic life." It was no doubt easier for a man like Goering—who liked individuals if they were useful or flattering to his vanity, and on occasion even liked Jews—to use a collective noun like "Jewry." On February 21, 1939, he signed the decree compelling Jews to surrender whatever they owned of gold and silver and platinum and jewelry.

Goering's signature appeared on such documents, but he had known of and participated in far worse measures than those published in the *Reichsgesetzblatt*. He knew about the lethal vans into which men, women, and children were loaded ostensibly for transport and then gassed; he knew about the gas chambers. It was his order to Heydrich that started the beltline of extermination in motion. Goebbels, in his diary entry of March 2, 1943, reported his saying, "Especially in the Jewish question, we are so involved that there is no escape . . . a movement and a people who have burned their bridges fight with much greater determination than those who are still able to retreat." [21] As early as March 12, 1933, Goering had announced that the Jews could not look for protection of life or property in the Third Reich: "Certainly I shall employ the police and quite ruthlessly, whenever the German people are hurt; but I refuse the notion that the police are protective troops for Jewish stores. No, the police protect whoever comes into Germany legitimately but it does not exist for the purpose of protecting Jewish usurers." [22]

In 1938 he said, "We can't let the Jews starve," but he signed the laws and wrote the decrees that took away their livelihood. "These swine," as he called them, had to be driven from German economic life and from the German community.

At the meeting that followed the *Kristallnacht*, Goebbels and Heydrich pressed Goering to determine what further anti-Jewish measures should be undertaken and how the Jews should pay for the damages. Heydrich reported that 7,500 Jewish stores were destroyed, and that 101 synagogues were destroyed by fire and 76 demolished.[23] Goering, with some clowning, matched Heydrich's and Goebbels' ferocity. The meeting, with Goering as chairman, took place in the Air Ministry on November 12, 1938, and lasted two hours and forty minutes. The pogrom had followed the murder of a member of the German legation in Paris, vom Rath, by a young Polish Jew. It was far from a spontaneous demonstration. The killing was used by Goebbels, Heydrich, and company as a pretext for taking further measures against the Jews. Bands of Nazi hooligans systematically looted Jewish stores of jewelry and furs or whatever else they could lay their hands on. The pogrom had long been prepared, and the murder of vom Rath was merely a pretext to unleash it. Goebbels appeared at the meeting prepared to justify the anti-Jewish acts, for he had been one of the chief instigators of the riots.

GOEBBELS: "I advocate that Jews be banned from all public places where they might cause provocation. It is still possible for a Jew to share a sleeper with a German. Therefore the Reich Ministry of Transport must issue a decree ordering that there shall be separate compartments for Jews. If this compartment is full, then the Jews cannot claim a seat . . . They must not mix with the Germans; if there is no more room, they will have to stand in the corridor."

GOERING: "I think it would be more sensible to give them separate compartments."

GOEBBELS: "Not if the train is overcrowded."

GOERING: "Just a moment. There will be only one Jewish coach. If that is filled up the other Jews will have to stay at home."

GOEBBELS: "But suppose there are not many going, let us say on the long-distance express train to Munich. Suppose there are two Jews on the train, and the other compartments are overcrowded; these two Jews would then have a compartment to themselves. Therefore the decree must state, Jews may claim a seat only after all Germans have secured a seat."

GOERING: "I would give the Jews one coach or one compartment, and should such a case as you mention arise, and the train be overcrowded, believe me, we will not need a law. He will be kicked out all right, and will have to sit alone in the toilet all the way." [24]

Goebbels then complained that Jews were using German holiday resorts and a decree should be issued to keep them out. Goering's hearty solution was: "Give them their own." When the discussion turned to the use of parks, Goebbels again wanted the Jews simply forbidden to use them. Jews, he said, had to be removed from the public gaze; their presence was provocative. To which Goering answered, "We will give the Jews a part of the forest, and Alpers will see to it that the various animals, which are damnably like the Jews—the elk too has a hooked nose—go into the Jewish enclosure and settle among them." [25] The meeting, which had been called to settle how much the Jews must pay for the damages, continued. Goebbels relentlessly pursued the subject of the intolerable presence of the Jews in German public places. He spoke of the whispering propaganda of Jewish women at the Ferbeliner Platz in Berlin.

GOEBBELS: "There are Jews who don't look so Jewish. They sit near German mothers with children and begin to complain and to pick everything apart."

GOERING: "They don't say they're Jewish."

GOEBBELS: "I see a great danger in it."

The Jews, Goebbels continued, need to have special places and can sit on benches marked "For Jews only." [26] He wanted no Jewish children in German schools. Goering declared at Nuremberg that Goebbels went so far as to say that he considered Goering's attitude provocative, but Goebbels, as is clear in the text, was referring to the Jews when he used the word "provocative," not to the second man in the Reich.

The meeting then came down to the business that had brought it together. How were the Jews to pay for the *Kristallnacht*? One man present said they might find a way to pay the fine demanded of them by dumping their Reich bonds. Goering's booming voice broke through the talk. He said, "The solution is quite simple. I will merely issue a decree making it illegal for Jews to sell bonds or for others to buy from them."

Throughout the meeting Goering played the role of the witty, terrible, but righteous viceroy who would do justice in his own way. In the end his decision was to impose fines for the damage on the Jews and the insurance companies were to pay in addition. A billion-mark fine was levied on the Jews. The insurance companies had a bill to pay of six million marks for the broken windows alone. The glass came from Belgium; to pay for it would take foreign currency, which was in short supply. This sum did not go to the Jewish proprietors of the shops or to their mostly Aryan owners who had taken out the insurance but, on Goering's ruling, to the State. Goering said he was tired of these riots and disturbances, which, in the last resort, were attacks not on the Jews but on him as the man responsible for the success of the Four-Year Plan, which was seriously damaged by this destruction of property.

The meeting reveals a good deal about Goering. His anti-Semitism was not far from the conventional German variety. Jews were to be permitted a minimal existence. When their enterprises were taken over by state trustees to be sold to Aryans, the Jewish owners were to be given securities and live on the interest yield. But they had to pay the billion-mark fine and the costs of the damage. Goering did not want to have to travel with Jews or to see them in public places, but he would let them live, he would even let them use German hospitals, at least for a time. He would move them out of the economic life of the Reich, but if they managed to survive, perhaps by trading with one another, they could travel on trains in special compartments or sections or, he said, slapping his fat thigh, sitting on the toilet. His directive from Hitler to settle the Jewish question meant, at this point, introducing harsher economic measures, but Goebbels and Heydrich needled him into taking a harder noneconomic line. It was Goebbels who had ordered the *Kristallnacht*. At the meeting he and Heydrich represented the Streicher brand of anti-Semitism. Jews were a moral and physical offense to the Germans. Just below the surface of what Goebbels was saying, the next wave was rising, wherein the Jew would disappear completely from sight and from the living. Goering ran through the various roles at the meeting. He was the mighty viceroy: "I will write a decree and everything will be arranged." He was the clown getting laughs from his audience with his remarks about the hooked-nose elks, but he was pushed by Goebbels toward the more violent measures soon to be adopted against the Jews. Goering was ready to fine them, to make them suffer through their pocketbooks. At one point he said he would rather have 200 Jews killed than so much property damage done the German Reich. Heydrich replied that thirty-five Jews had been killed. The two remarks revealed the character of each man. Goering was parading his authority as head of the Four-Year Plan. To him, 200 Jews were nothing compared to the task he had to perform of conserving German property while the Reich rearmed. Heydrich, talking of death and not of property values, was the real killer to whom thirty-five Jews were a small token of what was to come.

As the dialogue continued, the Austrian economist Hans Fischboeck, who had been one of Seyss-Inquart's collaborators, told of the plans for Vienna: 10,000 of the 12,000 Jewish workshops and 4,000 of the 5,000 Jewish retail stores were to be closed finally. The remainder were to be Aryanized. Thus, of these 17,000 businesses, Fischboeck said, 13,500 or 14,000 would be shut down. All that was needed was a short law.

Goering said, "I shall have this decree issued today." [27]

Buyers were already on hand, Fischboeck said, for half of the 3,000 businesses that were to be Aryanized, but if by the end of a year no buyer appeared for the remainder, the Government could decide whether or not to liquidate them. They would be turned over to a trustee (acting for the State) and the visible Jewish businesses would be finished.

> GOERING: "That would be splendid."
> FUNK: "We can do the same thing here. I have prepared a Law elaborating that. Effective January 1, 1939, Jews shall be prohibited from operating retail stores and wholesale establishments, as well as independent workshops. They shall be further prohibited from keeping employees or offering any ready-made products on the market; from advertising or receiving orders. Whenever a Jewish shop is operated the police shall shut it down . . ."
> GOERING: "I believe we can agree with this law." [28]

Fischboeck described how Jewish property had been expropriated in Austria, and Funk asked why, when their enterprises were taken over, they should not be able to keep bonds. Goering declined this idea because in that way they would actually be participating in the economy.[29]

The discussion turned to isolating and identifying the Jews. Heydrich said they would have to wear a certain badge. Goering asked, "A uniform?" and Heydrich replied, "A badge. In this way we could put an end to foreign Jews being molested who do not look different from ours." Goering then proposed that ghettos be created. The authorities could determine what stores could operate there, and the delivery of goods from German sources could be controlled. "You cannot let the Jews starve," he said. At the close of the the meeting, he summed up his sentiments: "I demand that German Jewry as a whole, as punishment for the abominable crimes, etc., make a contribution of one billion marks. That will work. The swine will not commit a second murder so quickly. Incidentally I would like to say again that I would not like to be a Jew in Germany." [30]

Three years were to elapse before Goering sent Heydrich the order to work out the Final Solution. In the process there was the long step from wanting the Jews to be put into ghettos where they would have industries and stores and be supplied on a limited scale from German sources to gas ovens. That was perhaps the reason why Heydrich opposed the ghettos in the November 12 meeting. The establishing of ghettos either by law or custom, including economic sanctions and limitations on travel and the use of public places, was not new in Europe. Pogroms like the *Kristallnacht* were not new either. What Goering would invent with his directive to Heydrich was the systematic, "legal," cold-blooded annihilation of a race. His own sentiments played but a small part in what was planned and later accomplished. If Goering had not given the order to Heydrich, the Fuehrer or Himmler would have done it. The order did not originate in Goering's mind; nothing in his psychological makeup or in his *Weltanschauung* would lead him to make the slightest resistance to those in the Party who wanted the extermination. A witness for him at the trial, General Karl Bodenschatz, told how he had at times protected individual Jews: at Hans Frank's urging he had stopped the deportation of Polish Jews into the General Government in 1940, and he had allowed the families of Jews working for Reich munitions industries to remain in Germany for a year after the transports to the East began in 1941. However, when the time came for the order of extermination to be written, it was Goering who, in the transparently veiled language of the Final Solution, wrote it. His anti-Semitism was at first of the run-of-the-mill prewar Nazi kind, as shown in his decrees driving Jews from the economic life of the Third Reich. But in the space of three years it had become more and more virulent, until he finally sent Jews to the gas chambers. Individual Jews he was on occasion willing to save, but "Jewry" he condemned to death.

Goering became just as ruthless when dealing with the Russians or the Poles. "I intend to plunder," he declared, speaking of Russia, "and to do it thoroughly." He told his assistants on the economic staff, "Whenever you come across anything that may be needed by the German people, you must be after it like a bloodhound. It must be taken out of store and brought to Germany."[31] He told the Reichskommissars for the Occupied Territories on August 6, 1942, "If anyone goes hungry, then it won't be the Germans but others." [32] His Green Portfolio was a plan for the ruthless exploitation of Russian resources prepared before the German attack on Russia, and his economic Staff East on May 23, 1941, foresaw "a cessation of supplies to the entire forest zone [of Russia], including the essential industrial centers of Moscow and Leningrad." [33] On September 16, 1941, he issued an order: "Only these people are to be supplied with an adequate amount of food who work for us. Even if one wanted to feed all the other inhabitants, one could not do it in the newly occupied Eastern areas. It is, therefore, wrong to funnel off food supplies for this purpose if it is done at the expense of the army and necessitates increased supplies from home."[34]

In pursuit of the goal of making the Reich self-sufficient, he told the Reichskommissars:

God knows you were not sent out here [to the East] to work for the welfare of the people in your charge but to squeeze the utmost out of them so that the German people may live . . . This everlasting concern about foreign people must cease once and for all . . . It makes no difference to me if you say that your people are collapsing from hunger. Let them do so as long as no German collapses. One thing I shall certainly do. I will make you deliver the quantities asked of you, and if you cannot do so I will set forces to work that will force you to do so whether you want to or not. Now let us see what Russia can deliver. I think, Riecke,* we should be able to get two million tons of cereals and fodder out of the whole of Russia.

RIECKE: "That can be done."

GOERING: "That means we must get three million, apart from Wehrmacht supplies."

RIECKE: "No, all that is in the front areas goes for the Wehrmacht only."

GOERING: "Then we bring two million."

RIECKE: "No."

GOERING: "A million and a half then."

RIECKE: "Yes . . ."

GOERING: "Gentlemen, I have a very great deal to do and a great deal of responsibility. I have no time to read letters and memoranda informing me that you cannot supply my requirements, I have only time to ascertain from time to time through short reports . . . whether the commitments are being fulfilled. If not then we shall have to meet on a different level." [35]

It was dangerous to cross Goering. His anger was most easily aroused when his vanity was wounded. He held Jews and Slavs in low esteem. He could, however, turn on anyone, no matter what his nationality, when what he demanded was not forthcoming. "In the occupied regions," he said, "I am interested only in those people who work to produce armaments and food supplies. They must receive just enough to enable them to continue working. It is all one to me whether Dutchmen are Germanic or not." [36]

With regard to the partisans, he never opposed the measures that were standard in the Eastern areas. He told with satisfaction how, after an attack was made on German soldiers in one village, the men were lined up on one side of the street, the women on the other. The men were threatened with immediate shooting if the women did not identify the strangers among them. The women always pointed out the nonresidents, he said, in order to save their own men. Those who were not shot were sent to concentration camps, the children were placed in childrens' camps, and then the villages were burned down.

* Hans Joachim Ernst Riecke, appointed Reichskommissar for Schaumburg-Lippe, 1933. Food expert in Goering's Ministry.

Goering liked adventure and cowboy-and-Indian stories and easy-to-follow movies that were run for him on his private train and in Karinhall. The Czech Ambassador to Germany before the war reported that he saw in Goering's bedroom at Karinhall the works of Karl May, a renowned German writer of adventure stories about the American Indians, and also a set of Jules Verne's books in a German translation. One of his plans for the campaign in Russia came close to the tactics of the redskins. He proposed recruiting convicts who were first offenders, poachers, and outdoor fellows of the kind he so easily romanticized and sending them behind the Russian lines to commit murder, arson, and rape. Both at his interrogation of October 8, 1945, where the matter was brought up, and in the courtroom, Goering objected only to his ever having countenanced rape. He tended to be sentimental about women, although he was never heard to express much sympathy for those who were not German. As the commanding officer of the Luftwaffe, he intervened to increase the severity of the penalty imposed for rape, changing sentences of imprisonment to death.[37]

As a routine matter Goering transmitted Hitler's scorched-earth order for Russia, which he as the Reichsmarschall issued on September 7, 1943. It read:

> 1.) All agricultural products, means of production, and machinery of enterprises serving the agriculture and food industry are to be removed. 2.) The factories serving the food economy, both in the field of production and of processing, are to be destroyed. 3.) The basis of agricultural production, especially the records and establishments, storage plants, etc., of the organization responsible for the food economy are to be destroyed. 4.) The population engaged in the agricultural and food economy is to be transported into the territory west of the fixed line.[38]

By the autumn of 1943 the campaign in Russia had become for both sides a war of naked survival, where food and shelter had as much military importance in the bitter weather as the guns, but the scorched-earth order was characteristic of the Reichsmarschall when he dealt with the enemy, whether his own personal enemies or those of the Fuehrer and of the Third Reich. He thought highly, for example, of Joseph Terboven, a man whose cruelty and participation in wholesale murder in Norway could easily be compared to the rule of Heydrich in Czechoslovakia. Goering liked barbarians, being one himself—the poachers who would kill and lay waste; the Gauleiter who burned the houses and slew their inhabitants on behalf of the Greater Reich.

From the time the German armies invaded Poland he went after forced labor on behalf of his Four-Year Plan. "In a struggle for the existence of the German people one cannot afford to be too scrupulous in the observance of treaties," he said. And while this is a statement of how nations may act in emergencies despite agreements solemnly signed and is a doctrine that at one time or another had been practiced by everyone of the four powers sitting in judgment on the Reichsmarschall, none of them (with the exception of the Soviet Union, which had been using the forced labor of millions of its own people) had conscripted labor on such a scale or under such inhuman conditions as developed in the Reich. At the end of the war both France and Russia took German prisoners of war and put them to work, often under conditions almost as bad as those the Germans had inflicted on their captive workers. The United States, which had turned over hundreds of thousands of German prisoners of war to France, was forced to protest over how the French treated them. German civilian labor was liable to be called up. Proclamation No. 2 of the Allied Control Council in September, 1945, ordered: "The German authorities must place at the disposal of the United Nations labor, personnel and expert and other services for use inside and outside Germany as they may be ordered by Allied authorities." Under this proclamation 200,000 Germans were "legally" shipped off to the Soviet Union after the cessation of hostilities. The Allies told one another the justification lay in the fact that it was right that Germans should repair the damages the Third Reich had caused. But actually nothing in international law countenanced such use of forced labor.

Goering had undoubtedly acted illegally when he called on Fritz Sauckel, whom he greatly admired for his energy, to recruit the millions of workers needed to carry out the Reich's economic program and when he used prisoners of war in the armaments industry and in the Luftwaffe antiaircraft companies. When his lawyer wanted to introduce the German White Book as background to show how the Russians had treated German prisoners of war and thus to attempt to explain in part why Goering had made such use of Allied war prisoners, the President of the Court said, "Well, we are here to try major war criminals; we are not here to try any of the signatory powers." After further discussion the President added, "The question is, how can you justify in a trial of the major war criminals of Germany evidence against Great Britain, or against the United States of America, or against the USSR, or against France? If you are going to try the actions of all those four signatory powers, apart from other considerations, there would be no end to the trial at all." [39] Despite this one-sided consideration of the evidence, Goering cannot be exculpated. Forced laborers for the airplane industry (including concentration-camp workers) lived under terrible conditions and died by the thousands of malnutrition and inadequate shelter in the packed transports shuttling to and from the Reich. Goering had little directly to do with such atrocities, but he certainly knew of them.

In addition, a series of captured German documents identified Goering with the shooting, without trial, of captured enemy "terror fliers." Toward the end of the war, when the Germans could put up only weak fighter resistance, Allied planes did vast destruction in their saturation bombing of German cities. In hedge-hopping and dive-bombing raids, they also attacked any car or train or horsecart that came before their sights. They went after any live target—people working in the fields, or huddled on the sides of roads, or walking or running for their lives. In a conference held in May, 1944, attended by Goering and high Air Force officers, the minutes read as follows: "The Reichsmarschall wishes to propose to the Fuehrer that American and English crews who shoot indiscriminately over towns, at moving civilian trains, or at soldiers hanging on parachutes should be shot immediately at the spot." [40] Goering denied on the stand having said this and instanced the fact that the phrase "hanging on parachutes" was unusual, but other orders besides this one connected him with the "shoot-on-capture" order.

Another German document, a note signed by General Walter Warlimont on June 6, 1944, placed Goering at a conference with Kaltenbrunner, Himmler, and Ribbentrop in which it was decided that lynch justice would be the rule where direct attacks had been made by Allied fliers shooting at civilians.[41] Hitler had already ordered, on May 21, 1944, that English and American air crews be executed without trial if they had fired on German civilians, railroad trains, or German airmen bailing out with parachutes or who had been forced to land and were in the immediate neighborhood of downed planes that Allied gunners were trying to destroy. A top-secret note from Warlimont of June 30, 1944, revealed that both Ribbentrop and Goering had approved the proposed measures to be taken against enemy fliers.[42]

The judgment did not mention these matters, although Mr. Justice Jackson had cross-examined Goering at length on the subject. Half the space given by the judgment to its reasons for finding Goering guilty on all four counts was devoted to his having committed crimes against peace—that is, having plotted to commit aggression and having waged war. "He was the planner and prime mover," the judgment said, "in the military and diplomatic preparation for war which Germany pursued." And it summed up: "There is nothing to be said in mitigation. For Goering was often, indeed almost always, the moving force, second only to his leader. He was the leading war aggressor both as political and military leader. . . ." [43]

Nevertheless, the charges against Goering for having taken part in the shooting of Allied airmen without a trial were serious, and despite his denial he seems guilty of having participated in the crime. In his defense it might be urged that what the Allied airmen were doing was also a crime, but in any case it was a crime that could have been tried before a German court-martial. By 1944, not much was left in Goering's mind of the notions of legality, not to mention the notions of chivalry he may have had in World War I and by fits and starts early in World War II, when he had sent Luftwaffe soldiers to protect Allied fliers who had fallen into the hands of an enraged civilian population.

All these events were diversionary for the Reichsmarschall. What he wanted was an unceasing flow of prestige, to be reminded daily that he was one of the great men of the world. Goering had lived well, even royally. In the course of his first interrogations his financial position and sources of income were carefully gone into by the Allied prosecution. During Germany's occupation of France he had bought jewels in Cartier's in Paris. He had his agents buy paintings for him in Switzerland. But outside his Berlin bank, he had no accounts, no money in foreign countries, none buried except in Karinhall, where his American interrogators would have to deal directly with the Russians to find out where it was. He told his questioners he could only show them the spot if he were there; he could not describe it, nor was there a plan available. He had once owned a property in Bavaria, he testified, but after the unsuccessful putsch and his flight from Germany, his car had been confiscated by the Bavarian State and later his wife had to sell the property to pay bills. But this sacrifice for the cause had been richly compensated when the Party took power. As late as 1959, property in West Berlin that had belonged to him was valued at 756,000 DM (it had been confiscated in denazification proceedings), and this did not include the ducal houses and estates he had owned or the collections of art he had assembled by way of his own agents and with the help of the Einsatzstab Rosenberg, which had orders to pick out especially meritorious works that might appeal to the Reichsmarschall. The Berlin property evaluated in 1959 consisted only of bank accounts, stocks, and sculpture.

One of his subordinates, Field Marshal Milch, got a present of 250,000 RM on the occasion of his fiftieth birthday from a grateful Fuehrer. Goering himself was given an art fund by Hitler to enable him to build up his gallery, which, he said at Nuremberg, he had planned to leave to the nation and therefore represented not only his taste in art but his generosity. He received 28,000 RM a month as Reichsmarschall, he told an American interrogator, and from a special fund he maintained a free residence in Berlin. His income from books alone, during the years he was one of the Nazi greats, came to between 1 and 1.5 million RM.* In addition, he received 5,000 to 7,000 RM a month in interest from annuities. The expenses of running Karinhall and his palace in Berlin were also paid by the State.[44]

Of his fidelity to the Fuehrer, despite the latter's suspicions, there can be no question. Goering pursued the delights of the table and of the princely landlord with the same appetite he had for the lighter jobs among his military and economic assignments. He was rightfully awarded his renaissance role, as he liked to think of it in his years of eminence, by a grateful Hitler, and he was paid on the monumental scale awarded the favorites. These men were generous to one another, both in the rewards and the punishments which were lavishly bestowed. Goering loved to command; he loved, too, to prostrate himself, to bask in the reflected glory of the Fuehrer.

---

* These were the figures he gave at Nuremberg, but he may have exaggerated. Goering had hastily written a short book, *Aufbau einer Nation* (*Germany Reborn*), published in Berlin and London in 1934. It was a boastful story of Nazi successes. Goering dictated the manuscript in a matter of hours with a British audience in mind. A number of his speeches had also been published, and he laid claim to part of the royalties of the Gritzbach biography, but his figures, even allowing for the forced sales of books by the Reichsmarschall, seem high.

To his subordinates he could be ruthless. At meetings he displayed his power by cutting off discussions: "Gentlemen, enough. I will decide this question later." Or, "The solution is quite simple. I will merely issue a decree making it illegal for Jews to sell bonds or for others to buy from them."

The role of number-two man of destiny suited Goering. He constantly referred, even during the trial, to the intimacy of the collaboration between himself and Hitler. Speaking of the charge of conspiracy against the twenty-two defendants, he said there could only be one such charge: against him and the Fuehrer, for no one else could have conspired, no one else was close enough to the throne. He explained to his American interrogators at Nuremberg that as Reichsmarschall he could not resign nor could the title ever be taken from him: "I shall have it as long as I live." No command rights went with it; it was simply the highest military title in the Reich. Asked whether he regarded himself as a military man, he said he did. He thought of himself as the only man in Germany, aside from the Fuehrer himself, who combined the highest military and political functions and capacity.

A number of witnesses testified to Goering's attempts to keep the peace. The Swede Dahlerus, who was the only foreign witness allowed to the defense by the court, told of his flying back and forth between Goering and the British Foreign Office in the days before the Polish campaign on behalf of the Reichsmarschall, who hoped, he said, that the war could be avoided. An assistant of Dr. Stahmer, a lawyer who saw much of Goering during the Nuremberg trial, received some documents from a Swedish lawyer which were placed at the disposal of the defense.[45] These documents came from a Swede, Baron Knut Bonde, who had been in touch with Goering through a Swedish friend, Erik von Rosen (a relative of Goering's first wife). Goering had confided to Bonde his hope, even after the war had started, that he might act as intermediary between Germany and England. Goering had been delighted, Bonde said, with the opportunity to try to make peace between the two countries.

At that time the following events took place: In the middle of December, 1939, Bonde flew to England, where he talked with Lord Halifax, who said England had never refused to try to come to a peaceful settlement with Adolf Hitler's Germany, and if a Polish state could be reconstituted and more freedom given Czechoslovakia he thought something might be arranged. Halifax said: "If there is one man in Germany who could make peace it is Goering." [46] Bonde's efforts ended early in 1941, after Hitler's declaration that the possibility of reconstituting Poland was discussable but nothing could be done for the Czechs. By 1941 Goering's influence with Hitler was already diminished, Bonde said, and efforts at negotiation were ended.

At the request of Dr. Stahmer, Lord Halifax signed an affidavit about his visits to Karinhall, where he had talked with Goering before the war. He said, somewhat frigidly, that he thought Goering would have liked to have avoided war if the Germans had been able to gain what they wanted without it. Although Goering, in 1936, had told a meeting of German airplane manufacturers he was certain war would come, the stories of his reluctance to see war break out are undoubtedly true. They can be accounted for in part by Goering's rivalry with Ribbentrop, who had nothing to do with the missions of Dahlerus and who certainly wanted war because he thought that was what Hitler expected of him. Dahlerus wrote, in his *The Last Attempt*, that Goering had warned him that Ribbentrop might attempt to place a bomb in his plane to sabotage the peace efforts. At Nuremberg Goering denied having said this, and it seems likely that Dahlerus misinterpreted him.

The rivalry and differences between Goering and Ribbentrop were of considerable dimensions. Ribbentrop, as Ambassador to Britain, had prevented Goering's attending the coronation of King Edward VIII. He had told the Fuehrer that the English would prefer another representative. In reality, Goering thought, his own presence was opposed because he and his wife, since he was a Field Marshal, would have outranked the Ribbentrops.* Goering was never allowed to take part in the negotiations in Bad Godesberg that led to the Munich Agreement. He had gone on his own account to Munich for the signing of the agreement, and he told his lawyer that Ernst von Weizsaecker, State Secretary in the Foreign Office, who greatly mistrusted Ribbentrop, had said to him, "Thank God you are here." At Nuremberg, Ribbentrop, casting about for any help he could get, wrote a note to Goering, asking him to testify that he had tried always to get a diplomatic solution of the problems before them. Goering struck out the suggested answer with a bold stroke and wrote in its place: "I have only heard that Ribbentrop advised in favor of war." [47]

Goering had nothing to gain from a war. True, he was the ranking military officer of the Nazi hierarchy as well as chief of the Luftwaffe. He was intelligent, he had the second highest IQ among the twenty-one defendants (the highest was Schacht, with 141; Goering was close behind, with 139), and he was aware that a war would put everything at stake that had been won—the succession of brilliant uniforms, the receptions, the hunting, the Party celebrations with their streaming lights and banners, and the perfumes of adulation that rose not only to the Fuehrer but to his faithful paladin as well. Goering was no coward. His war record was a brilliant one, and his conduct at Nuremberg, although posturing, showed none of the terror that seized Ribbentrop. He accepted risks when he had to. When decisions were made by the Fuehrer, he went along with them without visible misgivings. But he wanted to enjoy the amenities of the victory after the long struggle to power. He preferred the lush life of Karinhall to the private railroad train that bore him to the field of battle. (A plane regularly took off from his private train to return with rare fruits and wines in the midst of the war.)

For a time Goering had considerable success on the witness stand. He had

* After Carin's death, he married an actress from Hamburg, Emmy Sonnemann, in 1935.

no difficulty defending himself against the implacable ideology of the American prosecutor, who was himself put so on the defensive that he had to appeal to the President of the Court for help. Mr. Justice Jackson demanded of Goering, who declared he had disapproved of the war against Russia, why, if that was so, he had not told the German people of the plan to attack the Soviet Union and why he had not resigned when the decision was made. Goering pointed out that he was a soldier and that he had never heard of a case when, in time of war, a soldier could appeal over the head of his commander in chief to the citizenry merely because he did not approve of a decision his superior had made. Mr. Justice Jackson asked about a document that seemed to him to show that Goering, in connection with the German plans for mobilization in the mid-thirties, had prepared or helped to prepare for the occupation of the Rhineland when this was expressly forbidden by the Versailles Treaty. Goering pointed out that there was an error in the translation of the document, that what the mobilization plans called for was not occupation of the Rhineland but the clearing of river traffic from the Rhine. But Mr. Justice Jackson was not to be put off so easily.

> JACKSON: "Well, these preparations were preparations for the armed occupation of the Rhineland, were they not?"
> GOERING: "They were general preparations for mobilization, such as every country makes and not for the purpose of the occupation of the Rhineland."
> JACKSON: "But they were of a character which had to be kept secret . . . ?"
> GOERING: "I do not think that I can recall reading beforehand the publication of the mobilization preparations of the United States."

Jackson (turning to the President of the Court) denounced what he called this witness' "arrogant and contemptuous attitude toward the Tribunal which is giving him the trial which he never gave a living soul, nor dead ones either." The President agreed that Goering's remark was irrelevant, but when Jackson wanted to press the matter, saying that Goering was getting propaganda statements into the record and was successfully turning over control of the trial to the defense, the President coldly asked him, "What exactly is the motion you are making . . . are you submitting to the Tribunal that the witness has to answer every question yes or no and wait until he is reexamined for the purpose of making any explanation at all? Surely it is making too much of a sentence the witness has said, whether the United States makes orders for mobilization public or not . . . Every country keeps certain things secret."

> JACKSON: "Let me say that I agree with your Honor that as far as the United States is concerned we are not worried by anything the witness can say about it—and we expected plenty. . . . And it does seem to me that this is the beginning of the Trial's getting out of hand."
> THE PRESIDENT: "I have never heard it suggested that the counsel for the

prosecution have to answer every irrelevant observation made in cross-examination." [48]

Mr. Justice Jackson, convinced of the rectitude of his high mission, repeated clichés of Allied war propaganda that were refuted by the documents he had read or should have read. At one point he demanded of Goering: "You have testified . . . on interrogation that it was Hitler's information that the United States would never go to war, even if attacked, and that he counted on the isolationists of that country to keep it out of war?" Goering replied: "Such nonsense—I hope you will excuse me— . . . I could never have uttered, because if a country is attacked, it defends itself." [49] Hitler had a considerable store of misinformation about the United States, its decadence and subservience to Jewish influence, but both he and Goering had believed from the beginning that if the war lasted the United States was certain to join it. This, in fact, was given by the Fuehrer as one of the reasons for his attack on Russia. As early as July 31, 1940, he told the assembled company of generals and admirals that England continued its hopeless fight against Germany only because she was counting on Russia and the United States to enter the war.[50]

The reporters in the courtroom, as well as the defense counsel, were impressed with the adroitness of Goering's replies to Jackson's cross-examination. He had far less luck, though, with Jackson's questions about his part in the anti-Jewish measures and with the British prosecutor, Sir David Maxwell-Fyfe, who brought out the vulnerable points of Goering's past: the treatment of prisoners of war, the shooting of fifty British officers who had escaped from a prisoner-of-war camp at Sagan, the background of the German attacks on Holland and Belgium and Yugoslavia, the war against the partisans, the system of concentration camps, and the extermination of the Jews.

Goering had to listen to some unflattering judgments from his fellow defendants. When Speer spoke of his vanity, his corruption, and his morphine addiction, Goering impatiently told his assistant counsel that Speer had always been a traitor.*

* No one could wound his vanity without his reacting, sometimes viciously. One of his young officers to whom he had taken a great liking was falsely accused by a superior—a general—of having reported to the SS that so great was the chaos in the Air Force that a successor to Goering was being discussed everywhere. Goering, when told of this alleged remark, called a court-martial to try the young officer and said he expected a sentence of guilty to be handed down by six o'clock that evening. He also ordered that preparations be made for the execution. Owing to the diligence of the court president, Freiherr von Hammerstein, the proceedings, however, were continued, the young man's innocence was established to Goering's as well as the court's satisfaction, and Goering admitted he had been wrong. That was the young officer's good luck; Goering would certainly have had him shot had he believed him guilty. Goering had bursts of warmth and good feeling, but he did not suffer adversity easily and as his troubles multiplied he turned increasingly to morphine and the wild hopes that led to his promise to provision the Sixth Army at Stalingrad by means of an airlift. This was the same shallow optimism that had led him to say that no bomber would get through to Berlin. (Christian Freiherr von Hammerstein, *Mein Leben* [Private printing, 1962], pp. 171–73).

The reliability of his testimony depended largely on whether his replies were in accord with what he regarded as his prescribed loyalties to his Fuehrer and country—his roles of the faithful, brave soldier. He freely admitted on the witness stand that he had wanted to rearm Germany, to get rid of Versailles, and to attach Austria to the Reich and that he had said in 1935, "I intend to create an airforce which, if the hour should strike, shall burst upon the foe like a chorus of revenge. The enemy must have a feeling of having lost before even having fought." [51] He was sure these were the right words to use, as they had been, to indoctrinate young Air Force officers who were building up the Luftwaffe. He also admitted that he had known that the hair shorn from concentration camp inmates was to be used for practical purposes. But he denied, when Maxwell-Fyfe questioned him, that he had ever heard of the Bullet Decree under which Allied prisoners in Mauthausen were killed by an apparatus that seemingly was designed to measure them but actually was so arranged that it fired a shot into the victim's head when it was adjusted.

Goering's magnificent art collection of 1,300 or more paintings, worth, he reluctantly calculated at Nuremberg, some 50 million RM (Allied experts placed the figure at 180 million dollars), had come in part from property confiscated from Jews who had emigrated or had died in the gas chambers. It is doubtful that Goering had much genuine feeling for art. What he liked was collecting, having a renowned museum as part of his estate, living in style. He wrote to Rosenberg: "I have now obtained by means of purchase, presents, bequests, and barter perhaps the greatest private collection in Germany at least, if not in Europe." [52] Some of the bartered paintings were from the collections of so-called "degenerate art" confiscated from the museums and private collections of the Third Reich. They included the works of great contemporary painters: Beckmann, George Grosz, Chagall, Klee, Van Gogh, Signac, Cézanne, Gauguin, Picasso. Most of these paintings were sent to Switzerland to be auctioned off to bring in needed foreign exchange. Some of the confiscated paintings were burned, just as the evil books that offended the tastes of the National Socialists were burned.* Goering did not dare to hang the "degenerate" paintings, even if he had been so disposed. It is not easy to separate the overriding political considerations and the need for pleasing Adolf Hitler from what Goering might otherwise have chosen. What he liked was opulence. He had some thick carpets transported from museums to Karinhall. In 1937 he took a leading part in the "cleansing" of the German art galleries by having "degenerate art" replaced by posters—such as the grotesque poster of the Fuehrer mounted à la Saint Joan on a charger, wearing armor and carrying a banner. Goering had himself photographed admiring

* Such burnings were symbolic. Not all the proscribed books or paintings were destroyed. Those chosen for destruction, in a ceremony of rejection, were the Jewish or pacifist or antinationalist works.

the new, healthy paintings. An art school was named after him. Here painters were trained in the approved National Socialist style, and promising students were given financial help. His name was also attached to a prize of 5,000 RM to be awarded to the painter who in the year 1942 produced the best work of art dealing with Germany's defense forces.[53]

The high quality of his collection at Karinhall and in his seven other residences was due to his buying or stealing the sure things—Rembrandt, Goya, Velásquez—and to his having employed experts who seem to have acquired few fraudulent pieces. Only two fakes were mentioned at Nuremberg—a Vermeer and a Rembrandt. He had been advised by some of the Third Reich's most renowned experts.

Few Germans dared to resist the plundering of French art by Goering's agents as did, for one, the Rhenish Conservator Franz Wolff-Metternich. Goering had paid for some of the pictures he acquired, he told his interrogators at Nuremberg, out of the art fund Hitler had given him and sometimes out of his own pocket. Einsatzstab Rosenberg acquired large numbers of paintings and *objets d'art* on his behalf. (Goering never got around to paying for them.) * He also had substantial gifts from the Hermann Goering Division, from German cities, from private individuals, and from industrial firms. A lot of people knew of his expensive tastes and hoped to benefit by indulging them.† When Goering did pay for pictures he acquired, he did so always in cash. He boasted to an interrogator, "I was the second man in the Reich and always had plenty of money. I would give an order to the Reichsbank and they would get the money." When asked, "Could you get foreign exchange in this way?" Goering replied, "Yes, I was the last court of appeal."

His failure to pay Rosenberg did not disturb the relations between the two men, for both were declared art lovers. On Goering's fiftieth birthday Rosenberg sent him a seventeenth-century Dutch painting.

In his acquisition of paintings Goering was by turns extravagant and mean. He once acquired a collection of pictures for the sum named by a dealer, had them shipped to Karinhall, and then refused to pay more than half of the bill, saying it was too high. His wife, Emmy, who had been with him in the

* The Rosenberg staff organized twenty-nine large transports of paintings. The meticulous German reports showed that more than 130 freight cars and 4,000 crates were used. The collections included more than 5,000 paintings (including icons and hundreds of miniatures) from Russia, Poland, France, and Holland; costly pieces of furniture, textiles, Gobelin tapestries, and rare carpets; thousands of pieces of porcelain, bronzes, and faience, along with a great collection of bronzes from East Asia. Among the painters were masters from the entire Continent. Goering got his pick of these (N XXVI, pp. 527, 529). He also obtained many paintings from Italy, causing the German Ambassador in Rome, Hans von Mackensen, some unpleasant interviews with Italian authorities, who complained about Goering's collecting methods. (Roger Manvell and Heinrich Fraenkel, *Hermann Goering* [London: Heinemann, 1962], p. 275).

† Berlin, for example, one year sent him as a birthday present a painting worth 250,000 RM (*Ibid.*, p. 277).

gallery when he had agreed to pay the price named, secretly paid the other half.[54]

Goering felt compelled to own certain pictures. Whether they were paid for, and by whom, did not matter much, as long as the transactions did not pinch his style of living. One of his advisers was Dr. Hermann Bunjes, an art historian. He told Goering, as they were looking over art confiscated from Jewish collections in Paris in the Jeu de Paume, that the French Government was making trouble. Vichy was protesting the seizures being made by the Einsatzstab Rosenberg, calling them a breach of the Armistice of Compiègne. Goering said to Bunjes, "My orders are controlling. You will directly follow my orders." He then ordered the plunder he had chosen put in freight cars to be attached to his private train. When Bunjes pointed out that Army jurists attached to the Military Commander in France would make objections, Goering answered, "My dear Bunjes, let this be my trouble. I am the highest jurist in the state." [55] At Nuremberg Goering denied that he could have said this, since he was not in fact the highest jurist in the State.

The Reichsmarschall's nearest competitor was the Fuehrer, who intended to found a museum for his native Austria in Linz. Goering often held back from acquiring a picture he wanted, he told his interrogators, because the Fuehrer had expressed an interest in it. Actually, he acted on behalf of both Hitler and himself. He performed for the Fuehrer in his order of November 5, 1940, which read:

> In conveying the measures taken until now for the securing of Jewish art property by the Chief of the Military Administration, Paris, and the Einsatzstab Rosenberg . . . the art objects brought to the Louvre [later to the Jeu de Paume] will be disposed of in the following way:
> 1. Those art objects the decision as to the use of which the Fuehrer will reserve for himself;
> 2. Those art objects which serve the completion of the Reich Marshal's collection;
> 3. Those art objects and library materials which seem useful for the establishment of the Hohe Schule and for the program of Reichsleiter Rosenberg;
> 4. Those art objects which are suitable for sending to the German museums . . .[56]

Thus Goering appeared in another guise as the number-two man of the Reich. Since Hitler's interest in art collecting was sporadic and he had more on his mind than did the Reichsmarschall, Goering had the field pretty much to himself. He admitted during his interrogations that he had not given the paintings and other art he had acquired to the Reich, although he had talked of his public spirit in acquiring them. He said he had planned one day to leave them all not to the Reich but to the German people.[57]

It should be borne in mind that Goering was not the first among those conquerors in history who pillaged enemy *objets d'art* and brought them back to their native countries. Other museums in Europe have from time to time enriched their collections with paintings and sculpture confiscated from foreign countries. But Goering was working not for the museums of the Reich but for himself. His was a job of private plunder on the greatest scale ever recorded. Fifty million marks is a low estimate of what the collection he had assembled was worth. Goering had moved beyond the marketplace to where he could command a picture without putting a price on it merely by telling Rosenberg or some other person that he wanted it. This is what nourished him: the prestige of the picture, its value as a prized commodity or as decoration, and a background for his uniforms.

Goering's special train, as he sought to live out the war in as grand a style as he could command, was second only to Karinhall in his pride of possession. It consisted actually of two trains: the first, known as "the bomb clearer," with eight regular passenger cars; the second, with the armor and the luxury befitting the second in command of the Reich. His bathroom (one of three) was reserved for his sole use. While he bathed, the train stopped regardless of what this did to the timetable of other trains using the same tracks. At each end of the train (it had a crew and guards of 171 men) were the air-defense batteries, manned by twenty men. Behind the first battery came the baggage cars and then Goering's car, which had two sleeping rooms, with full-sized beds. One bedroom was for his wife, who never used the train. The ceiling woodwork and the furniture were of cherry. A library stocked mainly with detective stories sported heavy carpets. The following car was used as a living room. In the early days of the war, movies were shown every night, including *Gone with the Wind* and captured films like Garbo's *Ninotchka*, which was otherwise forbidden in Germany. Goering liked criminal films best of all, and he would sometimes leap up to shout the identity of the murderer before the film had ended: "There he is!" The next car was the command center, in which staff conferences were held at 11 A.M. It was dominated by a large picture of Hitler. Goering's first telephone call daily was to the Fuehrer's headquarters, the second to his wife. The food was of an elegant kind: strawberries might be flown in from Italy by the accompanying courier planes, rolls and cakes could be baked in the ovens of the train, and an ordinary lunch often included lobster and caviar as well as Italian fruit. The ten railroad cars had space for the automobiles that might be needed for shorter journeys; among them, after the fall of France, were two captured American automobiles, a LaSalle and a Buick, which the Reichsmarschall liked to use.

Everything had to be in plush style. Goering's kimonos were of brocade and silk, and the fifty or so uniforms of his own design included fur-lined overcoats. He received countless presents from admiring friends, but many were contributed by more reluctant givers, on whom the bite was put. One gift, presented to him in 1940, when he was forty-eight years old, was a gold box inlaid with jewels, which an observer calculated to be worth in the neighborhood of 20,000 or 30,000 RM. Another present, a brick of pure gold, was estimated to be worth as much as 2,000,000 RM.

A full-time technician was in charge of the playroom at Karinhall, where the toy railroad was housed. It measured half the size of a football field—240 square meters. It contained a scene that would delight the heart of any child, with its miniature mountains and hills, valleys and meadows, towers and castles, farms and roads. Planes could take off on wires that crossed over the landscape and drop their loads of bombs, which went off with a satisfactory bang while flak shot at them. Electric automobiles ran on the Autobahnen. Goering could cause collisions and derailments on the railroad. The sport was beloved by his visitors, among them the Prince of Wales, Mussolini, Miklós Horthy, Count Galeazzo Ciano, and Yosuke Matsuoka, who had once been in charge of the Manchurian railroads. He and Goering kept a group of high officers waiting for an hour while Matsuoka ran the railroad and later played in Goering's bowling alley, which could double as a shooting range.

As time went on, Goering retreated further and further from the war. One of his aides said that what interested Goering was bringing good news to the Fuehrer. The chances of doing this diminished steadily with the years; indeed, they went down almost immediately after the fall of France, with the failure to knock out the British planes, which proved to be faster and more maneuverable than the German aircraft. One of the reasons for this may well have lain in incidents such as the one that occurred when Goering kept the aces of his entourage—Ernst Udet, Bodenschatz, and Milch—waiting for three days while he went shopping in Paris and was unavailable for the necessary consultations and decisions on how to improve the German planes in accordance with the recommendations of the men who flew them. Hitler knew all too well of Goering's laziness and ineptness. What he believed in, and with reason, was Goering's faithfulness. He was, however, quoted as saying to a visitor, "You should visit Goering at Karinhall, a sight worth seeing."

Goering's responsibility for the loss of the German strength in the air was diminished by the Fuehrer's decision to put manpower and resources to work on the new wonder weapons rather than on the jets the Germans were producing in the underground factories in 1944. The gasoline shortage, too, became acute.* There was no point, said Speer, in building planes that could not be fueled. Goering told Werner Bross, one of his lawyers, that his planes had not been able to supply Stalingrad because of the lack of gasoline. This was only part of the story, but Goering was not one to let the facts deter him from coming to a conclusion favorable to himself or his cause. Talking

---

* Professor Percy Schramm wrote an opinion for the Remer trial, held in March, 1952, in which he said that the destruction of oil resources, beginning with the successful Allied air attacks on the Rumanian Ploesti airfields in April, 1944, alone must have brought the war to an end. The air raids on Ploesti and its neighboring refineries, together with the mining of the Danube by Allied airplanes, cut the transport of oil to the Reich in May, 1944, by 56 per cent—from 430,000 tons to 240,000 (Institut fuer Zeitgeschichte, Munich [hereinafter referred to as IZG], Gb 10.03, 357/52).

of the Battle of the Bulge, he said the Germans might have won it and driven the invaders from the Continent had it not been for some incompetence on the part of the military leaders and the lifting of the fog that had lasted for four days and had enabled the Allied planes with their overwhelming numerical superiority to strafe the German troops. But Goering was the commanding officer of the Luftwaffe, and its failure was his failure, no matter who else might share the responsibility. The Fuehrer could make no mistakes. Only his subordinates could lose battles and make wrong decisions. Goering, by 1944, had lost the battle of the air in the West, and his planes had no effect on the course of the struggle in the East. It was his planes that were not flying against the enemy.

For a short time Goering had succeeded in creating the most powerful air force in the world. It had cleared the skies over Poland, France, Norway, Yugoslavia, and Greece. In Crete his paratroopers, for the first time in the history of warfare, captured the major military objective of an island against an entrenched enemy that had control of the seas. Signs of the limitations of the Air Force had appeared early, for example, in the failure to defeat the British Air Force and the failure to prevent the embarkation at Dunkirk. But the real trouble started in 1941. German calculations greatly underestimated Russian strength in all arms, including air strength, and while the Luftwaffe long dominated the skies over Russia, it was never able after the first major successes to give the ground troops the support that so greatly aided the victories won before the invasion of the Soviet Union. It was Goering's optimism that helped to confirm Hitler in the decision to keep the Sixth Army where it was at Stalingrad and to stand adamant against the pleadings of the Army generals to let General Friedrich Paulus break out in time. As much as anything, however, numbers defeated his Luftwaffe. American and British production could in no way be matched by Germany, which, in addition, was increasingly open to air attack. Despite the excellent German jets, Goering had not kept up with the technical requirements of the air war. Bombers had to be converted to fighters and all sorts of deficiencies remained unremedied, because Goering had not taken the time to listen to his technicians and to see to it that new models were provided. By the time of the Allied invasion of Normandy, the Germans defending the French coast had only a handful of planes to send against the American and British bombers. So overwhelming was Allied air superiority that the OKW orders said that any planes operating in the skies over the French coast must be regarded as enemies.

Maxwell-Fyfe, in his cross-examination, told Goering that he knew him to have been a brave fighter in World War I. So he had been, and he never forgot it. His photographer saw him in France during World War II at the site of the airfield where his World War I planes had been based and noted how different his expression was as he went back over the scene and memories of the solid exploits of his career as a flier. In the last years of World War II he flew little, although two planes were at his disposal. He kept away from the front, continued to take morphine, and lived the life of a feudal prince to whom the conferences with the Fuehrer and the time given to the details of being commander in chief of the Air Force were trying. They were diversions from his collecting trips and hunting. He even went on hunting trips in Russia while the front-line troops, praised so unstintingly in his speeches, were dying by the thousands, only hundreds of kilometers to the East.

Was Goering the man of peace he described at Nuremberg? There is no evidence that he wished to risk his life or comfort. He did only what the formalities of being the second in command of the Reich armed forces demanded. Hitler increasingly bypassed him in the conduct of the war. Their relations, however, remained intermittently cordial until close to the Fuehrer's death, although the Fuehrer time and again attacked him for the failures of the Air Force. They met on July 20, 1944, the day of the attempt on Hitler's life. As a kind of expiation for the part the generals and Army had played in the attempt to kill the Fuehrer, Goering introduced the raised arm as the official salute in the armed forces. Only at the very end, when Goering did no more than he thought his duty in taking over the reins of government, when it seemed that Hitler had decided to remain in Berlin and die with the city, did the final break come. Other men had supplanted him in power, and during the last weeks all he retained was the title of Reichsmarschall, which he and Prince Eugene in the eighteenth century alone had borne. The surrender took that from him.

A few hours before he was to be hanged, he bit into a cyanide capsule that had been smuggled to him and died. His ashes were strewn into the Isar along with the ashes of the men executed. The Allies wanted no cult of Nazism to have a center around the graves of the dead, but Goering had few followers left and no disciples.

NOTES

1. Werner Bross, *Gespraeche mit Hermann Goering* (Flensburg and Hamburg: Christian Wolff, 1950), p. 143.

2. *Ibid.*, p. 176.

3. *Ibid.*, p. 223.

4. Christian Freiherr von Hammerstein, *Mein Leben* (Private printing, 1962).

5. Charles Bewley, *Hermann Goering* (Goettingen: Goettinger Verslagsanstalt, 1956).

6. Roger Manvell and Heinrich Fraenkel, *Hermann Goering* (London: Heinemann, 1962).

7. Erich Gritzbach, *Hermann Goering Werk und Mensch* (Munich: Zentralverlag der NSDAP, Franz Eher Nachf., 1939), pp. 239–40.

8. Charles Bewley, *Hermann Goering and the Third Reich* (New York: Devin-Adair, 1962), pp. 33–34.

9. Manvell and Fraenkel, *op. cit.*

10. Count Lutz Schwerin von Krosigk, *op. cit.*

11. N IX, p. 307.

12. Theodor Eschenburg, *"Zur Ermordung des Generals Schleicher,"* in *Vierteljahrshefte fuer Zeitgeschichte,* Vol. I, No. 1, 1953, pp. 71–95.

13. Hermann Mau, *"Die 'Zweite Revolution'—Der 30. Juni 1934,"* ibid., Vol. I, No. 2, 1953, pp. 119–37.

14. N XXXII, 3442-PS, pp. 289–90.

15. Hammerstein, *op. cit.,* pp. 107–9, 146–47.

16. J. K. Zawodny, *Death in the Forest* (Notre Dame: University of Notre Dame Press, 1962), p. 66.

17. Sir Winston S. Churchill, *The Second World War,* Vol. IV: *The Hinge of Fate* (Boston: Houghton Mifflin Company, 1950), p. 759.

18. N XXXII, p. 411.

19. NCA VI, 3575-PS, pp. 367–70.

20. N XXVI, 710-PS, pp. 266–67. NCA III, pp. 525–26.

21. Louis P. Lochner, *The Goebbels Diaries 1942–1943* (Garden City, N.Y.: Doubleday & Company, Inc., 1948), p. 266.

22. N IX, p. 526.

23. N XXVIII, 1816-PS, p. 508.

24. *Ibid.,* p. 509.

25. *Ibid.,* p. 510.

26. *Ibid.,* p. 511.

27. *Ibid.,* p. 524.

28. *Ibid.,* p. 525.

29. *Ibid.,* p 529.

30. *Ibid.,* p. 538.

31. N IX, p. 634.

32. N XXXIX, 170-USSR.

33. N IV, p. 5.

34. *Ibid.,* p. 551.

35. N XXXIX, 170-USSR, p. 407.

36. *Ibid.,* p. 387.

37. N IX, p. 683.

38. NCA VII, EC-317, p. 405.

39. N IX, p. 688.

40. *Ibid.,* p. 569.

41. N XXVI, 735-PS, pp. 276–78.

42. *Ibid.,* 740-PS, pp. 279–80.

43. N XXII, pp. 526–27.

44. NCA, Supp. B, pp. 1143–45.

45. Bross, *op. cit.,* p. 211.

46. *Ibid.,* p. 213.

47. *Ibid.,* p. 121.

48. N IX, pp. 506–11.

49 *Ibid.,* p. 444.

50. Franz Halder, *Kriegstagebuch,* Vol. II (Stuttgart: W. Kohlhammer, 1963), p. 49.

51. NCA II, p. 425.

52. N VIII, p. 63 .

53. Joseph Wulf, *Die Bildenden Kuenste im Dritten Reich* (Guetersloh: Sigbert Mohn, 1963), pp. 116, 364.

54. Edith Stargardt-Wolff, *Wegbereiter grosser Musiker* (Berlin and Wiesbaden, 1954), p. 284. Quoted in Wulf, *op. cit.*, p. 394.

55. N XXX, 2523-PS, p. 593.

56. N IV, 141-PS, p. 82.

57. NCA, Supp. B, p. 1137.

4

The Party in Action and Theory

MARTIN BORMANN

The hard core of the Party was formed by men who made both a career and a religion of the movement. The petty hopes of thousands of the rank-and-file brethren for jobs and political preferment were not for this fanatical inner circle. It was the will, the personality, the *mana* of the Fuehrer that gave substance to the core. Through Hitler, a man like Martin Bormann was given a historic identity and was able to rise from helping to run a farm to becoming one of the mightiest men in the Reich and to transform his life into a crusade for the ideas he and the Fuehrer shared. Without Hitler, Bormann the personage hardly existed. His *persona* became a projection not of himself but of himself in relation to the Fuehrer.

In 1933 Bormann was Rudolf Hess' *Stabsleiter*—that is, the second in command to the Fuehrer's deputy. He was in charge of the Party's aid fund (Hilfskasse) and a deputy in the Reichstag. It was easy to distinguish men like him from the rank and file of the Party, who, rejoicing in the victory of National Socialism, set out to make new careers. Hungry businessmen, manufacturers, workers, and the unemployed stormed the Party in 1933 with proposals that would make them all rich. One man wanted to manufacture a soap on which the form of a swastika would be pressed. Another had a plan for a shoe-polish factory, to be manned only by National Socialists; he had already had stationery printed on which appeared the red-and-white Party emblems he had in mind for the package. Busts of Hitler were turned out to be sold for seven marks. A silver pin was offered with the Fuehrer's likeness on its head; its designer had already, he wrote the Party headquarters, sold many of these and he now quoted wholesale prices for mass consumption. Offered for sale were swastika handkerchiefs; "Heil Hitler" stickers to be attached to cigarette packages; Jamaica rum in a bottle adorned with a swastika flag; swastikas as Christmas tree ornaments; and a Christmas tree in the shape of the hooked cross. A calendar was designed with the anti-Semitic slogan "Germany Awake." A confectioner wanted to make "German chocolate" and turn over 5 per cent of the profits to the Party.[1]

Bormann was as gross a man as any of these suppliers of trinkets, but he wanted to reform Germany with fire and sword and mighty symbols, not with gadgets and money-making devices. His ideas were the inner core of what would, under him, become the Party Chancellery, which screened out proposals before they reached the Fuehrer. With the same determination and ferocity that characterized Hitler and the SS, Bormann set out in the Fuehrer's name to cleanse or take over the courts, the state bureaucracy, and Germany's economic, political, and social life. It was the Party, said Hitler, that would control the State, not the other way around. And the man who would control the Party was Martin Bormann, who would get rid of every rival, even those who had been Hitler's closest advisers. At the end only he and his Fuehrer were left in command, and the Fuehrer's will was his too.

Walter Schellenberg, head of the secret service of the Reich, said that Bormann looked like a prizefighter who measured his opponent for the kill.[2] Of medium height, with thinning black hair, thick shoulders, and a stooping gait, he was a man with the same inexhaustible energy that animated Hitler, and he worked like a demon, often at the most trivial assignments that he gave himself. Nothing was too small or too large for him to be concerned with. He kept a record of Hitler's table talks at the daily lunches. The Fuehrer had only to mention casually a book he was interested in or a person or subject, and a little while later Bormann would put the book or a note of information on his table. Everything that brought him closer to Hitler was important and kept his rivals away. And all were his rivals—Himmler, Goebbels, Hess, Speer, Goering, Rosenberg, Keitel, even the Fuehrer's doctors. Bormann looked them over from the moment he got close to the throne, getting ready for the kill.

He was born on June 17, 1900, in Halberstadt in central Germany, the son of a sergeant, a trumpeter in a cavalry regiment who later became a post-office official. His father died two years after Martin Bormann's birth, and Frau Bormann moved up in the social scale soon thereafter, marrying a bank director. Bormann attended the Realgymnasium for a few years but did not receive a diploma, leaving school to work on an estate in Mecklenburg. He returned to his agricultural pursuits after World War I, when he became an inspector of the farmlands owned by the Treuenfels family in Herzberg. He had been called up for army service only in the last months of the war, serving as a cannoneer in a field-artillery regiment. In 1920 he joined an anti-Semitic group called the Society Against the Supremacy of the Jews. At the same time, he joined the so-called Rossbach organization, which was under the command of a former first lieutenant, Gerhard Rossbach. This group was descended from one of the many free-corps companies, whose mission had been to liberate Germany from the traitors and weaklings who had been the cause of her defeat. As a member of the Rossbach group, Bormann— together with Rudolf Hoess, the future commandant of Auschwitz—took part in the murder of Walter Kadow, the man who allegedly had betrayed, to the French, one of the great among the Nazi folk heroes, Albert Leo Schlageter (he had been executed as a saboteur during the French occupation of the Ruhr). While Hoess was sentenced to ten years, Bormann as a mere collaborator spent only a year in a Leipzig prison for his part in the killing. (It was this deed that made him eligible many years later to receive the well-named "blood order" from the Fuehrer.) In 1925 he joined another semi-military organization, the Frontbann. Two years later he joined the National Socialist Party, where, despite his previous allegiance to all its principles, he had a relatively high membership number, in the sixty thousands.

Bormann's rise in the Party was steady but unspectacular. He was no man for front-page publicity. Even later, when he was never long away from the Fuehrer's side, he was rarely photographed, and the public mainly saw him in group pictures as a nondescript stocky figure accompanying his master. Before he got his job with Rudolf Hess, he was attached to National Socialist newspapers in Thuringia. In 1928, he was promoted to the staff of the Supreme Command of the SA. He had the good fortune in 1929 to marry a woman as devoted to National Socialist principles as he—Gerda Buch, the daughter of a Nazi Reichstag deputy who had been a major in the Army, had undergone his National Socialist indoctrination with Julius Streicher, and was very highly regarded by the Fuehrer. Hitler was a witness at the wedding. Sixteen years later Bormann would act in the same capacity at Hitler's wedding with Eva Braun, for which he made all the arrangements. With Goebbels and Generals Wilhelm Burgdorf and Hans Krebs, he signed the marriage certificate as a witness.*

The Bormann pair were in many ways perfectly matched. Both lived passionately by and for the National Socialist creeds; both detested Christianity in all its forms, whether Protestant, Catholic, Jehovah's Witnesses, or any other. They shared every tenet of the most radical Nazi *Weltanschauung*, whether about the terrible evil of the Jews and the Slavs or the duty of the German woman to procreate in or out of wedlock. Bormann said:

> The Slavs are to work for us. Insofar as we do not need them, they may die. Therefore, compulsory vaccination and German health service are superfluous. The fertility of the Slavs is undesirable. They may use contraceptives or practice abortion, the more the better. Education is dangerous. It is enough if they can count up to one hundred. At best an education

* Hitler named Bormann executor of his will, with the right to make all final decisions concerning it.

which produces useful coolies for us is admissible. Every educated person is a future enemy.[3]

Gerda echoed him. In a letter of September 8, 1944, she wrote:

My dearest Heart: Every single child must realize that the Jew is the Absolute Evil in this world, and that he must be fought by every means, wherever he appears [Bormann scribbled "Quite true" on the margin]. . . . As long as there exists somewhere in the world Germanic people who want to work hard, cleanly and faithfully and to live according to their own laws, in a State befitting their breed, the Eternal Jew will try to prevent it and to annihilate all positive life.

To this Bormann added: "You are my dear, kind, good girl!"

Gerda Bormann bore her husband ten children, of whom the first was named Adolf after his godfather, the Reich Chancellor. The fourth son was named after Himmler, his godfather. Frau Himmler and Frau Bormann saw a good deal of each other while their husbands were away; and Himmler and Bormann used *Du* with each other, but no love was lost between them. Bormann was one rival Himmler feared. Gerda was such a National Socialist that even her relationships to her husband and family were ordered by the Party notions of the duty of the German woman. In one letter to his wife Bormann told her how he had overcome the resistance of the actress M, who was a friend of the family, and Gerda urged him in her next letter to have a child by M. Gerda proposed that she herself be pregnant one year and that the actress take her turn the next year. In this fashion the Fuehrer would be presented with the priceless gift of the increase of sound German stock. Gerda said it was a thousand pities that such fine girls as M should be denied children. In gratitude for his wife's understanding, Bormann sent her all the letters his mistress had written to him. The affair with the actress dwindled away, and the correspondence then took account of the state of the Fuehrer's health and the state of the Reich.

On September 18, 1944, Gerda told her husband of the visit of the woman novelist Dagmar Brand, who declared that Germany would fight within her own frontiers to gain strength for the time when the United States and Britain would revolt against the Jewish wire-pullers. Then the Germans would sally forth, and the small nations would welcome Germany jubilantly as a rescuer from Roosevelt, Stalin, and Churchill—the puppets of a powerful Jewry that had been working for centuries toward the establishment of a Jewish empire. On September 30, 1944, Bormann wrote that the Fuehrer, suffering terribly from stomach cramps, had been taking castor oil and had lost six pounds in two days. In December Bormann told Gerda that the trembling which had started in Hitler's leg after the bomb exploded on July 20 now affected the left arm and hand. In a letter of October 7, Gerda told her husband how incredible it was that a handful of Jews should be able to turn the whole world topsy-turvy. And on January 1, 1945, she wrote: "I am boundlessly furious that we, with our innate longing for light and sunshine, should be compelled by the Jews to make our abodes as if we were beings of the underground world." [4]

Bormann rose to eminence by making himself indispensable. He had a remarkable memory. He wrote hundreds of memoranda on every subject close to his heart: on the church, the Jews, the Slavs, the treatment to be accorded prisoners of war, the behavior of Gauleiters. Everything had to be supervised, controlled, made harsher. He worked his way up the Party ladder with a series of limited alliances, which were lightly held or dissolved as soon as they had served their purpose—alliances with Hess, Rosenberg, Himmler, Keitel, and, among others, Eva Braun, who was his assigned dinner partner at the Berghof. Hitler said that Bormann made decisions easy for him. Bormann was the tireless clerk who got material together and prepared it so the Fuehrer could deal with it quickly. When Hitler built the Berghof, it was Bormann who took over all the details, paying the bills from the Adolf Hitler *Spende,* providing the furnishings, seeing to the construction of the greenhouses that were to provide the Fuehrer with the fresh vegetables that were his only gastronomic indulgence, evicting the villagers, and putting in their place the SS men of the Leibstandarte (his bodyguards) and their barracks.

He had a passion not so much for Hitler as for the means the Fuehrer afforded him to become a figure the world would remember. In the last days at the Reich Chancellery in Berlin, when Hitler was issuing his final orders to nonexistent armies, Bormann was still stolidly making notes of what went on. After he had finished making his notes, he dreamed of a better living after the war was over, and, like many of the other inhabitants of the macabre bunker, he drank. One of the last visitors from the outside world saw him stretched out cold after too much wine with two companions.[5] An eyewitness wrote:

> Bormann moved about very little, kept instead very close to his writing desk. He was "recording the momentous events in the bunker for posterity." Every word, every action went down on his paper. Often he would visit this person or that to demand scowlingly what the exact remark had been that passed between the Fuehrer and the person he had just had an audience with. Things that passed between other occupants of the bunker were also carefully recorded. This document was to be spirited out of the bunker at the very last moment so that, according to the modest Bormann, it could "take its place among the greatest chapters in German history." [6]

Bormann lived wholly within this historical drama that had to be played around the persons of Hitler-Bormann. The threat of the Russian advance never disturbed him nearly as much as whether he could overcome his domestic enemies, the generals, the Party rivals. He allowed no one, said Keitel at Nuremberg, to interfere with the Volkssturm, and the High Command had to keep out of its affairs.[7] Although in theory he shared its command with Himmler, it was in fact his own army. When Hitler ordered its founding on September 26, 1944, Bormann said he felt like a young mother who had just given birth, exhausted and happy.[8] The fact that it was an army of boys—some of them twelve years old—and of old men made no difference.*

Bormann's scorched-earth orders went beyond those issued by anyone else. Nothing at all was to be left of food, clothing, water, power plants. Everything was to be destroyed. Himmler and Goering were to be destroyed too. He could convince Hitler that Himmler too was betraying the Fuehrer. And it was Bormann who sent the order for the arrest of Reichsmarschall Goering.

In the midst of great decisions of war, Bormann was concerned with protocol: whether Party members had applauded at the right spots during a Fuehrer speech; who was responsible when the Nazi salute was given for some minor song instead of for the "Horst Wessel Lied," or whether the Hitlerjugend should be permitted to raise their arms and merely shout "Heil" instead of "Heil Hitler." Such rituals were deeply symbolic for him. After the attempt on Hitler's life, the Wehrmacht, too, had to give the Nazi salute and say "Sieg Heil" as a greeting when its members were not carrying arms.†

In the minutes of a conference held on July 16, 1941, he noted that "this partisan war . . . enables us to eradicate everyone who opposes us." [9] He approved of the lynching of Allied airmen who had been shot down. His round-robin letter to group leaders was headed "Justice exercised by the people against Anglo-American murderers." [10] He urged on Hitler, and on the staffs, ever more brutal measures: more severe treatment of prisoners of war, stronger measures against the churches. And it was Bormann as much as any man in the Reich who kept the anti-Semitic apparatus in motion from the time of its first sanctions against the Jews up to the Final Solution. Bormann had a hand in all the 450 anti-Jewish laws, decrees, and orders that were issued. It was he who, fearing that some Jews might escape the net because they had changed their names, wanted "Yid" to be a compulsory middle name. Instead, a decree was issued making it obligatory for Jews to add "Israel" to men's names and "Sarah" to women's, which was not all that Bormann had demanded but would help prevent mistakes.

He was a bloodhound for Jews. Hitler, in Berchtesgaden, for a time took pleasure in the visits of a blond child, the daughter of a former officer who

* The Volkssturm called up all men between the ages of sixteen and sixty. They were to bring their own clothes and weapons, calling on their neighbors for anything lacking. (*Deutsche Allgemeine Zeitung*, October 19, 1944. See also Juergen Thorwald, *Die grosse Flucht* [Stuttgart: Steingrueben Verlag, 1949].)

† Bormann pointed out to the Gauleiters that the rescue of the Fuehrer was the rescue of the German people. He therefore ordered public demonstrations, preferably out of doors, of popular rejoicing over the failure of the attempt. He told them, too, that the Fuehrer did not want them to give the impression that the front-line army was involved; he wanted them to say that it was only a small group of reactionary generals. Neither the nobility nor the generals as such were to be attacked. (United States Document Center, Berlin [hereinafter referred to as BDC], Bormann folder 242.)

had won the Iron Cross. Bormann discovered from a zealous Party member that the little girl had Jewish blood and forbade her mother to bring the child to see the Fuehrer. He went so far as to try to confiscate copies of a book in which the child's picture had appeared. Hitler heard the account of why the girl no longer came to visit him from his photographer Heinrich Hoffmann, because it was his book that Bormann wanted to keep from being sold.[11] Bormann also conducted a relentless but unsuccessful campaign to have quarter and half Jews be legally considered full Jews under the Nuremberg Laws, so that the extermination process would get them too. His representative was present at the Wannsee Conference (see Goering, Chapt. 3). It was Bormann who told Schirach that 60,000 Jews in Vienna should be shipped to the East because their apartments were needed (see Schirach, Chapt. 8). In July, 1943, he placed the Jews outside all law, in order that they might be legally treated as dehumanized objects to be destroyed. Their property would automatically fall to the Reich. He had told visiting Hungarian Minister Bela Lukacz, in March, 1943, when he was urging Hungary to take more severe measures against the Jews, that Europe would only be free of bolshevism when it was free of Jews.

He was tireless, too, in his efforts to rid Germany of Christian influence. Like Rosenberg, he wanted a new scientific National Socialist religion. The churches were to be conquered with a new ideology. He and Rosenberg were in agreement on this, as they were on the need for preserving European and Eastern art by removing it to the Reich, but their collaboration stopped at this point. Bormann disliked Rosenberg's high school, which never was more than a blueprint (see Rosenberg, in the present chapter), because it meant increasing Rosenberg's importance. In April, 1943, he forced Rosenberg to deliver the art he had collected to the Party Chancellery.

Bormann liked to have a hand in anything that had to do with killing the enemies of German blood. He helped get the euthanasia factories going where the feebleminded or those suffering from incurable diseases were shot in the back of the neck or given lethal injections. He aided the plans for sterilization of those who, whether on racial or social grounds, were held by the Party to be unfit to procreate (see Frick, Chapt. 7).[12]

He worked quietly and unobtrusively. When he was Hess' second in command, he carried out policy, made appointments, and signed checks, for the visionary Hess had no liking for the clutter of details of his office but was interested only in the grand perspectives offered by an alliance of Northern peoples against the Jews, the Communists, and other mysterious enemies. Bormann worked hard at the details of everyday matters; he delighted in them. Soon no Gauleiter could be appointed without his approval, nor could any major decision be handed down by a Party court or any decree issued. The Fuehrer could not find his papers or sometimes even remember to order a decree drawn up without the help of Bormann, who was always at Hitler's elbow or scurrying to fetch something for him.

After Hess' flight to Britain in 1941, Bormann came into his own. He saw to it that Hess' name disappeared from Party records and monuments and that his picture was taken down in public places. He immediately set out to widen what had been Hess' domain as Hitler's deputy. Hess' office had been merely a center of Party activity, but Bormann turned it into the Party Chancellery, the opposite and far more potent number of the Reich Chancellery under Hans Heinrich Lammers. "The Party gives orders to the State," was proclaimed in 1933. Therefore the SS paralleled the Army; the Foreign Office had as a rival the Ribbentrop bureau and Rosenberg's Foreign Policy Department; and alongside the local and national administrative offices were the Gauleiters, the Kreisleiters, and all the rest of the Party apparatus under Bormann. Since Party and State were combined in the person of the Fuehrer, Bormann could use his key position to invade non-Party territory. A year after Hess' flight, Bormann became Secretary to the Fuehrer. He respectfully nudged the Fuehrer to write decrees but undertook this onerous job himself, merely getting approval from the Fuehrer, who had a good deal on his mind. He concerned himself with everything, whether it was the courts, the Army, or the rectitude of all Germans. It was dangerous for any judge to impose a sentence less than death if Bormann sensed treason or defeatism in the background of the accused. Bormann ordered the Gauleiters to act as judges in the last months of the war so there could be no question of the sentences handed down when towns were evacuated or when any soldier suspected of desertion was picked up.

In the superheated atmosphere of the Third Reich, death sentences were handed down for any kind of critical remark. One woman reported to her Gauleiter that a lifelong friend of the family had made slighting remarks to her about the Fuehrer and had left without saying "Heil Hitler." The man was arrested and sentenced to death. A pianist who came to Berlin in 1943 to give a concert stayed at the home of a childhood friend of his mother's. At breakfast he said she should take down the Fuehrer's picture and the British should drop more bombs so that the war would be over quickly. She reported the matter to her Gauleiter. Her visitor was arrested, brought before the Volksgericht (People's Court), and beheaded. A group of boys listened to the forbidden foreign broadcasts, and one of them told another in the spirit of Wild West adventure that he was in touch with foreign agents. In the plant where one of their number worked as an apprentice, the boys printed bulletins of what the foreign radio reported, and they were all arrested. Although their ages ranged from sixteen to eighteen, one was sentenced to death and executed; the others got long terms of imprisonment.[13]

Bormann decided who was to see Hitler and when. Without his permission, no one from the world outside the Fuehrer's bunker could get to the Presence. He kept faithful paladins like Hoffmann, Lammers, Rosenberg, and Goebbels, as well as high-ranking generals, from seeing the Chief, as he called him, until such time as he had impressed them with the fact that they must work through him. He once refused to let Heydrich, who had flown from Prague to report on the economic situation in Czechoslovakia and to present his proposals, have an audience. He walked with Hitler past the door where Heydrich had been waiting for hours, but the Reichsprotektor had no chance to speak with his Fuehrer, who merely looked at him and walked on. Bormann coolly told Heydrich the next day that the Fuehrer was not interested in seeing him.[14] * When his rivals did manage to get an audience, Bormann arranged to be present. He succeeded in attaining his goal—namely, to isolate Hitler, who, especially late in the war, wanted no part of reality. The life in the Wolfsschanze, where Bormann lived with him (Bormann also had a house provided by the State in Hitler's immediate neighborhood in Berchtesgaden), was entirely cut off from the devastation of cities like Berlin and Hamburg. Bormann and Hitler preferred not to talk about such matters and to avoid meeting those who had unpleasant news. Their way of dealing with it when it had to be confronted was to arrest someone and if possible shoot him. Generals were executed for being unable to defend their positions with the odds against them. Hermann Fegelein, an ex-jockey and SS general (he was Bormann's friend and Eva Braun's brother-in-law), had left the Fuehrer's bunker without permission; he was discovered in his house in Berlin in civilian clothes and was summarily shot.

Bormann had no difficulty in persuading Hitler that he was surrounded by traitors, and he had torpedoed many of them by the end of the war: Himmler; Goering; Rosenberg, whose high school he would have approved of had it not been the project of a rival; Schirach, of whose American relatives he informed the Fuehrer; Hans Frank, whose black-market dealings (see Frank, Chapt. 11) served as a weapon against him.† Although his attacks on Goebbels were unsuccessful, he had terrified the Propaganda Minister too, despite the close friendship Hitler professed for the entire family that was to die with him.

At Nuremberg, Bormann's lawyer, Friedrich Bergold, worked against formidable obstacles. His client was missing. In addition, he had no case of any kind, for Bormann was guilty of more crimes than the court would be able to take account of. So the defense became simply an effort to prove that Bormann was dead.‡ In this Dr. Bergold was unsuccessful, and the court condemned Bormann to death *in absentia*. Rumors have never died down that he is still alive. On May 5, 1961, during the Eichmann trial, former Argentine Ambassador to Israel, Gregorio Topolewski, said at a press conference that Bormann had been living in Argentina and was now in Brazil.

* Schellenberg suspected that either Bormann or Himmler had arranged for the murder of Heydrich (Walter Schellenberg, *Memoiren* [Cologne: Verlag fuer Politik und Wissenschaft, 1956], pp. 256–57).

† Bormann was also behind the trial of Frank's fellow black marketeers in Poland (Karl Lasch, *et al.*). (See Frank, Chapt. 11.)

‡ Bergold was himself convinced his client was no longer living. (Interview with the writer.)

Others have maintained that Bormann was the man who had been a Communist plant in the Fuehrer's headquarters and had been spirited into protective custody by the Russians at the end of the war. Such evidence as exists for this is less than slight, though the Russians certainly had an agent close to the highest echelons in Hitler's headquarters, and the ability of Soviet espionage to learn accurately of highly classified information in a short time is unquestionable. Bormann did from time to time make statements that his hearers remembered as showing how impressed he was with Communist power. But this was also true of Hitler, who, during the war, expressed his admiration of Stalin. Bormann's career as well as his private letters breathe a fanaticism and devotion to his master not to be reconciled with a court conspiracy of any kind, certainly not with the Jewish-Bolshevik conspiracy he lived to slay.*

Bormann, according to rumors, has been seen in Italy, and even in Germany. One story says that Gerda had a letter from him after Germany's collapse. She died of cancer in Merano, Italy, in 1946, and the rumor could not be corroborated. The stories have persisted ever since Bormann made his way out of the Fuehrer's bunker in an attempt to get to Admiral Doenitz at the new seat of government in Flensburg. He had gazed for a little while at the funeral pyre of Eva Braun and Adolf Hitler and given his last Nazi salute. Eyewitnesses have said that they saw him come under the fire of a Russian tank on the Weidendammer bridge and saw him hit. Two of them said they had seen his corpse. Because of the persistence of the rumors, the West Berlin Government ordered that the grave be opened where he was supposed to have been buried. It was found to be empty.[15]

No statute of limitations exists for Bormann dead or alive. The International Military Tribunal sentenced him to death, but how such a verdict would be carried out, should he ever be found, is not very clear. He is still wanted in West Germany, for his crimes against the German people compare with those he committed against the Jews and Slavs. In the event that the sentence of the International Military Tribunal could not be carried out, Bormann would be tried under German law. His name, along with the names of hundreds of others whose whereabouts are not known, has been duly recorded by a German judge, and he is subject to prosecution should he ever appear. The competition for his capture is truly international, from Israel to the Soviet Union.

His own war he had won. He had remained with the Fuehrer until the end, sharing his last hours and then outliving Goebbels, who had voluntarily shared the fate of his leader. Bormann's enemies in the Party were defeated or scattered; he was finally the only one left in authority in the bunker. Goering had thought that Hitler would name Bormann as his successor.

* General Gehlen, former chief of German intelligence for the East Front, writes in his memoirs that Bormann was a Soviet agent, survived, and was living in the USSR in the fifties. This view remains difficult to reconcile with Bormann's personality (Reinhard Gehlen, *Der Dienst* [Mainz: Hase u. Koehler, 1971]).

Instead, Hitler appointed Admiral Doenitz as President of the Reich, and Bormann as Party Minister in the Doenitz Cabinet. Bormann sent the Fuehrer's testament on to Admiral Doenitz and told him it was in force.[16] He informed Doenitz of the Fuehrer's death more than twenty-four hours after Hitler had killed himself. During that time it was he who ruled in the shadow of Hitler and who tried to deal with the enemy. Even if the Jews and the Bolsheviks and the Christian Church still remained, his domestic victory was well-nigh complete.

RUDOLF HESS

Rudolf Hess and Martin Bormann held the same ironclad principles in completely different ways. Hess, like Bormann, considered communism and Jewry the major evils besetting the world and Hitler the major prophet who would rescue it. Both were unshakable in their determination to conquer the evils and exalt Hitler. To this end they worked in the same office, but there the similarities ended. Hess was a disturbed mystic, an idealist, a man with a considerable range of quirks. One day Himmler's physiotherapist, Felix Kersten, found Hess with a large magnet swinging over his bed—to draw away the malign influences which always threatened him. Later Hess showed Kersten a dozen more under his bed. One of the psychiatrists who examined him after his flight to Scotland diagnosed him as schizophrenic but stated that his illness had not invaded his entire personality and that clear areas were often apparent in which Hess could function well. It was no doubt owing to his ability to perform for longer or shorter periods without showing patently abnormal signs that Hess could hold down his important job in the Nazi Party and could be tried for his life by the International Military Tribunal, which held him legally sane. When his mind was free to operate without delusions, he was intelligent and often remarkably shrewd in his judgments. The tests given him while he was in Britain placed him in the upper 10 per cent bracket of intelligence. (The American psychologist who tested him at Nuremberg found him only slightly above average intelligence.) But his periods of normal functioning were intermittent, and the psychiatrists who examined him during the months of his captivity in England had no hesitation in pronouncing him a schizoid personality, suffering from paranoia with hysteric inclusions. Some years later the panel of Allied psychiatrists selected by the Nuremberg court, after an examination of a few hours only, found that he suffered from amnesia—a diagnosis that needed amplification to explain his rambling speech at the end of the trial and his behavior during it.[17]

Hess was fifty-two years old at the time the trials started. He was born in Alexandria, Egypt, on April 26, 1894. There he attended a German school for six years. At the age of twelve he was sent to a Lutheran school in Bad

Godesberg. When World War I broke out he volunteered and served for a time in the same company as Hitler, in the 16th Bavarian Regiment, but the two did not meet until after the war. Hess later served as a pilot in the Army Air Force, rising to the rank of first lieutenant. After the end of the war he attended the University of Munich, where, wearing his Army uniform because he could not afford to buy civilian clothes, he attended a number of lectures given by the world-renowned *Geopolitiker* Karl Haushofer. Haushofer's theories had a profound influence on Hess' mind, as they did on Hitler's. Haushofer believed in the necessity for *Lebensraum* for Germany, and the East was the obvious place to expand. He and his son Albrecht, who taught at the University of Berlin and with whom Hess also became well acquainted, wanted friendship with England to be the cornerstone of German policy. The Munich agreement in 1938 seemed to be the high point of their influence on Hess and Hitler. (Hess, according to Karl Haushofer, held "a protective hand" over Haushofer's wife, who had some Jewish blood.)[18]

Hess wanted more than *Lebensraum* for Germany; he wanted the Reich purified of its contaminating elements. He joined the ultranationalist Freecorps Epp and, in June, 1920, the National Socialist Party, where he had a membership number only a little higher than Hitler's, who had No. 7 while Hess had No. 16. Hess became head of the National Socialist Student Organization at the University of Munich as well as an SA leader. He took part in the Beer Hall Putsch of November 8–9, 1923, with the Fuehrer (see Frank, Chapt. 11). He was essentially a passive man, glad to be instructed in his duties and to place himself without question under Hitler's orders.[19] When asked once what the future program of the Party would be, he said that he could not give an exact answer, but that the Communist Party must of course be eliminated and the strength of the Government increased. "The right thing," he said, "will occur to the Fuehrer at the decisive moment. He is always given the right thing by providence."[20] The National Socialists were the Party that sustained his mystical notion of the way the world must progress. "The time," he told one of his friends some years later, in 1930, "of monarchies and democracies in Europe is over, the time of Caesarism has come."[21] It was not enough to wait for the Fuehrer, or to call upon his name. One had to will him to be the Caesar.

In 1924 Hess was sentenced to eighteen months in Landsberg prison, where his Fuehrer was also a prisoner. Hitler dictated *Mein Kampf* to him in his cell, and Hess wrote later to his wife, what was undoubtedly true, that the book had many of his own ideas in it. The two men were released from Landsberg on the same day, and Hess was more than ever the Fuehrer's private secretary and adjutant. It was a close relationship—as close as Hitler was likely to come to any of his associates. Hess (along with Streicher) was one of the few men whom the Fuehrer addressed as *Du*. They had a great deal to give to each other. Though Hess could correct Hitler's grammar and spelling, he knew the Fuehrer to be one of the great men of all time—the Caesar for whom he and Germany had been searching. He willed that Hitler be the chosen man. He was eager, with transcendent purposes in his mind, to seek to reconcile the disparate elements in the Party; to bring the Socialists like the Strassers together with the conservative wing and the former German nationalists; to use people wherever they might be fit to serve. Even the *Lumpen* (dregs), he said, have their unique qualities.

Hess lacked the swagger and luster of Goering, but he nevertheless became the third man in the Reich after Hitler was named Reich Chancellor, and he narrowly missed being the designated successor to the Fuehrer. (According to Otto Dietrich, the Reich press chief, the Fuehrer decided in 1934, after visiting Hess' new house in the Isartal on the outskirts of Munich, that he would not designate him as his successor. The tasteless furnishings had offended Hitler's aesthetic sensibilities. A little later he chose Goering for the post.) [22]

When Gregor Strasser left the Party in December, 1932, Hess was appointed to take charge of the Central Political Committee of the Party, a newly created body designed to take the place of the Party's Political Organization, which had been headed by Strasser. The Fuehrer made Hess his deputy in April, 1933, and in December of that year gave him the rank of Reichsminister. Hess performed his duties with utter devotion and some skill. It was he who coined the phrase "Guns before butter." His speeches on the whole were no more than short hymns of praise of the Fuehrer. "There is one man," he said, "who is always above criticism, that is the Fuehrer. This is because everyone knows and feels he is always right and always will be right. . . . We believe that the Fuehrer has a higher calling to the shaping of Germany's fate." All that was needed was "faith without criticism, surrender to the Fuehrer, not to ask why but the silent carrying out of his orders." [23] Hess, the master of ceremonies who walked stiffly to the podium before the tumultuous masses of Brownshirts and Blackshirts, called for and eventually obtained from the disciplined faithful a short preliminary worshipful silence and then shouted: "Comrades! The Fuehrer!"

At one of the great Party rallies he presented Hitler to the packed phalanxes impatient to hear the voice of the Fuehrer. With an incantation, "Hitler is the Party, the Party is Germany. Sieg Heil," he turned toward the Fuehrer his grim, heavy-featured, beetle-browed face. Then he relaxed, and an expression almost of tenderness came into his face. Years after, the Allied psychiatrists would speak of Hess' latent homosexuality, although it is unlikely that they had ever read his speeches or seen newsreels of the two together. According to one story, Hess' wife was chosen by Hitler. The three were sitting in a restaurant, the Osteria Bavaria, in Munich, and the Frau Ilse Hess-to-be said she was undecided what to do, whether to study further at the university or to take a trip to Italy. Hitler asked Ilse why she did not marry Rudolf Hess.[24] It was apparently an idea that had not occurred to either Hess or Ilse, but they were married a few weeks later.

Bormann wanted to use the Fuehrer as a means of expanding himslf, of gaining an identity, but Hess thought of Hitler as an agent of higher powers, a nimbus, a pure symbol of racial rectitude. He lived in a twilight world of enormous imaginary conflicts. Both he and Rosenberg believed that Heinrich Bruening was a secret agent of dark forces who would bring the Communists to power in the Reich and then, after ridding Germany of Protestant Prussia, would establish a Catholic dictatorship.[25] When Hess came down from his world of fantasy, he was simple and modest. He never wore decorations, and he spent hours taking his young son for walks along the Isar. He had few if any close relationships except with people like the Haushofers, whose ideas were especially congenial to him. He lived by prescriptions which to a large degree were those of the Party. He wrote a letter to an unmarried mother whose fiancé had fallen in battle, offering to be the godfather of her child. The highest law of the Reich, he told her, was to maintain its people. What, he asked, would the Prussian Army have been without the bastard Yorck? He acknowledged the hard lot of women, but it was better, he said, to have the child than not to have it.[26]

Hess' flight to Britain was the logical outcome of his structured *Weltanschauung.* Far from being a betrayal of Hitler or the Reich, it was a voyage on their behalf and on behalf of the whole civilized world. A few weeks before he took off, he told Count Lutz Schwerin von Krosigk, the Minister of Finance in Hitler's Cabinet, that the two Germanic nations, England and Germany, were fighting for the benefit of the laughing Bolshevik nation. He was in despair because England and Germany were tearing one another apart instead of coming to an understanding and because the British had not responded favorably to the Fuehrer's offer of peace. He was sure that if someone could talk to authoritative Englishmen—make clear to them the Bolshevik danger to Western culture and the fact that Hitler wanted nothing from England—an agreement could be reached. When Schwerin von Krosigk pointed out that the British could scarcely trust Hitler after so many broken promises, Hess was as unimpressed as when Albrecht Haushofer had told him the same thing.[27]

Hess was uninterested in the lesser aspects of Party politics and confused by them. He was a puritan by National Socialist standards, and he had only contempt for the corruption and small-mindedness of many of the Party functionaries. Memoranda piled up in his office while he brooded over the state of Aryan mankind. When World War II began, he wanted to fly for the Third Reich as he had flown for Imperial Germany in World War I, but Hitler not only ordered him to stay at his post but forbade any kind of flying as too perilous. Hess managed to visit the front line in Belgium and rejoiced in being but a few meters away from the firing. But more important than fighting the war was making a peace—bringing the war between the Germanic brothers to an end. In this he saw himself carrying out the deepest wishes of the Fuehrer, who certainly wanted peace with Britain if he could get it on his own terms. Hitler could not understand why the British kept on fighting a war they could not possibly win unless they confidently expected aid from both Russia and the United States.

The need for some dramatic move to bring about a peace seemed overwhelming to Hess, as it did to the Haushofers. Hess was the man through whom they could influence Hitler and conceivably avert the catastrophe of a German invasion of Britain. Albrecht Haushofer told Hess that he sought a "friendship intensified to fusion, with a joint fleet, a joint air force, and joint possessions in the world," but, because the English hated Hitler, had no confidence in his promises, and mistrusted Ribbentrop, he saw little chance "in the present stage of development" for the possibility of a settlement between the Fuehrer and England. Nevertheless, he was ready to undertake a mission to talk with the Duke of Hamilton on neutral soil if he could be given "precise directives from the highest authority." Hess had asked Haushofer to come to see him to discuss the possibility of ending this war, which was "suicidal for the white race," and Haushofer had the impression that the conversation took place with the knowledge of Hitler and that Hess would discuss the matter further with the Fuehrer.[28] It is likely that he did. (Ulrich von Hassell stated that Hitler agreed with Hess' attempting to get in touch with English representatives.)[29] Such a meeting would have been in line with Hitler's policy toward England and, since he already had the attack on Soviet Russia in mind, had more importance than heretofore.

The upshot of the discussions between Hess and the Haushofers was that the Haushofers were to attempt to get in touch with the Duke of Hamilton, whom they knew and whom Hess had met at the Olympic Games in 1936, and to arrange his meeting with a German representative in neutral Portugal. Albrecht Haushofer wrote the letter on September 23, 1940, but it never reached Hamilton. It was intercepted by the British censor, who made a copy of it, and the original disappeared. Only months later did a British intelligence officer give Hamilton a copy of the letter and suggest that he go to Lisbon to discover the intentions of the Germans. Before Hamilton could make any move in this direction, Hess landed in Scotland. Hess had decided, when an answer did not come, to undertake the mission himself by flying directly to Scotland, where he would see Hamilton, who would put him in touch with the King and the British peace party.[30] The logical arguments against such a flight had no weight with him.

Being addicted to aberrant schools of medicine, Hess landed in Scotland with a large assortment of drugs and homeopathic medicaments, which British chemists analyzed and found so dilute that they could not tell what was in them.[31] He was also addicted to astrology and dream books and prophecies, and the clinching reason for his making the trip was a recurrent dream in which he was flying over water on an errand of great importance. Haushofer, too, had prophetic dreams, and in one of them he saw Hess in a plane flying on a historic mission. Hess told the American psychiatrist Dr. Douglas M. Kelley in Nuremberg that Professor Haushofer had seen him in a dream walking through tapestried halls in British castles on a mission to bring peace to the entire world and that an astrologer had predicted he was destined to arrange a world peace at the end of 1940.[32]

Not only was the flight rooted in Hess' own need to be a savior of the Western world but was also, he believed, in line with the Fuehrer's intentions. Like Napoleon, Hitler had to conquer either England or Russia, and if he could not get at the one he could certainly reach the throat of the other. England, he was convinced, remained in the war solely at the behest of third parties and of its own Jews and warmongers. If she would make peace, it would simplify an attack on the Soviet Union; and if she persisted in remaining a belligerent, he could in any event defeat Russia in a lightning campaign of the kind he had waged in France, and then turn his attention to Britain and her empire. Hess, on his part, merely wanted England out of the war; Russia's role as either friend or foe was secondary. The attack on the Soviet Union had been in Hitler's mind since the fall of France. But Hess, like so many others, opposed it. If England continued in the war, Germany would again be fighting on two fronts, and having been a soldier in World War I, he knew a two-front war to be ruinous. Haushofer had pointed out, and Hess agreed with him, that for the war with England to continue could only be a disaster for both countries. It would mean needless bloodshed. And if Russia won a war against Germany, communism would be victorious on the entire continent, the Reich would be destroyed, and the British Empire would be endangered.[33] It was on these assumptions that the scholarly Haushofers touched off the tic of the world preserver in Hess. At one stroke he could do an enormous service for his Fuehrer, who wanted peace with Britain; for the Germanic race; and for Germany's *Lebensraum*, whether through war or treaty with the Soviet Union. Thousands of precious Nordic lives would be spared and Evil given a death blow.

Hess' farewell letter to the Fuehrer, according to Hess' secretary, Hildegard Fath, who had read a copy of it, said nothing about making peace with England in order to attack Russia but stressed only the need to prevent further bloodshed in the war against Britain. Hitler's press chief, Otto Dietrich, who also described the contents of the letter, made no mention of Russia.[34]

Favoring the flight was the fact that Hess knew Wilhelm Messerschmitt and, despite the order against his flying, had readily persuaded the airplane builder to let him have a plane for practice flights. He was after all the deputy of the Fuehrer. Later, when Messerschmitt was sternly brought to task by Goering for letting Hess have the new two-engined ME in which he flew to Scotland, Messerschmitt reminded the Reichsmarschall of Hess' official status. Goering then was foolish enough to tell him that he should have known Hess was crazy, to which Messerschmitt made the reply that was delightedly quoted by all the irreverent who learned of it: "How could I be expected to suppose that one so high in the hierarchy of the Third Reich could be crazy? If that was the case, you should have secured his resigna- tion." [35]

Hess made three attempts to fly to Britain. Twice he had to return because of engine trouble, but the third flight, on May 10, 1941, was successful. He had made careful preparations: he got hold of a top-secret map, which was provided by Hitler's own pilot, showing the forbidden air zones, and he had extra fuel tanks and a special radio added to the Messerschmitt's equipment. Only his adjutant, Karlheinz Pintsch, was taken into his confidence. Neither Frau Hess nor the Haushofers knew he was attempting the flight.

Hess parachuted to earth not far from his goal, the residence of the Duke of Hamilton at Dungavel House near Busby in Scotland. He carried with him visiting cards of Albrecht and Karl Haushofer, his large supplies of medicaments, and notes for the conferences he planned to hold in Britain. Unarmed and dressed in the uniform of a Luftwaffe captain, he was im- mediately taken into custody. Aside from putting him in safekeeping, no one knew exactly what to do about him either in Britain or in Germany. His treatment in England was always that accorded an invalid—at first because he had hurt his back and foot, which had been struck by the tail of the plane after he plunged from the cockpit, and later because of his mental condition. On landing, Hess asked his captors politely to permit him to see the Duke of Hamilton, and in due course the Duke and other highly placed visitors—among them a member of the Churchill Cabinet, the Lord Chancel- lor Sir John Simon—journeyed to the hospital where Hess was held, to listen to his hour-long monologues delivered in German.

Churchill did not want to see Hess, for it might look as though he were discussing peace terms with him. Sir John Simon visited Hess under the pseudonym of Dr. Guthrie. In the transcript of their one-sided and top-secret conversation, Hess appeared as "J." The British Government was naturally interested to learn all it could from its visitor: whether he had come with Hitler's knowledge, whether (as the intelligence reports increasingly indi- cated) Hitler was determined to attack Russia, and just what had brought Hess to make the flight. In early interviews, explicitly and again indirectly, Hess denied that Hitler intended to attack the Soviet Union [36] or had known that he was coming to Britain. He merely knew how much the Fuehrer wanted to come to an understanding with England. He read to Dr. Guthrie for over an hour from the voluminous notes he had brought along, telling him and Dr. McKenzie (the cover name of Ivone Kirkpatrick from the Foreign Office) of the iniquities of the Versailles Treaty, of England's share of guilt for World War I, and of Germany's aspirations for colonies in Africa (a subject he had often discussed with the Haushofers, who thought England might be willing to make concessions in this area).

The heart of Hess' long harangue was that England should control her empire without interference from the Reich, and Germany should control the continent of Europe without interference from Britain. Hitler, he assured his listeners, wanted the British Empire preserved but would not tolerate British interference in the German sphere of interest. Dr. Guthrie gently pointed out that these were not quite parallel patterns for nonintervention. "The domestic affairs of the British Empire are British," he said, and then asked Hess, "Are all the domestic affairs of the continent of Europe German?" Hess struggled to make the whole picture clear: England was faced with increasingly heavy air attacks, and the U-boat war would become more effective. Hess said he saw plainly the long lines of coffins and the weeping mothers. It was all so simple to him: stop the civil war between the two Germanic peoples, let each stay in its own sphere, give Germany its colonies back, and all would be well. He had flown into the camp of the enemy, he said, so that he could clarify such matters and make it easier for the British to negotiate without loss of prestige. He came back a number of times to the question of prestige; it was obviously something he considered especially precious to the proud Britons.

Dr. Guthrie, between times out for rest after the uninterrupted flood of talk, wanted details.

> GUTHRIE: "May I ask one or two things: 'Rueckgabe der deutschen Kolonien' [return of the German colonies]. Well, now, am I to understand that includes German South-West Africa?"
> J: "Yes, all German colonies."
> GUTHRIE: "Because sometimes the statement has been made that the German claim did not include South-West Africa. I am authorized then, by you at least, to say to General [Jan Christian] Smuts that it does include German South-West Africa?"
> J: "Yes."
> DR. M (in German): "And the Japanese islands too?"
> J: "Not the Japanese islands."

This was the partly serious, partly Gilbert-and-Sullivan dialogue, which went on for months with many different interrogators, political and medical. Lord Beaverbrook, under the cover name of Dr. Livingston, came to talk with Hess after the invasion of Russia, and Hess told him a victory for England would be a victory for bolshevism.[37]

Hess had hoped to be back in Germany within a few days with the British acceptance of his offer and their counterproposals, but he was out of touch with reality. Neither the British nor the Germans were pleased with him. Churchill was puzzled, Hitler was enraged, and the press of both countries said he was insane. Churchill did not want it known that the third man in Germany had come to Britain bearing peace offers. A peace party did exist in England, and it was unpolitic to have a public discussion about the purpose of Hess' visit. A great propaganda coup conceivably might have been made of the curious event that disclosed something of the kind of personalities that were ruling Germany, but the British authorities cautiously decided to treat the matter as a medical-political affair. Churchill directed on May 13, three days after the landing, that Hess be considered a prisoner of war, isolated, interrogated, examined, and well treated.[38]

Hitler, too, had to treat the incident carefully. His deputy, his secretary, had flown off without his knowledge on a peace mission, and all he could do was arrest Pintsch and cause a statement to be issued that Hess had been deranged by overwork and by consulting astrologers and had taken it onto himself to make an unauthorized flight to the enemy. Witnesses reported that they had seldom seen Hitler in such fury as when he heard the news. "I hope he dives into the ocean," Paul Schmidt heard him say.[39] It was a propaganda blow of the first magnitude. Hess knew, of course, of the preparations for the attack on the Soviet Union, and there was no telling what he might divulge to the British. All the German press and radio could do was to repeat that Hess had been in poor mental health for some time, had consulted astrologers and soothsayers, and had flown off on a wild errand of his own. The Fuehrer called the Party leaders together at the Berghof and told them insanity ran in Hess' family.[40] But the question that was asked silently—as well as openly by men like Messerschmitt—was how someone so high in the councils of the mighty could have remained so long in his position when the Fuehrer himself said he was insane. Witticisms went the rounds: "The Thousand-Year Reich is now the Hundred-Year Reich. Why? One zero less." Or, "A new office has been created—Reichs-emigrantenfuehrer [head of emigrants from the Reich]," a play on the titles Reichsmarschall, Reichsfuehrer SS, etc.[41]

It seems likely that Hess had flown to Britain without the Fuehrer's knowledge, although many people in Germany were unconvinced of this. Goering believed that the Fuehrer had sent Hess, as did Schellenberg, who was an expert in matters of intelligence. They thought it would be easy to disavow his mission if it failed. According to Frau Hess, who had read a copy of the letter her husband sent to the Fuehrer, Hess had told Hitler he could always announce that his deputy was crazy if the trip was unsuccessful. This seems unconvincing in view of the bad propaganda effect the Hess mission would be bound to have for the Reich, both in Germany and abroad. Peace feelers could readily be made without sending the deputy of the Fuehrer to land by parachute in enemy country. Hitler's press chief, Otto Dietrich, who saw the letter, said that Hess told Hitler the flight was made not from cowardice or weakness, for it took more courage to go to Britain than to stay in Germany, but from a desire to establish a personal contact with Englishmen he knew (Hess was born in Egypt, in British-held territory), to reestablish Anglo-German relations in the interest of both peoples, and to end the war. Hess told Hitler he had the definite impression when they had last talked together that the Fuehrer too, from the bottom of his heart, wanted a German-English understanding. Hess had never said a word to Hitler about the flight because he knew the Fuehrer would have forbidden it.[42]

All the British could discover was that Hess believed that Hitler would make peace under certain conditions. The Reich, it seemed, was a strange and wonderful country that could be run with a combination of the efficiency of the Wehrmacht and the delusional system of a lunatic who had been the ever loyal companion and deputy of the Fuehrer. Hess was technically a prisoner of war, although he was treated with far more consideration than is usually accorded such a person. He had a house to himself, was guarded beyond the usual security measures after his first attempt to commit suicide, and for a time dined every evening with his captors, the commander being served first and Hess second. This, however, did not allay Hess' conviction that his food was being poisoned, and he would sometimes rapidly exchange his plate with that of the commanding officer to avert the danger. He was examined carefully over a long period of time by a panel of psychiatrists and other physicians. Their diagnosis, which declared Hess a schizophrenic personality with hysterical overlay, referred to his dysplastic physique, the stigmata of degeneration, the misshapen ears, the primitive skull formation, the split personality. The British doctors declared that the first amnesia they observed, which lasted from November, 1943, to June, 1944, was genuine. There seems small doubt of this, since Hess during that time submitted to an Evipal test, which put him in a state of seminarcosis that would presumably induce him to answer questions without the natural defenses afforded him when he was in possession of his full powers. The psychiatrists also discerned what was not infrequently evident in many of the higher-ups of the Nazi Party and State—namely, a large feminine inclusion in the jumbled personality. Part of the security staff guarding him were members of the Guards—examples of the *jeunesse dorée* of England—who ate by themselves and not as members of the mess attended by Hess and the political officers assigned to him. The British doctors thought that the homosexual in him responded strongly to these young men, whom he saw as representatives of the chivalrous King of England, whom he had come to save. On the other side were the political and medical officers, a very different kettle of fish from Hess' point of view. His first suicide attempt was called in the medical report at attempt at murder, since Hess had seemed prepared to hurl himself on the psychiatrist. The projection of his own incapacities had not been complete in Hess' mind, the psychiatrists thought, and at the last moment he plunged not at the doctor but over the bannister.[43] (Later he stabbed himself in the chest and also tried to starve himself.)

In time, Hess grew increasingly ill-tempered and confused. His reception in Britain disappointed him. More and more, the Jews exercised their malevolent influences. The good King of England and the good Duke of Hamilton were unhappily confounded by many wicked men who tried to poison him every day. His enemies practiced black arts upon him, using such commonplace devices as making noises all night to try to rob him of his rest and his sanity. As he had explained to the Duke of Hamilton, he had come to Scotland on a mission of humanity and had expected the King to grant him a parole because he had come of his own free will. But now magic and deviltry were being inflicted on him.

"He was convinced he was surrounded by secret-service agents who would accomplish his death by driving him to commit suicide, committing a murder staged to look like suicide, or administering poison in his food," wrote one of the British psychiatrists. Hess sometimes lay on the floor of his room writhing in pain from real or imaginary stomach cramps, which were stimulated by his supposed oppressors.[44] Writing to his wife on January 15, 1944, he said: "I have been sitting here for literally several hours, wondering what I can write to you about. But I get no further; and that I regret to say is for a very special reason. Since sooner or later, you will notice it or find out about it, I may as well tell you: I have completely lost my memory. . . . The reason for it I do not know. The doctor gave me a lengthy explanation, but I have meanwhile forgotten what it was." [45] He told his doctors the Russians were hypnotizing German troops from mysterious centers. Strange hypnotic influences were also at work on him in his captivity a thousand miles away.

This is the man who was flown back to Germany—to Nuremberg—to be tried on all four counts of the indictment. Churchill had declared in his first memorandum, written just after Hess landed, that Hess was liable to be tried as a major war criminal, but the British also feared that they might have to repatriate him under the Geneva Convention before the end of the war because of his mental state. Switzerland, the protecting power of the Reich in Britain, had sent representatives to visit Hess, and if they had made the recommendation to repatriate him, this would have presented embarrassing political complications—not that the British on their own had much interest in Hess. The Russians, however, did have an interest in him, and their mental operations were not entirely dissimilar from his. They had always suspected a British plot to raise a coalition against them, and when Lord Beaverbrook visited Stalin in Moscow, the Russian Premier had promptly inquired into the Hess case. Why had he flown to England? Why was he not executed? At Potsdam, Stalin asked questions again, this time of Mr. Attlee, who assured him that Hess would be produced for the forthcoming trials.

The court at Nuremberg appointed a medical panel from the four powers. The reports were somewhat conflicting, although the panelists all said that Hess could stand trial. The British called him a psychopathic personality but not at the moment insane. (The report of the British psychiatrists was signed by, among others, Dr. J. R. Rees, the chief Army psychiatrist, who had seen Hess over a period of months.) The American and French doctors found him hysterical and suffering from loss of memory but added that this would not interfere with his comprehension of the proceedings, though it would interfere with his response to questions relating to his past and to undertaking his defense. Three Soviet physicians and a French doctor said, "At present, he is not insane in the strict sense of the word. His amnesia does not prevent him completely from understanding what is going on around him, but it will interfere with his ability to conduct his defense and to understand details of the past, which would appear as factual data." [46] The report by the Soviet doctors who examined him called his malady "hysterical amnesia, the basis of which is a subconscious inclination towards self-defense as well as a deliberate and conscious tendency towards it." [47]

The tribunal asked to hear Hess on his own behalf, and he made a statement of the kind that would have been familiar to his British doctors during one of his clear periods:

> In order to forestall the possibility of my being pronounced incapable of pleading, in spite of my willingness to take part in the proceedings and to hear the verdict alongside my comrades, I would like to make the following declaration . . . : Henceforth my memory will again respond to the outside world. The reasons for simulating loss of memory were of a tactical nature. Only my ability to concentrate is, in fact, somewhat reduced.[48]

Hess' first lawyer, Guenther von Rohrscheidt, cited not only the medical evidence against Hess' sanity, which was considerable despite the short period of time he had been examined by the doctors at Nuremberg, but also his own experiences with his client, who, he said, was manifestly abnormal and unable to present a proper defense. (Some months later Rohrscheidt broke his leg and had to withdraw from the case. Hess's defense was taken over by the able Munich lawyer Alfred Seidl, who also represented Hans Frank.)

The President of the Court declared that Hess could put forward amnesia as part of his defense and could say, "I should have been able to make a better defense if I had been able to remember what took place at the time." The tribunal, after deliberating, decided he could stand trial, although it would later again have doubts.

Despite his statement to the court that he wished to be tried, Hess never took the stand. Once he had made his speech, he lost interest in the proceedings, denied the authority of the court to hold such a trial, refused to testify, and took to reading books during the sessions. He did, however, participate, in his fashion, in the more informal atmosphere of the interrogations. These took place over a considerable period, beginning with his arrival in Nuremberg and extending past the end of the trial. Hess was interrogated in the presence of his former secretary; a naturopath whom he had formerly consulted, Ludwig Schmitt; and others—none of whom he could clearly recognize.[49]

He had trouble remembering much of his past, as the President of the Court had predicted, but when the word "Jew" came up he said, "There stirs in me something that is dislike, or that they are not sympathetic to me, or rather that I have no sympathies for them." But he could not recall any reason, he said, why he should dislike them. He knew there had been a war because he had seen the ruins when he was in Brussels only the day before he was interrogated in Nuremberg.[50]

When, to test his memory, he was confronted with Goering, he professed to have only a dim idea of who he was. When Goering tried to remind him of the way Hitler had talked, Hess said he could not remember and that the picture he had of Hitler in his cell did not speak. Goering was most cooperative, for the meeting gave him an opportunity to recall his own splendid past.

> GOERING: "Don't you know me?"
> HESS: "Not personally, but I remember your name."
> GOERING: "But we talked a lot together."
> HESS: "That must have been the case . . . as the Deputy of the Fuehrer . . . I must have met the other high personalities like you, but I can't remember anyone."
> GOERING: "First I was a Field Marshal and later a Reichsmarschal, don't you remember that?"
> HESS: "No." [He added that if the doctors had not assured him his memory would return, he would be driven to desperation.]
> GOERING: "Do you remember that I lived just outside Berlin, in a great house in the forest, at Karinhall; don't you remember that you were there many times? [And then, speaking of the 1923 putsch] Do you remember that you arrested the Minister?"
> HESS: "I seem to have a pretty involved past, according to that."
> GOERING: "Do you remember that you moved to the Wilhelmstrasse, into a palace which really belonged to me, as the Prime Minister of Prussia, but I enabled you to live there?" [Goering was still boasting of his palaces, for the benefit, no doubt, of the Allied interrogators.]
> HESS: "I don't know."
> GOERING: "Do you remember Mr. Messerschmitt? . . . He constructed all our fighter planes, and he also gave you the plane that I refused to give you . . . with which you flew to England. Mr. Messerschmitt gave that to you behind my back."
> [The American] INTERROGATOR [to Goering]: "All right. You move over here." [51]

A procession of people, also designed to revive Hess' memory, followed: Karl Haushofer, Papen, Messerschmitt, Ernest Bohle (he had been leader of the Party's Foreign Organization). Bohle reminded Hess of his having been shot in the lungs as a lieutenant in World War I and talked about his letter to the Duke of Hamilton, which Bohle had translated for him. Haushofer called him by his first name, gave him news of the Hess family, of his wife and young son, and told him that Albrecht had been killed by the Nazis. But all this was of no use. Hess repeated that he could not remember.

A little later, however, on November 30, 1945, he was to tell the court and his interrogators that he had been acting all this time, that the films shown him and the people who had reminded him of his past had indeed been familiar to him, and that he had been feigning a loss of memory. The American psychologist G. M. Gilbert, who visited the prisoners regularly, noted Hess' pleasure at having fooled everyone and apparently accepted Hess' own befuddled estimate of himself.[52] But he and other specialists, including the American psychiatrist who had Hess under observation, soon had to admit that Hess was showing unmistakable signs of deterioration in his thinking: his amnesia had returned; he was apathetic toward the proceedings; he refused to cooperate with his lawyer; and he refused to take the stand or to play any part in the defense of his life.*

Seidl made the best defense he could. He had chanced to overhear a conversation between Goering and Ribbentrop in which the Russian-German secret treaty of August 23, 1939, was mentioned, and he set out on a search for it. A copy of the document came into his hands, given him by an unknown American officer, but he was unable to introduce it as evidence because it was a copy, and the Russian judges and prosecutors did not want to hear about it. What Seidl could do was to call witnesses, among them Friedrich Gaus, former chief of the Legal Division of the German Foreign Office, who testified on the secret protocols of the August pact in which Ribbentrop, after telephoning Hitler for approval, had declared the Reich not interested politically in Latvia, Estonia, and Finland. Only Lithuania was to come into the German sphere. Later, Gaus said, Hitler had approved Lithuania's going to the Soviet Union.[53]

Since Hess could have taken no part in the exterminations, in war crimes, or in crimes against humanity, the case against him had to be based solely on his having been a member of the conspiracy to plan and wage aggressive war. What Seidl attempted to do was to introduce into the courtroom a *tranche de vie internationale* that would show something of the way affairs between great powers were often actually conducted when they were stripped of their rhetoric and exhortations. Hess had nothing to do with the Russo-German pact, but Seidl tried to show how relations between the accused Germans and the representatives of one of the four peace-loving nations on the bench had in fact been conducted.

Hess took part in the proceedings only one more time—in his final statement. He asked the tribunal if he could address it from his seat, because of his ill health, and in this position he might have gone on for a long time

---

* Gilbert, who detested all the defendants, was later, in August, 1946, asked by the court to give a second opinion on Hess' sanity and whether a panel of psychiatrists should reexamine him. Gilbert said that he had no doubts about the sanity of Hess, who was suffering from a hysterical amnesia, and that there was no need for another psychiatric examination. (N I, pp. 166–67. Cf. also Douglas M. Kelley, 22 Cells in Nuremberg [New York: Greenberg: Publishers, Inc., 1947].)

had the President not cut him short after twenty minutes. What Hess said was disjointed, earnest, paranoid:

> Some of my comrades here can confirm the fact that at the beginning of the proceedings I predicted the following:
>
> 1. That witnesses would appear who, under oath, would make untrue statements while, at the same time, these witnesses could create an absolutely reliable impression and enjoy the best possible reputation.
>
> 2. That it was to be reckoned with that the Court would receive affidavits containing untrue statements.
>
> 3. That the defendants would be astonished and surprised at some German witnesses.
>
> 4. That some of the defendants would act rather strangely: they would make shameless utterances about the Fuehrer; they would incriminate their own people; they would partially incriminate each other, and falsely at that. Perhaps they would even incriminate themselves, and also wrongly. . . . I made these predictions, however, not only here at the beginning of the Trial, but had already made them months before the beginning of the Trial in England to, among others, Dr. Johnston, the physician who was with me in Abergavenny. . . . I said before that a certain incident in England caused me to think of the reports of the earlier trials. The reason was that the people around me during my imprisonment acted towards me in a peculiar and incomprehensible way, in a way which led me to conclude that these people somehow were acting in an abnormal state of mind. Some of them— these persons and people around me were changed from time to time. Some of the new ones who came to me in place of those who had been changed had strange eyes. They were glassy and like eyes in a dream. This symptom, however, lasted only a few days and then they made a completely normal impression. They could no longer be distinguished from normal human beings. Not only I alone noticed these strange eyes, but also the physician who attended me at the time, Dr. Johnston, a British Army doctor, a Scotsman.
>
> In the spring of 1942 I had a visitor, a visitor who quite obviously tried to provoke me and acted towards me in a strange way. This visitor also had these strange eyes. Afterwards, Dr. Johnston asked me what I thought of this visitor. He told me—I told him I had the impression that for some reason or other he was not completely normal mentally, whereupon Dr. Johnston did not protest, as I had expected, but agreed with me and asked me whether I had not noticed those strange eyes, these eyes with a dreamy look. Dr. Johnston did not suspect that he himself had exactly the same eyes when he came to me. . . . Concerning my oath, I should also like to say that I am not a churchgoer; I have no spiritual relationship with the Church, but I am a deeply religious person. I am convinced that my belief in God is stronger than that of most other people. I ask the High Tribunal to give all the more weight to everything which I declare under oath, expressly calling God as my witness.[54]

Hess was the first man in history to be found guilty of conspiracy to wage warfare and of having waged it. It was a remarkable judgment. In finding him guilty, the court declared:

> Hess was an active supporter of the preparations for war. . . . His signature established military service. . . . he expressed a desire for peace and advocated international economic cooperation. But . . . none knew better than Hess how determined Hitler was to realize his ambitions, how fanatical and violent a man he was. . . . With him on his flight to England, Hess carried certain peace proposals which he alleged Hitler was prepared to accept. It is significant to note that this flight took place only ten days after the date on which Hitler fixed, 22 June 1941, as the time for attacking the Soviet Union. . . . That Hess acts in an abnormal manner, suffers from loss of memory, and has mentally deteriorated during this Trial, may be true. But there is nothing to show that he does not realize the nature of the charges against him, or is incapable of defending himself. . . . There is no suggestion that Hess was not completely sane when the acts charged against him were committed. . . .
> Defendant Rudolf Hess, the court sentences you to imprisonment for life.[55]

Counterevidence did, however, exist. It was in the report of the psychiatrists who had examined Hess in Britain and had found that his aberrations were of long standing. The court chose to ignore such evidence. At least two of its members—the Russian judges—were unshakably convinced (and no doubt had been before the start of the trial) that Hess had flown to Britain for the express purpose of arranging a combined Anglo-German attack on the Soviet Union. This is perhaps why the court took pains, in sentencing Hess, to refer to his flight's coming only ten days after Hitler had set the date for the invasion of the Soviet Union. Nevertheless, over the protests of the Russian members of the tribunal, Hess' life was spared.

In his cell in the Palace of Justice, Hess wrote voluminously but destroyed what he wrote. He refused to see his wife or son when visiting privileges were allowed the prisoners after the sentences had been pronounced. He showed no interest in the verdict, and he went to the prison at Spandau no more concerned than when he had come to Nuremberg. He had expected, he said, to be sentenced to death. Despite his refusal to see his family, he wrote sporadically from Nuremberg and then from Spandau prison to his wife, as he had from England. His letters were affectionate and often detailed, as when he recounted his flight to England, but they evidenced many of the same symptoms he showed in the course of the trial. In his first letter from Spandau, written August 3, 1947, he described his newly painted cell, with its head cushion and cord mattress, and his gardening in the prison soil, where he raised tobacco and tomatoes.* He also said he had not written more from England because, since he had allegedly lost his memory, he was afraid

---

* The Spandau prisoners may raise vegetables, but not for their own consumption.

of disclosing in the letters that this was not the case. It had been a great swindle on his part, and the British, he said proudly, had admitted they had been taken in. They would probably think the sentence was bad enough, he wrote, but he himself only smiled, and he had written to his lawyer, Seidl, to prevent his asking for a pardon. Seidl had explained to him that he was not asking for a pardon, but pointed out that Hess had been the only person convicted on Points One and Two of the indictment—that is, of plotting to wage, and then having waged, aggressive war, and that the sentence was out of proportion to the offenses.

Obviously his enemies were still at work. In March, 1948, Hess wrote to his wife that he had not written for some time but could not give the real reason. But not only his world was irrational. Although, as Hess had explained in his letter to the Duke of Hamilton, he had gone to England on a mission of humanity, he was now sentenced to spend the rest of his life in the Spandau prison for his part in planning the attacks on Poland, Norway, Yugoslavia, the Low Countries, and the others—including, by implication, the Soviet Union. Not much could be said on his behalf after his conviction except to point out that in normal times he would have been judged insane. Even under the circumstances it was a curious verdict. The Western powers since that time have suggested that his sentence might be commuted, only to run up against a veto of the Soviet Union.

After the attack of the armed forces of England, France, and Israel on Egypt in November, 1956, Hess' attorney, Alfred Seidl, wrote to the British Foreign Office asking whether Anthony Eden, who was then Prime Minister, was to be brought before a court to answer for his part in an aggression that had been denounced in countries as far apart as the Soviet Union and the United States.

ALFRED ROSENBERG

The chief ideologist of the Party from the beginning was Alfred Rosenberg, a man far more erudite than Streicher and as implacably anti-Semitic, anti-Church, and anti-Slav as Bormann. Rosenberg came into his own on April 20, 1941, two months before the start of the Russian campaign, when Hitler named him Commissioner for the Central Control of Questions Connected with the East European Region. On July 17, after Germany's invasion of Russia, he was appointed Reich Minister for the Occupied Eastern Territories. Actually, the conquered provinces of Russia, which were to be his satrapy, turned out to be only another of his succession of failures in the practical world of National Socialist brass-knuckle politics. Rosenberg was defeated in Russia, as he was in the Reich, by ambitions and hopes out of proportion to his talents.

He always overestimated himself. At the end of the war he wrote a letter to Field Marshal Montgomery from Admiral Doenitz's headquarters at Flensburg, placing himself at the Marshal's disposal. He never received an answer. Instead, two British officers came to arrest him. They told him they had not heard of the letter. Rosenberg limped off to his captivity (he had long had trouble with his joints, had injured his ankle, and could only walk with difficulty) and to his trial as a major war criminal. His diary was found by American soldiers in a castle in Bavaria where he had hidden it. Because he was a voluminous writer, the author of many books and pamphlets, and because the records of his administration of the Eastern Territory as well as of his gigantic plundering of European art were preserved, little remains unknown about the part he played in the Third Reich.

Rosenberg's importance was far more formal than real. In Germany he had resounding titles: Reichsleiter, Chief of the Foreign Office of the Party, Commissioner of the Fuehrer for the Safeguarding of the National Socialist Philosophy. In actual practice, he was elbowed aside. In theory he was to exercise supreme civil authority in the territories won in battle from the Soviet Union [56] and to legislate for the entire area.

The administration of the Occupied Eastern Territories was a rat's nest of competing agencies with overlapping jurisdictions. Goering's staff for the Four-Year Plan was in charge of economic affairs, but the Army too had an economic staff, and Rosenberg's Reichsministry for these territories had both long- and short-range plans for the Soviet economy. Bormann and the Party apparatus, Goebbels and his Propaganda Ministry, Ribbentrop and the Foreign Office, the Army, and the SS—all were empire builders in Russia. Also, Todt and Speer had assignments for traffic and construction that conflicted with what Rosenberg considered his domain.[57]

Rosenberg signed the decree of December 19, 1941, for recruiting forced labor in the Eastern Territories. He approved, on behalf of his Ministry, the so-called Hay Action, which was a plan never carried out for bringing children from ten to fourteen years old from Russia to the Reich so they could work and at the same time reduce the biological potential of the Soviet Union. (See Schirach, Chapt. 8.) On paper Rosenberg was the civilian Czar of the East, but key men were appointed by the Fuehrer and often they were appointed over his head, as was the Gauleiter Erich Koch, who headed the Ukraine. Rosenberg's own men had to compete with appointees of other agencies, including Himmler's SS leaders. Since Himmler, unlike Rosenberg, was always in close touch with Hitler, who made the decisions when authorities conflicted, it was Himmler's men who became the real rulers of the occupied territories. Some of Rosenberg's theoretical subordinates—the practical men like Koch—could match in their brutality the SS police officials and the Einsatz commandos, but they were not carrying out Rosenberg's orders. They were merely the logical extension of his basic doctrines. He objected over and over again to the brutality, beatings, and killings that were alienating the people of the Ukraine and Russia and the other nationalities from the German cause. However, they were only *Untermenschen*, likable perhaps and useful, but in the case of the Great Russians, primitive and dangerous.

Rosenberg's tedious writings were the source of his preferment. His speeches and articles (he was editor of the *Voelkischer Beobachter* and of the *Nationalsozialistische Monatshefte*) and, above all, his *Myth of the Twentieth Century* impressed Hitler by their bulk and pure doctrinal purposes. (Rosenberg said at Nuremberg that he and Hitler had rarely discussed philosophy, but he knew they shared the same opinions.) Rosenberg, however, was more doctrinaire than Hitler, who sometimes commented sarcastically on Rosenberg's addiction to his *Germanen* cult.[58]

In 1929 Rosenberg founded the Militant League for German Culture, which became the National Socialist Cultural Community under which the "Strength through Joy" movement operated. In 1934 he was named Deputy of the Fuehrer for the Supervision of the Entire Ideological Training and Education of the NSDAP.[59] In February, 1940, when Hitler appointed him Commissioner for the Safeguarding of the National Socialist Philosophy for the Party and State, his responsibilities included the indoctrination of the Wehrmacht. A few days before, on January 29, 1940, Hitler gave Rosenberg the job of founding the so-called high school, the *Hohe Schule,* which was to be established after the war as the Central National Socialist University.[60] A great cathedral of Nazi education was planned to rise on the banks of the Chiemsee, south of Munich. For the benefit of his high school, Rosenberg set aside a large portion of the confiscated libraries of Jews and Masons. More than half a million volumes were confiscated and sent to the Central Library at the Tanzenberg Monastery in Carinthia for safekeeping until they could one day be sent to the Chiemsee. Rosenberg constantly prepared for historic roles, both inside and outside the Reich (he had long aspired to be Foreign Minister and was bitterly disappointed when Ribbentrop was named). He had hoped to be the learned chief of German education and the proconsul of the East, but these dizzy heights, described in the prospectuses, were never climbed. The tough men of affairs of the SS and the commissars, who either paid no attention to him or, like Koch, fought him tooth and nail, ruled the Russian provinces, and Bormann did his best to see to it that the high school remained a mock-up of what was never to be built.

Like Hitler, Rosenberg was one of the non-Germans who far outdid the native-born in their patriotic passion for their adopted country. Born in Reval, in Estonia, on January 12, 1893, he came from a family of German-speaking artisans and small business people acutely conscious of their Germanism in the midst of an alien culture. Rosenberg's father had a job in a Reval business firm; his grandfather was a shoemaker and head of his guild. Gossip in the Party said the family was not German at all but was descended from Estonian agricultural laborers who had taken the German name of their landlord and kept it after they migrated to the city. Others said that Rosenberg was a mixture of French or Slavic and Estonian ancestors. Some thought he had Jewish blood and remarked, when Rosenberg published a list of prominent Russian officials who were Jews, that he must consider himself to be the only Aryan Rosenberg in the world.[61] Rosenberg looked German, although he was dark-haired and had a round skull. He was handsome in a grim way.[62]

Rosenberg attended the Technical Institute (Technische Hochschule) in Riga, where he studied architecture and joined a student corps, the Rubonia, made up of German and pro-German students. Although Estonia was part of the Czarist empire, students were not drafted into the Russian Army. Rosenberg thought the reason was that Russia had enough manpower without them. When on the approach of the German Army in the war of 1915, the school was moved to Moscow, Rosenberg went along with his classmates and married a student he had known for a number of years. His wife, Hilda, soon fell ill with tuberculosis and had to go to the Crimea for her health. She seems to have been of a lively intellectual disposition. Through her Rosenberg was introduced to the works of Nietzsche, and together they read Balzac, Tolstoy, and Dostoevski while the rest of the population concerned itself with the war. Rosenberg followed her to the Crimea but had to return to Moscow to take his examinations, and there he found the revolution in full tide. What his political views were at this time is not clear, but the relative ease with which he moved from one country and allegiance to another suggests they were not strongly held. Some of his Nazi critics thought he was pro-Russian, at least up to the time of the revolution, and some thought he had served in the Russian Army. One of the critics who knew him says that Rosenberg always avoided the subject.[63]

Until 1918 Rosenberg concentrated mainly on architecture and painting. While in Estonia, he applied himself to being a member in good standing of the German community, in the midst of the Letts and Slavs and Jews. When the revolution came, he shared the belief—widely current in the Baltic States, Poland, and Russia—that the Jews had been responsible for it. He welcomed Estonian independence, which came as a result of the revolution, but he did not join, as did most of the young German Balts, the *Landswehr* to defend the country against bolshevism. Instead, after making a few speeches to his fellow countrymen, he emigrated to Paris, as did most of the Russian *émigrés*. There he read for the first time Gobineau and Houston Stewart Chamberlain, and in his enthusiasm for England, the center of the Northern races, he tried to get to London. The British, however, were suspicious in 1918 of the infiltration of Czarist and Communist agents and refused Rosenberg an entry permit. It was only then that Rosenberg turned toward another Nordic country and moved to Munich, which, like Paris, was a center of White Russian *émigrés* as anti-Bolshevik as Rosenberg. In Munich in 1918 he explained to the Baltic Independence Commission, which was recruiting soldiers to defend his native land, that his wife was ill and he had other pressing duties that must keep him in Germany. (Rosenberg and Hilda were divorced in the spring of 1923. She had left the Soviet Union to live in Paris, where she later died.)

Rosenberg's visions were (1) the racial superiority of the Northern peoples (to which he later added as a corollary the German need of living space); and (2) the establishing of a new religion, National Socialism, to replace the sterile dogmas of Christianity as well as the conspiratorial beliefs of the Jews. For Christian love he wanted to substitute National Socialist comradeship. He began to get a sense of his public mission in 1918, when, during the period of the short-lived Raete Republic of the Communists, mainly Jews, who seized control of Munich for a few bloody days, he discovered that he could speak to a German audience and that people listened. Actually, the times were explosive, and audiences were more than ready to be instructed. Rosenberg was never an eloquent speaker. He was humorless, dry, and long-winded, but his denunciation of Jews and Communists fell on willing ears, in both Estonia and Munich.

In Munich he almost immediately became a member of the German Worker's Party, which a few months later became the National Socialist Party. He joined it ahead of Hitler. Later he wrote that when he first met the Fuehrer he was not overly impressed, but he quickly came under Hitler's spell. His unshakable loyalty withstood the severest tests, such as Hitler's neglecting him for his rivals and the signing in August, 1939, of the non-aggression pact with Russia. Rosenberg dreamed intoxicating dreams of a German Reich that would take over its needed living space from the Soviet Union, breaking up for all time the Slav dominion over the vast stretches of the Eastern marches and the dangerous concentration of Great Russians, who were the main support of the Czar's empire and of the Communist State as well. This was to be done by means of colonization, and by making alliances with Finland and with the subject peoples of the Ukraine, the Caucasus, Galicia, White Ruthenia, and Turkestan, who had long been chafing under the dominion of Moscow.

Russia had always been essentially an Asiatic power, Rosenberg believed, and with its hordes could only be held in check by German force and guile that would divide and rule. To this end he wanted relatively good treatment for the non-Communists and for the minorities of the Soviet Union, who could produce food and goods and an additional line of defense for the Third Reich against any future Russian state. In this view he soon came into sharp conflict with the SS and with the administrators Himmler and Bormann sent to the East.* These men, like Rosenberg, were single-minded in their racial mission. They were also men of action, who were not seeking allies among the natives but obedient slaves who could be liquidated at any time. When

---

* Rosenberg even opposed the wholesale slaughter of commissars. Only high-ranking ones, he said, should be killed in accord with Hitler's order; the others should be spared and used to administer the occupied territory (see Keitel, Chapt. 9).

the Gauleiter of the Ukraine, Erich Koch, was met by a humble delegation sent to greet him with salt and bread, he dashed the gifts to the ground, shouting that it was an affront for such people to dare to offer anything to an official of the Reich. Koch's emissaries were not allowed to sit down at the same table with Slavs, not even with those collaborating with the German occupation. Rosenberg thought it possible to have an arm's-length relation with a Ukrainian, possibly to give him a drink in a friendly fashion, but not to get drunk with him. He fancied himself as an expert, not only on how to deal with the people of the Soviet Union but on all matters that had to do with foreign countries, and he wished to impress subject nations with German superiority without using a club to do it. In his diary entry of May 22, 1934, he recorded his protest against the manner in which the Jewish question was being handled, noting the bad propaganda effect on the outside world of the attacks instigated by Goebbels' speeches and Streicher's writings.

Rosenberg was as fanatic in racist matters as any members of the SS, but he objected to their methods as well as to their competition. He said that the beatings and killings and needless humiliations they inflicted on the populations were bound to create undying enmity for the Reich, and that Einsatz commandos had alienated even the pro-Germans in the Ukraine, who had first welcomed the German troops as deliverers. Nevertheless, Rosenberg's own instructions to the brown-uniformed representatives of his Ministry in the East were harsh by almost any standard but Himmler's. On June 20, 1941, he told an audience of his closest co-workers, "We see absolutely no reason for any obligation on our part to feed the Russian people with the products of this surplus region [southern Russia and the northern Caucasus]. We know this is a hard necessity that lies outside any feelings . . . the future will hold very hard years in store for the Russians." [64] In 1942 he told an audience of Reichskommissars, "The question is: What spares us most in German men and what brings us best to the political result . . . that thousands are badly cared for or are badly treated is taken for granted. You don't have to grow grey hairs over that." [65]

Despite such views, he never had in mind the mayhem and wholesale slaughter that took place. When they occurred, he spoke of the superior efficacy of more humane methods and looked the other way. Not that he was more humane than his rivals. He merely wanted to assert his authority and to impose his own program. Rosenberg, the Balt, hated the Great Russians—the core of Russia as he thought of them. And he had no love for the Ukrainians, the White Russians, or the other nationalities of the Soviet Union. These, he thought, should become the peoples of autonomous states, so that the Moscovites, as he called them, could be held in check. The separate nationalities could then be treated well enough to bind them to a German alliance. For this purpose he would use whatever methods were necessary. The problem was only to convince Hitler that Rosenberg's plans were superior to those of Koch, Goering, Bormann, Himmler, and the others. It would be necessary to take as hard a line as they, and to want what Hitler wanted. Thus, when Hitler wanted Germans to be resettled in the Crimea, Rosenberg told the Fuehrer that he had given earnest thought to the problem of renaming the cities: Simferopol was to be called Gotenburg, Sevastopol changed to Theoderichhafen.[66]

In a memorandum of March 6, 1942, he wrote:

> After continuous observation of the state of affairs in the Occupied Eastern Territories, I am convinced that German politics may have their own, possibly contemptuous opinion of the qualities of the conquered peoples, but that it is not the mission of German political representatives to proclaim measures and opinions which could eventually reduce the conquered peoples to dull despair instead of promoting the desired utilization of manpower to capacity. . . . If at home we had to announce our aims to the whole nation most openly and aggressively . . . the political leaders in the East must remain silent where German policy calls for necessary harshness. . . . Yes, a clever German policy may in certain circumstances do more in the German interest through alleviations which do not affect policy and certain humane concessions, than through open, inconsiderate brutality.[67]

He knew what Bormann was doing, for he got a memorandum from a member of his staff, a Dr. Markull, on the subject of Rosenberg's correspondence with Bormann that said in part:

> Any person reading this correspondence is struck, first of all, by the complete agreement of concepts. . . . The Minister [Rosenberg] not only raises no objections against Bormann's principles or even his phraseology; on the contrary, he uses them as a basis for his reply and endeavors to show that they are already being put into practice. . . . Imagine the formulas of Bormann's letter translated into the language of a member of the German civilian administration, and you will get, roughly, the following views: The Slavs are to work for us. Insofar as we do not need them, they may die. . . . Education is dangerous. It is enough if they can count up to 100. . . . Religion we leave to them as a means of diversion. As for food, they will not get any more than is necessary. We are the masters; we come first. These sentences are by no means overstatements. On the contrary they are covered, word by word, by the spirit and the text of Bormann's letter. . . . The above-mentioned concept of our role in the East already exists in practice. . . . there is no divergence of opinion. The Minister's [Rosenberg's] reply . . . might be considered to point in this direction.[68]

On the stand at Nuremberg, Rosenberg said what he had done was to write an "appeasing" letter to Bormann and then had gone on to issue decrees setting up schools and health control. That was Rosenberg's way: to agree with the extremists like Bormann and Himmler in an attempt to ward off the constant attacks upon him, and to end up by accepting the policies his enemies imposed both on the subject populations and on him. Rosenberg had vast geopolitical aims: he wanted Great Russia—any Great Russia, whether of the Czars or the Soviet Union—to be forced to remove its center of gravity to Asia. The best means for accomplishing this, he thought, was to make use of the Slavs' yearning for a firm and masterful hand, and to treat the native populations with the vigor and justice that were essential for asserting German moral superiority.[69] The natives were to be permitted to work for the German overlords, to take part in the anti-Semitic and anti-Bolshevik crusade, and to help keep the Moscovites in their place.

Rosenberg's aspiration to be Foreign Minister of the Reich was so strong that he had brought himself to express his disappointment to Hitler when the post went to Ribbentrop in 1938. He was in fact at least as well qualified for the job as was Ribbentrop, whose ideas on foreign policy were just as clouded as Rosenberg's.

On May 12, 1934, Rosenberg had written a memorandum to Hitler declaring that England's Air Force was really built against France. England, like Germany, he said, was vulnerable to air attack, and he recommended that Germany and England plan to cooperate in a combined air service to Calcutta through Berlin, Budapest, and Ankara, and to work together in the event of a Russo-Japanese war.[70] In his diary entry for December 26, 1934, he noted that England feared the French Air Force and that, when Germany had more planes, discussions could take place on how the two countries could work together.[71] In 1940 he sent Quisling to have an audience with Hitler. Rosenberg had met the Norwegian in 1933, and he kept in touch with him, as he did with scores of people in foreign countries he thought might be useful.[72] His appointment as Reichsminister for the Eastern Territories was a compensation for his not becoming Foreign Minister, and it was disappointing to Ribbentrop, whose responsibilities were obviously invaded with this newly created job administering and, as it was then thought, deciding on policies that would concern the Foreign Office.

The rivalry between Ribbentrop and Rosenberg was intense. Rosenberg was head of the Foreign Affairs Office of the Party (the APA, Aussenpolitisches Amt), one of the parallel organizations designed to provide competition for, and (should the occasion arise) to supplant, the existing State Office. Rosenberg, in fact, had gone to London in May, 1933, not long after Hitler had come to power, to represent National Socialist views in what he regarded as influential British quarters, and no trip (not even any trip made by Ribbentrop) was ever more disastrous. "A ponderous lightweight," Sir Robert Vansittart called him, and the English press saw in him a symbol of Nazi boorishness—something Rosenberg made easy for his critics in his pontifical press conferences (he spoke little English) held in his hotel. When he laid a wreath on the Cenotaph it was spirited away. Accompanied by Count Gottfried von Bismarck as interpreter, he was received at the Foreign Office on May 8 by Sir John Simon. Rosenberg explained how Nazism would be a stabilizing factor in Germany and on the Continent against communism. He said that if Hitler disappeared, communism would take his place. Simon told him with what concern England viewed certain aspects of the National Socialist revolution, especially the measures against the Jews. Rosenberg's answer was to repeat his charges against the Communists and to say that the German Government's real aim was the preservation of liberty, which would be destroyed if the Communists had their way. He acknowledged that Jews had been deprived of their jobs but said they had unrightfully governed Germany since World War I. Nothing came of his visit except outcries of indignation, and he was never to return.[73]

Rosenberg's Foreign Affairs Office of the Party survived all such episodes as well as the steady hostility of the German Foreign Office. He ascribed the success of the Norwegian campaign solely to his department, for it was he who had put Quisling in touch with the Fuehrer and Admiral Raeder, and it was *his* agents who warned of the imminent Anglo-French intervention in Norway, while the German Foreign Office officials were sending reassuring reports to Berlin. The victory in Norway, Rosenberg wrote, was "a confirmation of the historical task fulfilled by the Foreign Affairs Office of the Party" and another gratifying proof of Ribbentrop's incompetence.[74]

His early writings were not very different from Streicher's. In 1920 Rosenberg published *The Trail of the Jew in the Course of Time (Die Spur der Juden im Wandel der Zeiten)* and *Immorality in the Talmud (Unmoral im Talmud)*, and in 1923 *The Protocols of Zion and Jewish World Politics (Die Protokolle der Weisen von Zion und die juedische Weltpolitik)*. In these books Jewish depravity and the plan to conquer the world were exposed with the full apparatus of pseudoscholarship. Rosenberg was the original draftsman of the Party programs that traced the source of German woes to Jewish-Bolshevik Marxism and to the Jewish materialist influence on the Christian Church. In his grand synthesis he demanded living space from the Soviet Union and a return in the Reich of the Germanic pagan myth of the blood. His *The Myth of the Twentieth Century* was in the home of every "decent Party member," as the phrase went. In 1934 he noted in his diary that 250,000 copies had been sold. By the time the war started, the sales figure had gone to over a million, although letters in the files of the Party and the testimony of witnesses at Nuremberg often confessed an inability to get through the book. Goebbels laughed at it; Goering said he had never read it; the Fuehrer had only looked at it.

What made him important was the image he presented of the erudite, dedicated interpreter of the National Socialist mystique. His *Myth of the Twentieth Century*, despite many importunities from bewildered readers and shrewd editors, he would never allow to be abridged. One of his admirers, Alfred Baeumler, wrote a book about it [75] in which he told his readers that *The Myth* was a hard book to read because such monumental ideas could not be easily grasped. Rosenberg's style lacked rhetoric, he said, but this was a virtue, for Rosenberg did not believe in smoothing over differences but believed in fighting them out in political battle. "The Myth"—the myth of blood, the new secular sacrament of race (Baeumler wrote, paraphrasing Rosenberg), cannot be created; to win it back is not a deed but an experience.*

Rosenberg continued to make speeches until the very end. In 1945 he was still addressing the troops on the Eastern front. At one speech in Duesseldorf, the mayor introduced him with a trace of unconscious irony: "The name Rosenberg is a program." And indeed it was. Rosenberg took his ideas from all the wide stock of books that confirmed his notions. He told his audiences of Party leaders that what the hour demanded was a deepening of their racist and biological thinking. The primary importance of race in the making of history was the great discovery of the National Socialist revolution. The German mission, he said, was to defend with its Nordic blood the divine essence of man. Race was far more important than the state and its forms, and when the racist doctrine was combined with the mystical powers of the Fuehrer to express the German soul, it led inexorably to the need for Hitler's assuming complete authority over the Reich and the Germanic peoples.[76] The Fuehrer possessed the collective will of the people within himself. The true will of the people was the Fuehrer. Rosenberg was sure he had gotten hold of something deeply revolutionary for the whole life of man in all its phases. "The new grasp of the world," he told an audience, "is not a dogma but an attitude." He also made the following pronouncements:

"Soul means race seen from the inside. . . . Race is the outside of the soul." [77]

"Man as a personality is forming will, will is racially determined." [78]

"Every form is deed, every deed is basically discharged will." [79]

"The State is outside our ideal. The ideal is the inner side of the State." [80]

Rosenberg never changed after 1918. In May, 1945, he told his British captors that what went wrong with the Nazi State was due to the machinations of the Himmlers and Bormanns; that he believed the ideas of National Socialism to be as sound as ever; that the organization simply had not been up to the ideas. Even in defeat, he believed that the Nazi Party had forced the British and Americans at long last to see the necessity for an alliance with Germany.[81]

Despite his mystical devotion to the Fuehrer, Rosenberg had been sorely tried by the pact with the Soviet Union. To his diary (entry of August 22, 1939) he confided that "the journey of our Minister to Moscow is a moral loss in the face of our twenty-year battle, in the face of our Party days, in the face of Spain." The attempt of the English and French to win a Soviet

---

* This was a widely quoted Rosenbergian dogma: "The myth has to be experienced and not merely understood" (see Harry Griessdorff, *Unsere Weltanschauung* [Berlin: Nordland Verlag, 1941], p. 12.). The *Mythus* was regarded with awe even by supposedly learned men. One professor wrote a book that did no more than define 850 words of the vocabulary (Otto Gros, *850 Worte Mythus des 20. Jahrhunderts* [Munich: Hoheneichen Verlag, 1938]).

alliance was not as bad because they had never identified the Soviet Union with the Third International, which for twenty years the Nazis had characterized as "Jewish criminality." The Fuehrer had said only four years earlier, in Rosenberg's presence, that he could never make common cause with Moscow because it was not possible to forbid the German people to steal and at the same time make friends with the thieves. Rosenberg blamed the whole affair on Ribbentrop and his hatred of England. The German-Russian embrace over which the German press was so enthusiastic, wrote Rosenberg sadly, "is more than painful." He had the feeling, he confided in his diary (entry of August 25), that one day the Moscow agreement would avenge itself upon National Socialism, and he asked himself, "How can we still speak of the rescue and shaping of Europe when we must ask the destroyer of Europe to come to our aid? . . . And again the question poses itself: . . . was it necessary to settle the Polish question now and in this form? No one can give the answer today. I at least hold Ribbentrop to be the criminal Iswolsky,* who out of his sick jealousy creates the grounds for his political ideas." Rosenberg's bitter cup overflowed when he heard that Ribbentrop had said that he felt himself among Party comrades when he was with the Russians in Moscow.[82] But Rosenberg soon made a partial recovery from his disappointment at the signing of the pact. He was assuaged when Goering sent him a friendly telegram and when occasionally the Fuehrer asked his advice. And early in 1942 the Fuehrer appointed him to the high office of Chief Indoctrinator for the Ideological Unity of Party and State.

During the period of Russo-German friendship, Party agencies continued to collect material from informants in Poland on the inferiority of the Russians.[83] The following reports, among others, came in: A Soviet soldier in Poland said that Germany would undoubtedly win the war against the West but would end up Communist. The Russians bought or stole everything they could lay their hands on in Poland. Money had little importance for them. Soviet soldiers paid the equivalent of 250 RM for a watch worth a fraction of that. Boots costing 20 RM went for 150 RM (one Russian said of his purchase, "Now I have *two* pairs of boots"). Poles complained that the Russians stripped the leather upholstery from trains. A woman said that Russian officers, acting under orders, were not friendly to the Germans. They were reported as saying to Germans they met, "We'll see you again," and this the Germans took as a dark hint of a later military conflict.

Among the reports sent to Rosenberg were stories of the Russian soldiers' ignorance of the ways of other countries. (Such stories would be repeated years later by the Germans under Russian occupation.) One soldier was said to have bought a brassiere and was seen to have used it for earmuffs; another bought flypaper, which he allegedly took to be honey; another

---

* Alexander Petrovitch Iswolsky, Russian Ambassador to France from 1910 to 1917, was widely thought to have been one of those chiefly responsible for Czarist Russia's anti-German policy before World War I.

brought back a meat grinder complaining that he had thought it was an organ. Russians always, the reports said, declared that what they saw in Poland they had at home too. One Ukrainian lady told her Russian visitor she was sorry she had no lemon for tea and the Russian said, "That's all right, our factories are working night and day and you'll soon be able to get them."

Rosenberg digested such information and on May 3, 1940, wrote that the Russian question had to be treated circumspectly, and it was not to be neglected even if it remained in the background for the present. But when he was told in April, 1941, of Hitler's plan to invade Russia, he returned to his predominant notion: the overwhelming danger of the Bolshevik allied with the Jew and the Moscovite and the need to make them harmless.

While race was all-important, a proper environment was important too. Like many other Nazis, Rosenberg referred to the "filthy human masses" in the big cities. Few of the Party great loved the large cities. Many of them came from the provinces or from small cities. Many Party stalwarts, with their longing for the "folkish" roots of Germanic culture, regarded the metropolis as inferior, unhealthy, degenerate. Prevalent as this belief was, not all held it. Roehm, for example, writing to a friend in Berlin from South America, praised Berlin—especially its Turkish baths, which seemed to him in his exile the best place in the world. Roehm's reasons for liking Berlin were precisely those denounced by his colleagues.

Rosenberg always clung to the belief that the racist conflict alone was decisive, with the lower races warring against the spiritual, superior ones. There were other evils too. Germany had been rescued from the destruction wrought by democrats and Marxists and plutocratic false gods under the Christian heresy by the new religion of race and blood. All parliaments, Rosenberg thought, were dependent on high finance and were affiliated with the big intercorporate trusts, or cartels, which had enslaved the German people. The war, he wrote in the *Voelkischer Beobachter* of March 29, 1941, was the last desperate attempt to force the white race to march against Europe in an internecine conflict for the benefit of Jewish finance. The war would be also the cleansing biological world revolution. He was sure that in time other nations would recognize that the German task in bringing it about was being accomplished on behalf of the whole European continent. Liberalism, he wrote, sinned against the law of nature. The old effeminate liberal world would have to be replaced by authority and discipline. "The significance of world history was radiated out from the north over the whole world borne by a blue-eyed blond race which in several great waves determined the spiritual aspect of the world."[84] The contemporary world revolution lay in the awakening of the national types. There would be no Franco-Jewish pan-Europe. Instead, a Nordic Europe with a German center would arise. Race determined everything. The Japanese, the Negro, and the Jew could only be what they were; they could never be European and would therefore have to pursue entirely different intellectual and political aims, although the Japanese could be useful as an ally against the Soviet Union.[85]

Rosenberg's assignment of founding the Central National Socialist University was a characteristic distinction. It was a grandiose dream and a sanction for plunder. The university was to be divided into a number of institutes: one for the study of the Jewish problem, one for geopolitics, and one for research into racial matters. It was for the high school that the great libraries of the Rothschilds and of Baron van Zuylen and the Jewish banker Fuerstenberg in Berlin were ransacked. Hitler, planning for the reenergizing of European thinking, declared in a letter of January 29, 1940, that the school was to be a center of research and education under Alfred Rosenberg. Despite the prodigious efforts demanded on behalf of the war, Rosenberg could announce on January 7, 1943, that institutes had already been organized in Frankfurt am Main for the investigation of the Jewish question, in Halle for religious research, in Hamburg for overseas and colonial research, in Kiel for German living space, in Munich for Indo-Germanic cultural history, in Stuttgart for biology and race, and in Tannenberg for German studies. A few months later, in April, 1943, Rosenberg said matters were so far advanced that one institute would be opened in Marburg on May 1.[86] But the whole program remained in the blueprint stage for a postwar Europe.

In these educational programs Rosenberg had competition. Himmler had a macabre research organization founded "to explore the geographical extent, spirit, achievement and heritage of the Indo-Germans of Northern race." His organization—the Ahnenerbe (ancestral heritage)—had among other things a notable collection of skulls. Himmler also planned to found a National Socialist Academy of Sciences with many institutes, which would parallel the high school. With more than fifty departments and a budget of a million marks, the Ahnenerbe undertook research and teaching in the social and natural sciences; in history, archeology, and folklore; even in military colonization. It confiscated books and manuscripts of Jewish scholars that seemed in any way useful to its vast purposes. Himmler's organization was next to Einsatzstab Rosenberg in combing Europe for suitable cultural objects.[87]

In his interrogation on April 14, 1946, Rosenberg said he had thought of the books and paintings and miscellaneous objects of cultural value his Einsatzstab collected not as private property but as something belonging to hostile organizations fighting against Germany. His job, he had written on April 7, 1942, was to secure all the material that would be useful for National Socialist research and to prevent its becoming useful to Germany's enemies.[88] A Fuehrer decree announced that Rosenberg would accomplish his task in cooperation with the chief of the High Command of the Wehrmacht.[89] The special units carrying out his orders in the East were subordinate to the service branches of the Army, to which they were attached. Like the SD units, they had the right to use the communications of the Wehrmacht and to be supported by the Army under the orders issued by General Eduard Wagner for the High Command, but actually Rosenberg's influence in the East was largely limited to his "collections" on behalf of the culture of the Reich.

Along with his apparatus of plunder for the benefit of the high school, Rosenberg's Einsatzstab also had the task of confiscating art treasures in France and the other countries of occupied Europe, mainly for Goering's private collection. In addition to "cultural goods," Rosenberg's men collected furniture, wash basins, rugs, kitchenware, bottles, medicines, clothes—anything that could be carted and carried away. On October 3, 1942, he was able to report to the Fuehrer that "Action M"—the furniture action—directed against Jews and Freemasons in France and the Low Countries, had placed 19,500 tons of furniture at the disposal of Germans who had suffered losses from Allied bombs and that 40,000 tons had already been loaded on trains bound for Germany.[90] In August, 1944, he reported that up to then 69,619 Jewish apartments had been taken over, and that 26,984 freight cars (674 trains) had carried the goods to Germany.[91] All the furniture movers in Paris had been put to work: 1,200 to 1,500 men, who daily loaded 150 trucks. In Paris alone, 38,000 apartments had been cleared of their owners' belongings. The Military Governor of Occupied France, General Karl Heinrich von Stuelpnagel, complained that Rosenberg's staff in France made no payment for the Jewish property taken over.[92] Rosenberg regarded it as being without an owner, and Stuelpnagel demanded in vain that this be stopped.*

Rosenberg at Nuremberg (interrogation of August 30, 1946) called the accomplishments of his Einsatzstab Rosenberg "the biggest art operation in history." † It was aimed, he said, only against Jewish and Masonic collections and was not intended primarily to add to the pictures in Goering's museum, since the Reichsmarschall already had a great collection. Goering, however, turned out to be the chief beneficiary. Rosenberg testified, too, that neither he nor his organization were ever paid a cent by Goering for the pictures turned over to him. Rosenberg still thought this correct. He had felt that such matters should be kept for Hitler's postwar decision and as bargaining counters at an eventual peace conference. His vast operation, he testified, began in July, 1940, with the objective of bringing together historical works and of protecting them against the vicissitudes of the war. In this fashion the Germans would be able to get a complete inventory of what was available for their research purposes. He added that the art objects brought to the Reich might otherwise have been destroyed.

* For the Army's resistance to Rosenberg's operations, see Wilhelm Treue, "*Zum nationalsozialistischen Kunstraub in Frankreich,*" in *Vierteljahrshefte fuer Zeitgeschichte,* Vol. XIII, No. 3, 1965, pp. 285–337.

† It is likely that Rosenberg exaggerated. Napoleon's collections, which included paintings assembled from all Europe as well as the bronze horses from the façade of Saint Mark's in Venice and the armories from Naples, Munich, and Vienna, were probably made on a still larger scale.

A report on the activities of the Einsatzstab Rosenberg for the period between October, 1940, and July, 1944, summed up what had been taken as "ownerless Jewish property": 21,903 art objects of all kinds, brought to the Reich in 29 shipments, including 137 freight cars. Among them were 5,281 paintings, including works by Rembrandt, Rubens, Velásquez, Murillo, Goya, Boucher, Watteau, Cranach, and Reynolds; 684 miniatures; 583 textiles (Gobelins, rugs, embroideries); 5,825 handmade art objects (porcelains, bronzes, faiences, coins); 1,286 East Asiatic art works; 259 art works of antiquity (sculpture, bronzes, vases); also several hundred icons and a collection of degenerate Bolshevik art. Among 2,477 articles of furniture was a collection of French furniture of the seventeenth and eighteenth centuries, which, the report said, "is perhaps even more highly to be evaluated than some of the pictures."[93]

At Nuremberg, Rosenberg defended his confiscation of Jewish and Masonic property by pointing out that German property worth 25 billion marks had been taken by the Allies after World War I, and that now, in August, 1946, all German libraries were in the hands of the Allies. He himself, he said, had never received anything of value from the confiscations. But the prosecution reminded him that three Dutch paintings, including a Franz Hals, had been rescued from his house in Berlin when it was bombed. Rosenberg said these had been presents, that his second wife loved antiques, and that they got a great number of gifts. He stressed that during his whole life he had tried to fight for what he called a healthy development of mankind and had tried to inculcate this in his children, but he admitted that even the great ideas in Nazism had been in some sense perverted in their development.

He confessed that he operated under different standards in the East than in the West—that he had kept the thought of the Polish persecution of the Germans in mind when he first undertook the collection of art objects in Poland.[94] A report of September 29, 1941, from one of his subordinates, Reichskommissar Wilhelm Kube, protested to Rosenberg against the looting by the rival squads of the SS in Minsk and even told of the need to get hold of a Nazi painter who would be able to repaint the pictures that had been "thoughtlessly damaged with knife slashings." Unfortunately, Kube said, millions of marks worth of art had been destroyed. He asked Rosenberg to take up the problem of this vandalism with the armed forces to prevent future repetitions and to see to it that those responsible be severely punished. A museum of prehistoric artifacts had been completely devastated; semiprecious jewels had been stolen; and in the university, instruments worth hundreds of thousands of marks had been destroyed or stolen.[95]

Rosenberg, in his Olympian fashion, tried to act on such pleas. In the first place, in matters of art he felt his jurisdiction was being challenged.*

---

* The Wehrmacht, like the British and American forces, had officers who were art experts assigned to the job of safeguarding monuments and art in occupied territory. Their activities had nothing in common with Rosenberg's Einsatzstab.

And in the second place he objected to the treatment of the native peoples by his enemies in the Party, just as he opposed the creation of a Russian army of liberation under General Andrei Vlasov which would fight on the German side. He wanted the "protection" and collection of art to be solely under his command. And he wanted to use the conquered space to free it from bolshevism and from any future nationalistic threat to the Reich. But he had no influence on decisions. He saw Hitler only twice after the war with Russia started. Hitler had his own plans and his own problems. Rosenberg could go on writing his memoranda and making his speeches and protests.

Addressing a meeting of Reichskommissars in August, 1942, after a speech by Goering, Rosenberg talked about his philosophy of the relations of Germans to the Eastern peoples. He made the following points: The old Slavic toughness is now combined with a fanatical, primitive philosophy. Bolshevism has swept aside the elements really capable of culture in Russia. What the Germans are now seeing is a bedraggled people. But the Germans nevertheless have duties toward them. Then he said:

> Many a little peasant has established himself in this area, this new ordering of space and he feels himself a little master and a little king. That is correct. . . . In this broad area of the East . . . he must be hard and he must be . . . just. . . . The peoples of the East . . . have always had an authoritarian government . . . [but] they always cried out for justice. . . . We have to find the psychological points where we can dominate them with less strength and get the same results as though we had a hundred police battalions. . . . Crime and punishment must be brought into a relationship.

The population must not be driven to the partisans. This does not mean weakness as against toughness; it is a question of sensible politics.

> It does no harm if one or another Commissar acts in a decent fashion once in a while to one or another Ukrainian. He should, however, not be comradely with them. . . . But he can . . . clap a man on the shoulder and give him good advice . . . and buy them a bottle of schnaps. But he must not get drunk with them and must keep his distance; that is essential for a proper master in the East. . . . A master is one for whom a man placed under him allows himself to be beaten to death. . . . The population must realize there is no way out but to accept German leadership. . . . The question for us is: What spares us most in German manpower and what brings us best to political success? . . . The blanket is short and everyone tries to pull as much as possible over to his side. The Army . . . strives to keep itself ready for battle . . . Speer . . . demands production. We have the job not only of raising production in the occupied Eastern territories, but of raising it considerably. Gauleiter Sauckel on the orders of the Fuehrer calls for workers . . . The Russians took 14 to 15 year old boys from factories and shot them so they could not be used by the Germans. . . . Sometimes when

the [Sauckel] Commissars were clever . . . the workers were brought to the railroad station to the accompaniment of music as they departed for their assignments in Germany. But sometimes other, harder methods are used too, sometimes thought out and correct, and sometimes not thought out and unjust. . . . In these cases they [the natives] get the impression that there is nothing to distinguish the trip to Germany from the trip to . . . Siberia. . . . I know of course that if you bring one and a half million people to work, you cannot take care of them beautifully. But in order to obtain a good performance don't bring in three quarters of them frozen, don't let them just stand waiting for ten hours, and give them much more to eat so they have reserves of strength. . . . All the people of Europe are working in Germany . . . and [tell them] since the German soldier fights and bleeds for you, you have the duty at least to work here. . . . But there is no harm if they play the accordion at night, and sing and paste newspaper and magazine clippings on the walls. . . . The East has already saved Germany. All the heads of the farm economy, the Kreisleiter, the young Party leaders, the SA and SS leaders . . . have been tireless in this last hard winter. . . . History will one day disclose that this was a prodigious accomplishment of the National Socialist revolution. . . . The Commissar who works there doesn't think of leaving. He says: here is my little kingdom; here I want to work for the rest of my life.

The conflict (between Germany and Russia) has been 1,600 years abuilding, he said. "It must never again be taken from German hands . . . on this space a greater German Reich must rise. . . . [stormy applause]." [96]

Since Rosenberg was battling against a host of enemies, his co-workers could be critical. Some of the reports submitted to him by members of his staff were far more perceptive than most German appreciations of the situation.[97]

One of his liaison men, attached to the headquarters of Army Group North, wrote in December, 1942, that Russian military strength was by no means broken; that Slav fighting power must be used to win the prolonged war; that not enough food was given the Russians; and that the German combat soldier would pay in blood for the policies being pursued, including the recruiting of forced labor. He recommended land reform (which was permitted sporadically and always welcomed by the peasants), pointing out that the Russian farmer was land-hungry. The kolkhozes should be divided and their land given the farmers. He protested against the beatings and mistreatment of the population, which made them take to the woods. He said that the bonus system (that is, paying for work well done or performed in extra hours) was useful where it was in force. He thought the Germans were making the same mistakes Japan had made in China. He objected to the prohibition of the native population to use the German language, which, he thought, was a sign of weakness, not of strength, and made the population think the Germans intended to retreat. The Russians, he wrote, thought the Germans meant to put them on a level with the Negro and to exterminate them. He recommended a complete change in policy, which Rosenberg would certainly have been glad to adopt had he not always been overruled.[98]

Everyone ranged himself against Rosenberg. Sworn enemies made alliances to do him in. Ribbentrop and Himmler in 1944 worked out an agreement whereby Himmler would recruit SS units from among the Soviet nationalities and Ribbentrop would have authority over any foreign policy matters connected with these SS legions. Rosenberg was completely excluded under this pact, and Hitler refused to receive him. Rosenberg and the Fuehrer met last in November, 1943. In October, 1944, Rosenberg abjectly asked Hitler if he had any more use to make of him. "I beg you my Fuehrer," he wrote, "to tell me if you still want my services in this direction. . . . I must in view of the developments leave open the consideration whether you, my Fuehrer, see my services as no longer necessary." [99] But Rosenberg stayed on in his Ministry (as one man said, "of the no longer occupied territories"), fighting his battles to the bitter end—not against Bolsheviks and Jews and Moscovites but against his colleagues.

Passive, corroded by jealousy, living in his world patched out of other people's ideas obtained from scraps of reading, Rosenberg was an easy victim of the men of action. His rivals were always closer to the throne than he, for he was dull and verbose and constantly forced Hitler to make difficult decisions. He sent the Fuehrer memoranda and reports on the misdeeds or ineptitudes of Goebbels and Ribbentrop; he feuded with Ley and Himmler and Bormann and Koch and countless others; he made enemies of everyone he met, for they were all competitors in one way or another for his territories. But he often had a good word to say for Hess before his flight to England and for Goering. Hess could be depended on against Bormann, and Goering against Ribbentrop and Goebbels.

Everyone was trying to gain something from his preserves: Goebbels invaded culture, Bormann anti-Christianism, Himmler the Hohe Schule. Field Marshal Keitel's orders of August 29, 1942, said the Army was to be fed as far as possible from the East; Goering was pressing his staff to send more grain, more produce of all kinds, to the Reich; and Himmler was in charge of the punitive and security measures that drove the population to the partisans. Everywhere Rosenberg turned, he met men more able and ruthless than he and with the practical means at hand of accomplishing their missions.

Rosenberg had remarried in 1925. His wife, Hedwig, and small daughter (another child had died) were not much more in demand than he. When his wife and daughter took refuge toward the end of the war in a relatively safe German town, Frau Rosenberg was asked to leave because her presence, it was thought, brought on Allied bombing attacks. He was a good family man. When Rosenberg went off to his captivity, his wife told their daughter,

"We lose a good comrade in Papa," [100] and this was doubtless no exaggeration.

When the war was lost, Rosenberg was bewildered, but he clung to his National Socialism: "The leadership of Hitler was the necessary result of a great national self-awareness; the Fuehrer state an organically understandable, new concept of the Reich." [101] He told his captors that he had been right about race and the Jews, whom he had only wanted to send to Madagascar, not to exterminate. This was true. He had opposed an independent Jewish state as too dangerous a center of subversion, but Jews collected on some island under police surveillance seemed to him a proper solution of the problem. He was certain that Hitler had been right. Fate had defeated them both—Fate, Bormann, Goebbels, Ribbentrop, *et al.*

How to account for him? For one thing, he had lived and written as a half-educated theoretician working out the acute problems of his early years. He had spent his childhood and youth as a self-conscious German in a foreign land that had suddenly, while he was still a young man, taken a revolutionary course—a course that took no account of Germanic culture or the leading role of the Germans in the Baltic States or any of the other articles of faith he had lived by. The Baltic States were traditionally as anti-Semitic as Germany and Poland and Russia. They were always to provide willing helpers for the Einsatz Commandos, and Rosenberg had no need of German models to develop his anti-Semitism. He, the displaced Nordic, found himself in a post-World War I fevered, unstable society—a society in which it was enough to be German in order to feel martyred and superior.

He was never to regret the role he had played, because, like Eichmann and so many others, he had believed in the necessity for fighting on behalf of the highest manifestation of the human race—the mystical Nordic, represented at his best by the Germans. He had ordered his thinking around this racial myth. Like the Bolsheviks he so detested, he could see in Christianity only the enemy, the sorry survival of a past that had prevented the Germanic race from attaining its true stature.

Rosenberg learned nothing much in the course of the trial. He still thought Nazism was what he called the European answer to the problems of the twentieth century, "the most noble idea for which a German could use his strength." He stated that Nazism had given the German nation its unity and substance.[102] "I have served it faithfully and despite all errors and human inadequacies. I shall also remain true to it as long as I live."[103] When his British captors asked if he still believed in the *Mythus*, he said that, although parts of it had been overtaken by events, it was still true on the whole, and if the Fuehrer had chosen him instead of men like Goebbels and Bormann, the outcome would have been different. This he thought Adolf Hitler's major failure. The court found him guilty on all four counts and sentenced him to hang.

NOTES

1. United States Document Center, Berlin (hereinafter referred to as BDC), SA 493.

2. Walter Schellenberg, *Memoiren* (Cologne: Verlag fuer Politik und Wissenschaft, 1956), p. 285.

3. *N XI*, 36-R, pp. 542–43.

4. H. R. Trevor-Roper, ed., *The Bormann Letters* (London: Weidenfeld and Nicolson, 1954).

5. Gerhard Boldt, *Die letzten Tage der Reichskanzlei* (Hamburg and Stuttgart: Rowohlt, 1947).

6. *NCA VI*, 3734-PS, p. 561.

7. *N X*, p. 597.

8. Trevor-Roper, ed., *op. cit.*, p. 123.

9. *NCA VII*, L-221, p. 1086.

10. *N XXV*, 057-PS, pp. 112–13.

11. Heinrich Hoffmann, *Hitler Was My Friend* (London: Burke, 1955), pp. 193–94.

12. Léon Poliakov and Josef Wulf, *Das Dritte Reich und seine Denker* (Berlin-Grunewald: Arani, 1959), pp. 148–49.

13. BDC, Volksgericht.

14. *NCA VII*, D-753-A, pp. 214–19, and D-753-B, pp. 219–21. Also Schellenberg, *op. cit.*, p. 257.

15. Josef Wulf, *Martin Bormann—Hitlers Schatten* (Guetersloh: Sigbert Mohn, 1962).

16. *Ibid.*

17. J. R. Rees, ed., *The Case of Rudolf Hess* (London and Toronto: Heinemann, 1947).

18. Walter Stubbe, "*In Memoriam:* Albrecht Haushofer," *Vierteljahrshefte fuer Zeitgeschichte*, Vol. VIII, No. 3, 1960, p. 238.

19. Albert Krebs, *Tendenzen und Gestalten der NSDAP* (Stuttgart: Deutsche Verlags-Anstalt, 1959), p. 26.

20. *Ibid.*, p. 149.

21. *Ibid.*, p. 170.

22. Otto Dietrich, *12 Jahre mit Hitler* (Munich: Isar Verlag, 1955), p. 204.

23. *N XXX*, 2426-PS, p. 345.

24. James Leasor, *The Uninvited Envoy* (New York: McGraw-Hill Book Company, 1962), p. 84.

25. Krebs, *op. cit.*, p. 151.

26. Institut fuer Zeitgeschichte, Munich (hereinafter referred to as IZG), MA 330.

27. Schwerin von Krosigk, *op. cit.*, p. 241.

28. *Documents on German Foreign Policy, 1918–45*, Series D, Vol. XI (Washington: Department of State), pp. 78–81.

29. Hassell, *op. cit.*

30. *N* XXXVIII, 116-M, pp. 174–76.

31. Rees, ed., *op. cit.*

32. Douglas M. Kelley, *22 Cells in Nuremberg* (New York: Greenberg Publisher, Inc., 1947).

33. Stubbe, *op. cit.*, pp. 236-56.

34. *N* XL, Hess-13, pp. 278–79. Also Dietrich, *op. cit.*, pp. 76–77.

35. Leasor, *op. cit.*, p. 72.

36. NCA VIII, M-117, p. 43.

37. *N* XL, Hess-15, pp. 279–92.

38. Winston S. Churchill, *The Second World War*, Vol. III (Boston: Houghton Mifflin Company, 1951).

39. Paul Schmidt, *Statist auf diplomatischer Buehne 1923–1945* (Bonn: Athenaeum, 1949), p. 538.

40. Dietrich, *op. cit.*, p. 78.

41. Hassell, *op. cit.*, p.169.

42. Dietrich, *op. cit.*, p. 77.

43. Rees, ed., *op. cit.*

44. *Ibid.*

45. Ilse Hess, *England-Nuernberg-Spandau: Ein Schicksal in Briefen* (Leoni am Starnberger See: Druffel-Verlag, 1952).

46. *N* II, pp. 487-88.

47. *Ibid.*, p. 491.

48. *Ibid.*, p. 496.

49. Nuremberg Staatsarchiv: 9/12/46 Joseph Koretz; 11/25/46 Ludwig Schmitt; Fraeulein Hildegard Fath, Fraeulein Sperrs, n.d.

50. NCA, Supp. B, p. 1158.

51. *Ibid.*, pp. 1160–63.

52. G. M. Gilbert, *Nuremberg Diary* (New York: Farrar, Straus & Young, Inc. 1947), p. 53.

53. *N* XL, Hess-16, pp. 293–98.

54. *N* XXII, pp. 368–70, 372.

55. *N* I, pp. 283–84, 365.

56. NCA II, p. 609.

57. Alexander Dallin, *Deutsche Herrschaft in Russland 1941–1945* (Duesseldorf: Droste-Verlag, 1958), p. 96.

58. Hans Buchheim, Martin Broszat, Hans-Adolf Jacobsen, and Helmut Krausnick, *Anatomie des SS-Staates*, Vol. II (Olten and Freiburg i. Br.: Walter-Verlag, 1965).

59. NCA I, 2886-PS, p. 176.

60. *N* XXV, 136-PS, pp. 229–30,

61. Krebs, *op. cit.*, p. 180. Also, Schwerin von Krosigk, *op. cit.*, p. 262.

62. Serge Lang and Ernst von Schenck, eds., *Portraet eines Menschheitsverbrechers* (St. Gallen: Zollikofer, 1947).

63. Krebs, *op. cit.* Also Alfred Rosenberg, *Letzte Aufzeichnungen* (Goettingen: Plesse Verlag, 1955).

64. *N* XVI, 1058-PS, p. 622.

65. *N* XXXIX, USSR-170, p. 421.

66. Henry Picker, *Hitler's Table Talk*, Norman Cameron and R. H. Stevens, trans. (London: Weidenfeld and Nicolson, 1953).

67. N XI, 045-PS, p. 540.

68. *Ibid.*, pp. 542–44.

69. NCA I, 2426-PS, p. 187.

70. 049-PS (IZG).

71. Hans-Guenther Seraphim, *Das politische Tagebuch Alfred Rosenbergs 1934–35 und 1939–40* (Goettingen: Musterschmidt-Verlag, 1956).

72. N XI, p. 455.

73. E. L. Woodward and Rohan Butler, eds., *Documents on British Foreign Policy 1919–1939*, 2nd Series, Vol. V, 1933, Nos. 118 and 380 (London: Her Majesty's Stationery Office, 1956).

74. Seraphim, *op. cit.*, diary entries of April 13, 27, and 30, 1940.

75. Alfred Baeumler, *Alfred Rosenberg und der Mythus des 20. Jahrhunderts* (Munich: Hoheneichen-Verlag, 1943).

76. N XXVIII, 1814-PS, pp. 435–39.

77. S. Th. Hart, *Alfred Rosenberg* (Munich: J. S. Lehmanns Verlag, 1933), p. 17.

78. Baeumler, *op. cit.*, p. 52.

79. Alfred Rosenberg, *Der Mythus des 20. Jahrhunderts* (Munich: Hoheneichen-Verlag, 1930), pp. 316–17.

80. Seraphim, *op. cit.*, p. 253.

81. Lang and Schenck, eds., *op. cit.*

82. Seraphim, *op. cit.*, diary entry of October 5, 1939.

83. MA 48 (IZG).

84. Rosenberg, *Mythus*, *op. cit.*, p. 28.

85. NCA V, 2433-PS, p. 99.

86. BDC, Rosenberg material.

87. Fritz T. Epstein, "War-Time Activities of the SS-Ahnenerbe," in Max Beloff, ed., *On the Track of Tyranny*, (London: Wiener Library, 1960), pp. 79–81.

88. 145-PS (IZG).

89. N XXV, 149-PS, p. 235 and NCA III, 151-PS, pp. 191–92.

90. NCA III, 041-PS, pp. 80–82.

91. NCA VII, L-188, pp. 1025–26.

92. NCA VI, 3766-PS, pp. 646–52.

93. N XXVI, 1015(b)-PS, pp. 524–30.

94. Amen interrogation of September 29, 1945 (IZG).

95. NCA III, 1099-PS, pp. 781–82.

96. N XXXIX, USSR-170, pp. 412–25.

97. NCA III, 1381-PS, pp. 932–58.

98. *Ibid.*

99. Dallin, *op. cit.*, p. 646. Also N XLI, pp. 185–94.

100. Lang and Schenck, eds., *op. cit.*, p. 345.

101. *Ibid.*, p. 322.

102. Rosenberg, *Letzte Aufzeichnungen*, *op. cit.*

103. Lang and Schenck, eds., *op. cit.*, pp. 338–39.

5

The Diplomats

JOACHIM VON RIBBENTROP

Nazi diplomacy as such scarcely existed. In the first years of his power, Hitler concentrated on domestic tasks: the relief of unemployment, reorganizing the state apparatus, getting rid of the known opponents first in the non-Nazi parties and then in 1934 among the National Socialists themselves, priming the pumps of the economy, and starting rearmament.* Only with military strength behind him could he begin his systematic destruction of the Versailles system, and then would follow the major expansion. How far it would go would depend on eventual power relations and what use could be made of them. Hitler was to win bloodless, diplomatic victories on an unprecedented scale—even with a particularly ungifted amateur at the head of his Foreign Office—mainly because the seemingly overwhelming superiority of the system of security that France had built up on the Continent was a rope of sand and because Hitler was ready to take risks and his opponents in England and France were not. Up to a point he operated with great brilliance. He also operated with great brutality and had no need of a Foreign Minister in the traditional sense. He merely needed a man who would run his errands and confirm his judgments. For this Ribbentrop was perfectly adapted.

Almost no one had a good word to say for Ribbentrop. Neither the representatives of the Western Allies nor the representatives of the neutrals or of Germany's allies—or even his fellow defendants at the trial—thought

* In Austria alone Hitler, making use of the Austrian National Socialists, pursued a vigorous policy designed to bring that country immediately into the German orbit.

147

anything of his abilities. Goering, Schacht, Neurath, Papen, all of whom had had to deal with him, thought him incompetent, boastful, and vainglorious. All those who described him—whether it was Goering, who had competed with him for the ear of the Fuehrer when war threatened, or Neurath, who had been undermined and succeeded by him, or the Allied and neutral diplomats who had listened to his tirades—used the same epithets: arrogant, tactless, humorless, and, above all, incompetent. But because Ribbentrop had only one desire—to say what his Fuehrer wanted to hear—he was precisely the man for Hitler.

Joachim Ribbentrop was born April 3, 1893, in Wesel, a small garrison town on the Rhine in Westphalia, near the Dutch border. He came from a respectable middle-class family. His father, Richard Ribbentrop, was an Army officer who retired with the rank of lieutenant colonel; his mother came from a Saxon family of landowners. Ribbentrop told the court at Nuremberg that his father had resigned because of "differences connected with the person of the Kaiser." His listeners must have found it difficult to understand how such serious differences could have developed, given the disparity of rank between the Supreme Commander of the Prussian Army and a lieutenant colonel of artillery. In his autobiography, written in his cell in Nuremberg, Ribbentrop clarifies the matter somewhat: he says his father resigned because he disapproved of the Kaiser's dismissal of Bismarck. Ribbentrop always inflated circumstances that had to do with himself or his family. It may be that his father's retirement had to do with resentment of the Kaiser's action, for Richard Ribbentrop did not ask, as was usual, for permission to wear his uniform on suitable occasions after he resigned. In any event, the father took a job with a bank and the family moved to Switzerland, where they lived for a year and a half in Arosa before returning to Germany.

Joachim, with no ambitions of a scholastic nature, quit the Gymnasium at the age of sixteen. He liked travel and sports. Since the family was not very well off, and since he had no serious intellectual interests, he concentrated on making a career for himself with whatever came to hand. He did well. He was to marry Annelies Henkell, the rich daughter of the owner of the champagne firm whose wares he represented. He added the "von" to his name by getting himself adopted at the age of thirty-two by an aunt whose husband (a lieutenant general) had been knighted in 1884. By his own standards, he was a considerable success long before he met the Fuehrer at Berchtesgaden in 1932 and began his rapid rise to take his place among the statesmen of the world.

Although of modest formal education, Ribbentrop had an aptitude for languages. He picked up French fluently—first in Metz, to which his father had been assigned, and then during the family's stay in Switzerland. At the age of sixteen to seventeen, he spent a year in London, where he lived with an English family, and the following year he went to Canada. He became reasonably fluent in English, although his facility was often overrated by Germans who spoke of his perfect English. Actually it was full of Germanisms and phrases he obviously thought sounded like those of the upper class he so admired in every country. At the end of World War II, he addressed a letter to Winston Churchill (despite his years in England he wrote Vincent for the first name) and Anthony Eden, sent by way of Field Marshal Montgomery, which was remarkable not only for its unusual syntax but for its total incomprehension of the sentiments of the non-Nazi world and of the Anglo-Saxon character in particular.

The letter, marked "Personal and Confidential," read as follows:

> Radio reports, etc., which I do not quite understand but which, if they were true, would come to it, that former collaborators of the Fuehrer are at present soiling their own house, are trying to depreciate the Fuehrer, falsify his ideas about England, . . . compel me to do, what I really only wanted to do later on: to place myself at the disposal of the British Commander in Chief. I shall do it now. If I did not do so, false impressions owing to unclear or biassed statements or misunderstandings might arise.
>
> If I went during the advance of the British troops in the British occupation zone and not to some other place I did this in the hope of being able to reach you easier—but only at a time when the wars of hatred between victors and vanquished would have calmed down . . . —to inform you about my last political conversation with Adolf Hitler.
>
> This conversation—during which—as so often lately—the Fuehrer's deep disappointment and embitterment about the failure of a political conception was evident, culminated in a kind of last appeal and a message to the leaders of the British Empire. This appeal represents at the same time—one may well say—the last political will of a man, who as a great idealist has loved his people above all . . . and in whose conception of the world the English-German question has always been the central point of his political meditations.
>
> I do not know, if the old and noble English custom of fair play is also applicable for a defeated foe. I also do not know if you wish to hear the political testament of a deceased man. But I could imagine that its contents might be adapted to heal wounds . . . [and] in this perilous epoch of our world be able to help bring about a better future for all people.

Ribbentrop went to to say that he would be grateful for the opportunity to bring Churchill and Eden the message that had been entrusted to him "personally and verbally." He said he had been a close collaborator of the Fuehrer and had sworn loyalty to him, but he prudently added, "although I have for a long time already not been able to carry my points and views through with him. . . ." He also said that he had wanted to join the fighting in Berlin, he had been ready to fly there by a "Storch Airoplane," but the Fuehrer had sent him

> a message, saying that he appreciated my intention, but as he had already expressed his opinion on former occasions—he did not want me to take part

in the fights even now. One needed me later and I should therefore go outside the fighting zone and keep myself ready for further instructions. Such instructions did not come any more, as events began to precipitate. But I know that the Fuehrer in giving that order has meant our last conversation for the passing on of which I should keep myself prepared.

"In spite of the diversity of opinion which existed between the Fuehrer and me on foreign politics as well as on questions of world perception," Ribbentrop continued, he had had the personal confidence of the Fuehrer up to the last. They had both striven to attain German claims by diplomatic means, and his own work had been devoted to "concentration of the greater part of the Germans in Europe within the Reich . . . and evolution of the principles of world perception of the party in such a way that the existence or carrying through of such principles would not endanger or even make impossible the peaceful living together and collaboration of Germany with the other nations." So Ribbentrop had favored toleration in dealing with the churches and Jews and had also tried to build a bridge between National Socialism and communism, but unfortunately the "world perception" of the Party had been too much for him. One thing, however, on which the Fuehrer and he had always been agreed was

> that a strong and united Germany as a preliminary condition, for a stable and flourishing Europe could only exist in the long run by a close collaboration with Great Britain. . . . In spite of all disappointment and embitterment about the repeated English rejection of the German offers the English-German collaboration has to this last hour always been the political creed of the Fuehrer.

Ribbentrop asserted further that although the Fuehrer obviously did not understand British politics (that being where he himself came in), still "in an almost prophetic way" he had seen the need for Germany's establishing a stable balance of power in the new Europe. Ribbentrop spoke highly of everyone—of the English and the Russians and of the United States—but always came back to the need for good English-German relations. On this point (so dear to the heart of Ribbentrop), he and Hitler, he wrote, had had one of their most harmonious conversations. He himself, he added, had always considered England his second home, and the hatred now felt against Germany by the outside world was incomprehensible to him. When Germany had been victorious on the Continent, neither he nor the Fuehrer had wanted to violate English prestige and esteem in the world. And as for the concentration camps, he had had no idea of what was going on in them and had always wanted prisoners of war treated well. "When once I heard from a diplomatic report that ill-treatment of Jews in a concentration camp in Poland was discussed vehemently in diplomatic circles abroad, I took the report at once to the Fuehrer urging immediate change, if it were true. The Fuehrer kept the report to look into the matter but gave me clearly to understand that this was a question of the interior authorities."

In closing his letter, Ribbentrop repeated that he had always wanted an English-German alliance without war, but that the Fuehrer had been skeptical about such plans after the fruitless attempt in 1940 to make peace with England. Ribbentrop was still stout-hearted though; he told Churchill that despite the lost war "I am of the holy conviction, that the bringing about of a real friendship between the English and the German people is a fundamental necessity. . . . In order to fulfill this last mission I lay my fate into your hands." He ended with an appeal: "I would be grateful if this letter could not be published." [1] This was the man whom Hitler had often compared to Bismarck.

The letter was long. Ribbentrop, when aroused or when he was on safe ground, was very loquacious. Count Bernadotte once surreptitiously timed him with a stopwatch and reported that he talked for over an hour without letting his guest get a word in.[2] Whenever he recited Hitler's opinions, he talked at great length, but when he was on his own (before he became Foreign Minister) he often hid behind a mask of silence that portentously concealed the fact that he had nothing to say.[3]

Ribbentrop was industrious and had a sense of order. He worked hard, fourteen and more hours a day. He wore out his secretaries with the avalanche of work he gave them. Since he had so little gift or training for his job, he could only master it by overwork and multiplying his personnel. When he became Foreign Minister there were 2,300 officials in the Foreign Office, and this number he raised to 10,000. He created new departments with hundreds of employees. The former three officers of the Department of Protocol he increased to fifty, the Press Division from seven to two hundred. Both these departments represented two of his chief interests—who sits next to whom and publicity.[4] With zeal and devotion Ribbentrop tried to cover up his complete lack of qualifications for the job he held. It was a job for which he had not the slightest training or capacity. When he got the appointment it surprised even his wife, who had devoted herself to advancing his fortunes. In fact, Ribbentrop said it surprised him, and this is probably true too.

Curiously enough, he took the side of the old-line diplomats against the Party. Under the Reich Civil Service Law, the deputy to the Fuehrer, Rudolf Hess, had the right to veto appointments to the Foreign Office. His representative, E. W. Bohle, was assigned to the Auswaertiges Amt as Staatssekretaer. Bohle was chief of the Party's Auslandsorganisation, which Ribbentrop saw, and rightly so, as a rival to the Foreign Office, for it dealt directly with Party organizations and German citizens in foreign countries. Ribbentrop fought against Bohle's influence, and in 1941, after Hess' flight to Scotland, succeeded in getting rid of him. Ribbentrop, who feared more than anything else the invasion of his jealously held domain, had one main requirement for his underlings: unquestioning obedience. When he was considering appointing Weizsaecker as Staatssekretaer, he asked if he could take orders. He informed another of his subordinates, Adolf von Steengracht, that foreign policy was made not by the Foreign Office but by the Fuehrer and himself. The subordinates, he said, had no voice; they were there to carry out orders.[5]

While he retained the old career officers of his Ministry in their posts, he insisted that they join the Party and give evidence of their enthusiasm for it. He arranged for Weizsaecker and Ernst Woermann to join the SS, and the entire corps of Beamte had to march past him at Tempelhof field while he gave the Nazi salute. By 1940, 71 of 120 higher officials of the Foreign Office had joined the Party. A good portion of the rest had applied but for one reason or another had been rejected.[6] * In adding new officials to the mushrooming departments, Ribbentrop appointed activists—old fighters, like Freiherr von Killinger, who had been Minister President of Saxony. And he appointed SS Standartenfuehrer Bertling as head of the SS Junkerschule in Brunswick, to school and discipline the younger men from the Hitlerjugend, the SA, and the SS who were being trained as attachés.

As a young man Ribbentrop had chosen to make a career of business,[7] but what he actually did was to try his hand at anything that turned up. When at the age of eighteen he went to Canada, where he spent two years, he worked as a timekeeper, on road gangs and bridge construction, in a bank, and at all sorts of odd jobs. He was a pleasant-looking, friendly young man who liked amateur theatricals and music, and people took to him. Later, when he felt the need of asserting his authority, he assumed theatrical poses: he received foreign notables with folded arms and the diplomatic flunky's mask of impassivity. His face twitched on one side, and he often closed pale, watery blue eyes as he harangued his visitors. As a young man he was merely socially ambitious, and with his Old World accent he succeeded in winning the friendly acceptance of prominent Canadians in the cities of their young and booming country. He appeared at receptions of the Governor General in Ottawa and on the tennis courts and dance floors and might have remained in Canada to the end of his days had not war come in 1914. Feeling, as he said, his patriotic duty as a German to return to his fatherland, he made his way through the then neutral United States and past the British blockade to Holland and to Germany. He fought the war as a lieutenant, was wounded, got the Iron Cross First Class, and as an officer serving under one of General Hans von Seeckt's adjutants was present during the negotiations leading to the armistice of November 11, 1918. After being mustered out he became one of the thousands of ex-soldiers milling around in the chaos of postwar Germany with no plans for the future nor any clear idea of how the catastrophe had occurred.

With his knowledge of French and English, he got a job in the summer of 1919 with a cotton-import firm in Berlin and soon afterward met Annelies

---

* Dr. Heinz Guenther Sasse, in "Das Problem des diplomatischen Nachwuchses im Dritten Reich," in Forschungen zu Staat und Verfassung (Berlin: Duncker und Humblot, n.d.), pointed out that such figures can be misleading. Many of the Party members were considered dubious and unenthusiastic National Socialists. They joined in order to keep their jobs or to get promoted, and the Party knew it.

Henkell, whom he married the following year. The marriage was a happy one. Ribbentrop gave up his job with the cotton importers and joined the agency Schoeneberg and Company, representing Henkell in Berlin. Soon Schoeneberg became Schoeneberg and Ribbentrop. Along with Henkell Sekt, they sold large quantities of Johnny Walker and Chartreuse and good brandies, for in the hectic postwar years the thirst of the Germans increased with the political and economic uncertainties. Ribbentrop again set out on his travels, selling the products of his company in England and France and talking about the muddled problems of the postwar period with others no better and no worse informed than he.

With more money at hand and with the "von" that he had attached to his name in 1925, Ribbentrop stepped into the fashionable world that delighted his soul. Years later, in a form he had to fill out for the SS, who insisted on details, Ribbentrop wrote that he had got himself adopted and added the "von" to his name because he did not want the old noble line of the Ribbentrops to die out[8]—the old noble line that had been established forty years earlier. He played with the idea of running for the Reichstag as a candidate for the Democratic Party or for the nationalistic Deutsche Volkspartei but then sensed that the Nazis were the coming party and took steps to join them in 1932, just before they took power and after he succeeded in getting himself introduced to Hitler.

His elaborate house, his connections through his marriage, and his presumed knowledge of foreign countries and languages impressed the Fuehrer, who knew nothing first hand of the world outside Germany and had no desire to learn except through a man like Ribbentrop, who adroitly confirmed the Fuehrer's notions. Thus the English could be anything Hitler wanted them to be: a people who had brought civilization to many countries; a people who had borne the white man's burden; the degenerate descendants of the Germanic race, who would no longer fight for their heritage; a Jew-ridden people; or a people run by the plutocracy. Ribbentrop had been in England at the time Oxford students had publicly declared they would not fight for their king and country. This was enough to convince him that England would avoid war at any cost.

In his trial testimony, in the interrogations, and in the posthumous book edited by his widow, Ribbentrop declared that he had always worked for peace with England and that he had always admired and sympathized with the British and French and had never underestimated them. But the testimony against him was overwhelmingly to the contrary. Goering said that at the time of Munich Ribbentrop had wanted war and was disappointed by the treaty that divided Czechoslovakia without war. Ciano maintained that the German Foreign Minister echoed the war plans of his Fuehrer. On August 11, 1939, Ciano's diary entry read: "The decision to fight is implacable. He [Ribbentrop] rejects any solution which might give satisfaction to Germany and avoid the struggle." [9] Ciano asked him whether Germany wanted the

Corridor or Danzig, and Ribbentrop replied, "Not that any more. We want war." [10] Sir Nevile Henderson made similar accusations, as did men who worked under Ribbentrop, like Weizsaecker and Erich Kordt. The latter told of Ribbentrop's trying at the last in Munich to get Hitler to step up his demands and so "to rescue his war." The foreign observers—Robert Coulondre, André François-Poncet, Jacques Davignon, Birger Dahlerus (he had to deal with Goering in his well-intentioned if amateurish attempt to act as an intermediary between London and Berlin)—all spoke of Ribbentrop's belligerence.

Ribbentrop had convinced himself that the pact with Russia in August, 1939, made English and French intervention impossible. He believed that the pacifism and weakness of both England and France would force them to accept the German conquest of Poland without regard to any guarantees they had given. Britain would never dare oppose Hitler, he told Kordt, and if she did she would lose her empire and France would bleed to death on the Siegfried Line. "If I hear any official express a different view I will shoot him myself in his office and will be responsible for my action." [11] He liked to demonstrate his National Socialist ardor. He told Weizsaecker that he would shoot any subordinates who took a dim view of the foreign situation.[12]

He was always able to believe what he wanted to or, better still, what the Fuehrer wanted him to. On February 16, 1942, discussing the American contribution to the cause of the Allies with two members of the Italian Grand Council—Giuseppi Bottai and Dino Alfieri (the Italian Ambassador to Germany)—he pointed out that the United States had no military tradition, no officers or noncommissioned officers, no armaments industry, and no workers who, like those in Europe, had been trained artisans for generations. Furthermore, he said, the United States had a population of 125 million, while the Axis and the occupied countries could draw on a population of between 500 and 600 million people who could produce four times as much as the Americans. Thus, by reducing the population of the United States by 25 million, leaving out the production and populations of its Allies, and adding to the Axis war potential the unwilling slave laborers who were working at gunpoint and within bombing range of the Allies, Ribbentrop managed to work out a wholly spurious Axis superiority of four to one.[13] Before the United States came into the war, he said that its intense isolationism would be strengthened by Japan's becoming a belligerent.[14]

Ribbentrop had one moment of truth, on April 28, 1941. He had Staatssekretaer Weizsaecker write a memorandum (the sentiments were Ribbentrop's own) opposing the Russian campaign. It read:

> I can summarize my opinion on a German-Russian conflict in one sentence: if every burned out Russian city was worth as much to us as a sunk English battleship, then I should be in favor of a German-Russian war in this summer; I think though that we can win over Russia only militarily but that we should lose economically. One can perhaps find it enticing to give the

Communist system its death blow and perhaps say too that it lies in the logic of things to let the European-Asiatic continent now march forth against Anglo-Saxondom and its allies. But only one thing is decisive: whether this undertaking would hasten the fall of England.

The memo said further that either England was close to collapse, in which case she would only be encouraged by the Reich's taking on a new opponent, or, if England was not close to a collapse, one could get the idea that Germany had to obtain its food supply from the Soviet land mass by force.

> That we will advance militarily up to Moscow and beyond victoriously, I believe is unquestionable. But I thoroughly doubt that we could make use of what was won against the well known passive resistance of the Slavs. . . . A German attack on Russia would only give a lift to English morale. It would be evaluated there as German doubt of the success of our war against England. We would in this fashion not only admit that the war would still last a long time, but we could in this way actually lengthen instead of shorten it.

The memorandum showed insight and prescience of a kind that Ribbentrop was not to repeat during his years in office. Perhaps it was as much a product of his dislike for England as of his political forebodings.

Otherwise Ribbentrop lived in a dream world where anything that comported with his wishes could happen. Early in 1945 he sent Werner von Schmieden to Switzerland to establish contact with the British and Americans and to warn the Allies against an alliance between "radical Nazis and Communists." He instructed Schmieden to say that Germany would be satisfied with a peace settlement that would bring all Germans within one border and would be ready to cooperate toward a solution of the Jewish problem. Its economy would be redesigned to conform with the principles of free world trade, and religious freedom would be guaranteed.[16]

Ribbentrop got and held the Ministry job only because Hitler wanted to be his own foreign minister and to feel that he was being supported in his decisions by a man who knew the world better than the professional diplomats the Fuehrer trusted no more than he did his generals. In Ribbentrop he found the man he needed. The two met first in August, 1932, when Ribbentrop asked future Police President of Berlin, Count von Helldorf, whom he had known in World War I, to introduce him to Hitler.* Ribbentrop thus came late to the Nazis. When he had wanted to run for the Reichstag, in the days before the Nazis were piling up the large votes of 1931 and 1932, he had not considered running as a candidate of the National Socialists. Helldorf arranged the meeting with Hitler through the then powerful Roehm, and Ribbentrop met the Fuehrer at the Berghof.

A few months later, early in 1933, a meeting of crucial importance took

---

* Helldorf, at this period a convinced Nazi, was appointed Police President by Hitler but quickly became disillusioned. He joined the Resistance and was executed after the attempt on Hitler's life in July, 1944.

place at the manorial house the Ribbentrops had bought in Berlin-Dahlem. It was there that Papen, Goering, Staatssekretaer Otto Meissner, and Oskar von Hindenburg met with the Fuehrer for the final negotiations that led to Hitler's becoming Chancellor. It was a historic moment for Hitler, and for the others present too, as Hitler gave his terms for succeeding Schleicher. (Papen thought that, with a conservative nationalist majority in the Cabinet, he, not Hitler, had won.) The meeting took place at a time when the Party was woefully short of funds. Salaries could not be paid, nor could the printing costs of the *Voelkischer Beobachter* be met. In the rich bourgeois atmosphere created by the Henkell money, Ribbentrop was the self-effacing host and man of the world—a man with precisely the same ideas as the Fuehrer.

As soon as Hitler became Chancellor, he turned to Ribbentrop for counsel on foreign affairs. In 1933 he made him adviser on such matters to himself and to the Party. Ribbentrop was at home in the languages and politics of two of Germany's chief adversaries and judged them in the same light as the Fuehrer did. He read the Paris newspaper *Le Temps* and *The London Times* and translated relevant items for Hitler—something that Rudolf Hess, the Fuehrer's deputy and head of the Foreign Department of the Party, was unable to do. Hitler, using one of his favorite devices for undercutting the established Ministry, permitted Ribbentrop to set up a bureau to advise him on foreign policy. It had small beginnings, using three or four rooms near Hess' offices, and was paid for by Ribbentrop. Hitler was pleased with the results and soon supplied the bureau with funds of 20 million RM from his own treasury. The Ribbentrop Bureau was installed opposite the Wilhelm-strasse. It started with fifteen men in 1934, then rose to fifty, and finally to three hundred. It was made up of amateurs like its founder—young men who spoke foreign languages, who could in many cases place a "von" or flashier title before their names, and who could furnish their chief and eventually Hitler with the oversimplified well-digested information he wanted. They used the reports of news correspondents and other material gathered from foreign newspapers, as Neurath would later testify. Since Hitler read only German, their translations were his only means of getting such foreign news. The library of the bureau came from confiscated collections—among others, those of the Deutsche Hochschule fuer Politik in Berlin (it had formerly been subsidized by the Carnegie Foundation), the Hamburg Institute for Foreign Affairs, and Haushofer's Geopolitisches Institut in Munich.[17]

With the exception of letters addressed to the Foreign Minister and the Staatssekretaer, Ribbentrop was given the correspondence addressed to the Foreign Office before the Wilhelmstrasse got it. Hitler gave him permission to answer it—a situation that would have caused a stronger personality than Neurath to resign as Foreign Minister long before Hitler asked him to step aside in 1938. When Ribbentrop was appointed Special Ambassador, he was not placed under the Foreign Office but was made responsible to Hitler only.[18] In 1934 Hitler made Ribbentrop Special Commissioner for Disarmament Questions, a post in which he could take part in discussions in Paris, London, and Berlin.* Like all his predecessors, Ribbentrop failed to persuade the Allies to sign any agreement, although he had a small *quid pro quo* to offer: the disbanding of the SA in return for an increase in the Reichswehr. But France was basically unwilling to concede to Germany (whether the Weimar Republic or any other German government) the equality that would inevitably one day have to be granted. It made no difference whether a Ribbentrop or one of the old-line diplomats represented the Reich. The conferences achieved nothing.

Ribbentrop had, however, a considerable success at the Naval Conference in London on June 18, 1935, where he represented Germany as Special Ambassador. Taking place three months after the British note of protest against Germany's rearming, the conference marked a turning point in British policy. It was the first of Britain's efforts to limit Hitler's drive for the domination of the Continent by reasonable concessions. At long last there was recognition of the inevitability of accepting Germany as a power with equal status in Europe.

In the Anglo-German naval agreement reached at the conference, a ratio of 100 to 35 was accepted for the respective strengths of the two navies. Ribbentrop behaved as he was always to do—pushing the German claims, as the English said, as though the first day of the conference were the last and as though his demands had already been agreed upon. In his role as mouthpiece of the Fuehrer, he repeated the rigid formulas that had been furnished him. Fortunately for him, the British Government was desperately striving to prevent a war it believed could only be a disaster for Britain. So the British gave countenance to this man who only four or five years back had been selling them champagne. Though they were unimpressed by him as a person or negotiator, he returned to Germany in triumph, flourishing the first acknowledgment of Germany's right to rearm.

The agreement, as everyone knew, would be a blow to France, clinging ferociously to "legality" and still in a state of shock over the reintroduction of universal military service in the Reich. Ribbentrop at the close of the conference made the preposterous suggestion to the British (one they could scarcely turn down out of hand) that he stop off in Paris on his way back to Berlin to explain the whole matter to the French, with whom, he said, he had excellent relations. And this in fact he did, volubly instructing the French diplomats, whose manifold troubles, with the Stresa front broken, could only be multiplied by his appearance. He told the court at Nuremberg that he thought his visit had helped the French understand the situation.

Hitler, now completely persuaded of the abilities of his adviser, made him

* Hindenburg had hesitated to approve Ribbentrop's appointment, but Neurath convinced the President that this was a post Ribbentrop could fill. (Gordon Craig and Felix Gilbert, eds., *The Diplomats 1919–1939*, [Princeton: Princeton University Press, 1953], p. 423).

Ambassador to Great Britain. There Ribbentrop made his memorable *gaffe* when he appeared at the reception of the diplomatic corps and greeted the King with outstretched arm and a "Heil Hitler." (Writing in his cell in Nuremberg, Ribbentrop declared that Hitler had ordered him to give the Nazi salute, but in an interrogation of September 20, 1945, he said he had not been instructed to give it but had intended it as an honor to the British sovereign. The only certainty is that he had no notion of how the British would react, nor was he much interested. His sole concern was to give evidence of his zeal to his master in Berlin.)

In England the Ribbentrops were the very cut and pattern of the Nazi regime. Winston Churchill told of a conversation he had with Frau von Ribbentrop. To his remark that he hoped no serious difference would arise between their two countries, she replied, "This is up to you." This story was denied by Frau von Ribbentrop in the volume of her husband's notes that she edited.

While Ribbentrop was in London between November, 1936, and November, 1937, he made eleven trips to Berlin, for England was not nearly as much on his mind as were his relations with Hitler. He had no friends at court. Neurath feared and disliked him, as did the rest of the professional diplomats, and the Party regarded him as an interloper who had joined up far too late. For Ribbentrop, everything depended on his relations with Hitler. He did all he could to foster a closeness: He named one of his children Adolf, and he hovered as near to his master as possible. The only importance of London was the opportunity it gave him of impressing the Fuehrer with his indispensability.

Ribbentrop did not practice the arts of traditional diplomacy. He had the skill of the courtier, the sycophant who carefully noted what his master said and then repeated it later to the preoccupied Fuehrer, who was always pleased to hear his judgments echoed. Ribbentrop would express an opinion he already knew to be Hitler's or would bring him evidence from the foreign press that confirmed the Fuehrer's low esteem of Germany's opponents. Never once in the twelve years of their relationship was there any trace of serious difference. At Nuremberg Ribbentrop tried hard to portray himself as Hitler's counselor, as one who had often expressed an opposing view. But no evidence supports him aside from his expressed doubt of the wisdom of the Russian campaign.

In all the voluminous records of the Nuremberg trials and in the testimony of his contemporaries, no one had a favorable word for him. Mussolini, although coming more and more under the spell of Hitler in 1939, told Ciano on March 30 that Ribbentrop is "a truly sinister man because he is an imbecile and presumptuous." The German Counselor of Embassy in Rome, Prince Otto von Bismarck, talking to Ciano, used the same words: "He is such an imbecile, he is a freak of nature." [19] Swiss professor Carl Jakob Burckhardt, High Commissioner of Danzig, said that Ribbentrop was endowed below the average and that one could only expect stupidities from him. Bernardo Attolico called him a pure dilettante who had no concepts and no idea of either international law or history and was dangerous because of his inferiority. Ribbentrop, he said, always tried to terrorize.[20] Count Bernadotte called him a man "of very small mental stature, and moreover, rather ridiculous." [21]

Otto Skorzeny, the SS colonel who in 1944 rescued Mussolini from his Italian captors, told of a luncheon at which Ribbentrop sat on a kind of throne while the lesser members of the gathering sat stiffly under him.[22] As for Ribbentrop's wanting Hitler to go to war, his demanding the persecution of the Jews, his involvement in genocide, and the other capital crimes charged against him at Nuremberg—Ribbentrop had participated in them all because he was the eager creature of the Fuehrer, who had raised him from a member of the striving middle class to the company of the great. It was impossible to be unaware of his ignorance. Skorzeny, Ciano, and the German officials of the Foreign Office all noted how little he knew of matters under discussion. François-Poncet asserted that Ribbentrop had never read either the Versailles Treaty or the Kellogg-Briand Pact.

Like so many of the amateur diplomats of this time (they were by no means confined to the Axis powers), Ribbentrop had a few pat notions with which to justify the decisions of the Fuehrer. The fact that these "explanations" were often self-contradictory did not disturb him. One such notion was that England in the years before the war was merely trying to gain time to rearm, find allies, and eventually crush Germany. A second was that a decadent England would not fight. Another was the turpitude of the Jews. A fourth, subject to change, was the necessity of a war to the death with communism. Nevertheless, Ribbentrop eagerly journeyed to Moscow in 1939 to sign the Russo-German Nonaggression Pact and the secret treaty delineating the areas the two countries would occupy in the Baltic region and in Poland. Although it is true that he ran through his paces there as the messenger of the Fuehrer, it had been, he told Mussolini on March 10, 1940, like talking with old Party comrades in the Reich.[23] He informed the explorer Sven Hedin, an admirer of National Socialist Germany, that Stalin wanted no war with Finland, that the time of bolshevism was past, and that something new and better would rise in Russia. He unstintingly praised Stalin as he had heard Hitler praise him.

He loved and hated obediently in accordance with what he thought Hitler wanted. He ran his master's errands, whether in Paris or London or Rome or Moscow, parroting Hitler's phrases. At the trial, Ribbentrop asked Goering to testify on behalf of his desire for peace. Goering crossed out the line in the affidavit prepared for him by Ribbentrop that declared that the Foreign Minister "was always zealous [bestrebt] to help the Fuehrer attain his ends by diplomatic means" and wrote in its place: "I have only heard that Ribbentrop counselled in favor of war." As Ribbentrop continued to urge him to testify, Goering told their go-between, his assistant-counsel Bross, "I can only say what I can witness to, Ribbentrop should leave me in peace." [24] Weizsaecker testified at his own trial in 1948 that at the time the British Ambassador to Berlin, Sir Nevile Henderson, had the last desperate meetings with Ribbentrop and Weizsaecker, the Foreign Minister had said Weizsaecker should have thrown Henderson out instead of trying to clarify matters for him.[25]

Ribbentrop's one concern was to maintain his influence with the Fuehrer. When Herbert von Dirksen, the German Ambassador to London at the time of the Munich crisis, brought a personal letter from Chamberlain to Hitler, Ribbentrop refused to let him deliver it. He also prevented British Ambassador Henderson from seeing Hitler to tell him personally about the state of British public opinion. Ribbentrop had told the Fuehrer repeatedly that England would not fight, and any evidence to the contrary might weaken his reputation with him.[26]

The Nazi bureaucrats, like the Russians, had a style derived from the head of State and Party. Ribbentrop aped Hitler's monologues and saw his visions. After disaster had been narrowly averted in the winter of 1941–42, Ribbentrop told Ciano on April 29, 1942, that the ice of Russia that had defeated Napoleon had been conquered by the genius of Hitler.[27] He told Italian Ambassador Alfieri that the Russian offensives after Stalingrad had in reality resulted not in victories but merely in territorial gains, that Russian losses had been enormous, and that the present offensive would be one of the last the Russians would be capable of.[28] Until 1943, according to Ciano, Ribbentrop kept repeating that the war was won. After that he changed the tune a little, saying, "We cannot lose this war." He told Weizsaecker that the Fuehrer could never be mistaken. At Nuremberg, after the motion pictures were shown in which he saw his Fuehrer again, he told the prison psychologist, Gilbert, that he had wept at the film. "Can't you feel the terrific strength of the personality?" he asked. Confused and broken, Ribbentrop thought everyone but Hitler was to blame for the atrocities and the catastrophe—Himmler for the exterminations and the Allies for attacking Germany when she was defending civilization. He wrote in his cell:

It has always been the tragic fate of Germany that it had to stop the onstorming East with its own blood. It was so from the battle of the Catalaunian plains, over the wars with Turkey that France brought to Europe,* and up to the present world war in which the Western powers by the measures they have taken against Germany have opened the door to the East. Adolf Hitler to the very end was convinced that it was the great tragedy of this war that in the conflict between two worlds, between East and West, that the West fell upon the back of the people who were fighting for the entire world of culture.[29]

* This refers to the alliance of the French and the Turks in the war against Charles V.

Ribbentrop was unable at Nuremberg to tell a straight story even when he had nothing to conceal. In the last years of the war he had taken large doses of sleeping pills, which he thought had affected his memory. He floundered, took refuge in verbiage and in forgetting, and lied when he had to. During one of his interrogations he said that Schuschnigg, after being deposed as Austrian Chancellor, had been placed under house arrest (actually Schuschnigg had spent most of his captivity, although he was comparatively well treated, in the Sachsenhausen concentration camp) because very likely he had done "something against *Staatsraeson*." This word (the German translation of *"raison d'état"*) has many meanings, but it is unlikely that Ribbentrop knew what they were. Perhaps he merely meant that Schuschnigg had done something to injure Germany. When he was questioned about having said that the chances that England would not go to war were 100 to 1, he explained that he was using diplomatic language. In his interrogations, he kept using stock English phrases he had picked up, such as "quite impossible," "you know," "you see," "well, I mean." An example of his answers: "I must say I was less foreign minister than a sort of diplomatic adviser to the Fuehrer. So I had to take a very strong stand against the Party, you see. For instance I had a frightful row with Streicher about the Jewish question in 1935." [30]

Actually, he was as strong an anti-Semite as Streicher himself. The memoranda and notes of his views preserved statements that could have appeared in a *Stuermer* editorial. At Nuremberg he assured the Allies that he had been no anti-Semite, that he had opposed the mistreatment of the Jews, that one of his chief adjutants and the wife of another were partly Jewish, that he had thought of the concentration camps as a kind of prison—some sort of prison, he said, where people worked. Then, turning to his interrogator, in this case Mr. Justice Jackson, he added, "Quite frankly . . . I was not satisfied with quite a number of things." Mr. Justice Jackson was more at home with this kind of questioning than when he crossed swords with Goering on the problems of preparing to wage aggressive warfare and did a skillful job on the floundering Ribbentrop. According to the testimony of General Erwin Lahousen, who had been with Ribbentrop on a private train in Poland, Ribbentrop had wanted to see houses and villages go up in flames and the Jews killed. [31]

Because Ribbentrop insisted on having a voice in everything that had to do with foreign countries, the Foreign Office was deeply involved in the extermination of the Jews and the importing of slave labor. Ribbentrop had not the slightest objection to Himmler's exterminations; he insisted only that he be represented. To missions sent abroad by the Foreign Office, he added an expert on the Jewish problem. [32] He appointed Martin Luther, a fanatical anti-Semite whom he had known in his liquor business, to head up the Referat Partei—the section of the Foreign Office that dealt with Party agencies, among them the SD. The section grew to be a division with 200 employees, and by 1942 Ribbentrop had made Luther Undersecretary of State. Luther, who was in constant touch with Eichmann, conducted the negotiations with the satellite countries on the Jewish deportations.*

Although Ribbentrop had had cordial relations with rich Jews before he joined the Party, he quickly adopted the Nazi tone. On August 12, 1938, he confided to the French Foreign Minister Georges Bonnet that the Jews were without exception pickpockets, murderers, and thieves. The property they possessed had been obtained illegally in the first place, he said, and should be taken from them; they should be forced to live in criminal districts where they would be under police observation like other criminals. Late in the war he exhorted the Regent of Hungary to move along with the solution of the Jewish problem in Hungary, demanding that he kill the Jews or put them in concentration camps.[33] Nor were his fulminations confined to the Jews. An enemy was an enemy, and he said the Germans in Greece had to be brutal "to show the Greeks in iron fashion who is the master." He told Ciano and Marshal Ugo Cavallero that Draža Mihajlavić's *chetniks* had to be exterminated. And, speaking of the partisan warfare, he told Ambassador Dino Alfieri that the bands had to be destroyed, including men, women, and children, because they endangered the lives of German and Italian men, women, and children.[34] He favored the lynching of Allied fliers shot down over Germany. In fact, none of the measures taken by Hitler found him anything but anxious to carry them out.

In his appearances before interrogators he attempted, as he did in his letter to Winston Churchill, to project a *persona* of the upper-class diplomat as his real identity. Adolf Hitler, he said,

> didn't like diplomats at all. The Foreign Office was called the club of the defeatists so you can imagine the difficult position I had and the strong lines which I had to take. . . . With the French we made a sort of treaty. I don't know whether you know that I had been in Paris in 1938 and we closed a sort of non-aggression treaty . . . then the Fuehrer sent me to Moscow . . . I had a long discussion with Stalin and Molotov.[35]

The phrase "all measures short of war" he thought had been used "by Mr. Roosevelt or somebody." The reason Hitler had not met with Stalin, he said, was that the Fuehrer did not think Stalin would leave Russia and he did not want to leave Germany. Asked whether the Fuehrer had ordered the atrocities committed against the Jews in the concentration camps, he said, "I have thought about this again and again. I am quite convinced he did not order them; if possibly he knew about them I do not know." He thought there must have been "tremendous outrages somewhere in Poland" but added, "I don't remember exactly." As for himself, he had told the Fuehrer it was "quite impossible to carry out the racial program." Himmler would not let him see

---

* Martin Luther had a criminal record and was charged with misappropriating funds while he was in the Foreign Office. Ribbentrop prevented his being tried. In 1943 Luther told Himmler that Ribbentrop was crazy, and Himmler reported this conversation to Ribbentrop. Luther was sent to a concentration camp and died there in 1945.

the concentration camps, and when he learned the truth he had asked himself over and over, "What can the reason be for killing so many people? But why? What for? What is the reason?" [36] Asked by one of the American prosecuting staff, Colonel Brundage (September 13, 1945): "Do you know a man named Hodža, Chancellor of Hungary [sic]?" Ribbentrop, as confused as his questioner, answered, "Let me see now—a Czechoslovak. No, I don't know the name." *

Without Hitler, Ribbentrop was befuddled and lost. During the interrogation of September 10, 1945, he said, "The Fuehrer made a treaty with Poland perhaps a little under my advice . . . If the Fuehrer were here today he'd say, 'I take the entire responsibility.'" He had sought to guide Hitler in small ways, he said, and had told him, for example, that it would be "quite impossible" to come to an understanding with England without coming to an understanding with France. After the Allied landings in Africa, he had told the Fuehrer, "I think this situation is serious, very serious. Allow me to make peace with Russia at any sacrifice." But the Fuehrer had said, "No," and six weeks before the end he had said, "Ribbentrop, we're going to win this war by a nose." Ribbentrop said he had an idea at the time this might be true, for he had heard that the Germans had some ray planes. "I'm not well up," he told his interrogators, "on technical matters, wasn't it ray planes, airplanes sending out rays? I was amazed."

Ribbentrop believed whatever was necessary to help him keep his job. At the end, after Hitler's death, Admiral Doenitz told him over the telephone that he was drawing up the list of a new Cabinet and intended to make Schwerin von Krosigk, who was Minister of Finance, Foreign Minister. To soften the blow, he suggested to Ribbentrop that he think over other possible candidates and make a suggestion. An hour later Ribbentrop called back and said he had a candidate—himself.

Like so many of the leaders of the Third Reich, Ribbentrop professed to have a great love for the arts and to be a passionate collector of paintings. At Nuremberg he engaged his questioners in a discussion of Utrillo, who had been stigmatized in the Third Reich as a degenerate artist. Now, said Ribbentrop, he greatly admired Utrillo and had bought his pictures. He added that he had given Hitler a Cranach, which he had seen in the Fuehrer's bunker only a few months earlier. He had collected houses too. Of the six that he owned one was near Berlin on 750 hectares† of land with a golf course. Another was a castle in Fuschl, Austria, not far from Salzburg; he had taken it over from a sister of Fritz Thyssen and her husband, who had been put in a concentration camp. He also had a horse-breeding farm near Aachen and hunting lodges in Slovakia and in the Sudetenland, where he entertained foreign diplomats. These functions continued during the entire period of the war, for Ribbentrop's notions of the place of sports in high diplomacy took only theoretical

* Milan Hodža was Prime Minister of Czechoslovakia, 1935 to 1938.
† One hectare is equal to 2.47 acres.

account of the millions of men fighting on a front hundreds of kilometers away.*

Ribbentrop's usual methods were peremptory and often brutal. (Ciano was always suspicious of him when he was courteous.) When he read to Sir Nevile Henderson the final German terms Hitler offered to Poland, the British Ambassador took umbrage at his saying the matter was "damned serious" and at his reading the communication at such a speed that the words were unintelligible. He asked for a copy of the document, but Ribbentrop refused to let him see it. The skilled translator for Hitler and the Foreign Office—Paul Otto Schmidt—who was present at the meeting, said later that both men were nervous and that Ribbentrop read the document at a normal rate of speed. Ambassador Henderson had a good knowledge of German but was not fluent in it, and Schmidt had hoped that Henderson would ask him to provide a translation. This Henderson did not do. The final German offer reached England by way of Goering, who reluctantly gave the text to Birger Dahlerus to pass on to London. Ribbentrop had had categorical orders from the Fuehrer not to hand over to Henderson the terms he was ostensibly offering to the Poles, which were generous enough on the surface.

Hitler was incensed over the intransigence of the Poles, who, as the Polish Foreign Minister, Colonel Józef Beck said, expected that a revolution would break out in Germany should Hitler go to war and that an armistice would be signed in Berlin a few weeks after the outbreak of hostilities. Hitler's hypothetical offer to Poland had only a propagandistic significance at this point, after he had made his treaty with the Russians. He had never wanted another Munich, and this time, he said, no swine would deprive him of a military victory. Like Mussolini, he yearned for the sound of the guns, and Ribbentrop yearned along with him. What they both had on their side was a complete willingness to go to war—a willingness shared by no one else except the Poles, who had no means of winning a war without the aid of the Soviet Union. The Polish dreams of grandeur matched those of Ribbentrop and his master. A Polish empire stretching from the Baltic Sea to the Black Sea; the weakening of both its great neighbors, leaving Poland with the effective balance of power; the confident expectation of a revolution that would enable the Poles to occupy Berlin—of such stuff was their foreign policy made, and it dovetailed into the similarly grandiose schemes of Hitler, who planned to make a nation of helots and slaves out of the Poles, a people without an intellectual class, who could only count high enough and read enough to be able to serve their conquerors.

* In October, 1939, he asked the German Ambassador to Moscow to find out from Stalin or Molotov if he could not be given hunting grounds in Carpathia. Earlier he had asked Stalin that the demarcation line be so fixed that the Reich would be given the Suwalki area in Poland, where Ribbentrop had heard there was excellent hunting. Stalin had agreed, and Ribbentrop, having dispatched an official of the Foreign Office to reconnoiter the territory, had discovered to his intense disappointment that the game was poor there.

Ribbentrop's lawyer at Nuremberg told the prison psychologist that Ribbentrop was denying to him that he was present at meetings the records showed he had attended. According to a British observer who saw the defendant in prison, Ribbentrop was a nervous and physical wreck who did not sit down until told to. One day he wanted to come into court without a necktie because, he said, he could not button his collar (it had not occurred to him that he could wear the tie without buttoning the collar; the tie apparently had uncomfortable associations with a noose). He kept saying one thing that was obviously true—that he was against this trial from the start. He had written Mr. Justice Jackson, he said, to offer to be tried before an American court. Of the spectacle of Germans denouncing Germans he said, "It is really not very nice." [37]

He was distressed that so many of his co-workers were testifying against him, but he should have been used to contempt. Goering, at the time of the attempted assassination of Hitler on July 20, 1944, had struck at him with his marshal's baton as Ribbentrop had uttered some stupidity and had called him "Ribbentrop" without the "von." "You champagne peddler," Goering had shouted, "shut up." The Foreign Minister dodged the blow and shouted back, "I am still Foreign Minister and my name is *von* Ribbentrop." [38] What disturbed him more than anything else was any questioning of his role. When Ivone Kirkpatrick interviewed him at Ashcan (the Allied collecting depot used before the prisoners were sent to Nuremberg) and suggested that perhaps the Foreign Minister was not so important under Hitler, Ribbentrop, although he would later use this line as a defense, could not bear the suggestion. "I was a man of very considerable importance," he said.[39]

Sometimes he was in fact important, although not in a sense he would have accepted. As the Cicero documents (see p. 216) were being evaluated, he prevented some of the reports of L. C. Moyzisch, the German attaché in Ankara who was dealing with Cicero, from reaching Schellenberg. Ribbentrop said it was "intolerable" that Schellenberg should get them. Ribbentrop's unwillingness to have Amt VI of the RSHA share the credit for providing what would have been, had they been properly evaluated, priceless documents for Germany caused them to be sidetracked and never properly used.[40]

Ribbentrop was a frightened man at Nuremberg, and he had little defense to offer. He drew the tatters of his diplomatic finery around him as best he could, striving wildly to remain true to the Fuehrer and at the same time to appear to have been opposed to the policies—the treatment of the Jews, war with Britain and France, war with Yugoslavia, and the others—he had so loyally and uncomplainingly pursued. The cross-examination was relentless, because the documents in his case were as clear as his ineptness. In the furor of his daily attempts to master the intricacies of his office, everything he said had been taken down and copies made, and so, when he spoke at Nuremberg about his friendly feelings for the Jews and enemy prisoners of war and for the French and the British and the Hague Conventions, a dozen statements he had made could be cited against him.

He was never up to the kind of defense that might have been made for much of the foreign policy. The records from the Quai d'Orsay captured by the Germans furnished evidence of the quasi-neutrality of Belgium and Holland; of the need for the German invasion of Norway to forestall a British and French landing; of the irresponsible policies of the Poles, who had clung to the letter of Versailles but had also invaded their peaceful neighbors and had helped dismember Czechoslovakia; of the *Machtpolitik* of the Russians. But Ribbentrop could make no use of any of these matters because they had in fact little to do with the crimes he had committed. In the later case of one of his subordinates—Weizsaecker, a man of the old Foreign Office—the defendant's German lawyer was able to make sensible use of the words of Clemenceau to the cadets of Saint-Cyr after the end of World War I. Clemenceau said, "Don't fear for your careers gentlemen, the peace we have made guarantees ten years of disorder in Europe for you." The whole system of the post-Versailles collective security was bound to break down of itself, with its futile attempt to glue together a series of alliances based on nothing more than the desire to hold down a *status quo* dominated by a weak France. And this was to be done with states like Czechoslovakia, where the minorities warred among themselves. The revolt of Slovakia against Prague was a real one and needed little help from the Germans to intensify the resentment of the Slovaks. The revolt needed only the possibility of tearing loose from the Prague Government, which, since 1919, had arrogantly governed what was to have been a federation on the Swiss model. Polish and Hungarian attacks on the territory of Czechoslovakia were made possible by the Germans, just as was the Russian attack on Poland. Neither Ribbentrop nor Hitler created the conditions that demanded the partitions, for the conditions were part of a long history of misgovernment and wrong calculations and unkept promises.

Ribbentrop had in fact done all the things charged in the indictment. He had planned to wage "aggressive war," and, so far as his nonbelligerent office permitted, had helped to wage it. He had participated both in war crimes and in crimes against humanity, with no thought as to Hague Conventions or any of the international or other agreements about which he knew so little. His puerilities and disabilities caught up with him at Nuremberg. His letter to Churchill and Eden; his fatuous attempts to establish a camaraderie with his interrogators; his desire to show that he was no anti-Semite, no warmonger, but a man with peace in his heart toward both East and West who had wisely counseled his beloved Fuehrer and then at the end had borne his last message to Churchill to set aside the results of the war that had cost so many millions of lives—these were part of the disorderly wishful thinking that had characterized his term in the Foreign Service of Adolf Hitler. In another

time Ribbentrop would doubtless have lived out his years as a tolerable businessman, talking about the need for a strong Germany, just claims to living
space, and the wickedness of the Jews. He had the bad luck to find in Hitler
someone who took him almost at his face value.

CONSTANTIN VON NEURATH

Two other defendants represented the Reich's Foreign Office: the former
Foreign Minister and Ambassador to England and Italy, Freiherr von Neurath;
and the former Chancellor and Ambassador to Austria and Turkey, Franz von
Papen.

When Neurath heard of Ribbentrop's appointment as Ambassador to
England in July, 1936, he immediately offered his resignation as Foreign
Minister, but Hitler did not accept it at that point. Ribbentrop, from his
post in London, was to report directly to Hitler. This bypassing of Ribbentrop's nominal superior, in the manner of his appointment and in the conduct
of his office, understandably irritated Neurath, especially since, the year
before, Ribbentrop had been appointed Undersecretary in the Foreign Office
by the Fuehrer, also without consulting Neurath, who had offered to resign
then too. But these appointments were only samples of the many bitter doses
Neurath was to swallow in the course of the next years. His actual resignation
would take place two years later, when Hitler, with tears in his eyes, Neurath
said, told him that Ribbentrop was to succeed him as Foreign Minister.

As for Papen, he would drink the same unpalatable brews as Neurath and
would continue to serve the regime he came to loathe and—in more active
ways than Neurath—to oppose. He, too, would serve out his time in high
office as long as the Fuehrer permitted. Ribbentrop was jealous of both these
men, as he was of everyone—whether Goebbels, or Himmler, or Goering, or
Rosenberg—who in any way threatened to invade his cherished position as
the adviser on foreign affairs to the Fuehrer. When he heard that Papen,
after the fall of Poland, had discussed Germany's foreign relations with
Hitler, he instructed his staff henceforth to give Papen no information.

The infighting had complicated patterns. Papen was convinced that
Neurath, despite his attempted resignation, had actually wanted Ribbentrop
as ambassador in London in order to weaken his influence with the Fuehrer
and to prevent the appointment of Papen to this post. The machinations of
men like Neurath and Papen, who were never part of the genuine resistance
movement, tended to be nothing if not opportunistic. They were held together
in their uneasy alliances only by a common dislike of the Ribbentrops and
by a desire to stay in office and to continue to influence decisions or events,
no matter how feebly. As Neurath testified at Nuremberg, the question for
him had been whether to remain the rock on the side of the bank or the rock

in the stream. The metaphor was not inappropriate: he had chosen the stream, and it had easily flowed over him. He had affected the current little if at all. He had only become part of the riverbed.

Both Neurath and Papen were conservatives so far as they were anything more than self-serving. Neurath, on his father's side, came from a long line of state officials. His mother's family were mainly officers in the Austrian Army and members of the Swabian nobility. Born on February 2, 1873, Neurath was brought up in the manner of the small nobility of Wuerttemberg. He was raised on the family estate by parents who inculcated rockbound Protestant principles that sustained him fully until the Nazis came to power. He studied law in the universities of Tuebingen and Berlin to prepare himself for the diplomatic service. François-Poncet (who dealt with him while Neurath was Foreign Minister) liked him. He characterized Neurath as a man of irreproachable courtesy, an unassertive, correct, urbane gentleman who had undoubtedly opposed the war. He thought of him, as did the Nazis themselves, as one of the old-school diplomats who would like to see Germany accepted as an equal among the powers but who wanted to proceed according to the rules.

Neurath joined the Foreign Service in 1901. He was a member of the consular staff in London from 1903 to 1908, when he returned to Berlin. He fought in the war of 1914–18 as a captain in a grenadier regiment and was decorated with the Iron Cross First Class. As a result of being wounded late in 1914, he returned to diplomatic service, with Germany's Turkish ally.[41] Because he did not get along well with Chancellor Theobald von Bethmann Hollweg, he resigned from his diplomatic post in 1916 to become head of the Cabinet of the King of Wuerttemberg, a job he held until the end of the war. The Republican Government appointed him Minister to Denmark in 1919, and in 1921 Ambassador to Rome. He was Ambassador to Britain from 1930 to 1932, when Papen appointed him Foreign Minister, a post he continued to hold under Chancellor Schleicher and Adolf Hitler until 1938.

Neurath was a man of no conspicuous talents or vices. He testified at Nuremberg that he stayed on as Foreign Minister at the express wish of President von Hindenburg. As one of the so-called conservatives around Hitler, his role was to help tame the Nazi revolutionaries and to keep the foreign policy peaceful. Hindenburg felt so strongly about his continuing as Foreign Minister, Neurath said, that he made his remaining in office a condition for the appointment of Adolf Hitler as Reich Chancellor.[42] Neurath regarded the Versailles Treaty with as baleful an eye as every other German statesman, but he said—and his testimony was corroborated by the Swiss Minister, the Papal Nuncio, and the French and Belgian Ambassadors, among others—that he had wanted to change it by negotiation, and the records of his proposals and diplomatic conversations bear this out.

Although everything he did had to reflect Hitler's basic policy of taking one step at a time to dismantle the Versailles system, he was always reasonable and easy to deal with, and seems to have been persuaded this could be done by peaceful means. He presented the German case coolly and reasonably without any table-pounding. On April 16, 1934, he announced that Germany would accept the British disarmament proposals in principle and suggested that Germany be granted an air force with short-range planes and without bombers. In return, he said, Germany would permit a control commission to assure the nonmilitary character of the SA and SS.[43] A few days later, replying to French accusations that Germany was inflating its arms budget, Neurath pointed out that during the preceding year France had spent 16 billion francs on her armed forces and now was complaining over the 890 million Reichsmarks that Germany was spending. The French called Germany's increase of 220 million Reichsmarks "a threat to peace," despite the fact that their own armaments increase had been far greater than the Germans'.[44] When in 1936 France made her military alliance pact with Russia, Neurath pointed out the vast extent of the French system of security: Metropolitan France with its colonies had a population of almost 100 million; in addition she could count as allies Great Britain, Poland, Belgium, and Czechoslovakia, not to mention the guarantees of the Locarno Pact that were intended to involve Italy in the case of any violation of French frontiers by Germany. Now, to these formidable numbers aligned against Germany would be added 175 million Russians—all of them together deploying the most overwhelming force in history on the German borders. In March, Neurath proposed military restrictions for both Germany and Belgium along their common border, to be guaranteed by Britain and Italy. He also said that Germany was ready to enter an agreement to limit air forces; to ban poison gas in any future war along with incendiary bombs and any kind of bombing of towns and villages; and to renounce heavy tanks and heavy artillery.[45]

Hitler was probing the soft spots in the seemingly impregnable system of encirclement that France had built around Germany. He had no interest whatever in disarmament but was willing to make any agreement with the Allies that might recognize Germany's right to increase its army and air force. Then he could take the next step. In the Europe of the mid-thirties there were always inequalities enough to enable Hitler to make further demands, whatever reasonable concessions might be made to him. He told not only the Allies but also his own advisers that he wanted peace, and Neurath believed him. When at the Hossbach conference of November 5, 1937,* the Fuehrer disclosed his considered intention to go to war, Neurath had a heart attack, but he kept on at his job and kept telling himself that as the rock in the stream he might dam or direct the current, for on the bank he could do nothing.

He was never a strong man, and he avoided unpleasantness and trouble as far as possible. Though ready to resign on Ribbentrop's appointment, he

* Lieutenant Colonel Friedrich Hossbach was Hitler's military attaché who recorded what the Fuehrer said.

made no move when Hitler disclosed that he intended to go to war. He had no causes for which he would do or die, not being the stuff of which heroes are made—or Nazis either. The Party thought him timid. François-Poncet and Weizsaecker thought him anything but dynamic. He saw little of Hitler, and Hitler, with his love for improvisation and surprise, paid no attention to him when he wanted to act quickly. Neurath clutched at straws. After Lord Halifax and Ivone Kirkpatrick had had a thoroughly depressing time with Hitler, whom they had found in an evil mood, he told them that their visit had nevertheless been useful: "It was an excellent thing to bring the Fuehrer in contact with the outside world." [46] He could easily indulge in such glib hypocrisies, not only for the benefit of his foreign visitors but also for himself.

Up to the time Hitler came to power, Neurath's career was unexceptional. Observers who knew him well—Ulrich von Hassell, whom he had appointed Ambassador to Rome, François-Poncet, and Davignon, the Belgium Ambassador—thought he was lazy and conventional. Davignon said he was eloquent enough à deux, but that he made a poor speech. Physically he was imposing, with a heavy, expressionless face. He impressed his visitors and co-workers with his honesty and good intentions and solid ability to deal in a routine way with the matters at hand. He spoke English, French, and Italian fluently, and the representatives of foreign countries liked and respected him. It was only when the going turned rough that his defects became apparent.

He accepted his reappointment as Foreign Minister from Hitler, whom he mistrusted, and then the establishment of the Ribbentrop Bureau, which paralleled the Foreign Office but was independent of it. He accepted the Roehm purges (he was to say at Nuremberg that he had heard that he and Fritsch had been "on Roehm's list").[47] He accepted the Kristallnacht and the pogroms against the Jews, although he undoubtedly opposed them and thought that they did great harm to Germany's credit in foreign countries. When Ribbentrop succeeded him as Foreign Minister, Neurath accepted the wholly honorific expedient of becoming President of a Secret Council that held no meetings. He never protested against any of the Nazi excesses, whether against the Jews or the "Aryan" Germans or anyone else. He disliked barbaric behavior, but he wanted to keep whatever important job he held. So he comforted himself with the consoling notion that without him matters would certainly be no different and might well be worse. When Ribbentrop was appointed Foreign Minister, Neurath told some of his staff that war could probably no longer be avoided, but he nevertheless remained, eager to be called on by the Fuehrer for any decorative post to which he might be assigned.[48]

Whenever Hitler was successful, Neurath congratulated him and went along with the new de facto situation, however doubtful he may have been about it originally. "You may deplore the fact that Hitler is in power," he told a French diplomat, "but this is the fact." He conducted himself accordingly. "A weak nation," he said, "is either booty or a danger," and nothing that

Hitler did either in building up Germany's military strength or in putting pressure on its neighbors seemed to him to contradict this principle. Hitler's diplomacy as well as his coups had his full support as long as no large-scale war resulted.

Neurath's major mistake came in 1939, when he accepted the job of Reichsprotektor of Czechoslovakia. The other charges against him at Nuremberg he could plausibly refute, since the roles he had played in Hitler's assault on Europe were of a passive kind. But the position he accepted in Czechoslovakia was in its nature that of a proconsul of National Socialism. While Neurath carried out his tasks with relative humanity, he fell into the trap of being the correct representative of a criminal state demanding the most brutal policies. He was unable or unwilling to change their basic character or to influence them except in minor ways.

He did whatever he thought necessary to hold down an important post. He drafted one of those adulatory messages dictators love—a telegram on behalf of President Emil Hácha and the entire population of Czechoslovakia assuring Adolf Hitler of their allegiance. When disorders occurred among Czech students, it was his name that appeared on a decreee of November 11, 1939, that closed all Czech universities for three years. His name also appeared on the orders to shoot nine of the students who had taken part in the uprising, although he had known nothing of the incident and had not even been in the country when it occurred.

According to Czech sources he said to the population, "I shall not hesitate to set up a military dictatorship if necessary. The spirit of the Czechs must be broken." [49] Whether or not he used these precise words, he bore the responsibility for those whose business it was, as he well knew, to break the spirit of the conquered. The Gestapo and the Security Police operated not under him in Czechoslovakia but under Himmler. His State Secretary, Karl Hermann Frank, who had been one of the chief Nazi leaders of the Sudetenland, had been appointed to formulate the German occupation policies and to act as the trigger man when the Czechs retaliated against them. However, the German decrees and countermeasures appeared under the name and authority of the Reichsprotektor. And in Czech cities signs reading "Reserved for Neurath" appeared on the lampposts.

He was a man who found ready explanations, convincing to him, for any course he took. Although he testified at Nuremberg that the synagogues remained open in Prague while he was there, and that far from being anti-Semitic he had helped the Jews as much as he could in Germany, he had also thought that they had penetrated too deeply into the German social structure and that the laws directed against them in the professions and the business and artistic life of Germany were justified. In a speech of September, 1933, he said, "The stupid talk about purely internal affairs, as for example the Jewish question, will quickly be silenced if one realizes that the necessary cleaning up of public life must temporarily entail individual cases of personal hardship but that nevertheless it only serves to establish all the more firmly the authority of justice and law in Germany." [50]

That German life had been too greatly dominated by the alien Jews he still believed, he said at Nuremberg, but he thought they should have been dealt with in other ways. And he held much the same views on Czechoslovakia. The vicious decrees may have been written by Himmler's representative, Karl Frank, but Neurath, too, believed in the "sugarbread and whip" policy, as he said, in treatment of Czechs. The Czechs were there to serve the Germans. In order to carry out their assignments they should be able to speak fluent German, and their marriage laws should follow the German pattern because the country was to become a colony. When a Czech committed a crime against a German resident, the entire Czech nation was to be held responsible. If any Czech did not see the necessity for this, he was to be regarded as an enemy of the Reich.[51]

Neurath asserted at Nuremberg that he had delayed as long as he possibly could in issuing the anti-Jewish laws in the protectorate, in order to give the Jews an opportunity to prepare for them, but he had accepted and agreed with the racial doctrine that declared both Czechs and Jews inferior peoples. Nevertheless, he thought that any Czechs who were capable of being Germanized could be upgraded. He wanted a hard-working, pro-German Czechoslovakia of artisans and proletarians, and for this reason he favored the expulsion of the intellectual class, which, he said, had developed in the past twenty years, and of those other Czechs who from a racial point of view should not live in proximity to Germans.[52]

He suited no one in his role of being the conservative, old-school German in the new order dominated by the SS. The Czechs wanted to hang him, and Hitler found him too lenient.

At Nuremberg Neurath testified that under his rule Czech theaters, concert halls, opera houses, and movies remained open; no compulsory labor existed;* Prague had a Czech mayor and a German assistant mayor. In an article in the *Europaeische Revue* of March 29, 1939, he wrote that in Bohemia and Moravia Hitler had created conditions for justice, that his own job as Reichsprotektor was to foster them, and that the Czechs were to develop undisturbed. But his letter of August 31, 1940, to Reich Secretary Lammers revealed a different point of view. He enclosed a memorandum from Karl Hermann Frank, with which he said he was in full agreement. The memorandum made the following points: The seven million Czechs were a source of working power for Germany. They could not be deported, there was no

---

* When the Czech universities and other institutions of higher learning were ordered closed, two members of Neurath's staff suggested sending the 18,000 students to forced labor either in Germany or Czechoslovakia. Neurath apparently took no position in the matter. In an interrogation of September 12, 1946, he said that Czech students had been given forty-eight hours to find manual work. If unsuccessful, they were to be sent to Germany. (National Archives [hereinafter referred to as NA], Interrogation of 9/12/46. Also N XVII, pp. 15 and 71.)

place for them to be sent, and some of them were of a blond Germanic type and showed signs of assimilability. These should be Germanized and their standard of living raised. Farmers should be given the advantages of German agricultural policy, the middle class and workers assisted, youth reeducated. The Czech "historical-myth" was to be obliterated, and no one would get on without a perfect knowledge of the German language. The Czech language would become a dialect, as it had been in the seventeenth and eighteenth centuries. With almost 8,000 urban and rural administrative units, the Germans had to make use of Czech administrators on a large scale in order to govern. The relationship was a sensitive one: the Czechs should not be completely degraded to the status of Askari or of a ' purely auxiliary race." They were to be destroyed not as a people but as a nation; they were to be assimilated into Germany. Any elements who opposed this process of Germanization would be roughly handled. Racially unassimilable Czechs and the intelligentsia, who were anti-German, would be expelled or given "special treatment" —that is, executed.* Politically Bohemia and Moravia were to be part of the Reich, and for racial reasons they were to be populated by Germans and Germanized Czechs.[53]

Neurath did not write this memorandum, but he did express concurrence with its views and asked Lammers to arrange an interview with the Fuehrer for him together with his State Secretary Frank.[54] At Nuremberg Neurath told the court he had had to say he agreed with the Frank memorandum as a tactic to persuade Hitler toward moderation. The evidence, however, did not support him, for Hitler had in fact decided in favor of the policy favored by Neurath and Frank—namely, Germanization of the Czechs. And in a memorandum he did write, Neurath expressed similar ideas: "It will . . . be a case . . . of keeping those Czechs who are suitable for Germanization by individual selective breeding, while on the other hand of expelling those who are not useful from a racial standpoint or are enemies of the Reich, that is, the intelligentsia which has developed in the last twenty years." [55]

Neurath was not a man who would favor a policy of exterminating racially undesirable elements or the anti-German Czech intelligentsia. He would never have ordered the destruction of Lidice, for he disliked violent reprisals and killings. He just wanted Czechoslovakia and its people to become as useful to Germany as possible. It was Frank who wrote about "special treatment," and it was Neurath, wanting to impress Hitler with his zeal, who said he agreed with what Frank wrote. When the Fuehrer informed him in September, 1941, that he was sending Heydrich to Prague because Neurath's policies were too lenient, Neurath refused to return to his post and went on leave. His official resignation did not take place until October, 1943—an example of his clinging to a job and the shadow of respectability.

The testimony of George S. Messersmith, former American Consul Gen-

* Neurath did not at the time know the meaning of the term, he testified at Nuremberg. (N XVII, p. 104.)

eral in Berlin and later Minister to Austria, was categorically denied by Neurath, as it was by the other defendants whom Messersmith testified against. Messersmith's affidavit palpably exaggerated in important places, and his testimony that Neurath and Papen, both of whom had known him slightly, had disclosed to him the Nazi plan for the domination first of Austria and then of Czechoslovakia was unlikely on the face of it. The trials at Nuremberg, and later Eichmann's trial in Jerusalem, were to elicit such testimony on the part of witnesses who not only wanted to inflate their own roles but were determined to take part in bringing the accused to justice. The court does not seem to have given much weight to testimony that was obviously part of a fantasy in which the witnesses played momentous roles against tyranny. The tyranny was real enough, whether or not the accused had played the part he was charged with. In denying Messersmith's charges, both Neurath and Papen pointed out that they would scarcely have disclosed such confidential information, even if it had existed, to a man they knew so slightly and who was avowedly anti-German.

But Neurath's defense could not gainsay what he himself had written, nor his years of collaboration with the regime he knew to be criminal. It was true that he had made no use of the handsome gift the Fuehrer had made to him of 250,000 RM and that he had only accepted a German painting of no great value sent to him on his seventieth birthday. He had made little use of the Party's Golden Badge of Honor bestowed upon him or of the SS uniform provided for him as for the other high members of the Reich's diplomatic service. It was true, too, that his efforts to treat the Czechs with some decency and humanity led to his being replaced by Reinhard Heydrich, who would know how to carry out the measures of the SD without any attempt to win the Czechs over with "sugarbread." But Neurath had deserved the dubious honors he accepted. He had been one of the bridges between the old Germany and the new. Things could not be so bad, many critics of Hitler's policies would say, if the Neuraths and Papens were there. In April, 1947, months after the Nuremberg trial was over, Neurath told an Allied interrogator looking for information for other prosecutions that he had known nothing of the existence of Auschwitz. His testimony may well be believed, for he had no curiosity about unpleasant matters.[56]

Neurath had been most useful to Hitler in his place and time. In 1932, when Hitler was trying to persuade Hindenburg to make him Chancellor, one of the promises he made to prove his moderation was that he would keep Neurath as Foreign Minister. Neurath had not only added respectability to Hitler's government, but had also on occasion given him shrewd advice. In 1936 he told the Fuehrer he did not think France and England would react if a German division reoccupied the Rhineland. He was well thought of in England and France. He was known to be a gentleman of the old school, patriotic but opposed to war and to excesses against the Jews or anyone else. When he later continued to defend the regime and accepted the office of one of its chief proconsuls, when he spoke of the necessity for Germany's setting its own house in order without foreign interference and incorporating the hard-working people of central Europe in its new order, he did much on behalf of Hitler's credit among certain conservative circles in Germany if not in foreign countries. He was always willing, even if he found it distasteful, to work with Himmler's man Karl Frank, and to have orders for the execution of Czech hostages go out under his name, along with other decrees of reprisal that he did not write.

Neurath was the man England would have liked the German Government to send as representative of the Reich at the coronation of Edward VIII. He had many friends in Britain and had been received in private audience by George V. Everyone had confidence in him except the men of the German Resistance. The Resistance knew he disliked Nazism but also knew he would do nothing about getting rid of it. Instead, he would continue to serve it in his uncomplaining, cautious way. Weizsaecker in 1940 thought him lost in dreams of victory with no knowledge of the sector of the war that was not going well for the Reich—for example, the high losses of submarines— nor was there any serious complaint to be heard from Neurath about the outrages. Neurath certainly did not want the Czechs, the Poles, or the Jews to be dealt with as he knew them to be, nor had he wanted war, but, like Papen, he could never get off the red carpet until it was jerked out from under him.

He told the court in his final plea that it should act in the spirit of Franklin Roosevelt, the father of this trial, whose lamentable early death had been a loss for the entire world. Roosevelt, he said, had laid the groundstone for the temple of peace of the people of the world. But despite such efforts to talk the language of Germany's conquerors, he could be sharp in his rejoinders to Allied cross-examiners. Maxwell-Fyfe at one point implied that Neurath was not telling the truth, and a moment later Neurath called him a liar. When the Russian judge Nikitchenko asked him whether he had ever expressed in the press or at any public meetings any disagreement with Hitler, Neurath replied, "No . . . there was no freedom of the press any longer, any more than in Russia." [57] Nikitchenko said he was not asking him about Russia.

The judgment of the court said that Neurath had advised Hitler in connection with the German withdrawal from the Disarmament Conference of 1933 and the League of Nations and on the passage of the law for universal military service. It stated that he had been a key figure in the negotiation of the naval accord with Britain and had told Hitler German troops could reoccupy the Rhineland without reprisals from France. He had also told the United States Ambassador to France that the German Government would do nothing in foreign affairs until "the Rhineland had been digested," and that once the fortifications there had been constructed and France could not invade Germany at will, the other European countries would begin to feel differently about their foreign policies. With knowledge of Hitler's aggressive plans, Neurath had retained a formal relationship with the Nazi Government as Reich Minister Without Portfolio, President of the Secret Cabinet Council, and member of the Reich Defense Council. He had told the British Ambassador at the time of the *Anschluss* with Austria that this had not been brought about by a German ultimatum, and he had told the Czechoslovakian Minister that Germany intended to abide by its arbitration convention with Czechsolovakia. He had participated in the last phase of the negotiations preceding the Munich pact.

If one accepts the judgment's statements as fact, it is difficult to see what was criminal in anything Neurath did as Foreign Minister. His advice to Hitler on the Rhineland occupation and his statement on its refortification were borne out by the events and were no more than the kind of appreciation of the situation that any foreign minister might be expected to make. It is unlikly that Neurath knew of the German ultimatum to Schuschnigg (see Seyss-Inquart, Chapt. 11); in any event, he was no longer in office when it was sent. His statement to the Czechoslovakian Minister doubtless seemed to Neurath true at the time, and he played a smaller part in the destruction of the country than the British and French.[58]

Neurath was convicted on all four counts and sentenced to fifteen years in prison, of which he served eight, being one of the few to leave Spandau before the end of his sentence. An old man of eighty-one and in ill health, he returned to his estate at Leinfelder Hof near Stuttgart on November 6, 1954. He died there on August 14, 1956. Unlike Papen and Ribbentrop, perhaps because of his age, he made no effort to write his memoirs or to justify his course of action.

FRANZ VON PAPEN

Three defendants at Nuremberg were found not guilty of the charges against them and were freed by the tribunal from the custody of the Allied governments. One of them was Franz von Papen. It took a long time, however, before any of the three were out of prison. Papen, like the others, was promptly arrested after he left the Nuremberg jail. The German authorities in Wuerttemberg and Bavaria brought charges against him, and he was put on trial as a "major offender" under the denazification laws. Two German courts found him guilty. The first sentenced him, early in 1947, to eight years in prison. The second, in January, 1949, pointing out that he had been in confinement since May 8, 1945, placed him in a lesser category of "offenders" and freed him with a fine of 30,000 marks, which were to be a contribution to the restitution funds given people who had suffered under the Nazis, and with further penalties that deprived him of the right to vote, to get a pension from the State, to hold office, to work at anything but ordinary labor, or to drive a car.

The feeling against Papen among large sections of the German public—especially among the anti-Nazis who held political office under the Allied occupation after the war—was intensely hostile. The staff of the main hospital in Nuremberg drew up a resolution saying they did not wish to have him as a patient when he sought to go there after his release from jail. In a German prison, a former SS man later judged insane attacked him and broke his jaw and nose. As in the case of Schacht, a wave of indignation rose over his acquittal by the International Military Tribunal. People like the SPD (Sozialdemokratische Partei Deutschlands) Minister President of Bavaria, Wilhelm Hoegner, professed themselves unable to understand how the man who had played a leading role in bringing Hitler to power and then had collaborated with him by accepting important offices during all the years Hitler was Chancellor should be freed by the International Military Tribunal or any other court.*

At Nuremberg, Papen was formally accused on only one count of the indictment: of having taken part in the preparation for the waging of aggressive warfare in violation of international treaties. In the course of his trial the main charge developed against him was that he had prepared the way for Hitler to become Chancellor and then played a crucial role in helping the Fuehrer get his stranglehold on the political life of the country. But Papen could be formally charged only under Count One of the indictment, and he had no difficulty in showing that he had in fact always opposed the war and had regarded it as a catastrophe for Germany. What the German courts accused him of had little to do with the preparations to wage war but a great deal to do with his moral responsibility—something the Allies could only touch on at Nuremberg. Papen, like Neurath, had thrown his full support to the Nazis at critical times. Without his help, Hitler might never have succeeded in becoming Chancellor through legal means. And this matter of legality was of great importance; it was always to play a decisive role both in Hitler's thinking and in public opinion. It was one of the counters in the defense of the regime by the respectable and apolitical officers and bureaucrats who had been brought up to serve the head of state, whether they liked him or not and whether or not they approved his policies.

Papen came from an ancient Westphalian family. He was a devout Catholic, a career officer, a monarchist by conviction (although he was a member of the Center Party and one of its representatives in the Prussian Landtag). He had the outward aspects of conservative respectability: he was graceful in manner, liked horses, and rode as a gentleman jockey, and had married the daughter of a rich industrialist. He believed in the benevolent leadership of the *Obrigkeit;* in decent wages for workers who fitted into their place in a Christian society of order and mutual good feeling where management made

* Hoegner said, "The verdict is a scandal. I will see to it that these gentlemen are re-arrested at the prison gates" (Franz von Papen, *Der Wahrheit eine Gasse* [Munich: Paul List Verlag, 1952], p. 652).

wise decisions gratefully accepted by the underlings; and in higher farm prices for bankrupt landowners both small and large. A general staff officer, he had an undistinguished but meritorious military career in World War I, during which he also served as military attaché to Washington with lamentable results. The United States Department of State requested his recall for having attempted to organize sabotage of American armaments production for the Allies, including a plan to blow up two Canadian railroad bridges in order to slow down the reinforcement of the British Army in France.

A strong anti-German sentiment had been built up in the United States by skillful Allied propaganda on a thin layer of alleged war crimes. Papen contributed to this sentiment. His amateurish dealings with German agents and with adventurers who aspired to become agents (the man to whom he gave $500 to blow up one of the Canadian bridges was arrested when he crossed the border into Canada) were failures. He did achieve one thing for his country: he established a munitions factory working for Germany in Bridgeport. Since it could not ship anything to Germany, it had the purpose of consuming quantities of scarce raw materials, such as gunpowder, so as to prevent their going into war production for the Allies. The firm did succeed in buying up scarce commodities, but its operations had no appreciable effect on the flood of arms and ammunition going overseas.

Papen's worst failure came in connection with this dummy company. A member of his staff, Dr. Heinrich Albert, traveling on the Sixth Avenue elevated in New York, fell asleep with his briefcase alongside him full of material including letters compromising Papen for involvement in activities on behalf of the Central Powers. The aide woke up befuddled, and forgot his briefcase when he left the train at the 50th Street station. Suddenly remembering it, he started back for the train, only to see a man going off with it, racing to a taxi, and getting away. Three days later the New York *World* told the story of more German cloak-and-dagger machinations in the United States. The article told about Papen's attempt to organize workers of German and Austrian descent in plants working for the Allies to persuade them to slow down production, and about his sending information to Germany on shipping movements to England and France—through correspondence on what seemed to be commercial transactions. Nor was this all. A few weeks later Papen wrote a letter to his wife in Germany, which he entrusted to an American journalist to deliver past the Allied blockade. It read in part: "They stole unluckily from the good Albert in the Elevated, a whole thick portfolio . . . How splendid on the Eastern front! I always say to these idiotic Yankees that they should shut their mouths or better still express their admiration for all that heroism." [59] English officers found this letter as they searched the journalist's luggage at Falmouth and it was published in the United States.

Papen was always to have trouble with his papers. When he was declared *persona non grata* by the United States Government and sent back to Germany with a British safe-conduct on the Dutch ship *Nordam,* British officials searched his baggage as the ship stopped at Falmouth and over Papen's violent protests took away personal papers filled with further details (including canceled checks given the men who were to blow up the Canadian bridges) of his attempts to set up a spy network. This material soon appeared with devastating effect in Allied propaganda and in accounts of German onslaughts against American neutrality. Later in the war, when serving in Palestine, Papen went on leave from Nazareth to Germany and left behind in his quarters another batch of incriminating documents. When the British captured the ancient town, they found the papers in Papen's luggage and made good use of them. One of Papen's collaborators, Captain von Rintelen, later charged that as a result of the study of these documents, which concerned, among other things, rebellion in Ireland and India and sabotage in the United States, a number of the plotters were picked up by the British and Americans and either imprisoned or executed.[60]

Casting about for a place in the disorganized political life of post-World War I Germany, Papen chose the Catholic Center Party for his allegiance, and in 1923 bought 47 per cent of the stock of its leading paper, the *Germania,* thus becoming chairman of its board of directors. Though a monarchist at heart, with little confidence in the struggling democracy of Weimar Germany, Papen saw that the Center Party, with its strong Catholic ties and its middle-of-the-road position, had far more appeal to a wide base of the electorate than one of the nationalist parties he might also have chosen as his own. In his memoirs Papen said that his gaining control of the *Germania* came as a bombshell to the Center Party leadership. He promptly fired the editor of the paper and set out to impose on the party members his version of the line the party should follow, setting off a struggle that was to continue for eight years. Papen, the dilettante politician with a vague program, was never accepted by the party as a valid spokesman, nor even as a dependable member. A few weeks before he became Chancellor, the party disavowed him as a deputy in the Prussian Landtag. And although he had promised Monsignor Kaas, the head of the Center Party, that he would not accept the chancellorship in the place of Bruening, he did accept it and was immediately repudiated by the Centrist members of the Reichstag, as he had been in the Landtag, who voted not to support his government.[61]

Papen's completely unexpected appointment to the chancellorship on May 31, 1932, seemed absurd and scandalous to observers like François-Poncet as well as to Papen's colleagues. It seemed to them that in addition to his political inexperience and ineptitude, the most primitive political ethics would have prevented him from succeeding a member of his own party. His only political experience had been as a deputy in the Prussian Landtag, where, although nominally a Centrist, he had been supported in the elections by members of other parties—farmers and landowners making a comfortable if precarious living from their farms in Westphalia. They were mainly nationalists, fearful of both the radical Right and Left that threatened the stability they yearned for, and picked their way among the platforms, programs, and candidates of the thirty-two parties, each with its private solution for the woes of the nation.

The prices of farm products were catastrophically low in Germany at the time of the depression, as they were in the rest of the capitalist countries, including the United States. German farms and estates were heavily mortgaged, and the attempts by way of farm loans and subsidies to bail out the landowners resulted in repeated scandals owing to the misuse of the money loaned to the large estates. Instead of improving their farms, many owners took trips to the Riviera or otherwise disported themselves in nonagricultural pursuits. The farm problem remained unsolved.

Papen shared the confusion of the agrarians and, as one of them, opposed Bruening's efforts toward a land reform that would have broken large and inefficient estates into small holdings. Hindenburg's toleration of Bruening's farm policy cost him the undivided allegiance of the Right-wing nationalist parties, which, in the first presidential balloting of 1932, ran a rival candidate —the Stahlhelm leader Theodor Duesterberg. His candidacy forced the Field Marshal, who received 49.6 per cent of the votes, into a runoff with Hitler, whom he could scarcely bring himself to speak to. Hitler got 30.1 per cent of the votes, Duesterberg 6.8 per cent, and the other candidates a scattering of votes.

Hindenburg's rejection of Bruening and his choice of Papen came at a time when the aging President was showing increasing evidence of senility. Hindenburg at eighty-five was still capable on his "good days" of writing a concise estimate of the general political situation, but on other days he was uncertain about the identity of his Reich Chancellor.[62] In this period Hindenburg turned back more and more to his old habits of thought, reciting the military precepts of obedience and duty and *Treue* to justify his often arbitrary decisions, and violating them himself when he was caught in the welter of policies he could no longer master. In these last years he relied on four or five people he trusted to advise him in the face of the constantly growing threat of the extreme Right and Left: General Wilhelm Groener, an honorable and intelligent man with no gift for politics or for appearing before the public, who was both the Minister of Defense (since 1928) and of the Interior (since October, 1931); Kurt von Schleicher, one of the inept political generals in German life, a kingmaker with burning ambitions of himself one day becoming king; Otto von Meissner, the President's Staatssekretaer, cautious and knowledgeable; Hindenburg's son Oskar, a man of limited understanding whose chief talent lay in being the obsequious and devoted son of an illustrious father; and Heinrich Bruening, a sober, scholarly, and scrupulous man who, as a former officer, although a former lieutenant of reserve, had Hindenburg's respect but never his full confidence. On the other hand, he liked and trusted Papen.

As Hindenburg's problems multiplied and the other advisers slowly lost favor, the role of his son became more and more important. Who was to see the President was decided by Oskar rather than by the far more sophisticated Meissner, who had been Staatssekretaer under Friedrich Ebert and continued to serve in that capacity under Hindenburg and Hitler. Oskar became the main bridge between the President and his other advisers. Groener, the former staff officer, had little political shrewdness. Hindenburg could overlook this failing, but he could not forgive Groener's hasty marriage followed five months later by the birth of a son, who was nicknamed Nurmi, after the Finnish runner, in ribald Army circles. Hindenburg was a Prussian puritan, and it was not far from treason for a high officer to do anything that could bring public ridicule on the Army or the head of state.

In the runoff election when Hindenburg was chosen President in 1932, for the second time defeating Hitler, with 53 per cent of the votes cast (19,360,000 to 13,418,000), he owed his re-election to the parties of the Center and the Left. The Right had put two candidates in the field against him—Hitler and Duesterberg. It was the Center and the Social Democrats (Hindenburg's chief opponents in the election of 1925) who now in their fear of the Nazis provided the crucial support against the radicals of the Right and Left. Loss of the election was a hard blow to the National Socialists, who had set high hopes on it. Hitler had expected to win with his new allies in Alfred Hugenberg's party, which voted for the unknown Duesterberg on the first ballot but was instructed to vote for the Nazis in the runoff. All the election had done for Hitler was to make him a citizen. As a stateless person he could not run for the Presidency, and an obliging National Socialist, Dietrich Klagges, a Minister in the Brunswick Government, had arranged for his appointment to a minor post in the state administration on February 25, 1932. (See Chapt. 7.) This act conferred German citizenship on the Fuehrer.

Hindenburg was uneasy in his alliance with Bruening. He resented his dependence on forces that had formerly opposed him; the socialism of the SPD was anathema; the correct intellectual parliamentarian Bruening was never sympathetic to him. Bruening's foreign policies had failed to gain recognition of Germany's right-to-arms equality, and he had failed to get a customs union with Austria. He could command no stable coalition in the Reichstag, and the plans to settle war veterans on derelict estates had cost the support of the Right. Among the handful of men who now were close to Hindenburg was General von Schleicher, who had served in the same regiment as his son Oskar. Schleicher, although he had flirted with the Left, including the Communists, since the early days of the Republic, remained a monarchist. As an officer of the general staff he was concerned with politics but seemingly, as Hindenburg thought, was untainted by them. When Schleicher proposed Papen as Bruening's successor, he picked a man who also appealed to Hindenburg—a man the President could both trust and understand.

Papen's choice was in a sense apolitical. One of Bruening's last acts had been to ban the wearing of uniforms by the SA and SS, whose incessant parades with accompanying street fighting were an essential part of the Nazi strategy to impress the electorate and to paralyze their opponents. Neither Schleicher, nor Groener, nor Hindenburg had fully approved of the decree demanded by Bruening. Important in Schleicher's strategy was the plan for strengthening his own and Germany's military position by using the SA and the SS as a militia (their numbers had risen to 600,000 in 1932) to augment the Army of 100,000 men, which was inadequate to protect the German borders even against the Poles. The Poles, using the disorder created by the Nazis as a pretext, might at any time, the German High Command feared, march into East Prussia as they had into Vilna and the former Russian provinces on their eastern border. So Hindenburg, Schleicher, and Papen were united in their willingness to see the SA back in the streets. They considered the ban on them onesided, since the uniformed bodies of the other parties— the Stahlhelm, the Reichsbanner of the Socialists, even the Frontkaempfer-bund of the Communists—were not forbidden, although the Nazis had been mainly responsible for the violence that came out of the propaganda marches.

A few months after Bruening had become Chancellor, the Nazis had raised their vote from the 800,000 obtained on May 20, 1928, to almost 6.5 million in the election of September 14, 1930, where 4.6 million new voters cast their ballots for the first time. With 107 seats in the Reichstag, the National Socialists were the second largest party. The Social Democrats polled over 8.5 million votes and, although they were reduced from 152 seats to 143, were the largest party. The Communists had 77 deputies; the Center, 68. Bruening was unable to get this well-organized, raucous, heckling, brawling National Socialist minority off his back, and also was unable to organize a parliamentary majority. He represented everything the radicals hated: he was religious and moderate, and fearless in denouncing the Far Right and Far Left. He ruled through the unstable alliance cemented by a common fear of the Nazis and the Communists and by the writ of Hindenburg. The Socialists of the SPD were the unnatural allies of his half-authoritarian Centrist regime. Because he commanded no parliamentary majority, he had to rule by presidential decree. His enemies were all the rest of the parties.*

When, in July, 1931, the banks closed and the savings departments shut their windows, reparations (in theory) had still to be paid the countries that

---

* Bruening's Cabinet of April 30, 1930, had representatives from five parties: Center (Zentrum), Democrats (Demokraten), German People's Party (Deutsche Volkspartei), Bavarian People's Party (Bayerische Volkspartei), and People's Conservative Party (Konservative Volkspartei). This gave him a total of 200 out of 491 votes in the Reichstag. After the National Socialist victory in September, he attempted in October, 1931, to form a cabinet "above the parties," in which Hindenburg's friend Groener was both Minister of Defense and Minister of the Interior.

had won the war and were in the grip of the same depression. No Western nation succeeded in mastering the worsening depression, and Bruening no longer had any kind of economic or political base to operate from. On May 30, 1932, the day he resigned and Papen was appointed, Hindenburg summoned Hitler and Goering to the presidential palace to tell them the news and to say in a bid for their support that the Reichstag would be dissolved, new elections held, and the ban on the SA lifted if Hitler would promise to "tolerate" the Papen regime. Hitler did not hesitate to say he would; he had confidence in the result of new elections. Hitler and Papen met for the first time on June 9, 1932,* a week after Papen had become Chancellor, and both affirmed the promises made when the Fuehrer had met Hindenburg: Papen would lift the ban on the Brownshirts, Hitler would tolerate the Papen Cabinet, the Reichstag would be dissolved and new elections held.

That was all Hitler needed. Papen had no popular political support, and without the backing of his former Center Party a voter could not cast a ballot in his favor even if he wanted to. With the Nazi uniformed formations free to flood back on the streets, in a Germany where one-third of the population was living meagerly from public funds (Bruening, in an effort to stabilize finances, had cut relief allowances of families with children from 20 RM a month to 10 RM and had lowered the salaries of government officials by 20 per cent), and no part of either economic or political life was functioning normally, Papen was very nearly the chosen instrument to clear the way for a great Nazi victory. He and Hitler met not in the Reich Chancellery but privately in the home of a friend of Schleicher's—Werner von Alvensleben, a brother of the president of the Herrenklub and an admirer of Hitler. The Fuehrer agreed to keep his Brownshirt deputies in the Reichstag quiet while Papen journeyed to Lausanne to meet with the Allies. This concession was in no way inconsistent with Hitler's purpose of tolerating Papen's government for a short time. Papen, a man without a party, with borrowed policies no different from those of the half-authoritarian, half-parliamentarian men of the Right and Center against whom Hitler campaigned so successfully, could not last long. The National Socialists were certain to increase their numbers at his expense. And more important than the Reichstag were the streets.

Following Papen's lifting of the prohibition against the Nazis wearing uniforms, a fresh wave of rioting broke out. Between June 1 (permission to wear the uniforms was given on June 14) and July 20, 72 people were killed and 497 badly wounded.[63] In the midst of these signs of revolution, the Reichstag was a sounding board. Papen, like Bruening, had to govern without a parliamentary majority, and both had to resort to the device of invoking Article 48

---

* This is the date given by Papen. Goebbels says they first met on May 31, and a number of writers say a second meeting took place on June 13 (Otto Meissner and Harry Wilde, Die Machtergreifung [Stuttgart: J. G. Cotta'sche Buchhandlung, 1958], pp. 88, 279).

of the constitution, under which emergency legislation—later to be approved by the Reichstag—could be enacted by the Chancellor under a presidential decree. Bruening's cabinet had been based not on Parliament but on Hindenburg. From 1925 to 1930 no use of emergency decrees had been made. From December, 1930, to April, 1931, 19 laws were enacted by the Reichstag and 2 emergency laws were decreed; from April to December, 1931, 40 emergency laws were decreed under Article 48 and no law was enacted by the Reichstag; in 1932, 5 laws were approved by the Reichstag while 59 emergency laws were decreed. The Reichstag held 94 sessions in 1930, 41 in 1931, and only 13 in 1932.[64]

Bruening had had to use Article 48 increasingly toward the end of his first term as Chancellor, which began in April, 1930, and in his second term, which began in October, 1931. He had stayed in office with the help of the SPD, which (however much it disapproved of his party and policies) wanted at all costs to avoid a Hitler dictatorship of the Far Right that might come at any time, either through a general election giving the Nazis and their allies a majority or through Hindenburg's appointing Hitler as Chancellor. Bruening's attempt at agrarian reform, as many writers have pointed out, was the final blow to his relationship with the old President, who was under great pressure (from his friends and landowning neighbors in East Prussia with estates often mortgaged for more than they were worth) to get rid of the "agrarian Bolshevik" who wanted land redistributed for the benefit of the unemployed more than he wanted to bail out the landowners. Bruening was never more than a tolerable expedient for Hindenburg, and when it had become clear that he could only continue to govern by means of emergency decrees, the President had turned to one of the last measures open to him: creating, as he thought, through Papen, a regime that this time would be truly "above the parties," conservative, God-fearing, and would conceivably bring about a unity of the Right, including the National Socialists, in a coalition.

Papen, with a coalition cabinet, had to use the same tactics as Bruening, but he lacked the parliamentary support of the Center and Left that had backed Bruening, and also of most of the Right. He had a scattering of votes among the nationalist parties but no popular support, no political organization of any kind. Hindenburg had told him he wanted a cabinet "above politics"—meaning a presidential cabinet that would not have to try to govern with a majority in Parliament. What he got was a cabinet without a following in or outside the Reichstag. Papen and his cabinet of barons, industrialists, and landowners (it included Freiherr von Neurath as Foreign Minister and Count Schwerin von Krosigk, who would later serve Hitler as Minister of Finance) had the short-lived support of the unpredictable Schleicher, who was nursing his own ambitions, and of the President, who liked the former general staff officer's pleasant and courteous manner, his "conservative" belief in an authoritarian state with due regard for the proprieties, and above all his desire for a restoration of the monarchy. Papen seemed to Hindenburg, in the welter of the German parliamentary system, "a sound man." Papen's religion was also thought to be an advantage, for it showed that Hindenburg was not, as people sometimes said, anti-Catholic. But Papen could never possibly obtain a working majority in the Reichstag and Hindenburg could not long support him against the political realities.

Bruening had been the victim of rising unemployment, of low prices for farm commodities, of the deepening economic crisis engulfing the Western world. The crisis seemed most hopeless in the Germany of a lost war and postwar inflation. Everything Bruening had attempted seemed doomed to fail or to come too late: the customs union with Austria; a solution of the farm crisis with controlled prices and an agrarian reform that sought to divide up the uneconomic estates in East Prussia; the recognition of German equality in armament, either by an increase in the German forces or by a reduction of the forces of the other powers; and the effort to end reparations. Both in his foreign and his domestic policies, he lacked the success that sparks a popular following. He was far from being the demagogue who, like Hitler, could promise everything.

Papen's solutions were merely tactical. He sought to move the weight of the coalition that had been behind the Bruening Government from the Left and Center to the Right, but in order to do this he had to gain the support, not only the toleration, of Hitler. He had to bring Hitler into cooperation with a government without a party. It was a hopeless task. Papen came back from the Disarmament Conference at Lausanne on July 9, 1932, with no more to show for his efforts at gaining arms equality for Germany than Bruening had shown before him. As he made the case for German arms equality at Lausanne, he indulged in a characteristic Papenian gesture.[65] He told Herriot that since France would always be afraid of German rearmament, a kind of common general staff should be established: French officers should be assigned to duty in a German general staff and would thereupon know all Germany's military plans once such a staff (forbidden by Versailles) were recognized along with Germany's right to arms equality. Herriot, according to Papen, succeeded in getting the preliminary approval of his cabinet for this revolutionary proposal, but England cast a firm veto, for if this cooperation of German and French general staff officers should work out, unlikely as that might be, it would lead to an overwhelming military force on the Continent and permanently upset the balance of power. Neither France nor Germany was prepared for military collaboration after the bitter war. Like so many of Papen's solutions, the scheme was a fantasy, a *deus ex machina*, a device. He then sought to have at least the war-guilt clause expurgated from the Versailles Treaty, but the proposal at Lausanne to annul this article was unanimously defeated. What was decided was that Germany was to make a final reparations payment of three billion marks at a time when the almost bankrupt Reich could not pay the salaries of its employees. That was the positive result of the conference and a victory of sorts. On the negative side, equality of armament was still denied. There was to be no increase in Germany's armed forces, and no decrease in the forces of her neighbors.

Papen's offers to the French of a consultative pact and a combined general staff were no more than gestures. Germany had nothing to give. Her requests could easily be turned down, for Papen, unlike Schleicher, was not the man to raise the ghost of Rapallo, of a German shift to the East.

What could Papen offer the seven million unemployed, the owners of closed factories, the desperate farmers, that had not been promised and failed before? Even if large numbers of voters had wanted to cast a ballot for him, what was his party and his platform? For which deputies should they vote? When he and members of his Cabinet appeared on the hustings after the Lausanne conference, they were greeted with showers of rotten apples and eggs. The well-organized opposition of the parliamentary system had no trouble furnishing the manpower for such demonstrations. Futhermore, Papen's own devotion to the parliamentary system was lukewarm. On July 20, just before the elections, he had become Reichskommissar of Prussia. The appointment (with Hindenburg and Schleicher in agreement) was made possible by the use of a presidential decree "For the Restoration of Public Security and Order in Prussia." Papen replaced two Socialists—Minister President Braun and Minister of the Interior Severing—and the Centrist Welfare Minister Hirtsiefer. This coalition of three Ministers had lost its long-standing parliamentary majority by a combination of Nazi and Communist votes but had continued in office, as did so many of the German administrations, including Papen's, without a majority in the legislature, since the Nazis and Communists could scarcely collaborate in forming a government.

Karl Severing was a well-known anti-Nazi who had ordered house searches of members of the SA and was anathema to Hitler. Using as a pretext the disorders of Altona, where on July 17, 1932, a bloody battle between National Socialists and Communists had resulted in the death of fifteen men, including two uniformed Nazis, Papen took over the Government of Prussia. He accused Severing and Braun of being unable to guarantee the security of the State and of having made a deal with the Communists, who, he said, were infiltrating the police department. This was an act of pure force, of the kind the Nazis would later adopt, and it won support from none of the parties. Papen's act, completely illegal under the Prussian constitution, dissolved the Prussian Landtag. Without consulting the Ministers responsible to that body, he did away with the parliamentary system in that state. Whatever his motives—whether to make a show of strength with Hindenburg's help or to impress Hitler and to get rid of a Socialist government—Papen's act was as arbitrary and authoritarian as anything the Nazis might have done. It lacked only the National Socialist methods of terror.

When Papen came back from Lausanne with the small trophy of a final settlement of reparations but without equality of armament and without having succeeded in getting rid of the war-guilt clause, no alternative existed to bringing the Nazis somehow into the Government. The opposition to the National Socialists had nothing left but their will to oppose. They had not a single success to show in their attempts to revive Germany's internal or external credit, or to counter the promises the Nazis made to the electorate. If either Papen or Bruening had been able to return from a conference with the Allies with permission for the Germans to have an army of 300,000 men (Papen had promised at Lausanne that the Germans would make no immediate use of the right to the increase but merely rejoice in the moral victory it represented), the issue with the Nazis might have been joined. But that moment never came. Much too late, Schleicher, when he became Chancellor, was able to obtain a statement of the Allies' theoretical willingness to grant the Germans arms equality. When that happened, the Nazi tide was at flood.

The elections of July 31, 1932, gave the Nazis their greatest victory: a popular vote of 13.7 million out of 36.8 million, 37.3 per cent of the electorate, and 230 seats in the Reichstag (more than double what they had had before). The nine middle parties were down from 112 seats to only 25, and the German Nationalists had lost 4 of their 41 seats. The Communists were up too, from 77 to 89 seats. Together, the Communists and the Nazis had an absolute majority. The elections left Hitler with far less than a majority, even with the addition of the other nationalist parties, but together with the Communists, who had elected 14.6 per cent of the new Reichstag, the antidemocratic parties now had almost 60 per cent of the votes.

Flushed with this monumental victory, the Fuehrer asked the President to receive him. Powerful forces were urging that Hitler be named Vice-Chancellor. It was one way to bring the Party from the streets into the government, to have it accept responsibility. Among those who urged the appointment were Monsignor Kaas, head of the Center Party, Papen, and Schleicher. A meeting took place on August 13 in Papen's presence.* Hitler came in the company of Roehm and Frick, neither of whom had made a favorable impression on Hindenburg. Without offering his visitors his hand or an invitation to sit down, Hindenburg stood leaning on his cane during the twenty-minute meeting. Hitler told him what he thought the old Field Marshal would want to hear: that he wished only to come to power legally, to rebuild the economy, and in foreign affairs to seek full equality for Germany with sovereignty over her own territories. This, of course, must be secured by peaceful means, and to achieve these goals he should be Chancellor. Hindenburg listened gravely and then brought up his objections to naming Hitler as Chancellor: the acts of gangsterism of the Party—and the murders in Koenigsberg and Silesia—which had increased since the elections. He said that Hitler would have to show that he could work with others, with the Center and the Right, in a coalition government where power was divided and not concentrated in one person. Hitler said he did not want or demand all power in his hands. He would be

---

* Hitler had talked with Papen the day before, when Papen had tried to persuade him to become Vice-Chancellor.

ready to name non-Party specialists to key jobs, and did not expect all the posts in the cabinet to go to the Nazis. But he came, he said, to present his case as the leader of the largest party. He would not be Vice-Chancellor or head a coalition government under a mandate of the Reichstag. He needed to be freed of the debates and footlessness of the Parliament and therefore wanted the President to appoint him as Chancellor of another "presidential" cabinet.

Nothing Hitler said at this meeting would be likely to alienate Hindenburg, who thought no more of the powerless, nonfunctioning Parliament than Hitler did. The only thing lacking at the moment was Hindenburg's confidence in him. The first time they had met, on October 10, 1931, Hindenburg had been unimpressed by the obsequious little man who would campaign against him. Hitler might be appointed Minister of Communications at the most, he had told Schleicher after that first meeting (Schleicher, with his love for maneuver and his dream of controlling Hitler, wanted the Nazis brought into the Government), but he would not make him head of the Government. Now, five months and one election later, he was still of the same opinion. Papen would change his mind before the President did.

The immediate occasion of Papen's downfall was the sentencing to death of five Nazis who had killed a Communist in Potempa during the night of August 10, 1932. The killing had been a heinous crime, even for a murderous time. The victim, a coal miner named Konrad Pietrzuch, had been trampled to death—worked over for a half hour before he died, with his mother looking on. The only defense for the SA men was that they were drunk. Papen, just before the crime was committed, had succeeded in getting a presidential decree that provided for the death penalty for political murders. The court, under the circumstances, could do nothing but find the chief culprits guilty and to sentence them to death under the decree. The case produced an outburst of fury from the National Socialists. When the verdict was announced, Hitler sent a telegram: "My comrades, in the face of this monstrous judgment of blood I feel myself bound to you in limitless loyalty. Your freedom is from this moment a question of our honor, the battle against a regime, under which this is possible, our duty." The defense lawyer compared the SA men to brave soldiers; they were acting, he said, under superior orders in attacking an enemy insurgent. Liberal non-Nazi papers that were opposed to capital punishment also protested against the death penalty, and Papen, who had denounced the former Prussian Government for its evenhanded treatment of Right and Left, commuted the sentence to life imprisonment on September 2.[66]

But this was not enough for Hitler. The SA men were martyrs, and he could have no pacts with a regime that permitted such heroes even to be arrested. When the Reichstag reconvened on August 30, Goering, as the representative of the largest party, had been elected President with the help of the votes of the Center, whose strategy now, like Papen's, was to attempt to bring the National Socialists into a coalition government. Papen had prepared a report of his administration to be delivered at the first working session of the Reichstag, which was held on September 12, but to his consternation Goering immediately gave the floor to the Communist deputy Ernst Torgler, who proposed a vote of no confidence in the Papen Government. Papen tried in vain to forestall the vote by dissolving the Reichstag before it could act, using a presidential order Hindenburg had signed and sent posthaste during a half-hour adjournment. The order of dissolution was in the red portfolio that traditionally contained such decrees. But Goering steadily looked in the other direction as Papen held the portfolio before him, and when the ballots were counted Papen had been voted out 512 to 42, probably a not inaccurate reflection of his popularity in the country at large. New elections were set for November 6. Since the Reichstag had been dissolved by Hindenburg's decree, Papen remained in office.

The election of November 6 for the first time reduced the Nazi vote—by almost two million in the popular vote and by thirty-four seats in the Reichstag. National Socialism was a party of discontent and desperation, and, aside from the fanatical inner core, it won and lost millions of votes in proportion to the seeming hope or hopelessness of returning to the norms of society. The election was held after a slight drop in the rate of unemployment (it went down 123,000 in October), and after Papen, acting under an emergency decree, had allocated 2,200,000 RM to make work. Just before the election there had been a transport strike in Berlin, in which Nazis and Communists had combined to paralyze the city. The Potempa murder had also occurred, and in the brawls of July and August 300 people were killed and 1,200 wounded as a result of acts of political terror that dramatized the drive of violence of the Party.

Papen now turned again to Hindenburg, asking him to breach the constitution. An emergency existed, he said, that had not been foreseen when the document was written. He needed a few months to govern without a parliament and without another election, and in that time he would propose fundamental changes in the structure of the Government and in the constitution. He predicted that in the plebiscite that would follow, the Nazi wave would subside further than it had subsided on November 6.[*] In other words, he was proposing an interim dictatorship that, since it had no visible popular support, could only depend on the President and the Army to keep it in power. But now Schleicher revealed his own ambitions. Like Papen, he wanted a new constitution, and he would find his mass following in the Left. He declared his willingness to take over the chancellorship. He could

* Papen wanted a return to the Bismarckian era: Prussia and the Reich would be united through the person of the President. There would be a bicameral parliament, the upper house to be appointed by Hindenburg and the lower elected, but with the voters exercising unequal franchises; heads of families and war veterans would get more than one vote; and the Government would be independent of the Reichstag (Meissner and Wilde, *op. cit.*, p. 281).

split the Nazis, he said, with his close relations with Gregor Strasser and other Socialist dissidents inside the Party, and when the Reichstag reconvened get a majority from the orthodox Right and from the Left wing of the divided National Socialists. Papen declared that Schleicher could not possibly accomplish this, and Hindenburg agreed. Papen was to go ahead and form his new cabinet. As Papen and Schleicher parted after the meeting, each kept his illusions. The two were reduced to a struggle for the fading mind of the President, who alone would determine how and whether the Reichswehr would be used to support a government he constituted. As they parted, Schleicher said to Papen (what applied to both of them as well as to the shade of Martin Luther): "Little monk, little monk, you have chosen a hard road."

Now Schleicher played a card Papen could not match. When the Cabinet met on December 2, Schleicher said the appointment of Papen as Chancellor in another presidential cabinet would mean civil war; the Nazis would rise and the Reichswehr could not guarantee public security in a civil war. Nothing could have been better calculated to affect Hindenburg than such a warning. It was backed by a study a general staff officer, Lieutenant Colonel Eugen Ott (later Ambassador to Japan), had made of the forces at the disposal of the Army in the event of a National Socialist uprising, which might involve another general strike on the part of the Left. The Army always had great respect for the power of the masses. The disorders at the end of the war, the wave of strikes in the first years of peace, and the mass demonstrations of the Right and Left had stamped the thinking of men like Lieutenant Colonel Ott and Hindenburg. Ott thought that policing the Reich in the event of large-scale disorders, which would give the Poles the opportunity of invading the Corridor and the French of again occupying the Rhine-Ruhr area, presented too many dangers for the Army to risk.* In addition, Schleicher pointed out that the Prussian police in particular were badly infected with Nazi propaganda; and, if the Communists should also use the occasion to rise (they were now the third largest party in the Reich, having won 89 seats in the Reichstag in the last election), the army could not guarantee the order or the safety of the country. Hindenburg had to reverse his decision. On December 2 he appointed Schleicher the new Chancellor and Defense Minister. Papen got a photograph from the President, with an inscription reserved usually for military burials: "I had a comrade."

Papen was offered the ambassadorship to France, which under most cir-

* Ott's calculation, although exaggerating the likelihood of the Nazis and Communists staging a rising, was not far off with regard to Poland. On March 6, 1933, Marshal Józef Pilsudski ordered a Polish marine infantry battalion to march into the Westerplatte, situated at the entrance to the Danzig harbor, without permission of the High Commissioner. This was interpreted in some quarters as an attempt to provoke a German countermeasure, which in turn would lead the French to join the Poles in taking action (Hans Ross, "Die 'Praeventivkriegsplaene' Pilsudskis von 1933," in *Vierteljahrshefte fuer Zeitgeschichte*, Vol. III, No. 4, 1955, pp. 344–63).

cumstances he would have been glad to accept, but Hindenburg asked him to stay in Berlin to be on hand to advise him in these uncertain days. Papen continued to live in the Wilhelmstrasse. The house he now occupied was formerly assigned to the Minister of the Interior. It adjoined the Reich Chancellery, where Hindenburg was temporarily staying while the presidential palace was being repaired. Schleicher, newly married, continued to live in a house on which he doted in the Alsenstrasse. The gardens at the back of the houses in which Hindenburg and Papen were living adjoined, and the two could meet often, without ceremony or the knowledge of others. Now that Papen was no longer in office, the President believed he could rely more than ever on his disinterested judgment.

Schleicher had only one small success in his short term of office. He had always taken the point of view held by many of the Reichswehr officers of the Seeckt period that Germany must be the balance between East and West. He had conducted a good part of the negotiations with the emissaries of the Bolshevik Government when, after World War I, the two pariah powers made their quasi-military alliance, with Russian officers being schooled in Germany and the forbidden German tank and air cadres being trained in Russia. Schleicher, though, was fundamentally a Westerner, deeply religious, friendly to Socialists like Ebert and the moderate labor-union leaders. In regard to the Soviet Union, he was a supporter only of the Russian military counterweight that, properly used, would enable Germany to match the power of France and the Little Entente.

He told his friends in London and Paris—among them, François-Poncet—that this was their last chance to preserve a non-Nazi Reich. Either Germany would be freed of the onesided disarmament provisions of the Versailles Treaty or Hitler would come in. The result was the Five-Power Declaration of December 11, 1932, in which Germany was given the theoretical right to arms equality.

But this was a straw tossed into a whirlwind. Theoretical equality could not build a political resistance to Hitler, nor could the Nazis be split with what Schleicher had to offer. Schleicher had two cards to play. He offered the vice-chancellorship to one of Hitler's chief critics in the Party, Gregor Strasser, who had long been disaffected by the sharp turn to the Right that Hitler had made in his desperate search for funds and support from the conservative men of affairs in heavy industry and banking. Strasser was urged to accept Schleicher's offer by an influential group in the Party—Frick, Feder, and Rosenberg, all of whom, with the exception of Feder, were loyal to Hitler—for the Defense Minister had something to offer the Left wing of the Nazis. Schleicher promised them that the Reichswehr would pay the Party debts, which had grown so huge that the payroll and printer's bills of the *Voelkischer Beobachter* could no longer be met.

The troubles of the Party were many. The reduced vote in the November election, Hindenburg's adamant refusal to name Hitler as Chancellor, and the internal Party struggle gave some color to Schleicher's dream that this was the time to bring the movement down with part of its own weight. Strasser, cautious and undecided, told Schleicher he would accept the vice-chancellorship only if Hitler gave his permission, but Hitler instead read him out of the Party. The Fuehrer stormed into Berlin and the Hotel Kaiserhof to overpower his Left-wing critics with the tumult of eloquence and energy that had brought him from the beer halls to become Germany's most powerful political figure, with that fanatical conviction and rhetoric that so many audiences would never be able to withstand. Hitler, in his new orientation, had had to discard Feder's doctrine of the slavery of interest—the only tie that bound Feder and National Socialism.

That the Party, bankrupt and held together only by the iron will of one man, was in precarious shape is clear from the testimony of men who, like Goebbels, were wholly devoted to Hitler's cause. Hitler said, in one of the moments of despair he was given to, that if the Party fell to pieces it would take him only three minutes to finish himself with a pistol. Before his Gauleiters in the Kaiserhof he shouted and wept, and a greatly devoted follower like Streicher wept with him at the thought of the possibility of betrayal. Later, in other times of crisis, especially during the war, Hitler would give the same evidence of his uncanny ability to convince even those who had the most serious doubts of the wisdom of his decisions. The 1932 plot against his leadership was mastered, as so many crises would be, by the overwhelming tornado of oratory of the man who had brought them all, from Strasser to Goering, to the threshold of power. But in the background other potent forces were working for Hitler. The conservative Right was bankrupt, not in money but in ideas. A letter written in November, 1932, to Hindenburg and signed by Schacht, the Cologne banker Baron von Schroeder, the former Reich Chancellor Cuno, and great magnates and industrialists like Krupp, Siemens, Thyssen, Bosch, Woermann, and Voegler, asked the President to appoint Hitler as Chancellor. It was an enlightening list of signers. Thyssen had supported Hitler since the 1920's, but others, like Krupp and Schacht, had disliked and distrusted him until recently. One by one, they had become convinced that there was no longer an alternative between the extreme Right and the extreme Left.

The letter referred to the regime of the former Chancellor. It praised Papen and his Cabinet for their good will but pointed out that, as the election of November 6 had shown, they had no popular support. In order to overcome the class struggle, to unify Germany, and to bring an end to the fruitless and endless elections, Hitler had to be brought in as Chancellor. The signers noted that if the Communist Party were excluded, the combined nationalist forces had a majority in the electorate. They attacked Papen's plan to change the constitution, charging that this would only increase the economic and political unrest. They said they were writing because they felt it their bounden duty to ask Hindenburg to form a presidential cabinet, this time under leadership of the man with the greatest number of followers in the country—a man who would appoint the best non-Nazi technical and political advisers available.[67]

While Papen could not have signed this letter, it was not long before he came to have precisely the same views as those of his fellow conservatives who had sent it. Since the conservative parties had not been able to supply an alternative to Hitler, they could only defeat him in 1932 by convincing Hindenburg and the Army that they had to move against him. An easier, more plausible course was to try to capture him, to bring him to reasonable policies by giving him limited power and surrounding him with dependable advisers while the President was still alive to help hold him in check.

Papen now saw Schleicher as his enemy. Schleicher was the man who had turned him out of office—the man who, conspiring with the Left wing of the Nazi Party, had forced Hindenburg's hand in appointing a regime without Papen and without any purpose other than that of a naked military dictatorship. However, Schleicher's attempt to buy his way into the support of the National Socialists with Reichswehr funds could not have much success when the resources of the signers of the letter to Hindenburg could be placed at Hitler's disposal.

Papen, on his part, had both the ear of the President and a forum in the Deutscher Klub, commonly called Herrenklub. This was an organization in Berlin to which belonged many leading industrialists, high officials, and landowners; also many conservative politicians who kept in close touch with the politics and leadership of the chief parties, mainly of the Right. It published a magazine called *Der Ring* (*The Circle*), in which Papen had had an article on the need for the unification of the nationalist forces. Schleicher had called the article to the attention of Hindenburg when Papen was the President's candidate for the chancellorship. Now Papen used the Herrenklub against Schleicher. In a speech given before some three hundred of these leading members of the conservative parties, he reviewed the events of his own term of office as well as the present state of Germany, and in the view of many of those present he "called in" the Nazis, for his speech made it clear that only with the collaboration of Hitler could the essential changes be made and stability be assured.[68] No copies of the speech have survived. The reports on its text conflict, but at the very least it can be said that it caused the pro-Nazi Cologne banker Schroeder, who had been one of the signers of the letter to Hindenburg, to ask Papen to have a talk with the Fuehrer.

The Herrenklub speech was given on December 16, 1932. On December 19 Wilhelm Keppler, a friend of Schroeder's and a Nazi, wrote to Hitler that Papen in his talk with Schroeder had said he now realized that Hitler's becoming Chancellor was essential and he would back the Fuehrer's candidacy fully. Papen had told Schroeder that he had come to see how undependable Schleicher was and that Hindenburg, too, now realized the unworthy part that Schleicher had played in many matters, including the ending of Papen's chancellorship. Papen saw the need for a political change, wanted Hitler to become Chancellor, and wanted to have a meeting with him at Schroeder's home.

Papen declared that Keppler's letter was written only to overcome Hitler's aversion to him and that he had never spoken to Keppler, who had used this means to get Hitler to come to the meeting, for Keppler preferred Papen to Schleicher and in a letter of December 26 wrote Schroeder that he hoped Hitler's dislike of Papen might be overcome. Schleicher, not Papen, he said, had really been responsible for the failure of Hitler's talk with Hindenburg on August 13—a failure that Hitler had ascribed largely to Papen.

But Keppler would scarcely have told the Fuehrer categorically that Papen would back the Fuehrer's candidacy only to have Papen tell Hitler, when they met on January 4 at Baron von Schroeder's, that he was proposing another vice-chancellorship or, as he called it, a condominium with Schleicher as Chancellor. The meeting was obviously held because Papen, as he himself said, was convinced that Hitler and his Nazis had to come into the Government, under conditions that so far as possible would keep the Fuehrer in check. Neither Schroeder nor Keppler would have been so much in favor of the meeting if all Papen intended to offer Hitler was merely a strengthened version of what the Fuehrer had already refused when Papen on August 12 had tried to persuade him to go in his Cabinet. A vice-chancellorship, even with assurance that it was a condominium, would scarcely have appealed more strongly to Hitler than the offer Papen had made before, when he had promised that he would step down after a period of collaboration had demonstrated Hitler's willingness and ability to work in a coalition.[69]

The highly secret meeting between Hitler and Papen took place at Schroeder's house on January 4. Hitler was accompanied by Hess, Himmler, and Keppler. So careful had the security measures been that the rest of Hitler's escort waited two hours in their automobiles on the road to Duesseldorf, without knowing his whereabouts.[70] As Papen entered the house, he noticed that he was being photographed. So was Hitler when he arrived, although Papen did not see the cameraman. Then, as it turned out, a photo was taken of the two men by a hidden photographer as they were shaking hands on their departure. The newspaper Schleicher had been subsidizing from his Ministerial funds, the *Taegliche Rundschau*, had paid one of Hitler's SD men to keep them informed of his plans for travel, and it had sent photographers and reporters to the scene.* The next day the *Taegliche Rundschau* carried the story on its front page.

At Nuremberg Papen testified that he had talked with Hitler about participating in Schleicher's Government—not of Hitler's coming in as Chan-

---

* Berndorff says the SD man received 3,000 RM for the information he sent on (H. R. Berndorff, *General zwischen Ost und West* [Hamburg: Hoffmann and Campe, n.d.], p. 225).

cellor but of the Party's entering the Government and of his accepting the same vice-chancellorship he had kept declining. Papen's account of the meeting cannot be true, nor can his explanation of his Herrenklub talk be true. There would have been no point in asking Hitler again to become Vice-Chancellor. The belief of some shrewd observers at the time, that Papen offered Hitler a duumvirate, an equal sharing of power with himself, is the most plausible account of what went on.* Papen wanted to be Chancellor, and if he could not he hoped to come as close to the occupancy of the office as possible. In any event, Schleicher's dark suspicions when he incredulously saw the pictures of the meeting were certainly justified, despite the letter that Papen wrote him that afternoon, after he knew a photograph had been taken, telling him of the meeting and how he had acted on Schleicher's behalf.

Schleicher asked the President not to receive Papen except in his presence, after what he regarded as black treachery, but Hindenburg was not to be told by a subordinate what visitors he could receive and with whom he could consult. He not only continued to see Papen but also listened to his advice, which now was flatly to bring Hitler into the Government as Chancellor. All that was left to Schleicher was again to try to make a coalition with splinter groups, either with Hugenberg and his small nationalist faction, or with Gregor Strasser and the dissident Nazis, for these two could not be combined. But Strasser told Hindenburg (Schleicher had succeeded in arranging a meeting between them) that the National Socialists could not be split. The one possible source of a mass following for Schleicher had disappeared. He could only rule under Article 48 of the constitution—a means which, he had only recently told the President, would bring on civil war if it was attempted by Papen.[71]

The election in Lippe held on January 15, 1933, was used by Hitler as a major test of strength. The Fuehrer campaigned with all the panoply and ferocity he could conjure up, and the National Socialists won 9 out of 21 seats (47.8 per cent) in the state legislature and 39.6 per cent of the popular vote (up 17 per cent over November).[72] In 1929 they had not had a single seat. The conservative Right, including Hugenberg's German Nationalists, lost a third of their votes, and the Strasser following inside the Party had obviously shown itself to be without influence on the rank and file of the voters. It would have been a minor election in another time; now it was blown up as a nationwide major victory.† Hitler had shown his Party to be

* Papen said he offered Hitler a duumvirate with Schleicher. But see Otto Meissner, *Staatssekretaer unter Ebert, Hindenburg und Hitler* [Hamburg: Hoffmann and Campe, 1950], p. 261; and Erwin Wichert, *Dramatische Tage in Hitlers Reich* [Stuttgart, 1952], p. 22; also Schroeder 3337-PS (IZG).

† As Wucher points out, however, the Nazis received only 5,000 more votes than they had received in the November 6 election in Hesse and were 10 per cent under their July, 1932, total (Albert Wucher, *Die Fahne hoch* [Munich: Sueddeutscher Verlag, 1963], p. 142).

united behind him. On the 17th he met with Hugenberg, who was confronted with a choice between finding some way to accept collaboration with Hitler or being swamped in the political tides that, as the election in Lippe had shown, were running strongly against him. Hugenberg had told Schleicher he was willing to participate in the Government as Economics Minister, but Schleicher could only accept that offer by dropping the master plan he still clung to, of splitting Strasser's Left-wing Nazis from Hitler. The last opposition to Hitler was crumbling. Hugenberg's party had 51 seats in the Reichstag, not enough to be of any great help to Schleicher, to whom even the SPD seemed a possible ally, for it had 121 seats, which would be a substantial backing. Conceivably, the SPD would make an alliance with him rather than see Hitler come to power, but it declined any offers from Schleicher.

The parliamentary system was through, whether Papen or Schleicher or Hitler was called in as head of the Government, but in the case of Hitler no breach of the constitution would occur—at least not at the start of a Hitler chancellorship. Papen or Schleicher could rule only under Article 48, and under a presidential decree designed for emergencies that now had no foreseeable end. In Schleicher's case this would have meant a naked military dictatorship. With Hitler, a coalition government commanding all the forces of the Right, of the so-called "National Rising," and some two-fifths of the Reichstag would be in office. Schleicher's last card was a weak one and played much too late in the game: he tried to secure French consent, through François-Poncet, to adding 200,000 SA men to the armed forces, and he told Hindenburg he would enlist this number of volunteers and use them if necessary against the National Socialists. But this was merely a variation on the very tune he had rejected. He was offering nothing new. He was merely offering to remain in place of Papen, and he had had no more success in winning popular support or political backing in the Reichstag than Papen and far less than Bruening.

On January 22, 1933, another meeting took place, this one at Ribbentrop's luxurious house in Berlin-Dahlem. Hitler, Frick, and Goering met with Papen and the President's two other close advisers—Hindenburg's son Oskar and Staatssekretaer Otto Meissner. Meissner talked with Goering, who was very conciliatory. Goering said that the National Socialists by no means demanded sole power, that they would collaborate with the other parties, and that they asked for only two Ministries out of twelve in a Hitler Cabinet, which would be a working coalition of the National Socialists and the other nationalist parties. The National Socialists would respect the constitution; their goal was to come to power and to remain in power legally and after that the monarchy might be restored. Oskar, who had always opposed naming Hitler as Chancellor, came away from the meeting he had alone with Hitler silent and preoccupied. He said little to Meissner during their drive back, but what he said revealed that he had been won over: there was no avoiding naming Hitler as Chancellor. The Fuehrer was making enough concessions and solemn promises to give a plausible reason for appointing him.[73] Colonel von Hindenburg, who had met Hitler before, when the Fuehrer had presented himself to his father, now was certain that bringing Hitler into the Government was a grim necessity.

Papen played the leading role from the time of his Herrenklub speech until Hitler became Chancellor. The Fuehrer some years later, in 1937, in the presence of Austrian Chancellor Schuschnigg, thanked him: "In the decisive hour of 1933, you saved the Reich from chaos by making it possible that the controls were placed in my hands."

PAPEN: "Indeed my Fuehrer."

HITLER: "I shall never forget it, Herr von Papen." [74]

On January 23 Schleicher phoned Meissner and asked him how he had enjoyed his meal at Ribbentrop's house. Having given this evidence of the competence of his intelligence service, Schleicher met with Hindenburg and talked with him for two hours. He told the President the Nazis were through, that many of them in their disillusionment were ready to go over to the Communists, and that he and the President had only to show their teeth to set them in full retreat. The British and French would approve an increase in the Reichswehr, and with the flood of young volunteers the Army could put down any uprising. All Schleicher needed from the President was a blank check: the full power to rule and to use the Army. These were notions Hindenburg could not accept; he had rejected them when they were presented by Papen. Civil war was anathema to him.

Now he was warned against Schleicher on every side. Not a newspaper, with the exception of the *Taegliche Rundschau*, supported Schleicher and the military dictatorship he would install. The Center and SPD leaders told Hindenburg that Schleicher's plans meant a breach of the constitution. Schleicher wanted the dissolution of the Reichstag, which was to convene on January 31, and he wanted new elections to be indefinitely postponed. But under the constitution the latest possible date for an election after the dissolution of the Reichstag was sixty days, and the competent Reichstag committee had just voted against any further postponement of the session. Furthermore, the Nazis continued to make promises, and the most appealing of them came from Goering, whom Hindenburg could trust more than the other National Socialists including Hitler, for he was a war hero, a holder of Germany's highest decorations. Goering told Meissner that it might prove possible to reestablish the monarchy at some time in the future, thus nurturing one of Hindenburg's fondest dreams after he had reluctantly told the Kaiser he must abdicate.

On January 26 two military men called on the President: Generals Kurt von Hammerstein-Equord and Erich von dem Bussche. Bussche had to make a routine military report to Hindenburg, and Hammerstein made use of the occasion to go along at a time when he knew no civilians could be present, since Hindenburg would permit only soldiers to discuss military matters. Hammerstein apparently told Hindenburg the Army would not tolerate Hitler as Chancellor, but he (as well as Schleicher) was also opposed to Papen, whose appointment might well mean civil war. What Hammerstein seemingly was trying to do was to keep Schleicher in office, as well as to shut the door to Hitler and Papen, but he had no success. The aged Field Marshal told him and Bussche he knew what the Army would accept, and they should prepare for the next maneuvers and stop meddling in politics. But before they left, Hindenburg said, "You can't possibly believe, gentlemen, that I will make the Austrian corporal Reich Chancellor." In the course of the next few days, Hindenburg would discover he had no choice but to do just that.*

The visit was the ambivalent start of the generals' conspiracy against Hitler. Schleicher resigned on January 28, when, with nothing to lose, he accused Hindenburg of the final crime, *Treubruch* (breach of faith), in dealing behind Schleicher's back with Papen and Hitler. The next day, in a meeting at the Reichswehrministerium at which Generals Wilhelm Adam, von Hammerstein-Equord, and von dem Bussche (and one other officer, probably Colonel Kurt von Bredow) were present, Schleicher was urged to set up military rule—even, if necessary, to arrest Hindenburg, to call out the Potsdam garrison with orders to shoot.†

* Compare Wheeler-Bennett and Wolfgang Sauer (Karl Dietrich Bracher, Wolfgang Sauer, and Gerhard Schulz, *Die nationalsozialistische Machtergreifung* [Cologne: Westdeutscher Verlag, 1962]), who believe that Hammerstein, acting for Schleicher, wanted Hitler to be named Chancellor to prevent the appointment of Papen. See also Schwerin von Krosigk (*op. cit.*), Berndorff (*op cit.*), Meissner (*op cit.*), Hermann Foertsch (*Schuld and Verhaengnus* [Stuttgart: Deutsche Verlag-Anstalt, 1951]), Meissner and Wilde (*op cit.*), Gerhard Ritter (*Das deutsche Problem* [Munich: R. Oldenbourg Verlag, 1952]), Francis Carsten, and the account of Hammerstein's son Kunrat Freiherr von Hammerstein, "*Schleicher, Hammerstein und die Machtuebernahme*," in *Frankfurter Hefte*, Nov., 1956. See also General Freiherr von dem Bussche, *Frankfurter Allgemeine Zeitung*, February 5, 1952. The testimony is conflicting. Hammerstein's aversion to Hitler and Nazism was long-standing. Bussche says flatly that Hammerstein spoke against naming Hitler. Hammerstein's own memorandum (written in 1935 after Schleicher's murder), which declared he had urged Hitler's appointment, was dictated, certainly in large part, by prudence. In January, 1934, Schleicher, too, wrote in the *Vossische Zeitung* that since the summer of 1931 he had steadfastly been in favor of a National Socialist government. Hammerstein did not want Hitler as Reich Chancellor (in 1939, at the time of the Polish campaign, he was prepared to arrest him when Hitler planned to visit Hammerstein's headquarters on the Rhine), but he wanted civil war even less than he wanted Hitler. On the afternoon of January 29, 1933, he went to Hitler to express his concern over the situation and to find out whether Hitler thought the President was serious in negotiating with him or was going through motions. If the latter, Hammerstein said he would again attempt to influence decisions in order to prevent a heavy misfortune for the fatherland.

† Egon Kubuschok, Papen's lawyer at Nuremberg, stated in 1947 that Goering had told him that Schleicher, in an effort to remain Minister of Defense in Hitler's Cabinet, had offered on January 9, 1933, to call out the Potsdam garrison to arrest Hindenburg if he continued to oppose naming Hitler as Chancellor. Kubuschok's statement was confirmed by Neurath, who was present, as was Keitel, when Goering informed Kubuschok of the matter (Kubuschok affidavit, January 26, 1947). In the light of Schleicher's complicated

At Nuremberg two witnesses said that Schleicher had wanted to arrest Hitler as well as the President in a last effort to stop the Nazis. A rumor that a military coup was in the offing, that the Potsdam garrison had been alerted and given orders to shoot, reached Goering and Hitler. The story undoubtedly played a role in the killing of Schleicher by an SD detachment the next year during the murders that accompanied the liquidation of Roehm and his high officers of the SA. But Schleicher never made such a decision. That he played with the idea, discussed it with General von Hammerstein-Equord and Colonel von Bredow and others, is undoubtedly true (it was corroborated by Wilhelm Leuschner, former Minister of the Interior in Hesse, who said that even in February, 1933, Schleicher was still planning a revolt), but no orders reached the Potsdam garrison, and none was ever sent out to raise the Army against Hitler, not to mention the President. Schleicher could not have played that desperate card against Germany's greatest war hero, although he might have played it earlier against Hitler and won (cf. Goering, Chapt. 3).[75]

It is not known who made the suggestion, but it was in any event turned down, for this could only be the height of folly, as Schleicher knew. To call out the Army against its greatest war hero and the most popular political figure in Germany could be nothing but disastrous. Nor was the Army itself of one mind—far from it. Many of the generals detested the Party and its leader and saw clearly where Hitler's coming to power would be likely to lead, but even as supposedly cool-headed an officer as General Hans von Seeckt had advised his sister to vote for Hitler in the elections of 1932. General von Blomberg, who was soon to be chosen Minister of Defense, was an admirer of the Fuehrer, as were many of the younger officers.* Schleicher was left with nothing but his will to be Chancellor, and as for the Reichswehr, he and everyone else knew that in any emergency it would obey the Field Marshal who was also the President.

Schleicher tendered his resignation on January 28, and Hindenburg asked Papen to conduct the negotiations with Hitler for establishing the new government. In principle this presented no great difficulty: Hitler must be Chancellor, for that was his major condition; he must preside over a presidential cabinet, as had Papen and Schleicher before him; the Reichstag must be dissolved; and new elections must be called for. The elections were a stumbling block, for Hugenberg, with fifty-one German Nationalist deputies behind him, had to be brought into this Cabinet of so-called National Regeneration, and, still smarting under the defeat of his party in Lippe, he

last-minute intrigues, Goering may well have been speaking the truth. Schleicher at the end was wildly seeking any means to keep a decisive voice in public affairs, and he may have made the offer. But he did nothing beyond that.

* Bruening said that Blomberg was the only Nazi general in 1931; that he had had a bad fall from a horse and was in a critical nervous state; and that Bruening had intended to retire him. Blomberg was sent to Geneva as head of the German military mission as a prelude to his leaving active service (Wucher, op. cit., pp. 149–150).

wanted no new elections that would be all too likely to reduce its strength still further. Hitler was to have two National Socialist Ministers: Frick as Minister of the Interior for the Reich and Goering as Minister Without Portfolio and Minister of the Interior for Prussia, the latter a post that would place the Nazis in charge of the police of the largest state and the one in which the capital was situated. The rest of the Cabinet were the kind of men both Hindenburg and Papen liked and trusted: Franz Seldte, a leader of the Stahlhelm, and conservatives like Neurath and Schwerin von Krosigk, who had been in Papen's Cabinet, as had Franz Guertner, the Minister of Justice.

The rumor of a coup by the Potsdam garrison under Schleicher gave the final impetus to Papen's efforts to form a cabinet on Hitler's new terms. Now there seemed no time to be lost for him, or for the President, or for Hitler. Hindenburg's last doubts were dispelled by Papen, who told him what the President's son Oskar and Staatssekretaer Meissner had been saying these last days—that no sensible alternative existed to Hitler's heading a coalition Cabinet in which he would be greatly outnumbered by the conservatives and he and his movement put to constructive work. Furthermore, said Papen, Hitler had given signs of his reasonableness in agreeing to head such a cabinet, which would bring about the long-desired unity of the Right after the Center and the Social Democrats had failed.

Hindenburg had to choose between these alternatives: (1) war against the National Socialists or the possibility of a civil war with either Papen or Schleicher as Chancellor heading a government without a popular following and denounced by all the parties in the Reichstag; and (2) a cabinet under Hitler, in a government that would rule legally and with a vast popular following. Hindenburg would still have preferred to appoint Papen Chancellor. However, if Papen were Vice-Chancellor, as the second man in a kind of duumvirate, and Hitler chief of a coalition that could appeal to the President against him, the Fuehrer might be tamed. If Hindenburg could not have Papen, then he would have Hitler and Papen, and he would appoint as Minister of Defense a man who would, if necessary, command the Army to move against either Hitler or Schleicher.

Papen was delighted. He was to be not only Vice-Chancellor but also the deputy of the Fuehrer; and Hindenburg, who was still wary of Hitler, was to meet the latter only in Papen's presence. The Foreign Minister was Papen's own appointee, as were two other members of the Cabinet, Schwerin von Krosigk and Guertner. Papen and his friends had not lost, he told himself. On the contrary, they had captured the demagogue who would now be put to work to serve the cause of Germany's regeneration by joining the forces of the conservative Right.

On January 30, when the man whom Hindenburg had chosen as the next Minister of Defense, General von Blomberg, arrived at the Anhalter station in Berlin, having been ordered back by the President from the Disarmament

Conference at Geneva, he was met by two officers with different orders. One of them was there on behalf of Schleicher, ordering him to report to Blomberg's superior, General von Hammerstein-Equord, immediately. The other was the President's son Oskar, sent to bring Blomberg directly to Hindenburg. The chain of command began with the President as Commander in Chief of the armed forces, and Blomberg was driven to the presidential palace, where, when Hindenburg administered the oath of office, he became the first member of the Hitler Government. Schleicher had played his last card. Blomberg might have been arrested had he reported to Hammerstein-Equord. Papen told him he had made the right decision.

At 10:45 A.M. the Cabinet met in Meissner's office, but it was not sworn in by the President at 11:00 as had been planned. Hitler did what he was so often to do in the years to come when he thought he had the opposition in a corner: he presented new conditions. He irritably told Papen that Goering should be Reichskommissar of Prussia as well as its Minister of the Interior, and then he sullenly agreed to wait as Papen promised him that the President would appoint Goering to this office when, after a little while, the Fuehrer had won his confidence. But Hitler refused to budge an inch on the dissolution of the Reichstag and the new elections. Hugenberg, too, was adamant, while Papen, Goering, and Hitler did their best to overcome his objections. Hitler promised he would keep his present cabinet in office no matter what the results of the elections might be, and he would even add members of other parties, of the Center and the Bavarian Volkspartei. Finally Hugenberg gave ground. He agreed to let the President make the decision. Then the Cabinet filed in, twenty minutes late, to be presented to the President and to be given the oath of office. Papen again found reasons for letting Hitler have his way. New elections, he thought, would give the conservatives a chance to improve their position in the Reichstag and in the Cabinet, forgetting how well the Nazis had done in the recent past when their street fighters had been held in leash by the police and public resistance. He took no account of what they would be able to do now with the prestige of office, with Hitler the legal head of government, and with Goering in control of the Prussian police.

Hitler's taking over the Cabinet and then the Reichstag as well as the mind of the President came step by step but very rapidly. As Papen was to say later, he was the representative of a Fuehrer who would tolerate no representative. On the night of January 30 Hitler stood at the window of the Chancellor's palace snuffing up the homage of the shouting, singing, jubilant SA and SS as they marched by with their flaming torches. It was one of the two or three great moments of the life of the half-educated, Austrian-born, former corporal (Gefreiter) in the German Army, who had lived in flophouses and had dreamed of taking his revenge on the rich and powerful who had once defeated him. They were the same forces that had defeated Germany—the Jews, the plutocrats, the Communists—and now he would confound them all as Chancellor of the Reich. While the following story is apocryphal, it reveals a large kernel of truth. Hindenburg, standing at his window in the presidential palace watching the Brownshirts parade, was said to have commented: "I did not know we had taken so many Russian prisoners."

The atmosphere in the Cabinet in the first days was relatively friendly, and discussions were lively. Hitler did not force a showdown on any issue once the stage was set for the elections. The new government must go before the country as one of nationalist unity as well as revolution. Other things had to be arranged before the role of the Cabinet would become clear. The revolution was to be made not in the Cabinet but in the Reich. The roles of the Reichstag and the Ministers were small by comparison, for they would quickly fall into line when the work to be done in the streets, on the ranks of the opposition, on the press, and on the bureaucracy had begun and heads had begun to roll. Papen had thought in terms of the offices held by the conservatives and their majority of non-Nazis, but the Cabinet was a cork in a whirlpool. The free discussions continued for a little while, but Hitler's eventual decisions were made without any consultation. Hugenberg, although he was Minister of Economics, found out that the trade unions had been dissolved after the Party had taken them over. And after mild objections were raised in the Cabinet session, the first officially tolerated attacks on the Jews began. The conservative members of the Cabinet soon found themselves debating only with one another, for they were ignored as far as practical matters went. Goebbels and Hess were named Ministers in March and April, and by the end of June Hugenberg had resigned.[76]

Hitler concentrated on the key objectives: winning the uncommitted masses in an election, now that the police and the apparatus of the State were under his control, with means of coercion and propaganda never before open to him; and subduing the opposition by legal, semilegal, and illegal means. Every concession made to him was irreversible, and usually he asked for only a little at a time, taking care, until he was ready for the kill, not to show the full length of his claws. Papen, who deluded himself that he was a lion tamer, was never a match for him. "They make a mistake," he said, speaking of the Nazis. "We have hired him [Hitler] for ourselves [*Wir haben ihn uns engagiert*]."[77] But soon Goering was Reichskommissar for Prussia in place of Papen, and Hindenburg met the Fuehrer without Papen. Furthermore, Papen could only support the regime in the election campaign, for as the Vice-Chancellor and deputy of the Fuehrer he could scarcely criticize the Chancellor, even if he had been so disposed, and Papen at that point was no critic of a government he served with so many vain hopes and in whose coming to power he had played a leading role.

Hitler moved with dazzling speed, with the released energy of his years of preparation for this moment. He took every advantage of the mistakes of the enemy, acting with firm decision—something, as the war would show, that was not easy for him in moments of acute crises. But he was on firm ground at this moment of the destruction of his enemies and of accreting power for his revolution. On February 1 the Hamburg Red Front fighters issued a call to arms to their Communist brothers and to all who were not National Socialists: "The day is not far distant when our victorious Red Army that needs no police to protect it, weapon in hand will drive the deadly enemy of the working people to the devil." [78] Hitler knew how to deal with such manifestos—he had been writing them himself for ten years. On February 6 the Reichstag was dissolved and new elections were called for March 5 (the fifth balloting within nine months). The following day Goering, as Minister of the Interior for Prussia, forbade Communist demonstrations and any press attacks against the National Socialist regime. By February 24 the SA and SS and Stahlhelm had been authorized to act as auxiliary police. On February 25 the SA broke into the Communist headquarters in Berlin, the Karl Liebknecht house, and got hold of what they stated to be a large list of incriminating documents written in the same vein as the Hamburg manifesto. Then, on February 27, occurred the event the Nazis knew precisely how to use—the burning of the Reichstag building.

At Nuremberg it was confidently asserted, and for many years thereafter universally believed, that the Nazis, in all likelihood Goering, had engineered the burning in order to use the event precisely as the Party used it— as the pretext for the wholesale arrests of the Communists and for their exclusion as a party from the Reichstag. The following day 4,000 Communists were put in jail. Although the evidence is still unclear as to precisely how the fire was set and whether Marinus van der Lubbe, the anarchist who confessed to the crime, acted alone or had help, there is considerable doubt as to whether the Party engineered the blaze. But it knew what to do with the news of the burning. It was to be a propaganda proof for the President and the electorate that they were being saved by the National Socialist legions, by the Fuehrer and his followers, from a Communist attempt to overthrow the forces of law and order and to do what the Hamburg call to arms proclaimed: "Prepare the way for the victorious Red Army, the victorious Revolution of the Left." On February 28 Hindenburg issued the order his Chancellor asked him for, the Decree for the Protection of the People and the State, setting aside the constitutional guarantees of freedom of speech and freedom of assembly and giving the Hitler Government the right to invade the privacy of the mail, telephone, and telegraph, to make house searches, and to take over police duties formerly exercised by the states.

In the space of two weeks Hitler toured ten cities in his whirlwind campaign, and Papen, along with the other conservatives in the coalition Cabinet, spoke on behalf of the regime they now served together. The great ceremony at the Garrison Church in Potsdam opened the new session of the Reichstag on March 21. No members of the SPD or of the Communist Party were present, but the other parties were all represented. Hindenburg and Hitler were the chief actors in what seemed to be for the first time a unity of the

State under all the forces of the Right—with a vacant place on the platform for the Hohenzollern Emperor, who still haunted Hindenburg, the monarchist who had exiled his King.

In the election of March 5, the National Socialists won 43.9 per cent of the popular vote and 288 seats in a Reichstag of 647 deputies—a majority if the 52 votes if the nationalist parties were added. On the same day an amnesty was announced for the Nazis who had been jailed in the course of the years of terror and battle on the streets of the German cities and towns, including the murderers of Potempa, who only a few months before had been sentenced to death and then had their sentences commuted to life imprisonment.

Important people by the thousands flocked to Hitler now that he was Chancellor of Germany. On March 28 the Catholic bishops' conference at Fulda declared the previous warnings and prohibitions against joining the National Socialists rescinded. Five days earlier, on the fateful March 23, the Enabling Act had been passed, with the Center Party of the clerics and of Bruening voting along with the National Socialists and the Nationalists in favor of turning over to Hitler the powers of the Reichstag. The necessary two-thirds vote would thus have been secured even without the device of using the fire to exclude the Communists from the Reichstag. Only ninety-four members of the SPD voted against the law that delivered Germany, including its Parliament, into Hitler's hands, and 444 deputies voted for it. Papen was in favor of the law, and Hugenberg's deputies voted for it (his party would be dissolved along with all the other parties only three months later). Within two weeks Papen was to lose his post of Reichskommissar of Prussia when Goering took over that function on April 10.

As early as July 6, 1933, Hitler could announce that the revolution was ended, although in fact it had just begun. But the chief laws he had demanded for so many years were enacted or proclaimed. Jews were no longer German citizens, and their participation in the public and private life of Germany was limited; the *Laender* had been brought under the control of Berlin; the Stahlhelm had been made part of the SA; the labor unions had been dissolved at one stroke and brought into a single National Socialist Union; the farmers had been organized; and all parties other than the NSDAP (National Socialist German Workers' Party) were prohibited.

It was mainly conservatives like Papen who made this possible. Their help was critical and decisive. Monsignor Kaas and a caucus of the delegates of the Center Party decided to vote the plenary powers Hitler demanded. Theodor Heuss, the future President of the Bundesrepublik, who detested Hitler, voted for the law against his own will but following the decision of his Democratic Party. Papen, although warned by his advisers, among them Edgar Jung, was for it too. The reason was apparent: The parliamentary system was clearly finished; a large majority of the country had voted against it in the elections of the last year. If the Communists' votes were added, as they should be. to the antiparliamentary bloc, the only democratic parties left were the SPD with 121 seats in the Reichstag and possibly the Center with 74, plus a scattering among the splinter parties. The antiparliamentary parties counted 288 votes of the National Socialists plus 52 of the Black-Red-White front of the nationalist parties and 81 Communists.

Not much morale was left among the wavering, basically uncommitted opposition. The Socialists remained bitterly opposed to Hitler and to any extension of his power, but the Center and the Right could and did go along when he made the dose easy enough to swallow. And precedents existed for the Enabling Act. During World War I the Upper House, the Bundesrat, had been empowered to take any needed steps to make good any economic damage caused by the war. The Reichstag had surrendered its powers for this purpose. And during the Weimar period the use of presidential decrees under the continuing emergency of the postwar years and the depression had become increasingly frequent. Bruening, the democrat, had been forced to rely on this makeshift, as had Papen and Schleicher. Even in 1923 it had been found necessary to give the confirmed democratic statesman Gustav Stresemann emergency powers "to take measures which they [the Government] regard as essential in economic and social matters." Frick's draft of the Enabling Act, which he prepared as Minister of the Interior, was taken almost word for word from the text of the powers granted Stresemann. The power demanded by Frick on behalf of the Fuehrer was: "To take the measures that are necessary for the needs of the people and the State." The only difference was that Stresemann was given the power to promulgate *Verordnungen* (decrees), while Hitler could proclaim laws. Hitler could also feel free to order the arrest of the bitter opponents of the Nazis, and Severing, among many others, was promptly clapped into jail after passage of the Enabling Act.[79]

The same limitation was voted as in the Stresemann case: The power granted was only to last "until the present government was replaced by another." This enabled those who were turning the authority to legislate and to govern over to Adolf Hitler to convince themselves that they were controlling him. The Enabling Act was a grant of powers to the Cabinet, not to the Chancellor, and the Cabinet was a coalition. If Hitler attempted too much, Papen, as Vice-Chancellor, and a majority would vote against him, and the President would sustain them, for he had the right of veto. Thus went the reasoning. The leaders of the Center told themselves that without the grant of power Hitler could govern by his naked will, but the Enabling Act put legal bounds to what he could do by granting the power to the Government, not to one man. Furthermore, Hitler promised he would not misuse the authority, that he would respect the integrity of the *Laender,* and the Center comforted themselves with the knowledge that Hindenburg would not tolerate a one-party Cabinet. Hindenburg had insisted on the coalition, on a division of the Ministries, and if Hitler attempted to take over the entire

Cabinet for the Nazis, the conservative President would intervene. But even with the law of February 28 Hitler had the power under Hindenburg's decree to dissolve a party that threatened the security of the State. When differences grew acute inside the Cabinet and Hugenberg said he would resign and go into opposition, Hitler told him he would dismiss all the members of his German Nationalist People's Party in the government bureaucracy and retire them without their pensions. Hundreds of men who, like Gisevius, had been German Nationalists had already gone over to the Nazis. Anyone with an eye to his own advancement or even to his retirement with a pension could note the direction of a wind that was becoming a gale. By the time Hitler was ready to get rid of Hugenberg and his party on June 27, he could do two things at the same time: accept Hugenberg's resignation and dissolve the German Nationalist People's Party along with all the other parties. No one in the Cabinet could make a last-ditch stand on any one issue. Blomberg was both reassured and confirmed in his belief in Hitler's greatness when the Fuehrer told him the Army would not be used against the Communists. The Army was to protect Germany solely against the foreign enemy. That of course was the deeply held opinion of the Army and of Hindenburg: the police and the armed forces were two separate weapons of the State. A general strike, with its prospect of revolution, presented a far more complicated military problem than any campaign against an external enemy. Thus the decrees and laws following the Reichstag fire were accepted by Blomberg and the higher officers. They made no objection to the dissolution of the legislature and prerogatives of the *Laender*. Bavaria, Wuerttemberg, and the rest of the states were to be governed by Reichskommissars, as Prussia had been since Papen assumed that office, and the constitutional regimes of the *Laender* went overboard without dissent from Blomberg or Hindenburg. Blomberg ordered the Army not to interfere when local officials called for help.[80]

Hitler informed the Cabinet he wanted the swastika flag to supplant the Republic's black, red, and gold. Papen opposed the move and tried to rouse the Cabinet against it, but Blomberg supported Hitler and the matter was settled. Hitler's care to please the President paid off quickly, and by April, Hindenburg told Papen he need no longer be present when he received Hitler. The Fuehrer had viewed this dual audience as evidence of Hindenburg's mistrust and had asked the President to be received alone.

The SA, the Fuehrer told Army officers, was a political organization and had a role in the Government separate from the Wehrmacht. He spoke, as he had done in *Mein Kampf*, about winning *Lebensraum* in the East, about tearing out the Marxists root and branch, and, above all, about Germany's need to rearm. Army officers were not likely to disagree with any of this, and the Army had had enough of politics after Schleicher's futile attempt to govern. As early as February 6, 1933, one of the few pro-Nazi generals, Reichenau, could say, "Never was the Wehrmacht more identified with the State than today." Hitler declared that this was a unique phenomenon in history, when the forces of revolution and the responsible leaders of the most disciplined army in the world united in so hearty a fashion for the service of the people.[81]

Papen made one bold attempt to do what he had promised himself and his friends he would do: bridle the radicalism, the lawlessness of the revolution. In Marburg, on June 17, 1934, he delivered a speech written for him by a young assistant, Edgar Jung, that courageously attempted to rally opposition to the Party fanatics. Papen used the University of Marburg as a platform to reach the ear of the Fuehrer more efficaciously than he could when the two of them were alone or in a Cabinet meeting. As usual, Papen tried to disarm Party critics with a statement of his lofty purposes. He told his audience (and indirectly Hitler) that his sense of duty to the Fuehrer was so great, and so devoted was he to Germany's regeneration, that it "would be a deadly sin not to speak out in this decisive period of the German revolution." Then he plunged into waters that were very nearly to cost him his life a few weeks later, and were to save his life after the war was over.

In the packed auditorium of the university, Papen told the students and faculty:

> We know that rumors and whispering propaganda must be brought out from the darkness where they have taken refuge. Frank and manly discussion is better for the German people than, for instance, a press without an outlet, described by the Minister for Propaganda "as no longer having a face." This deficiency undoubtedly exists. The function of the press should be to inform the Government where deficiencies have crept in, where corruption has settled down, where grave mistakes have been committed, where incompetent men are in the wrong places, where offenses are committed against the spirit of the German revolution. An anonymous or secret information service, however well organized it may be, can never be a substitute for this task of the press. For the newspaper editor is responsible to the law and to his conscience, whereas anonymous news sources are not subject to control and are exposed to the danger of Byzantinism. When therefore the proper organs of public opinion do not shed sufficient light into the mysterious darkness, which at present seems to have fallen upon the German public, the statesman himself must intervene and call matters by their right names.

Such intervention, he continued, would demonstrate that the regime was strong enough to bear honest criticism, something only weaklings could not tolerate. If foreign countries said freedom was dead in Germany, his own plain speaking would, he said, be a proof that the German Government was ready to permit debate on vital (*brennende*) questions.

Next he attacked narrow Party doctrinaires:

> It is a matter of historical truth that the necessity for a fundamental change of course was recognized and urged even by those who shunned the path of revolution through a mass-party. A claim for revolutionary or nationalist monopoly by a certain group, therefore, seems to me exaggerated, quite apart from the fact that it disturbs the community.

After warning against the "misuse by young revolutionaries especially" of the word "reactionary" for those who were conscientiously carrying out their tasks, he commented on the State and the social order:

All of life cannot be organized; otherwise it becomes mechanized. The State is organization; life is growth. . . . The real revolution of the twentieth century . . . is that of the heroic god-bound personality who struggles against . . . the mechanization and collectivization which is only the last degeneration of bourgeois liberalism. . . . The meaning of the new time [*Zeitenwende*] is clear: it concerns the decision between believers and nonbelievers, whether all eternal values would be secularized or not . . .

The time of the emancipation of the lowest class against the higher classes is over. It is not a question of holding one class down—that would be reactionary—but to prevent one class from dominating the State and trying to achieve total control. In that case every natural and divine order would be lost; the permanent revolution would threaten. . . . The goal of the German revolution, if it is really to be valid and a pattern for Europe, must be based on a natural social order . . . true authority [*Herrschaft*] cannot come from one group or class.

The antidemocratic revolution must return to the natural and divine order, he said, and emphasized how much Hitler wanted the German people to retain its feeling for "a genuine, responsible, just authority."

He expressed his thoughts on the single-party system:

Domination by a single party replacing the majority-party system, which rightly has disappeared, appears to me historically as a transitional stage, justified only as long as the safeguarding of the new political change demands it and until the new process of personal selection begins to function.

On the religious question he said:

It is my conviction that the Christian doctrine clearly represents the religious form of all Occidental thinking and that with the reawakening of religious forces the German people also will be permeated anew by the Christian spirit, a spirit the profundity of which is almost forgotten by a humanity that has lived through the nineteenth century. A struggle is approaching: the decision as to whether the new Reich of the Germans will be Christian or is to be lost in sectarianism and half-religious materialism. . . . It would be easy if every attempt on the part of the State to force a reformation were to cease. It must be admitted that there is a political element in the opposition of Christian groups to State and Party interference. But this is merely because political interference in the religious sphere forces those concerned to resist on religious grounds such unnatural pretensions to total power in this area. . . . a battle against the church would unleash counter forces that would in the end defeat brute power. . . . How can Germany fulfill her task in Europe if we voluntarily place ourselves outside the ranks of the Christian peoples. . . . We cannot seal ourselves spiritually within our borders and place ourselves voluntarily in a ghetto. Here lies the real reaction . . .

He defended intellectualism:

> But once a revolution has been completed, the Government only repre-
> sents the people as a whole and is never the champion of individual groups.
> . . . National Socialism has always fought to replace the Party book with
> the principles of human conduct and achievement. . . . It is not permissible,
> therefore, to dismiss the intellect with the catchword of "intellectualism."
> Deficient or primitive intellects do not justify us in waging war against
> intellectualism. And when we complain frequently today about those of us
> who are 150 per cent Nazis, then we mean those intellectuals without a
> foundation, people who would like to deny the right of existence to scientists
> of world fame just because they are not Party members. . . . We should
> protect ourselves from the danger of placing such men of the spirit outside
> the community. . . . Nor should the objection be made that intellectuals lack
> the vitality necessary for the leading of a people. . . . the mistaking of
> brutality for vitality would reveal a worship of force which would be dan-
> gerous to a people.

He attacked Party fanatics:

> They oppose equality before the law . . . These people suppress that pillar
> of the State which always—and not only in liberal times—was called justice.
> Their attacks are directed against the security and freedom of the private
> sphere of life which the Germans won in centuries of hardest struggle. . . .
> No people can endure an eternal revolt from below if it is to answer to
> history [*wenn es vor der Geschichte bestehen will*]. The Movement must
> come to a standstill sometime; a solid social structure must sometime come
> into existence which is held together by an impartial administration of
> justice and by an undisputed governmental power. Nothing can be achieved
> by means of everlasting dynamics. Germany must not go adrift on uncharted
> seas toward unknown shores. . . . No organization and no propaganda, how-
> ever good, will in the long run be able to preserve confidence. . . . Confidence
> and readiness to cooperate cannot be won by provocation . . . nor by threats
> against helpless segments of the people, . . . The people know that great
> sacrifices are expected from them. They will bear them . . . if every word
> of criticism is not taken for ill-will, and if despairing patriots are not branded
> as enemies of the State.

The doctrinaire bigots of the Party had to be silenced:

> If we deny the great inheritance of culture . . . we again shall miss the
> chance that Europe has given its central people. . . . If Europe wants to keep
> alive its claim to world leadership not an hour can be lost to use its powers for
> a spiritual rebirth and to bury its petty quarrels. . . . Only a responsible,
> disciplined people will lead it.[82]

It is revealing to note the textual differences between Papen's speech and
the account he gave of it in his memoirs. In his memoirs he wrote that he
told his audience that National Socialism had come to power by democratic
means and that the coalition in the Cabinet had never foreseen that in the

place of the parties an unchecked dictatorship would rule against Justice, Law, and the Church. Actually, he made no such statement in his speech. Comparison can readily be made, since the printed text of his speech was included among his defense papers and was published in the volumes of the Nuremberg trials. One must conclude that Papen was convinced when he wrote his memoirs that this was what he had meant to say; that this was what he had believed and was perhaps what an astute listener to his courageous talk might get out of it. But he had not actually said it.

Just before his Marburg speech, Papen had made similar comments in addressing a gathering of students at Bonn University on May 29. He told them that the problem of freedom was not essentially solved by the use or nonuse of measures that limited freedom. "It has much more to do with a religious rebirth of personality that grows out of the free devotion [*Bindung*] of the individual human being to God." [83]

Both these speeches were typical of Papen's philosophy, which in general was that of a Christian, Catholic conservative. They deeply impressed not only people of similar views but also those who were glad to hear such untrammeled sentiments among the disorders of German life. But the convinced Nazis reacted differently. The speeches gave them the ammunition they needed to drive Papen as quickly as possible from his place in the Cabinet. Hitler and his convinced Nazis had no interest in Germany's leadership in a Christian Europe. They had been fighting for twelve years against these very sentiments, which repeated what Bruening and the bourgeois parties had been forever saying—that here was something to tide the people over from Sunday to Sunday while the Parliament debated, while the Allies promised that some day Germany would have equal rights, and while the ranks of the unemployed grew.

The Marburg speech was received by the Party in shocked silence. The *Voelkischer Beobachter* printed not a word of it. Only the *Frankfurter Zeitung* carried the text, and Goebbels, as soon as he read it, forbade its publication. Hitler merely referred to it in an offhand way in a talk with Papen and attempted, Papen wrote later, to mollify him. Papen protested against Goebbels' forbidding publication, and Hitler promised to discuss the matter with Hindenburg when he visited the President at Neudeck, but he never mentioned the subject again, nor did Papen.

It was a dangerous speech coming from a member of the Government, and the Party hierarchy knew this well. When Papen appeared at the racetrack in Hamburg a few days after the speech, the crowds shouted "Heil Marburg." Himmler and the SS kept him and Jung in mind for the chance that came a few days later. Jung, who had no high opinion of Papen, had written the speech, saying he would use Papen in the way Papen had thought of using Hitler, to play a useful role.[84] But Papen was certainly aware of what he was doing and aware of the dangers, and therefore was careful to cover himself with praise of the Fuehrer and to concentrate his fire on the rabid followers. This was Papen's first and last act of high civil courage.

On June 30, 1934, Hitler moved to liquidate Roehm and his coterie of the SA high command, and the SS thus became the chief military arm of the Party. Papen was immediately arrested and was confined to his house for three days, and the man who had written the speech for him was killed along with Papen's secretary Herbert von Bose and his enemy General Schleicher. (In his memoirs Papen proudly listed the Conservatives who had worked with him when the Enabling Act was adopted: Bose; Wilhelm von Ketteler, who was to be killed by the Nazis in 1938; and Tschirschky, who emigrated to England in 1935 because the Gestapo threatened his life. Papen wanted his readers to understand how anti-Nazi these men were. So they were undoubtedly. But they were either liquidated or sent into exile, and Papen continued to serve the regime that had done away with them.)

Papen busied himself with serving the cause of the revolution, at the same time consoling himself that what he did was also the work of the Lord. In July, 1933, he had negotiated a concordat with the Vatican, which for a time effectively blunted Catholic opposition to Hitler's regime. But the continued flagrant attacks on both churchmen and institutions brought some of the clergy and laymen into an opposition that was not to be quieted by flourishing a treaty. On January 15, 1934, Papen declared in the *Boersenzeitung*: "The Third Reich under the leadership of Adolf Hitler . . . is the first state in the world in which the higher principles of the Pope are not only recognized but carried out in practice." Papen was always concerned for Hitler's formal observations of the proprieties where the Church was concerned. Just after Hitler became Chancellor, Papen persuaded him, against Bormann's objections, to send a representative to Trier on one solemn ecclesiastical occasion. He protested to the Fuehrer when he received complaints about some outrageous attack on the clergy, but he continued to serve the Government.

Like Neurath and Schacht, he was distressed over the hooliganism of the SA, with its onslaughts against the Jews. After the SA had been made auxiliary police, their anti-Semitic activities had an official character. Though Papen himself believed that too many Jews were in public office and in the professions, he counted as victory the fact that the Fuehrer was persuaded to exempt, among the non-Aryan officials who must resign their posts, those who had served their country in the front line in World War I or had been government officials before the start of the war. The exemption was a respectable achievement, but it was due far more to Hitler's need to move slowly in the face of Hindenburg's allegiance to German frontline soldiers and old officials than to counsel or protests from the conservative faction in the Cabinet. The Nuremberg Laws of 1935 were anticipated in the non-Aryan clauses that were extended to the Army in the decree of June 1, 1933. By

February, 1934, no Jewish officer could serve (even if he had been in the front line in World War I) in a rank of battalion commander or higher. The Cabinet and the Army went beyond these proscriptions. In July, 1933, Blomberg and the Army High Command allowed Party propaganda to circulate in barracks, libraries, and service centers, and by the spring of 1934 Blomberg ordered instruction on political problems to be given the armed forces. The Wehrmacht, as the protector of Nazi Germany, he said, needed appropriate background for its task.[85]

Men like Papen always had a *quid pro quo* for their conscience. When the Church was attacked, Papen could point to his concordat, the first such treaty with the Vatican that Protestant Germany had had in centuries. When the Army without protest allowed a fraction of its officer corps to be dismissed and political propaganda to become part of its training program, officers who might question such orders could point to the decision of the Fuehrer that the Army alone was now the nation's bearer of arms and the SA was no longer a rival, for the SA had only a political function, and its leaders might be liquidated if they became unduly ambitious or overstepped their functions. In similar fashion Papen swallowed the bitter dose of being arrested for three days when the executions of Roehm and of SA leaders were going on and two men among his close collaborators were murdered. These were apparently evidences of the growing pains of the revolution.

Papen found it intolerable that he had been under arrest, that the SS had sealed off his office and gone through his papers. He told Hitler he could not attend the Reichstag session in which the Fuehrer explained to the nation how narrowly he had rescued it from the machinations of the conspirators. Papen said his honor had been compromised when, although a member of the Government, he had been arrested. He also demanded that the body of the murdered Bose be returned to his family so it could be properly buried, and he sent the widow of Edgar Jung the sum of 1,000 RM. But then Frau Jung heard no more from him nor did he attend the funeral of her husband, who, like Schleicher, had been hunted down by the SS. It would be unwise to show too much sympathy. The Army generals too accepted the murder of its éminence grise and former Minister of War along with that of his wife. However, a meeting of the Schlieffen Society, made up of distinguished senior officers, passed a resolution declaring that Schleicher had not committed an act of treason. With the 1,000 RM to Jung's widow and the resolution on Schleicher the dead were safely interred.

After June 30 Papen never again took part in a Cabinet meeting. He tendered his resignation as Vice-Chancellor to take effect in September. In his letter of July 12 to the Fuehrer, Papen praised him for having taken full responsibility for everything that had occurred in putting down the revolt. "Allow me to say," he wrote, "how manly and humanly great of you I think this is . . . your courageous and firm intervention have met with nothing but recognition throughout the entire world." He assured Hitler of his unchanged admiration and devotion, and asked him to tell the Reichstag that Papen's honor and authority were unimpeached. He also asked that Bose's case be cleared up publicly.[86] The day after Hitler made his speech of July 13 to the Reichstag, a session which Papen had declined to attend, Papen wrote him again, telling him how he would like to clasp his hand to thank him for his rescue of the country and to congratulate him "for all you have given anew to the German nation by crushing the intended second revolution." The praise accompanied Papen's plea for Hitler to make a statement, this time on behalf of Papen's loyalty, because preposterous charges were being made against him, including the calumny that he had a plan to murder men like Goering and Goebbels.[87]

A few days later, on July 25, the attempted coup of the National Socialists in Austria took place. It failed, but not until Chancellor Dollfuss (against whose authoritarian regime Austrian Socialists had also attempted a rising, including an unsuccessful attack on the Chancellor's life) had been killed (see Seyss-Inquart, Chapt. 11). Hitler needed someone who would mollify and reassure the new Austrian Government, a Catholic and non-Nazi, and Papen accepted the post of Ambassador Extraordinary. The prosecution lawyers at Nuremberg attacked him sharply for his behavior, but Papen had the standard answer: Going to Austria enabled him to work for a peaceful settlement in the interest of both countries.

Hindenburg died just before Papen left for Vienna, but Papen did not see him. Hitler got to the deathbed while the old man still had moments of consciousness. The Chancellor had to be in attendance on this solemn occasion. One of the chief reasons for his being there was to prepare the way for his succeeding Hindenburg as President. Papen had drawn up a testament for Hindenburg with accompanying documents that, he said, Hitler had approved in principle, in which Hindenburg called on the German people to restore the monarchy. Hindenburg, according to Papen, decided on reflection to address the documents not to the German people but to the Fuehrer as a recommendation. Hitler, being extremely anxious to get hold of these documents, sent Papen to Neudeck after the President's death. Papen promptly gave both papers to Hitler. The one, the official will, was published. It praised Hitler for his work as Chancellor and called on the country to be loyal to him. The other statement, which had to do with the possible establishing of a monarchy, simply disappeared. Hitler, by unanimous vote of the Cabinet, became President as well as Reich Chancellor, and the armed forces took their oath of fidelity to him only hours later, for this was a crucial matter in Hitler's mind. Once the oath was taken, the Army was his, the officer corps bound to him in the unconditional obedience it owed the head of state, whether king or president. From that day until Hitler's death, the oath was a controlling obligation for the majority of Wehrmacht officers and soldiers.

In Austria another Papen associate was murdered. Baron von Ketteler, who was violently anti-Hitler, had been entrusted by Papen with secret papers, which Ketteler had taken for safekeeping to Switzerland. From there he went on to Vienna, where the Gestapo murdered him at about the time Papen was viewing the victory parade of German units as the *Anschluss* was being celebrated. Papen protested, offered an award of 20,000 RM for the arrest of the perpetrators, and asked Hitler to help find them. But the Fuehrer never answered his letter. Instead, Papen was given the Party's Golden Badge of Honor. Later a woman testified that he had called it a dog tag, but he did keep it. His role, as seen by the prosecution at Nuremberg, in the preparations for the *Anschluss* was a major but quasi-legal one. No incriminating evidence was brought against him. The underground work was done by the Austrian National Socialists themselves and by the agents with which the German party and secret services flooded the country. The chief cause of the overwhelming Austrian sentiment in favor of the *Anschluss* came from the post-World War I circumstances in which Austria found itself chronically bankrupt, and dependent on the traditional enemy, Italy, to keep the Nazis from taking power. Chancellor von Schuschnigg, who had succeeded Dollfuss, could not hope to maintain his country's independence once Italy and Germany came to an understanding. (See Seyss-Inquart, Chapt. 11.)

In 1938 Papen accompanied Schuschnigg to Berchtesgaden when Hitler, in the presence of his generals, forced the Austrian Chancellor to sign the document making Seyss-Inquart Minister of Public Security, with the power of controlling the police, freeing any Nazis under political arrest, adding one hundred German officers to the Austrian Army, and making it legal to join the National Socialist Party, which became coequal with the other Austrian political organizations. In return, Hitler guaranteed Austrian independence— at least until he could claim that one of the clauses of the agreement had been violated. Papen had told Schuschnigg that only subjects on which the two governments were agreed would be brought up at the meeting. He probably was acting in good faith. Years later, Schuschnigg thought that he had been, but Hitler did not pay much attention to Papen, nor did he conceal his willingness to use force if Schuschnigg did not sign. When, a few weeks after the signing of the agreement, the Austrian Chancellor called the ill-fated and ill-planned plebiscite, which he intended to be a great public affirmation of confidence in his policies, he supplied the pretext for the *Anschluss* the Fuehrer was waiting for. The voting was clearly rigged: Only those over twenty-five could vote, thus excluding the youth who were the mainstays of Nazi strength. The plebiscite was to be held four days after it was announced. It would be almost as hard to vote "No" as it was in Nazi Germany (see Seyss-Inquart, Chapt. 11).

Papen had had nothing to do with the suddenly improvised plans for the German divisions crossing the Austrian border—an invasion that resulted only in "The Flower War" as the German soldiers marched past the jubilant population, with Austrian troops happily joining the German formations.* Hitler had given his army no advance notice either. No General Staff plan existed for an Austrian campaign, nor were the troops prepared for one. Tanks broke down. The march plans were improvised. But the soldiers were greeted with delirious enthusiasm by the Austrians, who were thoroughly tired of their drab, unhopeful life and yearning for the boom and glitter and future offered them by the Third Reich.

Papen had earned his place in the reviewing stand with Hitler, but it cost him dearly. He was excited over this relatively peaceful solution of the Austrian problem in Germany's favor, his mission to Austria was crowned with success, he had been honored with the dubious gewgaw of the Party. But another of his co-workers and friends, Baron von Ketteler, had been murdered by the regime he had helped bring to Austria. Papen stood with Hitler, accepting the homage of the crowd after the Fuehrer's triumphal entry into the city where the Chancellor (now of both countries) once had sold postcards and eaten in soup kitchens that fed the unemployed.

It was a moment of soul-searching for Papen. His choice of the regime to serve seemed right in many ways. A German and Catholic country had been added to the borders of the Reich, and Papen had done his duty in representing in legal fashion the legitimate interests not only of Germany but of Austria too. But the murders were counting up, and it took some effort to attribute the beatings and the persecution of the Jews that started immediately to the lunatic fringe of the Party, or to the intoxication that accompanied the great victory of National Socialism in undoing the work of the Allied treaty-makers who wanted to condemn both countries to weakness and destitution. The excesses, Papen still hoped, would not last. He and men like him held fast to this hope, or ignored such events, for even the Austrian Cardinal Innitzer and the rest of the higher Catholic hierarchy welcomed the *Anschluss*—the union of the two German countries—and enjoined their parishioners to accept it with enthusiasm.

Papen saw with sorrow the violence of the attack on the Church that followed the period of rejoicing. Soon after the *Anschluss*, Cardinal Innitzer's palace was invaded by Nazi hoodlums and looted, and the Cardinal was barricaded in one of its rooms. Priests and nuns in Austria, as in Germany, were hauled before courts to be accused of homosexuality or subversive political views or both. The Cardinal and the Vatican protested as did Papen. The protests were waved aside, and the attack on the Church never ceased. Hundreds of priests as well as Protestant ministers were sent to con-

---

* The Tavs plot (see Seyss-Inquart, Chapt. 11) included a plan to murder Papen in the German Embassy in Vienna. This would be an excuse for German intervention (Oswald Dutch, *The Errant Diplomat* [London: Edward Arnold, 1940], pp. 249–50. Also Papen-Spruchkammer interrogation of February 27, 1948 [Munich, Amtsgericht].)

centration camps, some of them because they preached against the regime, others because they were denounced, still others because they were members of the Resistance.

When World War II started, Papen accepted the last post he would hold for the Third Reich—that of Ambassador to Turkey. He had fought in Turkey during World War I and was highly esteemed there. He performed his ambassadorial duties as well as might be expected, perhaps better. It was he who discovered and made use of the remarkable spy called Cicero, who, through Papen, provided the German intelligence with the place and time of the Allied landing in Normandy. His information would have been priceless had it been properly evaluated and acted upon in Berlin. Papen had some discreet relations, too, with the German Resistance. One member, Count Pfeil, who testified for him at his first trial in a German court, said Papen was considered for the post of Foreign Minister by the leaders of the con- spiracy, and Papen declared at the trial that he would have been glad to cooperate if the *Attentat* (attempt on Hitler's life) had been successful. But he was never a member of the Resistance except in theory. He was never con- sidered reliable enough or bold enough by the men who were risking their lives in the July, 1944, plot to be included in any of their serious discussions or plans for a post-Hitler government. Papen's name appeared on none of the lists prepared by Carl Goerdeler or his co-conspirators; he was an out- sider there too.

Papen's guilt could only be decided by a German court, by men and women who had lived through the time when he had made his decision on whether to speak up against the Hitler tyranny or to bear with it. On March 25, 1933, soon after Hitler had taken over full power, Papen had sent a tele- gram to *The New York Times* in which he said that Jews could live com- pletely unmolested in Germany if they stayed out of politics, but in his opinion there were too many Jews in public life, in literature, theater and films, and especially in law.[88] This was published four days before the boy- cott of Jewish business took place and before the widespread publicity given the acts of hooliganism committed by the SA thugs. But countless episodes of the same kind had occurred before the telegram was sent, although not on so great a scale. The SA and SS were establishing their own unofficial concentration camps. The first ones appeared in March, 1933, where Jews were worked over and held prisoner. Papen could not have been unaware of these acts of terrorism, because he said later that he protested to Hitler against them.

In Nuremberg he tried to justify his activities. He believed himself to be a reasonable man. He had been in favor of a pure race, as he had said in January, 1934, but did not every country have the right to protect its blood? Papen wanted the Jews to be treated as foreigners in Germany. They were not to be citizens, but their rights would be defined and safeguarded by law, and when excesses occurred one could protest against them. In his view, it must be kept in mind that too many of them had positions of prominence and that they were a foreign body within the German community.

Papen saw all these matters in a mild, genteel light. "There can certainly be no objection to keeping the unique quality of a people as clean as possible and to awaken the sense of a peoples' community," he had said in a speech at Gleiwitz in 1934.[89] And in writing to Hitler he had stressed the similarity of their views: "Especially pleasing is the growing revulsion particularly of the workers to Jewish dominance." [90]

In a word, Papen was weak. He held no views that were not subject to modification when it seemed expedient to change them. But he was no moral coward. His speech at Marburg was an act of great courage, and in the first Hitler Cabinet he stood up to Hitler more than any of his colleagues did. Nor was he without generosity: He told Severing, who was testifying against Papen at his trial in the German court, that their political differences did not affect his high esteem of Severing as a man. The remark resulted in a half-hearted compliment from Severing, who had just called him a liar, to the effect that he was attacking not Papen personally but only his political career.[91]

All in all, it was a shabby career for a man who, with every formal advantage of family position and with many of the sound instincts of the German conservative, simply could not bring himself to face the deeper realities of his own and his country's predicament. His heart bled for his coreligionists, for the persecuted Jews, for the men and women deprived of due process of the law, for the war that he knew in 1939 was surely coming, for all the suffering and injustices the National Socialists were inflicting, but he served the Fuehrer and accepted the Party's Golden Badge of Honor, the ambassadorships, the rewards of high place.

At Nuremberg, telling about the preliminaries to his meeting with Hitler while Schleicher was Chancellor, he said the Herrenklub was called that to distinguish it from a woman's club.[92] Actually, as he and every German-speaking person in the courtroom knew, *Herren*, as the name was used for this club, was as close an approximation as the members could devise to "Gentlemen." Papen's other attempts to describe its functions to the Allies were equally fatuous. Socialists and even Communists, he said, were invited there. He meant as speakers, for the club was concerned with politics, but it sounded as though they might have been members, and the Herrenklub was the inveterate enemy of such elements. Papen certainly had every right to belong to the Herrenklub, but his attempts to explain away its function were part of the disingenuousness that plagued him all his life.

In one outburst of pride he said in a speech made while he was still Vice-Chancellor on November 3, 1933, that he had been the pathbreaker for the Nazis. "I have tried, with all my strength, to take part in the reconstruction and rebirth of our homeland." [93] The Nazis for him, once he decided to join Hitler, were "the young fighting freedom movement." The good Lord had blessed Germany by giving it, in times of deep distress, a Fuehrer who would lead it through all crises and moments of danger with the sure instincts of the statesman to a happy future.[94] While it is true that he was soon disillusioned, he continued to praise Hitler. After the murders of Bose and Jung, he thanked the Fuehrer for his speech in the Reichstag explaining why he had been forced to take such measures. He would be most grateful, he said, if Hitler would make a public announcement that Papen was a worthy person, loyal to the Fuehrer and his work.[95]

This was Papen. If he could rescue some shreds of respectability he could accept almost anything, even his own arrest and the murder of his friends. All he wanted was the restoration of his honor, the opportunity to keep face. He ventured no further than the fringes of the Resistance; he wanted to get in touch with Roosevelt; he talked of European solidarity and the long tradition of European culture. But he shrank from the idea of actually holding Hitler to account—arresting or if necessary killing him—for enormities committed. Papen wanted to stay alive, not only as a human being but as a person of importance. He succeeded in the first and to some degree in the second goal. But the Germans, after Nuremberg, turned their backs on him, refusing to accept the stories, which he certainly believed himself, of his efforts to bring Hitler and the Party to some semblance of Christian morals. His native city, which had once bestowed honorary citizenship upon him and named a street after him, refused him the right to live there. A hospital in Nuremberg refused him admission. The Bundesrepublik refused him a pension. And yet he had done more than many who fared better in West Germany after the war. He had spoken at Marburg.

NOTES

1. NCA VII, L-74, pp. 839–47.

2. Count Folke Bernadotte, *The Curtain Falls* (New York: Alfred A. Knopf, Inc., 1945).

3. H. R. Berndorff, *General zwischen Ost und West* (Hamburg: Hoffmann and Campe, n.d.).

4. Margaret Boveri, *Der Diplomat vor Gericht* (Berlin and Hannover: Minerva Verlag, 1948), p. 40.

5. Gordon A. Craig and Felix Gilbert, eds., *The Diplomats 1919–1939* (Princeton: Princeton University Press, 1953), p. 435.

6. Paul Seabury, *The Wilhelmstrasse* (Berkeley: University of California Press, 1954).

7. *Germania*, February 6, 1938.

8. N XXXV, 636-D, p. 233. Also NCA VII, D-744-A, pp. 198–99.

9. Count Galeazzo Ciano, *Ciano's Hidden Diary 1937–1938* (New York: E. P. Dutton, & Co., Inc., 1953), p. 119.

10. *Ibid.*, p. 582.

11. Erich Kordt, *Nicht aus den Akten* (Stuttgart: Union Deutsche Verlags GmbH., 1950), p. 332.

12. Weizsaecker Vernehmungsprotokoll 7912. Also Walther Hofer, *Die Entfesselung des Zweiten Weltkrieges* (Frankfurt a.M.: S. Fischer Verlag, 1964), p. 167.

13. F-15172, Bonn, Auswaertiges Amt.

14. Michael Freund, ed., *Geschichte des Zweiten Weltkrieges in Dokumenten*, Vol. I (Freiburg: Herder Verlag, 1953), p. 275.

15. Hans-Adolf Jacobsen, *1939–1945 Der Zweite Weltkrieg in Chronik und Dokumenten* (Darmstadt: Wehr und Wissen Verlag, 1961), p. 236.

16. NO 2618, Interrogation Summary Werner von Schmieden, June 26, 1947 (Rijksinstituut voor Oorlogsdocumentatie, Amsterdam; hereinafter referred to as Amsterdam).

17. Seabury, *op. cit.*, pp. 52–53.

18. Craig and Gilbert, eds., *op. cit.*

19. Ciano, *op. cit.*, p. 151.

20. Carl J. Burckhardt, *Meine Danziger Mission 1937–1939* (Munich: Deutscher Taschenbuch Verlag, 1962), p. 307.

21. Bernadotte, *op. cit.*, p. 39.

22. Otto Skorzeny, *Geheimkommando Skorzeny* (Hamburg: Hansa Verlag Josef Toth, 1950), p. 163.

23. *Documents on German Foreign Policy 1918–1945*, Series D, Vol. VIII (Washington: Department of State), p. 886.

24. Bross, *op. cit.*, p. 121.

25. *Trials of War Criminals Before the Nuremberg Military Tribunals Under Control Council Law No. 10, Nuremberg 1946–49*, Vol. XII (Washington: US Government Printing Office), p. 927. Hereinafter referred to as *TWC*.

26. Paul Seabury, "Ribbentrop and the German Foreign Office," in *Political Science Quarterly*, December, 1951. Also Hoffmann, *op. cit.*, p. 116.

27. Ciano, *op. cit.*, p. 477.

28. N XXXV, 741-D, pp. 458–61.

29. Joachim von Ribbentrop, *Zwischen London und Moskau* (Leoni: Druffel-Verlag, 1953), p. 268.

30. Interrogation, August 29, 1945 (National Archives, Washington, D.C.; hereinafter referred to as NA).

31. N II, p. 448.

32. Seabury, "Ribbentrop and the German Foreign Office," *op. cit.*

33. N XXXV, 736-D, p. 428.

34. *Ibid.*, 735-D, pp. 423-25, and 741-D, p. 462.

35. Interrogation, August 29, 1945 (NA).

36. Interrogation, September 10, 1945 (NA).

37. Gilbert, *op. cit.*

38. Eberhard Zeller, *Geist der Freiheit: Der 20. Juli* (Munich: Gotthold Mueller Verlag, 1963), p. 422.

39. Ivone Kirkpatrick, *The Inner Circle* (London: The Macmillan Company, Ltd., 1959), p. 197.

40. Schellenberg, *op. cit.*

41. N XVI, p. 594.

42. *Ibid.*, p. 608.

43. N XL, Neurath-69.

44. *Ibid.*, Neurath-74.

45. *Ibid.*, Neurath-112 and Neurath-116.

46. Kirkpatrick, *op. cit.*, p. 98.

47. N XVI, p. 611.

48. *Ibid.*, p. 604.

49. *Czechoslovakia Fights Back* (Washington: American Council on Public Affairs, 1943), pp. 118, 123.

50. N XIX, p. 447.

51. N XVII, pp. 59–73.

52. *Ibid.*, p. 61.

53. NCA, Supp. A, 3859-PS, pp. 598–614. Also N XVII, pp. 61–65.

54. N XVII, p. 59.

55. *Ibid.*, p. 61.

56. Interrogation, April 17, 1947 (NA).

57. N XVII, p. 101.

58. N I, pp. 333–34.

59. Oswald Dutch, *The Errant Diplomat* (London: Edward Arnold, 1940), p. 61.

60. Franz von Papen, *Der Wahrheit eine Gasse* (Munich: Paul List Verlag, 1952), p. 107. Also Dutch, *op. cit.*, p. 78.

61. Meissner and Wilde, *op. cit.* Also Papen, *op. cit.*

62. Erich Matthias, "Hindenburg zwischen den Fronten 1932," *Vierteljahrshefte fuer Zeitgeschichte*, Vol. VIII, No. 1, 1960, pp. 78–82.

63. Heinrich Bennecke, *Hitler und die SA* (Munich: Olzog, 1962).

64. Otto Meissner, *Staatssekretaer unter Ebert, Hindenburg und Hitler* (Hamburg: Hoffmann and Campe, 1950), p. 210.

65. Wilhelm Deist, "Schleicher und die deutsche Abruestungspolitik im Juni/ Juli 1932," in *Vierteljahrshefte fuer Zeitgeschichte*, Vol. VII, No. 2, 1959, pp. 163–76. Also Papen, *op. cit.*, pp. 202–7. Also Edouard Herriot, *Jadis*, Vol. II (Paris: Flammarion, 1952), p. 347.

66. Paul Kluke, "Der Fall Potempa," in *Vierteljahrshefte fuer Zeitgeschichte*, Vol. V, No. 3, 1957, pp. 279–97.

67. Berndorff, *op. cit.*, pp. 220–22.

68. Theodor Eschenburg, "Franz von Papen," *Vierteljahrshefte fuer Zeitgeschichte*, Vol. I, No. 2, 1953, pp. 153–69.

69. Thilo Vogelsang, *Reichswehr, Staat und NSDAP* (Stuttgart: Deutsche Verlags-Anstalt, 1962). Also Franz von Papen, *Einige Bemerkungen zum Buch "Reichswehr, Staat und NSDAP" von Dr. Thilo Vogelsang* (Private printing, n.d.).

70. Dietrich, *op. cit.*, p. 185.

71. Meissner and Wilde, *op. cit.*, p. 158.

72. *Ibid.*, p. 159.

73. *Ibid.*, p. 163.

74. Kurt von Schuschnigg, *Austrian Requiem* (New York: G. P. Putnam's Sons, 1946), p. 26.

75. N IX, p. 249.

76. Anton Ritthaler, *"Eine Etappe auf Hitlers Weg zur ungeteilten Macht,"* in *Vierteljahrshefte fuer Zeitgeschichte*, Vol. VIII, No. 2, 1960, pp. 193–218. Also N XL, Papen-87 and Papen-88.

77. Karl Dietrich Bracher, *"Stufen totalitaerer Gleichschaltung: Die Befestigung der nationalsozialistischen Herrschaft 1933–34,"* in *Vierteljahrshefte fuer Zeitgeschichte*, Vol. IV, No. 1, 1956, pp. 30–42. Also Schwerin von Krosigk, *op. cit.*, p. 147.

78. Adam Buckreis, *Politik des 20. Jahrhunderts*, Vol. I, *Weltgeschichte 1901–1936* (Nuremberg: Panorama-Verlag, n.d.), p. 579.

79. Hans Schneider. *"Das Ermaechtigungsgesetz vom 24. Maerz 1933,"* in *Vierteljahrshefte fuer Zeitgeschichte*, Vol. I, No. 3, 1953, pp. 197–221.

80. Karl Dietrich Bracher, Wolfgang Sauer, and Gerhard Schulz, *Die nationalsozialistische Machtergreifung* (Cologne: Westdeutscher Verlag, 1962), pp. 720 ff.

81. *Ibid.*, p. 717. Also *Schulthess' Europaeischer Geschichtskalender*, Vol. LXXV (Munich: C. H. Beck'sche Verlagsbuchhandlung, 1935), p. 44.

82. Hans-Adolf Jacobsen and Werner Jochmann, *Ausgewaehlte Dokumente zur Geschichte des Nationalsozialismus 1933–1945* (Bielefeld: Verlag Neue Gesellschaft, 1961). Also N XL, Papen-11; and N XVI, pp. 292–95.

83. Franz von Papen, *Der Wahrheit eine Gasse*, p. 343.

84. Papen Spruchkammer: Affidavit Edmund Forschbach of January 31, 1947 (Munich, Amtsgericht).

85. Bracher, Sauer, and Schulz, *op. cit.*, p. 919.

86. NCA, Supp. A, D-716, pp. 938–39.

87. *Ibid.*, D-718, pp. 940–41.

88. N VI, p. 88. Also N XVI, p. 274.

89. N XVI, pp. 274–75.

90. Papen Spruchkammer (Munich, Amtsgericht).

91. Papen Spruchkammer: Severing testimony of January 28, 1947 (Munich, Amtsgericht).

92. Papen interrogation of September 17, 1946.

93. Papen Spruchkammer (Munich, Amtsgericht).

94. N XVI, pp. 343–44. Also NCA II, p. 930.

95. NCA, Supp. A, D-715, pp. 936–37; D-718, pp. 940–41.

6

The Party and Big Business

HJALMAR SCHACHT

The Western as well as the Soviet prosecutors at Nuremberg were deeply convinced that German big business—the industrialists and bankers—were the real forces behind the movement that had brought Hitler to power and kept him there. In this classic Marxist view, widely shared by non-Marxists of a generation brought up on the notions of the paramountcy of economic over political forces, of the guilt of the munition makers for instigating wars, Hitler was the puppet, not the industrialists and bankers. And of the men held responsible for making Hitler Chancellor and then aiding him in his anti-Communist and antilabor purposes, Hjalmar Schacht was among the most prominent. The prosecution called him the wizard of Germany's autarky and the respectable front for the activist hoodlums who clubbed the opposition off the streets. But this view was a considerable distortion of what went on, for neither Schacht nor any other of the big-business leaders was a match for Hitler. For brief intervals they might indulge themselves in the illusion that they were influencing or even controlling the Fuehrer ("I have got Hitler by the throat," [1] Schacht boasted to a friend in the mid-thirties, the same sentiments Papen expressed when he joined Hitler's coalition Cabinet), but in fact it was always the Fuehrer who used them, and a good number, including Schacht, ended up in concentration camps.

Schacht came from a middle-class family that for generations had lived in Schleswig-Holstein. His father emigrated to America in the 1870's and became an American citizen. Schacht's mother, twenty-one years old when she married, followed. But Germany, after the victory in 1871 over France, seemed as promising for a young businessman as the Land of Promise itself, and after spending six years in America the Schachts returned to the Reich to seek their fortune. They had a hard time, but managed to educate three sons, one of whom, born January 22, 1877, was named Horace Greeley Hjalmar Schacht in honor of a man the father greatly admired. Greeley, a friend of Carl Schurz and a democrat with literary embellishments, was the kind of man the culture-loving Germans of that period took to be the very pattern of the free enlightened man of the New World, and after the Schachts returned to Germany they kept alive the memory of their New World hero. Hjalmar always considered himself a "democrat"; after World War I he helped found the German Democratic Party, although characteristically he thought of himself as a monarchist at the same time. He saw no inconsistency in these political positions, just as he would discover none in his notions of the compatibility of free enterprise and National Socialism.

Hjalmar Schacht was a man of many aptitudes. After attending the Gymnasium at Hamburg, he first studied medicine at Kiel, then German philology at Berlin and political science at Munich before taking his degree at the University of Berlin in economics. As he said of himself, his bent was practical not theoretical.[2] With his considerable intelligence—he had the highest IQ among the Nuremberg defendants—and his quick grasp of the essence of monetary problems he made his way rapidly in the banking world. He became a director of the National Bank at the age of thirty-nine, after having worked for thirteen years in the Dresdner Bank, where he was one of its chief officers, between 1908 and 1915, and having headed a private bank. Vain, ambitious, and shrewd, he had interests unusual in an aspiring banker. As a young man, in addition to his university studies, he wrote criticisms of plays and art exhibits for newspapers; all his life he composed verses and maxims that displayed a mild literary talent, although never as great as he himself believed. The verses were written for all occasions, and in his autobiography the author proudly prints a good many stanzas on his travels and rhymed commentaries on political and business occasions that would not otherwise have seen print. These verses, and maxims such as "Eating keeps body and soul together, drinking separates them," are no better and no worse than many businessmen write for their own pleasure and, as they like to say, for their friends.[3]

During World War I Schacht, on leave from the Dresdner Bank, had a temporary job in the economic section of the efficient German-occupation administration in Belgium. He was no table thumper but a conscientious bureaucrat seeking to obtain as high a Belgian contribution to Germany's war production as the circumstances permitted. Germany's defeat left Schacht incredulous. Above all, the disorders in the streets, the open threat of revolution, appalled this man of system and figures that balanced.

Schacht, who became president of the Reichsbank in 1923, at the age of forty-six, was mainly responsible for devising the means of stopping the catastrophic inflation of that year with a new currency backed by foreign loans. After World War I the Reichsbank had permitted the printing presses to run night and day, turning out worthless marks (zeros were added daily), because the bank's directors said they had no way of knowing what reparations would actually be required by the Allies and at what conceivable rate they could stabilize the mark against foreign currencies like the dollar. Schacht went to England and persuaded the governor of the Bank of England, Montagu Norman, to make the loan against which the new mark was to be secured.

Self-confident and with a useful touch of irritability, Schacht did not easily tolerate the arrogance and incivility of many of the Allied officials with whom he had to deal after World War I. He once abruptly left the office of the French Foreign Minister because he was kept waiting twenty minutes, and he had to be hauled back by a panting functionary who ran after him and promised an immediate audience. But Schacht and Montagu Norman got along well from the start, and after World War II Schacht could not understand why he was denied an English visa to attend the funeral services for his old friend. Schacht never had any sense of guilt about anything he did; he could never understand why he was brought to trial either by the Allies or by the Germans. The only imprisonment he found comprehensible, at least *post facto*, was when the Gestapo picked him up on July 23, 1944, after the attempt on Hitler's life and kept him jailed until the Americans rescued him. But if the Nazis had won, Schacht might well have been just as aggrieved as he was by his later arrests, for he was always a prudent opponent of Hitler, even when he violently disagreed with his policies. Schacht had done much on Hitler's behalf in the early 1930's when the cause had been greatly in need of his services, and he kept a discreet distance from any plot against Hitler demanding his active participation. He left direct action to the military and to others bolder of heart, but he urged the plotters on— once, in 1943, so hotly that his host had to intervene between the banker and one of the conspirators, General Fritz Lindemann.*

Schacht was a stalwart nationalist in politics who, like the rich German industrialists and like Hitler, too, said he wanted a strong economy in a strong state. He was angered by the French attempts after World War I to divide Germany, their invasion of the Ruhr, and their demand for reparations that could not possibly be paid. Schacht pointed out that the amount demanded was twelve times the six billion gold francs Germany had obtained from France in 1871. Germany had demanded then what amounted to 110 RM per head in French currency of 1869, the year before the Franco-Prussian War, or 3.2 per cent of the capital of the population of France as of that year. But the amount to be exacted from Germany at the end of World War I came to 38 per cent of the population's capital, or 1,350 RM per head for each German as of 1913. French reparations had amounted to 25

* The time to act was now, Schacht told Lindemann; the generals were delaying too long. But it was eventually Lindemann, not Schacht, who was executed for his part in the July 20 revolt (N XLI, p. 300, Gronau affidavit, Schacht-39).

per cent of the French income of 1869, but the German reparations were 220 per cent of the German income of 1913 (French reparations amounted to 100 per cent of the monetary metal of France, German reparations were 2,200 per cent of the monetary metal of the Reich).[4]

Schacht and men like him were outraged not only at the economic and political treatment accorded Germany but at what they regarded as the undeserved contempt with which the Allies treated them. When, during the first meetings where Frenchmen dealt with the German economic delegation, Schacht complained to a French general of the poor food and lodgings assigned the Germans, the general said, "You forget you lost the war." Woodrow Wilson had spoken with a golden tongue of many laudable things, including self-determination, the German delegation said, but neither that principle nor any other that might benefit them applied to the Germans.*

"A sound economy in a strong state," was what Hitler said he wanted when he talked to the men of industry and to the chief businessmen of the Ruhr. Not only was the state to be strong and the economy sound, but there would be no strikes, for as Schacht was to say in his memorable Koenigsberg speech of August 18, 1935, after he became Minister of Economics, the employers and the workers had the same obligation as the soldiers, to work for the entire society: "Just as the soldier in the Wehrmacht does his duty, so must each *Volks* comrade have the feeling that in the economy too he stands in the service of the whole." [5]

As a witness at one of his later trials said (after his acquittal at Nuremberg, German courts were to be busy with him for five years), Schacht was a member of only one party, the Schacht party. He was impressed with Hitler, perhaps not as deeply so as his fervent letters of praise to the Fuehrer in the early thirties would suggest, but rather along the lines Schacht indicated in a speech he made in New York City in 1931: "I am no National Socialist, but the basic ideas of National Socialism contain a good deal of truth." [6] In Germany he was to praise National Socialism far more fulsomely than in New York, but he was always cool to the idea of war; he could never accept the giddy noneconomic policies of Goering that appealed to Hitler's political thinking. Having done an enormous service to the Party by making it look respectable when it desperately needed money from the solid industrialists of the Ruhr, he quickly broke with it as far as active participation in the regime was concerned, and his outraged feeling that it was he who had been rejected by Hitler led to contempt for and then hatred of the Party. He explained his remaining as Minister Without Portfolio to himself as well as to the Allied and German judges by maintaining that the Resistance had urged him to keep this post, a defense that was corroborated by a number of witnesses.

---

* Approximately 60 per cent of the people of Upper Silesia, despite an Allied army of occupation and great pressure on the part of the Poles, voted in a plebiscite in March, 1921, for the territory to be part of Germany, but four-fifths of that valuable industrial area was nevertheless awarded to Poland.

This, however, was a stock Schachtian explanation of the kind he used at Nuremberg. He had reluctantly accepted the Party's Golden Badge of Honor, he said, because he had found it useful during the war for getting automobiles and railroad transportation otherwise hard to come by.

Like almost all bankers, Schacht was opposed to any major war. Jodl and Keitel testified that his economic measures, the money he made available for rearmament from his ingenious credit devices, would have provided no more than twenty-seven or twenty-eight divisions, scarcely enough for purely defensive purposes in a Germany surrounded by the armies of a potential coalition that included Poland, Czechoslovakia, France, Russia, and Great Britain. American visitors, including Sumner Welles, William C. Bullitt, Ambassador Dodd, and the consular officer S. R. Fuller, Jr.,[7] as well as people Schacht talked to in the United States, were convinced he was a man of peace. Nothing in his career contradicts this conclusion despite the prosecution's charges at Nuremberg that he not only had plotted to wage war but had made the war possible by his financial black magic. In fact, he had to leave his posts as Minister of Economics, Reichsbankpraesident, and Plenipotentiary for the War Economy, giving way to Goering and Funk, because he regarded the rate and size of German armament dangerous to the economy as well as to the peace of Europe. He wanted to cut down on the armament program as early as 1935 and, as he told Gisevius, to prevent the catastrophe of an inflation and a war.[8]

Schacht was solidly behind Hitler up to 1935 despite the doubts that arose in his mind during the Roehm putsch and his banker's revulsion at the humiliating and illegal measures of the Gestapo, which went as far as to put a microphone in his office. His first serious complaints aside from those having to do with economic policy were directed against the Gestapo, which he believed with reason to be suspicious of him. His friend Gisevius brought to his office an expert from the same secret police that had installed the microphone, who promptly found it. But Schacht's wincing at the Roehm murders and his well-grounded suspicions of the Gestapo did not prevent him from attending the September Party Days in 1935, and from declaring there, "For this Third Reich that our Fuehrer has made us a gift of we will work together as long as breath is in our bodies." Nor indeed, as late as March, 1938, did his revulsion stop him from telling the employees of the Vienna bank that "no one can find his future with us who is not with a full heart behind Adolf Hitler." [9]

Although a Freemason, he made an oblique attack on the Masons when he said in his Koenigsberg speech, of which he was always so proud, that not all who had been Freemasons were scoundrels.[10] In his Leipzig speech of April 4, 1935, when he opposed individual "actions" against Jews, he declared that not every Jew was to be killed, nor was every Mason guilty of high treason. He added that his foreign friends were of little help when they said he was against Adolf Hitler.[11]

His speeches were often studded with anti-Semitic sentiments, although all through his trial and in his autobiography he stoutly denied that he was an anti-Semite. Nevertheless, on November 11, 1933, he talked before a women's club in Berlin of which his wife was president and quoted Luther to show the necessity and justification for anti-Semitism at the time when the Jews were first beginning to feel the lash of the Nazi whip. Luther, too, Schacht said, had rightly seen the "folkish incompatibility" of the Jew in German society and had grasped the fateful essentials of the Jewish problem. Schacht added that it was not a contemporary problem, that over the centuries the same complaints had been made of the Jews.[12]

The solutions Schacht sought for the Jewish question were harsh, but only in an economic sense. He wanted to exterminate not the Jews but their political and economic influence in Germany. In 1934 he concluded the "Paltreu agreement" with the World Zionist Organization, permitting Jews who could pay 15,000 RM to emigrate. Jews in Palestine were to accept German exports so that the equivalent exchange would be released.[13] By 1938, 170,000 Jews reached Palestine under this agreement.[14] Late in 1938 Schacht proposed a plan for 150,000 Jews (in the course of three years the number would rise to 400,000) who wanted to emigrate from Germany to leave the country. One-fourth of the Jewish property confiscated in the Reich, or about 1.5 billion RM, would be set aside as a trust fund. Against this fund "International Jewry" would make a loan that would enable the Jews to emigrate. Germany was to repay this sum and meet the interest charges by increasing exports; that is, the stolen funds were to be made antiseptic through an international consortium and put to work on behalf of the people they had been taken from—another practical solution. But this plan, worked out by Schacht after he was no longer Minister of Economics, was prevented from becoming operational by the war.[15]

Schacht's shrewd practicality led him to support Hitler in the first place. Early in 1930 he wrote a letter to the *Berliner Tageblatt* in which he said that Hitler was no political leader and was capitalizing on the unrest in the country. But Hitler won a major political victory in the September, 1930, elections, when the Nazis became the second largest party in the Reichstag. Schacht had resigned his post as president of the Reichsbank in March because he increasingly opposed the economic and political policies of the Weimar Government, especially the growing foreign debt (he was always impatient of people who disregarded his advice; to be worth working with, people had to be either members of the Schacht party or at least in a potential coalition with it). In that year of unemployment, Schacht read *Mein Kampf* during a trip to the United States and became convinced of Hitler's political genius, as well as of the ineptitude of the leadership opposing him. He had met Goering, and early in 1931 he was invited to the future Reichsmarschall's apartment in Berlin for dinner. Fritz Thyssen and Goebbels were there, and Hitler came in late to talk to the small gathering for two hours. Schacht found him "completely acceptable." Hitler's program for Germany's economic recovery sounded reasonable even by Schacht's sober standards, for the Fuehrer always had a gift for telling listeners who were important to him what they wanted to hear. He confirmed Schacht's image of a man of enormous energy and a born political leader who could restore the depression-ridden, deeply corroded economic and political structure. Schacht was still formally the non-Nazi, but he was ready to use his influence to raise money for the Party. He set forth on journeys in and outside Germany to talk, as he said, to "leading circles," going as far as Copenhagen, Bern, Stockholm, and New York to tell the people of influence and substance about the plight of the Reich, the need for ending reparations, and the Nationalist movement under Hitler. In New York he explained to an audience highly critical of National Socialism that he personally did not take Adolf Hitler too seriously, but the movement was constitutional, and he assured the Jews among his listeners that they had no reason to fear for their coreligionists in the Reich.[16]

Although Bruening called on him for financial advice during the deepening depression, Schacht's talents, his National Socialist biographer Franz Reuter pointed out, were solely at Hitler's disposal.[17] He undoubtedly hoped to influence Hitler on the side of "conservative" economic policies. Like Funk, Schacht declared that he wanted to retain as much of the free market as could be rescued; like Papen and the other bankers and industrialists who were edging toward the Party, he wanted the Government to take a variety of so-called conservative measures: to rearm within prudent economic limits but to keep out of war at all costs, to reduce the number of Jews in the arts and professions and government, to restore employment through useful public works, to defeat the threat of communism, to put an end to strikes and to the hopelessness of millions of German workers.

Before 1930 Hitler had few pipelines to the funds of big business. Fritz Thyssen had been won to the cause of the Party as early as 1923 and had contributed, he wrote later, about a million marks to it.[18] Emil Kirdorf, director general of the Rhenish-Westphalian Coal Syndicate, was another rich Nazi sympathizer. Hitler's financial support in the early days, however, had come not as large sums from big industry but as small contributions from Party members and men like Munich piano manufacturer Carl Bechstein and Munich publisher Hugo Bruckmann. Big business was cautious and dubious—Krupp lost his misgivings only in 1931—but Schacht's endorsement of the Fuehrer undoubtedly helped the Party to tap sources of money that had hitherto been fearful of its economic "radicalism." It was in the period after the election of September, 1930, that Schacht, Baron Kurt von Schroeder of Cologne, and the prominent industrialists Otto Wolff, Georg von Schnitzler of the Board of Directors of I. G. Farben, Albert Voegler of the United Steel Works, and August Rosterg of the potash industry began to be active with both their checkbooks and their influence on Hitler's behalf. The chief businessmen of northern Germany attended a meeting arranged by Thyssen at the Industry Club in Duesseldorf a year before Hitler became Chancellor to hear the Fuehrer's views. Like Schacht, they were favorably impressed, although many of them were reluctant to commit themselves. They were favorably impressed largely because they had so few alternatives.* [19]

Most of the men of big industry continued to drag their feet. In a letter to Hitler of April 12, 1932, Schacht said he had not, unfortunately, been able to get the help he had hoped for from the industrialists, to persuade them "to come out for you openly," although he had received many expressions of sympathetic interest. But, he told Hitler, "they are unclear on your economic program." Some of them had expressed their willingness to finance, along with Schacht, an economic center where National Socialist principles could be studied and brought into agreement with those of a prosperous private economy. The battle against socialism was simple, Schacht said, and he thought it could be successful. There was an apparent conflict, he wrote in 1932, between individualism and socialism, but paraphrasing Hitler, he said that they could be reconciled in the higher demands of the whole society. Schacht was ready to take over the supervision of such a center. He ended his letter by expressing hope that the increased strain of these last days had not impaired Hitler's health.[20]

Whatever doubts about Hitler Schacht may have had, he never after September, 1930, saw any alternative to Hitler as Chancellor.† He thought Hitler would be tamed by becoming Chancellor and by the conservatives who would be part of his government, and that the Fuehrer could be taught the principles of a sound economy, an opinion shared by Papen and the conservative members of the Keppler circle.‡ By November, 1932, Schacht and his friends were ready to sign the fateful letter urging Hindenburg to appoint Hitler Chancellor.[21] (Cf. Papen, Chapt. 5.) Schacht was unquestionably one of the key people to rescue Hitler when the tide could have turned against him. In 1932, after the crushing expenses of two elections within a few months, Party funds were at an all-time low. After phenomenal gains

---

* Some support of Hitler came from foreign countries. The Dutch oil magnate Henri Deterding, who had an estate in Mecklenburg, made sizable contributions. The Nazis also tried to get support from Henry Ford, but had no success.

† Schacht himself was the candidate for Chancellor proposed to President Hindenburg by the Reich Association of German Industries in 1932, but this was the only following he had.

‡ A group of wealthy businessmen was formed in the autumn of 1931 at the suggestion of Adolf Hitler by Wilhelm Keppler. Keppler, a successful entrepreneur and pro-Nazi, was appointed Hitler's economic adviser at a time when Feder's activities (see Papen, Chapt. 5) were reduced. The purpose, Hitler told Keppler, was to "bring together a circle of business leaders who have proved themselves in industry. Hitler suggested that I should form these men into a circle so that they could advise me. He mentioned also that it was in no way necessary that these people be members of the Party." (Arthur Schweitzer, *Big Business in the Third Reich* [Bloomington: Indiana University Press, 1964], pp. 100–101. TWC, Flick case VI.)

in the July election, the National Socialists lost thirty-four seats in November. Hitler could not even raise the funds to pay for the next weeks' Party activities, the costs of meetings, the printing bills, the rallies. It was with the help of men like Schacht that the considerable sums needed to tide him over were obtained.

Schacht wrote to the Fuehrer on November 12, 1932, congratulating him on the firm stand he had taken after the election and expressing the belief that Hitler would be Chancellor. "It seems," Schacht added, "that our attempts to get subscriptions from the economy have not been in vain." Schacht sorrowed over the unwillingness of heavy industry (*Schwerindustrie*) to go along with National Socialism and said they got their name from *Schwerfaelligkeit*—being hard to move. Schacht also sent along a genteel banker's admonition and expressed his hope that the little exaggerations necessary in the propaganda of the next few weeks would not give Hitler's enemies the chance to disarm him. "The stronger your internal position," he told the Fuehrer in his avuncular fashion, "the more dignified can be the form of battle. The more the situation is decided in your favor, the more you can avoid personalities in the campaign. I am filled with confidence that the whole present system is with certainty leading toward oblivion." [22]

On February 20, after Hitler had become Chancellor, Schacht acted as treasurer of a meeting of twenty-five leaders of the Reich Association of German Industry that took place at Goering's residence. Three million marks were collected. Krupp, who was President of the Reich Association, was present, as were Voegler, Schnitzler, and Bose from I. G. Farben. Schacht, according to Schnitzler, acted "as a kind of host." Schacht later sent all the funds collected to Rudolf Hess for the Nazis, although the money raised was in theory to be divided among the three nationalist parties in Hitler's coalition Government—the German People's Party, the German National People's Party, and the National Socialists. This would be a long-term investment, Goering told the industrialists, for if Hitler were given the powers he would demand of the Reichstag it would be the last election for at least ten years and perhaps a century. Goering was prophetic as far as election contributions were concerned; big industry would give no more money for the winning of voters after February, 1933. It would, however, through the Keppler circle and by direct contributions, make many and handsome gifts in the future to the Party and to members of its high command: to Himmler and Goering, as well as to Hitler.* [23]

---

* In order to stop the "wild collection drives" of the Party, Gustav Krupp, after the burning of the Reichstag, arranged for a "Hitler Donation" to be made through the "contribution" of 0.03 per cent of the salaries and wages paid employees of the German trade associations. A half billion marks were collected by this means and placed at Hitler's disposal during the Nazi period. Krupp could well afford to make his own gifts; profits of the firm went up from 108 million marks in 1932 to 232 million in 1935 (Arthur Schweitzer, "Business Policy in a Dictatorship," in *The Business History Review*, Vol. XXXVIII, No. 4, 1964, pp. 413-38).

On March 17, less than two weeks after the March 5 election, in which Hitler received 43.9 per cent of the votes, Schacht was again named president of the Reichsbank, a post he had held under the Weimar Government. Hitler felt that the very man to send to the Economic Conference in London and to the United States was Schacht, a banker of probity and common sense who could discuss ways and means of countering the worldwide depression with the experts and politicians of many countries. In New York Schacht told his audience that many people made the mistake of thinking of Germany as a dictatorship, but nothing could be more democratic than the present government. And, he said, it should be easy for the governments of Franklin Roosevelt and Adolf Hitler to collaborate because of the close similarity between them. The crisis, he said, was moral, not economic. *The New York Times* hailed the speech as "humane and courageous." Schacht made some forty speeches in the United States, he talked over a nationwide radio hookup, and his articles appeared in newspapers as widely separated as the New York *Herald Tribune* and the Omaha *Bee*.[24]

The accounts of Schacht's relations with the Roosevelt Administration are conflicting. Schacht reported that the President received him cordially in May, 1933, and when Schacht told him Germany might have to default on the interest payments (he meant transfer payments)[25] of her American loans, Roosevelt, he wrote in his memoirs, laughed and slapped his thigh. "It would serve the Wall Street bankers right," the President said.[26] But the American Ambassador to Germany, William E. Dodd, recorded in his diary that Roosevelt disliked Schacht's arrogant bearing.[27] Cordell Hull found Schacht "simple and unaffected," but he was outraged at the announcement Schacht had made on May 8, the day before they met, that the German Government would cease payments abroad on the Reich's foreign debts. All Schacht could say was that he was extremely sorry and he had not foreseen Hull's reactions.[28] Actually Schacht had been given the authority when he left for the United States to determine when the moratorium would begin. He had strongly disapproved of Germany's taking out the loans in the first place; now one way of helping to finance the rearmament, which he, like Hitler, regarded as all important, would be to stop transfer payments on foreign loans.[29]

Schacht, no doubt, was genuinely of the opinion that the Fuehrer planned no war, because that was what Hitler kept saying and that was what Schacht wanted to believe. In his financial calculations for the future he allowed for a limited rearmament that he thought Germany could afford. He believed a degree of autarky to be thrust upon Germany, which lacked credit and gold and faced boycotts because of its anti-Semitic measures. If he had been left to himself, his program of public works would have relied heavily on constructing irrigation projects and building factories. But he agreed with Hitler that a vast program of public works, including housing developments and the building of the Autobahnen, would be a powerful answer to the depression. Rearmament, he knew, must be the center of the German economic effort under Hitler. Partly because of Schacht's skill, the economy began to pick up rapidly despite its burden of price controls, quotas, and import and export restrictions. He undoubtedly would have preferred dropping these restraints, for like most German bankers and economists he liked a free-market economy that relied only as needful on government intervention. He also undoubtedly would have preferred to do without the basic shift of the economy to rearmament for a huge military machine. Price controls could dampen the inflation, but Schacht feared that rapid and exaggerated rearming was an excessive drain on raw materials and the Reich's resources; what he wanted was a strong, efficient German Army, not the nation in arms that was Hitler's goal.

For some time he and Hitler saw matters in the same light. In August, 1934, the Fuehrer appointed Schacht as acting Minister of Economics, and less than a year later, when he was Minister of Economics, he was named General Plenipotentiary for the War Economy. Up to a point Schacht did all he was expected to do. He devised an extraordinarily complicated and successful series of banking measures designed to spark the rapidly expanding economy—"a daring credit policy," he called it. In order to prevent printing money, he financed rearmament in part through so-called Mefo bills (Mefo was an abbreviation for Metallurgische Forschungsgesellschaft, a dummy company formed by four great concerns: Siemens, Gutehoffnungshuette, Krupp, and Rheinstahl, with a capital of only one million marks). The Mefo bills were guaranteed by the Government and could be discounted at any German bank. They ran for six months but could be extended, and the Reichsbank would rediscount them at any time within the last three months of the earliest date of maturity.[30] Thus the Reichsbank in effect loaned money to the Government, a practice which was illegal under existing statutes, but credit to the amount of twelve billion marks was provided the munitions industry in this fashion without floating new loans or increasing the money supply.

Schacht had thought correctly that the Mefo bills, which paid 4 per cent interest, would bring out a good deal of money lying fallow in the vaults of German business concerns that because of the financial uncertainties had been uninvested. But the 4 per cent interest and the readiness of the Reichsbank to exchange the Mefo bills for money at any time put these hidden funds to work, and six billion marks were unearthed from this source.[31] In addition, Schacht used blocked funds (of foreigners) deposited in the Reichsbank, which gave him added pleasure for, as he said, "The Reichsbank invested the major part of Reichsbank accounts owned by foreigners . . . in armament draughts. Our armaments are therefore being financed partially with the assets of our political opponents." [32]

When he became Minister of Economics, Schacht set out with what he called "the New Plan," designed to streamline and control everything the Reich bought abroad and everything that was imported. Twenty-five supervisory bodies were formed, which had authority over all foreign trade. A series of bilateral barter agreements were conducted, mostly with southeastern European countries and South America, through which more than half of Germany's trade was channeled. In addition, restrictions were imposed on the demands for foreign exchange and on export licenses, and German travel abroad was for the most part prohibited. Schacht set up clearing agreements through which German importers paid the costs of their transactions by depositing marks with the German clearing agency; these sums were transferred as a credit to the clearing agency of the exporting country. The exporter was thus paid in his own currency; and since the countries of southeast Europe and South America had large raw material and agricultural surpluses they desperately needed to get rid of on almost any terms, they did business.

Schacht's plans for bilateral trade agreements were partial answers to the boycotts against German goods. Any boycott, Schacht pointed out, would hurt the Australian sheep raiser, the Spanish orange grower, the American cotton planter, the Scottish herring fisherman, as well as Germany. He was ready to deal with every country that would make a satisfactory trade agreement, including the Soviet Union, and in 1935 he succeeded in securing a credit from Russia for 200 million marks to run over a period of five years. A year later the Reichsbank had a favorable balance of trade with the Soviet Union of some 15 million marks.[33] Schacht could write proudly three years after he became Economics Minister, "The success of the New Plan can be proved by means of a few figures. Calculated according to quantity, the import of finished products was throttled by 63 per cent between 1934 and 1937. On the other hand the import of ores was increased by 132 per cent, of petroleum by 116 per cent, of grain by 102 per cent and of rubber by 71 per cent." [34] Within the Reich, allotments were stringent; in September, 1934, Schacht issued a decree declaring: "All raw materials in Germany are allocated and their use for processing for other than war, or otherwise absolutely vital goods is prohibited." [35]

Thousands of decrees were required to administer the system. Schacht requisitioned all German foreign-exchange reserves; his Ministry controlled in effect every mark spent in foreign trade as well as German exports. The New Plan was so successful that John Maynard Keynes later declared that England might have to imitate it after the war.[36] But although Schacht said many of the same things that Hitler did about the primacy of spirit over economics and echoed the sentiments of *Mein Kampf* about the need for worker and capitalist to put their abilities at the service of the entire German community, he knew and cared about a sound fiscal policy, and Hitler had no interest whatever in such matters. Schacht's Mefo bills were intended to be repaid after five years from the taxes paid in from the expanding economy; and they could have been, Schacht said at Nuremberg, had Hitler and Goering not wanted everything plowed into new armament.

A number of events disturbed Schacht during this period. He said at

Nuremberg that while he was shocked by the killings at the time of the Roehm putsch, he was even more deeply upset by the Fritsch affair (*cf.* Goering, Chapt. 2, and Frank, Chapt. 11). Nevertheless, he went down the line with Hitler as long as he thought the Fuehrer's economic policies could be made amenable to his own. In his speech to the Central Association of Banks and Banking Concerns of February 26, 1934, he said, "The task of the men now at the head of banking affairs can be fulfilled only when they devote themselves to the spirit of the new state. If this should not be the case with one or another of you, he must disappear from the scene as quickly as possible." [37] Although in 1935 Schacht began his campaign to cut down on armament spending, he had nothing but public praise for what was being done. On March 4, 1935, he said at the Leipzig Spring Fair:

> My so-called foreign friends do neither me nor the situation nor themselves any good when they try to bring me into opposition to the allegedly impossible National Socialist economic theories and declare me to some extent the protector of economic reason. I can assure you that everything I say and do has the complete approval of the Fuehrer and that I would not say or do anything that does not have his approval. Therefore, it is not I but the Fuehrer who is the protector of economic reason. The strength of the National Socialist regime lies in the unified will directed through the Fuehrer and in the enthusiastic and unconditional devotion of his co-workers and of the people to him.[38]

In his Koenigsberg speech of August 18, 1935, Schacht dealt with matters that were troubling him. Talking warily to his Fuehrer and to his conservative admirers, as did Papen in his Marburg speech, Schacht mixed fulsome praise and guarded criticism. He said:

> In a time in which many circles abroad are pleased to stamp every smashed windowpane in Germany as a cultural infamy, disregarding the fact that those circles themselves have smashed more windowpanes than the political leaders of the world can ever pay for with their peace efforts, in such a time I should like to emphasize . . . that we have the heartiest desire to conduct peaceful economic and cultural exchange with all people and nations of the earth. . . . Whose heart would not beat higher when he reads these sentences: "The flag is more than a bank account," "The people is primary, not the economy?" Such sentences are disarmingly correct but can the economist use them for his practical work? . . . My view that the re-armament of our people demands the concentration of everyone, as well as all economic and financial forces, was countered by the argument that only old women would wring their hands and ask: "Who will pay for all this?" . . . Adolf Hitler has called the German people to this new, almost impossible effort with boundless courage, statesmanlike skill, and with an unerring sense of responsibility toward history; and the impossible has become fact. . . . The politics of our Fuehrer can only be successful when the people in unanimous solidarity, in a single concentration of will, place themselves behind them. Just as the soldier in the Wehrmacht does his duty, so must

each citizen have the feeling that in the economy, too, he works in the service of the whole community. . . . Unfortunately, not all of our compatriots are conscious of this. . . . Then there are those of our contemporaries who are best remembered by the saying "Lord, save me from my friends." Those are the people who heroically smear windowpanes in the middle of the night, who brand every German who trades in a Jewish store as a traitor, who condemn every former Freemason as a worthless character, and who, in the just fight against priests and ministers who talk politics from the pulpit, cannot themselves distinguish between religion and misuse of the pulpit.

"The goal of such people," Schacht added, however, with his banker's preference for the middle of the road, "is generally correct and good." There was no place for secret organizations in the Third Reich, he said, and the priests should take care of the souls, not of the politics, of their parishioners. He continued:

> The Jews must realize that their influence in Germany has disappeared for all time. We wish to keep our people and our culture pure and distinctive, just as the Jews have always demanded this of themselves . . . But the solution of these problems must be brought about under state leadership, and cannot be left to unregulated individual actions, which have a disturbing influence on the national economy, and which have therefore been repeatedly forbidden by governmental as well as Party agencies . . . The economy is a very sensitive organism. Every disturbance, from whatever direction it may come, acts as sand in the machine. Since our economy is closely allied with that of foreign countries, not one of us . . . can be indifferent to what consequences these disturbances can have at home and abroad. It is absolutely necessary for the leadership of our economic policies that confidence in Germany as a constitutional state remains unshaken.
>
> No one in Germany is without rights. . . . The Jew can become neither a citizen nor a fellow German. But . . . he must not be under arbitrary action, but under the law . . . I emphasize now that all of us are in the same boat, and no one will be given the opportunity to get out. There is only one thing. Confidence in the seaworthiness of this ship and in the captain's leadership of the German ship of state.[39]

This was a skillful speech aimed at Schacht's critics, at those who caused disorder and property damage, and above all at the Fuehrer, who had to learn to listen more closely to what Schacht said.

At a meeting two days later, Schacht again denounced "the unlawful activities" against Jews, which were hurting German exports. He was especially incensed over Streicher's having printed in *Der Stuermer* the picture of a manager of the Reichsbank, calling him a traitor because he had traded with a Jew. The Jew, Schacht said, was the holder of an Iron Cross from World War I, and Schacht demanded an apology from Streicher. He told the gathering that since he himself was not a Party member he would buy wherever he wanted to.[40] Schacht always flourished a measure of independence where the market or the Reichsbank were concerned, and the Streichers were detestable to him. But any criticism of Hitler or high policy was out of the question.

In a conversation with the American S. R. Fuller, Jr., on September 23, 1935, Schacht said that Hitler was necessary to the German people, who were 95 per cent behind him, that "they want and need Hitler." * Schacht said that he was conservative, the Army was conservative, and Hitler, too, was turning to the conservative side—because that was essential for a statesman. In answer to Fuller's question as to whether the Army really wanted Hitler, Schacht replied, "Without a doubt. Hitler is a necessity to them and to Germany." Schacht told Fuller that Germany needed colonies and that Germans opposed as did Hitler a socialist state where the impulses of development came from the Government. In answer to Fuller's remark that Germany's treatment of the Jews was resented in the United States, Schacht said he had just explained to Mr. Warburg that the Jews must stop making such an outcry—they would always be inferior to the Germans in the Reich and should accept the government protection being offered them. He told Fuller he was at liberty to repeat to President Roosevelt all that Schacht was telling him.[41]

George Messersmith, the veracity of whose testimony by affidavit at Nuremberg was sharply attacked by the defense lawyers (he was given to using high colors in depicting his relations to the Nazi great), reported that Schacht had told him between 1930 and 1934 that the Nazis would plunge Germany into war and the rest of the world, too, if they were not stopped—words that Schacht probably would not have used to a foreign acquaintance. Messersmith thought that Schacht was no captive of the Nazis, but an opportunist, a view shared by a far more reliable and astute observer, François-Poncet.[42]

Schacht masked his increasing differences with Goering by doggedly praising Hitler; there was no other way to reach the Fuehrer. On January 30, 1937, on the occasion of his receiving the Party's Golden Badge of Honor, Schacht expressed his gratitude: "We must devote ourselves with all our hearts and strength to the Fuehrer and to the Reich. The German future lies in the hands of our Fuehrer." [43] On April 21 he added, "Our Fuehrer, Adolf Hitler, upheld by the veneration of a whole nation . . . has won for himself the soul of the German people . . . Only those closest to him know how difficult the burden of responsibility is, how sorrowful the hours during which decisions have to be made . . ." [44]

On March 21, 1938, after the *Anschluss* with Austria, Schacht, who had already resigned as Minister of Economics but was still President of the Reichsbank, made a speech in Vienna in which he stressed that of course Austria had a special mission, as did Bavaria and Prussia, but that there was no German mission outside Germany. Schacht said that the method of

* Fuller, according to Ambassador Dodd, had been sent to talk with Schacht and other leading Germans by President Roosevelt.

achieving the *Anschluss* had been adopted as the result of countless perfidies, Wilson's fourteen points, and the frustrated readiness of both Austria and Germany for the customs union that could not be made. He told how the Austrian National Assembly had asked for union with Germany after World War I, and when the treaty of St. Germain was signed in the museum room for extinct races, Clemenceau said that the site fitted the Austrians perfectly. He reiterated that in February, 1921, the Austrian National Council had again voted for the *Anschluss* and 98.5 per cent of the voters in the Tyrol and more than 99 per cent in Salzburg had voted for it. He concluded that the grumblers should be told that everyone cannot be satisfied; that this deed was accomplished only "by our Adolf Hitler." And Schacht asked his audience to swear allegiance to the Fuehrer.[45]

Schacht had broken with Hitler, he said at Nuremberg, as soon as it became evident that Germany was going to build armed forces far beyond its economic capacity and when he realized that Hitler was preparing not to bring Germany as an equal to the conference table but to wage war. This posturing was an exaggeration. What he had done was to try over a period of years to make concessions and to bring Hitler to the Schacht party. The battle was never directly with Hitler but with his faithful paladin Hermann Goering, and in 1937 Schacht's differences with Goering became so acute that the two no longer could work together. Goering was slavishly following the will of the Fuehrer with no more regard for economics than his master, while Schacht was stubbornly trying to be a banker as well as a devoted follower. It was inevitable that Schacht and Goering would clash. Schacht never had liked Goering. He disliked his ostentation, his theatrical costumes; Schacht was not the man to appreciate Goering's appearing at social gatherings as a primitive German hunter carrying a spear or dressing in a Roman toga, rouging his cheeks, and displaying painted toenails through his sandals.

Schacht in his frosty way came to despise him after Goering was given charge of the German economy in 1936 as head of the Four-Year Plan. He brought to this position grandiose notions about a subject on which Schacht thought him completely ignorant. When Goering was made Commissioner of Foreign Exchange and Raw Materials in May, 1936, the two men claimed jurisdiction over the same economic fields—and they approached their tasks with diametrically opposed views. Schacht thought it would be ruinous to step up production on the scale now being ordered by Hitler and Goering, and he told Goering in a meeting in May, 1936, that it was Hitler's intention that the pace of rearmament be maintained only through 1936. Goering was incensed and declared that he had never heard of any limitations to be imposed on rearmament. As the tension between the two men increased, Goering said he would personally examine the records of Schacht's departments to make sure he was not guilty of bad judgment.[46] When Schacht stubbornly repeated that to produce uneconomically was to waste the substance of the people, Goering replied laconically, "I tell you, if the Fuehrer wishes it then two times two are five." [47] Schacht's notions of fiscal solvency seemed old fashioned and absurd to the revolutionaries he had determined to advise. In order to provide the foreign exchange to obtain raw materials like copper and lead, Schacht wanted the Reich to export more goods. Otherwise, he said, the Reich would go bankrupt. Goering was merely impatient of such old-hat orthodox banking notions. Credit would be decreed; the economy was what he and Hitler wanted it to be.

In 1937 Schacht received the Party's Golden Badge of Honor, but a few months later he was effectively removed from the official life of the country in everything but title. The paper agreements he and Goering arrived at were soon disregarded by Goering, and Hitler had no hesitation—when the two men clashed—in backing his faithful paladin over the shriveled banker in a frock coat. Schacht had never even been a Party member; men like Himmler from the first had opposed his appointment; he was only useful as a show-piece for the Army and big business and to devise ingenious methods for providing credit and foreign exchange. The Army backed Schacht's attempts to limit rearmament against Goering's headlong measures, but Goering's policies were Hitler's, and by November the struggle between Goering and Schacht had come to a crisis. Goering, in his measureless vanity, said to Schacht, "But I have to be able to give you directives," and Schacht, dis-dainful as always of the pretense of the man, answered, "Not to me but to my successor." [48] That was the last time he saw Goering until they met again at Nuremberg, though Goering telephoned him after the incident to tell Schacht he was sitting in his chair in the Ministry of Economics.

Schacht resigned both as Minister of Economics and as Plenipotentiary for the War Economy in November, 1937, but Hitler solaced him with much the same device he used on Neurath: he appointed him Minister Without Portfolio—a post, Schacht told a friend, he could not risk refusing.[49] He remained president of the Reichsbank—Hitler reappointed him in March, 1938—but his relationship with the Fuehrer steadily deteriorated, and a memorandum Schacht sent in early January, 1939, in which he again opposed the excessive expenditures for armament, was the last straw. Hitler asked him to resign on January 20, but Schacht continued to receive the full salary he had been paid as president of the Reichsbank—60,000 RM a year. He retained the title Minister Without Portfolio and received the 24,000 RM annual salary of that position.[50] In the autumn of 1939, at the start of the war, Schacht tried to get from his American acquaintances an invitation to visit the United States, where he hoped to persuade President Roosevelt to act as mediator between Germany and the Allies, but he received neither the invitation nor permission from the Fuehrer to undertake such a mission.[51] After the fall of France, Hitler triumphantly asked Schacht at a reception what he thought of the great military success, and Schacht reported in his memoirs that he merely replied, "May God protect you."

Despite his growing disenchantment Schacht was much too cautious to involve himself irretrievably in a conspiracy against Hitler. In 1938 he talked and plotted with most of the generals who were determined to overthrow Hitler in the event of war with the great powers. He agreed with General Edwin von Witzleben, one of the chief conspirators, that a military regime should be established by a coup to be followed by a popular vote. But in 1942, when he received the speech a member of the Resistance, Reichsregierungsrat Dr. Hans von Dohnanyi, was prepared to give when a coup succeeded, Schacht read only the first words—"Hitler is dead"—and said he would read the rest when the event really took place.[52] Asked by Ulrich von Hassell, German Ambassador to Italy and one of the men who would be killed as a result of the July 20 plot, if he would join the Cabinet of the new Government, Schacht said that it was too early to talk of such matters, although he offered to try to use his influence with the Allies on behalf of the proposed Government. At the time of Schacht's involvement in these intrigues, Carl Goerdeler, Fabian von Schlabrendorff, and others were trying to get a commitment from London and Washington for something less than unconditional surrender if Hitler was overthrown.

Schacht joined nothing dangerous to his life or the future of his family. Until 1938, when he was fifty-five years old, he was married to a woman who was so pro-Nazi she would tolerate no criticism of the the Fuehrer or the Party. Since Schacht was unmistakably a critic and his wife repeated what he said outside the family circle, the relationship became increasingly strained, and they separated that year. Schacht remarried in March, 1941. His second wife was thirty years younger than he, and they had two daughters. They were not long to have a peaceful family life together.

In November, 1942, Schacht wrote a barbed letter to his old enemy Goering, objecting to conscripting fifteen-year-old boys and telling the Reichsmarschall that this would be a burden on the fighting morale of the German people. In addition, he pointed out to the chief of the Luftwaffe that the anticipated quick victory over England by the Air Force had not materialized, nor had Germany been free of enemy air raids. "The repeated announcements," Schacht wrote, "that the Russian resistance was definitely broken have been proved to be untrue. . . . Allied supplies of arms to Russia, and the manpower reserves of Russia . . . have been sufficient to bring continuous counterattacks against our Eastern front." Schacht then commented on the Allied landings in North Africa and the failure of the German U-boats to prevent the transport of enemy war material.[53] It was a bold and foolish letter, for Goering had said that the German people could call him Meyer if a single bomb dropped on German cities, but it was the Fuehrer who had prematurely announced the victory over Russia. The reply to Schacht came in the form of letters from Lammers and Goering. Lammers informed Schacht that on January 21, 1943, because of Schacht's attitude "to the fateful battle of the German nation," the Fuehrer had decided to dismiss him as Minister Without Portfolio. Goering wrote, "My answer to your defeatist letter, that undermines the powers of resistance of the German people, is that I expel you herewith from the Prussian State Council." [54]

Schacht was arrested on July 21, 1944, the day after the attempt on Hitler's life, and he was to spend the next four years in twenty-three prisons, German and Allied. Before the end of the war he was imprisoned in three Nazi concentration camps: Ravensbrueck, Flossenbuerg and Dachau; the Americans took him into custody in Pustertal, Austria, where a number of former Gestapo prisoners had been shipped.

At Nuremberg, Schacht said, he and the other defendants were treated as though they had already been found guilty. He complained that the American commandant of the prison would not permit him to climb on the chair in his cell to look out of the window, that he was not permitted to sleep on his side, that the radios of the GIs played "Don't Fence Me In" too loudly, that visitors came as to a zoo, chewing gum and loud and contemptuous. Once, when he was photographed without a collar while he was eating, he threw the contents of a coffee pot over the cameraman—an action the commandant of the prison called a defamation of the American uniform. The American guards, however, loved the episode and happily replaced the coffee—which was officially denied him—with all he could drink.*

After the Nuremberg tribunal found Schacht not guilty of the charges brought against him, the German courts brought him to trial. He was sentenced to eight years' imprisonment as a major offender under the denazification laws. Though the full sentence was never served, he was not freed until September 2, 1948, and he was not completely cleared until September, 1950.[55] Two years of his prison terms he spent in solitary confinement.

Schacht, like Goering, had an easy time with those of his cross-examiners who struggled to fit onto the stubborn facts their stereotypes of German big business, the conspiracy to commit aggressive warfare, and Schacht's connection with the great plot. The indictment against him was drawn up in a scrappy fashion; it accused him of having been a member of the Reichstag, and the prosecution said that as such Schacht had voted for the Enabling Act to give Hitler full powers. But Schacht had never been a member of the Reichstag and thus could not have voted for the Enabling Act. Mr. Justice Jackson, cross-examining Schacht on the latter's demands for a return of the former German colonies, swiftly took umbrage at Schacht's calling them German property. "And your property, as you call it," said Jackson, "were African colonies." Schacht replied that the use of the word "property" was not invented by him but appeared in the text of the Versailles Treaty.

Since in some cases confusion was combined with an uncertain familiarity

* Everyone involved in the American occupation at this point was likely to be in uniform, which facilitated identification since it helped to distinguish from the native population many of the occupation officials who spoke English with marked accents. Once, when Schacht apologized to an American member of the prosecution staff for his bad English, the man replied, "It's a lot better than most of my colleagues'."

with the English language, the sense of some of the interrogations is not always easy to follow. An American prosecutor, questioning Schacht about the costs of German rearmament, asked on October 13, 1945, "You would not say that the figure of 35 billions was fantastic like the figure of 90 billions that Hitler said? [56] In a question about aggression, the prosecutor asked Schacht on October 16, 1945, "When did it first come to your mind that the extent of the German armament was in such a position as to cause the danger of war in itself?" [57] Proceeding to the international situation preceding the war, Schacht's interrogator staggered onto the problem of Austria and the *Anschluss*, which the prosecution often spoke of as "the rape of Austria" although no country had ever more willingly come under the domination of another than the impoverished and strife-ridden Austria came to the embrace of Hitler's booming Reich. The prosecutor struggled mightily with this rape of Austria. He said, "Austrian reservists were called up . . . Does that come back to your memory? I am just trying to get the framework on the situation." Schacht replied that he did not know. The prosecutor said, "Well, but you were a living man at the time. We all were, and we were very influential, as a matter of fact. What I am trying to do is to ask you whether you remember . . . the tension that existed in Europe . . ." [58] A day later he returned to the subject: "There was," he told Schacht, "at that time already a tension in Europe . . . There were statements and declarations by the powers, with respect to guaranteeing integrities, and all the implications that we knew from the last war . . ." Schacht replied, "Yes."[59]

During the course of these interrogations Schacht explained one role an army plays in international politics. In 1932, he said, the Allies had forbidden the customs union proposed by Austria to keep the country from bankruptcy and complete despair as to its enonomic future. But in 1938 the Allies had accepted the *Anschluss*—this was the difference between confronting a strong and a weak Wehrmacht. The American prosecutor was obviously confused not only by the complexities of the international situation with which he was struggling, but also by the meaning of some of the words in the working vocabulary. "Vis-à-vis," especially, troubled him, and he could not always distinguish it from "against" or "versus." The following dialogues took place:

PROSECUTOR: The position you took, as I understand it, was that the Wehrmacht was important not so much as an aggressive weapon against strong countries, Austria and Czechoslovakia, as against, or vis-à-vis, if you will, the larger powers, the concert of nations in Europe. . . .[60]
PROSECUTOR: In other words, the army stood there . . . as a weapon . . . vis-à-vis the Austrians.
SCHACHT: Not vis-à-vis the Austrians but vis-à-vis the Allies.
PROSECUTOR: I am a little naïve about these things, I must say. You say . . . not vis-à-vis Austria but against the Powers?
SCHACHT: Not against the Powers but vis-à-vis the Powers.[61]

PROSECUTOR: The *Anschluss* with Austria was not certainly by virtue of any international agreement, was it?

SCHACHT: No, but they tolerated it.[62]

Schacht then said that the *Anschluss* had been achieved by propaganda and political pressure, that military force had nothing directly to do with it but that the very existence of the Wehrmacht as a power behind the propaganda and political pressure had a lot to do with the success of the coup. He added that he did not know how far the pressure would have succeeded if no Wehrmacht had been there.

PROSECUTOR: What I mean is did you at that time credit the Wehrmacht as an instrument for the achievement of Hitler's march into Austria? . . .[63] Was there a mobilization? Do you remember?

SCHACHT: I don't know. Was there?

PROSECUTOR: I am just wondering what you remember about it.[64] Would you deny that there was tension in Europe and the threat of a war prior to the Austrian *Anschluss*?

Schacht replied that Hitler intended to force the *Anschluss* but there was no threat of war from the German side. The prosecutor then asked, "You realize, of course, that the Czechs had an army, and the Czechs had munition works, as well, did they not?" [65] Questions on other subjects could be equally inane. Referring to a meeting between Schacht and Ambassador Bullitt, the American prosecutor said ". . . to refresh your recollection, I will tell you that that was in November of 1937. You don't doubt that, do you?" Schacht replied, "No, I don't doubt it at all." [66] Speaking of Schacht's wavering relations with Hitler the prosecutor asked, "This meeting that you had after Munich . . . this attendance that you had, was that a voluntary attendance on Hitler . . . ?" [67] "Now, did you again renew that situation in 1941?" [68]

The man with the highest IQ among the twenty-one defendants had no trouble answering such questions. There were others, however, that did not come so easily. Schacht had certainly approved of the principles of the anti-Semitic laws, including depriving Jews of German citizenship. He, too, thought the Eastern Jews who had come to Germany after World War I were a poor lot with no morals who preferred to do no useful work. He wanted the jobs open to Jews to be limited by percentages—a protective device he thought should be adopted by countries other than Germany. That he opposed, however, the rowdyism of the Nazis, the broken windows of the *Kristallnacht*, the destruction of Jewish property and then of the Jews themselves goes without saying. Schacht was no radical. He chose Hitler calculatedly and with forethought as the only one of the nonleftist political leaders who could be elected by a sizable minority of the German people, as the sole alternative to chaos and communism and a world in which Schacht would play no role.

None of his thinking had disposed him against the main tenets of the

Nazis. Although at the age of thirty-two he had been deputy director of the Dresdner Bank, his doctoral dissertation on mercantilism had dealt with "the morphine of the trust, but the elixir of life of the cartel," one of those philosophical-economic distinctions that the non-German world finds so hard to follow. The German inflation, which had reached the point where one gold mark was worth a billion paper ones; the threat of communism; the protracted depression; and above all Hitler's victories at the polls, together with his apparent reasonableness when he spoke at such functions at the Goering dinner—all these elements led Schacht to think that new measures were essential and Hitler might well be brought into a coalition where his political magnetism could be retained but the noisy propaganda and unsound ideas removed. In any event, Schacht thought that there was no alternative to him—without the relatively disciplined and nationalistic Nazis the country would automatically fall prey to the Left, to communism.

Hitler's program of housing and Autobahnen to counter unemployment was Schacht's, too, and when he visited Franklin Roosevelt in 1933 there seemed to have been no essential differences in the economic solutions the two men discussed. Schacht reported in his book that Roosevelt told him he made a fine impression. Schacht also met and attended a dinner given by David Sarnoff of the Radio Corporation of America. Ten of Sarnoff's dozen or so guests were Jews, and Schacht reported that he spoke as carefully and circumspectly as possible and that no discussion followed the speech. Afterward Sarnoff said, "Doctor, you've been a very good sport." Schacht declared that Sumner Welles, too, had a good opinion of him, and when Welles came to Germany in 1940 he had asked to see Schacht alone, a request that Ribbentrop opposed. But Welles and Schacht nevertheless did have a talk together, and Schacht said he put his life into Welles' hands by telling plainly what he thought of Hitler, with whom by that time he had broken. Schacht felt later that Welles could certainly have demolished the charges against him at Nuremberg by testifying for him and that the Department of State could have made the record of the talks available, but neither Welles nor his superiors saw fit to do this. Ambassador Dodd, knowing of Schacht's aversion to the Nazis, urged Schacht in the late 1930's to emigrate to the United States instead of remaining in Germany, where his life was in danger.

But the record of Schacht's support of Hitler when he thought the Nazis could be brought within a conservative, strong, nationalist state was clear enough. In 1932 Schacht had written to Hitler, "Your movement is carried internally by so strong a truth and necessity that victory in one form or another cannot elude you for long."[69] Goebbels, too, attested to Schacht's reliability; he had written in his diary, "Schacht absolutely represents our point of view. He is one of the few who accepts the Fuehrer's position entirely." [70] Hassell noted in his diary the incongruity of Schacht's remaining as a member of Hitler's Cabinet when he in private conversations was so critical of the regime. Schacht came to hate Hitler, but he continued to serve him until he was dismissed from one after another of his various posts. He thought Ribbentrop extraordinarily stupid and incompetent, Goering dishonest, and Funk alcoholic and homosexual; but he did not leave such company of his own free will.

The Nuremberg court freed him—although the Russians voted for finding him guilty. In its judgment the court said that it had not been proved beyond a reasonable doubt that Schacht had known of Hitler's plan for aggression.[71] Although his German jail sentence was annulled, he was never to get a clean bill of health from many of his critics. In 1951 a Canadian who met him in Indonesia refused to shake hands with him. Karl Severing (see Papen, Chapt. 5) said Schacht was the one man for whom he could not subordinate feelings of personal animosity, and other members of the Resistance felt the same way. Among the Americans his stock was not high either. Mr. Justice Jackson found his acquittal "regrettable." [72] The Military Governor of Wuerttemberg Baden, Charles M. La Follette, said his comments when he heard that Schacht was freed by the German appellate court would be unprintable.* The United States denazification officer for that state said the decision was "incomprehensible." † Either Schacht was a big war criminal or he was nothing.[73]

When Schacht was released after his last prison term, in 1948, he had two marks fifty pfennigs in his pocket and seemingly no hope of soon bettering his fortunes (he testified he had one million marks when the Nazis arrested him in July, 1944), for he could not practice his profession nor was he to be allowed to drive a car. But his rise after he was again able to return to business was rapid. He was invited to consult on economic matters with governments East and West—even in Nuremberg the American prosecution had him draw up a memorandum on a solution for the economic plight of Germany, and his services were immediately in demand as soon as he was able to use them. For there was no question of his abilities.

The Wehrmacht properly expressed its appreciation in 1938 for all he had done in making possible the rearmament of the Reich. His workable system of controls of what went out of and came into Germany and his cautious attempt to keep rearmament within the capacity of German industry without causing inflation made him one of the key figures of the decade when the financiers and economists of the world were struggling with unemployment and blowing on the embers of the recovery from the depression that had hit all the nations of the West.

There is no reason to doubt the essential truth of what Schacht told the court at Nuremberg. He had supported the Fuehrer until he became con-

* La Follette was also Deputy Chief Counsel at the later trial in Nuremberg of the German judges.
† The court reversed its decision to free Schacht a little while later, but by then Schacht had moved to the British zone.

vinced that Hitler would lead the country into war, he said, and he had always opposed the excesses of the Party rowdies, and of the Fuehrer himself. He had hoped in his hubris to be able to harness the hurricane but had been carried along with it until he himself very nearly fell victim to it and ended up in the concentration camps of the SS with other conservatives from the Army and official life of whom Himmler and the Gestapo had any doubts. His failure to see deeply into events or to see unpleasant realities was the same as Jodl's, but in a minor civilian key, and he had broken with the leader in time—or, better said, the leader had broken with him in time. Like Schacht, Hitler found it easy to choose between his purposes and another's. Despite the mutual words of praise there had never been any genuine sympathy between the two. Hitler said once that Schacht had always opposed him, and Goering's testimony bears this out despite his conflicting statement that Schacht must have gone along with the rearmament program or Hitler would not have tolerated him in office. Schacht undoubtedly approved of the general program of rearming, but he tried to brake it, to keep it within German resources. Goering says, too, that Schacht always painted things in extreme colors, once even telling Hitler that what the Fuehrer proposed would bankrupt the country.

Schacht, in a word, had been an opportunist, as so many observers said he was, but a cautious one who never involved himself in anything beyond repair. His anti-Semitism was of the cautious, conventional kind, too. The exterminations were a horror to him, as they were to all respectable people in Germany. But his nationalism, his offended pride as a German after the defeat of World War I, and his belief in the maleficence of the Eastern Jews and in the necessity of getting Jews out of the healthy German communal life permitted him to take an important part in the regime that was to exterminate them. Schacht did not break with the Party on the Jewish question, although he undoubtedly deplored the broken windows and the rabble in the streets preying upon the Jews, but because Goering was invading his domain and the economic risks of Hitler's policies were becoming too great. Even so, he stayed on in the Cabinet until he was told to leave, with the conventional excuse that without him matters would be worse. For he was always right, always incapable of making a mistake, and the worst turn Hitler or anyone else could take was to turn away from the Schacht party.

WALTHER EMANUEL FUNK

Walther Funk, the man who succeeded Schacht as Minister of Economics in 1938, was the final cause of Schacht's dismissal in 1939 as president of the Reichsbank. On January 7, 1939, Schacht had written a memorandum to Hitler, telling him that the too rapid pace of rearmament would have disastrous consequences for the German economy. The memorandum had irritated Hitler, but it was not until he heard the tidings Funk brought to him a few days later that he could bring himself to dismiss Schacht. During a meeting with Funk and Schwerin von Krosigk soon after Schacht had written the memorandum, Schacht said that the Reichsbank would not grant a short-term credit of one hundred million marks at the end of January, that the Reich was bankrupt and Krosigk should tell this to Hitler. Krosigk prudently declined to bring such a message to the Fuehrer, but Funk reported the conversation to Hitler the next day, and Schacht's active career on behalf of the Reich's economy was over.[74] On January 19, 1939, Funk took over the post of president of the Reichsbank, as he had assumed the other offices Schacht had held. Schacht thought little of his successor. He said that Funk was a harmless homosexual, an alcoholic.* He felt that Funk was inept in financial matters and too easily led by the Fuehrer in his economic decisions. Since the latter charge was also leveled against Schacht, it may properly be regarded with suspicion, but it is nevertheless true.

Funk was another of the self-styled free enterprisers who, like Schacht, said he had joined the Party in order to preserve the market economy. The notions of German big businessmen and of the bankers like Schacht easily accommodated themselves for a time at least to those of the Party. Almost all German businessmen believed in therapeutic doses of government intervention and in a powerful, well-disposed government to administer them. In 1925 the same Reich Association of German Industry that was to back Schacht's candidacy for the chancellorship was addressed by Carl Duisberg of I. G. Farben as follows: "Be united, united, united! . . . We hope that our words of today will be heard, and will find the strong man, for he is always necessary for us Germans, as we have seen in the case of Bismarck . . ." In 1926 Duisberg told the same group: "If Germany is again to be great, all classes of our people must come to the realization that leaders are necessary who can act without concern for the caprices of the masses." In 1930 he attacked the principle of the democracy of the marketplace, of the ability of the consumer to choose well among competing products: ". . . the masses who neither were expert nor were able to become expert in economic matters." [75] These men were accustomed to cartels, to trade agreements, to the traditional mechanisms by which the market is rigged on behalf of order and sound business morals, but more important, perhaps, their philosophy and training made them suspicious of the caprices of the unregulated market which bought their products and made them men of business instead of bureaucrats.

After the war a number of communications from Hitler were found in the Krupp files. One said: "Private enterprise cannot be maintained in the age of democracy; it is conceivable only if the people have a sound idea of

---

* Belgian Ambassador Davignon said that Funk was so drunk at one of his own parties that he could not say good-bye to his guests; and others, too, corroborate Schacht (cf. Curt Riess, *Joseph Goebbels* [Baden-Baden: Dreieck Verlag, 1949], p. 150).

authority and personality. Everything positive, good and valuable that has been achieved in the world of economics and culture is solely attributable to personality." [76] Such sentiments were echoed by Gustav Krupp and by many other entrepreneurs. Everything in German economic life was organized from the top down. The competing industries of the Ruhr, the firms that supplied them, and agriculture, too, had cartels—and the workers, of course, had unions. Unionism had begun in Germany, and the majority of German workers approved of cartels, which they believed made for job stability. The free play of the democratic market led to all kinds of uncertainties, such as price cutting, which led to wage cutting and layoffs. The cure for the depression was sought by both capital and labor in government action on a grand scale.

In the world of German big business, Funk, who never opposed any measure Hitler favored, was not much more erratic than the entrepreneurs of I. G. Farben and Krupp or than Schacht, who for all his ingenious price controls and quotas and efforts toward autarky always regarded himself a free enterpriser. Funk, like Schacht, had close relations with some of the great industrialists of Germany and used his influence with them on behalf of the Party. In the classical pattern of German conservatives, Funk saw Hitler as the sole alternative to the Communists taking over the bankrupt economy and the impotent Weimar parliamentary democracy. Funk after 1931 was another front man for the Party. He, too, knew a lot of influential people, including the President of Germany, and during his frequent visits to Hindenburg in the crucial year of 1932 he was one of the conservatives who assured the old man that Hitler was not as black as reports painted him.

Funk was born in Koenigsberg on August 18, 1890, the third child of a Prussian family of businessmen and artisans. He grew up to be a man of many talents, interested in a wide variety of subjects including political economy, law, philosophy, literature, and music—all of which he studied at one time or another. Like so many of the top Nazis, he loved music and played the piano extremely well. Before World War I he took courses in philosophy at the University of Berlin, then shifted to law, and later took up political economics. At the same time, he wrote financial articles for Leipzig and Berlin newspapers. When World War I began, he was drafted into the Army but was discharged in 1916 because of ill health (he had a defective bladder that troubled him the rest of his life).

Following his release from the Army, he took a job on the conservative *Berliner Boersenzeitung*, one of the foremost financial newspapers in Germany, and by 1920 was chief editor of its business section. Funk had a few ideas that appealed to his businessmen readers, was passionately anti-Marxist, and was an able financial reporter. In 1922 he became editor of the paper, a post he kept until he resigned to devote all his time to Party work. His articles followed the line of the flexible postwar economists, declaring the workers' demands for higher wages to be inflationary but also favoring taxing away any war profits that remained after the German collapse. Like Schacht, he was strongly nationalist; he attacked the French invasion of the Ruhr, opposed the ineffectual Weimar parliamentary system, and wanted what his National Socialist biographer characterized as a "national, constructive, integrated economic system tied into the social structure and responsible to the needs of the general public." [77] Funk knew Gregor Strasser well and approved of his theories. Strasser, he said at Nuremberg, was a man who favored free enterprise, a statement in accord with Funk's woolly thinking, for Strasser, as he must have known, was actually one of the few convinced socialists among the Nazis. It was through Strasser that he met Hitler in 1931 and became a Party member.[78] Funk was another of the men with "conservative" economic principles and connections—like Keppler—whom Hilter could make good use of, and he was soon named Hitler's personal economic adviser and chief of the Party Office for Private Economy.

With the head of every third German family unemployed in the late twenties and early thirties, Funk offered the standard solutions for reviving the economy that were to be adopted by most of the countries of the industrial West. He proposed public works, a vast road-building program, the stepping up of automobile manufacture, and mechanization of German farms. These programs, with easier credit to be obtained through the Reichsbank and a sound currency, he believed would bring Germany out of the depression. Funk had many talks with prominent Nazis who told him they held the same views. Goering told him he, too, believed in the role the creative, that is, the entrepreneurial, personality must play in the economy—scarcely anyone in the Party did not. Funk, for his part, accepted the *Fuehrerprinzip*; for how else was a strong, nationalistic, solvent Germany to emerge from the depression? By 1932 he was chief of the Party's Committee on Economic Policy, with its strange array of advisers, including the entrepreneur Wilhelm Keppler, Gottfried Feder, and Gregor Strasser, for whom on occasion Funk wrote speeches. Funk's main job, however, was liaison between the Party and big business, and he was admirably adapted for it since he spoke the language and held the views of both at the same time. At Nuremberg he said he joined the Party to convert it to free enterprise.[79] He very likely told the same thing to the industrialists he knew in 1931. In any event, the Ruhr industrialists were much in favor of his acting as an adviser to Hitler, for they felt that with men like Funk and Schacht informing the Fuehrer on economic problems, he would become more reasonable.[80]

Funk was elected to the Reichstag in July, 1932. In March, 1933, after Hitler came to power, he was given posts under Goebbels as Undersecretary of the Reich Ministry for Enlightenment and Propaganda, Press Chief of the Government (Reichsregierung), and Chairman of the Board of Directors of the Reich Broadcasting Company.[81] He held these jobs until he returned to his economic duties in 1938, when he succeeded Schacht as Minister of Economics. In the course of the next two years he took over Schacht's other posts as president of the Reichsbank and Plenipotentiary of the War Economy.

Funk never had Schacht's difficulty in getting along with Goering. He accepted the Reichsmarschall's preeminence in the economic sphere—as in all else—and whatever economic program Hitler decided on was good enough for him. Funk declared that he wanted the economy to function as a whole; food production, industry, forest and agricultural lands were to be bound together with strong central controls over wages and prices, financing and credit. In speech after speech during the war he propagated the doctrines of a controlled economy in a Reich that would lead Europe after the war and be independent of blockades and the machinations of the imperialist democracies and their unholy alliance with Soviet Russia. He denounced the "money imperialism" of Anglo-American capitalism and repeated what Hitler had always declared, that money gets its value from the authority of the state and the labor of its people.[82]

Gold, with its base in finance capital, Funk said, would be the key to American postwar plans. The United States would carry on the British imperialism of the nineteenth century. But Europe would now be independent of such abracadabra.[83] The countries of Europe had the chance to work together in a common market that had never existed before, he said, and it would be rationally organized under the auspices of the German victory. Funk hammered on Nazi prewar themes of the world economic disturbances caused by countries like the United States. The value of money was determined not by the interplay of international forces and influences, but by national and social values; work was the key to a sound currency. On the other hand, Funk pointed out, Germany after the war would have enough gold to pay its international obligations in this metal if need be. Thus, he adopted from Hitler the strategy of preaching whatever doctrine was needed to convince his audience at the moment. Europe was to live it up with Autobahnen safeguarded against accidents, and its economy was to be made proof against the vicissitudes of the capitalistic competitive price changes without the unwieldy, massive bureaucratization and collectivization of the Bolshevik system with which the Western democracies were allied.[84] The views Funk held were not only those of Hitler but those, with minor variations, of the industrialists he had helped persuade to make contributions to the Party. Funk said in one of his interrogations that three groups of industrialists had formed in the Party: one around Himmler, one around Roehm, and a third around the Fuehrer. The last group made their chief contributions either to Hitler directly or to one of Funk's agents.[85] The methods of contributing were the only differences among the groups; but it was an honor and a considerable advantage to be one of the insiders in the Himmler or Hitler circle.

The two main charges against Funk at Nuremberg were based on his part in drafting the laws to drive the Jews from the German economy and on his dealings with the SS in which, as president of the Reichsbank, he was accused of having received personal objects of value taken from the Jews before they were slaughtered. From 1942 on, the SS made unusual banking deposits of gold teeth, eyeglass frames, platinum and gold rings, diamonds, watches, earrings, spoons, knives, and forks, as well as foreign currency and stocks and bonds. Twelve kilos of pearls alone had been deposited in the Reichsbank after one delivery.[86] The jewelry was sent to the official Berlin pawnshop, and the deposits were used as security for loans for special purposes —of which Himmler had a great many. The deposits were used mainly to finance the wide-ranging SS economic enterprises manned by concentration-camp labor (see Speer, Chapt. 12).

Such shipments had been delivered to Emil Puhl, vice-president of the Reichsbank, who declared in an affidavit that he had told Funk about them and that Funk had seen them when he visited the vaults from time to time.[87] Puhl, who later appeared as a witness, formally retracted the statements he had made in his affidavit, denying that either he or Funk had known of the contents of these "closed deposits" which had been placed in sacks or boxes. But Oswald Pohl, an SS Gruppenfuehrer who headed the SS industrial empire of concentration-camp workers, told of discussions about the deliveries with both Funk and Puhl, to whom the contents of the SS booty were described in detail. Pohl said he had accompanied Funk and Puhl in a visit to the vaults of the bank after which they and the SS men had gone to lunch together.[88]

On the stand at Nuremberg and in the course of sixteen interrogations, Funk denied that he had known anything whatever of the contents of the deposits. He said he had thought that they were the usual coins and foreign exchange the SS routinely brought in. The prosecution, however, had made motion pictures of the deposits of gold teeth, jewelry, and pearls that made the Reichsbank look a good deal more like a hock shop than a bank. It could be shown also that the SS had sent Funk a letter thanking him ceremoniously for the understanding he had shown toward their enterprises, including a loan of eight million marks he had arranged, "so workers in the concentration camps can be useful both economically and in their reeducation."[89] Even at Spandau, Funk denied that he had known what kind of security he was getting at the Reichsbank, and it is possible he was telling the truth. But this point seems of small moment compared with the knowledge which he did not deny having. Whether or not he permitted himself to investigate the contents of the SS shipments, he certainly knew that he was accepting the property of murdered people to finance the SS use of concentration-camp labor.

Funk helped looting in other ways too. He was in charge of the funds of the Roges Gesellschaft (see Seyss-Inquart, Chapt. 11), used for buying goods in France on the black market. The money came from the excess occupation costs paid by France; and thirty million marks in French francs, according to the testimony at the trial, were needed every ten days when the purchases were at their height.[90] Nor was there any denial of his close identification with other ways in which the Party and its friends operated to reward the faithful. On the occasion of his fiftieth birthday he was given a 110-acre estate in Bavaria by a group of industrialists who always seemed to be on hand to supply the Nazi *Bonzen* with what they needed. When, despite his comfortable salary (which with extras came to 60,000 RM a year[91]), the running expenses and taxes of the gift house proved too high for Funk, Goering obligingly presented him with 300,000 RM to which Hitler added 520,000, and thus the Minister of Economics was bailed out of his financial troubles. He explained at Nuremberg that he had used the money to create two foundations for the benefit of the war needy among the families of the employees of the Reichsbank and the Ministry of Economics, but he had obviously regarded himself as coming under the foundations' provisions.

When questioned about the treatment of the Jews, Funk was so overcome at one of his early interrogations that he wept as he confessed his guilt. He admitted that he had known of the plundering of Jewish property. This was a considerable understatement, for he had drawn up the laws of November, 1938, that expelled the Jews from German economic life, prohibiting them after January 1, 1939, from taking part in any wholesale or retail trade, from the craftsmen and tradesmen in small shops to the managers of large-scale enterprise. He had been a conspicuous member of the meeting that took place after the *Kristallnacht*[92] (see Goering, Chapt. 3), and it was he, the handy journalist, who gave the occasion its name. He said at Nuremberg that he had deplored the *Kristallnacht*, as had Goering and Schacht and Papen and everyone, it seemed, but Goebbels. If so, it did not prevent him from drawing up the law that punished the Jews for having their shops raided.

Nevertheless, he was one of the more humane Nazis. An affidavit secured in his defense related how as Reich Press Chief he had permitted Jews to remain on the staff of the *Frankfurter Zeitung* after 1933, and another witness told how Funk maintained friendly relations with Richard Strauss even after Strauss had fallen into disgrace with the regime because he had written a letter on behalf of a Jewish colleague.[93] Another affidavit, that of Ministerial Councilor Kallus, told how Funk had tried to help a Jewish composer, Leo Blech, who had been a director of the Berlin State Opera.[94]

Funk's relations with the Party fanatics were not always completely harmonious. Streicher had once written to warn him: "You are looked upon in certain Party circles as the secret exponent of certain powers that have no place in the Party. I have always defended you against the various prominent Party members who have attacked you—but your letter of October 31, 1934, raises doubts." (Funk had written to Streicher to protest the rude treatment accorded a Norwegian vice-consul by Nazi hoodlums, treatment recorded with praise in *Der Stuermer*.)[95] He thought of himself as a man of infinite sensibility, a man of feeling and fine taste—qualities conspicuously lacking in brawlers like Streicher. Funk preferred more genteel National Socialists.

Funk's testimony at Nuremberg threw some light on the relations between industry and the Party. He pointed out that big German firms, like big industry in other countries, gave funds to competing parties whether or not they approved of their principles, and that the amount given the Nazis was small in comparison to the sums given some of the other parties—the German People's Party and the German Nationalists, for example. Even the Social Democrats were heavily supported by industry. Up to 1931, Funk said, he doubted that big industry had given more than one million marks to the National Socialist Party.[96] In 1932 the Flick firm gave 950,000 RM to President von Hindenburg to help his campaign in the presidential election and also 50,000 RM to the Nazis. In 1933 they gave 100,000 RM to the Nationalist People's Party and 120,000 RM to the Nazis. Big business, however, soon made both peace and an alliance with the National Socialists. For a time industry and the Army worked together, supporting Schacht in his efforts to control the inflated arms budget, to restrain the economic and social programs of the radical Nazis, and to establish at the same time military, political, and economic independence for the Reich.[97] After the dismissal of Schacht, such conservative forces had to deal with Funk, who docilely did what Hitler ordered. Big business survived and flourished in a fashion under the Nazis, but the word "under" must be emphasized. Men of business either became Nazified and made their peace with the Party, as did Gustav Krupp, or fled the country, as did Thyssen. A few, such as Schacht, played a small, prudent role in the Resistance; others, like Funk, just went along.

Some of the directors of the large firms were pro-Nazi, including directors of Siemens, I. G. Farben, Krupp, and several Hamburg shipping companies. These firms, Funk said, in 1933 raised seven million marks for the Party.[98] This amount, however, was raised after Hitler was Chancellor, and Funk calculated that big business as a whole contributed three billion marks—after the Fuehrer was established in power—to the Adolf Hitler Spende, a fund used for the relief of the poor and indigent, of whom there had been millions until unemployment began to be whittled down. On February 27, 1935, I. G. Farben gave 400,000 RM to the National Trust (*Nationale Treuhand*), which was to be administered by Schacht as trustee, and on September 30, 1938, the same concern made Hitler a present of 500,000 RM for use in the Sudetenland after it had been returned to the Reich. Hitler presented this money to the Sudeten Relief Fund.

Hitler actually did not like industrialists any more than he liked generals. The Reichswirtschaftsrat, a council of representative industrialists who were supposed to advise the Government on economic matters, had but one meeting. In the thirties, the Fuehrer invited prominent businessmen and their wives to a reception and concert once a year only. These occasions were known to the initiates as "money arias," and every guest who attended had to pledge a contribution. Those invited gave up to 100,000 RM each, and on one occasion the collection came to over three million marks.[99] Only one industrialist balked at the strong-arm measures, and Funk said that the Party took immediate reprisals against him; for once the Nazis came into power no business could be carried on without government approval and license. Economic chambers existed in each Gau, and first Schacht then Funk controlled foreign trade, while Goering, as Minister Without Portfolio for the Four-Year Plan, devoted his energies specifically to organizing German industry for war.

As many economists have pointed out, the German economy before Hitler came to power was ready to be taken over by a strong man.[100] Under the Weimar Republic prices of raw materials were controlled; government loans, or as it turned out gifts, were made to the owners of great estates in East Prussia; key public utilities, telephone, telegraph, the railroads, gas and water supplies were government-owned; agriculture was bolstered by subsidies and tariffs; government funds were made available to private banks that had no capital left after the 1923 inflation; and the banks in turn controlled much of German private industry. The great vertical trusts, the 2,500 cartels, the labor unions far more powerful than those in the United States, all looked to the State to revive the economy after the inflation was followed within a few years by the depression. After World War I, Germany had lost 13 per cent of its territory, 74 per cent of its iron ore, 26 per cent of its coal. Its entire merchant fleet, all vessels of more than 1,600 tons displacement, had been taken by the Allies, as had a quarter of its fishing fleet; 5000 locomotives and 150,000 railway cars had been surrendered; all Germany's colonies had been given up. Added to everything else, the Reich was saddled with the reparations, including the costs of the occupying Allied troops. John Maynard Keynes estimated that Germany was called on to pay about three times more than its utmost capacity.[101] With problems of these dimensions before them, everyone, from the worker out of a job to the industrialists, looked to the Government, whether Bruening was its head or Hitler.

Funk and his friends wanted what a later economist would call "organized capitalism." Its organization led some of the best-known firms in the Reich to employ slave and concentration-camp workers, and it brought about such voluntary associations as the Circle of Friends of Heinrich Himmler. This circle, which included among its members the head of the Potash Syndicate and other major industrialists, put millions of marks at the disposal of the Reichsfuehrer SS. The donors neither expected nor received any accounting of the funds' use. Witnesses in the Flick trial testified that businessmen offered large sums to become members of the circle, but such requests were refused; it was a closed circle. Being a "friend" of Himmler brought not only prestige but practical advantages, such as allocations of concentration-camp workers when labor became very scarce. The Friends met every second Monday in Berlin, and attendance records were sent to Himmler. The money given the Reichsfuehrer was used for expenses he could not finance out of his own official budget. The group visited Dachau in 1937 and the High Command headquarters in 1943. In return for their largesse some of them received high ranks in the SS. Baron von Schroeder, for example, became a Brigadefuehrer, the SS equivalent of a brigadier general; Otto Steinbrinck, who had been a submarine officer in World War I and was now an important figure in the coal industry, held the same rank.[102] The Circle of Friends had originally been an advisory group that was supposed to help the Fuehrer plan measures against unemployment, but it was diverted to participate in Himmler's manifold hobbies.

On May 8, 1942, Schroeder gave Himmler one million marks on behalf of the Friends for his use for "scientific" purposes. Himmler thanked him for his generosity and said that the Baron knew he could not make plans for more than three days ahead but he hoped to be able to get to the next evening meeting. When Himmler became Reichsinnenminister, Schroeder congratulated him on August 27, 1943, expressing his joy on the occasion, which he further brightened by sending another million marks from the Circle of Friends. The sum was contributed by Siemens, I. G. Farben, the Middle German Steelworks, the Deutsche Bank, the petroleum group, and others.[103] By April 4, 1943, the Circle had forty-four members, and although the secretary had to note that Himmler had been away for two years, he added that a good many meetings had been held in his absence and all sorts of enlightening talks had been given. His report of that evening, sent on to Himmler, said that one SS man had told of his experiences, and then everyone had had dinner; included was a list of those absent and the information that thirty-eight invitations had been issued and that a man named Bingel had been absent eight times; Count von Bismarck, three times; Rheinhart, chairman of the board of directors of the Commerz Bank, twelve times; an SS major general, eleven times; an SS brigadier general, twenty-three times; and Secretary of State Kleimann, thirty-one times.[104]

When the group was first formed on his behalf, Himmler had explained that he lacked funds for various cultural purposes in which he was interested, as well as for benefactions and for certain emergencies. In accord with the cultural program, lecturers came not only from the ranks of the SS but from men who had climbed or were experts on the Himalayas, excavators, ethnologists, historians who told of their research on the life of Henry the Lion and Charles the Great, archeologists who reported on their diggings in the Lueneburg Heath. Himmler needed money for all this cultural activity and for the advancement of science as well, for he was interested in many kinds of research, from the torture experiments in the concentration camps to a brandnew and wildly implausible theory on the Ice Age.

The Nazis, once they came to power, ruled with a heavy hand—although they had said they wanted merely to direct the economy, not administer it. Thyssen failed to attend a meeting called by Goering; he left the country instead. Such meetings were not called compulsory, but Thyssen had taken the only other road if one did not choose to show his solidarity with the purposes of the Party. After he left Germany, Thyssen's property was confiscated, and when the Nazis eventually caught up with him, he was put in a concentration camp, where he remained until the American forces arrived.

Funk acknowledged his guilt at Nuremberg. He said, "I placed the will of the State before my own conscience and my inner sense of duty." [105] This statement sums up well what he did and wherein his guilt lay. He was found guilty of having taken part in waging aggressive warfare and of having committed war crimes and crimes against humanity. He had aided in the exploitation of occupied territories and had participated indirectly in the slave-labor operations both by lending money to Himmler and by being a member of the Central Planning Board. But, as the court said, he was never a dominant figure, and it was this that saved him from the hangman. He was sentenced to life imprisonment.

In Spandau he read Kant—his real present concern, he said in 1947—and he and Speer worked in the garden and washed the laundry of the other prisoners. He had diabetes, but American doctors were doing well treating it and told him he could live to be a hundred. In prison he said he thought he should never have accepted the job as head of the Economics Ministry, because it was against his nature. And when nature is assaulted in this fashion, he added, she revenges herself. His wife, he told his interrogator (Kempner) in 1947, lived in a small inn in a small town; all their worldly wealth had been taken or stolen from them.[106]

Every two months he could talk to a visitor approved by the prison authorities, in the presence of two guards for fifteen minutes. He could write and receive every four weeks one letter of no more than 1300 words.[107] But his luck turned in the 1950's. The Spruchkammer proceedings in 1947 had confiscated all his property, valued at 590,183 DM in August, 1949. During the proceedings he had not been heard in his own defense because of his enforced confinement in Spandau. The Allied prison authorities would not permit him to leave the prison to testify, nor would they give his lawyer permission to visit him, for the conversation would have had to do with the Nuremberg trial, which was a forbidden subject. His lawyer in the German Court of Appeals, Hans Rechenberg, succeeded in getting the judgment reversed in 1957, by pleading that Funk was actually a prisoner of war and therefore his property could not be confiscated. Funk was an inmate of a military prison after having been tried by an international military court. Furthermore, when he had been arrested he had been immediately classified by his American captors as a prisoner of war and given a number as such. The Appellate Court agreed with Rechenberg's argument and reversed the decision of the Spruchkammer proceedings. In the same year, 1957, Funk was released from Spandau because of ill health—three years before his death.

Funk was another of those middle-class, correct time servers who were caught in the spiritual and intellectual chaos of post-World War I Germany. He came late to the Party, but he never had any criticisms to make of its doctrines, which he liked to think could be adapted to the more civilized purposes he had in mind. His pen and glib journalistic formulations were placed at the service of Hitler because Funk saw no one else who could rescue the Reich from bankruptcy and communism. He was a weak, not very intelligent man, and he gladly went along with a movement that included him among those who held high office and received princely gifts. Once the structure collapsed, he could readily see how jerry-built it had been, which is what every opportunist observes when his hopeful plans go wrong.

NOTES

1. N XII, p. 210.

2. Henri Bertrand, *Le docteur Schacht* (Paris: Gallimard, 1939).

3. Hjalmar Schacht, *Kleine Bekenntnisse* (Private printing, 1949).

4. Hjalmar Schacht, *Das Ende der Reparationen* (Oldenburg: Gerhard Stalling, 1931), pp. 29–30.

5. Hjalmar Schacht, *76 Jahre meines Lebens* (Bad Woerishofen: Kindler & Schiermeyer Verlag, 1953), p. 9.

6. Schacht Spruchkammer, Stuttgart, Vol. III, p. 48 (IZG).

7. NCA VII, EC-450, pp. 502–9.

8. N XII, pp. 188 ff.

9. NCA VII, EC-297-A, pp. 394–402. Schacht Spruchkammer, Stuttgart (IZG).

10. NCA VII, EC-433, pp. 486–94.

11. Schacht Spruchkammer, Stuttgart, Vol. I (IZG).

12. *Ibid.*, Vol. IV, p. 458.

13. Earl R. Beck, *Verdict on Schacht* (Tallahassee: Florida State University Press, 1955), pp. 75–76.

14. Buchheim, *et al.*, *op. cit.*, Vol. II, p. 320.

15. Schacht, *76 Jahre meines Lebens*, pp. 481–82. Raul Hilberg, *The Destruction of the European Jews* (Chicago: Quadrangle Books, 1961), p. 97. Beck, *op. cit.*, pp. 75–76, 131–33. *Documents on German Foreign Policy, 1918–1945*, Series D, Vol. V (Washington: US Government Printing Office), Document 661. Schacht Spruchkammer, Stuttgart, Vol. I, p. 223, Vol. II, pp. 436, 476 (IZG).

16. Beck, *op. cit.*

17. Franz Reuter, *Schacht* (Stuttgart and Berlin: Deutsche Verlagsanstalt, 1937), pp. 113–14.

18. Fritz Thyssen, *I Paid Hitler* (New York: Farrar & Rhinehart, Inc., 1941), p. 133.

19. Schacht interrogation, July 31, 1947 (NA).

20. Fritz Klein, "*Neue Dokumente zur Rolle Schachts bei der Vorbereitung der Hitlerdiktatur,*" in *Zeitschrift fuer Geschichtswissenschaft,* Vol. V, No. 4, 1957, pp. 818–22.

21. NCA VI, 3901-PS, pp. 796–98.

22. NCA VII, EC-456, pp. 512–13.

23. NCA VI, D-201, p. 1080. *Ibid.,* D-204, p. 1085. NCA VII, EC-439, pp. 501–2.

24. Beck, *op. cit.,* p. 43.

25. Gerhard L. Weinberg, "*Schachts Besuch in den USA im Jahre 1933,*" in *Vierteljahrshefte fuer Zeitgeschichte,* Vol. XI, No. 2, 1963, pp. 166–80.

26. Schacht, *76 Jahre meines Lebens,* p. 391.

27. William E. Dodd, *Ambassador Dodd's Diary, 1933–1938* (New York: Harcourt, Brace & World, Inc., 1941), pp. 4–5.

28. Cordell Hull, *The Memoirs of Cordell Hull,* Vol. I (New York: The Macmillan Company, 1948), pp. 237–38.

29. Beck, *op. cit.,* p. 42. Franz Reuter, *op. cit.,* pp. 128–31. NCA VII, EC-437, pp. 495–99. NCA III, 1168-PS, pp. 827–30.

30. Schacht, *76 Jahre meines Lebens,* p. 400. Hjalmar Schacht, *Abrechnung mit Hitler* (Hamburg and Stuttgart: Rowohlt Verlag, 1948), pp. 85–86.

31. Schacht, *76 Jahre meines Lebens,* p. 401.

32. NCA III, 1168-PS, pp. 827–30.

33. Beck, *op. cit.,* p. 59.

34. NCA VII, EC-611, pp. 589–602.

35. *Ibid.,* EC-128, p. 600.

36. Beck, *op. cit.*

37. Schacht Spruchkammer, Stuttgart, Vol. I, p. 18 (IZG).

38. N XXXVI, 415-EC, p. 488.

39. *Ibid.,* 433-EC, pp. 502–12. Also NCA VII, EC-433, pp. 486–94.

40. NG-4067, quoted in Hilberg, *op. cit.,* p. 21.

41. NCA VII, EC-450, pp. 503–9.

42. *Ibid.,* EC-451, pp. 509–10.

43. *Ibid.,* EC-500, p. 578.

44. *Ibid.,* EC-501, pp. 579–83.

45. *Ibid.,* EC-297-A, pp. 394–402.

46. Amos E. Simpson, "The Struggle for the Control of the Germany Economy 1936–37," in *Journal of Modern History,* 1959, pp. 37–45. NCA III, 1301-PS, pp. 879–82.

47. Simpson, *op. cit.* Beck, *op. cit.,* p. 85. Hans B. Gisevius, *Bis zum bitteren Ende,* Vol. I (Zurich: Fretz & Wasmuth Verlag, 1946), p. 211. N XXXIII, p 562.

48. Schacht, *76 Jahre meines Lebens,* p. 473.

49. Beck, *op. cit.*

50. N XXXII, 3724-PS, p. 538.

51. Schacht, *76 Jahre meines Lebens,* pp. 515–17. Beck, *op. cit.,* p. 146.

52. Schacht, *76 Jahre meines Lebens,* p. 532.

53. NCA VI, 3700-PS, pp. 404–5.

54. Schacht, *76 Jahres meines Lebens,* pp. 527–29.

55. Beck, *op. cit.*

56. NCA VI, 3727-PS, p. 480.

57. Ibid., 3728-PS, p. 485.

58. Ibid., 3728-PS, p. 487.

59. Ibid., 3729-PS, p. 506.

60. Ibid., 3729-PS, p. 529.

61. Ibid., 3727-PS, p. 483.

62. Ibid., 3728-PS, p. 491.

63. Ibid., 3727-PS, p. 481.

64. Ibid., 3728-PS, p. 487.

65. Ibid., 3728-PS, pp. 489–91.

66. Ibid., 3729-PS, p. 504.

67. Ibid., 3729-PS, p. 506.

68. Ibid., 3729-PS, p. 511.

69. NCA II, p. 740.

70. NCA V, 2409-PS, p. 83.

71. N I, p. 310.

72. Robert H. Jackson, Report to the President, in *The New York Times*, October 16, 1946.

73. *Jackson Report*, p. 254.

74. Schwerin von Krosigk, *op cit.*, pp. 191–92.

75. TWC, I. G. Farben, VII, pp. 172–73.

76. Ibid., p. 558.

77. Paul Oestreich, *Walther Funk, ein Leben fuer die Wirtschaft* (Munich: Zentralverlag der NSDAP, Franz Eher Nachf., 1940), p. 68.

78. Funk interrogation of November 5, 1945 (NA).

79. Funk interrogation at Ashcan Detention Center of June 28, 1945 (IZG).

80. A. Heinrichsbauer, *Schwerindustrie und Politik* (Essen-Kettwig: West Verlag, 1949).

81. N XXXII, 3505-PS, pp. 346–47. Ibid., 3533-PS, pp. 354–55.

82. Walther Funk, *Wirtschaftsordnung gegen Waehrungsmechanismus* (Koenigsberg, 1944).

83. Walther Funk, *Das wirtschaftliche Gesicht des neuen Europa* (Berlin: January 15, 1942). Walther Funk, *Wirtschaftsordnung im neuen Europa*, Rede gehalten vor der Suedosteuropagesellschaft in Wien on June 12, 1941 (Vienna: Suedost-Echo Verlagsgesellschaft, 1941).

84. Walther Funk, *Grundsaetze der deutschen Aussenhandelspolitik und das Problem der internationalen Verschuldung*, speech given in Bremen on June 16, 1938 (Berlin: Junker und Duennhaupt Verlag, 1938). Funk, *Das wirtschaftliche Gesicht des neuen Europa*.

85. Funk interrogation at Ashcan Detention Center of June 28, 1945 (IZG).

86. N XIII, pp. 580–81, 602–3.

87. NCA, Supp. A, 3944-PS, pp. 670–71. Ibid., 3947-PS, pp. 675–76.

88. N XXXIV, 4045-PS, pp. 110–13.

89. SS 2125, letter of July 21, 1942 (BDC).

90. N XIII, pp. 179–80.

91. I, 4215-34, Funk interrogation of June 4, 1945 (BDC).

92. N XXVIII, 1816-PS, pp. 499–540.

93. *N* XL, Document Funk-1, pp. 183–88. *Ibid.*, Document Funk-2, pp. 188–89.

94. *Ibid.*, Funk-15, pp. 196–98. Also Funk Spruchkammer, testimony by Anne-marie Schlusnus and Frau Kuennecke of September 15, 1956 (Munich: Amtsgericht).

95. I, 4215-34, letter of November 3, 1934 (BDC).

96. Funk interrogation at Ashcan Detention Center of June 28, 1945 (IZG).

97. Schweitzer, *op. cit.*

98. Funk interrogation at Ashcan Detention Center of June 28, 1945 (IZG).

99. *Ibid.* Funk Spruchkammer, Pietzsche affidavit of February 23, 1953 (Munich: Amtsgericht).

100. Gustav Stolper, *Deutsche Wirtschaft 1870–1940* (Stuttgart: Franz-Mittelbach Verlag, 1950). Louis P. Lochner, *Tycoons and Tyrant* (Chicago: Henry Regnery Company, 1954).

101. Stolper, *op. cit.*, p. 89.

102. *TWC*, Flick, VI, p. 278.

103. *Ibid.*, pp. 269–70.

104. *Ibid.*, p. 266.

105. *N* XIII, p. 120.

106. Funk interrogation, May 19, 1947 (IZG).

107. Funk Spruchkammer, Heinrich Hoffmann, Jr. (Munich: Amtsgericht).

7

The Law

Aside from Hess, the only one among the defendants at Nuremberg who failed to take the stand to explain his past was the former Minister of the Interior, Wilhelm Frick, one of the most notable among the early National Socialists. While still an official in the Munich police department, he took a leading part in the attempted putsch of November, 1923, and wore the highest of Party honor badges, the *Blutorden*, for his services on that historic occasion. Frick had been head of the political section of the Munich police, until 1923, when he took over the criminal section. It was he who had ordered the police not to intervene when Hitler proclaimed the revolution on November 8. There were too few police, he told his subordinates, to attempt to put down the uprising; they should do no more than act as observers and see that order was maintained. Hitler had assigned Frick to work with former Munich Police President Ernst Poehner to take over police headquarters on behalf of the revolution. But before Frick could act—indeed, hours before Hitler began his march on the Feldherrnhalle—both Frick and Poehner were arrested.

Everything went wrong with the putsch. Although Hitler announced that both the Reichswehr and the police were already serving under the swastika, neither one showed the slightest inclination to join the uprising. Frick was already in jail at seven o'clock on the morning of November 9, the time he had been ordered to take over the police. He spent four months in prison while he was being interrogated. He then was tried along with Hitler, Ludendorff, and the other members of the high command and was given a sentence, later suspended, of one year and three months. The court dealt in lenient fashion with these fanatics of a new order—no doubt impressed by the presence of Ludendorff and also by their nationalist idealism and their resolve to rescue Germany, even by illegal means, from its tumults and sorrows. Had the revolt been successful, Frick was to have been made Police President of Munich, a post that up to that time had seemed the most dazzling to which he could aspire.

Frick, the police official, was a devoted if crypto-National Socialist from the earliest days of the Party, when, as he said during his and Hitler's trial, he and Poehner could hold a protecting hand over the Fuehrer and the movement.[1] At least once Frick was able on his own authority to free Hitler from police custody after he had been arrested. Because of the job he held with the police, Frick formally was not a Party member; he joined officially only in 1925, when the Party was reconstituted after Hitler's release from the Landsberg prison. Hitler, however, had won his support the first time Frick met him, in Poehner's office, which the Fuehrer was visiting on one of his many errands to get help to confound the Communist Party (this time he had wanted a Communist publication forbidden). Both Frick and Poehner were strongly rightist, as were most of their colleagues and their superiors in the various Bavarian Government agencies. They hated communism, and parties that fought it immediately won their support. Frick's developing allegiance to the Nazis was readily tolerated by conservatives such as Bavarian Minister President Gustav Ritter von Kahr, who was a monarchist. Unlike Frick and Poehner, Kahr was willing to help the Nazis only up to a certain point; when the revolt started, he joined the forces that put it down.

Frick was made for the Party and the Party for him. He was an active and methodical man and was as convinced of the need for the revolution as any of the street brawlers in the SA. He brought the order and the *Wuerde* of the trained German bureaucrat to the Party hierarchy. No "T" was uncrossed in his memoranda, no "I" without a dot. The laws and decrees he would one day draw up had staying power. As his Party biographer said of him, he drafted the basic laws "classical in form and with epoch-making contents," under which the other bureaucrats of the National Socialist state could operate with the good conscience that everything they did was legally impeccable.[2] In 1943, when the Final Solution was in full progress, Frick could issue a decree in effect placing Jews outside the law and turning them over to the Gestapo; this decree was based on a law he had drawn up and signed in September, 1935, before the liquidation of the Jews had been dreamed of.

Frick was of peasant stock, as his admirers never tired of pointing out when he was introduced at Party gatherings; "sound, healthy peasant stock," was the phrase. He was born on March 12, 1877, in Alsenz in the Palatinate, the son of a schoolteacher and a farmer's daughter, Henriette Schmidt. He attended the *Volksschule* and Gymnasium at Kaiserslautern, then studied law at the universities of Munich, Goettingen, and Berlin; he wrote his doctor's thesis at Heidelberg, where he got his degree in 1901. His dissertation, on the complicated Bavarian laws dealing with the formerly privately run mail service, was never published because Frick could not afford to pay for the printing. Thus, his highly prized doctor's title could be questioned by strict constructionists of academic requirements. He was something of an athlete in his cautious way, cautious, possibly, because his constitution was not robust. (He had a weak chest, his biographer later wrote to explain why he had not fought in World War I. But he swam and rowed and snowshoed, his admiring chronicler also pointed out; he was an eminent man but a regular fellow.) His life was ordered around his stacks of papers. He often worked from eight in the morning until midnight ungrudgingly.[3]

Frick practiced law privately for three years before taking a post in the Munich police department, where from 1904 to 1907 he dealt with economic crimes. He then got a job in the County Legal Division as an assessor, an assistant *Landrat*, where he spent most of the war years. When a socialist critic asked him later why he had not been a soldier, he piously explained that he had done his duty where his Bavarian King had put him, which is to say he continued at his legal tasks and was put in charge of handing out the ration books. There were no scandals in his administrative precincts. He filled out forms, drew up the complicated legal documents German administrators delight in, and awaited the victory. He remained in this job for ten years, then returned, after the war, to the political section of the police directorate at Munich.

He experienced as a personal affront the riots in the streets of Munich that followed the defeat of Germany. They were an unwarranted attack on his carefully preserved order of files and documented security, where everything had its proper place and only needed a practiced hand to bring it to light, to annotate it, and to file it again among the other elaborately phrased and paragraphed formulations that kept the world tidy. At the time of the Raeterepublik, when a Communist government ruled Munich from mid-April to May, 1919, Frick the policeman was on their list of hostages. He was lucky; ten people who were taken as hostages were shot in the courtyard of the Luitpold Gymnasium before the revolt was put down.

Frick came to know a good deal about the Fuehrer and his National Socialists when they applied to the police for permits to hold their meetings. As he became better acquainted with Hitler, he knew that this man had many of the answers he and the staggering Weimar Republic had been looking for; here was the person to build the strong state where Communists and Left-wing demagogues would be put in their place, which was jail.

Always a man of strict duty, Frick knew the importance of proper draftsmanship on behalf of the great goals of the National Socialist State. At Nuremberg after he was sentenced he said:

I have a clear conscience . . . My entire life was spent in the service of my people and my fatherland. To them I have devoted the best of my strength in the loyal fulfillment of my duty. I am convinced that no patriotic American or citizen of any other country would have acted differently in my place . . . For to have acted any differently would have been a breach of my oath of allegiance, and high treason. In fulfilling my legal and moral duties, I believe that I have deserved punishment no more than have the tens of thousands of faithful German civil servants and officals in the public service who have already been detained in camps for over a year merely because they did their duty. I feel in duty and honor bound, as a former long-standing public minister, to remember them here in gratitude.[4]

He had drawn up his administrative charts, regulations, decrees, and laws as he knew they should appear, with no loopholes, no overlappings, and with an eye to the future. He recognized two authorities competent to decide their own principles: one was the State, when it was purged of its non-German afflictions; the other was his own bureaucratic conscience, which was strict within its departmental limits, but never found itself in conflict with any decision of the Fuehrer's. Hitler in turn could for years make good use of this devoted technician. In *Mein Kampf* he mentioned Frick and Poehner as the only two men in government positions who had the right to collaborate in the establishment of a Bavarian nation. "They alone," Hitler said, "had the courage to be Germans first and then officials."[5] Like his jurist colleague Hans Frank, Frick resisted the machinations of such savage rivals as Himmler and Heydrich (both of whom for a time were technically subordinate to him). When they flouted his authority while carrying out their own special and murderous missions and pursued their empire building, what they did became illegal, a threat to the high purposes of the new order.

Hitler never lost his powerful attraction for him. Only one month after being sentenced for his part in the 1923 uprising, Frick ran for a seat in the Reichstag, and he was one of the four down-the-line National Socialist deputies elected. The Party had been formally dissolved, but the crypto-National Socialists and their allies of the German Folkish Party (Deutsche Voelkische Partei) in an uneasy coalition called the National Socialist Freedom Movement had thirty-two delegates in the Reichstag following the election of May 4, 1924, nine of whom were National Socialists. The two elements had in common mainly a sworn enmity to the parliamentary system. The Freedom Movement delegates had as nominal leader not Adolf Hitler, who was in jail, but Albrecht von Graefe, who had none of the talents needed to bind his membership together or to appeal to the electorate.* In the following election, on December 7, 1924, the elected delegates from this coalition fell to fourteen, one short of the number required to form a recog-

---

* In addition to Graefe, Ludendorff and Gregor Strasser were leading members of the National Socialist Freedom Movement.

nized "fraction" in the Reichstag. The Freedom Movement was badly split; the members of the Folkish Party were divided, but they felt themselves superior in numbers and talents to the remnants of the National Socialists.

From the beginning Frick echoed Hitler's words, declaring it to be his task in the Reichstag not to support but to undermine the parliamentary system. Frick spoke with all the assurance of the ideologue who knows his cause must triumph. "Our participation in the Parliament," he told the Reichstag, "does not indicate a support but rather an undermining of the parliamentary system. It does not indicate that we renounce our antiparliamentary attitude but that we are fighting the enemy with his own weapons." [6] In 1924, immediately after his election, Frick introduced a bill, the first of the racial measures he would propose, to exclude Jews from public office and reduce their participation in German economic and political life. Radicals of the Right made headlines with their incessant attacks on their world of enemies; Frick told the Reichstag that behind all republics was nothing more than moneybags. He denounced both the capitalist exploiters and the materialists of the Left. "Not the economy but politics is our fate . . . the creative Folk," he said, and he warned the SPD Deputy Gerhart Seger, "When we are in power, we will put you all in jail." [7]

In February, 1925, two months after Hitler (who had been released from prison just before Christmas) reestablished his party, Frick and the three other Nazi delegates withdrew from the coalition. The Nazis again began their slow rise to power, attracting a few delegates from the other Right-wing parties, all of which lacked a personality with the dynamism and forensic power of Hitler. Hitler determined now to make use of the parliamentary system in order to destroy it. His attempt at revolution through an uprising had failed; from now on he would make much of legality. He would come to power by ceaseless propaganda by means that even his enemies must accept, by recruiting elements from any quarter, Left or Right, willing to support his revolution.

A new coalition called the Folkish Working Association (Voelkische Arbeitsgemeinschaft) was established in June and managed to reach the number of fifteen required for a fraction; eleven delegates were from the German Folkish Party (which gained a member, Deputy Best, from the German Nationalist Party), and four were National Socialists. The coalition of the Folkish Working Association dissolved in 1927. Frick then became undisputed floor leader of the tiny but now independent Nazi group of seven members, and, although a poor speaker, he was the most conspicuous leader of the antiparliamentary delegates. In the election of May 20, 1928, the National Socialists, now firmly under Hitler's leadership, sent to the 491-member Reichstag twelve delegates—among them, Goebbels and Goering, Feder and Strasser—not enough for a fraction but more than enough for a noisy propaganda apparatus.

In December, 1929, Frick was elected Minister of the Interior and Education in Thuringia by a vote of 28 to 22 of the Provincial Diet. This was a result of the Nazi upsurge in the *Land* elections, in which they polled the third largest vote and thus became members of the coalition government. Hitler chose him to be the first Nazi Minister of a German state, and Frick, as always, was eager to do his duty. He fought tenaciously in Thuringia on behalf of his National Socialist principles. He dismissed two-thirds of the higher officials in his Ministry; he appointed a Nazi racial theorist, one Dr. Hans Guenther, to the faculty of the University of Jena, overruling the vote of the professoriat; and he installed another National Socialist, Paul Schultze-Naumburg, as principal of the United National Academy of Arts in Weimar. He forbade the playing of "Nigger Jazz" in Thuringian beer halls and restaurants. He introduced Nazi-flavored prayers into the school system, three of which the Supreme Court of Leipzig found unconstitutional.* He infiltrated the police department with Party members, including a Nazi President of Police in Weimar.[8]

Frick not only sought to reform Thuringia, but also set out to make the Fuehrer a German citizen. Hitler had been stateless since 1924, and in 1925 he had formally renounced his Austrian citizenship in the event that he still had it.[9] He therefore could not run for the Presidency. No matter how many millions of roaring followers he collected, they had no chance to vote for him. Frick tried first in Bavaria at the end of 1929, but the Bavarians declined to act, partly on the ground that Hitler had been convicted of high treason. Frick tried again a few months later in Thuringia, by appointing Hitler as a Gendarmerie Commissioner in Hildburghausen, but the attempt fell through either because Hitler did not want to become a citizen by way of the Gendarmerie Commission or because the pressure on the Thuringian authorities to prevent the fake appointment was too strong. Frick had made a good case for his Fuehrer, citing Hitler's war record as a frontline fighter for Germany, but he had not gone through the right channels. Frick had appointed Hitler on his own during the summer, when colleagues were on vacation, and the Thuringian Minister-President, as well as the central government of the Reich in the person of the Chancellor Bruening, Minister of Defense Groener, and Staatssekretaer Puender, found that Frick's action had not been properly approved by the constituted authorities. Hitler, therefore, still was not a German citizen. But the matter was never pressed; Hitler had more decorous ways of becoming a citizen.

* One, called "A Prayer for Freedom from Betrayal and Treason," read as follows: "Father in Heaven, I believe in your complete power, justice, and love. I believe in my German people and fatherland. I believe that its freedom will come through the Father in Heaven if we believe in our own strength" (Hans Pfundtner, *Dr. Wilhelm Frick und sein Ministerium*, [Munich: Zentralverlag der NSDAP, Franz Eher Nachf., 1937], p. 188).

The prayers were denounced by both Protestants and Catholics; one pastor wrote: "We want a German and Christian education, but we know no Christianity without tolerance and a great-hearted mildness and no nationalism without humanity" (Hans Fabricius, *Reichsinnenminister Dr. Frick: der revolutionaere Staatsmann*, [Berlin: Deutsche Kulturwacht, 1939]).

Frick was forced to resign in April, 1931, a victim, Hitler said, of German treachery. His one-man campaign in the Thuringian Government, however, had created such resistance both in and outside the *Land* that Berlin for a time refused to pay the regular subsidies to Thuringia, where the majority of the Government and the Landtag were infuriated with Frick's strong-arm tactics.

Hitler got his citizenship with the help of Frick in Brunswick, where a National Socialist Minister of the Interior, Klagges, was a member of the Government, on February 2, 1932, when he was made a State Councilor by the Budget Committee of the Landtag. The Fuehrer was formally attached to Brunswick's Embassy in Berlin, where he took his oath of office on February 26, swearing to support the constitution of Brunswick and of the Reich. That was the last he saw of the Embassy.

Hitler's supporters had pointed out that with his political connections he could bring new industries to Brunswick's sagging economy, but he did nothing at all. Nor did he accept his salary of 320.70 RM a month but suggested it be given to the unemployed. There had been many attempts to make Hitler a citizen by way of some kind of state job. One such plan was to have him appointed a professor in the Technische Hochschule, and Staatsminister Klagges said on the Fuehrer's behalf that he was the author of a basic scientific work—*Mein Kampf*—as well as the leader of a great political movement. He would, Klagges said, bring great prestige to the faculty. Klagges was not able to convince the faculty.[10]

Long before Hitler came to power, Frick was clearly established as one of the foremost Nazis. A report of the Prussian police of 1930 called him the number-two man of the Party, ranking next to the Fuehrer. Hitler leaned heavily on his pedantic talents. Frick not only had led the Nazi deputies in the Reichstag, but had been called on by the Fuehrer at critical times to negotiate with the opposition. Hitler sent Frick with Goering to Schleicher when the general wanted to appoint Gregor Strasser as Vice-Chancellor in an effort to split the National Socialists. Frick favored Strasser's accepting the post, hoping in this way to drive a wedge into the Government's forces, but he unconditionally accepted Hitler's refusal to permit a National Socialist to enter the Schleicher Cabinet (see Papen, Chapt. 5). Frick also accompanied Hitler during the negotiations with Papen when the Fuehrer's coalition government was being discussed, and Hitler turned to him for dealing with the leader of the Centrist Party, Monsignor Kaas, whose votes were needed to give Hitler the full legislative and executive powers of the Enabling Act.

After becoming Chancellor, Hitler immediately appointed Frick as Minister of the Interior in his Cabinet. Goering, as Minister Without Portfolio, was the only other National Socialist in what Hindenburg and Papen had convinced themselves was to be a coalition government in which Papen, representing the President, would be able to veto any extreme legislation.

Frick promptly called for the enactment of the Enabling Law that would mean the end of any legislative or judicial control over anything Adolf Hitler decided to do. The veto was never to be used, never could be used; Hitler moved too quickly and too expertly. Frick was the fanatical technician chosen by the Fuehrer to prepare in final, legal form the hundreds of documents, decrees, laws, and regulations that would effect the centralization and racial revolution of the Nazi State, leaving Papen and all the other conservatives of the coalition no more than helpless bystanders.

Far less flamboyant than Frank, the wordy theoretician and trial lawyer, Frick was the well-trained official as well as the Party whip and political organizer, and he moved in on his task with a cold fervor. One law and decree ordered by Hitler and formulated by Frick followed another: *de facto* dissolution of the Communist Party and confiscation of its property; dissolution of the trades unions and of the Social Democratic Party and confiscation of its property; ban on new parties or reestablishment of old ones. On February 28, 1933, the day after the Reichstag fire, he promulgated the law for the Protection of People and State, which abolished civil rights, free assembly, and privacy of the mails and telephones, and permitted house searches without warrants. A month later, on March 24, 1933, Frick signed the Enabling Act, the law for Elimination of the Misery of the People and the Reich, that gave Hitler the legal right to promulgate laws—even if they were unconstitutional—without the approval of the Reichstag.

Frick had promised the opposition deputies in the Reichstag that they would all be put in jail, and he now was in a position to carry out his threat. The decrees he formulated and signed had been in his mind for many years; they were part of the long-planned Nazi legislation, and the Jews had not been forgotten. Frick and Hitler, on April 7, 1933, signed the law for the Reestablishment of the Professional Civil Service, the first of a series of Nazi formulations that prettified and made as plausible as possible to the non-Nazi world the onslaughts on the Jews. The law provided for the retirement from the civil service of non-Aryans and of those whose political records were dubious. It was a first step only, for with Hindenburg as President, the Fuehrer and Frick had to tread carefully when former soldiers were involved.

Hindenburg wrote a letter to Hitler on April 4, 1933, in which he told the Reich Chancellor that his attention had been called to the dismissal from the civil service of Jewish judges and lawyers who had fought for Germany. He objected to this and he said it was "personally insupportable," something he could not tolerate in the cases of Jews who had been wounded or who had been frontline soldiers. He told Hitler that if there was no special reason for the dismissal of such men, they should remain in the civil service. Hitler replied respectfully on the next day, and after pointing mechanically to the gross injustices Germans had suffered for these many years from the Jews, he nevertheless agreed that in view of the President's generous concern for such people he would tell Frick that he should draft the law to take care of such cases.[11] As a result, the dismissals were to affect no one who had fought for Germany in World War I or whose father or son had been killed in the war, nor those who had been in government employ before August 1, 1914. Non-Aryan officials who had been on a government staff since November 9, 1918, were to be dismissed immediately with three months' salary, but they might be given a pension of one-third of their salary if they had dependent relatives. No pension was to be paid for less than ten years' service.

This was a key law, the first legal step toward the Final Solution. Frick blandly defended it in a speech he delivered to the foreign diplomatic corps and newspaper correspondents in Berlin on February 15, 1934. He told them that Germany wanted only to be master in its own house; that Jews had held too many influential positions in leading posts and professions; that 48 per cent of the doctors were Jews, 54 per cent of the lawyers, 80 per cent of the directors of theaters; that they were disproportionately important in business and industry. Therefore, he said, foreigners got a wrong impression of Germany. He pointed out that both the United States and Australia had immigration quotas and that Greece and Turkey had exchanged populations in 1923, so there was nothing new in what the Germans were trying to do to promote the racial homogeneity of their country. They were not forcing the Jews to migrate, but were only reestablishing the civil service in a most generous spirit. The way chosen could not have been more legal or more mild. The Jewish officials had not been thrown out of their jobs but had been retired with honor and with pensions. The Germans' racial laws were no reflection on other races; the Chinese had their ancestor worship, the Japanese their ideal of the samurai. The German program, Frick told his audience, was long-range—only the Fuehrer would determine when and how the next steps would be taken.[12]

Frick was a stern anti-Semite. In a speech in the Reichstag on May 27, 1924, he quoted Streicher's lurid accounts in *Der Stuermer* of alleged Jewish sexual crimes, as well as the spurious texts Streicher loved so well. From so-called Talmudic sources he remarked that for the Jews the non-Jewish woman was an animal. Frick then proposed a law to protect German womanhood from the Jews that would forbid mixed marriages (ten years later he would sign it). Nevertheless, officials in Frick's Ministry and Frick himself took a relatively liberal position in the anti-Semitic measures proposed after the Nazis rose to power. Frick was a legalist. His anti-Semitism was orderly; it was to be construed within limits, in a context where racial considerations were paramount but where the attitudes of other peoples must also have consideration. Race was all-important, he told his foreign listeners in 1934, and in a speech he made in Luebeck two years later he told his German audience that their concept of race was difficult for foreigners to understand. It was not an article for export. The German racial laws were not to be seen separately but as part of the National Socialist philosophy, where freedom and honor held a central place in a racially conscious community.

On September 15, 1935, he signed the law forbidding marriage between Jews and Germans. No woman under the age of forty-five was permitted to be a servant in a Jewish household; Jews were not allowed to display the national flag. Only those of German or related Aryan blood could be German citizens. Two months later, on November 14, Hitler, Frick, and Hess signed the regulation that determined who was a Jew. It declared that a Jew was anyone descended from three Jewish grandparents, or from two if he practiced the Jewish religion. The *Mischlinge* were those with either one or two grandparents who were racially full Jews.[13] These *Mischlinge* were always to present an insuperable problem to the National Socialist State. Although Frick declared in an article on race, published in the *Deutsche Juristenzeitung*, that the sinking of the racial level had been the main cause of the dying out of cultures, he nevertheless favored not the exclusion of but a quota system for Jews in the universities and technical schools (which the law of April 25, 1933, provided for), and he also pointed out to his readers that the Germans were not a pure race. It was this latter argument that Frick's assistants used in making their case for treating the half-Jews and quarter-Jews either as a separate category or as Germans—not, as the extreme racists demanded, as Jews.

One eloquent memorandum from Frick's Ministry, written on October 11, 1935, pointed out that 40,000 to 45,000 of the 200,000 half-Jews in the Third Reich were eligible for the Wehrmacht. Many had war decorations—at least one had a Pour le Mérite—and if these *Mischlinge* were discriminated against, the half-Jews who had fought for Germany would be worse off than many foreigners who had fought against the Reich.[14] This problem would plague the National Socialists until the end. A later memorandum written during the war by Dr. Bernhard Loesener in Frick's Ministry mentioned the case of a first lieutenant, a half-Jew who had been recalled to active duty. He had been wounded twice and awarded an Iron Cross; he was now sixty-six years old and had been threatened with arrest by the police in the town where he lived because he had been seen talking to Aryans on the street and taking walks as freely as if he were a German.[15]

Loesener repeated in effect what Frick had written—the Germans for centuries had absorbed alien and undesirable blood from the East, and this *Mischlinge* group would be the last bearers of the Jewish bloodstream that would enter the German community, for marriage between Jews and Germans was now forbidden. Many of these *Mischlinge* felt themselves entirely German, and Loesener, summing up his case for their being recognized as Germans, said that this solution would silence foreign criticism; it would prevent families from being torn apart; it would close the gate to the enormous corruption likely to follow if local authorities could determine who was a

Jew; it would prevent the blackmail that also would surely be part of a system where the individual's racial status was uncertain. The 200,000 *Mischlinge*, if accepted as Germans, would be pro-German instead of enemies of the Third Reich—this, Loesener cannily pointed out, made a difference of 400,000 people. The problem was never to be resolved. Eichmann, and others like him, wanted half-Jews to be considered Jews with the exception of those married to Christians, and at a meeting on August 9, 1941, he said that all others should be sterilized without exception.[16]

The battle continued through the entire Nazi period; every solution was provisional. In the Wehrmacht, a commanding officer often protected the status of the *Mischlinge* under him against assaults of the racial purists; the more circumspect referred individual cases to the Fuehrer. Hitler alone could decide whether a *Mischling*, or in very rare cases even a full Jew, was to be officially declared Aryan. In theory it required a decree from him to make a *Mischling* eligible as an officer in the Wehrmacht or in the Government, and Hitler issued such documents with considerable reluctance. The files of Frick's Ministry show that 118 *Mischlinge* soldiers and their wives were declared German on September 10, 1942, along with 197 civilians working for the Army and 79 others. In addition, 258 *Mischlinge* were declared eligible to be officers and 339 Jews who were so-called *Geltungsjuden* (those with one Aryan grandparent) were awarded the status of *Mischlinge* [17] (see Chapts. 10 and 14).

Frick's Ministry was a center of the controversy. The Loesener memorandum and others argued that a decision to regard the *Mischlinge* as Jews would be destructive of the German community. Half of the *Mischlinge's* biological inheritance was German, and their parents and grandparents often had Aryan relatives, all of whom would be alienated to some degree by creating such a legal and psychological cleavage in their families. In the discussions in the mid-thirties, Frick and Schacht took the same position on behalf of their Ministries; the Jews must be eliminated from leading positions in the German community, but this must be done in a legal and orderly fashion. The Jewish problem would best be solved, in Frick's opinion, by emigration. He also pointed out in a dry and objective memorandum that it was unlikely that Jews would be permitted to enter other countries, whether in Europe, the Near East, or North America, and therefore, since the Jews had diminishing economic opportunities in Germany, the welfare agencies of the Third Reich must prepare to carry a vast burden of relief. The racial laws were extended from the civil servants, doctors, and lawyers to Jews engaged in industry and commerce. On September 23, 1935, in a conference attended by Frick and Schacht, it was decided that Jews were to be excluded from any positions in industry requiring special confidence; Jewish apprentices could only work for Jewish firms; only German citizens could hold leading positions in German economic life.[18] The consensus of the meeting was that *Mischlinge* in industry were to be regarded as Germans, and the conferees opposed the widely used placards announcing that Jews were not wanted in public places and also the attempt to exclude Jews from theaters.

Like many other German men inexorably bent on high purposes, Frick thought the Nuremberg Laws not only essential for Germany but good for the Jews. They gave the Jews legal status within the German State, which had the same right, Frick said, as all other states to determine who should be a citizen and who not. With the Reich's officialdom "restored," that is, purged of Jews, and the legal measures taken to rid the State of any opposition, the Law for Securing the Unity of Party and State took the last ideological step. Signed on December 1, 1933, it declared that the National Socialist Party was the bearer of the concept of the State and was inseparable from it. Frick had underwritten the revolution. The doctrine that the Party controls the State, not the other way around, was established; civil liberties were abolished, as were opposition parties; and the final attack on the Jews, which would deprive them not only of certain proscribed positions but of any jobs at all and finally of their lives and property, had been mounted.

In 1933 and 1934 Frick signed 235 laws and decrees; he could appoint or dismiss any mayor; he had turned the regular German police, formerly divided by regions, into a network controlled from Berlin; he had made the use of warrants for arrests and house searches unnecessary; and the way was prepared for the Gestapo and the police state that Frick opposed only when he was not the chief policeman. On June 12, 1934, he issued the only directive to which his counsel at Nuremberg could point that defended the legal principles which must have concerned him before the war. "Protective custody" had been introduced by the Gestapo; this device, like so many Nazi inventions or adaptations, was named so as to seem designed for the benefit of its victims. Almost as soon as Goering founded the Gestapo, it could at any time and without a warrant place under protective arrest anyone who endangered the State or who because of antisocial activities might be endangered by the indignant, healthy racial sense of the community retaliating against them.

One such arrest that disturbed Frick involved a lawyer representing a widow whose husband was murdered during the Roehm putsch and who could not collect her insurance because the victim had allegedly committed suicide. The lawyer, in order to bring pressure on the insurance company, had to go before a Spruchkammer (the equivalent of an American trial court) and charge that the man had in fact not committed suicide but had been killed during the purge. The lawyer was arrested by the Gestapo and placed in protective custody. Other similar cases distressed Frick, for he felt his authority challenged, and an order of March 11, 1934, for which of course he had to get Hitler's approval, stated his position. The order declared that a person might be placed in protective custody only if his behavior immediately endangered public safety; this form of arrest was not to be employed against people who were making use of civil or public law or against lawyers representing their clients' interests or against anyone for personal or economic reasons, such as against a person who wanted an increase in salary. Frick expressly rescinded the previous regulations permitting such arrests on the orders of district police; political arrests for the purpose of protective custody could now be made only by higher officials, and every case was to come to Frick's attention. "In the future," he wrote, "I will relentlessly punish the abuse of arrest." [19]

It was a bold move to assert his authority, but it had little effect. Frick appointed to police assignments under his Ministry of the Interior, or approved the appointments, of both Heinrich Himmler and Reinhard Heydrich; soon they, like the Gestapo (taken from the Ministry of the Interior in November, 1933), slipped away from his authority. For a time Himmler signed letters as coming from Frick's Ministry, but by 1936, as Reichsfuehrer SS, he became virtually independent. The secret police, as Goering and later Himmler argued persuasively with the Fuehrer, needed to be free of any department controls; they had to smite the enemies of Party and State without regard to such pettifogging measures as Frick had in mind with his March, 1934, decree. Hitler agreed; he would tolerate no legal paragraphs or reactionary notions of the rights of the accused that could interfere with making his enemies harmless. Frick was defeated in his effort to bring a legal code into the methods of the secret police, but he clearly had no consuming interest in the plight of those arrested. Other laws he signed abolishing civil rights and confiscating property for racial or political reasons were measures stripping the population or undesirable parts of it of personal and property rights. Only in the case of this one law did Frick appear as a defender of the German legal tradition. The chief witness called on his behalf at Nuremberg, Hans Gisevius, said that Frick had been appalled by the murders at the time of the Roehm putsch in June, 1934; but there was no doubt that Frick, together with Hitler and the Minister of Justice, had signed the law of July 3, 1934, that declared the executions on that occasion legitimate "for the self-defense of the State." [*] [20]

The portrait of Frick that Gisevius and Frick's lawyer, Otto Pannenbecker, presented at Nuremberg was that of a devoted administrator with essentially humanitarian principles, an official having no real power but functioning under the orders handed down by Hitler and Goering, a man doing his feeble best to protect the innocent and to carry out his assignments in the whirlpool of a permanent revolution. Gisevius said Frick even disclosed to him in 1934 that a Gestapo plot was afoot to murder Frick while he was on holiday in Bavaria. Gisevius testified that he had asked his friend Arthur

---

[*] On July 13 the Reichstag met, heard Hitler on the subject, approved the Cabinet decision, and expressed its thanks to the Fuehrer for his "energetic and resolute rescue of the fatherland from civil war and chaos" (Adam Buckreis, *Politik des 20. Jahrhunderts* [Nuremberg: Panorama-Verlag, n.d.] p. 606).

Nebe, an official in the Gestapo, if this were true and that Nebe had said the matter had been discussed. The story seems unlikely. Frick undoubtedly was nervous at the time of the Roehm killings—as were others in high positions, like Papen and Schacht—but Cabinet Ministers in the Third Reich were not as readily murdered as were opposition generals like Schleicher, political writers like Jung, and unruly members of the Party who were considered a threat to its leadership. Never for a moment was Frick an opponent of Hitler; no record exists of his having objected to any policy the Fuehrer approved; he was no danger to the merging Party-State, he was one of its pillars. And in his single attempt to assert his authority over the secret police he was simply overruled—protective custody continued to be invoked whenever the Gestapo wanted to make an arrest and keep a man in prison or a concentration camp without going through the courts.

There was no need to murder Frick. His love of paperwork could be ignored by Himmler after Frick appointed him Chief of the German Police and at all times by Goering, who was the more powerful personality and, with his fascinating plans for rebuilding not only a secret police but a German Air Force and the war economy, was far closer to Hitler. When, during the days of the Roehm executions, Frick asked Goering what was going on, Goering merely told him to go home and not to worry. Frick meekly accepted the advice. While Goering was conducting the purge operation and deciding on who was to be killed in Berlin and Hitler was taking care of the heart of the revolt in the Munich area, Frick stayed away from his office for three days. When he returned he was ready to agree that what had been done was legal and to continue to work at any jobs assigned him.

Frick played a characteristic role in the Party's war with the church. He had always thought of himself as a religious man; the Party seemed to him to be doing the Lord's work. In the running battles the Protestant pastors had with some of their ecclesiastical brethren, as well as with the atheistic movement of German Believers, Frick again represented the conservative wing of the Party: he wanted to act legally and he had considerable sympathy for the ministers who opposed the intervention of the Party actions.

Hitler was indifferent to religion; it had no mystical or transcendental meaning for him; but both the Protestant and Catholic churches were institutions, and as such they had to be taken into account. In the early stages of his rule he wanted no religious wars; he wanted the churches to support his policies. The Party's coming to political power released a parallel movement within the Protestant church that sought to establish the religious counterpart of the Party: the *Voelkische* church, which, as one of its supporters, Pastor Hossenfelder, said, was intended to be the "SA Jesus Christ." [21] Another National Socialist faction wanted a *Reich* church; both groups demanded a church that was politically oriented and National Socialist to the core. Germany was to rearm, to be free of Versailles; any Jewish converts were to be thrown out; they wanted Adolf Hitler's program with ecclesiastical trimmings. But from Hitler's point of view a *Voelkische* church could be dangerous, too; he preferred a state church, a political instrument he could wield himself. Frick, Goering, and Gauleiter Kube were honorary members of a group calling themselves German Christians who met in Berlin in April, 1933, to proclaim the right of Christian believers to a revolution and the need for a *Reich* church. They delighted in such statements as "God made us Germans. Germandom is a gift of God. God wants me to fight for my Germany . . . The state of Adolf Hitler calls on the church; the church must heed the call." [22]

Such pronouncements, Party surveillance of sermons and church publications, and dissolution of church youth organizations immediately gave rise to strong protests on the part of both Catholic and Protestant ministers. Hitler in March, 1933, named a crusading nationalist and anti-Semitic clergyman, Ludwig Mueller, as his plenipotentiary to the Protestant church. Mueller, whom Hitler had met in 1926 and admired for views identical to his own, was given the assignment of setting up a nationalist Protestant German church. Despite Hitler's backing of Mueller for the post of Reich Bishop, the Protestant synod meeting on May 27, 1933, defeated Mueller's candidacy by a vote of 13 to 11 and proceeded to elect Pastor Friedrich von Bodelschwingh, who represented the opposition. The militant German Christians went into action in true National Socialist fashion. Meetings of protest were held, called by the SA and SS; telegrams of protest were filed; press attacks were mounted; and Mueller denounced the election of Bodelschwingh as illegal, citing the law that any such appointment had to be approved by the Prussian State Government.

On Hitler's orders Frick had a talk with Pastor von Bodelschwingh, who felt himself obliged to resign on June 24, having held office for less than a month. Now protests flooded in from the other side, many of which reached Hindenburg, who was sorely disturbed at these evidences of internal Protestant conflict. The Fuehrer, eager to still any doubts on the part of the President, called on Frick to settle the matter. Frick for a time did nothing. A new church constitution was being written and he wanted to have the legal documents up to date before he acted. But history was in motion and events could not be stopped. Ludwig Mueller, using the well-tried Party methods of dealing with the opposition, occupied the buildings of the Church Union with SA men. He then dissolved the old committee that had been working on the constitution.

Frick and the Fuehrer were anxious to avoid open conflict in the church and they reproached the extreme wing of the German Christians. Frick, on July 11, said that the National Socialist task was greatly endangered when there was loose talk of continuing the revolution or of a second revolution. "Whoever talks in this fashion should be told that he opposes the Fuehrer and will be so treated," he declared. He was only echoing what Hitler had just said on July 6, when the Fuehrer told the Reichsstatthalter that the revolution was over, that the Party had become the State, and that other organizations must not exert separate authority. Hitler's and Frick's words could have referred to either the SA a year before the June killings or to the German Christians.[23] But Hitler openly supported the Mueller faction of the German Christians, who wanted the church brought into the state apparatus—to become, as they said, part of the outward order of the National Socialist Reich. The German Christians won a majority in the July 23 church elections, and in September Ludwig Mueller was duly elected Reichsbischof.

The struggle within the ranks of the German Christians continued, and a *Volkskirche* (people's church) group set out to rid the church of any taint of Orientalism, that is, of the Old Testament and the teachings of "Rabbi" Paul. Mueller, on his part, preached untrammeled love for the fatherland and the Fuehrer and the paramount duty of being a German. Lutheran ministers like Martin Dibelius and Martin Niemoeller were incensed. They were not only confronted by the Party's support of the German Christians but were attacked by the German Believers, a collection of pseudomystical, non-Christian, "folkish" elements with some 10,000 members. They, too, were enthusiastic National Socialists, and they believed that the pagan, northern Germanic elements in the German society, the Baldur-Siegfried, Indo-Germanic religion should take the place of the Eastern-Semitic type. Members had to swear they were free of Jewish or colored blood, that they were not Freemasons or Jesuits, and that they belonged to no other religion.

The Confessional Synod (*Bekenntnissynode*) of the Altpreussische Union of the Lutheran Church, a group founded by Pastor Niemoeller and other eminent Protestant ministers, meeting in Berlin-Dahlem March 4–5, 1935, accepted the challenge and drew up a proclamation. It read:

> We see our people threatened with a deadly danger. The danger lies in a new religion. The church has by order of its Master to see to it that in our people Christ is given the honor that is proper to the Judge of the world . . . The First Commandment says "Thou shalt have no other gods before me." The new religion is a rejection of the First Commandment.
>
> 1) In it the racist-folkish philosophy becomes a myth. In it blood and race, folkishness, honor and freedom become a false God.
> 2) The new religion demands belief in an eternal Germany in place of the belief in the eternal kingdom of our Master and Savior Jesus Christ.
> 3) This insane belief makes itself a God from man's image and being . . . It is anti-Christianism.
>
> In the face of the temptation and danger of this religion . . . we must bear witness to our country and people that:
>
> 1) The state has its authority and power through the commandment and the mercy of God who alone grants and limits all human authority.

Whoever places blood, race and *Volkstum* in the place of God as the creator and Lord over the authority of the state undermines the state.

2) Earthly justice fails to acknowledge its heavenly judge and protector and the state itself loses its sovereignty when it lets itself be clothed with the mantle of the eternal judge and makes its own authority the highest and final one in all the areas of life.

3) Obediently and thankfully the church recognizes the authority of the state founded and limited through God's word. Therefore it cannot bow before the total pretension to authority that binds conscience which the new religion of the state prescribes. Dedicated to God's word, the church is in duty bound to witness before state and people the sole authority of Jesus Christ, who alone has the power to bind conscience and to free it.

To him is given all power in Heaven and on earth.[24]

Frick forbade the reading of this proclamation from the pulpit, and some 500 ministers were arrested because they did read it.[25] After tedious negotiations with two representatives of the synod, *Praeses* Koch and Bishop Marahrens, Frick finally gave permission for the proclamation to be read on the condition that a paragraph be added, saying that it was directed against the neo-heathen religion and that the synod wished to warn the people and State of this threatening danger.

Frick was on the side of the Lutheran Christians; the pastors who talked with him were convinced of this. But his official view was Hitler's—that the State should be neutral in inner-church controversies, a bland position that attempted to avoid as long as possible the issues the conservative pastors thought a matter of life and death.[26] Up to 1935 Hitler was preoccupied with many things other than the church controversy. The opinion held of Germany in foreign countries was still of some importance to him, as were the protests that reached Hindenburg. When Neurath reported to Frick that the attacks on the traditional church were injuring Germany's reputation abroad, Frick could use this in his cautious support of the anti-Mueller position.[27] But by 1935 the situation had hardened, and the valiant band of stubborn Lutheran pastors with their stream of memorials and protests had to be silenced. Frick had to tell his friends in the church that the Government could no longer be neutral; that dark political forces lurked behind the flag of the defenders of the old church and were using a religious controversy for their own purposes. The Minister of the Interior, who for a short time had been the chief support of the religious function of the church, capitulated when Hitler tired of the badgering and the resistance to what he wanted done. A separate Church Ministry was established on July 16, 1935, and Frick was relieved of dealing with the problem.

All this, however, was not the chief trouble Frick had with the church. Since the beginning of the seizure of power, the National Socialists had wanted, in opposition to the deepest beliefs of both Protestant and Catholic churches, to sterilize or to kill the unfit.* Confirmed criminals, the feeble-minded, the insane, any threat to the racial integrity of the Volk was to be removed—either through sterilization or execution. The law for the Prevention of Offspring with Hereditary Diseases was issued on July 14, 1933. It provided for the sterilization of anyone suffering from a severe mental illness such as schizophrenia or a manic-depressive psychosis, from hereditary Saint Vitus's dance, or hereditary blindness, or a severe physical malformation. Each case would come before a eugenics' court on the application of the family, a civil-service doctor, or the head of a nursing home; and the court, over which a doctor presided, would decide by a majority vote whether or not to approve the application. An appeal might be taken to a higher eugenics' court, which was constituted in the same fashion as the original court. From time to time changes were made in the procedures; for example, under a Frick decree of August 22, 1936, no Party member could be sterilized without the approval of the Party authorities.[28] Frick said that the whole person must be taken into consideration when the decision was made; by that he no doubt meant that redeeming racial or other qualities highly regarded in Party doctrine should prevent a too literal following of the statute that he had signed along with Hitler and the Minister of Justice. If a Gauleiter disagreed with the findings of the eugenics' court, he was to put the matter in Frick's hands; all such cases were to be handled as "urgent and secret."

By 1942 all the Jews remaining at liberty in Holland were to be sterilized regardless of their mental or physical health (see Seyss-Inquart, Chapt. 11). Within Germany, the mentally sick and the feebleminded were no longer being sterilized; they were being killed.† Ten thousand Germans, witnesses later testified, were killed at Hadamar alone by lethal injections or pills; homes for the insane, the feebleminded, and the aged and all similar establishments in Germany and Austria by the beginning of 1940 were potential or active extermination centers. The victims were Germans—Aryans—and their families were usually told they had died of pneumonia or of other natural causes. But the real story could not be suppressed. Relatives assured the authorities of their loyalty and asked to be told how a brother or sister

---

* These actions were to be taken in accordance with a pre-Nazi doctrine of the so-called Social Darwinists. Adolf Hitler eagerly seized upon this theory, which maintained that the law of the survival of the fittest in the natural world applied to society, too. The unfit must be eliminated. Friedrich Lenz wrote: "The goal of socialism is not the individual but the race." Hitler in a speech to officer candidates in 1944 said, "In every part of her realm nature teaches us that the principle of selection governs her, that the stronger are the victors and the weak go under. She teaches us that what mankind often sees as brutality . . . is a basic necessity in order to bring about the higher development of living creatures . . . nature above all knows nothing of humanitarianism . . . on the contrary weakness is a ground for condemnation" (Buchheim, et al., op. cit., Vol. II, pp. 296–97).

† Frick said in an interrogation of September 16, 1946, that Hitler had ordered mercy deaths in a letter of September 1, 1939 (NA). By the summer of 1940 it had been decided that all incurable mental patients should be killed (Earl W. Kintner, ed., Hadamar Trial of Alfons Klein, Adolf Wallmann, et al. [London, Edinburgh, Glasgow: William Hodge, 1948]). Concentration camps were also combed for victims.

or son or daughter had really died. One mother had a son who was an epileptic and had been sterilized. Soon after she sent him tobacco, she received his ashes in an urn. Despite his illness he had been able to work a good deal of the time—he had done most of the farm chores when he had been at home—but an anonymous authority had decided on his death.[29]

The individuals in charge of such institutions protested, for the law that Frick had drawn up in the summer of 1940 on the Fuehrer's order was secret and the public had never heard of it. Being conscientious bureaucrats they objected to what they regarded as high-handed proceedings (one superintendent complained that if such measures had to be taken they should be done legally and that the patients should be given a hearing).[30] The provincial bishop of the Lutheran Church in Wuerttemberg, Dr. Wurm, writing a letter of shocked protest to Frick, said the local population saw the smoke rising from the crematorium near the home in Marbach, which the Samaritan Foundation had established to look after physically and mentally incapacitated persons. Sinister rumors, the bishop wrote, were going around; and among the victims, he said flatly, were wounded veterans of World War I, epileptics, and other people capable of working.[31] The Bishop of Limburg wrote a solemn condemnation of the killings at Hadamar to the Minister of Justice, Guertner, and sent a copy to Frick. The bishop said that children watching the hospital busses go by said, "Here come the murder wagons," and told one another that if they did not behave, they, too, would end up in the bake ovens.[32]

A sermon on August 3, 1941, by the Bishop of Muenster, Clemens August Count von Galen, forced the Government to a decision. The bishop had long been a critic of the Party; in 1934 he had spoken out against its racial policies and in July, 1941, had preached a sermon in which he denounced the unlawful arrests of the secret police. In the August sermon he told his congregation of the reports concerning the killings in the institutions—of the murders, he called them, of those who could no longer work. "These are our brothers and sisters," he said, and he asked his listeners how long the rest of them could expect to live if the measure of their life span was its productivity. No one's life was safe any longer, he told them, and he asked who now could have confidence in his doctor. It was a blistering sermon, and the decision had to be made either to arrest Galen and the others who were publicly protesting or to stop the killings. Bishop von Galen delivered his sermon at the start of the Russian campaign, when Hitler had troubles enough without taking on the outraged churchmen and their followers. The killings were suspended; but they were stopped only as a beltline production.[33] They went on sporadically until the end of the war; Nazi doctrine never changed, and whenever a local Party or SS leader thought it necessary the executions began again.

It sometimes seemed too much trouble to evacuate such a hospital; in one case near the end of the war, although trucks were at hand, the inmates of a home for the feebleminded were simply taken out and shot instead of being sent to safety before the advancing Russians. No one in authority objected to this; on the contrary, it was regarded as a sensible act of war and saving of scarce resources. Frick could frame the decrees, Hitler could order their suspension for propagandistic reasons, but everyone knew that "useless feeders" could always be gotten rid of. After the German patients in Hadamar had been executed, their places were taken by the babies of Polish and Russian women who were working for the Germans. The foreign babies were killed by injections. They, too, were useless feeders.[34]

The killing of weakminded or insane Germans and of the babies of inferior races was all one to the personnel of the hospital. One of the nurses was so devout that she brought in priests to hear the confessions of the German patients before they were killed, and so full of charitable impulses that she bought toys for the condemned children in her care.[35]

Frick's part in the killings of the Germans was clear enough (the other deaths at Hadamar and elsewhere occurred after he was no longer Minister of the Interior). Sometime in the summer of 1940, he had drawn up and signed the secret law providing for the killing of aged and incurably ill citizens of the Third Reich.[36] He had received report after report showing that its provisions were being carried out. One such report, written on May 6, 1941, to the director of the hospital at Kaufbeuren, said, "I have the honor to inform you that the female patients transferred from your institute on November 8, 1940, to the institutions in Grafeneck, Bernburg, Sonnenstein and Hartheim all died in November of last year." [37]

How many people were killed under the euthanasia law can only be guessed at; the prosecution at Nuremberg said 275,000 were put to death, including 75,000 old people, but later calculations were between 70,000-80,000.[38] The killings were meant to be kept secret, the personnel of the homes were sworn to silence, and only in rare cases were relatives told what had happened—when their devotion to the Party and their understanding of the necessity for purging the Reich of its incompetents seemed beyond reproach. Otherwise the condemned ones, like the inmates of the concentration camps, officially died of natural causes.

Frick was a remote but convinced participant in these killings. He did not delight in them, but he thought they were necessary, as he thought the laws he signed that placed the Jews outside the law and into the sole power of the police and guards of the concentration and extermination camps were necessary. In more than one speech he echoed Hitler, saying that race and blood were decisive for a people, that biological substance determined its fate, and that if this were so its physically or mentally inferior members as well as its enemies had to be disposed of. He saw as his supreme duty the carrying out the Fuehrer's decrees; for what Hitler proclaimed was law, the highest law of the land. That was why he unquestioningly signed the decree of July 3, 1934, declaring the Roehm murders a legal act of state. In the end his principles left him, too, defenseless against the whims of the Fuehrer. Hitler told Goebbels in 1943 that he was very dissatisfied with Frick, who, he said, was old and used up. But as in the case of so many others who had fallen from grace, Frick had no successor readily available and if Hitler dismissed Frick, there would be an immediate battle to be his successor as Minister of the Interior. Himmler, Terboven, and Stuckart, Hitler said, were all aspirants for the post, but the Fuehrer was thinking of appointing Arthur Greiser, Gauleiter of Wartheland, if he did dismiss Frick.[39] Hitler finally did get rid of Frick on August 20, 1943; he appointed him Reich Protector of Bohemia and Moravia to replace Neurath, but he took care to see that the real power remained in the hands of Karl Hermann Frank, one of Himmler's men. Himmler got another job he had been looking for: he was named Minister of the Interior.

Frick's duties in Czechoslovakia were routine. He asked for and received "suitable," that is, pretentious, residences in Prague and in the countryside; he had the power of pardon for persons convicted of crimes committed against the State, a privilege which he never appears to have exercised. He went through the motions of being the highest-ranking official in Czechoslovakia, issuing the regulations for providing the slave labor for Sauckel and for maintaining order among the hostile population. Frick continued to hold the rank of Reich Minister; and because by 1943 the basic laws and decrees for the Reich had been issued, it perhaps did not matter much to him whether he had one post or another. The main thing was to do his duty.

Although he did not testify in his own defense—he told Fritzsche it was useless—he seems to have been genuinely convinced of his innocence. What had he done that was wrong from the point of view of a true believer? He had obeyed the orders of the legal head of state; he had loyally served the cause of the Party, in whose principles he devoutly believed; he had drawn up the laws that were essential to its well-being and preservation. The concentration camps and the RSHA had been under his nominal control, but actually they were soon under Himmler and he had done his best to limit some of the illegalities he knew were taking place. He had never had much to do with the concentration camps, although an unconvincing witness at Nuremberg declared that he had visited Dachau, where he had shown great interest in the experiments performed on the inmates by Dr. Sigmund Rascher. Frick's guilt was of a kind that he could no longer comprehend. Perhaps the early Frick, the assessor in a provincial administration or a member of the economics division of the Munich police, would have understood the nature of his complicity in the crimes of the Nazi State, of his having made it legally possible for thousands of Germans and millions of Jews to be killed legally. But Frick—even at Nuremberg, even after the testimony of the survivors had been heard and the atrocity films had been shown —felt that he had only worked long hours, given the best of his talents to the ordained authorities, and always done his duty for them and for his people.

With the exception of his closing statement to the court, he was silent. He obviously thought it would not be possible to explain to a tribunal made up of the enemies of the theories and practices of the Third Reich that he had always believed in law and order, that he had administered both devotedly with the sole object of purifying Germany of its racial contagions and securing its future. He had done all within his power and within the limits of his *Weltanschauung* to further the renewal of Germany, to strengthen it by law and decree and to defend it against the hosts of evil. The court found him guilty on every count except that of having planned to wage aggressive war and sentenced him to death. He told the prison psychologist that was the only decision he had expected. The tribunal was operating on another system and wavelength of communication and he knew he could never reach its ear with the story he had to tell.

NOTES

1. Hans Fabricius, *Reichsinnenminister Dr. Frick: der revolutionaere Staatsmann* (Berlin: Deutsche Kulturwacht, 1939).

2. NCA V, 3119-PS, p. 893. Hans Pfundtner, *Dr. Wilhelm Frick und sein Ministerium* (Munich: Zentralverlag der NSDAP, Franz Eher Nachf., 1937).

3. Fabricius, *op. cit.* Also Pfundtner, *op. cit.*

4. N XXII, p. 385.

5. NCA II, 3125-PS, p. 655.

6. NCA V, 2742-PS, p. 383.

7. Wilhelm Frick, *Die Nationalsozialisten im Reichstag 1924–1928* (Munich: Franz Eher Verlag, 1928).

8. NCA V, 3132-PS, pp. 906–10. Hans Heinz Sadila-Mantau, *Unsere Reichsregierung* (Berlin: C. A. Weller, 1936). "Dr. Wilhelm Frick," in *Nationalsozialistische Monatshefte*, August 4, 1930, pp. 229–31.

9. D. C. Watt, "Die bayerischen Bemuehungen um Ausweisung Hitlers, 1924," in *Vierteljahrshefte fuer Zeitgeschichte*, Vol. VI, No. 3, 1958, pp. 270–80.

10. NCA V, 3132-PS, pp. 906–10. NCA VI, 3399-PS, pp. 116–17. Rudolf Morsey, "Hitler als Braunschweiger Regierungsrat," in *Vierteljahrshefte fuer Zeitgeschichte*, Vol. VIII, No. 4, 1960, pp. 419–48. Helmut Heiber, *Adolph Hitler* (Berlin: Colloquium Verlag, 1960). Cuno Horkenbach, *Das Deutsche Reich von 1918 bis heute* (Berlin: Verlag fuer Presse, Wirtschaft und Politik, 1930). *Schulthess' Europäischer Geschichtskalender*, Vol. LXXIII, 1932 (Munich: C. H. Beck'sche Verlagsbuchhandlung, 1933).

11. Johannes Hohlfeld, ed., *Dokumente der Deutschen Politik und Geschichte von 1848 bis zur Gegenwart*, Vol. IV (Berlin: Dokumenten-Verlag Dr. Herbert Wendler & Co., n.d.), pp. 47–50.

12. Wilhelm Frick, *Die Rassengesetzgebung des Dritten Reiches* (Munich: Franz Eher Verlag, 1934).

13. NCA IV, 1417-PS, p. 8.

14. F 71, Loesener Memorandum (IZG).

15. *Ibid.*, December 4, 1941. Walter Strauss, "*Das Reichsministerium des Innern und die Judengesetzgebung*," Aufzeichnungen von Dr. Bernhard Loesener, in *Vierteljahrshefte fuer Zeitgeschichte*, Vol. IX, No. 3, 1961, pp. 262–313.

16. F 71, *op. cit.*

17. *Ibid.*

18. *Ibid.*

19. NCA III, 779-PS, pp. 555–57.

20. Hohlfeld, ed., *op. cit.*, Vol. IV.

21. Hans Buchheim, *Glaubenskrise im Dritten Reich* (Stuttgart: Deutsche Verlags-Anstalt, 1953), p. 92.

22. *Ibid.*, p. 85.

23. Heiber, *op. cit.*

24. Buchheim, *op. cit.*, pp. 191–92.

25. *Ibid.*, p. 192.

26. Heinrich Hermelink, ed., *Kirche im Kampf* (Tuebingen and Stuttgart: Rainer Wunderlich Verlag Hermann Leins, 1950).

27. Walter Conrad, *Der Kampf um die Kanzleien* (Berlin: Toepelmann, 1957).

28. N XXXV, 181-D, pp. 40–42.

29. *Ibid.*, 906-D, pp. 685–86.

30. NCA, Supp. A, M-151, pp. 1216–18.

31. *Ibid.*, M-152, pp. 1218–25.

32. NCA III, 615-PS, pp. 449–51.

33. Annedore Leber, *Fuer und Wider* (Berlin: Mosaik-Verlag, 1961).

34. Earl W. Kintner, ed., *Hadamar Trial of Alfons Klein, Adolf Wallmann, et al.* (London: William Hodge, 1948).

35. *Ibid.*, testimony Irmgard Huber.

36. NCA IV, 1556-PS, pp. 111–12.

37. *Ibid.*, 1696-PS, pp. 202–3.

38. N V, pp. 362–63.

39. EG 83-1, Joseph Goebbels, *Tagebuch*. Vol. I, entry for February 23, 1943, p. 272 (IZG).

8

The Youth Leader

For boys and girls of Nazi Germany, the indoctrination into the world of Baldur von Schirach, youth leader of the Third Reich, began officially at the age of ten. Starting in 1939, on April 20, Hitler's birthday, the children who in the course of the year became ten years old were formally inducted into the Jungvolk and Jungmaedel. The boy, the *Pimpf* (the word is Austrian and means "lad" or "squirt"), was given his neckerchief and slip knot and a performance book that would be important to him for the rest of his life. It would record his progress for the eight years he remained in the Hitlerjugend; how he had performed in the *Pimpfe* test of his cultural and athletic achievements (the test was given him after his first four months in the organization and included his reciting the main events in the life of Adolf Hitler); and then through the years the badges he won and what his youth leaders thought of him. The Jungmaedel, too, had to undergo similar tests, but girls were the future mothers of the nation, and while they sang the same songs and denounced the same enemies of the Fuehrer as did the boys, their indoctrination was intended to prepare them to be the future helpmates of the warrior males and to beget new ones. At the age of fourteen the boys and girls went on from the Jungvolk and Jungmaedel to the more advanced Hitlerjugend for the boys and Bund Deutscher Maedel for the girls. At the age of eighteen they graduated into the adult world of the Party, in theory at least fully indoctrinated to live and die for the Fuehrer.

The youth movement had started in Berlin at the turn of the century and got its pre-World War I name when in 1901 a group of students and other young men christened themselves the Wandervoegel. The movement began soon after the migration of large numbers of Germans from the country to the city, and the Wandervoegel brought young people back to the out-of-doors. They left the cities behind, to commune with nature in the woods and at lakeside refuges as far as possible from the urban, industrial centers that were exploding all over Germany.* The youth movement was no week-end affair. The Wandervoegel was a way of life, a protest against the adult society of strict categories, of money and business success. It rejected class distinctions; a member had only to be young and a good comrade, to love nature and deny the city. The young people marched, but not in step; it was a movement of individuals, of nonconformists. Many of them were non-smokers and drank no alcohol; they felt themselves part of a secret order allied against the bleak world of their parents. The Wandervoegel were a Germanic phenomenon; they were strong in Austria and had groups in Switzerland as well as in Germany, but they never spread to the rest of Europe. Their idealism was of a romantic, Teutonic kind. The journey which was the center of the movement was a journey away from the the city but to no end. On the journey one might find the rare blue flower that grew in lonely places, but that was all; the journey itself was enough. Some groups among the Wandervoegel were nationalistic and anti-Semitic; they were all against intellectualism and for the "whole man," the healthy, self-sufficient future citizen of a better world.

The Buende, which succeeded the Wandervoegel after World War I, were better organized.† They had leaders and differing purposes, and they represented religious and political groups; there were nationalist, socialist, Protestant, and Catholic members of the Buende. The journey was no longer the center of the movement; the new center was the *Lager*—the discussion around a campfire, and if the Buende had a common symbol, it was this fire with a speaker standing in front of it to enlighten them. Women played only a minor role in both the Wandervoegel and the Buende. When women's organizations existed, they were usually separate from the men's, although girls were admitted to some of the male Buende.[1] At the start of World War I the Wandervoegel had some 25,000 members; 15,000 of them fought for Germany, some 7,000 of whom did not return from the war. In the Buende period the number of members was much higher; in 1932 the National Socialist youth alone had 20,000 paying and 20,000

* Between 1850 and 1900 Dortmund had grown from 7,500 to 140,000 inhabitants; Hamburg from 155,000 to 780,000; Munich from 35,000 to 500,000 (J. Freund, quoted by Pierre Bertaux, *La vie quotidienne en Allemagne* [Paris: Hachette, 1962], p. 186).

† The name designated the loosely organized youth movement of the Weimar Republic. The Buende's Reich Committee, which represented some 4.5 million members, included all the youth organizations aside from those of the Communists, National Socialists, and Jews (Karl O. Paetel, "Die deutsche Jugendbewegung als politisches Phaenomen," in *Politische Studien*, July, 1957, p. 3).

nonpaying members.[2] * This was a small representation, since the Party that year polled six million votes. Catholic youth in the various Buende numbered over a million and the Protestant Buende totaled 1.4 million.[8] Far from the simplicities of the Wandervoegel, where at the end of a journey a viscous, cheap broth called *Schleim* (consisting mainly of barley and water) was cooked up, the members of the many Buende led an organized life of planned political discussions; the members of Party organizations often took part in street brawls where so many of the issues of the Weimar period were fought out. The Nazi youths would invade Communist sections of the German cities; fighting was often fierce and sometimes boys were killed to become, if they were National Socialists, the revered martyrs of Baldur von Schirach's later pageants.

Schirach joined the Party in 1925, when he was eighteen years old. Born in Berlin, one of four children from a well-to-do family, he was too young to take part in World War I. He was the kind of young man the Germans call *schwaermerisch*—a lad with a sentimental longing for adventure linked to high pursuits and a love of poetry, tales of derring-do, and literary discussions that do not place too great a strain on one's intellectual capacities. He spoke English well; he was three-quarters American.† His father, Carl Bailey-Norris von Schirach, had been an officer in the Garde-Kuerassier-Regiment of Wilhelm II, from which he had resigned in 1908 to become director of the Court, later the National Theater, in Weimar, where Baldur grew up. In this environment Baldur early acquired a precocious love for the theater, music, and literature—especially, he told the court at Nuremberg, for Goethe. But he soon had things other than the theater on his mind. First World War I came, then his father lost his job during the revolution that followed; and the family knew the bitterness shared by so many middle-class people in those years of being downgraded in status as well as income.

In 1917, when he was ten years old, Baldur joined his first youth organization—the Young Germans' League, a group given to hikes and singing on the march and around campfires. At this time he also attended a country boarding school conducted by Hermann Lietz, one of the founders of the Landerziehungsheime movement, which also had a program for youth. Lietz had the idea that a school should mirror the state—and his students practiced

---

* By the end of 1932, membership in the Hitlerjugend rose to over 100,000 (Werner Klose, *Generation im Gleichschritt* [Oldenbourg and Hamburg: Gerhard Stalling Verlag, 1964], p. 25.)

† Baldur von Schirach's paternal grandfather had lived for a time in the United States, where he had fought as a major in the Civil War. He married an American girl, Elizabeth Bailey-Norris, in Philadelphia in 1869 and then returned to Germany with her. Baldur's father was born in Kiel, and he too married an American girl, Emma Tillou, during a visit to the United States (Max von Schirach: *Geschichte der Familie von Schirach* [Berlin: Walter de Gruyter Verlag, 1939]).

(for a time) self-government in a discreetly supervised fashion. At the end of World War I Baldur joined still another youth organization, the Knappen-schaft, a patriotic group of youths who talked about the iniquities of Versailles and the misdeeds of the Communists and the Jews, who had brought the revolution upon them. He eagerly heard the speakers visiting Weimar who said the same things, such as Count Ernst zu Reventlow, Rosenberg, Streicher, and Sauckel, and he began reading anti-Semitic literature—includ-ing Henry Ford's *The International Jew* and Houston S. Chamberlain's *The Foundations of the Nineteenth Century.*

In Weimar in 1926 he first met Hitler, who was visiting the city with his deputy Hess to make a speech. Baldur had read *Mein Kampf* in 1925, and from the first page, this book that confirmed everything he believed was a bible to him. Hitler advised him to go to Munich, to the city that was the beating heart of the Party, and Baldur, who aspired to write, decided to attend the university there. He had joined the SA when he was eighteen, and in the University of Munich he eagerly set out to recruit students for the Party. He was a conventionally attractive young man, serious, plump, well mannered, and voluble, although he spoke in a somewhat stilted, humorless style with solemn earnestness and in sentences that were studded with clichés. This flat oratorical style was unusual among Party speakers, but he was successful enough in talking to his student audiences that in 1929 he was made leader of the National Socialist Students' Union. Schirach was always proud of having been elected to the job at a students' meeting at Graz—Party posts were invariably bestowed only by higher authority—and Hitler had promptly confirmed his selection.

In 1931 Schirach was named Reich youth leader of the National Socialist Party. As such he was for a year on Roehm's staff of the SA Supreme Command, and from then on he gave full time to his Party duties. A year later Hitler, always lavish with titles and quick to promote those he thought worthy, made him in addition Reich Leader for Youth Education of the NSDAP. In 1933 he was made youth leader of the German Reich, a posi-tion he held for a time under his codefendant Frick, who was then Minister of the Interior. By 1936 Schirach, at the age of twenty-nine, was one of the leading officials of the Reich, reporting directly to the Fuehrer. He was a somewhat effeminate young man. His contemporaries spoke derisively of his girlish bedroom and living room decorated in white, and those who disliked him said he looked like a transplanted Berliner in his incongruous Bavarian shorts.[4] But it was not easy to please everyone in the Party. The main thing was to please the Fuehrer, and this Schirach did with odes of adulation in texts and rituals, and in endless ceremonials intended to make German youth into little samurai who, as the youth leader said, would not only ardently perform but also willingly die for Hitler.

Many people disliked Schirach; he was corny, and he clung ostentatiously to his upper middle-class origins (at one meeting of the Hitlerjugend in

Hamburg, the leaders stayed at the Teutonic and cheap hotel, the Hein Godewind, but Schirach spent the night alone at the deluxe Vier Jahreszeiten). He was objectionable enough that some of the Party leaders wanted to get rid of him, but Hitler was convinced of his choice and Schirach stayed. How could anything serious be wrong with a man who wrote:

> That is the greatest thing about him,
> That he is not only our leader and a great hero,
> But himself, upright, firm and simple,
> . . . in him rest the roots of our world.
> And his soul touches the stars
> And yet he remains a man like you and me.

To which in Schirach's verses Hitler replies:

> You are a thousand behind me
> You are me and I am you
> I have no thoughts that have not moved in your hearts
> And if I form words; I know none that are not one with your will
> For I am you and you are me and we all believe, Germany, in you.[5]

This is not far from what Hitler actually said in September, 1936, to the men of his *Kampfverbaende*: "This is the miracle of our time, that you have found me among so many millions. And that I have found you is Germany's good fortune." [6] Schirach and Hitler were clearly of one mind when they dealt with the mystique of the Fuehrer's leadership. Schirach's passionate devotion to Hitler swept everything before it, and only in the superheated atmosphere in which the young people paid their homage could his adulation be recorded without embarrassment. "One thing is stronger than you, my Fuehrer," he said on the occasion of the Reich Party Day in 1936, with Hitler listening gravely, "that is the love of young Germans for you. There are many happy hours in the year of the youth. This, however, in every year is one of our happiest. Because more than any other people, my Fuehrer, we feel ourselves to be chained to your person by our name. Your name is the happiness of the youth, your name, my Fuehrer, is our immortality." [7]

This was only the beginning. As Schirach warmed to his assignment, he had to reach even higher to express the ecstasy he felt. At another meeting of the Hitlerjugend he said:

> This Sunday morning ceremony doesn't aim at presenting arguments . . .
> but at imbuing life and men with courage and strength to fulfill their
> greater and lesser tasks through unqualified faith in the divine power and the
> ideology of the Fuehrer and his movement. . . . The service of Germany
> appears to us to be . . . the service of God; the banner of the Third Reich
> appears to us to be His banner; and the Fuehrer of the people is the savior
> whom He sent to rescue us from the calamity and peril into which we were
> actually plunged by the most pious parties of the defunct Weimar Republic.[8]

The parallels to Christian devotional themes were many. Young people recited such prayers as the following before an evening meal:

> Fuehrer, my Fuehrer given me by God,
> Protect and preserve my life for long.
> You rescued Germany from its deepest need.
> I thank you for my daily bread.
> Stay for a long time with me, leave me not.
> Fuehrer, my Fuehrer, my faith, my light
> Heil my Fuehrer.[9]

Even kindergarten children might recite a secular prayer when they began their day's activities: "Fold hands, bow heads; think always on the Fuehrer."

Schirach was a great man for pageants. To see one boy after another step up and deliver a burst of heroic or devotional lines brought him some of his most titillating moments, especially as he wrote many of the parts himself. The Hitler Youth was full of togetherness. While they marched, the boys and girls sang songs taken from approved songbooks in which a number of the *Lieder* had been written by Schirach. The ceremonies and indoctrination courses for boys and girls were designed to shape them in the new revolutionary mold, to detach them from the non-Nazi past, to substitute Hitler not only for the former heroes of German history and folklore but for the most sacred symbols of the Christian religion. Days of dedication were held, when the children would chant in responsive readings: "Where one walks his step is lost, where a thousand walk his step has its full weight." Then followed the words of the Fuehrer: "My will has to be the creed . . . that is your faith. My faith is to me as it is to you—everything in this world." The children of the Jungvolk and Jungmaedel then made their vows of allegiance: "I promise to do my duty in the Hitlerjugend in love and fidelity to the Fuehrer and to our flag." The elder brothers and sisters swore a "bodily oath" of loyalty. Their lines read: "The Fuehrer of Great Germany has many in the world who hate him; they have maliciously prepared his grave on land and water." None of this, however, would avail such forces of evil, for there were enough "sword bearers" and "true ones" to protect him. The children declared they would never speak of "I" but only of "we." They chanted that they were part of the "God-willed German community," that where they stood, stood faithfulness, "and our march is its order." [10]

On the days of these pageants there would be no school, and after the war started, Party reports said that parents came in increasing numbers, that these were now more family occasions than they had been in the past. More teachers came, too, the reports said, but unfortunately church attendance was also up. This undesirable development occurred, the observer thought, because of the increasing losses at the front and the alacrity of the clergy to take advantage of the many war deaths to hold services. People were now going to church who had never gone before, and, as the reports dolefully conceded, many Party members even preferred to have such memorial services performed by the church rather than by the Party.[11]

The shadow of war intensified Schirach's devotional exercises. Here is his "instructional description" of a program for Hitler Youth meetings in 1937, to be used for "flag parades, celebrations, etc."

A Flag Parade

The detail has assembled. The leader on duty announces this to the camp leader. "Heil Hitler, camp detail."

"Heil Hitler."

The leader on duty gives the parole for the day:

"Eyes front! The parole for today is: Herbert Norkus."

A boy says:

"We don't mourn at cold caskets,
We step up and say: there was one
Who dared that which we all dare.
His mouth is silent. We step up and say:
The comradeship is immutable.
Many die. Many are born.
The world is large which encloses them.
The word, however, which we have sworn to,
The word is not lost even to the dead.
That means: the duty is greater than the world." . . .

Then the camp leader speaks for the fallen comrade:

"On January 24, 1931, at Beuszelkietz in Berlin our fifteen-year-old comrade Herbert Norkus was slain by Communists. As a Hitler Youth he had done nothing but his duty and that caused the hatred of the Communists. We know that for the sake of our dead comrade, there will never be an understanding between Bolshevism and us!"

The leader on duty:

"Attention! We sing while raising the flag: 'A young nation is rising ready to storm . . .' Ready to raise the flag . . . Eyes right!

Raise the flag!"

The leaders of the camp units at once give the command for marching off.

Examples of suitable paroles for the day:

Arminius, Geiserich, Teja, Widukind, Heinrich I, Heinrich der Loewe, Braunschweig, Franz von Sickingen, Gneisenau, Bluecher, Verdun, Immelmann, Feldherrnhalle, Nuernberg.

Flag Mottos

He who loves the nation proves it only by the sacrifices he is ready to make for it. Adolf Hitler.

Thou art the most beautiful of all that waved for us,
Thou art the power which recruits every fighter,
Thou even sanctifiest the sinner who dies for thee,
Thou high hand with which the heroes pray.
Fervor and will thou art of us all.

Who fell for thee a symbol he becomes of thee.
Thou art the bridge between there and here.
Hail to those who fall in thy shadow.

Baldur von Schirach [12]

What Schirach was doing from the beginning was preparing the perfect SS man. He nourished himself and the boys and girls with fragments of wisdom and poetic tags taken from a large stock of Teutonic authors. Schirach himself in his student days used to meet with a group of young men under a portrait of Napoleon to read and discuss the runelike poems of Stefan George, and his love for Rilke at his least abstruse is plainly visible in Schirach's own contributions to the repertoire of the Hitlerjugend. He was filled with the aphorisms that delighted the hearts of the Party members. "Youth must be led by youth," "Youth knows no superiors, only leaders," he told his audiences, for the Nazi movement itself, like its Italian counterpart, was "a youth movement." "The Hitler Youth is not a founding of the State for youth, but a founding of youth for the State." [13] *Giovenezza* never was slighted by either Hitler or Mussolini—the Fuehrer always concealed the fact that he needed glasses to read by, and long after the young Fascists who had marched on Rome were middle-aged, Mussolini made his now corpulent followers leap about in exercises designed to show that they were still the lads who had captured the capital for the party. Mussolini and Hitler told their people and the world that they were the leaders of the young nations; they had cast off the errors of the weaklings of the past and thus would now lead their peoples to a thousand-year Reich or a new empire of the Caesars.

Schirach fitted perfectly into this design. "We are the soldiers of the future," he had the boys and girls sing.* And he could bring the house down when he told them what he had learned from his old headmaster Lietz: the Hitlerjugend were building a youth state, that is, a state for youth. It was the spirit of the SS he cherished, not its military postures—those would come later. Schirach never wanted his young men to do military drill, and despite what the Nuremberg indictment said, he never "militarized" his boys and girls. The most the boys got, in the way of weapons, were smallbore rifles and target practice. It was their souls he was after; their bodies were only to be made fit to carry out the assignments they would later be given to complete training in their heaven-sent mission of living and dying for the Fuehrer. But while the boys were in the Hitlerjugend they had little to do with military matters before the start of the war. Schirach himself preferred, one observer noted, poetry to steel helmets and guns, and even though one of the youth leaders said the boys must be able to handle a gun

---

* This was wrongly translated at the trial as "We are the future soldiers," and was cited as evidence of Schirach's desire to militarize the German youth. But the original text states what Schirach and Hitler wanted the youth to aspire to be: the militant shapers of the future.

as readily as they handled a fountain pen, they had to learn this aptitude with .22's, for Schirach resolutely held out against a specifically military training.

He nevertheless prepared the young people for the role that Hitler appreciated above all others: that of unconditional obedience to the Fuehrer. The youth, said Schirach, represent "not their own interest, but the well-being of Germany; the will of the Fuehrer is living for them." "Nothing for us ourselves, everything for Germany." They were soldiers not only of the future but of the idea, he told them; and he took over the old slogans of the Wandervoegel and Buende, merely giving them a new direction. "The working lad whose heart beats hot for the Fuehrer is more essential for Germany than the highly educated esthete. Higher than the sharpest intellect we cherish a true and brave heart. The ones who are cold and intelligent can make mistakes; the true ones are always right. The intelligent ones want advantages for themselves; the true ones want nothing; they know only their duty." [14] And what Himmler planned in the way of SS cadres formed from among the nations of Europe, Schirach wanted for the youth of Europe who were to unite in a mystical fashion under these principles of the Hitlerjugend. Visitors from all over the world came to see him; Boy Scout leaders, youth groups from France and England and Yugoslavia, from Italy and Finland and the United States.

There was much idealism in what he was doing and preaching. Like the SA uniforms of the 1920's, the brown shirt of the HJ and the white blouse and blue skirt of the BDM were intended to conceal any economic differences among members, to enable the poor and pure of heart to meet their more highly placed contemporaries as equals. The Hitlerjugend had drawn its membership largely from the proletariat or the proletarianized middle classes before the Party took power.* [15] Their rivals considered them activists, street fighters, and brawlers like their elders in the SA. They were regarded with derision by members of the more sophisticated Buende until the boys in the Buende, too, were forced to become HJ members. The Buende then found their own watchwords adopted, sometimes with minor changes, by those they had thought of as "hoodlums" on the march.

"Only what is eternally young is to find its homeland in our Germany," Schirach said, and the eternally young, if they took a properly reverent attitude, were given a warm and well-organized welcome when they visited Germany after 1933 from whatever country they came—except for Jews, of course. The songs of the Hitlerjugend were less than welcoming when they dealt with the Jews. One of them went to the tune of the student song "*Socrates, Socrates!*":

---

* In 1932 69 per cent of the HJ were factory workers or mechanics, 10 per cent were in business, 12 per cent in school, and the rest came from a scattering of occupations and many were unemployed. (Klose, *op. cit.*, p. 17. Arno Kloenne, *Hitlerjugend*, [Hannover and Frankfurt a.M.: Norddeutsche Verlagsanstalt O. Goedel, 1955], p. 11.)

O friends listen to the ballad,
Of what happened long ago,
When there governed here before us,
The system, the system.
Curly hair, crooked nose,
He ran around in this land,
And thought himself strong and powerful,
Isidor, Isidor.

After a few stanzas devoted to the misdeeds of the Catholics and capitalists came the climactic stanza:

Now Michel is master in his house,
And within it's comfortable again,
The others fled the country,
Emigrant! Emigrant! [16]

Such songs properly belonged to the movement, for the Hitlerjugend had been given its name by none other than Julius Streicher. Hitler himself, Schirach said, had thought of having a youth movement in the Party—all the parties in the early twenties had them, including the Social Democrats and the Communists, and in Austria they formed part of the National Socialist movement. Kurt Gruber, who had long been identified with nationalist youth organizations, in 1926 had founded the first group of young National Socialists. When Gruber first met Hitler, in the early twenties, he started a youth brigade he called the Jungsturm, and in 1925 he was head of the grandiosely named Greater German Youth Movement.

The story of the founding of the HJ is told somewhat differently by a man who knew the principal figures among the early Nazis. Albert Krebs, who was Gauleiter of Hamburg when Hitler cast him out of the Party in 1932, had been a member of the pre-Hitler youth movement, and he said that Arnold Peters, a seventeen-year-old boy from a worker's family, was the originator of the HJ. Peters had belonged to the Red Falcons and later to the Socialist Workers' Youth (Sozialistische Arbeiterjugend), and when at seventeen he became a convinced National Socialist he was too young to join the Party. Peters therefore proposed to the Party leadership that they establish a Union of German Working Youth without any direct connection with the Party, although the youth would be prepared for their future roles as Party members. Peters began to enlist his members at the same time as Party circles in Munich were planning a Hitler Youth. Peters declined to change the name of this group to any of those suggested by his elders (The Defense of Youth was one suggestion; another was The Youth SA). Hess and Krebs agreed with Peters as far as the organizational plan went, but Hess wanted the name "Hitler Youth" adopted, and eventually he turned the practical decisions over to Gruber and to Franz von Pfeffer, who between May, 1926, and 1930 was head of the SA. Pfeffer saw in the HJ an opportunity to feed new recruits into his legions of the SA, and Gruber, who was in the sporting goods business, saw the chance to sell more brown shirts, canteens, drums, and so on. Krebs, who was then leader of the Ortsgruppe Hamburg, was instructed either to bring the Hamburger Union of Working Youth into the HJ or to dissolve them. Krebs obeyed. But Peters refused, and that was the end of his organization.[17]

Gruber and Pfeffer's program for the Hitlerjugend was intended to make them "honorably hard," able to battle ideologically and with their fists against the members of the Buende, and they succeeded. Their boys were a raw group, outwardly disciplined and spoiling for a fight as they marched or filled the great tent encampment at the 1930 Party celebration in Nuremberg. Schirach saw the Hitlerjugend differently. Next to the Fuehrer, he best loved culture, and he had great faith in the power of high-sounding phrases, tableaus, and indoctrination through dramatics. He had never belonged to the Hitlerjugend, but he quickly made up for his lack of formal training by instinctive feeling for that which was necessary to accomplish what he and the Fuehrer so ardently desired—a huge cadre of German youth that would be prepared for the dangerous life of the single-minded, unquestioning Party member in the Third Reich. Gruber and Pfeffer wanted young SA men; Schirach wanted the soldiers of the future, the men who would one day, if all went well, rule Germany and Europe in the name of the Fuehrer and in unconditional obedience to him.

Schirach's ideological contribution, as far as he had one, was what he borrowed from Lietz—a youth state. The Hitlerjugend up to his time was merely a group of youth cells, an adjunct of the SA under men who, like Pfeffer, were far more concerned with the organization of adults than of the young. The SA had been the first seedbed of the HJ and thus Schirach found himself in 1931 under Roehm, who had succeeded Pfeffer as head of the SA. Schirach explained to Hitler the need for an independent youth movement, and he cited the various slogans he had picked up to further his cause— "youth must be independent," "youth must lead youth." Since Hitler always liked a multiplicity of organizations and was already becoming dubious of Roehm's pretentions to power, he was easily persuaded. It was Schirach who established the Hitler Youth in the image the Nuremberg tribunal and the world outside Germany found so obnoxious. The boys and girls paid membership fees until the start of the war, and until 1936 joined voluntarily. After 1936 membership was compulsory, but actually not all young people were forced to join until 1939. Even then this was true only for the small towns and villages; in the bigger cities it was sometimes possible to escape the movement or even to carry on a resistance within it, despite the close watch maintained by the HJ Streifendienst and other policing organizations.

After the Party came to power it did not take Schirach long to move in on the rival youth organizations. On April 5, 1933, in enthusiastic imitation of their elders' raids on the enemies of the Party, members of the Hitlerjugend began their invasions of the headquarters and local offices of the Buende. In Berlin on that day the headquarters of the Reich Committee of the German Youth Groups (Reichsausschuss der deutschen Jugendverbaende), which was headed by General Ludwig Vogt, were occupied. The organization had many Social Democrats in leading positions, but in any event no rival organizations in any form were to be tolerated. It was in part a ludicrous performance; one little Hitler boy who had the task of standing guard over a woman secretary of the Buende asked her permission to throw into her wastebasket the wrapping of a sandwich he had brought with him. The Communist Party and its youth organizations had already been forbidden and the leaders arrested. The center of the Socialist Workers Youth Movement was also taken over by a "roll commando" of the Hitlerjugend, who among other things made off with 160 weatherproof jackets. The members of the nationalist Scharnhorst Union were allowed for a time to keep their uniforms, but they had to wear HJ armbands. They, too, were forced to come under the control of Schirach, in the same way as their elders in the Stahlhelm—the organization of former German frontline soldiers—were incorporated into the SA.

The Grossdeutscher Bund under Admiral Adolf von Trotha, made up of a group of nationalistic youth organizations, was ordered dissolved on June 17, 1933, the day Schirach was named Reich youth leader. A great *Lager* of the Grossdeutscher Bund held in June was its last formal ceremony. The boys sang the old song of the resisters, "*Lever dot als Slav*," and "*Eine feste Burg ist unser Gott*," but the encampment was surrounded by police and SS and the boys were sent home.[18] Trotha, a friend of Hindenburg's, protested. He wrote a letter to Hitler and tried to persuade Hindenburg to intervene. As a result he became a suspicious person; his house was searched and his activities carefully scrutinized. But later, in 1936, Trotha made his peace; he accepted an honorary fuehrership in the Navy Division of the HJ. General Vogt, too, discreetly moved over from the headquarters of the German Youth Groups to the HJ and received the gold medal of the Hitler Youth in recognition of his decision.* The offices of these organizations of the former Buende were all occupied and their bank accounts seized.

Most of the leaders of the Buende had already taken cover. Five leaders of the Deutsche Freischar on March 8, 1933, announced they had joined the Hitlerjugend; its national leaders declared no one who had not found a place in National Socialist Germany could remain a member in the Freischar.[19] The executive committee of the Grossdeutscher Bund on April 15, 1933, decided that its members should join the Hitlerjugend, hoping in this way to keep their young people under their own leadership. Some leaders of the other Buende organizations quickly got jobs in the Hitlerjugend, which was sorely in need of leaders. Some joined the SA, some the SS, and some, a

* In 1934, 100,000 HJ who had attended the Potsdam meeting in 1932 received this honor (Klose, *op. cit.*, p. 25).

very few, went into the Resistance, where they continued to meet secretly with their boys. Many of these youth leaders and the boys, too, ended up in concentration camps.[20] The Boy Scouts were allowed to continue until 1934, because Schirach thought their connections with foreign countries might be useful to the HJ; but they, too, had to be dissolved and their membership taken into the HJ.

The Protestant youth organizations capitulated more quickly than the Catholic ones, because the latter were for a time protected by the concordat which Hitler made with the Vatican on July 29, 1933. But the Catholics, too, soon found themselves under heavy fire they could not withstand. Like the Protestants, many of them went over to the Hitlerjugend of their own accord; some of the priests and higher clergy urged their parishioners to let their children join the Hitlerjugend because they saw the danger of staying out or because they were carried away by the National Socialist fervor. There was much talk of the necessity of taking part in the new movement. One writer said it would be "deplorable if a young German were to stand aside now with his hands in his pockets . . . instead of participating with his whole heart in the new start of the nation." * [21] In one way or another the clergy accepted Schirach's statement of his own belief in the need for unity. He had said, "I belong to no confession, neither Protestant nor Catholic. I believe only in Germany." The Protestants sometimes asked for their own dissolution. The magazine *Evangelium im Dritten Reich* ran an article in September, 1933, declaring that the young peoples' organizations of the churches should be dissolved.[22] For it soon became apparent that Schirach and his Party were not going to permit a double membership in any youth organization—every notion of opposition had to be eliminated.

Double membership, which by then was allowed only to Catholic youth, was finally forbidden by Schirach on April 18, 1937, and that was to mean the end of the separate Catholic youth organizations.[23] Schirach's attack on his rivals was unrelenting. His most powerful propaganda weapon against a group he wished to destroy, against the so-called "cultural bolshevists" the Nazis detested, was characteristic of the National Socialist attack on the aesthetics of any non-Party members, on anyone who approved of modern art or painting or literature, or who did not show the proper enthusiasm for the cultural accomplishments of the Party. All Buende members were accused of "cultural bolshevism" and of the political variety too; both Protestant and Catholic organizations were denounced for harboring the remnants of the bolshevists, who had been driven underground. Schirach said in 1933, when he forbade membership in the Buende, that its youth movement was "bol-

* The Protestant surrender was speeded by the agreement made between Schirach and the Nazi Reich Bishop Ludwig Mueller (see Frick, Chapt. 7), in December, 1933, which declared that the Protestant youth groups were all to go over to the Hitlerjugend. Other Protestant ministers, such as Pastor Niemoeller and Wuerttemberg Landesbischof Wurm, openly opposed the Party and all its works, including its youth movement, but such outspoken men were few.

shevism," and as the attack mounted against the Catholics he repeated this accusation until in 1938 the Catholic youth movement suffered the same fate as the Protestant and was formally forbidden. But long before then the pressures were difficult to resist. In these years when unemployment was still a bitter problem, an apprentice got a job more quickly if he was a member of the Hitlerjugend. Only Hitlerjugend members got prizes for their school work.[24] In Hesse in 1933 the head of an artisans' guild of skilled workers told parents that their duty was to enroll their sons and daughters in the HJ— only those youth who did join, the statement said, could be expected to be trained as apprentices.[25] Any attempt to stay out of the HJ was dangerous. In Wiesbaden on May 3, 1941, the fuehrer of Bann 80 sent out the following summons: "The HJ comes to you today with the question: why are you still outside the ranks of the HJ? We take it that you accept our Fuehrer, Adolf Hitler. But you can only do this if you also accept the HJ created by him. If you are for the Fuehrer, therefore for the HJ, then sign the enclosed application. If you are not willing to join the HJ, then write us that on the enclosed blank." [26] This blank was a form calling for the signature of the father and son and a statement of where they both were employed. In effect, writing out reasons for not joining was applying to a concentration camp.

Contests were held among the schools, which obtained flags as soon as they had enrolled 90 per cent of their pupils in the Hitlerjugend. Signs in a factory warned young apprentices that they could be dismissed from trade schools if they had not joined the German Work Front (DAF, Deutsche Arbeitsfront), and to join the DAF one had to be a member of the HJ.[27] There was also a threat to impose a deadline for joining the Hitlerjugend; if one were not in it in time he or she might be barred forever from membership and then every career and every possibility of further study would be closed.

Leaders were needed to take care of the huge influx of new members. In 1932 there had been 12,000 leaders; by 1934 they numbered 367,000; by 1936 (when membership in the HJ became compulsory), 496,000; and two years later, in 1938, 720,000. These, however, were people who gave some spare time to leading the Hitlerjugend; some 8,000 were full-time, carefully trained members of its leadership staff.[28] These men and women were efficiently indoctrinated. They spent eight weeks working in a special training school, one year in a leadership academy, three weeks in an industry outside Germany, and six months in industry inside Germany. Schoolteachers flocked to the HJ in droves; it was not easy for them to stay outside the most important concerns of their charges, and the activities of the Hitlerjugend always took precedence over any notions of formal education. Nazi Germany vibrated with Party activity, and whenever drives were organized, marches were held. In any kind of Party or national celebration, the boys and girls were not supposed to bother about attending classes—that would have been intellectualism, something Nazis hated as much as cultural bolshevism.

Every young person was to be in the Hitlerjugend and it was to have something for everyone. The Jungvolk and Jungmaedel learned arts and crafts; the *Pimpfe* collected for the *Winterhilfe*; in 1938, 50,000 boys were enrolled in the Naval Unit; 90,000 in the Motor Corps; 78,000 in the Flying Corps, where model planes were made by the Jungvolk and the older boys learned to fly gliders and sail planes and studied the rudiments of navigation. An intensely active life was offered the boys and girls. Magazines were published: *Der Pimpf*, and *Das junge Deutschland*, *Jungvolk*; for the girls, *The German Girl (Das Deutsche Maedel)* and *Girls Your World (Maedchen Eure Welt)*; *The Young World (Die junge Welt)*, *Die Hitlerjugend*.[29] One publication appeared under the auspices of the Youth Hostel Association—*Youth and Homeland (Jugend und Heimat)*. Another appealed to the music lovers among the young—*Music in Youth and Folk (Musik in Jugend und Volk)*. *Will and Power (Wille und Macht)* was published for the youth leaders. There was even a publication for the deaf—*The Source (Die Quelle)*—and magazines were printed in braille for the blind.[30] The Hitlerjugend had its own news service, and as the boundaries of the Reich expanded, it established another one for the East, the *Ostdienst*, covering Austria, Czechoslovakia, the Baltic countries, Poland, Yugoslavia, and Rumania.

Both the female guardians of the Bund Deutscher Maedel and the male leaders were trained for their major task: indoctrinating their charges with National Socialist morality. They kept the children busy at a thousand small tasks intended to divert and entertain them, many of the kind they would have been engaged in any youth organization, but the one overriding purpose drilled incessantly into the Hitlerjugend was their ultimate duty of allegiance unto death to the Fuehrer. "We were born to die for Germany," was one of the watchwords, and this is what the boys learned to do. The SS Panzer Division Hitlerjugend, made up only of members of the organization, was almost totally destroyed in 1944 at Caen; thousands of them, Schirach related, had fought brilliantly at Sevastopol—and had died there, too.

The normal routine of the Hitlerjugend filled the week. In addition to the camps and hiking trips, evenings spent together at the youth homes (*Heimabende*) were devoted to lectures and hobbies and story telling; films were shown at small cost—20 pfennigs. When the war came, boys and girls collected old clothes and bones and paper; *Pimpfe* struggled under loads of blankets and overcoats sacrificed for the troops fighting in Russia; girls visited the wounded and sang for them, handed out coffee and food at railroad stations, took care of traveling mothers and their children. After Hitler took power, no public demonstration in the Reich could be held without the uniformed boys and girls. They marched, they ran errands, they trudged off to encampments, sometimes they went on long trips (*Grossfahrten*)—in 1939 from Westphalia to Vienna, for example—and some even went to foreign countries until the war put an end to such excursions.

The movement was intended to give a new meaning to the life of the children and young people, to loosen their ties to the church, to the family if they were not fanatical Nazis, and to the past. It had the same aims as the Communist youth movement, and in certain ways was modeled on it: the antireligious propaganda, the reverence for the leader, the idealized notion of the selflessness of the individual who takes on meaning only as part of a group, the emphasis on mass exercises. But the role of German women was very different from that of women in the Soviet Union. These German girls— in the small bourgeois image of women that Hitler had grown up with, to which were added the racial purposes of the Third Reich—were to be good and prolific German mothers; many a family was horrified to learn that a daughter was also getting a head start in responding to this exhortation of the Fuehrer. For Himmler and Bormann were not always preaching to deaf ears when they spoke of the duty of the German woman to bear racially sound children and the unimportance of whether this was accomplished in or out of wedlock. *Lebensborn*, the well-organized and efficient SS home for unwed mothers, who were vastly praised by the Himmlers and Bormanns and their female counterparts, got some of its clientele from girls of the Bund Deutscher Maedel who had come under the influence of a leader who urged them to do their share in the tasks assigned the women of the Third Reich.

One of the books Schirach wrote was called *Revolution in Education*,[31] in which this is what he said he was trying to accomplish: "They [the youth] represent not their interests but the well being of the nation . . . Nothing for ourselves, everything for Germany." "The Hitler Youth is a philosophical educational community . . . [the member] a soldier of an idea." The most promising soldiers of the idea, chosen from among the boys with outstanding records in the Jungvolk, were to be sent at the age of twelve to the Adolf Hitler schools, which were established on January 17, 1937, by the Fuehrer. These schools were part of the Hitlerjugend, part of the vast program of indoctrination, and the boys and their teachers appeared in classroom in uniform. All expenses of the boys in theory were paid.* When they got their diplomas at the age of eighteen, the decree founding the schools declared: "Every career of the Party and the State is open to them." The Adolf Hitler schools were intended to be the preschools for the Ordensburgen, which were the final training places for the elite cadres of the Party whose members would one day take part in ruling the Reich and, if all went well,

---

* This was true only in theory; in practice the parents were expected to make contributions to the Adolf Hitler *Spende* (Dietrich Orlow, *"Die Adolf Hitler Schulen,"* in *Vierteljahrshefte fuer Zeitgeschichte*, Vol. XIII, No. 3, 1965, pp. 274–84).

much of Europe. Three Ordensburgen were established: at Kroessinsee in Pomerania, Vogelsang in the Rhineland, and Sonthofen in the Allgaeuer Alps. In a spartan environment the students (*Ordensjunker*) were given a vigorous three-year training program to be followed by another half year in Marienburg in Prussia. The *Ordensjunker* were to marry as soon as possible— not later than twenty-five years—so the race could have the full benefit of their breeding.[32]

The Adolf Hitler schools had a varied curriculum. The boys were given the usual academic subjects, but in addition they had intensive courses in physical conditioning and Party ideology. Of the first group that got its *Abitur* in 1942, 67 per cent chose Party service as a career and only 10 per cent wanted to be Wehrmacht officers.[33] They were carefully chosen from *Pimpfe* whose families were racially and politically impeccable and who had been nominated by their local youth leaders to the territorial leader. Great emphasis was laid on tests of strength and courage, but the academic curriculum was much the same as that in the other *Oberschule*. Students were allowed considerable freedom in class; their teacher was not, as in most German schools, merely a superior but was supposed to be a friend and comrade as well. The boys got no marks but at the end of the year had to take part in a typically Nazi "performance competition." There was no religious education; as one of the chief Nazi pedagogues said, "The right of the people breaks the right of the church . . . the right of the Volk alone is God's right."[34]

The Hitlerjugend reached a membership in 1939 of almost nine million. A reasonably good performance in it was essential for a boy or girl to be allowed to enter any university or technical school, and many positions, before membership was compulsory, were dependent on having belonged to it. Teaching, for example, could not be left to those who had not been fully indoctrinated; every teacher who came into the school system who had been young enough to be eligible for the Hitlerjugend had to show his card.

The movement had its own police force—the Streifendienst—which was started in 1934 and which, by an agreement made in 1938 between Schirach and Himmler, was to be regarded as a pre-SS service that would lead its members directly at the age of eighteen into one of the branches of the SS: the Verfuegungstruppen (later the Waffen SS), the Junker schools, or the Totenkopf units. The latter, although the boys in the Streifendienst did not know it, were to be used as guards in the concentration camps. The Streifendienst was from the beginning a juvenile model of the SS police system intended to ferret out conspiracy among the young, to detect those who were critical of or who opposed the regime, and to spot children who failed to join the HJ. Members of the Streifendienst visited beer halls and patrolled railroad stations; they supervised encampments; they kept order. One illegal cartoon that appeared surreptitiously in 1937 showed the Streifendienst combing the countryside for youthful malefactors and four husky patrolmen guarding a skinny little boy who was being led by one of them with a rope. It was a youthful secret service and military police designed to do for the HJ what the Sipo and SD did for the country at large.[35]

Juvenile crime went down in the early years of the National Socialist take-over. Abortions almost disappeared (in 1940 there were less than a third of what there had been in 1931) as the Party preached the glory of motherhood in and out of wedlock. Secret reports give a great deal of space to homosexuality in the Hitlerjugend, which the Nazi experts blamed on the Buendist past of many of the Hitlerjugend and their leaders. Total crimes committed by young people in 1933 and 1934 were two-thirds of the number in 1932. The figures gradually rose, however, and new crimes were committed that had not been punishable under the Weimar Republic: *Rassenschande*, or shaming the race, that is, having sexual intercourse with any of the inferior races, such as Poles, Jews, Russians; and *lèse majesté*—making any kind of derogatory remark about the Fuehrer or the Party. Robbery went up with the blackouts; sexual offenses rose with the start of the war, when girls found it daring and exciting to visit the neighborhoods of factories and troop centers to find themselves a partner for the night. Money seems to have played a minor role in these encounters. The girls themselves were often well paid in factories where they were doing war work; many of them, as the confidential reports show, were very young, from thirteen to fifteen years old. Some of them committed *Rassenschande*, the reports said, with Poles in a nearby camp.[36]

On the whole the HJ did a thorough job of indoctrination of its youth. It selected whatever seemed useful from the Wandervoegel and the Buende— the journey, the campfire, the singing, the comradeship—and added the doses of idealism that were so dear to Schirach's heart. "Nothing for ourselves, everything for Germany," as he said. But it was not Germany that gave the youth their purpose, but Hitler. The magazine *Pimpf*, in its issue of September, 1940, presented its readers with a prose poem on "the gentle hand of the Fuehrer." It read: "Now all German hearts belong to the Fuehrer. His hand is the fate of our fatherland. All that happens, that determines our present, is his will . . . The hand of our Fuehrer leads us . . ." A book of tales, published in 1935 for the HJ *Gefolgschaft* (the *Retinue*), gave its readers as a battle cry: "No one shall live after the Leader's death." [37] That was what the Hitlerjugend was intended to produce—a *Gefolgschaft* for the Fuehrer—and every move the boys and girls made—even their play— was part of an ideological program.

The *Parole* of the *Sportsdienst* was: "Let us praise what makes hard" ("*Gelobt sei was hart macht*"). Hitler had said in 1935, "Youth must be swift as greyhounds, tough as leather and hard as Krupp steel." * [38] And

* The words also appear in *Mein Kampf*, when he was writing about the early Party members.

another time he told his listeners, "In my Ordensburgen a youth will grow up that will terrify the world." [39] Schirach and his organization did all they could to fit their charges to the prescriptions. "Your body belongs to your nation," the boys and girls were told; "You have the duty to be healthy." [40] Schirach, a master of *kitsch*, named 1939 as "the year of the duty to be healthy."

The Hitlerjugend could be a desolate succession of compulsory events for many members, but the Jungvolk and the Jungmaedel on the whole had a good time. Many of their leaders came from the Buende, and the old habits of solicitude for their young charges persisted. When a child tired on his march, his leaders often took the occasion to stop and rest and chat and sometimes to shoulder the heavy packs. The hike of the Jungvolk was less organized, less like a military formation than that of the HJ, and both the *Pimpf* and the Jungmaedel enjoyed the world of camping, with its camaraderie and its relatively light duties. The boys slept sometimes in barns, sometimes in tents, but tents were forbidden the Jungmaedel, who were assigned more substantial shelter. For all ages the campfire of the Wandervogel and the Buende remained the focus of the ritual, a magic center of light and shadow that made even the set speeches different from those of the *Heimabende*. In a forest clearing or on the shore of a lake or sea the children huddled together, singing often absurd songs about how they would deal with the rotten bones of the enemies of the Fuehrer; but they sat in the firelight with the night all around them, certain that they at least were warm and exalted among the children of the earth, part of a great movement that would bring ever more glory to their fatherland and its leader.

The Jungvolk and Jungmaedel especially were an obedient army of boys and girls; they escaped the tougher, more deeply indoctrinated leaders of their older brothers and sisters. It was mainly in the special services of the Hitlerjugend proper—in the HJ Navy, Motor Corps, and Flying Units—that something of the freedom and spirit of play of the Jungvolk still remained. For the HJ, the fire was not only a center of the camp, but also a place where school caps were burned to demonstrate the new solidarity of youth as opposed to the particularism of geography or income or status; and books could be burned in them, too, as the children learned.

Children of all ages were useful to the economy. Boys and girls worked on farms; they were needed especially during the war to help gather the harvest and to hand out ration books. Girls worked in stores that were shorthanded; they took care of children; they were trained in first aid and acted as medical assistants and as air-raid wardens. The boys, when the war started, were also on service during air-raid alarms and as fire fighters; their training led them easily to fit in wherever they were needed—finally into the soldier clothes that often were much too big for them, but in which they fought valiantly, far too well for their own or Germany's good.

Schirach was in charge of all youth education outside the schools, and, as typical of his sentimental notions, he established in 1937 a special branch of the BDM, the BDM *Werk*, or section, called Faith and Beauty (*Glaube und Schoenheit*). Girls from the ages of seventeen to twenty-one were intended to enter this branch of the HJ to develop their spiritual and physical graces. It was a volunteer plan that was never fully realized because of the war. The girls were to take part in a common program of work and play to become prize exhibits of the National Socialist ideal of woman. They could go to dances, but on such occasions they were supposed to wear the holiday dress of the BDM that was shown for the first time at the Nuremberg Party Days. Ten to fifteen girls belonged to a "work community" (an *Arbeitsgemein- schaft*), a number of which in turn made up a group. The girls wore BDM uniforms on all occasions, had calisthenics and sports together, performed health services, played music, and did house and farm work. The Faith and Beauty program was intended to permit the thoroughly indoctrinated girls to glide effortlessly into the Frauenschaft when they became twenty-one years old. It might have done so, were it not for the war and the need to engage in sterner tasks. The *Glaube und Schoenheit* handbook for 1943 has recipes in it; the calendar tells what day Goering and Frederick the Great were born, when France signed the armistice in 1940, when Herbert Norkus was killed; it is illustrated with pictures of Baldur von Schirach, his successor Arthur Axmann, and Adolf Hitler's mother; and the text has hints on how to wash materials and how to color Easter eggs and accounts of how one girl felt as she sang with her group to wounded soldiers. Other sketches tell how the power of Paris over women's fashions has been broken in favor of sensible clothes for women; another, combining both Faith and Beauty, advises the girls to look in the mirror a good deal, to study themselves so they can be convinced bearers of German culture. "The time of the small, middle-class, servile, modest German girl is over and *Glaube und Schoenheit* has under- taken the education of women so that the coming generations will be free to create from their sure instincts . . ."

At the far end of the spectrum of Faith and Beauty was the so-called Hay Action, a plan to bring boys between the ages of ten to fourteen from the occupied territories of Soviet Russia to the Reich. Although he had ceased to be active head of the Hitlerjugend in 1940, Schirach was accused at Nuremberg of complicity in this kidnapping operation, because in 1943, when the Hay Action took place, he was still on paper the highest official of the youth movement in the Reich (his title was Deputy to the Fuehrer for the Inspection of the Hitler Youth).

For six months in 1940 Schirach served in the German Army, rising from corporal to lieutenant. At the end of the French campaign he was summoned to a conference with Hitler, who told him he wanted him to be Governor and Gauleiter of Vienna. Schriach was to keep his Party offices, to continue as Reich leader of youth education, and to remain responsible for the Hitler- jugend to the Fuehrer. His assistant, Arthur Axmann, was chosen to take his place as full-time *Reichsjugendfuehrer*, and Schirach, his wife, and four children moved to the governor's palace in the city, which they quickly adopted as their own. Vienna's cultural tradition, the prestige of his office, the high style in which the Schirachs lived—seventeen servants, Schirach's enemies pointed out, were required to run his household, and this in wartime—soon made Vienna very dear to the Schirachs.

But Vienna was his downfall. Schirach had so many jobs, he could be accused of participating in almost all the iniquities that took place: of complicity in the Hay Action because he was still the youth leader, of the transportation of the Jews to the East from Vienna because he was Governor and Gauleiter of the city, and of the use of slave labor in his administrative area. His activities in Vienna also put him in deep trouble with the Fuehrer. The court in its judgment did not dwell on Schirach's responsibility for the Hay Action; it merely said he had known about it. Actually he had only the remotest connection with it. The action began in July, 1944; its name came from the initial letters of *heimatlos, elternlos, unterkunftslos*, which described swarms of Russian children without a country or families or shelter who were living somehow behind the German lines, begging, stealing, and staying alive as best they could. Their parents either had gone to the work battalions of the Germans or had fled to territory held by the Soviet Union or to the partisans. The children wandered in hungry droves through the countryside in much the same way the ragged bands of orphans after the revolution of 1917 had lived for years off the land and streets of the Soviet Union until the Government finally rounded them up. In 1944 these children were not only a problem for the German armies, they were a danger. Some of them were used by the partisans to bring information on the German units, and at best it was impossible to provide for their care and safety at a time when the Wehrmacht was feeling the full weight of the Russian counteroffensives. Older boys and girls had been recruited as helpers for the Luftwaffe, the Organization Todt, and the SS; they could move with the troops in the often precipitate retreats; but the younger ones were only a burden.*

Schirach had been in charge of founding settlements for German children as far as possible from the threat of the air raids and the fighting. In 1943 the Germans attempted to do much the same thing for the Russian children by establishing, under the Hitlerjugend, the Reich Welfare Organization, and Rosenberg's Organization East children's villages where the children would

---

* As late as the spring of 1944 the SS called on boys and girls to join up as "an SS helper for a new and more beautiful homeland in a united Europe with unity, freedom and justice . . . You can look forward to a happy and fortunate future . . . be in the advance guard in rebuilding your own country . . . Adolf Hitler calls you. Show yourself worthy of his confidence." If not enough young people volunteered they were drafted. In 1944–45 there were 21,000 of these SS helpers and 34,900 were in the Luftwaffe (Robert Herzog, *Besatzungsverwaltungen in den besetzten Ostgebieten* Studien des Instituts fuer Besatzungsfragen in Tuebingen zu den deutschen Besetzungen im 2. Weltkrieg, Nr. 19, Tuebingen, 1960).

live together and work on gardening and farm projects. But with the increasing violence of the Russian attack, the villages were constantly threatened; two of them were overrun by partisans, and German accounts said the children in them had been killed.[41] A report from the German Army Group Center (Heeresgruppe Mitte) said in mid-1944 that they had 40,000 to 50,000 of these children from ten to fourteen in their territory and they wanted them sent to Germany. There they could be trained as apprentices and work in various trades. In addition, the SS memorandum on behalf of the action pointed out that their loss would be a damage to Soviet Russia's biological potential.[42]

The Army refused to turn the homeless children over to Sauckel; apparently the notion of forced labor for children was too much for the officers of Heeresgruppe Mitte. But sending them back to Germany to learn a trade or to the Todt Organization was a tolerable idea. The Army also proposed that a number of mothers be sent with the children to Germany, but this was never done. Not many children were sent to the Reich; only between 2,500 and 3,000 arrived there before June 22, 1944, when the German front broke under the onslaught of the new Russian offensive and the project was abandoned. The only work the children ever did was performed in their own kitchens, in a camp set up in a barracks at Dessau and in a camp where foreign workers were stationed. Schirach's part in all this was only nominal, as was his connection with a similar youth operation in 1943. Some Yugoslav children had been brought to Vienna in that year from Serbia, where they had been housed in a police barracks; they performed odd jobs, working in the kitchen, shining shoes, taking over other small household duties—a precursor to the Hay Action.

Schirach, as the court said, had known of these cases. He was still head of the youth of the Reich and as such he had a formal connection with the part the Hitlerjugend played in the Hay Action. It had sent both male and female leaders to the East to help in the job of rounding up and taking care of the Russian children. With the lurid picture of Sauckel's "actions" before the court, as well as the explicit statement of Army Group Center that these children, too, were to be sent by force to work for German masters, the case on its face seemed black enough to warrant the charge against Schirach. In truth, however, neither Schirach, nor the Army, nor Rosenberg's organization, nor the German Welfare Organization seemed to have done anything in this instance that could be called criminal.

Schirach had a much closer connection with other crimes against humanity. As Governor, Defense Commissioner, and Gauleiter of Vienna, he took a leading part in the deportation of Jews from the city. At a meeting in October, 1940, at which Hitler and Bormann were present, Schirach told Frank, as the group was discussing the anti-Jewish measures and plans, that the General Government would have to take 60,000 Jews from Vienna.[43] Hitler wanted Vienna, which he had always thought especially "Jew ridden," to be

ABOVE: Palace of Justice and prison (*Hoffmann Photo*)

BELOW: Courtroom (*Hoffmann Photo*)

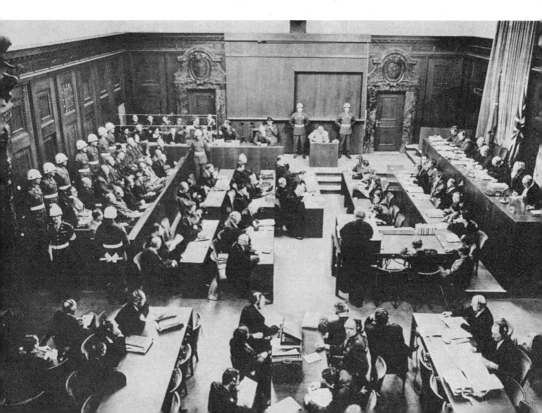

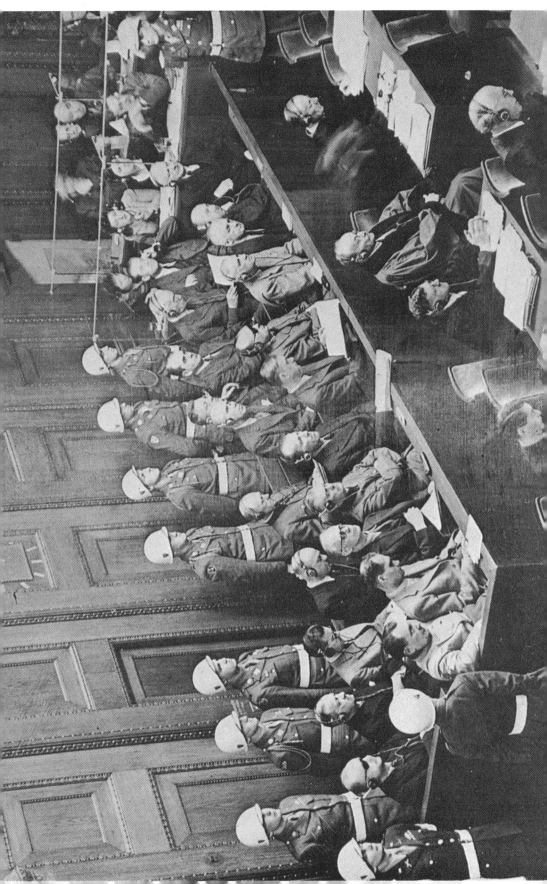

Lord Justice Lawrence (*Hoffmann Photo*)

PRECEDING PAGES

LEFT: The tribunal
from left to right: Volchkov, USSR; Nikitchenko, USSR;
Birkett, England; Lord Justice Lawrence, England; Biddle, USA;
Parker, USA; de Vabres, France; Falco, France (*Hoffmann Photo*)

RIGHT: The defendants
first row: Goering, Hess, Ribbentrop, Keitel,
Kaltenbrunner, Rosenberg, Frank, Frick, Streicher,
Funk, Schacht

second row: Doenitz, Raeder, Schirach, Sauckel, Jodl, Papen,
Seyss-Inquart, Speer, Neurath, Fritzsche (*Hoffmann Photo*)

Mr. Justice Jackson (*Ullstein Photo*)

Streicher during the trial (*Ullstein Photo*)

OPPOSITE:

Goering being congratulated by Hitler
on his forty-fifth birthday (*Ullstein Photo*)

RIGHT:

Goering in court (*Südd. Verlag Photo*)

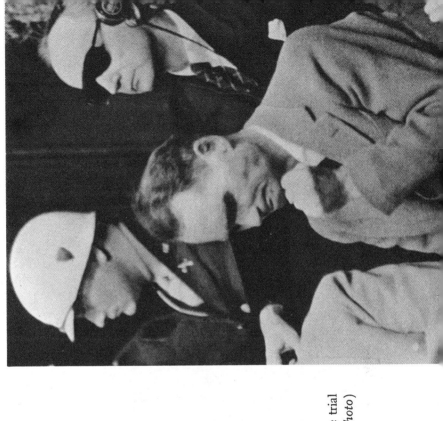

ABOVE: Martin Bormann, Rudolf Hess, and Robert Ley at a meeting of Reichsleiter in 1935 (*Ullstein Photo*)

Hess during the trial
(*Südd. Verlag Photo*)

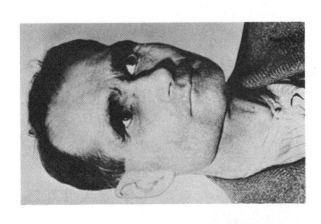

Rudolf Hess in Spandau
(*Wide World Photo*)

Alfred Rosenberg in London, 1933
(*Ullstein Photo*)

Rosenberg during the trial (*Hoffmann Photo*)

Ribbentrop at the signing of the "friendship treaty" with the Soviet Union, with Stalin (*right*) and Molotov (*seated*) (*Südd. Verlag Photo*)

Ribbentrop talking with his lawyer Martin Horn at Nuremberg (*Südd. Verlag Photo*)

Constantin von Neurath (*right*) with Hermann Goering at a reception for Count Ciano
(*Südd. Verlag Photo*)

Neurath with his daughter after his release from Spandau
(*Wide World Photo*)

ABOVE: Vice-Chancellor Franz von Papen with Hitler and Goebbels
(*Südd. Verlag Photo*)

BELOW: Papen after his arrest at Ninth Army Headquarters (*Südd. Verlag Photo*)

OPPOSITE: Papen, Ambassador in Ankara (*Südd. Verlag Photo*)

Schacht and his wife after the Nuremberg verdict (*Wide World Photo*)

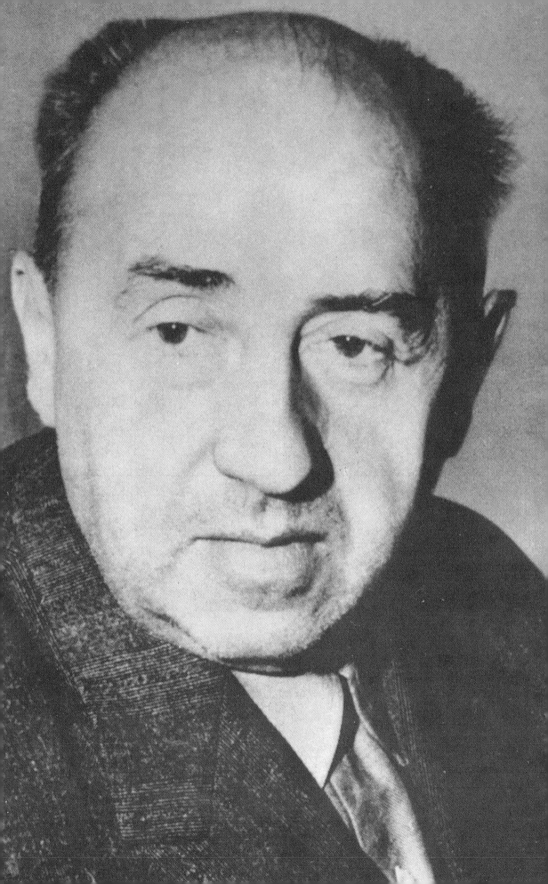

Funk taking office as Minister of Economics. Goering at left (*Südd. Verlag Photo*)

Wilhelm Frick, Minister of the Interior (*Südd. Verlag Photo*)

OPPOSITE: Baldur von Schirach with boys of the
Hitlerjugend, 1936 (*Ullstein Photo*)

RIGHT: Schirach at Nuremberg
(*Wide World Photo*)

BELOW: Ernst Kaltenbrunner after his sentence
(*Wide World Photo*)

Field Marshal Wilhelm Keitel (*right*) with Admiral Raeder and Field Marshal Milch greeting the Fuehrer in March, 1942 (*Südd. Verlag Photo*)

Keitel in the courtroom (*Wide World Photo*)

OPPOSITE: General Alfred Jodl (*Luise Jodl Photo*)

Jodl in the courtroom (*Wide World Photo*)

Admiral Erich Raeder
(*Südd. Verlag Photo*)

Frank as Governor General in Poland, 1940 (*Ullstein Photo*)

Seyss-Inquart after the *Anschluss* (*Südd. Verlag Photo*)

Fritz Sauckel after he was named Plenipotentiary
for the Allocation of Labor (*Südd. Verlag Photo*)

Albert Speer (*Wide World Photo*)

Hans Fritzsche (*Südd. Verlag Photo*)

"cleansed" of its non-Germanic elements (soon he would demand that all Czechs also be forced to leave the city). In 1941 the transports, that would by 1942 lead to the extermination camps, were well under way. The orders came from Hitler, the deportations were under the command of Heinrich Himmler, and Schirach was no more than a dutiful administrator in helping carry them out.

He readily admitted at Nuremberg that he had been an anti-Semite from the time he had read Houston Stewart Chamberlain's and Henry Ford's writings, and when the Jews of Vienna were shipped off he declared that the action was a contribution to European culture. He denied at Nuremberg, not only in court but privately to his lawyer, that he had known that the Jews were destined for the Final Solution; the shipments from Vienna, with the Nazis' passion for finding seemingly harmless phrases for obscene deeds, were called *Abwanderungstransporte*, emigration transports. The orders were explicit that the deportations must not be called evacuations or resettlements (*Umsiedlungen*), which were becoming tainted words for the Jews, and the collecting centers were to be known as emigration camps.[44]

Schirach was no doubt telling the truth when he spoke of the early stages of the evacuations of the period 1940–41—the Final Solution began only in 1942—and he had no reason to believe at the beginning that the Jews were being shipped to the East for any reason but to rid the Reich of them and to send them to ghettos or camps where they would work. But later, in 1942, Schirach as Defense Commissioner was on the carefully selected distribution list of people who received the weekly and monthly reports from Heydrich's office about the exterminations, and he had to admit at Nuremberg that he had eventually come to know what was going on. Schirach was, however, no violent anti-Semite; curiously enough, considering his high posts in the Party, he scarcely mentions Jews in his published speeches to the Hitlerjugend. The HJ sang anti-Semitic songs; they were instructed in their *Heimabende* in the malefactions of world Jewry; but Schirach seems to have had no great interest in the problem. Frau von Schirach was accused, in Party reports sent to Bormann soon after the Schirachs went to Vienna, of buying a pair of stockings worth twenty marks in a Jewish store—a serious misdemeanor for the wife of a Gauleiter.[45] Schirach accepted Hitler's and Himmler's decisions in this, as in almost all other matters, but he took no more than a passive, routine part in the transports and in the indoctrination of the German youth. He made no objections; he had none to make. He believed that Germany had to be freed of its Jews; and when the Fuehrer decided they were to be killed, he accepted that decision too.

But the Schirachs were mild-mannered if ambitious people, and they could be disturbed by brutality when they were eyewitnesses of it. In late June, 1943, when Schirach and his wife were visiting the Fuehrer at Berchtesgaden, Frau von Schirach, who had known Hitler since she was a young girl—she was the daughter of his photographer Heinrich Hoffman—told the Fuehrer how revolted she had been when she had chanced to see from her hotel window in Amsterdam a deportation of Jewish women who were driven onto trucks amid shrieks and blows. Schirach was already in disfavor with the Fuehrer for sponsoring an art exhibit in Vienna that had shown the work of painters proscribed in the Reich. Hitler coldly informed Frau von Schirach that she was sentimental and he wanted to hear no more of the story, which she had naïvely believed would be news to him. As for Schirach, Hitler turned savagely against him on this occasion, and everything Schirach said irritated him to the point of fury.[46] Goebbels, who was also staying at the Berghof, wrote in his diary that he felt sorry for the Fuehrer, whose many burdens were only added to by Schirach's blundering.[47]

It was on this luckless occasion, too, that Schirach ventured to speak to the Fuehrer about the great cultural tradition of Vienna and his hopes for the refurbishment of the city when the war was over. Everything Schirach said now was a red flag to Hitler; the Fuehrer shouted that Vienna could never compete with Berlin, that it was a city of second rank and would stay that way. Goebbels wrote that Frau von Schirach had tears in her eyes as all their hopes for a dazzling future for Vienna, and no doubt for themselves, were dashed. It was morning when Hitler went to bed, and the Schirachs left the Eagle's Nest that afternoon without seeing him again. Schirach never came back into favor. Rumors accumulated that he was to be dismissed from his post. Ley, who had friendly feelings for him, visited him in Vienna and warned him of his precarious position. Reports from the SD told how badly Schirach was performing his administrative functions; he was reacting, they said, to crisis situations as they arose but never leading, never taking the responsibility to be expected of a Gauleiter. The Party reports repeated the old charges that Schirach was interested in polite society, not in the people; he mistrusted them and they him.[48]

Ribbentrop at Nuremberg declared he was present when, at the end of 1943, Himmler told the Fuehrer he wanted to arrest Schirach and bring him before a people's court. A report had come from Bormann that Schirach had called war with the United States disastrous for Germany. The Fuehrer did not act on Himmler's suggestion, Ribbentrop said, because the arrest and trial of a Governor would make a bad impression; but Schirach remained in disgrace. Goering declared at Nuremberg that in 1944 he tore up a telegram from Schirach proposing that Ribbentrop be dropped and a new Foreign Minister be put in his place, because Hitler would have taken the proposal so ill that Goering feared for Schirach's safety.[49] Schirach was so doubtful of his own security that he had a squad from the Grossdeutschland Division, in which he had served in 1940, assigned to protect his person against a raid by Himmler's SS.[50] The rough and tough SS men took no pains to conceal their dislike of him. "A *Pimpf* in Vienna," they called him. One informer reported that Schirach said he could not live without his household help because otherwise he would have to polish his own shoes and get his own ration books; this remark was made at a time when Vienna was being flooded with refugees from the Eastern territories, the German front lines were collapsing under the Russian attack, and Vienna was not far from the rapidly advancing Soviet armies.[51]

Schirach was not a criminal; in another era he might have been a teacher, a director of dramatics, a boy's club leader, the scoutmaster of a local church. From 1933 on, he gladly took part in a regime that he regarded as leading a revolutionary crusade and rejoiced in the high life and the opportunity it gave him of persuading himself that he was not only a man of culture but one of the powers of enlightenment in a coarse, plebeian world. The criminality of the Hitler Government he chose to ignore. He did not like the *Kristallnacht*; he did not want war, nor did he want to train his boys as soldiers. The latter could come later, as could war, if the world were so foolish as to challenge the Fuehrer's desire for a strong Germany, a Germany which would lead Europe. He wanted to serve his adored Fuehrer and to teach others their duty toward him. The ready-made phrases that pleased him and thousands of other youth leaders seemed the ultimate wisdom to them. "Youth must be led by youth"—taken from Goethe—"Fuehrer order, we follow"—taken from Hitler: Schirach asked for nothing deeper or wiser or more telling than such profundities.

He was given occasionally to harsh statements that the prosecution used with telling effect against him. When Heydrich was killed in Czechoslovakia, Schirach proposed that in retaliation German planes bomb an English cultural center. Somewhat devious reasoning led him to this conclusion: the British were urging the Czechs to resist the German occupation, he said, whereas left to themselves the Czechs and the Germans got on well together; therefore, the British were responsible for Heydrich's murder. Since culture was always on Schirach's mind, the worst damage that could be done the British in his estimation was to bomb a historic city.

German estimates of his character were not far wrong. He was indeed no leader, except of people much younger than he. He was a polite, excited, uncritical, *schwaermerisch* admirer of the accomplishments of the standard authors and artists of Germany. He oversimplified a world that was too complicated for him with a sentimental imitation of Hoelderlin's compressed lines, producing such insipid and uninspired ideas as: "The flag comes before all." Believing in Hitler's greatness, he admitted at Nuremberg that he had misled a generation of German youth. He had accepted everything the Fuehrer decided. Forced labor was no problem for him; as Gauleiter of Vienna he cooperated gladly with Sauckel; the evacuation of the Jews presented only technical problems and cultural advantages.

The court dealt harshly with him. The tribunal stressed the *Anschluss* with Austria; the occupation of that country by the Reich, it said, was a crime that came within the jurisdiction of the tribunal. It found Schirach innocent of planning to commit aggression, although it said he had given premilitary training to the Hitlerjugend. The court found him guilty of having committed crimes against humanity and sentenced him to twenty years on that count. The sentence was based on Schirach's connection with the deportation of the Jews, slave labor, his knowledge of the Hay Action, his recommendation that a British cultural center be bombed. His main malefactions, however, had been directed against his own country, not against the Jews or nationals of other nations; Schirach saw this better than the court. The misleading of youth is always a serious crime, and it was Schirach's chief one. He had not trained his HJ for war, he had done worse: he had taught them for years that their highest duty was to say, "You order, my Fuehrer—we follow."

NOTES

1. Felix Raabe, *Die Buendische Jugend* (Stuttgart: Brentano Verlag, 1961).

2. Arno Kloenne, *Hitlerjugend* (Hannover and Frankfurt a.M.: Norddeutsche Verlagsanstalt O. Goedel, 1955).

3. Karl Knoll, *Die Gesellung der deutschen Jugend in der Gegenwart.* Dissertation, Munich, 1962, p. 76.

4. Krebs, *op. cit*, p. 232.

5. Baldur von Schirach, *Die Feier der Neuen Front* (Munich: Deutscher Volksverlag, n.d.).

6. Werner Klose, *Generation im Gleichschritt* (Oldenburg and Hamburg: Gerhard Stalling Verlag, 1964), p. 78.

7. NCA IV, 1458-PS, pp. 22–23.

8. N XIV, pp. 480–81.

9. Manfred Priepke, *Die evangelische Jugend im Dritten Reich 1933–1936* (Hannover and Frankfurt a.M.: Norddeutsche Verlagsanstalt O. Goedel, 1960), p. 94.

10. MA 48 (IZG).

11. *Ibid.*

12. N XXX, 2436-PS, pp. 488–502.

13. N XXVII, 1458-PS, p. 238.

14. Baldur von Schirach, *Revolution der Erziehung* (Munich: Zentralverlag der NSDAP, Franz Eher Nachf., 1938).

15. Kloenne, *op. cit.*

16. N XXX, 2436-PS, pp. 497–98.

17. Krebs, *op. cit.*, pp. 49–51.

18. Walter Z. Laqueur, *Die deutsche Jugendbewegung* (Cologne: Verlag Wissenschaft und Politik, 1962), p. 219.

19. Karl O. Paetel, "*Die deutsche Jugendbewegung als politisches Phaenomen*," in *Politische Studien*, July, 1957, pp. 9–10.

20. Arno Kloenne, *Gegen den Strom* (Hannover and Frankfurt a.M.: Norddeutsche Verlagsanstalt O. Goedel, 1957).

21. Priepke, *op. cit.*

22. *Ibid.*, p. 68.

23. Kloenne, *Hitlerjugend.*

24. Klose, *op. cit.*

25. Kloenne, *Gegen den Strom*, p. 45.

26. Klose, *op. cit.*, p. 47.

27. *Ibid.*, p. 47.

28. *Ibid.*, p. 79.

29. *Ibid.*, p. 151.

30. N XXXII, 3349-PS, pp. 195–97.

31. Schirach, *Revolution der Erziehung.*

32. Rudolf Benze, *Erziehung im Grossdeutschen Reich* (Frankfurt a.M.: Moritz Diesterweg Verlag, 1943).

33. Klose, *op. cit.*, p. 206.

34. *Ibid.*, p. 208.

35. Kloenne, *Gegen den Strom*, p. 124.

36. Reichsjugendfuehrer, ed., *Kriminalitaet und Gefaehrdung der Jugend* (Berlin, 1941).

37. Horst Wagenfuehr, ed., *Gefolgschaft* (Hamburg: Hanseatische Verlagsanstalt, 1935).

38. Klose, *op. cit.*, p. 108.

39. *Ibid.*, p. 122.

40. *Ibid.*, pp. 109–10.

41. Robert Herzog, *Besatzungsverwaltung in den besetzten Ostgebieten, Abteilung Jugend* (Tuebingen: Institut fuer Besatzungsfragen, 1960), p. 46.

42. *Ibid.*, p. 47. N XXV, 031-PS, pp. 88–92.

43. N XIV, pp. 509–10.

44. Eichmann 1152: "Report of December 29, 1941, on the conversations of the leader of the [Jewish] Kulturgemeinde with Obersturmbannfuehrer Brenner, signed Josef Loewenherz" (Jerusalem, Israel: *Eichmann Trial Record*, mimeographed, 1961).

45. FA 91/6-8, p. 1528 (IZG).

46. N XIV, pp. 427–28.

47. ED 83/1, Joseph Goebbels: *Tagebuch*, Vol. I, 1943 (unpublished) (IZG).

48. FA 91/6-8, pp. 1490, 1517 (IZG).

49. Sauter papers (IZG).

50. N XIV, p. 431.

51. FA 91/6, p. 1520 (IZG).

9

The Party, the Police Forces, and the Army

"WE HAVE BEEN BORN IN BATTLE"

Only a few years before the twenty-two were brought to trial, almost all of them at one time or another had attended a different kind of solemn occasion in Nuremberg—the Party days that took place every year for a week in September. These latter celebrations had started in the early years of the movement with parades of the Brownshirts and continued sporadically until the great victory of 1933, when the Party took over the Government. Then the Party days truly began. The bells of the great cathedrals rang, first when the Fuehrer arrived at the railroad station, then a week later as he departed in an aureole of adoration from the hundreds of thousands of members of Party formations from all over Germany. Probably no other country in the world could have suffered such oratory. The speeches were long and repetitive, and when they stopped, the parades started. The Hitlerjugend paraded, as did the Work Service with picks and shovels and delegations representing the new Gaue. Army regiments marched, and Hitler drove slowly in his open automobile past the ecstatic crowds. The onlookers, including foreigners, were often as impressed as the participants with the athletic, well-drilled pageant designed to celebrate Germany's reborn strength, although many foreigners and even Germans had difficulty keeping their breakfasts down.

These were the unforgettable days when the Fuehrer reported on the accomplishments of the year to his liegemen—a favorite word of the cult of the *Germanen* that was being established by the Rosenbergs and Himmlers—and they to him. On the huge Zeppelin field, where thousands could turn and wheel and other thousands look on, a great, 350-meter-long tribune was erected, for Nuremberg was the city of the Party days of the Reich as Munich was the city of the Party. In 1936, the Reich Party Day of Honor, as the celebration that year was called, took place in this field.* For two hours 45,000 men of the Work Service marched by, shouldering their shovels; later at night the torches of the 30,000 political leaders, accompanied by a sea of 25,000 flags, filed by, too, and all the Party great came to march or be marched by, to take the salute and to speak. They were all there: Himmler, Kaltenbrunner, Hess, Ley, Goebbels, Frank, Fritsch of the Army, Raeder of the Navy, and Goering of the Luftwaffe, Rosenberg, and Streicher, of course, for this was his home city. Since this was a people's holiday, half a million celebrants were spread out over the open spaces.

The speeches could be based on facts, although they could not mention any of the prices paid as the Party took over. By 1936 unemployment had gone down steadily until it virtually had disappeared; conscription started in 1935 and rearmament accelerated as the public-works projects and then heavy and light industry got under way for war production. The Jews and the Bolsheviks were denounced in Rosenberg's speech; the decisive world battle was being fought, he said. The Bolsheviks intended to destroy the world, to thrust it into a chaotic whirlpool. "Bolshevism is the preconcerted attempt of Jewry to establish its reign over all the peoples. The battle against it is a world battle, in the truest sense of the word, in which Adolf Hitler is the historical leader. There can be no reconciliation between these two extremes. Bolshevism must be destroyed if Europe is to be healed." [1]

The leader of the German women's organization, Frau Scholtz-Klink, a blonde, middle-aged woman with an unsmiling, taut face, told how indifferently despite the theoretical equality of the sexes the Russians regarded the position of women; how abortions had been freely permitted in the Soviet Union with such a consequent low birth rate that the laws had to be changed making abortions more difficult to obtain. Frau Scholtz-Klink related how in Russia Stalin called on the Soviet women to help in the struggle for the victory of bolshevism, and she in turn called on German women to do their share in the struggle of good against evil. Allied with the Fuehrer and other women of the non-Bolshevik world, they would be able to guarantee peace, she said. The Fuehrer replied, assailing the doctrine of equal rights for men and women; man's job, he said, was to protect the whole of the society, woman's was the family, her husband, her children, her home. The child, not the new factories, Hitler told them, was the symbol of the success of their work. No one, he shouted, could understand the National Socialist movement better than the German woman—and these words brought forth a thunderous outburst of applause. When it subsided Frau Scholtz-Klink promised in the name of all German women to try in the future to help lighten the Fuehrer's burdens as far as they could.

* The celebration of 1933 was called the Reich Party Day of Victory; 1934 was the Day of Will; and 1935, the Day of Freedom.

Next Hitler talked to the Hitlerjugend. He told them how lucky they were to be living in such momentous times, when a new prototype of beauty was emerging in Germany; in place of the corpulent beer drinker of the caricaturist's pen and the photographer's lens, one saw the slender, willowy young athletes. "It is a stirring time but we should not complain," Hitler told them, "we are used to battles, for we have been born in battle, we have emerged from battle, we want to plant our feet in our earth and will succumb to no attack. And you will be near me if this hour should ever come! You will stand before me, beside me and behind me and will hold our banners high! . . . We will be victorious again." [2] There was no lack of reciprocal praise and one-sided worship. To the 110,000 men in the "brown storm columns," the SA, the SS, the National Socialist Motor Corps, and the Party Air Corps, the Fuehrer shouted, "Hail, my men!" to which they shouted back, "Hail, my Fuehrer!" Then the Fuehrer said, "I know that I have built no useless work. It will stand fast and towering in the most distant times [cheers]. Believe me it is indeed wonderful for me to live in this time and to be able to be your leader, and the Chancellor of the German Reich [cheers]." [3]

The Minister of Defense, Blomberg, spoke too. Following the protocol of the meetings, he shouted, "Heil Soldaten!" to which the troops responded with a thunderous, echoing "Heil." He said, "In this hour we think of the man who gave us our fieldbadges and to whom in unshakeable fealty we are bound.* Adolf Hitler, our Fuehrer and Reichskanzler, the highest commander of the German Wehrmacht, of our German people and fatherland, Sieg Heil!" † [4]

The last speech at Nuremberg was always that of the Fuehrer, who in 1936 denounced the Bolshevik infection and the democracies and with ringing words reminded his listeners of all they owed him. "What would have happened to Germany," he asked, "if in 1919 an unknown soldier had not had the belief, the readiness to defend and to sacrifice, the courage and will to give of himself so as to rescue the German nation from its ignominy." [5]

Along with these mammoth ceremonies were others of less notoriety, but still of considerable importance because they represented the mystical but brutally realistic mumbo-jumbo of the rival of the Party and the Army—the

* The battle flags of the Wehrmacht appeared at the 1936 Nuremberg rally for the first time.

† Blomberg was the second-to-last Minister of Defense the Reich was to have. Hindenburg had chosen him because he thought Blomberg to be a nonpolitical general who had astutely conducted military discussions with the Allied powers at Geneva. Blomberg looked like a soldier; his military bearing was impressive. But his nickname was "Rubber Lion," and he soon became a convinced National Socialist. A field marshal of the Army as well as head of the armed forces, he was forced to quit his post some two years later, in January, 1938, because of his marriage to a registered prostitute. The Fuehrer, however, was able to soothe his own pride, which had been damaged when he learned the truth about the past of the bride after he and Goering had attended the marriage ceremony, by himself taking over the post of Minister of Defense.

SS. Aside from its oath to the Fuehrer, the SS was bound only to its leader, Heinrich Himmler. In 1934, when the order to put down the so-called Roehm putsch was given, no member of the SS had hesitated to shoot former comrades in the SA. Once a year, in a monastery in Webelsberg, the inner circle of the SS met in an atmosphere of secrecy and elegance (a silver plate with his name engraved on it hung on the back of each man's chair). This was the meeting of the twelve men who formed the Secret Inner Order of the SS and was a manifestation of the Himmlerian concept of a new aristocracy that would rule the German, then the European, peoples, and possibly the entire world.

Himmler, whose father was a greengrocer and a devout Christian, founded this order on the pattern of the Jesuits, and he believed fanatically in a future dominated by the SS and cemented by such slogans as "My honor is called loyalty." Himmler said that the word of an SS man to another, their handshake, was weightier and more binding than any legal document, and long before the Nazis took power, his approval was essential before SS men could marry. This was a precaution not only to make certain that the marriage was pure Aryan on both sides, but to prevent the infusion of any foreign blood (even French blood was undesirable). Walter Schellenberg, who rose high in the SS and SD despite his being married to a Polish woman, always had the threat of a reprisal for his *mésalliance* hanging over his head.

The SS man was supposed to defend his honor in a dispute with another SS man or another character worthy of such combat in a duel, according to the Himmlerian prescriptions, and his obligations included safeguarding the honor of the wives and daughters of other SS men. But unfortunately for some of the membership, the SS man could be sentenced to death for too great admiration of his comrades—homosexuality in the SS was punishable, said Himmler (and his word in this organization was law), by death or imprisonment where there were no mitigating circumstances. For the SS, too, so-called Junker schools were established for training SS officers, the future commanders of the empire that Germany was to create in Europe. The SS man had to be able to trace his Aryan lineage back to 1750 without a drop of profane blood and had to show that the bride of his choice could do the same. He had to be able and willing to kill at a moment's notice the enemies of his race and to steel himself against any unmanly or un-SS emotions when he saw the blood run in the trenches that his defenseless victims had to dig for themselves before they were shot.

In a speech to the Wehrmacht in 1939, Himmler told how with such high standards only 10 to 15 per cent of the applicants could be accepted by the SS. And even they had to go through a long apprenticeship. At eighteen, after having graduated from the Hitlerjugend, a young man could volunteer to become an applicant for the SS. He was tested over and over for his political and physical qualities; he had to show that his family suffered from no heritable disease, and he had to appear before a commission which included, along with SS officers, "specialists" in racial matters and medical doctors who knew about racial stigmata. The height and body build of the applicant were carefully correlated. No one could be under 1.70 meters, and if he were over 1.80 or 1.85, although this was in itself gratifying, the height must be balanced by the harmony of the rest of the body—the lower thigh, for example, must be in proportion to the upper. The hands, the gait, the bearing must be those of the desirable SS man, an ideal physical and psychological type on whose specifications they had been working since 1931, said Himmler.

After three months, the eighteen-year-old was sworn in, taking his oath of fealty to the Fuehrer, and became a candidate, an *Anwaerter*. In the course of the next year he had to win his SA sport badge. At nineteen he went to the Labor Service, and after that to the Wehrmacht. After his two years of service with the armed forces, he returned to the SS—but still remained a candidate. His indoctrination in the ideology of the movement was zealously continued and he was instructed in the racial and marriage doctrines, the rules that concerned his own biological inheritance and descendants, and the questions that touched on the honor of an SS man. Finally, on November 9 of the year following his return to the SS from the Wehrmacht, he became a full-fledged SS man.[6]

Himmler made use of the idea of the *Germanen* to extend the recruiting of the SS. When the war came, Finnish, Dutch, Norwegian, Danish, Flemish, and later Walloon volunteers were eligible to join SS formations and swear allegiance to the Fuehrer of the *Germanen*, Adolf Hitler.* Thus a supranational body, competing with the regimes of Terboven in Norway and Seyss-Inquart in Holland and the Bormann network of Party administrators, was established. If Germany won the war, the SS, not Bormann or the Army, would provide the leaders of the future Europe, as Himmler saw it. Many of these foreign SS units were as enthusiastic in fighting for the cause of Nazidom as any of the German leaders. Léon Degrelle, who commanded the Walloon legion, was one of them; he and his men fought throughout the war on the Eastern front, and of the original 800 Belgian volunteers, only three survived—of whom Degrelle was one. The censored mail of SS foreign volunteers is as filled with ecstatic praise of the Fuehrer and the racial purpose of the SS as that of any Reich German.[7]

The SS was essentially a police formation. Although the Waffen SS, which first saw action in the Polish campaign, gradually grew to number 600,000 men and took part with the Army in the frontline fighting, it fought under Himmler the policeman, and when it sought recruits among the Germanic brethren it started with the police of the northern countries. Technically it

---

* With time and the deterioration of the military situation, almost all the nationalities that came near or under the control of German arms were added: Frenchmen, Latvians, Estonians, Ukrainians, Croats, Bosnians, Italians, Bulgarians, Romanians, Turko-Tartars, Azerbaijanis, Hungarians, even a scattering of Britons.

was part neither of the police nor of the Wehrmacht, although its troops thought of themselves as an elite branch of the armed forces and were often better armed and equipped than the Army.* It was Hitler and Himmler's armed force. The protective duties of the SS as a whole were internal as well as external, and thus it was in competition with both the Army and the forces of administration in the conquered territories and through the SD in Germany.[8]

German generals in Poland protested against the activities of the SS. General Johannes Blaskowitz described the atrocities in a memorandum that reached the Fuehrer, who paid no attention to it. Other high officers also complained (see The Organizations, Chapt. 14). On November 23, 1939, General of Artillery Walter Petzel, reporting on the Warthegau (in Poland), said the situation was peaceful but that reconstruction was not being helped by the SS, which regarded itself as a state within a state. He complained of the arbitrary arrests and internment of Poles and of the SS plundering, driving Jews through the streets with heavy leather whips (*Ochsenziemer*) and beating them in synagogues, and forcing a man who had dirtied his pants to smear the faces of his coreligionists with his excrement.[9]

ERNST KALTENBRUNNER

The SS representative in the dock at Nuremberg in the place of Heinrich Himmler was Ernst Kaltenbrunner, who after 1943 had headed up the RSHA, the Reich Security Main Office, with the rank of SS Obergruppenfuehrer and General of the Police. Under the RSHA were the Secret Police of the Reich, with the authority of the concentration and extermination camps behind them; the Security Police (SIPO); the Gestapo; the Criminal Police (well shortened to Kripo); and the SD, or Security Service. Kaltenbrunner was directly responsible to Himmler, who was Reichsfuehrer SS, and as Eichmann's superior (Eichmann was chief of Amt IV B4 of the RSHA) was in charge of the "actions" against the Jews, that is, their organized extermination.

The RSHA had been founded by Kaltenbrunner's predecessor, Reinhard Heydrich, who by 1941 had taken over on behalf of Himmler one police organization after the other until they were all under the RSHA. Under RSHA too were the Einsatzgruppen, the special mobile units for use in the East which had first appeared in Poland. They had the mission in the Soviet Union of exterminating Jews, commissars, and other undesirables, as well as

---

* The formations of the Waffen SS fought with great courage as well as brutality. Their percentage of losses was considerably higher than the Army's, and Army generals like Eberhard von Mackensen often praised their courage and fighting qualities. Their political indoctrination, however, prepared many of the Waffen SS members to participate in the atrocities that flawed their military record (George H. Stein, *The Waffen SS* [Ithaca: Cornell University Press, 1966]).

fighting the partisan bands that plagued the German rear areas. A directive of March 13, 1941, signed by Field Marshal Keitel, said that the Reichsfuehrer SS, Heinrich Himmler, would carry out in Russia special duties by order of the Fuehrer and that Himmler would act on his own responsibility in this area. On April 4, six weeks before the attack on Russia, the Quartermaster General of the Army, Eduard Wagner, started negotiations on a written agreement with the RSHA, which was drafted by Walter Schellenberg of the SD. In this document the Army agreed that the Einsatzgruppen would be given food, transportation, and communication facilities by the Army, but the directives for the missions of these groups would come from the RSHA. The arrangements between the OKH, the High Command of the Army, and the RSHA were completed late in May, just before the attack on Russia had begun. The rear areas of the Army aside from tactical matters were placed under the Reichsfuehrer SS, and the realm of Himmler in the East expanded rapidly.

It was difficult for the civilian victims of the war in Russia to discriminate between the German units that were attacking them. In the following account from one of the witnesses at the Eichmann trial, members of the Wehrmacht and of the SA are almost certainly wrongly identified:

> One morning the Jewish quarter was sealed off; these were streets inhabited mainly by Jews. German soldiers and officers broke savagely into the houses; they shouted at the men to leave the homes, they threw everything out of the cupboards, they beat people up, they shot and killed many. . . . They assembled mainly elderly male Jews, and all of them were put in the great synagogue in Mielicz; there they were slaughtered—almost all the Jews were killed. Those who tried to escape through the windows were shot from the outside. In the morning units in black and green uniforms surrounded the place, and they took us out of our homes and ordered us to the marketplace. People who could not run, the sick, were shot sometimes in their beds; others were later placed in the center of the marketplace. Then young men were selected and ordered to step aside; the women, children, and old people were roped off in a long column and we were in the middle. These were SS, SD and SA people. . . . When we arrived there they surrounded us with such heavily armed units, the like of which I had only seen at the front. Then they told us to stand in a semicircle and told us that we were setting out on a march and that we had to hand over everything which we possessed—money, gold, silver, watches—only twenty zloty were left to each man. They ordered us not to speak, not to turn around, not to look at or come into contact with each other, and said that whoever violated these orders would be shot. . . . Then we were given the order to set out and march. One girl managed to run after the column and she shouted all the time, "Father, Mother." Here Chola Chenis [phonetic spelling], the girl, was taken away. We did not know what happened to her. All we heard was a shot. From time to time whoever halted and tried to arrange his clothes was told to leave the column and then we heard a shot behind us. That is how we marched, in the mud, because this was the heaviest rainy season. It was

in December. Then when we were already sitting or lying down on the floor, they came and argued with us, and told us that we were to blame for the war. They took all the sacred articles, and they took the two Jewish elders with beards. We heard that others were also taken. We knew that two hundred people were taken away. And we never saw them anymore. We did not know what happened to them. We still had hope that perhaps this was not a death march. The next morning we were placed in rows again. But there were only three people to a row now." [10]

How much the Army and the civilian, administrative, non-SS apparatus in the East knew of the mass murders committed by the SD, the Einsatzkommandos, and the other police formations would be the subject of long debate not only at the trials but also in the years to come. The RSHA worked by reason of its nature in secrecy. What actually went on in the concentration and later in the extermination camps was known to only a small group; from the beginning the inmates were sworn not to disclose what they had seen or experienced if they returned to their families, on pain of being sent back to the camps again. In the case of the extermination camps, for an official to disclose what he knew was punishable by death, and the train crews and guards who took the prisoners to these camps were changed at the outskirts of the camps. Frau Hoess, who herself lived in Auschwitz, asked her husband if the rumors she had heard of the gassings were true and was reluctantly told they were by her husband, the commander of the camp, who was himself responsible for the killings of hundreds of thousands of inmates. The executions conducted by the Einsatzkommandos, too, were ordered to take place far from Army units. The official mission of these units was described as being responsible for the security of the Army in the rear areas, a task that quickly involved them in the intense and bitter war against the partisans, as well as the "actions" against the Jews, which was their principal assignment.

But killings on the scale of those practiced by the SD and the Einsatzgruppen could not be kept secret; witness after witness from the Army and the civil administration testified at Nuremberg and later trials that they had seen or heard of them. The stories were horrifying, but they might be accounted for, these witnesses said, if a man was not too curious or did not care to speculate on other possibilities but accepted the explanation that the killings were part of the battle against the partisans and the infiltrators who more and more successfully operated behind the German lines. In this relentless war where no holds were barred, the Army was glad to get what help it could from the police and the SD—whatever its commanders might think of these formations—but even under these circumstances indirect evidence shows how little the Army enjoyed the presence of the Einsatz and the SS police forces. Himmler and his subordinates wrote many reports and protests about the little comprehension the Army had for their work, of the officers' avoiding them, of never being invited to Wehrmacht social gatherings, although they also referred to gratifying exceptions.* But in the nature of the assignment given Himmler, collaboration between the Army and the police units began with the Russian campaign.

The SD leader sometimes in fact had command over small Army units in the war against the partisans, although this warfare too was theoretically under the sole command of the Army in the operational areas. In specific actions, Army units were placed under an SS or SD officer, depending on which troop leader had the largest contingent.[11] After 1943 all partisan warfare was placed under the command of Himmler.† In addition, under the Commissar Order the Army was directed to turn over captured commissars and *politruks* to the SD for execution. Many troop commanders refused to do this. But there had to be close collaboration by the Army, Higher SS and Police leaders, and the SD in the battles against the partisans, who became an increasingly deadly menace to the communications of the fighting troops as the war went on. The Army played no active role in the SD and Einsatz exterminations of the Jews. In a number of cases, when a field commander learned details of what the extermination units actually did, he ordered them out of his territory and could enforce the order because these men were fed and supplied by the Army under the agreement Himmler and Heydrich had reached with Quartermaster General Eduard Wagner. The executions took place behind the frontline area of the Army under the direct command of Himmler and his SD subordinates, first Heydrich and then Kaltenbrunner.

Toward the end of the war even Himmler said he had to watch out for Kaltenbrunner. Kaltenbrunner would use any weapon to advance himself and anyone might be his victim. A giant of a man, heavy-set with a thick neck that went up like a block from his shoulders to his head, with piercing brown eyes, a deep scar that rose from the left of his mouth to his nose, and bad teeth with some missing, Kaltenbrunner looked like what he was— a killer. Himmler's skillful physiotherapist, Felix Kersten, who examined all the men the Reichsfuehrer SS appointed to high office, said he had never had such an ox of a man in his office, nor one so stupid. Kaltenbrunner, Kersten added, had to get drunk to become capable of reasoning. That is an exaggeration, for Kaltenbrunner operated in a jungle of enemies where some of the shrewdest and most ruthless members of the Reich's secret services were at home; and men like Heydrich and Schellenberg, who detested him, feared him, too. A Doctor of Law who early discovered a talent for combining police and political work in the Austria of post-World

---

* In some cases Army formations resorted to force against the SS when it tried to take Jewish workers away from the Army, as happened in Przemysl. *Cf.* Haengeordner Schriftgut persoenlicher Stab RFSS, SD reports SS-887, BDC. (See The Organizations, Chapt. 14.)

† After the attempt on Hitler's life on July 20, 1944, Himmler also became chief of the Home Army. He was thus in command of both the police and the military formations on German soil (Siegfried Westphal, *Heer in Fesseln* [Bonn: Athenaeum Verlag, 1952], p. 98). (See The Organizations, Chapt. 14.)

War I, he had as his ambition when the Nazis took Austria to be Staats-sekretaer for Internal Security for Austria—that is, head of the SD. But Heydrich prevented his getting that job and he was made Higher SS and Police Chief for Vienna. He was virtually unknown when, after Heydrich's death, he was unexpectedly appointed head of the RSHA. Schellenberg boasted in his memoirs that he would have been given the appointment but for his youth; in any event, Himmler proposed and Hitler approved the naming of Kaltenbrunner on January 30, 1943.

Kaltenbrunner, too, made his alliances with whatever strong battalions were available to him. Hermann Fegelein, the former jockey who had married the sister of Eva Braun, was one of his friends, and he got along with Bormann, who in turn was seeking allies against Himmler. Kaltenbrunner knew the war was lost after the German defeat at Stalingrad, and he made a number of attempts to get in touch with the Allies with the hope of saving his own neck. In 1944, working through the Austrian-born Gestapo man Wilhelm Hoettl and the wily Schellenberg, he tried to arrange for talks with representatives of the Allies. Hoettl was then in touch with Allen Dulles in Switzerland, and Kaltenbrunner seems to have believed that the SS under his direction alone could arrange for an armistice and perhaps he might make a deal for his own head. Kaltenbrunner also had his lines out in Sweden, and Bernadotte visited him the day before he had an appointment with Himmler to discuss the Reichsfuehrer's plans for a deal to end hostilities with the West.

Kaltenbrunner conspired against a world of enemies; he had feelers out to the Allies not only as a possible means of rescuing himself but in part at least to do in Himmler, who was also trying to open negotiations and find some way to save his own skin. Kaltenbrunner, like Himmler, had monumental plans, but Kaltenbrunner's were limited to feathering his own nest; his blueprints lacked the mystique, the mumbo-jumbo of Himmler's. Kaltenbrunner and other members of the top echelon of the SD hated and mistrusted Admiral Canaris and the Abwehr, which they believed not only to be engaged in treasonable activities but also to be a center of every vice; Kaltenbrunner said that 80 per cent of the Abwehr were sexually perverted and could be bribed, and that Canaris was a masochist, a sadist, and a homosexual of both active and passive character at the same time.[12] In February, 1944, Kaltenbrunner finally succeeded in taking over the Abwehr and making it part of RSHA. In March he had the further satisfaction, although he got no useful information, of interrogating Admiral Canaris before his execution. It was one of Kaltenbrunner's last moments of triumph over the forces ranged against him. Canaris was a pillar of the Resistance movement and for years had skillfully managed to elude Kaltenbrunner and the SD and to protect many of the plotters until the attempt on Hitler's life was made.[13]

Kaltenbrunner lived well according to his lights, but under the strain of his manifold duties he smoked about a hundred cigarettes a day and drank heavily. Schellenberg described finding him at his desk at eleven o'clock in the morning drinking one brandy after the other and said that Kaltenbrunner insisted that Schellenberg drink along with him. Even in 1938, when he lived in Vienna, Himmler had to bail him out of his debts and to warn that his *Lebensstil*, including his expensive apartment, was far beyond his means. Himmler, in addition to the warning, presented him with 2000 RM from special funds; Kaltenbrunner was his kind of operator and Himmler could in such cases overlook minor moral frailties.[14] For Kaltenbrunner's hatred of the Jews matched his and Eichmann's. Kaltenbrunner assigned two of the most notorious exterminators in Hungary, Vites Endre and Laszlo Baky to work with Eichmann in sending the Jews remaining there to the extermination camps.[15] When the fantastic negotiations were going on between Himmler and Joel Brand to trade Jews for Allied trucks, Kaltenbrunner, like Eichmann, did his best to sabotage them. Kaltenbrunner told the major of Vienna, SS Brigadefuehrer Karl Blaschke, to whom he used *Du*, that the Jewish women and children should be held for a few days in the concentration camp near Vienna and should not be allowed to leave because they were destined for a special action, which was transportation to an extermination camp—not to Switzerland. Only 30 per cent of the 12,000 Jews still alive after being shipped to Vienna would be fit to work, he told Blaschke, and nonworking Jews had a short life.[16] He was against any rescue operation, he said, because he thought it would turn Adolf Hitler against the SS.

Kaltenbrunner was tireless in hunting down Jews for the gas chambers. Shortly after he became chief of RSHA he had 5000 Jews under sixty transferred to Auschwitz from the relative safety of Theresienstadt. He then complained that the Jews over sixty in that ghetto city were disease carriers and that they also tied up the energies of younger Jews who might be doing some useful work. Kaltenbrunner asked Himmler for his approval to send these old people, too, to Auschwitz, assuring his chief that he would be careful not to choose any Jews with important connections in foreign countries or with high war decorations. Himmler, who was now busy trying to ingratiate himself with the neutrals and the Allies, told Kaltenbrunner that the Jews should be allowed to live and die in this old people's ghetto in peace.[17]

Toward the end of the war Himmler played an unaccustomed humanitarian role when Kaltenbrunner set out on his killing expedition. Again, in the autumn of 1944, he told Kaltenbrunner, according to another SS witness, that no further exterminations must take place. "I hold you personally responsible," he wrote, "even if this order should not be strictly adhered to by subordinate offices." [18]

Kaltenbrunner had no heroes, neither Himmler, nor the Fuehrer, nor the Germans, nor the Austrians. He was a gangster filled with hatred and resentment and plans for improving his own condition. He had the ear of Hitler because in the last year he was often in the Fuehrer's headquarters and with this direct line he could circumvent Himmler when necessary. But his varied ambitions—one was to supplant Ribbentrop as Foreign Minister—had no focus; he just wanted to get on in his jaundiced world. He could win the small battles; he could defeat Karl Wolff, the SS military governor in Italy under Kesselring, by reporting to Himmler on Wolff's dealings with the Allies; he could overcome one enemy after another; but at the end, on Himmler's orders, he was only put in charge of the hopeless operations to create the last defense of the Reich, the *Alpenfestung*.

His hopes that he could negotiate on behalf of the SS with the Allies after he had made an impression of humanitarian goodwill on them were preposterous. He ordered Mauthausen to be surrendered intact to General Patton, but the commander of the camp, SS Major Franz Ziereis, who was mortally wounded as he attempted to escape at the time of the camp's surrender, on his deathbed told an American officer that Kaltenbrunner had wanted to blow up all the inmates.[19] Similar testimony was given by two witnesses with regard to Dachau, Landsberg, and Muehldorf; Gauleiters testified that Kaltenbrunner had wanted the Luftwaffe to bomb these camps to kill the prisoners and had planned to poison the inmates of Dachau.[20] This action had been prevented by one of the Gauleiters, who pleaded lack of gasoline and bombs, and by a run of bad weather.[21] Even a few days before the end of the war, on April 27, 1945, according to a former SS colonel, Kaltenbrunner told the commandant of Mauthausen that 1000 inmates must die each day.[22]

How could Kaltenbrunner, it may well be asked, have been trying to curry favor with the Allies by such humanitarian acts as handing over Mauthausen to Patton, while at about the same time he was planning to kill its inmates, as well as those of other concentration camps? The answer may lie in his primitive character and his drunkenness. Kaltenbrunner's first instinct was to kill; but even more important than his sadism was his own skin, and in bursts of alcoholic euphoria he came to think he might be able to save it.

He could only squirm under the weight of the testimony at Nuremberg. He declared wildly that he barely knew Adolf Eichmann; although they had not only collaborated in the Jewish exterminations for years, they had been boyhood friends in Linz. He claimed that he had heard that the Jews were being killed in the concentration camps but had been told by Himmler that he should not be burdened with this problem. Kaltenbrunner had a cerebral hemorrhage on November 18, at the start of the trial, and was able to attend sessions only intermittently in December and January. His testimony, however, although completely unreliable, showed no other signs of mental deterioration.

He had always displayed the characteristics he evidenced at Nuremberg;

he was blustering and devious, and when he was confronted with unmistakable evidence of his perfidy, he simply denied it. One of Goering's lawyers said Kaltenbrunner had convinced himself that he had run nothing more than an intelligence agency in the RSHA. But self-deception on such a monumental scale was impossible.

Like Hitler, Kaltenbrunner was an Austrian; he was born on October 4, 1903, in the little town of Ried on the Inn, near Hitler's birthplace, Braunau. The son of a lawyer, he studied law at the technical college (Technische Hochschule) in Graz after attending the Realgymnasium at Linz. He took his degree of Doctor of Law in 1926 and worked for a year for the court at Salzburg and then in a law office in Linz. He married and begot three children. He joined the Party in 1932 and in 1935 became leader of the Austrian SS. Arrested by the Vienna Government when Dollfuss was murdered, he led a hunger strike of the jailed Nazis. At the time of the *Anschluss*, he proudly announced to Himmler, "The SS is in formation awaiting further orders." [23] After the death of Heydrich, he reached the summit of his career when he became chief of the Reich Security Main Office, with his sphere of interest in southeastern Europe, Bulgaria, and Greece, although, like Himmler, his concerns were far ranging. He thought it should be compulsory for all German women over thirty-five to have children; if the children could not be fathered by the women's husbands, the fathers of families with more than four children should be made available. Kaltenbrunner believed in the opposite course for inferior races; the Jews should be exterminated and the Slavs should gradually die out by way of sterilization and the annihilation of their leaders.

Kaltenbrunner wanted Allied airmen parachuting from their planes to be lynched, and he ordered the police not only not to interfere with the enraged populace but to encourage them.[24] When Heinrich Mueller, the chief of the Gestapo, asked him what to do with twenty-five French prostitutes who were suffering from syphilis, Kaltenbrunner said to shoot them. This was his formula for any problem involving enemies who fell into his hands. He signed the orders for executions at Mauthausen of officers and noncommissioned officers other than British and American, as well as foreign civilian workers who had repeatedly escaped, who were killed by a bullet in the back of the neck as they were supposedly having their height measured. When the International Red Cross inquired about the executions of British and American prisoners of war, Kaltenbrunner suggested that the deaths be explained by stories of bombing attacks on the camps or of prisoners shot while attempting to escape.[25] Juergen Stroop, SS Police Leader of the Warsaw district, who commanded the mixed forces that razed the Warsaw ghetto, testified that Kaltenbrunner gave the orders as to how the operation was to be conducted and for the executions.[26] When discussions were going on in February, 1945, as to whether prisoners of the Gestapo in Berlin should be transported elsewhere in Germany or shot, Kaltenbrunner made the decision for executions "in an extremely hasty and superficial manner" even by the easy standards of the Gestapo men present.[27]

Kaltenbrunner admitted to none of these charges despite all the witnesses and the overwhelming evidence against him. On the stand, under the searching questioning of British prosecutor Colonel Amen, he could only deny the authenticity of his own signature and declare that the witnesses were lying who said they had seen him in Mauthausen when killings were staged in his honor by gas, hanging, and shooting. Everyone was lying who said the head of the Secret Police of Germany had anything to do with the executions or the arrests that sent people in the occupied countries to forced labor or concentration camps. He admitted he had known about the existence of the "show camp" of Theresienstadt, where prominent Jews or those in preferred categories such as former German soldiers were herded together in a ghetto city with coffee houses and cultural and academic activities on display for the visits of the International Red Cross and other neutral investigators. Kaltenbrunner testified that he had repeatedly talked with the Fuehrer about the concentration camps, but that Hitler had as often told him they were none of his affair. "They are," the Fuehrer had said, "my arrangement with Himmler." He admitted he had known of the Einsatz formations but said their excesses were Himmler's fault. He thought that Ribbentrop was in a position to have influenced Hitler against war, and when asked a question again about the concentration camps, he said blandly that Himmler must have known of the mistreatment of the prisoners in them. Kaltenbrunner declared that Himmler after the death of Heydrich had directed the entire RSHA until he himself was forced to take over the job on January 15, 1943, Himmler retaining only the executive branches IV (Gestapo) and V (Foreign Secret Service). His own responsibility he said, had been one in name only and his real function was to make "objective reports." Perhaps, he said, Pohl had issued orders in his name, and Oswald Pohl and Richard Gluecks (both administrators in the concentration-camp system), and Himmler too, had been responsible for the "horrible rumors" that circulated about the activities in the concentration camps.[28]

Like so many others, Kaltenbrunner declared that he had tried to resign on the issue of the concentration camps. In 1938 he had remonstrated with the Fuehrer on the treatment of the Jews, but that was all he could do since he had to keep resolutely on with his part of the war effort. He said that he regarded himself as a soldier, as having been commanded to head up the RSHA.[29] In an interrogation of October 15, 1945, he confronted the former Hungarian Minister of the Interior, Gabor Vajna, who testified that Kaltenbrunner had promised every possible assistance to the Hungarian police in transporting Jews to the German extermination camps and had said the transport and feeding of the victims en route would be taken care of by the Army. Such testimony, Kaltenbrunner always said, was either mistaken or a lie. On the next day he denied having written a report which he had signed and sent to Goering, Himmler, and Ribbentrop, recommending the executions of enemy "terror fliers," nor was he able to remember a meeting of July 6, 1944, where, as the written records showed, he had agreed that lynching or execution by the SD should be the rule in such cases.[30]

Eichmann, in department IV B4, Kaltenbrunner said, had been responsible for solving the Jewish question, and he himself had known nothing of the persecution of the Jews when he took office as chief of the RSHA in 1943. He admitted knowing of the existence of the gas trucks in which Jews were asphyxiated, and speaking of concentration camps, he said, he believed Goering had first thought up the idea in 1933.[31] He was vague about the vast apparatus of the RSHA. His job, he said, had been to report mainly on the morale of the population, and these reports had been sent to Amt 11, headed by Otto Ohlendorf, which dealt with internal political questions. Kaltenbrunner had trouble identifying many documents he had signed; at a hearing on October 10, 1945, he could not, for example, identify his signature on a commando order and said perhaps a rubber stamp had been used without his knowledge. His questioner asked him how he could expect any reasonable man to believe him in the face of this denial of written evidence, and Kaltenbrunner could only reply, "That, I don't know."

These flounderings at Nuremberg contrasted sharply with the clear reports he sent on with accompanying notes to Bormann and Hitler after the arrest of the conspirators of July 20. The reports, although not written by Kaltenbrunner, were interrogations of his devising. They were precise accounts of why the attack on the life of the Fuehrer had been made, what the conspirators had found intolerable in the National Socialist regime and why. Between the lines may be discerned Kaltenbrunner's own vendettas, his personal attacks on his rivals: on Goering, who, the conspirators say, is enriching himself from public sources and in his manner of living and personal conduct is in no way adequate to the demands of the war; on Ribbentrop, the incompetent, who, the conspirators say, made his foreign policy at the point of a bayonet and with whom no foreign government will deal now, at a time when secret negotiations are needed and there is still the possibility of playing Germany's enemies off against each other. Kaltenbrunner said too that the conspirators thought Ribbentrop had wanted war against England because he had been received in an unfriendly fashion as ambassador, that his vanity had been hurt by a country that like all foreign countries had only contempt for his diplomatic abilities. Furthermore, he said, or said the conspirators believed, Ribbentrop had misjudged England; it was not decadent as he claimed. And as for Russia, Ribbentrop would be useless dealing with Stalin because it was he who had signed the nonaggression pact with Molotov.[32]

He knew his reports would be read carefully by Hitler, and keeping within the bounds of what the prisoners actually said, he skillfully played on motives that would be certain to arouse Hitler's resentment. Kaltenbrunner quoted the conspirators as saying:

> Look at the Gauleiter, look at the Kreiswalter and how they enrich themselves. Is it bearable in a war that high, and even the highest, dignitaries take over foreign property in Germany and the occupied territories in the most shameless manner and swim in well-being while millions of German families endure stark need? . . . While our soldiers are fighting, bleeding and dying at the front, men like Goering, Goebbels, Ley, and others live a life of luxury; they rob, fill their cellars and attics and demand that the people hold out while they themselves and their followers shy away in a cowardly fashion from the sacrifices of the front.[33]

The reports written by Obersturmbannfuehrer von Kielpinski and forwarded by Kaltenbrunner contain more than indirect attacks on Kaltenbrunner's enemies. The important passages were underlined, and in these as well as in the general text are ideas Kaltenbrunner and Himmler had been revolving in their minds. The reports—similar to what Kaltenbrunner was telling the Fuehrer in their daily conferences—quote only what is always referred to as "the clique of conspirators," but no attentive reader could miss the well-founded criticisms Kaltenbrunner passed along: that Cabinet meetings in the time of Bismarck were held where advisers were allowed to state their opinions, but now one man alone made the decisions; that "even officers who at first in a negative way had had an honorable concern with the war situation and the fate of the people had little by little been drawn into the whirlpool of the conspiracy." Kaltenbrunner, like Bormann, Himmler, and the others who got close to the Presence, was intent not only on getting rid of the opposition to his own empire building but in forcing Hitler to rely more on him and perhaps even to prepare the way for Hitler's recognizing one day the need for someone else—for Kaltenbrunner, for example—to negotiate in his stead with the Allies.

The reports pulled no punches; they contained the criticisms that had been made for years by the secret opposition that came to include even some SS men like the chief of the criminal police and a former Einsatz leader Arthur Nebe. Hitler lost many of his formerly devoted admirers as he lived more and more in the fantasies and intuitions that were no longer a match for the odds against him or for the objective calculations of the generals. The reports were coated with a light covering of flattery, telling of the indignation, with few exceptions, of the German people at the attempt on Hitler's life and of the admission of the conspirators that the death of Hitler would have meant the loss of the war for Germany. But the overwhelming impression given was of the widespread network of conspiracy reaching into every layer of German society and the reasonableness of the conclusions contained in the documents the conspirators had prepared for their appeal to the German people. The sugarcoating wears through very quickly. When the corruption in the Nazi regime was mentioned, the reports were careful to point out that the conspirators too lived well (government gasoline was used for nefarious enterprises; men like Stauffenberg had tobacco and alcohol in their homes), and they comment on the perfidy of the enemy—the United States, for example—thousands of kilometers from the field of battle, entering the war only for capitalist motives. A few paragraphs of such palatable comments appeared, followed by page after page of the most bitter attacks by the opponents of Hitler's tyranny.

Even the reports on the trials of the conspirators, while accompanied by descriptions of the approval of the population as the malefactors were brought to justice, nevertheless told of the resentment of some of the citizens—mainly among the intelligentsia—who said the trials were show trials, like those the Russians put on.[35] Other Germans said that Roland Freisler, the ferocious President of the Court, behaved in a way unbecoming to the highest court in Germany. Still other anonymous critics said that it was strange that men who were given the highest decorations by the Government and the Fuehrer and whose deeds were celebrated in the press were now regarded as foolish, abject, and uncertain. The foreign press, too, was quoted in a way that could give small comfort to Bormann and to Hitler. The *Neue Zuercher Zeitung*, for example, reminded its readers—and through Kaltenbrunner, the Fuehrer—that when Italy surrendered in September, 1943, Hitler had said that a treason like that of Badoglio would be impossible in Germany. And in some of its accounts of the hearings of the conspirators, the Kaltenbrunner reports pointed out that as an excuse these men said they were honorably concerned with the fate of Germany.[36]

The split between the Party and the Army was clearly described. The Wehrmacht, said the reports, was never pleased at being commanded by an outsider, one not a member of the corps and not even an officer. In the nineteenth century and under the Weimar Republic the Army had been expected to be nonpolitical, but now its officers felt they were commanded and influenced not only by Hitler but by people outside the officer corps. The Army was no longer the sole bearer of arms; the SS had come in as its rival. One of the conspirators, General Henning von Tresckow, said that not even small troop movements could be ordered without approval of high authority. And the Kaltenbrunner reports did not fail to point out that criticism among the public repeated that of the conspirators in complaining about the corruption and smoothness of the lives of the *Bonzen*.[37]

Kaltenbrunner hit where he knew it would hurt. Many of the conspirators had formerly been loyal Nazis who had gradually become enemies because the facts of life were not consonant with the Nazi principles of the general profit coming before self-profit (*Nutz vor Eigenutz*), because they lost the feeling of justice, of *Rechtsgefuehl*. One man said he was also dubious of the conduct of leading personalities, "especially of the Reichsmarschall, who in his personal life and leadership in no way is equal to the demands of the war." Another said, "My personal opinion continues to be the same as it was, and I still approve of National Socialism as we understood it and as it was taught to us during the years of struggle for power. But what appears today as its realization I no longer can call good. . . . The good foot-slogger [braver Landser] means little as against the vast number of corrupt Party members who hide out in the bases and in the homeland and have everything they can use." Another said, "I approve the Weltanschauung . . . including the Party program, but like every decent person, I condemn the encroach-ments [Uebergriffe] of the individual Party comrades. . . . We want a leader-ship that is an example in its conduct and deeds." [38] Speer, too, was identified as having talked matters over with members of the conspiracy, but the report said that he would have nothing to do with violence against the regime. Lesser men than Speer were arrested and executed merely for having heard of the plans for a revolt and not having reported them, but Speer's influence with the Fuehrer was able to withstand even such accusa-tions.

Kaltenbrunner and his police did a thorough job of laying bare the plot and its ramifications. The secret police, the courts, and Hitler himself knew everything the conspirators had thought and planned—and why—as well as how widespread the opposition was, including labor unionists, former enthu-siastic Party members, war heroes, and members of the SS. Kaltenbrunner, perhaps skillfully preparing the way for a future denunciation, reported that even he was thought by some of the German people to have been involved in the conspiracy. Since members of the SS had been trying to get in touch with the Allies (Himmler was, as Kaltenbrunner well knew), this suggestive statement may have been the first warning to Hitler that even his most trusted policemen were looking in other directions for their salvation.

The tribunal found Kaltenbrunner guilty on two of the three counts with which he was charged: war crimes and crimes against humanity; he was found not guilty of planning to wage aggressive war. No one, not even Kaltenbrunner, could have quarreled with the verdict. His only recorded complaint against the treatment of the Jews was that the concentration-camp inmates sent to forced labor died faster than they could be put to work. He was one of the phenomena of the Nazi period, a shrewd on-the-make lawyer with a touch of nostalgia at the end of the war, as appeared in his reports, for due process of law and a state where opinions like his own would be listened to by the Fuehrer. At bottom, he was a cold and ruthless killer who gladly did without any legal forms if the renunciation meant fewer Jews or Slavs, fewer Goebbelses or Goerings or Leys or Ribbentrops. Having no defense that could possibly stand up, Kaltenbrunner decided that the court was an enemy court and that he would deny everything. This at least was Goering's view of his attitude, and it perhaps comes as close to the explanation of Kaltenbrunner's behavior at Nuremberg as any other.

Kaltenbrunner regarded himself as a soldier, as did Eichmann and SD commanders like Walter Schellenberg and Einsatz commanders like Ohlendorf, who boasted that his unit had liquidated 90,000 Jews in the Baltic States. Kaltenbrunner said that as head of the RSHA he had received his soldier's pay and like a soldier had obeyed orders and stuck to his post. Soldiers they all were, so they told one another—and they finally came to believe it themselves—soldiers performing harder tasks than the men at the front but essential tasks on behalf of the purity of the race and its future. One British judge at a later trial indignantly said to a concentration-camp guard who had spoken of returning to the troops after having been on leave, "To the troops? You were no soldier, you were a concentration-camp guard!" But these were the views of the normal world, not of the dream world of the Nazi State. Schellenberg and Ohlendorf testified that the Army had known all about the SD and Einsatz activities; but both had to retreat under the sharp questioning of Laternser, the lawyer defending the High Command, and they finally admitted that their missions of killing Jews could be divulged to no one and that Schellenberg had never mentioned the exterminations when he drew up the contract with General Wagner (see The Organizations, Chapt. 14). It was clear, however, from the strong protests on the part of the Army in some sectors that many German generals did know. The question the court had to answer at Nuremberg had to do primarily with the guilt of Keitel and Jodl in the murders as well as in the other three points of the indictment against them. For Kaltenbrunner, no questions were left open.

WILHELM KEITEL

The prosecution, one of Jodl's lawyers said, treated Field Marshal Keitel and Colonel General Jodl as inseparable twins. But few in the Party or the Wehrmacht—and certainly not Adolf Hitler—judged them alike. Jodl was a Bavarian with few of the gay, careless "living-it-up" qualities popularly supposed to be *Bayrisch*; he was sober, intelligent, methodical, and practical, a thoroughly capable officer and one, moreover, with his own opinions. He became devoted to Hitler only gradually as the Fuehrer repeatedly dazzled him with intuitive flashes of when and how to act in both political and military affairs. Jodl had been dubious of Hitler, and only after such successes as the reoccupation of the Rhineland, the *Anschluss*, Munich, and the victories in the West did he develop his awed regard for Hitler's genius. But in the course of their relationship he argued stiffly with Hitler on a number of military decisions and stubbornly stood his ground when the Fuehrer reacted with *Sturm und Drang*.

Keitel, on the other hand, who had been schooled in the Prussian Army and who represented to the Allies at Nuremberg the prototype of a Prussian officer, was never much more than an efficient yes-man. Never during his five years as chief of OKW did he argue against a Hitler decision, although, like Ribbentrop, he did go so far as to write a memorandum advising against the Russian campaign before it started. According to a witness at Nuremberg, Admiral Canaris had regarded Keitel as a type of noncommissioned officer blown up to superhuman proportions and had felt that, despite his monocle and absurd swagger, he was essentially the obsequious military clerk, signing on the dotted line and dutifully initialing orders, even those he knew to be questionable if not criminal.[39] Neither Keitel nor Jodl had any power of command; as chief of the OKW, the High Command of the Armed Forces, Keitel was the channel through which Hitler communicated orders to the Army, the Air Force, and the Navy. It was clear not only from the testimony of witnesses but also from the structure of the Wehrmacht that orders going to either the Air Force or Navy could not originate with Keitel since their commanders, Reichsmarschall Hermann Goering of the Luftwaffe and Admiral Raeder and then Doenitz of the Navy, would have immediately resisted any interference with their authority on his part, however subservient they might be to the Fuehrer. They accepted orders from Keitel only because the orders came through him from Hitler.[40]

At Nuremberg Admiral Raeder's testimony on the Field Marshal's defects of character and professional capabilities deeply distressed Keitel—so deeply, in fact, that he wrote a note to his lawyer, Dr. Otto Nelte, telling Nelte that he must feel free to resign his mandate after Raeder's testimony, but pointing out that if Raeder really had believed him so incompetent as chief of OKW, he should have told the Fuehrer so and should not have collaborated with such a bungler for five and a half years. The Army, too, had its chief of staff and its own chain of command, and Keitel, despite the high rank of Generalfeldmarschall, given him after the fall of France, told the field commanders only what Hitler ordered him to pass along. In time, especially when orders became impossible to carry out, Keitel became known to his colleagues as Nickesel (a toy donkey that nods its head) and Lakaitel, a pun on the word "lackey"; it was this servile quality that enabled him to last out the war when so many able men were relieved of their commands or shot by order of the Fuehrer. Everyone knew that to head OKW was a thankless job; no one intrigued to win this post as they did the others. The criticisms of Keitel were inevitable, for no other kind of man could have held the job.[41]

Although Keitel had served in the Prussian Army, where the form and pattern of the general staff officer had its origins, he was as far from being the conventional Prussian officer as Jodl was from the stock figure of the jolly Bavarian. He looked the part, but the steel was lacking. The Keitel family came not from Prussia but from Hannover, and Keitel's grandfather had so disliked the Prussians that he would not let his son appear in his house in Army uniform. In 1871 Keitel's father bought a farmstead in Brunswick, a large tract called Helmscherode near Gandersheim in the western part of the state. Wilhelm Bodewin Johann Gustav Keitel was born there on September 22, 1882. His mother, Apollonia Vissering, came from a bourgeois landed family, and the young son wanted above any other career open to him to be a Landwirt, a large-scale farmer, like his ancestors. After the death of his mother and his father's remarriage, however, he was told that Helmscherode could not support two families. He was an obedient boy, and in the spring of 1900, having taken his *Abitur*, he cheerfully joined the 46th Field Artillery Regiment in Wolfenbuettel, in which his father had entered him. Keitel would have preferred the cavalry, but the family could not afford the added expense of supplying him with a horse. He had been an average student at the Gymnasium and had gotten along well with both his superiors and his schoolmates. He was tractable, not overly intelligent—average, they called him—and one of his schoolmasters said, "You'd do a hundred times better at taking Saint Paul out for a ride with some mettlesome horses than you would at understanding him."

Keitel developed into a solid, dependable type: a man who followed instructions and who was able to smooth over differences when they arose, a conciliator who avoided rather than overcame obstacles and who carefully repeated what his superiors had taught him. He served with his artillery regiment as a lieutenant in the march into Belgium and France in 1914 and was slightly wounded in September. In March, 1915, he was transferred to the General Staff of the Xth Reserve Corps, from which he was moved in July to the Great General Staff, where he was entitled to wear the General Staff trousers with their red stripes. As he wrote to his father on March 11, 1915, he could thank his preferment in part at least to chance; he had taken part during the prewar 1914 maneuvers in the General Staff inspection trip and had favorably impressed the visiting staff officers.[42]

Keitel stayed in the Army after 1918. His wife, Lisa Fontaine, whom he had married just before the start of the war, came from a well-to-do family of landowners and brewers. The Keitels, therefore, were not among the victims of the economic crises that rocked Germany in the postwar years. The Keitels were always careful with their money and always used what they had circumspectly. When they traveled to an official ceremony, Keitel used the automobile placed at his disposal, but his wife went by trolleycar. They were bourgeois people, and both had deep feeling for the land and the formerly well-to-do who had lived by it. Keitel sorrowfully reported in one of his letters that in *Kreis* Schlochau alone in the spring of 1931 forty-three estates of 46,000 *Morgen* (about 30,000 acres) had been taken over by creditors.[43] This was the year in which he, now a colonel and chief of the organization division of the General Staff, together with Major General Wilhelm Adam and Colonel Walther von Brauchitsch, made a two-week trip to Russia.* Keitel was greatly impressed with the Soviet Union, its immense spaces, its raw materials, and the eagerness and tempo of its workers.

* Adam was chief of T1 (operations), Brauchitsch of T4 (training).

Keitel was never a man to see what went on below surfaces. He was a hard worker who busied himself with innumerable burdensome details, and he stayed at his job from early morning until late at night usually seven days a week. His superiors valued him for his enormous industry and his ability to carry out assignments with considerable efficiency and dispatch. By 1934, at the age of fifty-two, he was a major general; he was a man who accepted all the conventional views of General Staff officers, and, in addition, he had a high tolerance for National Socialism but not for the SA's incorporation into the Army with its leaders as officers.* The Army was for Keitel not only the center of his own life but the center of Germany. The Air Force and Navy had their place, but only the Army would be the decisive factor if war came, he wrote in a memorandum appraising Germany's military position. That was what every General Staff officer believed, and Keitel's memorandum was as acceptable to the General Staff as to Hitler.

Hitler had chosen him as chief of OKW in February, 1938, because he seemed to be the kind of man he could trust to carry out his assignment. Field Marshal von Blomberg, whose chief of staff Keitel had been and who had known him since 1917, told the Fuehrer that Keitel would be no more than a good section chief, to which Hitler replied, "That's what I want." And in this matter, as in many others, the Fuehrer's intuition was correct.† In 1938 the chief of the General Staff of the Army, General Beck, along with other high-ranking officers, planned a *coup d'état* and the arrest of Hitler if he brought on a war against Czechoslovakia that would mean the inevitable defeat of the Reich by the overwhelming superior forces of the coalition against Germany. This was a key year in Hitler's takeover of the Army. Colonel General von Fritsch, who had been appointed Commander in Chief of the Army in February, 1934, and Field Marshal von Blomberg, who had been made Minister of Defense in Hitler's first Cabinet, both lost their offices.‡ General Ludwig Beck, who became chief of the General Staff in 1935, when it was reestablished, moved into open opposition to Hitler. Beck was the center of the conspiracy of Army generals, which included many of the men who would take part in the *attentat* of July 20. "A good

* His wife, Lisa, in March, 1933, after the Potsdam ceremonies, wrote to her mother that although she never could be a National Socialist she was enormously enthusiastic about Hitler; a few months later she said his speeches were masterpieces.

† Hitler had known little of Keitel; when he ordered him to report he referred to him as General von Keitel (Walter Goerlitz, *Keitel—Verbrecher oder Offizier?* [Goettingen: Musterschmidt-Verlag, 1961], p. 107).

‡ At the time when Blomberg made his ill-advised second marriage, his youngest daughter, Dorothee, was engaged to Keitel's son, Lieutenant Karl Heinz Keitel. When the unpleasant proof that Blomberg's new wife had been a registered prostitute was laid on the desk of the Police President of Berlin, Count von Helldorf, he went with the documents to Keitel. Keitel characteristically sidestepped; he sent Helldorf to Goering, who in turn went to Hitler with the bad news. Later, when Blomberg was honeymooning in Italy, he wrote to Keitel, asking whether if he divorced his wife he might be reinstated. Keitel, instead of advising him, turned the letter over to Hitler, who would have none of the idea (see also Goering, Chapt. 3).

section chief" was exactly what Hitler needed, for the chief of OKW would be no more than Hitler's personal chief of staff.

Keitel was not a member of this conspiracy; neither then nor later would he dream of being untrue to his leader no matter what catastrophe might befall his country. Both he and Jodl, opposing the advice of the generals at the front, would agree, when the time came, with Hitler's orders for the encircled Sixth Army at Stalingrad to fight on against hopeless odds. Keitel, in the autobiographical account he wrote at Nuremberg, told of occasions when he resisted Hitler. Once, in April, 1940, he reacted strongly against Hitler's taking the administration of Norway from the Army and putting it in the hands of Gauleiter Terboven. He threw his briefcase on the table, he said, and walked out.[44] This scene was also described by Jodl, who witnessed it.[45] Again, in the autumn of 1941 Keitel had a difference of opinion with Hitler, offered his resignation, and thought of suicide, but he overcame his despair and stayed on. In 1943 both he and Jodl took the part of Field Marshal Sigmund List, who had fallen into grave disfavor by his campaign in the Caucasus, and Hitler refused for months to shake hands with either of them. But such moments came seldom; and toward the end, when Hitler's fury had no limits, they never recurred.

Keitel's most important and historic assignments before the start of the war were appearances in an actor's role at two meetings with foreign statesmen. He was on hand when Chancellor von Schuschnigg was summoned to Berchtesgaden to hear Hitler's demands that Schuschnigg renounce his "anti-German policy" and collaborate with the Austrian Nazis; Keitel's presence was intended to impress Schuschnigg with Germany's determination to march if the Austrian Chancellor was unwilling to sign the agreement prepared for him. Keitel's second theatrical appearance came on March 14, 1939, when Emil Hácha, President of Czechoslovakia, was ordered to visit Hitler at the Reich Chancellery. Again Keitel was present, along with Goering, to act the part of the imperturbable military commander awaiting the final order to strike as Hácha in the early hours of the 15th was forced to sign the document that placed what remained of his country under the protection of the Fuehrer. Keitel admitted at Nuremberg that his presence in Hitler's office at a dramatic moment had been prearranged to step up the psychological pressure on Hácha. He had recited his lines in answer to Hitler's question, saying that the orders had gone out for the Army to cross the demarcation lines of rump Czechoslovakia and to occupy Prague. Thus he had played his part in the coercion of the exhausted and ill old man who had to sign the paper pushed before him.

Keitel went along with everything Hitler demanded of him. He owed his high preferment to the Fuehrer. As a young officer he had never dreamed of becoming a Field Marshal; he knew his limitations, and only by the grace of Hitler had he transcended them. He repaid the Fuehrer with unquestioning devotion. His signature appeared on orders and directives that were to help make the war in the East as ruthless as any in history. He had written in his order of December 16, 1942, dealing with the partisans:

> The Fuehrer has received reports that some members of the armed forces taking part in the actions against the bands have been held to account to their disadvantage for their behavior in battle. The Fuehrer has therefore ordered: The enemy is sending into the partisan battle well-trained, fanatical, communistically schooled fighters who shrink from no act of violence. More than ever before is it a question of to be or not to be. This war no longer has anything to do with knightly conduct or with the agreements of the Geneva Convention. If this war is not fought with the greatest brutality against the bands both in the East and in the Balkans then in the foreseeable future the strength at our disposal will not be sufficient to be able to master this plague. The troops are therefore empowered and are in duty bound in this war to use without mitigation even against women and children any means that will lead to success. Considerations of any kind are a crime against the German people and the soldier at the front. . . .[46]

Insurmountable objections existed, he said, to any chivalrous idea of warfare when the Germans invaded Russia. Keitel forwarded the orders to shoot prisoners of war if they were commissars or *politruks* captured in the uniform of the Red Army or Allied soldiers sent on missions of sabotage, even if they were in uniform.[47] On June 26, 1944, he signed the order that only Allied soldiers making parachute landings at the Normandy beachhead were to be spared from execution if captured; any others were to be regarded as saboteurs and were to be killed in battle or turned over to the SD, which meant execution.[48]

Keitel ordered that every village in which partisans were found must be burned down and all victims suspected of offenses against the German troops shot without trial. At the end of the war, he was to turn such directives against German generals. On April 13, 1945, with Heinrich Himmler he issued an order declaring that cities that were traffic centers had to be defended to the last man. The battle commander in each city was to be held responsible for carrying out the order, and if he did anything to weaken it, he was to be made harmless or to be condemned to death.[49] Keitel also signed the order for the killing of fifty to one hundred hostages for the murder of one German soldier in the East, although he told the Nuremberg court he had proposed ratios of only five or ten to one. Hitler had overruled him, so he sent out the order for the higher numbers. He was also accused by a witness, General Erwin Lahousen of the Abwehr, of having ordered the retaliatory killing of two French generals: the slaying planned by the SD of General Henri Giraud, who had escaped in 1942 from a German prison near Dresden; and the Abwehr's killing of General Maxime Weygand, who, Keitel thought, might become a center of French resistance in North Africa. Keitel denied these accusations, saying that Lahousen had misunderstood his concern with these cases; as a result of Hitler's constant inquiries, he had merely intended to place both generals under arrest. But if Lahousen, who was in direct touch with Keitel, had misunderstood him, who else would have known the men were only to be arrested?

Keitel ordered that Russian prisoners of war were to be tatooed on the buttocks because thousands escaped and were difficult to identify when they mingled with the local population in the East. The order produced such an immediate and vigorous reaction from commandants of prison camps and even from Ribbentrop, who in this case pointed to international law forbidding such practices, that Keitel rescinded it before it could be carried out. One camp commander told him that the Russians would retaliate by branding German prisoners on the forehead. That was language Keitel understood; a reprisal was something he respected.

Keitel's authority was actually limited to issuing the orders given him by Hitler. Since neither he nor Jodl had authority to give orders or directives on their own, they signed or initialed them on behalf of or on the authority of the Fuehrer. Keitel would apparently sign anything Hitler gave him. Witnesses testified to his passive ferocity: Lahousen wrote in his diary while they were traveling together in the Fuehrer's train in Upper Silesia on September 12, 1939, that Keitel had spoken of the need of exterminating the Polish intellectuals along with the priests, pastors, nobles, and Jews who would be the center of the Resistance. Hitler, said Keitel, had decided to break the will of the Polish people.* Keitel was echoing here the current Party line; the same words were being used by Himmler and Ribbentrop.[50]

General Nikolaus von Falkenhorst, who had commanded the German forces in Norway, testified that he tried to save the lives of British Commandos who had been captured at Stavanger, Norway, in November, 1942, but that Keitel told him they had to be shot. Falkenhorst had at least wanted the prisoners to be interrogated first, but they were killed at once.[51] Keitel told Falkenhorst that the Fuehrer had issued the order and Falkenhorst would have to abide by it. The same thing happened, Falkenhorst testified, when Norwegian seamen, trying to escape to England, were captured off the coast of Norway in March, 1943. These men, too, were shot without courts-martial.[52] Another witness, Joachim von und zur Gathen, testified in his interrogation of November 30, 1945, that Keitel had proposed the killing of terror fliers on the order of any Army or Air Force officer of a rank not lower than regimental commander. He said that the Luftwaffe staff was opposed to this, but Goering had ordered the Air Force not to intervene against the "well-justified fury of the population." [53]

Keitel fitted perfectly into the National Socialist scheme of things. When Blomberg resigned, the Fuehrer himself became, with the decree of Febru-

* Lahousen told Keitel that "the world would eventually hold the Wehrmacht under whose eyes such things had happened responsible for these deeds." Keitel replied that the Fuehrer had already decided on this matter. He made it clear to the Commander in Chief of the Army that if the Wehrmacht did not want any part in these occurrences, it would have to accept the SS and Gestapo as rivals (NCA V, 3047-PS, p. 769).

ary 4, 1938, head of the armed forces with no intermediaries. "From now on," Hitler declared, "I will directly and personally take over the supreme command of the entire Wehrmacht. The former Wehrmacht Office in the War Ministry becomes the High Command of the Armed Forces and comes immediately under my command as my military staff. At the head of the staff of the High Command stands the former chief of the Wehrmacht Office [Keitel]." At this point Keitel, as Chief of Staff of the Armed Forces, became not only chief of Hitler's working staff but, as representative of the Wehrmacht with the rank of minister, a member of the Council of Ministers for Defense of the Reich. But since no such council was needed (see The Organizations, Chapt. 14), because Hitler undertook to defend the Reich in his own capacity as head of the Party, the Government, the Armed Forces, the Foreign Office, and the Judiciary, Keitel's main duty was merely to obtain Hitler's decisions on all basic military questions and, after they were drafted and approved by the Fuehrer, to countersign them.

In the autumn of 1944, when for the first time it became legal for an Army officer to join the Party, Keitel received the Party's Golden Badge of Honor and contributed 1,000 RM to the Party funds. He never lost his faith in his master; he stated at Nuremberg, "Even today I am a convinced adherent of Adolf Hitler"; however, he added cautiously, "this does not exclude my rejecting some items of the Party program." [54]

On March 30, 1941, almost three months before the start of the Russian campaign, Hitler told Keitel, Halder, and other members of the High Command that the war to come was a clash of two ideologies, that bolshevism was criminality and communism an enormous danger to the future of the Reich. We must forget, the Fuehrer said, any concept of comradeship between soldiers in this war. A Communist is no comrade before or after the battle; this is a war of extermination. The generals were to overcome their personal scruples, for harshness today meant leniency in the future.[55] Therefore Hitler demanded what came to be called the Commissar Order (*der Kommissarbefehl*), the order to shoot any Party officials, commissars, or *politruks* captured in battle immediately, without a court-martial or legal procedures of any kind. Other generals immediately called it a criminal order, but Keitel never made the slightest objection to it; he accepted it as a matter of course. On May 12, 1941, General Warlimont, with the approval of General Jodl, sent to Hitler a draft of a proposed directive of OKH, including a memorandum of Alfred Rosenberg and OKW's proposals. OKH recommended in accord with Hitler's purposes:

1. Political officials and leaders [commissars] are to be liquidated.
2. Insofar as they are captured by the troops, an officer with authority to impose disciplinary punishment decides whether the given individual must be liquidated. For such a decision the fact suffices that he is a political official.
3. Political leaders in the troops [Red Army] are not recognized as prison-

ers of war and are to be liquidated at the latest in the prisoner-of-war transit camps.[56]

Rosenberg wanted the liquidation order limited to high party functionaries, and Warlimont's draft proposed liquidating only commissars who fought against the German troops and leaving unharmed those who took no part in hostilities. This was Warlimont's and Jodl's attempt to water down the order in some degree. Warlimont said later that the Army had known that if he did not draw up the Commissar Order, someone in the SS would.

The final Commissar Order of June 6 followed in the main the Warlimont draft: in the battle area commissars who fought against German troops were to be liquidated immediately. The others, for the time being, were to be left unharmed. In the rear areas, any commissars who had been seized because of doubtful behavior were to be turned over to the SD.[57]

Keitel obediently sent along the *Kommissarbefehl*. Very nearly every general except Keitel protested against it (see The Organizations, Chapt. 14). At Nuremberg he expressed mixed feelings about it. During one interrogation he called it a *Schweinerei*; at other times, he repeated what he had doubtless said at the time, that commissars were not soldiers but party functionaries, not bearers of arms but political inciters. The majority of the German generals and field marshals had strongly disagreed with this reasoning, however. They pointed out that commissars and other party functionaries wore military uniforms, fought alongside the Red Army, and could not legally be distinguished from any other prisoner of war. That this order was immediately recognized as illegal was clear when on May 14, 1941, Keitel ordered that it be transmitted by word of mouth only and the written records always be destroyed. At Nuremberg Keitel excused the fact that the *Kommissarbefehl* and similar orders were issued before the start of the Russian campaign by saying that the Germans had known before the war started what would happen. Yugoslavia, he said, had shown what Russian tactics might be like. The country was honeycombed with Bolshevik agents when the Germans invaded. All Hitler's orders and decrees, he said, were reactions and countermeasures to "misbehavior and rebellion in the occupied territories." [58]

And on May 13, 1941, Keitel signed a directive issued by the Fuehrer which was to be an additional reason for Brauchitsch's issuing his Maintenance of Discipline order (see The Organizations, Chapt. 14). It read:

> The application of martial law aims in the first place at *maintaining discipline*.
> The fact that the operational areas in the East are so far-flung, the battle strategy which this necessitates, and the peculiar qualities of the enemy, confront the courts-martial with problems which, being understaffed, they cannot solve while hostilities are in progress, . . . unless jurisdiction is confined, in the first instance, to its main task.

This is possible only if *the troops themselves* take ruthless action against any threat from the enemy population. . . .

I. Treatment of offenses committed by enemy civilians:
1. Until further notice the military courts and the courts-martial will not be competent for *crimes committed by enemy civilians.*
2. *Guerrillas* should be disposed of ruthlessly by the military, whether they are fighting or in flight. . . .
3. Where measures of this kind [killing partisans in action] are not followed or are not possible the *suspected persons are to be taken before an officer immediately. He will decide whether they will be shot.*

   In the case of localities where the Wehrmacht has been treacherously or maliciously attacked *collective measures of force* may be taken on the order of an officer of at least the rank of battalion commander if circumstances do not permit a quick identification of individual offenders. . . .

II. Treatment of offenses committed against inhabitants by members of the Armed Forces and its employees:
1. With regard to *offenses* committed *against enemy civilians* by *members of the Wehrmacht* and its employees *prosecution is not obligatory* even where the deed is at the same time a military crime or offense.
2. When *judging such offenses,* it must be borne in mind . . . that the collapse of Germany in 1918, the subsequent sufferings of the German people and the fight against National Socialism which cost the blood of innumerable supporters of the movement were caused primarily by Bolshevik influence and that no German has forgotten this fact.
3. Therefore the judicial authority will decide in such cases whether a disciplinary penalty is indicated, or whether *legal* measures are necessary. In the case of offenses against inhabitants it will order a *court-martial* only if *maintenance of discipline or security of the Forces* calls for such a measure. This applies for instance to serious offenses originating in lack of self-control in sexual matters, or in a criminal disposition, and to those which indicate that the troops are threatening to get out of hand. Offenses which have resulted in senseless destruction of billets or stores of other captured material to the disadvantage of our Forces should as a rule be judged no less severely. . . .

III. Within their sphere of competence Military Commanders are *personally* responsible for seeing that:
1. every commissioned officer of the units under their command is instructed promptly and in the most emphatic manner on principles set out under I above.
2. their legal advisers are notified promptly of these instructions and of *verbal information in which the political intentions of the High Command were explained to C-in-Cs.*
3. only those court sentences are confirmed which are in accordance

with the political intentions of the High Command.[59] [Emphasis in original.]

Keitel was as anti-Semitic as his being Hitler's mouthpiece required. He directed that no soft-hearted or even merely efficient commander use Jews in the military government or in any useful capacity even to aid the tasks of the Army. On September 12, 1941, Keitel said that isolated instances of disobedience made it necessary for him to remind the troops of the directives for the conduct of the Army in Russia, that the fight against bolshevism necessitated "indiscriminate and energetic accomplishment of this task, especially also against the Jews, the main carriers of Bolshevism. For such reasons, any cooperation of the Armed Forces with the Jewish population . . . as well as the use of any single Jew in any preferred auxiliary position, will have to cease." [60]

Keitel was a hard liner on every occasion when he was sure of Hitler's views. On September 15, 1941, when Admiral Canaris sent a memorandum strongly opposing the treatment accorded Soviet prisoners of war, Keitel wrote on the margin: "The observations correspond to the soldierly notions of chivalrous warfare. We are dealing here with the destruction of a philosophy. Therefore I approve the measures and sanction them." [61]

He signed Hitler's Night and Fog decree on December 7, 1941. This action, he said at Nuremberg, was one of the three he most regretted. Another was the execution of fifty RAF officers who had escaped from the Sagan prison camp in Silesia, had been recaptured, and then had been shot.* The third involved the orders for the conduct of the war in Russia.[62] The Night and Fog decree was designed to strike terror in the ranks of all resisters, particularly those in France and the Low Countries. Under it people suspected of crimes against the German occupation were simply to disappear after they were turned over to the Gestapo. Night and Fog (this was the Fuehrer's coinage) was a substitute for the death penalty; the prisoners no longer existed for the outside world. They were transported clandestinely to the Reich by the Gestapo and then to an anonymous place in a concentration camp. They went into the night and fog, and no word would be heard from them by their families and friends. Concerning Night and Fog, Keitel said at Nuremberg that he had inserted before the order the words: "It is the will of the Fuehrer after long consideration," to show to the commanders receiving it that he himself disapproved. This is as far as his criticism could go.

An order of Keitel's of September 8, 1942, called for the introduction of

---

* Eighty members of the RAF, including English, Belgian, French, Greek, Norwegian, Polish, and Czech officers, had tunneled out of Sagan. Four were promptly caught in the tunnel and seventy-six escaped. Of these, three were never found and fifteen were recaptured in the immediate neighborhood. Keitel ordered these sent back to the camp and thus saved their lives. The other fifty, captured in various parts of Germany, the Fuehrer ordered to be shot immediately. Keitel opposed the executions but could not prevent them (N X, pp. 564–67).

compulsory labor in the occupied territories and prohibited workers from changing employment without permission.[63] In addition, he approved shooting striking railroad men in Holland as a reprisal for this act of passive resistance. Many of the orders Keitel signed and sent on were so manifestly illegal under previous German military law that Keitel had to take the part of the lawbreakers. When the proposal was made in the latter part of the war that German civilians be allowed or encouraged to lynch Allied fliers who were forced to land, Keitel seemingly went along with the lynchers: "I am against legal procedure," he said, "it does not work out." [64] Actually, he strongly opposed killing Allied fliers; what he did was, as usual, to attempt to stall for time, and in this he was successful. No order to execute Allied bombing crews was ever issued.

Keitel's orders reflected no more than Hitler's mounting wrath. In June, 1939, the Army Service Regulations, expressing the traditional views of the Army High Command, declared that war was waged only against the armed forces of the enemy. Supplies vital to the troops could be obtained only against payment; cultural monuments were to be spared; prisoners were not to be mishandled and were to be allowed to retain their personal effects. They were to be killed only if they tried to escape. In January, 1940, before the partisan war had become the major threat it was to be in Russia, the German orders to troops fighting guerrillas corresponded almost word for word to the Hague rules on land warfare, under which guerrillas might be threatened with death and confiscation of their property if they could not be identified as soldiers but which nevertheless spelled out the offenses that made a partisan liable to such punishment. All this, however, changed even before the war with Russia started. And Keitel dutifully changed too, whether the orders he signed had to do with killing soldiers or civilians. The underlying lawlessness and brutality were always present—even after the defeat of France in September, 1940. Keitel declared that the Fuehrer wanted the French to be treated from the political angle only; it made no difference, he said, if the economy was destroyed. The Army should use force only if there were disturbances. To an objection that France would become a center of unrest, Keitel replied, "Then we'll shoot." [65]

But such threats and the shooting of French hostages were small events when compared to the major struggle of two world views in Russia. Not only the Russian economy was to be destroyed, but the civilian population as well if they were suspected of collaborating with the enemy forces in the German rear. But Keitel's direct influence in the conduct of the Russian campaign was slight since it was the High Command of the Army, not of the Armed Forces, that, under Hitler, directed the war in the East. Hitler, late in 1941, after dismissing Field Marshal von Brauchitsch, became Commander in Chief of the Army, in addition to being Commander in Chief of the Armed Forces. At this time, the OKH, like the OKW, became nothing more than his personal staff. Nevertheless, it was Keitel and OKW that issued or approved patently criminal orders such as the one signed by General Reinecke for use of weapons without hesitation against Russian prisoners of war. Keitel at Nuremberg could only defend these measures and the others that resulted in the death of hundreds of thousands of Russian prisoners by citing the advanced age of many of the German guards, who, he claimed, were often attacked by Soviet prisoners.

Keitel was also charged with having ordered the shackling of English prisoners of war on their way to prison camps and the execution of Allied Commando troops who were to be turned over to the SD by the Army and Navy even when captured in uniform. These orders Keitel defended as reprisals for the shackling of German prisoners at the time the British raided Dieppe and for the execution of others.* Keitel said that the Germans had proof both from the actions of the Commandos who had landed at Dieppe and from captured British orders that the Commandos were instructed to use every atrocious and illegal means to accomplish their mission.†

Toward the close of the war, in July, 1944, Keitel's signature was the last of three appearing on two orders concerning the chain of command that marked what a few years before would have been a revolution in the armed forces. As the enemy was about to invade Germany, Heinrich Himmler was put in charge not only of the SS, the Gestapo, and the Secret Police, but of the Home Army; in addition, the Gauleiters were to be the recruiters for the nondescript forces of the Volkssturm that were being gathered from among the very young and the old. Both Bormann and Lammers, on behalf of the Party, signed their names on these military orders before Keitel docilely affixed his.

Keitel was a member of the court of honor that expelled from the Army the accused officers who took part in the July 20, 1944, plot against Hitler; in Keitel's eyes, this was the gravest crime that anyone could commit. Yet he had liked Canaris, one of the chief members of the Resistance, and after Canaris' arrest he sent money to aid his family. It was Keitel who helped the slightly wounded Hitler out of the bunker that day, and he knew now that the Fuehrer felt he could trust him even if he aided the family of one of the would-be assassins. Keitel had deep personal loyalties, and Canaris' family had been guilty of no crime. When Keitel had first heard in 1943 that General Oster was involved in a conspiracy, he simply refused to believe it and forced the witness to withdraw his charges.[66]

If Keitel knew the war was lost—and one family report said he was doubtful of a German victory even in the autumn of 1941—he gave no sign of it. He told his Russian interrogator at Bad Mondorf that in the summer

---

* French prisoners were also shackled after two hundred escaped.

† The captured British *Handbook of Instructions on How to Conduct Irregular Warfare* bore out Keitel's defense: British Commandos were told "to use any weapons including broken bottles in hand to hand fighting against the enemy, . . ." These documents, however, could not be introduced at the International Military Tribunal trial, although they were brought into evidence two years later at the trial of Leeb, *et al.*

of 1944 he had thought that the war could no longer be won by military means, that the matter now had to be turned over to the politicians. If this statement has any clear meaning, it must be that he still thought a German victory somehow possible.[67] In a letter to his wife dated August 29, 1943, he wrote that the war had been going on for four years and "when the Bolsheviki will sink to their knees, one knows not but before then we can never have peace." [68] The letter was written following the devastating British air attack on Hamburg which the German Air Force could not prevent, months after major German defeats in Russia and Africa, and after Mussolini had been forced from office. In the last days of the war he and Jodl importuned the Fuehrer to leave his bunker in Berlin and to go south to Bavaria and the mythical redoubt. Only when Hitler ordered him to leave did Keitel go, for he needed the leader even when there was nothing to lead.

When asked at Nuremberg whether he would behave in the same fashion again, he answered:

> I would rather choose death than to let myself be drawn into the net of such pernicious methods. . . . I believed, but I erred, and I was not in a position to prevent what ought to have been prevented. That is my guilt. It is tragic to have to realize that the best I had to give as a soldier, obedience and loyalty, was exploited for purposes which could not be recognized at the time, and that I did not see that there is a limit set even for a soldier's performance of his duty. That is my fate.[69]

His fate had not been as high flown as his prose. He had servilely accepted the small and large ignominies of Hitler's scorn. Hitler said he had the brains of an usher in a moving picture theater, and Keitel, when asked how relations were between the Fuehrer and OKW, said, "I don't know, he tells me nothing; he only spits at me." [70] He had to do without smoking the cigars he was addicted to for hours at a time while he was with the Fuehrer, who would not permit Keitel to smoke in his presence. His proposal that General von Falkenhorst be given charge of the Norwegian campaign led the Fuehrer to interview Falkenhorst and then to appoint him, but he did so without consulting Keitel further. Keitel saw his brother officers defamed, called cowards, and some of them shot for disobedience when they ordered a retreat to save the lives of their troops. He sent the squad of SS men and Army officers to Field Marshal Rommel that gave Rommel the chance to poison himself or come before a people's court. And in a letter to his wife, he repeated the official story that this leader "blessed by God" had been critically injured in an automobile accident.[71] He was never permitted to criticize a proposal by the Fuehrer. His first loyalty was to Hitler, and he never deviated from his single-minded, blind, and numb devotion— and there is no evidence that he ever wanted to. He had begun by saying, "Yes, Sir," when the Fuehrer spoke, and at the end he was only a much-decorated and well-paid flunkey.

When he was found guilty and sentenced to hang, both Keitel and his wife refused to permit his attorney, Dr. Nelte, to appeal the sentence. Keitel admitted his guilt; the facts, he said, had been proven, but he hoped the court would understand that he too had been a victim both of the Fuehrer and of fate. A slightly different turn of the wheel and he would have been a farmer; another turn, an artillery officer or a general staff officer under Beck or Blomberg. He accepted his death sentence; all he wanted from the court was permission to be shot instead of dying by the rope. This symbolic token of a soldier's death was denied him.

ALFRED JODL

Alfred Jodl was resistant to the charisma of the Fuehrer and his National Socialism before Hitler became Chancellor. Even at the time of the solemn ceremonies at Potsdam, on March 21, 1933, where the President of the Reich and his Chancellor celebrated the rebirth of a German nationalist state, Hitler to Jodl was a mountebank, a charlatan. But Jodl struggled with conflicting emotions. Hindenburg, the revered Field Marshal and head of state, had chosen Hitler, and on February 1, the day after Hitler became Chancellor, Jodl told a group of officers that the Fuehrer had come to power legally; according to the constitution and the laws of the Reich he was the duly appointed political leader of the State. To criticize Hitler was to criticize Hindenburg.[72] That was the first time Jodl was forced to choose between duty and conscience so far as the Fuehrer was concerned, and this conflict gradually resolved as he came under the spell of Hitler after the bloodless victories of the years before the war and the lightning campaigns against Poland, Norway, and, above all, France. Jodl had fought in France in World War I, where soldiers had died by the hundreds of thousands to win a few yards of ground, but the Fuehrer's brilliant strategy conquered the entire country in a few weeks. He firmly believed Hitler to be what his most devoted admirers said he was, "the greatest military leader of all times" (*der groesste Feldherr aller Zeiten*), a phrase that gradually became more and more ironic as the victories dwindled and then turned into catastrophic defeats until the appellation itself was shortened to the derisive abbreviation Groefaz. But Hitler was never to become the Groefaz for Jodl, although he quarreled with the Fuehrer and he did something that few generals dared do—tell him he was wrong.

Not many such scenes took place. There could not be many, for a general who dealt with Hitler either obeyed or was retired or shot. But Jodl was one of the few ready to brave the Fuehrer's towering rages when Jodl knew a disastrous military decision was being made, although morally disastrous decisions were something else again. One head-on collision that nearly cost Jodl his job occurred in August, 1942. Hitler was furious with Field Marshal

List, commanding the newly formed Army Group A, for the campaign List was waging in the Caucasus. The Fuehrer had never liked List but had reluctantly appointed him on Keitel's and Halder's urging and because he had no likely candidate of his own at hand.*

Hitler, as always, was playing for high stakes: the oil area of Grozny and the mouth of the Volga at Astrakhan. Only the capture of Baku was he ready to postpone if necessary to the next year. But again it was getting late in the season and the Fuehrer was nervous and impatient. Hitler accused List of preventing an SS Panzerdivision from capturing Rostow and fumed at the uncertain progress of the operations on his mountain front. The Fuehrer sent Jodl by plane to a corps of List's army battling for the Caucasus passes, and Jodl, having talked with its commander, General Konrad, and the Field Marshal, agreed with them that the Fuehrer's orders to press forward at all costs were impossible to carry out. Jodl returned to the Fuehrer's headquarters and this conversation took place:

JODL: "I am convinced by my flight to the Caucasus that sending in parachute troops to Tuapse in all likelihood would lead to their destruction. The difficulty of the terrain is so great . . . that their being reinforced in time doesn't seem possible. A thrust of the mountain troops over the passes is just as unpromising. . . . While I was there the first snow had already fallen. The commanding general [Konrad] asked me to obtain permission to pull back the advance units that are two kilometers beyond the passes. I think that only a slow nibbling away on the road to Tuapse is possible. Whether that can be done this year seems very doubtful to me. Field Marshal List is of the same opinion"

HITLER: "Naturally, Jodl, the Field Marshal can scarcely be of any other opinion since this muddle is owing to his brilliant leadership. . . ."

JODL: "As far as I can see, List at the start did everything he should have. He had to expect the strongest resistance on the road and therefore he had to try to bypass it by going through the passes. The only mistake one can possibly reproach him for is that his forces are too massed and now oblique thrusts in the mountains are difficult to carry out. But that in the first place is the fault of the Army [OKH]."

HITLER: "Then his leadership was not stiff enough. . . ."

JODL: "One has to see these mountain roads, my Fuehrer, to be able to really judge all the trouble that a Panzerdivision runs into there."

HITLER: "I didn't send you, Jodl, to hear you report on all the difficulties. You were supposed to represent my view that paratroopers were to be landed in Tuapse. That was your job. Instead of that you come back completely under the influence of the front commanders and become the megaphone of these gentlemen. I didn't need to send you there for that. This morning the

* Colonel General Franz Halder was Chief of Staff of OKH. Goerlitz believed that Hitler's dislike of List went back to 1931, when List, as commander of the Infantry School in Dresden, had taken disciplinary measures against young officers (Faehnriche) for National Socialist activities.

mountain corps has already reported they have to bring back their advanced units on the passes. Apparently that's the only success of your flight. . . .

JODL (rising): "If you want to lose your paratroopers, then drop them on Tuapse. And the same thing will happen to the mountain troops if they have to go over the passes at this time of year. In addition I was not sent to carry orders but to examine the situation. If it was only necessary to transmit an order I wasn't needed."

HITLER: "You should have carried through my order against the resistance I so often encounter. That was your task, General Jodl. You haven't done it. Thank you very much." [73]

Jodl left the room without replying, and Hitler told his adjutant, General Rudolf Schmundt, that from then on he would not eat at the same table with Keitel and Jodl. Stenographers would henceforth be present so his words could not again be twisted. Keitel was sent to tell List that he was dismissed from his command, and Hitler planned to replace Jodl with Paulus as soon as Stalingrad was captured—which in August, 1942, seemed almost in Paulus' grasp. Hitler in his first rage thought of court-martialing Jodl, but he cooled off sufficiently to tolerate his presence. He refused to shake hands with either Jodl or Keitel, although all Keitel had done was to propose List as commander of the Caucasus Army.[74]

The more wrong decisions the Fuehrer made, the less opposition he could tolerate. On other occasions, too, Jodl took issue with Hitler. He heatedly argued against the Commando Order, although the Fuehrer was determined to issue it and was supported by Keitel.* Jodl also tried unsuccessfully to keep Halder at his post when Hitler decided to get rid of him. But these were sparse and minor differences over a long period of faithful collaboration, and when the attempt to kill Hitler was made on July 20, 1944, Jodl was appalled. He said he did not know whether he could bear to put on his uniform again. At the same time, he used the events of July 20 to teach the Fuehrer a lesson. Colonel von Bonin, who had been retired from the Army in 1933 for his unfriendly attitude toward National Socialism, was arrested as a suspicious character in July, 1944. Jodl liked and admired Bonin and he said to Hitler, "You cannot be surprised, my Fuehrer, if you throw a man like Bonin into jail without any proofs being found, and apparently only on the basis of rumor that the spirit of July 20 dominates the General Staff." [75]

Jodl never completely lost his National Socialist faith or his belief in its dogmas, nor did he ever learn to distinguish what was true from the Nazi claptrap. Even on September 6, 1945, in prison he said he thought that the mission of the Party had been to free Germany from the spiritual, cultural, and economic domination of the Jews. The Party had fought against com-

* According to the unpublished diary of Major General Engel, when Jodl was first told by Schmundt to issue the Commando Order, Jodl said, "Please give him my best regards but I will not issue an order like that." The Fuehrer thereupon drew up the order himself (N XV, p. 318).

munism and the Versailles Treaty, and although it had been without money or influence, it had won 96 per cent of the vote of the German people. It must therefore have had something, said Jodl, and he recited the standard justifications for the Nazi State of the thirties: National Socialism had brought unity to Germany, improved the health services and mother and child care, given vacations to workers, and restored Germany as a great power. It had produced "a friendly atmosphere" in England and France, and the hearts and the sympathies of all Germans had gone out to the Fuehrer. This, said Jodl, will always remain in the German memory.

He was still impressed with Churchill's praise of Hitler in 1938 and pointed out that any evidences of criminality in National Socialism obviously could not have been clear at that time. He thought, perhaps because he was so unskilled in these questions, that the fatal period had come with the political decisions of 1939, and he said he hoped the court would clarify the question of such guilt. Jodl said Hitler had feared the increasing strength of Russia. In any event, he had thought that what he called "the deep, methodical manner" of Hitler's thinking had prevented any rash action on the Fuehrer's part in 1939. But he added that in history and war, success alone counts and that this spoke against Adolf Hitler. He defended the seemingly unprovoked attacks that Hitler ordered under the doctrine of "national rights under an emergency," and said Germany had invaded neutrals only when it was known their territory would soon be made use of by the enemy. Jodl made no case for war, aggressive or otherwise; he said that people accepted it as a stroke of fate, as something like sickness or death, and the Germans loved war no more than any other people. They could only be blamed for electing a regime which they must have known would use force to regain their lost liberty and give the country a means for its development.[76] And he freely admitted he had shared these views. "My aims," he told the officers of the operations staff of OKW on July 24, 1944, "were by and large, the aims of the movement, since my thinking was always nationalistic, social and anti-Catholic." [77] His testimony in 1945 and 1946 was substantially the same as what he had written in the speeches and in his diary at the time the events took place.

Jodl was born in Wuerzburg on May 10, 1890. His father was a captain in the 2nd Bavarian Field Artillery Regiment; his mother was from an Austrian peasant family from Vilshofen on the Danube. The family was Catholic and thought of themselves as religious but, unlike most devout Bavarians, they did not go to church. One uncle was a professor of philosophy and another commanded the 4th Bavarian Artillery Regiment, which Jodl joined after he had taken his *Abitur* and attended the cadet school on a scholarship. His father's pension of 3839 RM a year as a retired artillery lieutenant colonel did not leave enough money over to pay his son's board, which came to 225 RM a month. Jodl's scholastic performance was satisfactory and unimpressive. At the Theresiengymnasium in Munich his marks were satisfactory to good—only in religion was he "very good." Later, as a cadet, he had an average record with a few punishments for minor escapades. Once he was given a twenty-four-hour house arrest and a cut in his rations for climbing out a window after the evening meal and smoking in the courtyard. The report noted as a mitigating circumstance that he had immediately admitted his guilt. Another time he came back from his Sunday leave twenty-five minutes late because he had missed a connecting train. The penalty this time was again less to eat and he was forbidden to leave the school grounds. His schoolwork here too was judged satisfactory, although he had to repeat the fourth class because, as he wrote in an autobiographical sketch in Nuremberg, he gave too much time to sports. His industry and attention were marked "great" and his general achievement "fair." [78]

In 1910 Jodl joined his artillery regiment as a Faehnrich or sublieutenant, and the next year he met his first wife, Irma Countess von Bullion, whom he married in 1913.* It was a successful marriage; the somewhat phlegmatic, intelligent young officer who liked women and dancing and society adored his attractive, vivacious wife.

At the very start of World War I, on August 24, 1914, Jodl, then a first lieutenant, was wounded by a grenade splinter. Partly recovered, he returned to his regiment in December but again had to be operated on and the splinter in his thigh finally removed. Jodl served as an artilleryman on both the Russian and the French fronts, but he found time between battles to read omnivorously in history, biography, and philosophy and to come to some conclusions about the future of Germany. He disapproved of the Kaiser's leadership and became antimonarchical; he felt that France and Germany must somehow settle their historic differences, that the eternal conflict was a disaster for both countries. After the armistice he thought of studying medicine but decided to stay on in the Army. His superiors thought well of him; an army report calls him "very thoughtful, decisive, energetic, a good sportsman [he was an enthusiastic mountain climber], eager, an excellent leader and suitable for higher command." [79]

Jodl was one of the few military men who was wholeheartedly in favor of the Ebert republican government; he had vague hopes for the development of a Social Democratic Party that would bridge the gap to the conservatives and bring unity to the country. But he was more directly concerned with the future of the Army. In 1920 he joined the secret general staff—camouflaged as the *Truppenamt*—that was forbidden under the Versailles Treaty. In 1927–28 he served as commander of a battery in the 7th Artillery Regiment; in 1929, then a major, he was assigned as an instructor to junior officers.

From 1932 to 1935 he was in the operations section of the Army; from 1935 to 1938, he was chief of the national defense section of the Wehrmacht-

---

* Near the end of the war, after the death of his first wife, Jodl married Luise von Benda.

samt—the office that later became OKW. In 1938 he was ordered to Vienna to become commander of an artillery division; in August, 1939, he was recalled to Berlin and OKW as chief of the operations staff (Wehrmacht-fuehrungsstab). He became general of artillery in 1940 and colonel general only in 1944, despite his proximity to the source of all promotions. Hitler never made him a field marshal, perhaps because Keitel already held that rank.

Jodl always was regarded as a competent officer.* General Ludwig Beck thought him the best of his age group, but they broke on what later developed to be one of the most vulnerable spots in Jodl's *Weltanschauung*: his naïveté in political matters. Jodl, unlike Beck, was able to accept the excesses of the Party and its formations after Hitler became Chancellor because he thought of them as the "children's sicknesses" of a revolution and he believed that only if the Army had the full confidence of the Fuehrer could it maintain its central importance in the German polity against the Party and the SS. Beck, on the other hand, after a brief period of optimism in 1933, regarded National Socialism as a threat to all the deeply rooted traditions of political order; and Hitler, it soon became clear to him, was basically an irresponsible, opportunistic leader who was likely to plunge the country into war by whim.

By 1938, Jodl found the Army's critical attitude to Hitler insupportable. Jodl's diary entry for August 10, 1938, read:

> I was summoned to the Berghof with senior officers of the Army. After dinner the Fuehrer talked for nearly three hours explaining his line of thought on political questions. Thereafter certain of the generals tried to point out to the Fuehrer that we were by no means ready. This was to say the least unfortunate. There are a number of reasons for this pusillanimous attitude which is unhappily fairly widespread in the Army General Staff. To begin with the General Staff is obsessed with memories of the past and instead of doing what it is told and getting on with its military job, thinks it is responsible for political decisions. It does get on with its job with all its old devotion but its heart is not in it because in the last analysis it does not believe in the genius of the Fuehrer.

> .   .   .

> It is tragic that the Fuehrer should have the whole nation behind him with the single exception of the Army generals. In my opinion it is only by action that they can now atone for their faults of lack of character and discipline. It is the same problem as in 1914. There is only one undisciplined element in the Army—the generals, and in the last analysis this comes from the fact that they are arrogant. They have neither confidence nor discipline because they cannot recognize the Fuehrer's genius. This is no doubt to

---

* In 1936, when he was a colonel, and again in 1937, he was offered the post of Chief of Staff of the Luftwaffe, which would have been a promotion. He declined because, he said, he felt bound to the Army (Letter to General Stumpf, July, 1936. Also diary entry April 10, 1937, 1780-PS).

some extent due to the fact that they still look on him as the Corporal of the First World War instead of the greatest statesman since Bismarck.[80]

Jodl, like Keitel, saw in Hitler a political and military genius; and as he stayed on year after year he could only keep increasing his own stakes in backing Hitler's gambles. The Fuehrer's headquarters, he said, was a cross between a monastery and a concentration camp, and he could bear to live in it solely because of his faith that the Fuehrer alone could rescue the Reich. The endless conferences, often with dilettantes like Goering overperforming, were hard to bear. At one meeting Goering complained that his Hermann Goering Division was being torn apart because of wrong decisions by the Army.* Jodl flared up. Every ensign, he told the Reichsmarschall, knew that it was sometimes necessary to break up divisions; they learned it in war school and anyone who has not understood such an elementary principle never learns it later. Everyone in the room looked at the Fuehrer to see how he would react, but all he said, turning to Jodl, was, "Please continue." [81] Jodl wrote to his wife from his cell in Nuremberg that he had known by 1942 that Germany could not win the war, but if this is true he did not permit the thought to affect anything he did or said. As the fortunes of war turned against Germany, Jodl could only write grimly that Germany must win and "if a soldier can't believe in that then he should shoot himself." And he bolstered his spirits with high hopes for the new weapons which, he thought, Hitler with his military genius would know how to use.

He talked with Hitler for the first time on the Fuehrer's train early in the Polish campaign, and he was with him steadily from then on. He came slowly under Hitler's spell, but gave his devotion unstintingly when he did. On October 28, 1939, he wrote to Karl Schwabe, the President of the German Police Force in Bruenn, Moravia, "You . . . will contribute your weighty share to keeping the Czechs at it and not letting them perk up." And then, thanking Dr. Schwabe for his words of appreciation, he deprecated his own "modest contribution in the shadow of the powerful personality of our Fuehrer." [82] On March 4, 1940, he wrote in his diary, "The Fuehrer gave his wonderful talk on the occasion of the heroes' memorial day." In Russia in the winter of 1941–42, when catastrophe suddenly threatened the German armies, Jodl said he had never had more admiration for the Fuehrer; the strength of his iron will had held the weakening front all along the line against a Bolshevik breakthrough.

* The Hermann Goering Division was formed in 1942 from the Reichsmarschall's personal regiment and was listed in typical Goering fashion as a "parachute-tank division." Since its officers mostly came from the Luftwaffe, they had little or no training in infantry warfare and it suffered high losses. Nevertheless, the division was later expanded to a corps, but in 1944, when Goering was no longer in favor, it was turned over to the Army. Before then it fought under Kesselring in Italy (Kesselring himself was a field marshal of the Luftwaffe), and Goering did not hesitate at times to give the division direct orders. (Frido von Senger und Etterlin, *Krieg in Europa* [Cologne-Berlin: Kiepenheuer and Witsch, 1960], pp. 162, 176. Westphal, *op. cit.*, p. 90.)

A year later in a speech to assembled Gauleiters in Munich on November 7, 1943, he said that the National Socialist movement had prepared the way for the liberation from Versailles, the reawakening of the will to fight, and the rearming of the German people. Then he said:

> My most profound confidence is however based upon the fact that at the head of Germany there stands a man who by his entire development, his desires, and striving can only have been destined by fate to lead our people into a brighter future. In defiance of all views to the contrary I must here testify that he is the soul not only of the political but also of the military conduct of the war and that the force of his willpower and the creative riches of his thought animate and hold together the whole of the German Armed Forces, with respect to strategy, organization and munitions of war. Similarly the unity of political and military command which is so important is personified by him in a way such as has never been known since the days of Frederick the Great. . . . A Europe under the whip of American Jews or Bolshevik commissars is unthinkable.

He testified, he told them, at this hour "not with the lips but with my deepest heart: that our trust and faith in the Fuehrer is boundless. . . . that we will cast off all who are soft and forget their duties. . . . that we shall win because we must win since otherwise world history would have lost all meaning." * [83]

Jodl was always pragmatic about the rules of war and international law, and he accepted, for the most part, Hitler's readiness to transgress them when it seemed necessary or useful. He thought Germany had made a mistake in World War I in admitting violations of international agreements; if, for example, a German hospital ship was sunk, a British hospital ship might be torpedoed as a reprisal, but the Germans should say it was a mistake. Even at Nuremberg he said that up to March, 1944—the time of the shooting of the fifty RAF fliers—the Fuehrer had never issued a criminal order. Hitler had done nothing that could not be justified under international law or as a reprisal.[84]

On the stand he made a good defense of many of his military activities—he had, like Keitel, opposed the Commando Order and the Sagan shootings—but as soon as the barbed questioning of his British cross-examiner dealt with other than military affairs, Jodl made a poor impression. Questioning Jodl on the *Anschluss* with Austria, the British prosecutor, Mr. Roberts, asked: "So the Armed Forces of Germany then marched into Austria? That is right?"

JODL: "That is right; the Wehrmacht marched in."
ROBERTS: "And Austria, from that day, received all the benefits of National Socialism, is that right?"

---

* Jodl said at Nuremberg that these were merely notes for a speech, but in any event his sentiments when he gave the talk were undoubtedly the same.

JODL: "That is a political question. At any rate it could perhaps have become the happiest country on earth."

ROBERTS: "I wasn't asking what it could have become, but what it received. It received the SS, the Gestapo, the concentration camps, the suppression of opponents, and the persecution of Jews, didn't it?"

JODL: "Those are questions with which I did not concern myself. Those questions you have to put to the competent authorities." [85]

The competent authority was, of course, the Fuehrer, and it was convenient for Jodl to believe that when Schuschnigg was deposed he was placed under "honorary arrest." Such notions enabled him to live in the military compartment of his mind, to rejoice in the reception of the German troops by the cheering, flower-throwing population of Austria and to ignore the Jews cleaning up the streets with toothbrushes. Competent authorities or the "children's sicknesses" of Nazism would account for such events, which in any case were insignificant compared with the historical moment of German reunion.

As time went on, Jodl's attitude, like Keitel's, reflected the mounting tension and brutality of the war Hitler was waging. In his diary entry of March 4, 1940, before the Norwegian campaign, Jodl noted that "Himmler or Canaris should provide personnel who are familiar with the Hague rules"—in itself an interesting observation—but to believe for a moment that Himmler, who was already operating savagely in Poland, might have people under him concerned with the Hague or any other rules of international law was at least naïve. Himmler, however, was also one of those who were competent in their specialized fields, chosen by the Fuehrer.

Once the war against Russia started, and with it the well-organized guerrilla resistance that was so important to the Soviet strategy, the no-holds-barred directives from OKW became explicit. On July 23, 1941, Jodl ordered on behalf of the Fuehrer:

> In view of the vast size of the occupied areas in the East the forces available for establishing security in these areas will be sufficient only if all resistance is punished not by legal prosecution of the guilty but by the spreading of such terror by the occupying power as is appropriate to eradicate every inclination to resist among the population. The competent commanders must find the means of keeping order . . . not by demanding more security forces but by applying suitable Draconic methods . . .[86]

On June 12, 1942, he noted in his diary:

> The German field gendarmes have arrested a Ustashi company for atrocities against the civil population in East Bosnia; they have disarmed and imprisoned them.* The Fuehrer has not approved this measure ordered by the commander of the 708th Division because it undermines the author-

* The Ustashi were Croat militia recruited by Ante Pavelić, chief of the Croat state, who fought on the German side.

ity of the Ustashi. . . . This will do more damage to peace and order in Croatia than the unrest caused by the atrocities.[87]

On September 16, 1944, he wrote:

The enemy is on German soil. Fanatical determination is needed. Every pillbox, city and village should become a fortress to make the enemy smash himself to bits and Germans should be ready to die in hand to hand fighting. We can no longer have large-scale operations. All we can do is to hold our positions or die. The officer corps is responsible for kindling this fanaticism. Anyone who fails, whether he is an officer or enlisted man, should be eliminated or called to account.[88]

Two months later he was echoing Hitler's savage orders to the Army:

If, as a result of negligence or lack of energy on the part of commanders or troops, the enemy succeeds in breaking into the fortified zone [of the Siegfried Line] that constitutes a *crime* of incalculable consequence. The Fuehrer is determined . . . to bring those responsible to justice immediately.[89]

Jodl was never to believe himself guilty of any of the crimes with which he was charged. The most he conceded even to himself was that the Germans had not clung to justice as they should have in the conduct of the war; even if the enemy had committed its wrongful acts first, the Germans would have done better to hold to what was right than to rely on force.[90] As his lawyer pointed out, Jodl had had three weeks to burn his documents before he surrendered to the Allies but he turned them all over to his captors. He said at Nuremberg, quoting General Eisenhower, that not only are soldiers presented with the war they must fight but with the check afterward. He regarded all the campaigns on which Germany embarked as basically justified. In Norway, he believed—and here the evidence bears him out—the Germans had merely landed a few days before the British and the French. He believed both Belgium and Holland to be unneutral, allowing French and British planes to fly over their territory, taking part in conferences with the General Staff of the Allies, and in his view thus making possible a strike at the vulnerable Ruhr. He had opposed aid to the Italians fighting Greece, his lawyer said, but here as elsewhere Hitler made the decision. He thought that General Dušan Simović's *coup d'état* in Yugoslavia, which resulted in a complete shift from a pro-German policy to an anti-German one, was instigated by British and Russian agents, that the German troops in Bulgaria were thereby threatened, and that the Russian telegram of friendship to Belgrade and the Yugoslav deployment of troops had justified Hitler's decision to attack. But he had urged that an ultimatum be delivered before the German armies invaded and before the German bombs came down on Belgrade. Its not being sent was another decision made by the competent authority.

Jodl was always convinced that Germany was fighting a preventive war in

Russia. A great many generals and observers, including Jan Masaryk, agreed that the German invasion had forestalled the Russian Army, that Stalin had every intention of ordering an attack on Germany, and that Hitler had surprised him on June 22, 1941. The main body of evidence is against this thesis but there was nevertheless seemingly a good deal of evidence to sustain it. The Russians had built air fields on the territory bordering the German lines, military roads had been constructed, and some German generals thought that the positions the Russians had overrun in their first attack had been designed as jumping-off places rather than defense points. Masaryk, bitter opponent of Hitler as he was, credited the Fuehrer's extraordinary intuition with having divined Stalin's plans, and anti-Nazi German scholars years after Jodl's execution believed as firmly as he that the German drive into Russia had merely anticipated a Russian attack on Germany.[91] In addition, the nature of the war in Russia, the fierce ideological struggle of two conflicting faiths, seemed to Jodl to justify the harsh measures that were adopted.

Correct and meticulous in carrying out his duties, Jodl acted always under the overriding belief that Hitler was a genius, the savior of a country that would have otherwise fallen prey to Jewry and Marxism, and his criticisms of the Fuehrer had to do only with the success or failure of specific military actions. Once unconditional surrender was announced as an Allied goal, Jodl said at Nuremberg, Germany had no alternative to fighting on, but he was for fighting just as desperately before Casablanca as after. He hoped vaguely that the fundamental contradictions between Russia and the West might bring some sort of compromise peace. But he had no notion of how the rest of the world had reacted to the diabolism and atrocities of the Nazi regime and, by extension, of the German Army, in which he played a leading part. He declared at Nuremberg that he had not known of the exterminations and the Einsatz killings; even if this was true, he had known of much else and had either looked the other way or countersigned the orders.

Jodl's anti-Semitism had no personal feeling in it; he could be polite, even friendly, to individual Jews. One Jewish woman offered to testify on his behalf at Nuremberg; a Mrs. Moskovitch wrote to Jodl's lawyer in November and said she would like to tell how General Jodl and his wife had tried to help her in March, 1939, when she was attempting to leave Germany. But Jodl had accepted the thesis of the collective responsibility of Jewry for Germany's troubles before and after World War I. At Nuremberg he referred to the Jews, "who wanted the destruction of Germany," and he was never to rid himself of this central article of the Nazi creed, nor was he able to comprehend his own part in the excesses of the war that Hitler conducted. After his arrest he wrote to his wife that he thought he might be required to be more than a witness in the forthcoming trials at Nuremberg, but he never for a moment regarded himself as a war criminal because he thought he had done no more than obey orders from the duly elected head of state, orders with which he had often disagreed and in some instances which he had attempted to circumvent. What else could he have done? he asked. He had not been allowed to resign; he could only protest and then obey. He pointed out, too, at Nuremberg, that the prosecution could thank its own obedient soldiers for being in a position to prosecute.[92]

One of Jodl's two lawyers, Professor Franz Exner, who like Hermann Jahrreiss—the associate counsel—was not a practicing lawyer but an Akademiker, a distinguished professor of law, had agreed to take the case only, he said, because he had known Jodl for many years and was convinced of his impeccable character. Exner and the general became closer friends in the course of the trial, when Exner employed Frau Jodl in his office, and Exner conducted a spirited and erudite defense of his client—and an impassioned one, for he believed deeply in the innocence of the man he was defending. Allied officers showed sympathy for Jodl. The American guards presented arms when he left the prison at Flensburg, a young officer told Frau Jodl that he wished her husband well, and an American colonel called him "a fine soldier." But following their capture and early imprisonment at Flensburg, Jodl and Keitel were sent to the collecting depot of the former Nazi great, with the code name of Ashcan, at Mondorf in Luxembourg. No longer were they treated as defeated but respectable military men or prisoners of war. At Ashcan and at Dustbin near Frankfort they officially became what they were to be until the end of their days: major war criminals. When they arrived at the Palace of Justice in Nuremberg, this verdict was confirmed: "You are no longer Colonel General Jodl, but war criminal Jodl," the commander of the prison told him, whereupon both Jodl and Keitel had their shoulder bars ripped off.

Frau Jodl and Frau Keitel shared the burdens of the wives whose husbands were to be tried; they lived together in Berchtesgaden before the trial started and Frau Jodl went to Nuremberg. The families of the accused had a grim time and received a mixed reaction from both the Germans and the conquerors. Frau Goering one day was looking with her little daughter, Edda, at a newspaper picture of her husband when an American woman journalist walked up to her and drew her finger across the neck of the Reichsmarschall. Germans were often openly hostile to all the accused, including these defeated generals who had lost their glittering uniforms and the war; they were easy scapegoats for the universal suffering. A German lawyer objected to eating with Frau Jodl because, he said, she was the wife of a war criminal; an American told her there was no difference between an SD man and her husband. But one day on her way to the prison Frau Jodl was introduced to an American captain and although she did not know whether to offer him her hand, he took hers in his and said, "Ma'am, I wish to God your husband gets through all this safely." Even victims of the Nazis could feel the same way. Frau Jodl received a letter from a French woman who wrote: "Jodl was a real soldier. He fought for his country as have soldiers of all times. Part of my family died in concentration camps. I ask you to believe in my profound and sympathetic sympathy. Anne Marie de Pontavice." And from other German officers awaiting their trials—Manstein, Wagner, Westphal, Kesselring, Brauchitsch—Jodl was given two precious packages of cigarettes addressed: "To our dear Jodl." Admiral Raeder, who had denounced Keitel, praised Jodl in his interrogation for his soldierly qualities and his courage in standing up to Hitler.

Jodl had married his second wife, Luise von Benda, on the day that General Patton crossed the Rhine at Remagen, but they had spent very little time together as the German war machine careened to its end. After Jodl's arrest, Frau Jodl had to find a room for herself in a battered house in Nuremberg, where she was fortunate enough to get a job on Exner's staff. She had to hitchhike on the Autobahn when she had to return to Bavaria to renew ration coupons. She paid for her transportation with the American cigarettes that were part of her pay.

Jodl, however, despite his inner certainty of innocence, had initialed clearly illegal orders, such as the one Keitel issued on May 13, 1941, for the shooting without trial of enemy civilians guilty of offenses against German troops.[93] He had forwarded Hitler's orders that a capitulation of neither Moscow nor Leningrad should be accepted if it were offered; he had passed along the order for executing Commandos; he had told the Gauleiters in November, 1943, that forced labor was to be recruited with remorseless vigor in France and Belgium, that too many people among the population were doing nothing.[94] He had proposed that the Commissar Order, issued before the war started, be defended as a retaliatory measure. He had sent along the order for a scorched earth policy in Norway that had resulted, according to the Norwegian Government's estimate, in damage to or destruction of 30,000 houses and the forcible evacuation of the population that lived in the northern districts.

A defense could be made for Jodl's part in such measures. In the case of Leningrad and Moscow, his lawyer pointed out, the commanders of those cities never offered to surrender so the charge was made for a crime that was not committed. As for the Commissar Order, he had had no part in drafting it, although he had been shown a copy. Jodl said the Germans were aware of how Communists operated—he mentioned the Munich Raeterepublik (see Rosenberg, Chapt. 4; Frick, Chapt. 7)—but he himself had wanted to wait to see what they did in this war before applying such measures, and if they acted as they had before, he would then take this as a reprisal measure. The translation, too, had shown Jodl's marginal note in an unnecessarily bad light. He had written: "*Man zieht es am besten auf als Repressalie.*" This had been translated in English as: "It is therefore best to brand . . ." whereas, as Exner said, the plain sense was "It is best to handle it as a reprisal." "*Aufziehen,*" said Jodl, meant arrange, not conceal, which would have been "*vortaeuschen.*" Jodl, in short, had expected the kind of savage warfare that developed in the East, but the orders which he initialed helped to produce it.[95]

Jodl had flatly refused to draft the Commando Order, but here again he was of two minds. He knew that many of the British Commandos were acting in an illegal fashion and thus, in his view, placed themselves outside military law; but he also knew that under the Hitler order all Commandos were to be executed no matter how they behaved. It was this order that Jodl objected to but nevertheless distributed, although he attempted to keep it confined to troops who had acted "in an unsoldierly fashion."

In every country, Jodl said, the population was forced to work; and in the case of fortifications in France and Belgium, the population had often worked with enthusiasm because they hoped they might thus spare the areas where they lived from the destruction of the invasion.[96] In the case of Norway, as the Germans were retreating to the still incompleted Lyngen Line, the order for the evacuation of the population, Exner said, was given to prevent endangering the population in the battle area; when houses were destroyed, he added, this was not done wantonly but to prevent their use by partisans and the advancing Russians. Such destruction may be carried out "legally" under international law when it is essential to military operations. Jodl's brother Ferdinand was a general in command of German troops in northern Norway. He protested heatedly against the order and discussed with his brother Alfred how it could be softened; the demolitions were carried out as humanely as possible under the circumstances. The Fuehrer had ordered the destruction on the advice of his civilian commissar, Terboven; Jodl had not been consulted but had only drafted and distributed the order and had done his best to hold the demolitions to a minimum.* [97]

The prosecution charged that Jodl had used his position, his personal influence, and his close relationship to the Fuehrer to help the Nazi conspirators come to power and consolidate their control over Germany; he had promoted the preparations for aggressive war in contradiction to international treaties, agreements, and assurances, and he had committed the kind of war crimes and crimes against humanity that have been described.[98] In his summary of July 26, 1946, Jackson accused Jodl, as a member of the Defense Council, of having made in January, 1934, a mobilization calendar for 240,000 industrial establishments and of wanting to keep to the Geneva Convention as a dodge—using its advantages but by no means being limited by it. [99] Jodl was one of the greatly needed experts, said Jackson, along with Keitel and Raeder and Doenitz and others without whom the Nazis could not have operated. He was one of those who wanted the land and goods of their

* A later American court at Nuremberg found Colonel General Lothar Rendulic, who had carried out the order, not guilty of having caused needless destruction in Norway and Jodl's brother, when tried before a Norwegian court, was not even charged with the crime (IZG Jodl, p. 35; Munich Spruchkammer, *U.S. vs. List, Trials of War Criminals*, p. 1296).

neighbors. No soldier, he said, stood above Keitel and Jodl in the military hierarchy. And who nourished Hitler's notion of Germany's invincibility if not these two and Raeder and Doenitz? [100]

Sir Hartley Shawcross, following Mr. Justice Jackson, accused Jodl and the other members of the High Command of having had a chief role in Germany's rearming, of having taken part in "the first step"—the reoccupation of the Rhineland—and in the next step—the occupation of Austria—and then in the occupation of the whole of Czechoslovakia, as well as in the later aggressions against Poland and other countries. "The killing of combatants in war is justifiable, both in international and in municipal law, only where the war itself is legal," he said. "But where a war is illegal, as a war started not only in breach of the Pact of Paris but without any sort of warning or declaration clearly is, there is nothing to justify the killing, and these murders are not to be distinguished from those of any other lawless robber bands." [101]

The defense not only of Keitel and Jodl but of all the accused in the matter of aggressive war was undertaken by Professor Hermann Jahrreiss, an authority on international law, one of Jodl's defending lawyers. Jahrreiss argued long and learnedly before a session of the court (when the chief prosecutors of Britain, France, and the United States were absent) that the whole system of collective security had broken down, as was evident in the American declaration of neutrality in 1939 and in the Soviet position with regard to the German-Polish conflict. The British Government itself had acknowledged in September, 1939, that the security machinery of the League had not functioned and in fact had broken down, and as a result, members of the League had declared their neutrality—a view that Neville Chamberlain had stated plainly on February 22, 1938, before the *Anschluss* with Austria.

The British, Jahrreiss pointed out, had made reservations to their adherence to the Kellogg-Briand Pact, retaining their right to a free hand in areas where they had a special interest. The right of any sovereign state to wage a defensive war and to decide whether it was a defensive war was "an inalienable right to all states; without that right sovereignty does not exist." The complete uncertainty about the meaning of the obligations of the treaty was clear in Kellogg's own statement in his note of June 25, 1928, to the nine signatories: "The right of self-defense . . . is inherent in every sovereign state and is implicit in every treaty. Every nation . . . is alone competent to decide whether circumstances require recourse to war in self-defense."

American senators in the debate over ratification of the pact declared it to be no more than an international embrace and a fruitful source of a future war, a gigantic piece of hypocrisy, a guarantee of the British world empire and of the unjust *status quo* of the Versailles Treaty on behalf of England and France. One American authority, Philip Marshall Brown, declared that the pact, with its ineptness, had indeed merely brought into the world the horrible specter of "undeclared war." But leaving aside the Italian-Ethiopian

War, where collective security had failed either to prevent the war or to prevent the Italian victory, nowhere had a possibility arisen of the punishment of a state for breach of the treaty—not to mention the punishment of individuals. A breach of the treaty would be any violation of international law—it was no more than a delict, an offense, but not a crime, not a punishable act. In any event, Jahrreiss said, sentences against individuals for breach of the peace between states would be "completely new under the aspect of law, something revolutionarily new." [102]

Answering the scholarly historical summary of Professor Jahrreiss, Sir Hartley said it might be true that a sovereign state alone could decide whether it was threatened by an enemy and thus take recourse to arms, and it might also be true that under international law a decision to go to war was an act of state and not a crime of individuals. But, he stated, under the charter of this tribunal the planning, preparation, initiation, or waging of a war of aggression or of a war in violation of international treaties was a crime, and Jodl and the others had committed it. They were unable to show that their wars were neither wars of aggression nor wars that had not taken place in violation of treaties. What were they trying to do, asked Sir Hartley, deny the jurisdiction of the tribunal in this matter? The right to self-defense could no more be misused by a state than by an individual, and a state like an individual made a decision to act on its own risk. The first man to have been accused of murder may have complained that no court had tried such a case before. The only innovation the charter had introduced was to provide the long-overdue machinery to enforce an already existing law. As for the acts of these individuals, they, like pirates or spies or blockade runners, could be punished under international law. If a state, said Sir Hartley, sent a body of people into the territory of another state to murder and rob, could anyone argue that the individual member of such a group would not be punished merely because he had acted on behalf of a state? [103]

The defense of superior orders was excluded by the charter. Under Article 8 a penalty might be made milder because of the necessity for obeying, but there was no rule for finding immune to punishment those who obeyed an order against the natural law out of which international law developed, even though the order might be legal in the country where it was given. If international law was to be applied at all, it must be superior to municipal law in this respect. And by any test of international law, of common conscience, of elementary humanity, such orders were illegal. These men had created the dictatorship under which they now sought to hide their responsibility. Even if, as Jodl said, they had been arrested for disobedience, would that not have been better than carrying out such orders? But in fact they had forged these plans as well as carried them out. They were the ones above all who might have advised, restrained, or halted Hitler instead of encouraging him. [104]

Shawcross was intent on hanging not only Keitel and Jodl, Doenitz and Raeder, but the German Army and Navy. The High Command and Kaltenbrunner, he said, bore responsibility for the Commando Order of October 18, 1942, that provided for the execution not of spies but of soldiers in uniform. Keitel had signed the *Nacht und Nebel* decree of December 7, 1941, and had made the curious comment when he appeared before the Nuremberg court that "penal servitude would be considered dishonorable by these patriots. By going to Germany they would suffer no dishonor." Keitel, too, Shawcross charged, had said in answer to a Luftwaffe general's objection that it was too complicated to hand over striking railway workers to the SD, ". . . other effective measures are to be taken ruthlessly and independently . . ." [105] Thus Jodl and Keitel's case and that of Doenitz and Raeder were equated to the lowest common denominator of Kaltenbrunner.

Jodl's chief defense counsel, Franz Exner, defended him with energy and skill. Jodl, Exner pointed out, had never been a "Party general." Aside from the officers among the accused he had known only Frick, whom he had met on official business, and he had tried to prevent the naming of a "Nazi general" like Reichenau to the post of Commander in Chief of the Army. He had tried to block off Himmler's SS and the Party apparatus from the Wehrmacht. Exner said that Jodl's job had nothing to do with plans for waging aggressive war and that up to 1938 Germany could put into the field not a sixth of the forces her likely enemies—France, Poland, and Czechoslovakia—could muster. In 1937 Germany had but one battleship and even in 1939 had not more than twenty-six ocean-going U-boats—less than one-tenth those of England and France. The only war plans were those for defending her eastern borders. No deployment plan existed against Austria. "Case Otto" referred to an intervention there in the event that a Hapsburg restoration should be attempted, but no plan was worked out—intervention was merely a possibility.[106] Jodl had not been present at the meeting at Obersalzberg of February 12, 1938, and Hitler's telephone call to be prepared to march into Austria two days later had taken him by surprise. The troops were completely unprepared to wage war; the Austrians had crossed the frontier to Germany to greet them and Austrian soldiers had joined them in the march to Vienna. Regarding Czechoslovakia, the Fuehrer had said, he would under all circumstances avoid a conflict with the West and would achieve a peaceful solution. Jodl's suggestion that an incident could be created as a motive to invade Czechoslovakia was no more than the *ruse de guerre* used by all armies, including those of ancient Greece, but in fact no such incident had occurred. The Sudetenland had greeted the arrival of the German troops with the same enthusiasm as Austria, and Jodl had taken no part in the invasion of the rest of Czechoslovakia ordered by Hitler in March, 1939.[107]

As for Poland, when Jodl left Berlin no plan existed for invasion, and when he returned on August 23, 1939, the plan in which he had taken no part was already prepared. The fact brought out by the prosecution that he had been on the Fuehrer's train that served as headquarters on September

3, 1939, is scarcely a serious charge against a soldier. The Germans had every legal right to send their freighters into Norwegian territorial waters, and the English interference with this traffic was a clear breach of Norway's neutrality. Jodl was convinced even after the war, said Exner, that the Germans had forestalled an English landing at the last moment, and the decision for the German invasion had been Hitler's, not his; Jodl had merely agreed that it was essential.[108]

The Italians had invaded Greece—or had attempted to—in early October, 1940. When Hitler came to the aid of Mussolini in late March, 1941, Greek territory was already being used by England, British troops having landed on the mainland on March 3, 1941, after Crete had come under British control. With Salonika and other Greek territory that could be used by RAF bombers in British hands, the danger to Germany's sources of Rumanian oil was acute. World War I had made the results of such an occupation clear. Hitler's decision to attack Yugoslavia, after the Simović putsch had drawn that country from its pro-Axis policy, was made the day following the coup. The German Army had made no preparations for this attack, and Jodl had wanted an ultimatum sent to Yugoslavia, "to make things unambiguous," but Hitler would not even consider the idea. Again Jodl thought Hitler had correctly estimated the Russian participation in the revolutionary change of policy in Yugoslavia—which Jodl thought was borne out by the Soviet telegram of friendship and the eventual pact of friendship established between Belgrade and Moscow.[109]

As for the Russian campaign, Exner said, the Germans in May and June, 1940, had only from five to six divisions in the East, while thirty Soviet divisions had marched into Bessarabia. Although Russia, it seemed to Jodl, should have been one of the countries making common cause against England,[110] relations between Berlin and the Kremlin had deteriorated as Soviet pressure increased in the Balkans and in the Baltic countries.* The ten infantry divisions and two panzer divisions Germany had sent to the General Government of Poland were there, Jodl said, to protect the oil regions of Rumania against a sudden Russian attack. The unpleasant evidences of Russian plans increased after the Vienna arbitration of August 30, 1940, when Germany had guaranteed the borders of Rumania—a move clearly directed against Russia. Jodl believed with Hitler that the Soviet Union had determined to destroy Germany at a time when the latter nation was fully engaged against England.[111]

A German intelligence report of September 18, 1940, tells of anti-German propaganda being used in the Red Army, the Russian assumption of German intentions to attack, and the thesis that the German-Russian conflict was

* Although Jodl did not say so, Molotov in his visit to Berlin had demanded what a later German historian was to call the equivalent of the trophies of a victorious war from Germany—control of the Skagerrak as well as the Dardanelles (Hans-Guenter Seraphim and Andreas Hillgruber, "Hitlers Entschluss zum Angriff auf Russland," in Vierteljahrshefte fuer Zeitgeschichte, Vol. II, No. 3, 1954).

inevitable.[112] Thus Hitler had reckoned with a Russian attack in the summer of 1941 or the winter of 1941–42. The failure of the talks with Molotov led the Fuehrer to order on December 18, 1940, the military preparations for the attack, but these were to be changed if the situation clarified.* Jodl, as a specialist, had pointed out the formidable military risk of a war with Russia, which should only be decided on when all political means of averting a Russian attack were exhausted. He was convinced that Hitler had exhausted such political attempts. In early February, 1941, Russia had 150 divisions, two-thirds of its entire forces on the German front. The telegram of friendship Russia sent to Yugoslavia after the anti-German putsch of March 27, 1941, was the last straw for Hitler.[113]

A genuine preventive war is one sanctioned even by the Kellogg-Briand Pact, and the German generals had trustworthy reports of Russian war preparations which were later confirmed when they invaded Russia. The large number of new air fields near the border and the German maps in the hands of the Russian staff led Field Marshal Gerd von Rundstedt and General (then Lieutenant Colonel) August Winter, among others, to the same conclusions. Jodl was certain Hitler would never had gone to war with Russia were he not utterly convinced no other alternative remained; the risks of a two-front war were abundantly clear to him. Jodl's job was to support the High Command through the operational leadership of the Wehrmacht. He was the adviser to the Fuehrer in all operational questions; as in the case of every country that has this system he served not in a commanding but in an advisory, assisting, executive function. He was not Keitel's chief of staff but chief of the most important department of OKW; he had nothing to do with the other departments of OKW. He was not Keitel's representative in Berlin; Admiral Canaris was. In the Fuehrer's headquarters was only the Armed Forces Operations Staff, for whom Jodl reported directly to the Fuehrer. He had no command authority whatever, and no soldier decides whether a war is to be fought or not, only how it is to be fought. The job of a general to prepare and if necessary carry out war plans is very different from inciting the political arm of the government to go to war.[114]

It was Jodl's duty to make plans, and whether or not they were used did not depend on him. As for his participation in aggressions, he first had to be able to recognize them as such. From the reports reaching him—and he believed them—the enemy either was acting in an unneutral fashion or was preparing to attack. It is a political question to be decided by the political authority whether or not to go to war. "One should consider," Exner said, "the extraordinary consequences which would arise from a different conception: the competent authority would declare war, and the Chief of the General Staff, who regards this war as contrary to international law, would

* Actually preparations started well before then. *Cf.* Gerhard L. Weinberg, *Germany and the Soviet Union 1939–1941, Studies in East European History,* Vol. I (Leiden: Brill, 1954).

fail to cooperate. Or the Chief of [the] General Staff happens to be of the same opinion as the head of the State, but one of the army commanders has objections and refuses to march, while another one has doubts and has to think it over first." Even for scholars of international law the concepts of aggressive and illegal war are completely unclarified; therefore, how can a general who lives far from these considerations make a legal investigation of them? And even if he has recognized the war as illegal, he finds himself in a tragic situation. Exner said, "On one hand there is his obvious duty toward his own country, which he has taken an oath as a soldier to fulfill, on the other side this obligation not to support any war of aggression, a duty which forces him to commit high treason and desertion, and to break his oath." In fact, he added, the situation is that as long as there is no superstate authority impartially prescribing the duty of an individual and protecting him against punishment for high treason, no officer can be held criminally responsible for a breach of the peace; on the one hand the prosecution reproached the generals for having been politicians as well as soldiers, and on the other it insisted that they should have opposed the political leadership, that they should have been not merely soldiers but also politicians.[115]

Jodl asked for nineteen witnesses at Nuremberg but he was permitted only four; the others testified by means of interrogations. The man who was slated to succeed him in 1942, Field Marshal Paulus, came to Nuremberg and told what he knew of the criminal war in which Hitler had engaged his country but did not implicate either Jodl or Keitel in any specific criminal acts. To the Germans who observed him closely in the courtroom Paulus seemed to be under heavy psychological pressure, owing no doubt in part to the fact that he would in due course return to the Soviet Union.

Jodl defended himself vigorously both on the witness stand and in interrogations on the first two charges against himself and Keitel and the General Staff. A soldier, he too maintained, cannot be held responsible for political decisions of the head of state; he cannot weigh the pros and cons of why he draws up war plans and carries them out. Discussing aggressive warfare, he said in his interrogation of August 30, 1945, it was never legitimate to attack a country of whose neutrality one is sure, such as Switzerland; but Belgium and Holland, he thought, were pro-Ally and their territory might be used and their sovereignty infringed upon by the English without serious resistance on their part. Asking about the attack on France, the American prosecutor said, "I take it that your attitude concerning the attack on France was that the most favorable operation should be used regardless of whether it meant the invasion of countries with which Germany was at peace." Jodl replied, "I do not hold this opinion unreservedly, but I do hold that when a nation is fighting for its life it has the right to use such means as it can to carry on warfare."

The prosecution, under its preconception of a conspiracy to commit aggression, reported in its account of the interrogation of August 27, 1945, that Jodl "admitted" he had tested the Czech defenses, which were similar to the Maginot Line, as a preliminary measure for the attack on France. Describing an interrogation of October 1, 1945, it said that he had "admitted" that Barbarossa was the code name for the Russian operation. Jodl had also "admitted" in an interrogation of August 29, 1945, "that he engaged in the planning of operations for the Russian campaign." A more serious charge, that he had said that as far as he was concerned partisans should be drawn and quartered, he admitted, too, in his interrogation of November 8, 1945, but he said this had been merely a joke, an attempt to make the needless destruction of villages Hitler had in mind seem absurd, and he pointed out that he had succeeded in persuading the Fuehrer to agree that villages would not be burned down once the local fighting was over.

Hitler's decisions, Jodl said, were final and they were his entirely; once they were made, no further discussion was tolerated. The Fuehrer got the material he needed from his subordinates, brooded over it sometimes for days, and then proceeded to give the order which would then be worked out by Jodl's chief of staff, General Warlimont. Jodl then would edit the typescript and give it to the Fuehrer, who made further changes.* The early plans for the Western campaign, for example, were changed completely by Hitler, who adopted Manstein's idea of breaking through the Ardennes Forest and then turning west to the coast, thus reversing the old Schlieffen plan of keeping the right flank strong and attacking Paris in an enveloping movement.[116]

Jodl's day in his Nuremberg cell began at 6:30 A.M. when his glasses and a pencil were returned to him, along with his suspenders. He then made his bed and read until 7:30, when he went to the barber shop to be shaved. Breakfast followed, after which he swept out his cell, cleaned his boots, and brushed his uniform, which was brought from the common room where the prisoners' clothes were kept. He then did sitting-up exercises, washed, and dressed. Neither he nor the other prisoners got the full American ration, and he lost fifteen pounds during his imprisonment. He spent his time reading and trying to think his way through the catastrophe. One of the books he read was A Tale of Two Cities, another was Hamsun's The Wanderer.

In a guessing game the newspapermen played, he was given a small chance of being found not guilty; only thirteen thought he would be sentenced to death, as against fourteen for Doenitz, thirteen for Raeder, and twenty-nine for Keitel. Jodl was able to bear his fate with considerable equanimity. He took sleeping pills only occasionally after sentence of death was pronounced upon him. He did not want to appeal his sentence, although at the urging of his wife and his lawyer he did eventually permit an appeal to be made.

* Jodl had been mainly responsible for the phrasing of the Wehrmachtberichte—the official war communiqués. He wrote well and the reports were carefully designed to be as factual as possible and to be adapted above all to the needs and morale of the German troops (Erich Murawski, Der deutsche Wehrmachtberichte 1939–1945 [Boppard: Boldt, 1962], Schriften des Bundesarchivs, 9).

When he had to appear at the last visit of his wife shackled to a guard, he apologized in a letter to her but said he actually felt as though the guard had been shackled to him rather than the other way around. He never had any sense of guilt.*

Like so many other officers and officials in the Third Reich, Jodl had looked the other way when he heard of the atrocious means with which Hitler was conducting the war and the extermination of the Jews, the Slavs, the Gypsies, and the commissars. Still, he was vastly overworked. During the entire war he had only one leave; 60,000 messages a year went across his desk, many of which had to be signed; and it was not possible, as he pointed out in his trial, to investigate the legality of each of these. Believing in Hitler, in the justice of the war, in the attack the Jews were making on Germany, in the nefariousness of the enemy who combined the forces of bolshevism and capitalism in its effort to overthrow National Socialism, Jodl gratefully accepted the golden Party badge in 1944 as something he had earned by single-mindedly serving his leader. But unlike Keitel and so many others, he never received any financial evidence of Hitler's gratitude. He was never given a penny by the Fuehrer.

Jodl, like the other military men, had the bad luck to revere the wrong head of state. He was not an evil man or a weak one, and those who knew him outside the Fuehrer headquarters liked and respected him. Exner said when he visited him after the verdict was pronounced, "We have to be ashamed to come to you," to which Jodl added in writing to his wife: "I must rather be ashamed to have brought him to this situation." His last letters contained much more feeling for his wife's suffering than for his own situation. He said he hoped when the day of execution came she would have a friend nearby whose arm could be around her. He who had sent so many men to their death, he said, could not himself be afraid of death, which would be a liberation with no more guards and no more prison.

It seems unlikely that Jodl would have been sentenced to death by a later court.† Generals as deeply involved in criminal orders as he had been had their lives spared and were soon free, including Manstein, Kesselring, and even Bach-Zelewski, who on behalf of the SS had led the attack against the Warsaw uprising. They all were released in the space of a few years. Jodl had the misfortune to be tried too early. His guilt was probably no greater

---

* "I have to look fate in the eye," he wrote his wife. "The Court is the Court of the victors and remains a political instrument. It will always have the appearance of justice but it has the task of punishing the major war criminals."

† Testimony was introduced at the Hauptspruchkammer proceedings in Munich in 1953, where Jodl in effect was found not guilty of the main charges brought against him at Nuremberg, declaring that one of the French judges at Nuremberg, Donnedieu de Fabres, had said in 1949 that the verdict against Jodl was a mistake (Affidavit by Erich Schwinge, Professor of Law, Marburg University). Alfred Seidl, who had been counsel for Rudolf Hess at Nuremberg, represented Jodl's widow in her successful attempt before the five members of the Hauptspruchkammer to rehabilitate him and to annul the German penalties against his property (IZG, Proceedings, Hauptspruchkammer).

than that of the Allied generals who told the Commandos to fight without regard to the rules of war and the Allied strategists who ordered the annihilation bombings of Dresden, Hamburg, Berlin, and other German cities. It is true that Jodl had proposed in June, 1940, long before the British had begun the mass bombing of German cities, that German "terror attacks" on English cities be declared a reprisal. But neither Jodl nor his opposite numbers among the Allies were interested in anything more than a justification for using whatever methods they believed to be essential to gain victory. Jodl said plainly that international law should be used as a means of battle and that illegal acts should be countered with illegal acts instead of by appeals to the law against the enemy's breaches of the law.[117] He used the same reasoning when the Commissar Order came before him. He was against it, but his only sign of resistance was again to suggest that it be justified as a reprisal— a reprisal before the war started.

Jodl's misfortune was that he had, one step at a time, become part of a criminal government; he took a leading role in its military establishment even when he knew that it had murdered one former chief of the Reichswehr and had degraded and humiliated another after bringing false charges against him. Jodl came to accept violence in public life as well as orders he knew to be illegal; he reacted only when irrational military decisions were made. The killing of the Jews may have disturbed him, but if it did no evidence exists; the beatings and killings of Russian prisoners of war, the use of slave labor, the deportations, the collaboration of the Army with the SD, the collective measures against civilian populations, very nearly everything was ignored or condoned and accepted if it led to victory. His soldierly qualities were absorbed in the *état criminel*, although with more luck he would have served a better cause with as much devotion and skill.

NOTES

1. *Der Parteitag der Ehre* (Munich: Zentralverlag der NSDAP, Franz Eher Nachf., 1936), pp. 103–4.

2. *Ibid.*, pp. 181–85.

3. *Ibid.*, pp. 245–50.

4. *Ibid.*, pp. 284–85.

5. *Ibid.*, p. 307.

6. "Himmler Rede," in *Sammelheft ausgewaehlter Vortraege und Reden* (Munich: Zentralverlag der NSDAP, Franz Eher Nachf., 1939).

7. Léon Degrelle, *Die verlorene Legion* (Stuttgart: Veritas Verlag, 1955), p. 177.

8. Hans Buchheim, "Die SS in der Verfassung des Dritten Reiches," in *Vierteljahrshefte fuer Zeitgeschichte*, Vol. III, No. 2, 1955, pp. 127–57.

9. Friedrich Meyer-Abich, ed., *Die Masken fallen* (Hamburg: Morawe and Scheffelt Verlag, 1949), pp. 43–45.

10. *Eichmann Trial, Session 111, August 8th, 1961* (Jerusalem: Eichmann Trial Record, mimeographed, 1961).

11. NCA VI, 3715-PS, p 431.

12. Kaltenbrunner interrogation of September 16, 1946 (IZG).

13. Karl Heinz Abshagen, *Canaris* (Stuttgart: Union Verlag, 1959).

14. Himmler letter of September 2, 1938 (BDC).

15. Gerald Reitlinger, *The SS: Alibi of a Nation* (London: William Heinemann, 1957), pp. 351–52.

16. NCA VI, 3803-PS, p. 738.

17. Raul Hilberg, *The Destruction of the European Jews* (Chicago: Quadrangle Books, 1961), pp. 283–84. Himmler files, folder 126 (BDC).

18. N XI, p. 334.

19. N XXXIII, 3870-PS, pp. 279–86.

20. N IV, 3462-PS, pp. 306–7.

21. NCA VI, 3462-PS, pp. 161–65.

22. N XI, p. 335.

23. NCA V, 2938-PS, p. 605.

24. *Ibid.*, 2990-PS, pp. 694–95.

25. *Ibid.*

26. N XI, pp. 354–55.

27. *Ibid.*, 3838-PS, p. 340.

28. Kaltenbrunner interrogation of September 21, 1945 (IZG).

29. Kaltenbrunner interrogation of October 5, 1945 (IZG).

30. NCA III, 735-PS, pp. 533–35.

31. Kaltenbrunner interrogations of Sept. 28, 1945, and Oct. 31, 1945 (IZG).

32. Archiv Peter, ed., *Spiegelbild einer Verschwoerung: Die Kaltenbrunner-Berichte an Bormann und Hitler ueber das Attentat vom 20. Juli 1944* (Stuttgart: Seewald Verlag, 1961), p. 355.

33. *Ibid.*, pp. 327–28.

34. *Ibid.*, p. 124.

35. *Ibid.*, p. 276.

36. *Ibid.*, p. 285.

37. *Ibid.*, pp. 525–28.

38. *Ibid.*, pp. 325–27.

39. NCA VIII, Erwin Lahousen Statement VI, pp. 682–83.

40. NCA VI, 3702-PS, pp. 411–12. Peter Bor, *Gespraeche mit Halder* (Wiesbaden: Limes Verlag, 1950).

41. Walter Goerlitz, *Keitel—Verbrecher oder Offizier?* (Goettingen: Musterschmidt-Verlag, 1961).

42. *Ibid.*, p. 29.

43. *Ibid.*, p. 47.

44. *Ibid.*, p. 230.

45. N XXVII, 1809-PS, p. 422.

46. N XXXIX, 066-UK, pp. 128–29.

47. N XXVI, 884-PS, pp. 406–8.

48. NCA III, 551-PS, pp. 440–41.

49. Kurt Detlev Moeller, *Das letzte Kapitel* (Hamburg: Hoffmann and Campe Verlag, 1947), pp. 64–65.

50. Lahousen interrogation of April 7, 1947 (NA).

51. Falkenhorst interrogation of November 22, 1945 (NA).

52. Falkenhorst interrogation of October 25, 1945 (NA).

53. Joachim von und zur Gathen interrogation of November 30, 1945 (NA).

54. NCA IV, 1954-PS, pp. 592–97.

55. Franz Halder, *Kreigstagebuch*, Vol. II (Stuttgart: W. Kohlhammer, 1963), pp. 336–37.

56. N XXVI, 884-PS, pp. 406–8.

57. Buchheim, *et al.*, *op. cit.*, Vol. II, pp. 225–27.

58. NCA VIII, pp. 681–82.

59. NCA VI, 50-C, pp. 873–75. Also N XXXIV, pp. 252–55.

60. NCA III, 878-PS, p. 636.

61. Buchheim, *et al.*, *op. cit.*, Vol. II, pp. 251–52.

62. N X, p. 627.

63. NCA III, 556-2-PS, p. 443.

64. N XIX, p. 477.

65. N XXXVI, 409-EC, p. 480.

66. Goerlitz, *op. cit.*, p. 433.

67. Wilhelm Arentz, trans., "Die Vernehmung von Generalfeldmarschall Keitel durch die Sowjets," in *Wehrwissenschaftliche Rundschau*, 1961, pp. 651–62.

68. Goerlitz, *op. cit.*, p. 323.

69. N XXII, p. 378.

70. Ulrich von Hassell, *Vom andern Deutschland* (Zurich and Freiburg i. Br.: Atlantis, 1946), p. 230.

71. Goerlitz, *op. cit.*, pp. 325–26.

72. N XV, Affidavit of General Nicholaus von Vormann, pp. 286–87.

73. Adolf Heusinger, *Befehl im Widerstreit* (Tuebingen: Rainer Wunderlich Verlag Hermann Leins, 1957), pp. 198–200.

74. Goerlitz, *op. cit.*, pp. 304–6. Kordt, *Wahn und Wirklichkeit*. Jodl Spruchkammer (IZG). TWC High Command Case, List interrogation of March 4, 1946, pp. 2684 ff. Luise Jodl, unpublished biography of General Alfred Jodl (hereinafter referred to as Jodl ms.).

75. Jodl Spruchkammer, Affidavit of Lieutenant Colonel Ernst John von Freyand, September 1, 1952 (IZG). Jodl ms. The scene was described to Luise Jodl by Major Buechs, who was present.

76. NCA VIII, pp. 662–69.

77. NCA IV, 1808-PS, p. 377.

78. Jodl documents in possession of Luise Jodl.

79. Jodl documents in possesion of Luise Jodl, Report of July 25, 1919.

80. Walter Warlimont, *Inside Hitler's Headquarters 1939–45* (New York: Frederick A. Praeger, Inc., 1964), pp. 13–14, 16–17.

81. Jodl Spruchkammer, Affidavit of Lieutenant Colonel Ernst John von Freyand, September 1, 1952 (IZG).

82. NCA, Supp. A, D-885, p. 1024.

83. NCA VII, L-172, pp. 923, 973–74.

84. N XV, pp. 496, 505–7.

85. *Ibid.*, pp. 457–58.

86. N XIX, C-52, p. 500.

87. N XXVIII, 1807-PS, p. 395.

88. MA 119 (IZG).

89. Warlimont, *op. cit.*, p. 479.

90. Joachim Schulz, *Die letzten 30 Tage* (Stuttgart: Steingrueben-Verlag, 1951), p. 120.

91. *Cf.* Hans-Guenter Seraphim and Andreas Hillgruber, "*Hitlers Entschluss zum Angriff auf Russland*," in *Vierteljahrshefte fuer Zeitgeschichte*, Vol II, No. 3, 1954, pp. 240–54.

92. Guenter Lewy, "Superior Orders, Nuclear Warfare and the Dictators," in *American Political Science Review*, March, 1961, p. 22.

93. *NCA III*, 886-PS, p. 637.

94. *NCA VII*, L-172, p. 961.

95. *N XV*, p. 10.

96. *Ibid.*, p. 495.

97. *Ibid.*, pp. 497–98.

98. *N I*, pp. 77–78.

99. *N XIX*, pp. 408–13.

100. *Ibid.*, pp. 426–30.

101. *Ibid.*, p. 458.

102. *N XVII*, pp. 464–94.

103. *N XIX*, pp. 459, 464–65.

104. *Ibid.*, p. 466.

105. *Ibid.*, pp. 479–80 and D-770, p. 482.

106. *Ibid.*, p. 5.

107. *N XVIII*, pp. 506–10. *N XIX*, pp. 1–7.

108. *N XIX*, pp. 7–9.

109. *Ibid.*, pp. 12–13.

110. *NCA*, Supp. A, 1776-PS, pp. 404–6.

111. *NCA VI*, C-170, pp. 977–1002.

112. *Ibid.*, p. 987.

113. *N XIX*, pp. 13–15.

114. *Ibid.*, pp. 15, 20–21.

115. *Ibid.*, pp. 20–22.

116. *Cf.* Hans-Adolf Jacobsen, ed., *Dokumente zum Westfeldzug 1940* (Goettingen: Musterschmidt-Verlag, 1960). Hans-Adolf Jacobsen, *Fall Gelb* (Wiesbaden: Franz Steiner Verlag, 1957).

117. *N XXXV*, D-606, p. 181. *NCA*, Supp. A, 1776-PS, pp. 404–6.

10

The Navy

ERICH RAEDER

Erich Raeder, the predecessor of Doenitz as Commander in Chief of the
German Navy, was of middle-class origins. The German Navy had never
had the Prussian-Junker tradition of the Army's officer corps. They recruited their officers mainly from nonaristocratic families (Doenitz came
from a Prussian line of farmers, civil servants, pastors, teachers, and a
sprinkling of officers). Raeder's father was a language teacher in a secondary
school in Hamburg before he became headmaster of the Friedrich Wilhelm
Realgymnasium in the little town of Gruenberg in Silesia. Raeder's mother
was the daughter of a musician, and the future admiral was brought up in a
humanistic, God-fearing atmosphere of learning and middle-class culture
with a considerable degree of what could be called permissiveness, for when
at the age of eighteen he announced that he wanted to become a naval
officer his parents made no objection. Although up to this point the young
Raeder had been studying Greek and Latin texts and other subjects remote from the life of a sailor, his father promptly took steps to enroll
him as a cadet.*

Raeder was a good officer from the start. He made one of the pre-World
War I cruises to the Orient with a flotilla of German warships under command of Prince Heinrich, and he later served as a watch officer on the
prince's flagship in home waters. With only fifteen other young officers he
attended the Naval Academy (Marineakademie) in Kiel for two years, a
preparation for high command in the Navy designed to give special train-

* Greek was not part of the curriculum of the Realgymnasium, and Raeder took private
lessons in that language.

ing to selected officers who would serve on ships of the line and on the admiralty staff. The Naval Academy did not aim, as did the War Academy (Kriegsakademie) on behalf of the Army, to turn out General Staff officers; it concentrated on the professional training of the German naval officers, with a good deal of emphasis on naval history and foreign languages. Raeder was sent to Russia for three months in 1904 during the Russo-Japanese War to further his knowledge of Russian, which he had chosen as his language study at the Naval Academy.

His early career was varied. He served two years in the naval intelligence bureau, a news-gathering and publishing service that had nothing to do with espionage, and after returning to sea was unexpectedly assigned to the Kaiser's yacht *Hohenzollern*, where he was navigation officer. There he learned to mix with the men who were running not only the Navy but the country. Returning to line duty, he served on the staff of Admiral Hipper, commanding the reconnaissance forces, and he took part during World War I in the early mining and hit-and-run raids of the German surface ships against the English coast. During this time his superiors were sufficiently impressed by him for the Naval Chief of Staff, Konteradmiral von Trotha, to ask his advice on the German operations in the Skagerrak—an unusual distinction for a junior officer.

He took part in the historic battle between the British and German high-seas fleets at Jutland, in which the Germans inflicted greater damage on the enemy than they received but were nevertheless forced to retreat to their massive inactivity in their relatively safe harbors, still facing the numerically far superior British fleet. Toward the end of the war Raeder was freed of his staff duties and given command of the light cruiser *Coeln*, which was used for reconnaissance and antimining assignments in the North Sea. While the *Coeln* was laid up for repairs, he was named a member of the German armistice delegation that met at Spa to prepare for what they hopefully thought would be an honorable peace with the Allies. But the terms of the armistice, as well as the revolt in the German Navy, took Raeder and a good many more like him by surprise. The spectacle of sailors mutinying, the one-sided conditions of the armistice, and then the peace treaty were a profound shock.[1]

Raeder could rationalize what had happened by ascribing the mutinies to the work of demogogues, the Left wing, and he remained in the service to help put the pieces together.* The question confronting him, as it

* Raeder, like most German naval officers, was appalled at the mutiny of the German sailors in 1918. This experience was one of the main causes, Admiral Assmann, who served under Raeder, believes, of Raeder's autocratic handling of naval affairs and of his emphasis on discipline. It was also one of the reasons for his backing the Right-wing Kapp putsch, led by a minor political figure, Dr. Wolfgang Kapp, and General Walther von Luettwitz, who in March, 1920, tried to depose the Weimar Government with the help of the naval brigade Ehrhardt. Because he had sided with the mutineers, Raeder was assigned for two years to inconspicuous duty in the Navy archives (Francis L. Carsten, *Reichswehr und Politik 1918–1933* [Cologne and Berlin: Kiepenhever & Witsch, 1964.]).

confronted the other Navy and Army officers who stayed on after the collapse, was how they could defend the country in the postwar violence and chaos with the limitations imposed upon them. Raeder testified at Nuremberg that the German Navy had followed on the whole the provisions of the Versailles Treaty and had dealt fairly with the Allied commission that supervised the disarmament provisions. No submarines were built for Germany, although dummy companies set up in Spain and Holland helped the Navy keep its hand in submarine construction by providing designs for undersea vessels for other countries. The Navy sent thirty engineers and designers to Holland where two 500-ton U-boats were built for Turkey in 1925, and a German U-boat designer went in 1924 to Finland, where submarines were built for Finland that were prototypes for later German U-boats. Still others were constructed under the supervision of the German technicians for Sweden, Holland, and Spain, but since the companies built none for the German Navy this construction was all within the provisions of the Versailles Treaty; German experts could act on behalf of other nations in neutral countries.[2] * The actual violations of the treaty were very minor and were clearly far more concerned with defensive than offensive emergencies. Practice antiaircraft batteries were set up, old mine sweepers were armed with 10.5cm. guns and one machine gun for use against aircraft. This was illegal since no antiaircraft guns were permitted the Weimar Republic. Some 43,000 gas masks were manufactured instead of the permitted 22,500, 185 movable guns were salvaged for the Army, and not all the prescribed demolitions were made at Heligoland.[3]

The violations were no menace to any country. Weimar Germany produced 3,675 mines (2,000 more than the 1,665 permitted under Versailles), and with them the Navy could close off an area of some twenty-seven nautical miles. The German defense at Nuremberg tried to show the number of mines needed for a thoroughgoing operation. Some idea of this, they pointed out, may be had from the fact that the British had laid from 400,000 to 500,000 mines in the North Sea during World War I, and the German Luftwaffe in one action alone at the start of World War II laid 30,000 to 50,000 mines. The Navy also moved guns of the coast-defense fortification farther apart so they could not be knocked out with one shot, which was a breach of the treaty, as was the replacing of the permissible six 15cm. guns with three 17cm. ones and keeping antiaircraft batteries. Another subterfuge was the Navy's retaining 96 guns, six of them of large caliber, which they were supposed to have scrapped.[4]

Most of these post-World War I measures were taken in the face of what

---

* The funds for such enterprises were provided by the Defense Ministry and were in the charge of Captain Lohmann of the German Navy. Lohmann also established a number of commercial companies including one for producing patriotic moving pictures. The result was a financial disaster and a great public scandal when the machinations were uncovered in 1927.

the Germans believed in the early 1920's to be imminent danger, Polish attack. The Poles had taken over Vilna without serious opposition from the Allies or the League of Nations, and Raeder testified at Nuremberg that the Germans knew that in the event of a Polish attack the French intended to support their allies the Poles. The Navy therefore had the task—with the insignificant forces remaining after surrender of the high-seas fleet and its scuttling at Scapa Flow—of stopping the French fleet from entering the Baltic.

The German Navy in many categories had not built up to the tonnages allotted it. Under the Versailles Treaty it was allowed eight cruisers (it had six) and thirty-two destroyers (it had twelve). The secret arms budget that had to be proof against the pacifist vigilance of the Social Democrats amounted to between five and six million marks, or a little more than a million and a quarter dollars, and even in the 1920's that did not buy much armament, naval or otherwise. Neither in the pre-Nazi period nor under Hitler did the Germans build to the tonnages allowed, for Hitler's concern was the Army and Air Force—the Navy was seldom uppermost in his mind. In allocation of resources for rearmament it ran third.[5]

Raeder was a considerable distance from the devout Nazi that Doenitz was, but after meeting Hitler in 1933 he considered the Fuehrer a greatly gifted man, endowed with a charisma so powerful that Raeder sought to avoid personal meetings. Like so many others, Raeder had seen evidence of the Fuehrer's ability to convince people of the soundness of his views against their will and better judgment, and he kept away from the occasions when he might have to be alone with Hitler. Doenitz told his lawyer that Raeder was present at conferences with Hitler only when ordered there and that he left as soon as possible.* When Hitler commanded the German troops to march into the Rhineland, Raeder was against the move, but when the French failed to react with decision, he agreed that Hitler had been right, as he was to be later at the time of Munich. Raeder wrote concerning the Rhineland: "We admit we were wrong, the Fuehrer was right. We won because we had the stronger nerves and stuck it out." [6]

Raeder had a son-in-law with one-quarter Jewish blood who emigrated from Germany and lived abroad, so his anti-Semitism was tempered compared with that of Doenitz, although he too did not hesitate to denounce the Jews or to accept the golden Party badge in 1937. In a speech on March 12, 1939, on the occasion of Heroes' Memorial Day, he spoke of National Socialism, which originated, he said, from the spirit of the German fighting soldier, and he praised "the clear and unsparing summons to fight bolshevism and international Jewry, whose race-destroying activities we have sufficiently experienced on our own people . . . the parasites of a foreign race." But Jews testified for him at Nuremberg, telling of his help in keeping

---

* Doenitz, after he became Grossadmiral, stayed at the Fuehrer's headquarters sometimes for days at a time.

them out of concentration camps. He also intervened with the SS on behalf of Pastor Niemoeller, who was then in Buchenwald, to attempt to get him freed.[7]

Raeder never was close to the Party bigwigs—he came to regard Goering as an implacable enemy of the Navy. The Reichsmarschall (then Colonel General) in his attempt to defend his domain against all comers had succeeded in reversing the decision made before Hitler came to power that allowed the Navy to have its own planes. Goering insisted that the Navy ask for support of the Luftwaffe when it needed help and make use of the Luftwaffe's pilots and planes, which were sometimes refused when the Air Force deemed other missions more important. Raeder said at Nuremberg that as a result countless errors were made that were extremely costly to the Navy. The Ark Royal was incorrectly reported sunk; in Norway a battleship was identified as a destroyer; on February 2, 1940, two German destroyers were sunk by an inexperienced Luftwaffe pilot; and the submarines were seldom given adequate help. Eventually he and Doenitz succeeded in convincing a reluctant Hitler of the necessity of the Navy's having its own planes.

Goering in jealousy of the Navy once said to Hitler that it was true that Raeder had the Navy in good shape but the admiral went to church and the Fuehrer could thereupon draw his own conclusions of Raeder's attitude toward National Socialism. The Reichsmarschall went to Hitler with the firsthand news gathered by his air-force reporting service and thus was able to give false and invariably optimistic reports to the Fuehrer, Raeder thought, on what had happened on land and sea and in the air. Nor did Goering ever let himself be slighted in the picture he drew.

Goering's close relationship to Hitler disturbed Raeder, because the combination of the Reichsmarschall's vanity and incompetence led him constantly to get what he wanted by intrigue or direct appeals to the Fuehrer regardless of the needs of the armed forces. Raeder was convinced that Goering had helped spring the trap on the German Minister of War, Blomberg, whose wedding to a prostitute both Goering and Hitler attended. The marriage could only result, once the facts were known, in Blomberg's resignation, and Raeder believed Goering had promoted the marriage and Hitler's presence at the ceremony so he could get Blomberg's job. Raeder sat on the court which tried the former Chief of Staff of the Army, Fritsch, who might have been Blomberg's successor, and here again Raeder thought the charges of homosexuality against Fritsch had been trumped up by Goering to get rid of a rival who also might be a successor to Blomberg. Fritsch was in fact Raeder's candidate for the War Ministry, but Hitler declined to name him even though the court (of which Goering was president) found him innocent.

Raeder was disquieted by Goering's appointment on February 4, 1938, as Generalfeldmarschall. Raeder had refused the equivalent rank in 1935, when

Hitler had wanted to make him grand admiral with a field marshal's baton (the first officer of that rank since World War I) because this would have meant his outranking Fritsch. Goering's promotion and his boundless ambition as well as his malign influence on Hitler caused Raeder to think much about resigning in the course of 1938. He again declined the promotion to grand admiral in 1938, but the Navy clearly needed an officer of equal rank with the increasing number of field marshals and when in 1939 Hitler again wanted to make him grand admiral he accepted the promotion. Up to the start of the war he still considered leaving the service, but once hostilities began, he could not resign. He left only in 1943, when his differences with Hitler on the strategy of the Navy became intolerable to both. His last words to the Fuehrer when he retired were: "Please protect the Navy and my successor against Goering."

Raeder did not get along well with the Party *Bonzen* and the SS. Heydrich too was an enemy. The man who headed the SD and ruled Czechoslovakia until June, 1942, had been a naval officer, and Raeder had dismissed him from the service in 1931 for the disreputable part he played in an affair involving a young girl. Heydrich had never forgiven him, and Raeder was sure he was an implacable enemy.

Raeder shared the widespread contempt for Ribbentrop, who he believed mainly responsible for Hitler's wrong ideas about England and the Fuehrer's doubts that the British would fight. Like the rest of the Navy men who had fought in World War I, Raeder knew and respected the fighting qualities of the English and never accepted the stock Nazi beliefs about Britain's decadence. But Hitler believed what he wanted to hear, and Raeder was as powerless against the imbecilities of Ribbentrop as against the decision to fight Russia—a country he also knew something about.

In general, Raeder held views characteristic of the Navy. He was an aloof man, tolerating no differences of opinion once he had made up his mind on any matter that had to do with the Navy. But officers were officers and comrades, regardless of what the Party said on the matter, and during the entire war many men who were *Mischlinge* continued at their posts. Raeder testified that he had lost only two officers under the Nuremberg Laws and both of them got good jobs in civilian life with the help of the Navy. In another case he made use of his friendly relations with Hess to keep a *Mischling* in active service. The Navy on the whole was freer than the Army of Party surveillance and could always plead its need for highly trained and specialized officers. Moreover, it was a service with which Hitler and most of the Party hierarchy had no experience. The Nazi movement was born in the mountains and villages and cities of South Germany and Austria; it had no connection with the cosmopolitanism of the sea. The Fuehrer himself always regarded the Navy with a mixture of respect and suspicion. Raeder had a furious response from Hitler when he refused to give the naval attaché at the Fuehrer's headquarters permission to marry. The officer, whom Hitler liked, had made false statements in his application, and Raeder wanted to cashier him as he had Heydrich. In the end the man left the Navy and Hitler had him taken into the Party bureaucracy.

The Navy was stiff-necked compared to the Army; its organization was far more compact, the chain of command demanding close personal as well as professional relationships, and it had more success in protecting its men and in maintaining its standards of discipline, regardless of the Party views. Although the Navy was fairly well represented in the July 20 plot against Hitler, only one naval man beside Admiral Canaris was executed. The others were protected anonymously by Doenitz's well-known National Socialist principles; since his loyalty to the Fuehrer was beyond reproach he was able to fend off the SD and the Gestapo. Even Doenitz, for all his devotion to Hitler, kept a man in service who could have been shot for what he had said. A captain told one of Doenitz's adjutants, Captain von Davidson, that he would be glad if his son one day were to sail on a ship named *Alfred Kranzfelder* (Kranzfelder was one of the conspirators in the July plot).[8]

But the main charges against Raeder at Nuremberg were of another kind. When he was accused of having conspired to commit aggressive warfare, the Allied prosecution had the Norwegian campaign mainly in mind, for Raeder at the start of the war in a conference of October 10, 1939, had urged on Adolf Hitler the case for establishing German bases in Norway to conduct the submarine war against Britain and to secure the vital transports of iron ore from Sweden. Raeder, influenced by studies made by Vice-Admiral Wolfgang Wegener, had been convinced for some years of the need, in the event of war, of acquiring bases in Norway and Denmark. In his conference with Hitler he proposed putting political pressure on Norway with the help of the Soviet Union to acquire Norwegian bases.[9] He also thought, and with good reason, that the English and French would attempt to stop the ore shipments to Germany by one means or another, including, if necessary, their occupying the Norwegian harbors where the supplies were loaded. He knew, too, that this blow would be as damaging to the Reich as the loss of the Rumanian oil fields at the other end of Europe—where the Western Allies were also bound to be active by sabotage, bombing, or invasion whether or not the oil fields were under control of a neutral country. General Maurice Gamelin and his staff had planned for four French and nine English air groups to be ready to attack Baku and Batum, using Turkish and French bases.[10]

The weight of the Norwegian campaign lay mainly on the German Navy, which had the task of transporting and protecting the landing forces against an overwhelmingly superior enemy fleet. With help of the Luftwaffe and surprise, it might succeed in its task, but it also would need luck. As events turned out it had all three. For both sides knew the importance of the Swedish iron ore and the long Norwegian coastline, within which freighters could move under the protection of Norwegian neutrality until they reached the short run across the Baltic to the nearest port and where they would have the cover of German air and naval support against Allied attacks. Winston Churchill wrote his first memorandum on the subject of Norway shortly after the start of the war. On September 19, 1939, he detailed "the importance of stopping the Norwegian transportation of Swedish iron ore from Narvik." By December he was ready to take stern measures against the neutrals under whose protection the Germans were getting supplies. On December 16 he wrote of the need to mine Norwegian waters and to occupy Norwegian bases and perhaps the Swedish minefields: "The final tribunal is our own conscience . . . Small nations must not tie our hands when we are fighting for their rights and freedom. The letter of the law must not in supreme emergency obstruct those who are charged with its protection and enforcement . . . Humanity, rather than legality, must be our guide." [11]

This was the period when the Allies had great hopes of winning the war without the carnage of World War I—by fighting at the edges, by denying the Germans essential commodities through their blockade or taking over the sources of supply. If Baku oil and Swedish ore could be denied the Germans, the war would be over before long. And when the Soviet Union attacked Finland at the end of 1939, taking advantage of the marvelous opportunity presented by its pact with Germany to improve the protection of its coast against a possible future change of policy on the part of the Reich, the Western Allies saw opportunity not only of helping the Finns, who had the sympathy of Europe, including the still uncommitted neutrals in Scandinavia and the United States, but of using the occasion to occupy the Norwegian ports. The French, anxious to keep the war as far as possible from their borders, were ready to act. They agreed without consulting the British to send 50,000 men and 100 airplanes, which they could ill spare, as an expeditionary force of volunteers to land in Norway and move across Sweden to Finland.[12] The British, too, although they felt that the French had somewhat forced their hand, agreed to send three to four divisions as well as air support. But the Swedes would have none of this; they were too conscious of German power; despite their sympathy for Finland they said no to the Allied request for permission to cross Swedish territory. The strength and courage of the flexible, individualistic Finnish defense, along with the massive ineptitude of the Russian attack, astonished and delighted the world. Even the Italians and Germans showed pro-Finnish sympathies. The Swedes were delighted more than most. But their neutrality was as deeply rooted as their respect for the might of the German Army.

Finnish capitulation, however, became inevitable once the Soviet Union brought its full power to bear. The Russians had first used troops mainly from the Leningrad garrison and were seemingly unprepared for the ferocity of the Finnish defense in the forest warfare their men were forced to fight. In addition, it is likely that they were victims of their own propaganda, which often affected even the Soviet officials who conjured it. The Russian high command had seemingly convinced themselves that their troops would be welcomed by the Finns as an army of liberation, freeing them from their imperialistic and capitalistic masters. The poor performance of the Soviet soldiers, even in victory, led many in the Allied camp to congratulate themselves in having escaped a Russian alliance. But for the Allies it was still necessary to deprive the Germans of the protection of Norwegian neutrality that let them get the iron ore past British sea power, and this had to be done with or without the plan to aid the Finns.

The chance came with the successful British attack on the German ship *Altmark*. The *Altmark*, a supply ship carrying British prisoners, had succeeded in eluding the British blockade and sailed from South America to the coast of Norway. There Norwegian officers inspected it and satisfied themselves that it was unarmed and that its presence in no way violated Norwegian neutrality; it therefore could sail legally along the neutral coast until it reached waters controlled by the German Navy and Luftwaffe. But Churchill and the British Admiralty ordered the destroyer *Cossack* to attack the *Altmark* and get the prisoners off. The crew of the *Cossack* boarded the *Altmark*. A number of the German crew were killed, including some trying to escape across the ice of the fjord. The prisoners were freed and, to the surprise of everyone, were found to be in good physical condition, although doctors and medical supplies were ready on the assumption they would be living skeletons. The Germans, as was customary with them at this stage of the war, had treated the prisoners well and there was no need for medical services.

A hue and cry rose over the attack. The captain of the British ship was decorated for his exploit, to the intense indignation of the Germans, who pointed not only to violation of Norwegian neutrality but to the dead sailors shot while trying to save themselves. The Norwegians protested on their own account, but they were unable and unwilling to press the case too far. Like every other non-Axis country in Europe, they were strongly pro-Ally; and they had not hesitated to lease their entire merchant fleet to the British on most favorable terms. The British knew they had the support of the world, including the United States, in whatever they did to defeat Hitler, and Churchill was sure the next steps too would be accepted and approved. These steps included the mining of Norwegian territorial waters, followed by occupation of Norwegian ports by a combined British-French landing force. The mining operation was set for April 4, and on assumption the Germans would react promptly, the British-French force was embarked for Narvik, with other contingents to land in Stavanger and Trondheim. But the Germans were there before them, by a matter of hours.

Raeder and the High Command of the Navy had long been aware of the strategic necessity for keeping the Norwegian harbors out of the hands of the Allies. On the whole they would have been glad to keep Norway neutral, thus to continue to use her territorial waters, but they doubted that this would be possible for long. The British were as fully aware of the importance of the shipments—the Germans got ten million tons of high-grade ore a year—and of the safe-passage route to Germany by way of ice-free Narvik, through which one-third of the ore came. The Germans soon received information from the pro-Nazi groups in Norway, headed by former Minister of War Vidkun Quisling, of British-French preparations for the landings. Quisling had been brought to visit Raeder through Rosenberg, who as Hitler's commissioner for ideological education of the National Socialist Party had been in touch with the Norwegian Nazi Party (Nasjonal Samling), headed by Quisling. The German legation was unimpressed by Quisling, reporting to Berlin that he was not to be taken seriously, but the Foreign Office of the Party, through Rosenberg, took a different view. Raeder recommended that Hitler see Quisling, and the Norwegian had helped to convince them both of the imminence of an Allied landing, although the German Minister to Norway doubted that it would be attempted in the near future.[13]

The Germans found French documents bearing on the preparations for war in the West, the Norwegian campaign, and offensive actions in the Balkans in a freight train on a siding in the little town of La Charité, as well as in the Quai d'Orsay. They included messages and memoranda from General Gamelin and Daladier, and the captured minutes of the Supreme War Council which were to be confirmed later by Winston Churchill when he published his memoirs. Raeder had these documents for his defense at Nuremberg, but the British primly refused defense attorney Siemers' request on behalf of Raeder for access to Admiralty files from April, 1939, to April, 1940. Any plans for Scandinavia had not been put into effect, the British wrote, because the decision had been made not to intervene unless the Germans did so first. "It is assumed," the letter said, "that the request relates to matters other than the laying of minefields in Norwegian waters by the forces of His Majesty's Government which action is a matter of public knowledge." [14] All the communication left out was the critical fact that the Allies knew the Germans would have to react and were determined to force the issue either by way of intervention in Finland or by direct action in Norway.

Raeder had in his possession the telegram Daladier sent to the French Ambassador in London, Charles Corbin, on February 21, 1940, about preparations for landing in Norway:

> . . . Our main aim . . . is to cut Germany off from its ore supply . . . On the other hand it is very likely that if we don't exploit the *Altmark* Case up to the point of taking over . . . bases in Norway, Sweden out of fear of Germany and in doubt of the effectiveness of our support will ignore Finland's call for help and shut us off from its territory . . .[15]

Raeder also had General Gamelin's notes of March 16, 1940, commenting on future conduct of the war: ". . . The first necessity is a sharpening of the blockade." This might force the Germans to attack Belgium and Holland if they were no longer a help to circumvent the blockade. Sweden's ore was essential to Germany, and Sweden and Norway could be threatened with reprisals. The Allies had to act quickly, said Gamelin, and with more vigor. "The experience of six months of war shows that the neutrals fear Germany. Without being as threatening we must let them feel our strength . . ." [16] In addition, Raeder had the German translation of the minutes of the sixth session of the Supreme Allied War Council, on March 28, 1940:

> The Supreme Council agrees that the French and British Governments on Monday, the 1st of April, will deliver a note to the Norwegian and Swedish Governments . . . [to the effect that] the Allied governments cannot permit any further attacks on Finland [she had made peace on March 12] by either the Soviet or the German Governments. If such an attack nevertheless takes place and the Norwegian and the Swedish Governments refuse to support the appropriate countermeasures of the Allied governments on behalf of Finland, and furthermore should these governments attempt to block such measures of assistance, then the Allies will regard this an act against their vital interests that will call for an appropriate reaction. Any exclusive political agreement that Sweden and Norway make with Germany will be regarded by the Allied governments as a hostile act even if such an agreement would have as its explicit aim the defense of Finland . . . Any attempt of the Soviet Government to obtain from Norway a port on the Atlantic coast contradicts the vital interests of the Allies and would call for appropriate countermeasures. The Allied governments must take appropriate measures . . . in the event that the Swedish and Norwegian Governments stop or reduce the delivery of goods and tonnage, which the Allied governments regard as absolutely necessary for the carrying on of the war . . . In consideration of the fact . . . that the Allies are conducting the war for aims that concern the small states as much as themselves, the Allies cannot permit that the further development of the war be endangered by the advantages that Sweden and Norway are granting Germany . . . After this note on April 5 the mine laying in Norwegian territorial waters and the action against German shipping is to take place in order to drive it out of territorial waters . . . Operation "Royal Marine" for the laying of mines in the Rhine estuary is to begin on April 4 and the air action on April 15 . . . The measures at hand are to be taken to cut down the German oil supplies coming from Rumania . . .[17]

Another document Raeder had was a telegram from the French military attaché in London to General Gamelin, dated April 2, 1940: "The British have reserved three places for General Audet on a cruiser . . . The first transport . . . leaves on April 5th . . ." [18] The date for the mine laying in Norwegian waters was changed on April 3 from the 5th to the 8th and only by this chance, Raeder pointed out in his memoirs, were the Germans first in Norway when they landed on the 9th.

In the attack on Norway, Raeder planned to make use of a *ruse de guerre*, a chicanery approved by international law whereby an enemy ship may disguise itself as a friend and fly a foreign flag if it lowers it and flies its own once the shooting begins. However, Raeder feared that with the English fleet in action, the German ships might be confused; the British flag was not flown. Raeder ordered the German blockade breakers to penetrate the Oslo fjord with lights on; the other ships were to be blacked out. The only personnel on deck were to be gun crews. Challenges were to be answered in English and the names of British ships were to be given when questions were asked. "Say, 'Please repeat last signal, impossible to understand.' Then if firing begins, say, 'Stop firing, British ship, good friend.' If the destination were asked say, 'Going Bergen, pursuing German steamers.' " [19]

Raeder's participation in a conspiracy to wage aggressive war was limited to defensive strategies. It was clear to him, as to any sailor in his right mind, that the German Navy could not successfully fight the British Navy together with its allies. Moreover, Raeder gave a talk just before the start of the war in which he told his audience in Swinemuende that war with the West would mean *Finis Germaniae*. Like Doenitz, he drew the conclusions he was looking for from among Hitler's many pronouncements, mainly from those in which the Fuehrer spoke of the need for an understanding with Britain. Although he attended top-secret meetings, including the so-called Hossbach conference on November 5, 1937, where Hitler told of his plans for gaining living space for Germany, Raeder preferred to accept Goering's explanation that the speech was only an incitement to the generals to speed rearmament.

Other Navy as well as Army officers took the November 5 speech at face value; Colonel General Beck planned to arrest Hitler if he ordered an attack which, as those of Beck's mind thought, could only end in destruction of Germany. Raeder merely doubted that it should be taken seriously. He never joined the Resistance, never thought of it. Basically Raeder got what he wanted from Hitler, a Navy prepared to defend the country against any power on the Continent. "Where I get my armored ships from is all the same to me," Raeder had once said. His whole career bore out this easy dictum. The Roehm putsch, the *Kristallnacht*, the concentration camps, Himmler's police—he could and did accept them all if he got his ships and freedom to use them in a sailorlike fashion, free from interference of men like Goering.

Once the war started, Raeder wanted it waged primarily against England; he thought a landing in Britain could have been made successfully in 1940, but that it would require complete support from the air. (On this point he and Hitler and the generals agreed.) But Goering's Luftwaffe was never able to win complete or even predominant control of the air over Britain. Should the invasion of England not take place, Raeder wanted to capture Suez and Gibraltar, depriving England of control and bases in the Mediterranean. This, he said, with his opportunistic habit of making the best of things, would be more important than capture of the British Isles. England was *the* enemy, Raeder believed, and he had no doubt of the necessity of ousting the British from the Greek bases they had taken over and occupying the country. He had the same reasons for this strategy as he had for invasion of Norway: either Germany or England would occupy the country. The British seized control of Salonika, as they did in World War I, and even if Italy had not launched the attack on Greece in early 1941, Germany would have had to invade that country if only to keep the British out. Raeder's memorandum to Hitler on Spain and Portugal emphasized the same alternatives. England's occupation of the Iberian peninsula was a grave danger; Raeder did not want to intervene there, he wrote in another memorandum of 1942. Germany was far too involved on too many fronts, but if England took over the Spanish and Portuguese ports, it would have catastrophic results for Germany's submarine campaign. A British occupation had to be prevented at all costs, he stressed.

Britain was always uppermost in Raeder's mind. When the question was being debated in the High Command in December, 1939, as to whether the plans for the *Bismarck* were to be sold to the Russians, Raeder said he favored letting the Russians buy them. He also later warned the Fuehrer against occupying Tromsö in Norway because he thought this might offend Russia, but Hitler paid no attention to either of his pieces of advice. Raeder's one fear was that the *Bismarck* plans might fall into the hands of the British. Britain remained the chief enemy for him, more so than for Doenitz, who was far more influenced by National Socialist ideology and whose ultimate enmity was therefore reserved for bolshevism. Raeder was taken prisoner by the Russians in Potsdam, brought with his wife to a villa near Moscow, and although he went a full day without food after his arrest, he was on the whole well-treated, he told the court at Nuremberg. Later, when neither he nor officials of the Western Allies could get in touch with his wife, who was being held in a Soviet prison, he may have felt differently, but Russia was never the chief antagonist for the German Navy except for the Nazified officers.

As soon as he heard of the plans for it, Raeder opposed the war against Russia. He wrote a memorandum to Admiral Kurt Assmann on January 10, 1944, marked for Assmann's own use, in which he repeated that he had never been convinced of the "compelling necessity" for Barbarossa, as the Fuehrer called the Russian campaign.[20]

The prosecution accused him of instigating Japanese aggression, of urging Hitler as early as March 18, 1941, to induce Japan to seize Singapore. Raeder had told Hitler:

> Japan must take steps to seize Singapore as soon as possible, since the opportunity will never again be as favorable (whole English Fleet contained; unpreparedness of USA for war against Japan; inferiority of US Fleet vis-à-vis the Japanese). Japan is indeed making preparations for this action, but according to all declarations made by Japanese officers she will only carry it out if Germany proceeds to land in England. Germany must therefore concentrate all her efforts on spurring Japan to act immediately. If Japan has Singapore, all other East Asiatic questions regarding the USA

and England are thereby solved (Guam, Philippines, Borneo, Dutch East Indies). Japan wishes if possible to avoid war against USA. She can do so if she determinedly takes Singapore as soon as possible.[21]

To charge the commander-in-chief of a belligerent navy with trying to gain an ally in the battle against the enemy was curious indeed. The Americans and British, who used all their eloquence to persuade the Russians to breach their non-aggression pact with Japan at a time when Japan was trying to get the Soviet Union to act as mediator in its war against the West, were never put on trial. Nor had the attempt to win an ally ever been defined as a crime before Nuremberg. Raeder of course would have been delighted to have Japan join the fight against his chief adversary, England, without bringing in the United States.

Although he was convicted of planning and waging aggressive warfare, the main charge against Raeder, as against Doenitz, was that he had committed war crimes. His method of conducting submarine warfare, including sinking of the *Athenia*, while condemned by the court was not legally held against him.* As in Doenitz's case, the tribunal cited the American and British orders to their submarine commanders, which balanced that account. The last and most serious charge against him involved his part in carrying out the so-called Commando Order.

The Commando Order was issued by Hitler on October 18, 1942, two months after the British attack at Dieppe on August 19, 1942 (see Chapt. 9). The order had been brewing in the Fuehrer's mind ever since the raid. First, to discourage such raids, Hitler authorized the German radio to broadcast that sabotage and terror units would be treated as bandits in the future and exterminated. Then he issued the Commando Order as a direct "Fuehrer order" to his armed forces. It was sent out with twelve copies, and unlike the Commissar Order, it directly affected the Navy. The Fuehrer wrote a prologue that declared: "For some time our enemies have made use of meth-

---

* Raeder's part in the sinking of the *Athenia* and its aftermath was minor despite his responsibility as Commander in Chief of the Navy. When he first heard of the incident he made inquiries and was told that no U-boat was nearer than seventy-five miles to where the *Athenia* had been sunk. Raeder therefore told the American chargé d'affaires in good faith (Americans had been lost when the *Athenia* went down) that the German Navy was not responsible. Some two weeks later, on September 27, when the U-30 returned to harbor at Wilhelmshaven, its commander, Oberleutnant Lemp, reported to Admiral Doenitz that he had sunk the *Athenia* in error. Doenitz sent Lemp by airplane to Berlin, where the U-boat captain explained to Raeder what had happened. Raeder reported to Hitler, who for political reasons ordered that the matter be kept secret. Raeder decided no court-martial should be held because the submarine commander had acted in good faith and had made an understandable error. A month later the *Voelkischer Beobachter* published an article blaming the sinking of the *Athenia* on the British. Raeder declared he knew nothing of this move beforehand and if he had he would have prevented the article's appearance. The log of the U-30, which was seen by many people, had to be changed if the official denials of the sinking were to be sustained. The tribunal apparently believed Raeder's defense; in its judgment it merely stated the facts, making no findings (N XIV, D-659, pp. 78–80). See pp. 392ff. and Chapter 13.

ods of waging war that are outside the Geneva agreements." [22] The Commandos, the Fuehrer said, were in part made up of criminals released from prisons, and captured orders showed that they were instructed not only to manacle any prisoners they took but to kill them when they threatened in any way to obstruct the mission. In addition, Allied orders had been found demanding the killing of any prisoners taken. Hitler's response was typical—he ordered extermination. He wrote:

> I therefore order that from now on all enemies on so-called Commando missions in Europe or Africa, challenged by German troops, even if they are to all appearances soldiers in uniform or demolition troops, whether armed or unarmed, in battle or in flight, are to be slaughtered to the last man. It does not make any difference whether they landed from ships or airplanes for their attacks or whether they were dropped by parachutes. Even if these individuals when found should apparently seem to give themselves up, no pardon is to be granted them on principle. In each individual case full information is to be sent to the OKW for publication in the OKW communiqué.

The Commandos, Hitler said, were immediately to be turned over to the SD. Any military protection, such as being sent to prisoner-of-war camps, was forbidden. The order did not apply to regular prisoners of war taken in the course of battle. And Hitler added that every commanding officer would be held to account before a court-martial "who has either failed in his duty to the troops in communicating this order or who acts contrary to it." [23]

Raeder's guilt, the court said, lay in his passing on this infamous order. In fact, the Naval High Command noted when two captured Commandos were executed in Bordeaux by a firing squad of the German Navy that this was done "in accordance with the Fuehrer's special order, but it is nevertheless new in international law, since the soldiers were in uniform." [24]

The naval war staff was right; the shooting was something new in international law. The problems raised by the Commandos were new too; they arose from the many uses to which new weapons might be put. Airplanes and gliders could land small units behind enemy lines; two-man submarines, rubber boats, parachutes could set the Commandos down in enemy territory with the mission of blowing up ships, harbor installations, railroads, or anything else of military value. The Commandos had to strike swiftly, to postpone any alarm as long as they could, and to get away as fast as possible. Their job was to destroy and to terrorize, to let Germans know they were never safe. Sometimes they wore civilian clothing under their uniforms (those who landed at Bordeaux had been captured in olive green uniforms under which were the anonymous garments they hoped to escape in).

When the British landed at Dieppe, the Germans captured many Commandos, and with them their orders as to how to behave. In addition, they had testimony of German survivors who had been held prisoner by the landing force. The picture was not a pretty one. The Dieppe landing took place after the war had considerably deteriorated from the forms of the fighting in France and in North Africa, where in the first battles neither Allied nor German planes machine-gunned an enemy on the desert after his plane was downed. Thousands of Germans in Russia, however, following the Fuehrer's directives issued through OKW, considered themselves justified in paying no attention to the military conventions they had observed in the West. Mass executions of civilians by SD and Einsatz groups took place behind the front lines; political officers captured in uniform in battle were shot by the Army. But the British had experienced little or nothing of this kind of German ruthlessness; the war at sea was fierce but kept within visible bounds of humanity; cities had been bombed on both sides with considerable civilian loss of life; but the Commando orders the British issued had no direct relation with any of these events. They apparently resulted from the same thinking as caused Churchill to approve saturation bombing of German cities; he wanted to break the German will to continue the war.

The anti-Nazi feeling in England was intense, and it easily led to a conviction that any means was justifiable that would defeat Hitler and the Nazi movement, in which the British placed the majority of the German people. Hitler this time had not exaggerated; the order issued to British sabotage troops was as brutal and primitive as anything the Nazis had dreamed up. It read:

> Your value to the war effort as a live and effective killer is great. . . . The only way to achieve this is never to give the enemy a chance, the days when we could practice the rules of sportsmanship are over. For the time being every soldier must be a potential gangster and must be prepared to adopt their methods whenever necessary.
>
> In the past we as a nation have not looked upon gangsters and their methods with favour; the time has now come when we are compelled to adopt some of their methods. . . .
>
> Remember you are not a wrestler trying to render your enemy helpless, you have to kill.
>
> And remember you are out to kill, not to hold him down until the referee has finished counting. . . .
>
> In finishing off an opponent use him as a weapon as it were, beating his head on the curb or any convenient stone.
>
> Do not forget that good weapons are often lying about ready at hand. A bottle with the bottom smashed off is more effective than a naked hand in gouging an opponent's face. . . . The vulnerable parts of the enemy are the heart, spine and privates. Kick him or knee him as hard as you can in the fork. While he is doubled up in pain get him on the ground and stamp his head in.

At least some of the Commandos were provided with an ingenious device: two guns strapped under the armpits of a trooper fired when his arms were raised in seeming surrender. The chains used on the prisoners who were trussed in the Dieppe raid were called "death slings" in the Commando handbook. A noose was passed over the head and around the neck of the man shackled, then the end of an attached chain was tied to his bent legs. Thus with every movement the victim helped to strangle himself. The time of death could be determined, for no human being could long lie in this position without being forced to stretch out his legs; the muscle tension became unbearable. This handbook, however, could only be produced in a later trial. The President of the Court at Nuremberg reminded the defense that they were not trying the victorious powers and the British Commando orders, and the events at Dieppe were brought into the trial record only by witnesses' reference to them.[25]

Doenitz and Raeder both testified that they had regarded the Fuehrer's order as a reprisal. Raeder went to Dieppe shortly after the British raid and heard firsthand evidence of how the Commandos had behaved. He saw no reason to protest the Commando Order, as the generals had the Commissar Order, because in fact it seemed to him perfectly legal. Moreover, the Navy was directly involved in only two or three episodes. One was the alleged handing over to the SD at the end of October, 1942, of a member of a British Commando unit that had landed in Norway with orders to attack the *Tirpitz*, lying in dock at Trondheim. The attack made by six Englishmen and four Norwegians had failed, and the entire group with the exception of one British seaman, Robert Paul Evans, escaped across the Swedish border. Evans was captured wearing civilian clothes, with a holster for carrying a pistol under his armpit and a knuckle-duster. He was shot by the SD according to Hitler's orders. The prosecution charged that the Navy captured him, but the arrest was made by the Sipo (the Security Police), the German records showed. A German admiral interrogated Evans before his execution, but otherwise the Navy had not been involved.

Another case, however, directly implicated the Navy. On December 8, 1942, at Le Verdon near Bordeaux two British sailors were captured who said they were shipwrecked. Their faces were painted green, and near where they were picked up a rubber boat was discovered, along with explosives and maps. Immediately after they were interrogated, the Navy commander ordered them shot for attempted sabotage. The shootings were delayed because of a request from Paris from the SD and a Navy captain who wanted further questioning. More interrogations were ordered by the Navy Command, Group West, and the shooting was postponed. When they were finished, the men were delivered to the professional questioning of the SD, since the Navy observed that routine interrogations elicited little useful information in such cases. Permission was asked by the SD on December 10 to delay the execution of the men for three days, but on December 11 they were shot by a Navy detail of one officer and sixteen men.[26]

The war diary of Admiral Johannes Bachmann, the German flag officer in command of western France, read: "Shooting of two English prisoners was carried out by a unit . . . attached to the harbor command, Bordeaux, in the presence of an officer of the SD on order of the Fuehrer." A note appeared in green pencil on the margin opposite this entry that said: "SD should have done this. Phone flag officer in charge in future cases."

The two Commandos, Wallace and Ewart, were the advance party of a group of five two-man sabotage units sent to the Gironde estuary; and while Bachmann was recording the proceedings against the two captured Commandos, one German ship after another reported damage from mines exploding against their hulls in the harbor of Bordeaux. Adhesive mines had been attached below the waterline.* Of the ten Commandos involved in this operation, four in addition to Wallace and Ewart were captured on December 12, one man was drowned in carrying out the operation, and the rest escaped to Spain. The four were executed on March 23 by the SD.

Raeder's lawyer brought up another case, which occurred after Raeder had retired, involving seven seamen (six of the Norwegian Navy and one of the Royal Navy) who were captured near Bergen in July, 1943. Although they were wearing uniforms and the SD man and the Navy Intelligence officers who interrogated them recommended treatment as prisoners of war, the Navy handed them over to the SD for shooting, apparently because Norwegian ships such as the one on which these men were captured belonged to the Norwegian motor torpedo-boat flotilla and were frequently used for sabotage operations. The Navy commander regarded the men, despite their battle dress, as saboteurs, therefore coming under the Fuehrer order. After the execution, their bodies were weighted and thrown into the sea with a depth charge attached to them.[27]

No direct evidence connected Raeder or Doenitz with any of these executions. Raeder testified, and witnesses corroborated him, that he had known nothing of these cases used by the prosecution as evidence against him. Killing of the two Bordeaux Commandos had not been reported to him, although he was familiar enough with the general instructions responsible for their execution. On February 11, 1943, a little more than a week after Raeder retired, the Navy Operations Division International Law and Prizes Section sent out an advice to the effect that a wrong impression seemingly existed in the Navy as well as in the Army, and all commanders in all theaters were threatened, following the Fuehrer's orders, with court-martial proceedings if they "have neglected their duty in informing the troops about the order against saboteurs." The communication went on to say:

---

* The chief of counterintelligence, Admiral Canaris, one of the key members of the Resistance movement who despite being an implacable enemy of Hitler remained in charge of the Abwehr until July 20, 1944, telegraphed the following message to the High Command at the Wolfsschanze on December 17, 1942: "Some five explosions mouth of Gironde at Bordeaux. Sabotage vs. ore ships *Alabama* and *Portland* and vs. ships *Tannenfels* and *Dresden*. In view of statements of the two men shot this probably must have been done with magnetic mines. [signed] Canaris" (NOKW-002 IZG).

Uniformed prisoners acting on military orders must be shot even after they surrender voluntarily and ask to be spared. On the other hand . . . the annihilation of sabotage troops in battle is not to be kept secret at all, but on the contrary should be published in the armed forces communiqué. The purpose of these measures, i.e., to discourage enemy sabotage operations, cannot be accomplished if the enemy Commando troops do not learn that certain death and not safe imprisonment awaits them. Since the saboteurs are to be exterminated at once unless for military reasons they are needed for a short time for interrogation, this office believes it necessary to inform all members of the armed forces at the front and all officers at home dealing with such problems that all saboteurs of this type should be annihilated even if they are in uniform.[28]

It was, the advice admitted, difficult to know what came under the term "saboteur." It did not apply to troops undertaking large-scale operations or to large-scale airborne landings or to open warfare. But if the troops' orders were to destroy factories, bridges, or railroad installations, the men involved came under the extermination order. The Navy Division said:

It can be assumed that security III is familiar with the Fuehrer directive and can therefore answer any objections of the OKH General Staff and the Air Force Operations Staff. With regard to the Navy the question is whether this case should not be used after a conference with the Commander in Chief Navy to make sure that all departments concerned are quite clear as to how Commando troops are to be treated.[29]

The Navy undoubtedly bore the responsibility for the executions in the case of the men who were shot in Bergen. They were captured by Navy units; Navy counterintelligence interrogated them and on direct orders from the sea command at Bergen turned the men over to the SD. A discussion then arose between the higher leaders of the SD to whom the interrogator had reported and the admiral in command; this discussion led to the admiral's decision that these men came under the Fuehrer order. In this unusual case both the SD man and the Abwehr officers who conducted the interrogation told their superiors that the captured men in their opinion should be treated as prisoners of war, but the admiral, disregarding this advice, decided they must be shot.

Sometimes, it should be observed, contrary decisions were made. In one case in late October, 1944, the OKW told the SD and Sipo that three men who had been captured near Verona had been improperly turned over to the SD and were in fact genuine prisoners of war.

The only event in the three cases that could be said to have occurred counter to Raeder's orders or expectations was the shooting of the saboteurs by the Navy firing squad at Bordeaux. Everything else, including the executions, he had approved in principle—as he said, he regarded the Commando Order as a legitimate reprisal. The commanding admiral at Bordeaux, Bachmann, was dubious too about the Navy's doing the killing.

On the whole Raeder took the same view of international law as did the chief officers and officials of the Western Allies. On October 15, 1939, at the start of the war, he wrote a memorandum that stated:

> Military success can be most confidently expected if we attack British sea-communications wherever they are accessible to us with the greatest ruthlessness . . . It is desirable to base all military measures taken on existing International Law; however measures which are considered necessary from a military point of view, provided a decisive success can be expected from them, will have to be carried out, even if they are not covered by existing International Law. In principle therefore, any means of warfare which is effective in breaking enemy resistance should be used on some legal conception, even if that entails the creation of a new code of naval warfare.[30]

Out of context these may sound like hard, canting words, but they match what Churchill and the British and French high commands said when they spoke of the need of depriving Germany of Swedish iron ore and on the other occasions when Norwegian neutrality was being discussed. Furthermore, Raeder's words express the philosophy behind what both sides did in the course of the war.

Raeder put up some resistance to the Nazi attempt to determine naval policies in ideological matters. As Goering said of him—and Raeder remarks with some pride in his memoirs that he made no secret of this—he went to church and he preserved church services in the Navy, although the Party zealots, especially Goebbels, tried to hinder or get rid of them. He was cautious, however; in 1937 he told a Navy pastor that he was not there to wage political warfare against Nazism but to show himself a genuine disciple of Christ with all earnestness and without compromise. Through him, too, the Navy managed to retain *The Naval Officer as Leader and Teacher*, its old manual of indoctrination for officers, written by Korvettenkapitaen Siegfried Sorge before the Nazis came to power. It was used until 1944, when OKW managed to make the Navy get rid of it because of its "humanistic foundations." [31]

Both Raeder and Doenitz had their only serious quarrels with Hitler when the Fuehrer attacked the Navy. Raeder's attempts to resign came as a result of such quarrels. Hitler impugned Raeder's professional judgment. In 1938 the Fuehrer criticized the Navy's plans for shipbuilding in general and for the *Bismarck* and the *Tirpitz* in particular, for their too weak armament and too low speed. This, together with Raeder's built-in mistrust of Hitler, was enough to cause him to leave the room where the Fuehrer was haranguing him in the presence of Keitel and to ask for his demission. Hitler cooled down, as he often did when the mysteries of the Navy were concerned, and asked Raeder to stay. In December, 1942, Hitler feverishly awaited a major success as the big ships attacked a large Allied convoy going to Murmansk; but the commanding officer decided that continuing the action that had resulted in sinking two English destroyers as well as damaging the German warship *Admiral Hipper* would be too precarious in the short northern day. He ordered the ships to return to their base, and Raeder backed up his decision. Hitler was furious and berated Raeder for his policies, again in the presence of Keitel, for a full hour until Raeder asked to see Hitler alone and told him he had to resign. Nor did Hitler this time relent. Although Raeder was nominally made Inspector of the Navy, a post in which he might have continued to exert some influence, his services were never called on again except for a few ceremonial occasions: he attended the funeral of King Boris of Bulgaria in Sofia, and later he presented a motor boat to Admiral Horthy in Budapest on behalf of the Fuehrer. Hitler did not present him with the usual oak leaves for his Knight's Cross on occasion of his retirement. The Fuehrer had been thwarted in his high expectations of a victory at sea in the dark days of the loss of the Stalingrad army, and he turned hopefully to Doenitz and the submarines.

Raeder never won the battle with Hitler on behalf of his ships. In the early part of the war he attempted to explain to a dubious Fuehrer that the big ships even in their harbors, whether in France or in Norwegian fjords, forced the Allies to keep large forces on hand—forces that would be freed if the German battleships were scrapped, as Hitler wanted them to be. Raeder explained that the Allies had to detach their own battleships for guarding convoys or keep them near the German coast for instant use in case a major battle of surface craft should develop. Britain could not take the risk of the German heavy cruisers and battleships breaking through, thus leaving Allied merchant ships and the British coast unprotected, even for a short time. Hitler was never fully convinced. The loss of major ships—the *Graf Spee*, the *Bismarck*—and the experience during World War I (which the Fuehrer was determined not to repeat) when the battleships tied up for most of the war led Hitler to outbursts of fury against the Navy when anything went wrong on the high seas. Inaction was wrong and so was any battle that was lost.

No serious moral issues came between Raeder and Hitler, although Raeder regarded the attack on Russia as a breach of the Soviet-German nonaggression pact; nor did he like the vulgar destructions of the *Kristallnacht* or the Nazi war on the churches. None of these things, however, led to any protests on his part. These came only when the Navy was the object of attack. He never thought of resistance. The Roehm putsch and the Fritsch affair left him perhaps saddened, but he was unwilling to take any countermeasures for his friend Fritsch. True, after Fritsch's acquittal on the charges of homosexuality Raeder ostentatiously had the Navy salute his visit to the flagship with a fifteen-gun salute. Otherwise the admiral was silent.

In his farewell talk to the conference of flag officers in mid-January, 1943, after his final quarrel with Hitler, he said:

> For the first time in *this* war the German people are fortunate enough to meet their enemies with a united philosophy by reason of an ideology which is predominant among the whole people . . . I believe it is one of the highest tasks of the officer corps to recognize these facts . . . and to ap-

preciate them as the sources of tremendous moral force . . . I ask you all to make every effort to occupy yourselves still further and more searchingly from a higher standpoint, with the National Socialist ideology. . . . Today *the life of the people* must depend on these tasks as primarily on the totality of National Socialist ideas. The nation personifies the ambition and substance of our whole life. Its thousand-year-old tasks and struggles reach to the Heavens, from which the influence of God governs all living creatures . . . National Socialism is what is held in common above all keenly desired personal convictions. From it alone, therefore, can grow the uniformity of ideas in the officers' corps which is necessary to sweep the nation and the services on toward the high aims which we wish to attain.

. . . It is quite obvious from the great common task of educating the German to his new aim, as indicated above, that there must be a complete mutual trust in the relationship to the Party which can only exist if both sides have recognized their duty.*

Although this was a ceremonial talk and Hitler and the Party would be sensitive to what he said, the words were nevertheless in accord with Raeder's conduct ever since Hitler took power. National Socialism might have some regrettable sides, but it was a means to an end and the end, which was a unified Germany presiding over a cooperative and blockade-proof Europe, could also be part of the Kingdom of Heaven.

Raeder was not without civil courage; he did use his influence in a number of cases to help Jews or part Jews whom he knew and on behalf of Pastor Niemoeller, a former submarine officer. Late in the war, too, he intervened with Himmler, whose police had jailed and tortured Raeder's friend Dr. Otto Gessler. Gessler, a former member of the SPD and Reich Defense Minister, had suggested some measures that might improve the failing civilian morale, and because this sounded like criticism if not defeatism and because of Gessler's political background he was arrested at the time of the attempt on Hitler's life along with hundreds of other men and women with suspicious political pasts. Raeder, at some risk to himself in those days of long knives, got in touch with Himmler and Hitler and tried to protect Gessler. Furthermore, he saw Gessler after the former minister was released from prison, and he even was able to provide Gessler with a remodeled truck for traveling (Gessler was not allowed to use trains). But Raeder accepted the rest of Nazism *faute de mieux*, and he also accepted the golden Party badge and on his sixty-fifth birthday a present of 250,000 RM from the Fuehrer. If he got not only his battleships but the means of protecting them from assaults of the amateurs, including Hitler, he could make his tacit pacts. But he was never self-seeking. His lances were broken for the Navy, not for himself.

* The final "Address of the Naval Supreme Commander Grossadmiral Dr.h.c. Raeder at the conference of Flag Officers and Commanding Officers of the Navy at the Supreme Command Headquarters of the Navy, Berlin, January 12–15, 1943." Grossadmiral Raeder had been given the title of Doctor of Philosophy, *honoris causa*, by the Christian-Albrechts University in 1926 for his *History of German Cruiser Warfare in World War I* (489-PS [IZG]).

Raeder was defended with great skill and devotion by his chief counsel, Walter Siemers, a Hamburg lawyer he had not known before. The admiral characteristically—for he was convinced of his unblemished character—thought it an advantage that he and his lawyer had not met previously; in this way Siemers could start without prejudice. Siemers, obviously convinced the charges against his client were without substance, called a succession of witnesses whose testimony on behalf of Raeder and the Navy was most informative, and like Doenitz's counsel, Otto Kranzbuehler, he was a dignified and learned figure in that hostile courtroom. Neither Siemers nor Kranzbuehler could get direct access to Allied orders such as those regarding Norway, but they patched the story together from material Kranzbuehler's assistant, Meckel, was able to get from well-disposed Americans and Britishers in London. Siemers was also able to put on the stand former SPD Minister of the Interior Karl Severing, who could remind the court, as a man who had bitterly opposed Hitler, how many prominent foreigners had dined with and praised the Fuehrer during the period Raeder was Commander in Chief of the Navy. Admiral Erich Schulte-Moenting, commanding admiral in France, was an excellent witness not only for Raeder but for the Navy as he explained how a non-Nazi officer looked on the trivial violations of Versailles in the face of the need for defending the country. A former state secretary in the foreign office, Freiherr von Weizsaecker, who had been a member of the Resistance and would soon be tried before another Nuremberg court, testified on the secret treaty that had accompanied the German-Russian nonaggression treaty. The Russian prosecutor objected—as he always did—to any mention of this sensitive subject. "We are examining the crimes of the major German criminals," Rudenko said. "We are not investigating the foreign policies of other states." [32]

Closely read, the defense successfully refuted the main charges or at least explained them in such fashion as to place Raeder, as far as his military career was concerned, in no worse light than his accusers. It was true that he had served a criminal regime, but he had never known it as such; he, like Doenitz, was busy with the war at sea. Nothing for which he was responsible—neither waging submarine warfare while he was Commander in Chief, nor accepting the Commando Order as a reprisal and a means of combatting a new form of atrocious warfare—was essentially different from either the theory or the practice of Allied naval commanders. The counts on aggressive warfare were without substance. As any naval officer would and must, Raeder took orders, analyzed the strategic situation—whether in Norway or on the high seas—astutely and objectively, and he fought decently.

After Raeder was convicted and sentenced to life imprisonment (a sentence he begged the court to change to shooting), a Norwegian officer visited him in Spandau. The officer, filled with resentment against all Germans, had to question him in connection with the impending trials in Norway of alleged collaborators. The following dialogue took place:

PELLESTAD: "Are you called Raeder?"

RAEDER: "Please, who are you?"

PELLESTAD: "First Lieutenant Pellestad."

RAEDER: "It would be more to the point to have said so at first as is customary between soldiers."

PELLESTAD: "But you're not a soldier any more."

RAEDER: "I've been an honorable soldier; I emphasize with all decisiveness that you are not following the general usages. I repeat: don't say Raeder to me. Only my superiors can do that."

PELLESTAD: "I've heard you. I ought to and will call you Raeder and nothing else."

RAEDER: "Then I won't answer you. What do you think, that you're my superior?"

PELLESTAD: "What do you think really?"

RAEDER: "I think I'll go right away. I have no reason to speak to you."

PELLESTAD: "You'll sit here until we're through with you. What do you want, and how do you want to be addressed?"

RAEDER: "I want to be called Herr Raeder."

PELLESTAD: "We know something about your countrymen and how we were addressed in Norway and you are being much more politely addressed than many of your countrymen did [sic] or talked to us."

RAEDER: "The Navy always treated the Norwegians decently and courteously . . . and the Norwegians recognized this."

PELLESTAD: "I think too the Navy by and large behaved decently."

RAEDER: "Then why are we quarreling? Will you call me Herr Raeder or not?"

PELLESTAD: "I can call you Sir. That will probably satisfy you."

RAEDER: "Certainly you can't call me *Du*." [33]

Raeder won his point and had earned it. They shaved his head after his conviction (he was over seventy then) and handcuffed him to an MP so that when he wrote a note to his visiting lawyer the soldier's hand moved with his across the paper. His wife, who had committed no crime that was ever identified, was imprisoned by the Russians until September, 1949. Not until March, 1950, could she visit her husband, and then only for fifteen minutes every two months. They talked with a double-mesh wire between them, under supervision of officers from the four nations that run Spandau and who often, Raeder said, interrupted the conversation. From his Berlin prison he could write one letter a month to his family. The prisoners were allowed no conversation with each other, and until the summer of 1954 they were forbidden to talk with one another during their work, whether they pasted papers, or did cleaning, or worked in the garden. They were not even allowed to talk, Raeder wrote, with the French prison priest, although they were given careful and "correct" medical attention. Permission was denied him to attend burial services of his only son who died while Raeder was in prison.

Raeder was suddenly released when he was eighty years old. Having no inkling of what was to come, he was brought to a room where his civilian clothing was laid out and was told he could leave. Raeder was released after indefatigable labors by Walter Siemers, his lawyer at Nuremberg. Siemers could have worked on the sympathies of the British, French, and Americans, who were by now doubtful of the usefulness of keeping Raeder in prison. It would have been easy to circulate a petition for clemency, and mighty voices would have been heard on Raeder's behalf. But Siemers worked quietly behind the scenes to convince the Russians, who are always the stumbling block at Spandau, that no threat to world peace would come from the old man leaning on two canes. His tactics were slow, but successful, and the Russians agreed with their three former allies that he could be released from prison.

Raeder survived long enough to write his memoirs and to attend a few ceremonies, including one with Doenitz on the occasion of dedication of the naval war memorial in Wilhelmshaven in 1957. There they were photographed, Doenitz, with his hand under Raeder's arm, unostentatiously helping to keep him steady. Both of them were free, but with many memories of deeds done and undone.

KARL DOENITZ

Both the German admirals on trial at Nuremberg, Karl Doenitz and Erich Raeder, were charged with the gravest crimes that could be laid to seafaring men. Not only were they accused of plotting to wage aggressive warfare and then having waged it (the latter was at least consonant with the profession of arms), but they were charged with war crimes, with *the* war crime of any naval officer: they had made no effort to rescue the survivors of torpedoed ships but instead had ordered survivors shot as they sat or lay in boats or floated in the water. In addition, Doenitz and Raeder had sent to their deaths, according to the prosecution, hundreds of noncombatants, including women and children, who had been passengers on merchant ships.

Karl Doenitz, who commanded the German submarines during World War II first as their immediate chief and then as Commander in Chief of the Navy had determined U-boat strategy from the beginning of the war until the end. He was primarily a submarine officer, so much so that his concentration on the U-boats rather than on the entire Navy and its over-all strategy led Raeder to recommend Admiral Rolf Carls ahead of Doenitz as commander-in-chief in 1943. In addition, Doenitz was one of the few convinced National Socialist officers in the German Navy. Over and over again he made ringing addresses with loud political overtones to the German sailors and to the nation, praising "the heaven-sent leadership" in the person of the Fuehrer. Doenitz not only never questioned the Party policies in any respect, but adopted its basic usages and spoke of the Jews in tones used by Gauleiters. He was completely devoted to Hitler. "We are worms compared with him," he told a cheering crowd in Berlin in 1943, adding that Hitler foresaw everything and made no misjudgments. Even at the end of the war Doenitz ordered the ubiquitous pictures of Hitler taken down from public view only a full week after the surrender.

Doenitz was the descendant of a long line of farmers who had lived in Westphalia for centuries and later moved to near Magdeburg. In recent times members of the family left the land to become pastors, professors, officers, businessmen, and industrialists, and to one such, the engineer Emil Doenitz and his wife, Anna, Karl Doenitz was born on September 16, 1891, in Berlin-Gruenau. The boy attended the Realgymnasium in Weimar and after getting his *Abitur* entered the training school of the Imperial Navy on April 1, 1910. In 1912 he was assigned to the light cruiser *Breslau*, which, at the start of World War I, together with the battle cruiser *Goeben* broke through the British Mediterranean fleet to the Dardanelles to join the Turkish forces fighting against the Russian fleet in the Black Sea. Doenitz remained in Near Eastern waters until October, 1916, when he was ordered to the submarine fleet, where he served first as watch officer of the *U-39* and then as commander of the *U-68*. In early October, 1918, Doenitz's submarine was sunk after he had torpedoed a British ship in a convoy near Malta; he was taken prisoner and remained in a British prisoner-of-war camp until July, 1919. Upon his release he returned to active duty as commander of a torpedo boat; in 1923 he was assigned to the staff of the torpedo-boat inspectorate in Kiel, and after that to Navy headquarters in Berlin. In 1927 he returned to sea duty as a navigation officer and in 1930 was made chief of a destroyer flotilla. From 1930 to 1934 he was head of the Admiralty staff division of the High Command of the North Sea and then was given command of the cruiser *Emden*. In 1935 he was assigned the job of rebuilding the German U-boat fleet, which he commanded at the outbreak of the war.*

As commander in chief of submarines Doenitz was a skillful, courageous, and often chivalrous officer. The increase in efficiency of communications and weapons since World War I had given certain advantages to the U-boats at the start of the war. They could be sent to operate in packs in the good hunting grounds that had been discovered by air reconnaissance or by other submarines; they could rendezvous with surface and U-boat tankers that could provide the life-giving fuel. Toward the latter part of the war the faster engine and the snorkel enabled U-boats to cruise for weeks at a time underwater at speeds high enough to enable them to overtake convoys. Their weapons were better too: the torpedo that showed no wake, that homed in on the sound of a propeller, and the magnetic mines that wrought considerable destruction in the early part of the war were formidable new devices

---

* In the spring of 1916, Doenitz married Ingeborg Weber, the daughter of General Erich Weber. They had three children, a daughter and two sons, both of whom were killed in the war (the elder a lieutenant senior grade whose speed boat was sunk in the English Channel in 1944, the other a junior lieutenant who lost his life on a submarine). The daughter married an outstanding U-boat commander, Guenter Hessler.

when they worked properly. There were new weapons against the U-boats, too; radar could pick up the low silhouette of the submarine through fog and night; depth charges were improved and new tactics of dropping them were developed; and above all there was the airplane that could spot the U-boats and bear down on them with such speed that they were often caught on or near the surface.

Although from the very start of the war Doenitz and his fellow officers of the submarine service chafed at the restrictions Hitler for political reasons placed on their activities, they observed them on the whole, but they argued against them as best they could. It was all very well, they said, if high policy required them to let Allied ships sail by their torpedo tubes, but Germany could not win the war with such tactics. A British ship carrying 20,000 troops had been allowed to run past a submarine that was in a position to torpedo her because the commander, in the night, could not be sure it was not a French ship and France was to be kept as quiescent as possible. From the beginning, Doenitz wanted an unrestricted submarine blockade around the British Isles, one that would allow the submarine commanders to sink on sight any ship found there. Not until January 1, 1940, however, was Raeder able to persuade Hitler to issue the order; it was the Fuehrer's strategy to keep hostilities in the *drôle de guerre* stage until he was ready to strike.

The German Admiralty's orders in the early stages of the war were for immediate attack on both enemy and neutral ships that zigzagged, were blacked out, or radioed the position of a submarine they sighted. Other ships were first to be visited and searched and their crews placed in a position of safety as demanded by the Hague Convention.* The sinking of the passenger ship *Athenia* a few days after the start of the war was an error, for the commander of the *U-30*, which sunk her, took her for a troop carrier. She was blacked out and following a zigzag course—and he had just let a real troop carrier, the *Duchess of Bedford*, of 20,000 register tons, go by on assumption that she was a passenger ship. British passenger ships were used, as needed, as troop transports, and it was not always possible for a submarine commander to tell which service they were in. Hitler was concerned enough with neutral opinion to order as a consequence of the sinking of the *Athenia* that no passenger ships, even in convoys, were to be sunk.[34]

On the whole, in those early days, the so-called legal forms of warfare were maintained at sea, as they were on the land, by the regular armed forces. The British Admiralty in 1938, a year before the start of the war, instructed all ships to wireless their position on sighting a submarine, thus

* The 1936 London Protocols, which repeated the provisions of the Hague Convention, also required that a merchant ship, whether armed or not, be visited and searched; if it was found to be carrying contraband, the crew had to be put in a place of safety before it was sunk. But it could be sunk without visit and search if it was in a convoy, defended itself, or was a troop transport.

making them, as the Germans pointed out, part of a sea-wide spotting apparatus. After the start of the war, British captains followed these instructions almost without exception Early in September, 1939, a German submarine sank the *Blairlogie* as it tried to escape while sending its position and, of course, that of the submarine. But along with routine sinkings went acts of a kind that traditionally had distinguished war from mere mutual butchery. When the British ship *Fanan Head* was torpedoed, the submarine, still on the surface, was attacked by British planes, one of which it shot down. A number of the German crew had been wounded as they manned the antiaircraft gun on the submarine's deck, and the British pilot of the downed plane was rescued by one of the men who had been hit in the attack; despite a shell splinter in his back, the German sprang into the water after the pilot and brought him on board the U-boat. The submarine then headed for Reykjavik, Iceland, to hand over the pilot for medical care, and only then continued what the Germans, who even at sea considered the Army the dominant service, called "the march East."

When on September 5, 1939, a German U-boat sank the British ship *Royal Sceptre*, the submarine commander stood by while the survivors were transferred to the British steamer *Browning*. A month later another submarine, which had sunk the Greek steamer *Diamantin* with its lifeboats up, picked up the entire crew and brought them to safety.[35] In another case in the early months of the war, a German submarine stopped a British ship and ordered the crew into a lifeboat, but when the commander of the submarine saw the poor state of the boat he told the skipper to reembark his crew of thirteen and make full speed to the nearest British port. He also gave him a bottle of German gin and told him, "You English are no good, sending a ship to sea with a boat like that.[36]

A month after the start of the war, U-boat captains, despite considerable losses and damage suffered from planes and armed ships, were still directed to aid in the rescue of crews of sunken ships if doing so did not endanger the submarine and not to attack passenger ships without warning even if they were armed unless they were carrying troops. Shortly after, the orders became more elastic and more difficult for a commander to follow: U-boats were not to torpedo unarmed passenger ships not in convoy and with more than 120 people on board (this number, the submarine commanders were told, could be calculated by counting the number of lifeboats; noting the number of decks, and estimating the length of the promenade decks would assist their calculations).[37]

But the war hardened rapidly. The desire to sink more ships without unduly endangering the submarine, which was as vulnerable to so-called defensive armament as to any other, coupled with British practices soon forced a change in U-boat tactics. Reports almost immediately came to the German Admiralty that British ships were using radio to summon aid from the air, and only a month after the start of the war came the order from Winston Churchill to ram any submarine sighted. "Ram it or attack it with depth charges, if equipped to do so." [38] This followed the announcement made by Churchill as First Lord of the Admiralty on September 26, 1939, that all British ships were to be armed.*

Not only British ships attempted to ram the U-boats; the Danish ship Vendia tried the maneuver on September 30, 1939, as did the Swedish ship Gun, and both were sunk. Doenitz said at Nuremberg that the German commanders at that time were still ordered to conduct their operations in accord with the rules of international law. They were provided with a "prize disk," a mechanical, portable legal adviser with information about what they could do under the naval conventions and which supplied the submarine commanders with the relevant paragraphs of the prize ordinances. The prize disk showed immediately whether, for example, a neutral ship with contraband should be sunk or captured or allowed to proceed on its voyage.[39] It was standard practice for U-boat captains to give position, medical supplies, and water to the survivors of ships sunk.

On the whole, the Germans reacted to what the British were doing. A German order of September 4, 1939, read: "On the Fuehrer's orders, no hostile action is to be taken against passenger ships for the time being, even when in convoy." [40] Then the British began to ship troops to France in such vessels, and on October 29, 1939, a different order was issued: "Passenger liners in enemy convoys may be subjected to immediate unrestricted armed attack by U-boats." [41] As submarines were fired on increasingly by merchant vessels, the German Admiralty ordered on November 7, 1939: "U-boats are permitted to attack immediately with all weapons at their command all passenger ships which can be identified with certainty as enemy ships and whose armament is detected or already known." [42] Even blacked-out passenger ships were not to be attacked; the order permitting their torpedoing came only on February 23, 1940.

The reasons for these orders are not difficult to see. Hitler hoped to keep France and England from full-scale participation in a war he preferred to fight by stages. The Navy understood his purposes; the Naval Operations Staff, echoing Raeder's memorandum, stated on October 15, 1939:

> It is still desirable to base military measures on the existing principle of international law; but military measures recognized as necessary must be taken if they seem likely to lead to decisive military successes, even if they

* The British orders issued in 1938 regarding cases of an enemy's observing international law read: "As the armament is solely for the purpose of self-defense, it must only be used against an enemy who is clearly attempting to capture or sink the merchant ship . . . Once it is clear that resistance will be necessary if capture is to be averted, fire should be opened immediately." And against an enemy acting in defiance of international law the orders read: "It will then be permissible to open fire on an enemy vessel . . . even before she [the merchant ship] has attacked . . ." (N XIII, pp. 256–57). Of course, in practice the submarine commander could not distinguish whether a ship was firing on him in order to escape or because its captain believed the submarine to be violating international law.

are not admitted by international law. For that reason, the military weapon which effectively breaks the enemy's powers of resistance must on principle be given a legal base, even if new rules of naval warfare have to be created for that purpose.[43]

But modern war tends to deteriorate rapidly because the job, however concealed by the traditional forms of chivalry, is to kill and destroy not only the soldiers but the will of a country to continue to fight. One submarine surfaced and the British ship it had torpedoed immediately opened fire. In another case, the Germans complained that soldiers were hidden all over the deck of a seemingly peaceful merchantman, which was ready for action and whose armament included depth charges on the deck. The German Navy behaved correctly, as do most branches of the armed forces of any country when the cost is not too great. Doenitz pointed out that the Navy always recognized the immunity of hospital ships, although in the early part of the war the Germans themselves had none except in the Baltic, where the Geneva Convention was not recognized between Soviet Russia and the Reich. According to the testimony of a German officer during the trials, not one hospital ship was sunk by the Germans during World War II, although a German hospital ship, the *Tuebingen*, was sunk (doubtless in error) by the British in the Mediterranean. On April 1, 1945, the American submarine *Queenfish* sank the Japanese passenger ship *Awa Maru*, of 11,259 tons. The *Awa Maru*, carrying Red Cross supplies to Allied prisoners of war, had been given a safe conduct by the Allies on her voyage to and from Malaya and the Dutch Northeast Indies. Only one man survived the sinking, which was certainly due not to ruthlessness but to a regrettable error on the part of the American submarine commander. He was court-martialed and found guilty of negligence.[44]

Doenitz testified that it usually took the German Admiralty four weeks to adopt measures to counter what the British were doing. But he also knew that the British blockade of the Reich "had to be broken one way or another," and the submarine arm, which he called "a respectable firm," had a huge task in fighting against an enemy who numerically was vastly superior. After the fall of France, the German Admiralty on August 17, 1940, ordered that any ship could be sunk that came within the zone the Americans had forbidden to their own vessels (an area of some 750,000 sea miles stretching from the Faeroes to Bordeaux and 500 miles west of the coast of Ireland). No nonsense now about visit and search, and Raeder ordered that if a neutral ship were sunk, a mine rather than a submarine should be blamed whenever possible. This was meant to confuse the enemy as well as to placate the neutrals, who were warned in effect not to trade with Britain on pain of losing their ships and the lives of their crews. This was a far cry from the concept of close blockade, which can only be enforced by a superior fleet within an area where it commands the exits and entrances to harbors. But the British were just as far from former notions of international law with their own measures of blockade and their definitions of contraband. Both sides regarded the other as lawless, and both were right. A nation, as the German Operations Staff report said, will always adopt measures that will lead to decisive results in a war.

The Reich started the war with a relatively small submarine fleet. The Germans had fifty-six U-boats, of which, Doenitz testified, thirty had completed their tests by July, 1939, and of these only fifteen were capable of navigating in the Atlantic.* By late 1940 and early 1941 the Germans, Doenitz said, were down to eighteen high-seas U-boats; and since only one-third of a submarine fleet can be in operational areas at a time (one-third is at home preparing to go to sea, the other third on its way to the battle stations), six or sometimes only three submarines were in action against the enemy. In other words, 120 to 240 men were actively fighting the naval war against England.

If the submarines' early success was out of all proportion to their numbers, so were their losses. A higher proportion of submarines was sunk in the early months of the war than at any other time, even when the Allied countermeasures were at their most efficient, during the times of the great convoys to England and to Russia of 1943 and 1944. This ratio was the result of the small number of submarines operating compared to later years. Nevertheless, in 1943, Doenitz was forced for some time to suspend operations in the North Atlantic since losses of German U-boats were insupportable. In December, 1942, 164 submarines were assigned to operations in the Atlantic, but of these only about forty were at their battle stations at one time. In addition, there were twenty-four U-boats assigned to the Mediterranean, twenty-one to the North Sea, and three to the Black Sea. The hardest convoy battle came in March, 1943, when out of a single convoy the U-boats sank twenty-one ships with 141,000 GRT and damaged one or two others. But the radar and air coverage became too much for the U-boats, and seven submarines were sunk fighting against one convoy, although they sank 55,761 tons. In another encounter, the U-boats sank almost 30,000 tons, but three were lost and such attrition over a period of time was unbearable, for the highly trained crews were not easily replaceable nor, with the strain on the German war effort, were the ships.†

---

* This was Doenitz's testimony at Nuremberg. Years later in his book 10 Jahre und 20 Tage he said the number of U-boats was twenty-two (Karl Doenitz, 10 Jahre und 20 Tage [Bonn: Athenaeum-Verlag, 1958], p. 49. N XIII, pp. 249, 309).

† German losses in 1939 were 17.5 per cent, in 1940 13.4 per cent, in 1941 11.4 per cent, in 1942 8.9 per cent. As improved radar and air protection were added to Allied defensive measures, they rose to 9.2 per cent in the three-month period from January to March, 1943. In May of that year Doenitz had to send his U-boats out of the North Atlantic. Despite every stratagem he could think up—ordering, for example, submarines in the Bay of Biscay to stay on the surface and to shoot it out with British planes, or diving to avoid the fight— he could not seriously menace Allied convoys again until June, 1944.

At that time the new and faster submarines were ready, equipped with the snorkel that enabled them to take in air and recharge their batteries while underwater. The new

Doenitz and the German Navy from their point of view were up against a virulent case of Anglo-Saxon pseudomorality. On the one hand, both England and the United States regarded with horror the sinking without warning of merchant ships carying noncombatants even though the ships were armed. These allies were powerful in surface ships and could hold to the traditional moralities of sea warfare far better than a country like Germany that had to rely on new weapons. In World War I, Americans were moved to a high pitch of indignation when the *Lusitania* was sunk even though she was a British ship, she was listed as an armed merchantman in the British Naval Pocketbook of 1914, and the most valuable single item of her cargo was ammunition.* On the other hand, first Britain and then both countries blockaded Germany in World War II as they had in World War I, without regard to international convention on contraband. In World War I they had tried to keep every commodity out of Germany including food and all nonmilitary supplies, and the civil population had suffered severely for eight months after the end of hostilities as the blockade continued. It was a way of putting pressure on the Germans to sign the peace treaty, which was ratified by Germany on July 10, 1919. The blockade was lifted two days later, on the 12th.

The Allies also used precisely the same tactics against enemy shipping that they officially complained of—a circumstance the court at Nuremberg took into account. It was the only time the tribunal permitted the defense of tu quoque. The British would not recognize the Red Cross markings on German planes seeking to rescue fliers who had bailed out over the English Channel, and the German Admiralty accepted their shooting at these planes without protest because no specific international arrangement on the status of such planes had ever been reached. But the orders to ram and to attack with depth charges and the decision to arm all vessels and to radio positions

---

U-boats could cruise for weeks at a time without surfacing; they could run submerged from the North Sea to Capetown and back and fire their torpedoes from a depth of fifty meters. They had an underwater speed of eighteen miles per hour. The snorkel could be installed on old submarines as well, and Doenitz ordered that no U-boat be used after June 1 without it. From the time of the invasion of Normandy, in June, 1944, to the end of August the Germans equipped thirty U-boats with the device; in this short period of the revival of submarine strength, they sank twelve ships of 56,845 tons, five war vessels, and four landing craft.

A weapon that never came into action was the XXI, a type of U-boat that an American commander called "so advanced no practical defense existed against it." By the end of the war, 119 of these were built. One was on its way to the Caribbean at the time of the surrender, but none fired a torpedo. They were 250 feet long with a low silhouette, and since they could fight entirely underwater were undetectable by radar. They carried twenty torpedoes on long patrols and twenty-three normally. They could fire a second salvo within five minutes of the first. Many of the features of these U-boats are still in use in the American Navy (Lt. Commander A. N. Glennon, U.S.N., "The Weapon that Came Too Late," in *U.S. Naval Institute Proceedings*, Mar., 1961, pp. 85–93).

* The *Lusitania* had 5,468 cases of ammunition on board, 4,200 of which contained a total of 10½ tons of gunpowder—five pounds to the case (Edwin Borchard and W. P. Lage, *Neutrality for the United States* [New Haven: Yale University Press, 1957]).

when a U-boat was sighted made it imprudent for a submarine to visit and search. In Norway and on the high seas, both the English and the Americans could act in ways that seemed to the Germans clearly illegal; not only did the British mine Norwegian territorial waters and attack an unarmed German ship inside them, but the commander of the British ship that breached Norway's neutrality was presented with a citation and a medal.

The United States, which was technically at peace with Germany for a year and a half after the start of the war, permitted American warships to shadow German submarines and to report their positions. British ships were repaired in American shipyards; fifty destroyers were turned over to England in return for the lease of bases in British possessions. President Roosevelt, Doenitz pointed out, sent a mission of naval officers under command of an admiral to London to work out means of cooperation between the Anglo-Saxon navies. In place of the three-mile limit formerly internationally recognized as marking a nation's sovereignty, Roosevelt imposed a 300-mile limit, which included both American and Canadian waters, within which no German submarine could enter. If it did, it was to be regarded as an enemy and if possible destroyed. On April 18, 1941, Admiral King announced an American security zone extending 2,300 nautical miles off the east coast to within 740 sea miles of Europe, thus including the Azores in the American security area, and on July 7, 1941, the United States took over the protection of Iceland.

On June 20, 1940, the German submarine U-203 sighted the battleship USS *Texas* in a British blockade zone. Since the U-boat commander was uncertain whether or not it had been lend-leased to England, he attacked, but the torpedoes missed. Hitler, who for all his loathing of Roosevelt and the democracy he headed was anxious to keep the United States out of the war, ordered that the performance not be repeated. The War Diary of the Naval Operations Staff for March 5, 1940, stated:

> With reference to the conduct of economic warfare, orders are given to the Naval Forces that US ships are not to be stopped, seized or sunk. The reason is the assurance given by the Commander in Chief to the American Naval Attaché, whom he received on 20 February, that German submarines had orders not to stop any American ships whatsoever. All possibility of difficulties arising between the USA and Germany as a result of economic warfare are thereby to be eliminated from the start.[45]

The American neutral zone of 300 miles off the coast was recognized in a directive of the German Admiralty of April 4, 1941.

On September 4, 1941, the U-652 was attacked with two depth charges and in return fired two torpedoes at an unknown destroyer that turned out to be the USS *Greer*. The submarine commander discovered only the day after the attack that the destroyer was American. Despite the facts, Roosevelt announced that the German attack on the *Greer* had been unprovoked and denounced the piracy of the U-boat. American warships sailed with British convoys, and two of the destroyers taking part in these actions, the *Kearney* and the *Reuben James*, were struck by torpedoes.* On September 15, 1941, the American Secretary of the Navy ordered American naval vessels to sink any German ship attacking Allied commerce, whether surface or underwater craft.[46]

The American Navy, according to Admiral King, took a realistic view of all this. It regarded attacks of the submarines as understandable under the circumstances and not as an aggression against the United States, but this was far from true of the administration. Roosevelt used the incidents to move the United States as close to war as he could without a vote of Congress. He declared an unlimited national emergency, something never known in American history before, and he ordered American warships to shoot first on sighting any German submarine. German U-boats were unleashed against American ships only on December 9, 1941, after the declaration of war, and they caused heavy losses off the American coast. The region between Cape Hatteras and south of Florida for a time saw some conspicuous submarine successes—the coastal ports were lighted, and even in the relatively shallow waters, only eight to ten meters deep, the submarines found targets for their torpedoes. These sinkings must have been balm to the Fuehrer's ego, for it was not like him to suffer aggressions without replying a hundredfold if he could, and his restraint with regard to American provocations, especially after he threw his armies against the Soviet Union in June, 1941, was owing solely to a desire to keep the United States out of the war as long as possible.

German success in the use of submarines was regarded with admiration by their allies in Italy and Japan, but neither country imitated the tactics successfully, although the Japanese submarine command asked for German instructors and German liaison officers journeyed to Tokyo. The strategy of the two navies, as of the armed forces in general, was never coordinated. The Japanese went their own way and the Germans theirs. The Italians, however, responding to a German request on July 24, 1940, joined the Germans in the Atlantic, sending twenty-two submarines to Bordeaux. Doenitz declared that they were most cooperative, but their training was simply not up to the job before them. The Atlantic was an alien sea to the Italians, and their reports of where they were and what shipping they spotted were inaccurate. Doenitz stationed the Italian submarines where they would be least threatened from the air, but they maneuvered inefficiently when they came to attack, or they failed to attack, or they came on the scene too late. The Italians had been trained to wait for ships to cross their paths. Individual

---

* The *Reuben James* was one of five destroyers escorting a fast convoy; after she was torpedoed, her depth charges apparently exploded and casualties were heavy. Out of a crew of 160 only 45 survived. The *Kearney* also suffered heavy losses. (Samuel Eliot Morison, *The Battle of the Atlantic* [Boston: Little, Brown and Company, 1950]; Langer and Gleason, *The Undeclared War* [New York: Harper and Row, Publishers, 1953]).

commanders attacking ships not in convoy often showed great daring and initiative. The tactics against convoys, however, were something else again. A total of only twenty tons of shipping a day for each U-boat was sunk by Italian submarines in 243 sea days. The Germans, in 378 sea days, sank in the same area 453,199 GRT or 1,115 tons per ship day. Moreover, as Doenitz pointed out, the Germans did not have the benefit of the years of training the Italians had, for submarines were forbidden the Weimar Republic. Some failures of the Italian submarine warfare were due to technical deficiencies; the submarines had no ventilator mast as part of the conning tower so when traveling on the surface they had to sail with the tower open, which was impossible in the heavy seas of the Atlantic though perfectly comfortable in the Mediterranean. Such defects could be repaired, but with few exceptions the Italian war effort at sea as on land was without enthusiasm or, indeed, much if any desire to fight. The war was never popular in Italy, nor were the Nazis.

The Germans with inadequate forces for the main theater of naval war in the Atlantic disliked diverting submarines to the Mediterranean, but with the mounting and eventually catastrophic losses of Axis ships supplying the North African Italo-German armies, the Admiralty was forced to send U-boats to these shallow, dangerous waters. There occurred one of the few atrocities committed by German submarines, the basis of one of the chief charges against Doenitz at Nuremberg.

The most serious charge leveled against Doenitz was his alleged violation of the customs and usages of war. He issued the so-called *Laconia* Order, in which he declared that the rescue of shipwrecked survivors after a sinking was contrary to the most primitive requirements of self-preservation. In talks to submarine crews he also allegedly issued most ambiguous verbal orders (for which one German submarine commander was later executed after a trial by a British court), that seemed to demand that a submarine captain shoot the crews of torpedoed enemy ships. The Commando Order affected Doenitz only tangentially, since when it was issued he was in charge of U-boats, which had nothing to do with either the capture or the later treatment of saboteurs, and when he became Commander in Chief it was already in force.

Otto Kranzbuehler, a captain in the German Navy and one of the ablest lawyers on either side at Nuremberg, made a brilliant defense. He cited testimony from Allied as well as German sources telling of Doenitz's chivalry; shipwrecked crews on his order had been given food and rum; an American captain had thanked the Germans for treatment accorded him and his crew; Allied and neutral ships had been given medical assistance; a submarine commander had helped to right capsized lifeboats despite the danger to his U-boat from attack by airplanes. The defense also cited Doenitz's messages before September, 1942, of approval for the rescue of survivors of a sinking (in one instance, six enemy survivors were taken on board a submarine, the U-206, where they had spent two weeks after their plane had been shot down in August, 1941).

One of the turning points of the submarine campaign and of treatment of survivors of torpedoed ships came with the sinking of the British passenger ship *Laconia*, an event that gave rise to a grave charge against Doenitz. The *Laconia*, of 19,965 tons, was torpedoed in the mid-South Atlantic between the West African coast and Brazil on September 12, 1942. She carried 2,732 passengers and crew, including some 1,800 Italian prisoners of war being transported to England from North Africa, where they had been captured. The *Laconia* was a legitimate target for a U-boat. She mounted two 4.7-inch naval guns of Japanese manufacture from World War I, six three-inch anti-aircraft guns, six 1.5-inch guns, four rapid-firing Bofors guns, and two groups of two-inch rockets—more than was needed to sink a submarine. Further, on previous voyages she had served as a troop ship. This time, in addition to the crew of 463 men, there were 286 British military men, 80 civilian passengers, including women and children (mostly returning home from Suez or the British colonies), the Italian prisoners, and 103 Poles, a company from a division formed in April, 1942, in Teheran. They were now acting as jailors for the Italians on board.

The weather was clear, the sea calm, and the *Laconia* sank slowly enough for everyone except the Italian prisoners of war to get off the ship. The majority of the Italians, who had been locked up in the hold, were caught there, but some 500 managed to break out, having fought off their Polish guards, and most of them got off the ship. Because of the *Laconia*'s list many of the lifeboats and rafts could not be lowered. After the ship went down, Kapitaenleutnant Werner Hartenstein, the commander of the U-156, who had sunk her, saw immediately that hundreds of the survivors would perish in the waters infested with shark and barracuda unless emergency rescue measures could be taken. He heard calls for help in Italian, and discovered to his dismay that a large number of Italian prisoners of war had been on board. He wirelessed Doenitz: "Sunk . . . Britisher *Laconia* . . . unfortunately with 1500 [actually 1800] Italian war prisoners. Up to now 90 fished out. Please instruct."

Doenitz, despite the standing rule of all navies that waging war takes precedence over rescuing, detached two submarines, the U-506 and the U-507, underway to missions in the area off Freetown to take part in the rescue operation and requested the Italian commandant stationed at Bordeaux to send the Italian submarine *Cappellini*, which was operating in the area.* The Vichy Government was also asked to send surface ships from Dakar.

---

* Doenitz also ordered a third U-boat, the U-459, to the rescue scene. She was a supply ship without torpedo tubes and was too far away, its commander thought, to be able to reach the survivors at the time the other U-boats would arrive. He also had to spare fuel so he could supply the submarines of this so-called Polar Bear Group. He accordingly decided not to attempt to take part in the operation—the kind of reasonable disobedience of orders permitted in Navy practice.

Hartenstein with Doenitz's permission sent a radio message in English *en clair* guaranteeing the safety of any Allied vessel that would aid in the rescue providing it did not attack his U-boat. The U-156 took 260 survivors on board, rescuing friend and foe impartially; half of them were transferred to the U-506 when it came a day later. The U-507, arriving soon after, picked up 157 others from the water and overfilled lifeboats, making its decks too crowded. The three submarines each took a row of lifeboats in tow, the U-156 flying a large Red Cross flag, four meters square, to identify the rescue work.

But a four-motor American Liberator bomber spotted the U-156, flew over the scene, and after circling the submarines and the lifeboats went away. When it returned a half hour later, it carried out five bombing attacks on the submarine from a height of eighty meters, despite a radio message from Hartenstein that he had English on board and signals from an RAF officer in a lifeboat using an Aldis lamp. One bomb struck a lifeboat the U-156 was towing, a near hit capsized another; there were killed and wounded, and the submarine was damaged by a bomb hitting amidships directly under the control room. The plane flying at a low level on its first bombing run over the submarine was an easy target for the U-156's antiaircraft gun but Hartenstein forbade its being used although he cursed his decision as the plane's last two bombs were aimed at his ship. He wirelessed to Doenitz: "Both periscopes are at present out of order. Breaking off rescue; all off board, putting out toward west, will report." The survivors were put back into the water near lifeboats that could take them on board and Hartenstein had to use what he called "mild force" to get some of the terrified Italians to leave his ship. The Italians, thin and half naked, were in poor physical shape. They had been put on rations of bread and water for days for having violated the no-smoking rule in the hold of the *Laconia* and for having tried to break into the ship's storeroom. But Hartenstein had to put them off his ship; he then was able to make emergency repairs to the U-156, and he remained on the scene.

Doenitz had to make a soul-searching decision. Hitler got copies of the exchange of messages with the submarine commanders. The Fuehrer had doubtless only approved the rescue operation in the first place because of its mollifying effect on German-Italian relations, but if one of the U-boats should be badly damaged or sunk, Doenitz would have to take full responsibility for the loss of German lives. At the beginning of the operation Admiral Kurt Fricke, telephoning Doenitz in his Paris headquarters from Berlin, told him, "The Fuehrer has been informed of the *Laconia* affair. He is displeased, and asks you urgently, if you continue the rescue operations, not to take any risks with the U-boats . . . no risks at all . . ." [47] Many of Doenitz's own staff opposed continuing the operation after the bombing of the U-156, but he replied, "I can't simply put these people in the water. I will go on as before." [48]

Doenitz ordered only Hartenstein to break off his rescue operations;

U-boat commanders Wuerdemann and Schacht in the *U-506* and *U-507*, carrying survivors, continued toward the rendezvous with the French ships from Dakar. Doenitz signaled Hartenstein: "Stop rescue. Check fuel, torpedoes, supplies and equipment, then report." This message was followed by a signal to the other submarines: "The Tommy is a swine, the submarine's safety must in no circumstances be risked even if rescue operations have to be stopped. Remember that protection of submarines by enemy is completely ruled out. Schacht and Wuerdemann give your positions." [49] Schacht replied that he had on board one British officer, sixteen children, and fifteen women, and was towing seven boats with 330 survivors in them. Wuerdemann had 142 Italians on board and nine women and children.

On the 17th, the *U-506*, with its 151 survivors, was bombed by a seaplane. Three bombs detonated near her, but she had dived in time, reached a depth of sixty meters, and was undamaged. Doenitz sent another order telling the two U-boat commanders that only Italians were to be kept on board. Schacht put his British passengers in lifeboats with the exception of two officers he kept as prisoners.* He then made off for the rendezvous, where he transferred the Italians and gave the French ships the position of the survivors. Wuerdemann delivered all his passengers to the French sloop *Annamite*, which had been sent to aid the rescue.

The Vichy Government, too, had a hard decision to make since sending ships to rendezvous with German submarines could easily have unpleasant consequences should the French ships be sighted by the British. Nevertheless, three French ships, the sloops *Annamite* and *Dumont-d'Urville* and the cruiser *Gloire*, were dispatched to the scene and carried out their assignment without untoward incidents, although the captain of the *Gloire* had some nervous moments when a Sunderland approached his ship. He had to decide whether to shoot at it when it came close to bombing range and was getting ready to give the order when it turned away.

The rescue operation as such was a success: A total of 1039 men, women, and children were brought on board the *Gloire*, 42 on the *Annamite*. The others were brought in by the submarines and lifeboats. The *Cappellini* rescued 70 or so, some of whom died of shark bites and exhaustion; the rest were transferred to the *Dumont-d'Urville*, keeping eight on board (two Englishmen and six Italians). Of 103 Poles, 73 were rescued, as were 450 Italians out of the 1,800, a few of whom died almost immediately. Pictures were taken of the survivors as they landed in Gibraltar and Casablanca; the German submarine captains were given testimonials of gratitude—they had turned over their officers' quarters to the women and children and had even provided them cold cream, eau de cologne, and the creature comforts they could supply. The submarines returned with their exhausted crews to their home port.

* Because he had orders to keep two British officers prisoner he took one man from a lifeboat.

But on September 17 and again on the 20th, as a result of the bombing of the *U-156*, Doenitz sent a signal to the commanders of all U-boats, telling them they were under no circumstances to attempt to rescue or to give aid to lifeboats. Submarine commanders were too prone to take a chance on air attacks; after the *Laconia* experience he felt he must give them no choice. He therefore issued the *Laconia* Order, which read:

1) No attempt of any kind must be made at rescuing members of ships sunk, and this includes picking up persons in the water and putting them in lifeboats, righting capsized lifeboats, and handing over food and water. Rescue runs counter to the most primitive demands of warfare for the destruction of enemy ships and crews.

2) Orders on bringing along captains and chief engineers remain in force.

3) Shipwrecked only to be rescued in case their information is important for the boat.

4) Be hard, remember that the enemy has no regard for women and children when he bombs German cities.[50]

Doenitz said at Nuremberg that two men on his staff, Captain Guenther Hessler and Admiral Eberhard Godt, had opposed sending the order. Godt denied this at Nuremberg, but it seems unlikely that Doenitz would have so testified if they had not in fact opposed sending it. It was clearly a hard order to send and to obey.

The lesson for Doenitz and the German Navy seemed clear. Obviously no rescue operation could be undertaken without grave danger to the submarines and their crews. That the U-boats had been dispatched to save Italians is plain from the radio exchange. When Schacht, commanding the *U-507*, reported that he had taken women and children on board and given warm food and drink to people in the lifeboats, the German submarine command had wirelessed back: "Your conduct was wrong. Boat dispatched to aid the Italian allies and not for the rescue of English and Poles."[51] Nevertheless, the U-boat crews had made no distinction in the nationality of the people they picked up. Doenitz's willingness to detach submarines from their battle stations for a rescue operation and Hitler's tacit approval can only be attributed to the presence of the Italians on board the *Laconia*, but once the rescue was started, the Italians were given no priority. The rescue was a spectacular one made under great psychological stress, and Doenitz was its chief organizer.[52]

The mystery of what had happened on the Allied side has not to this date been fully cleared up. No Anglo-American rescue ships ever appeared. The British and Americans knew immediately of the sinking. Not only had the Liberator reported it, but the *Laconia* before she went down had flashed, along with her position, an SSS that she was being attacked by a U-boat and Hartenstein repeatedly radioed his call for help in English. It is known that the messages were received by the British Admiralty and that Allied ships were in the neighborhood. A later British report said that rescue attempts were planned and that the Liberator attack had taken place because of a misunderstanding.* [53]

In the summer of 1963 in an interview with a reporter from the London *Sunday Express*, the American officer who was responsible for the decision to attack the *U-156*, Robert C. Richardson, now a brigadier general attached to the NATO forces, said he had done the right thing. Richardson was in command of the 1st Composite Squadron, U.S. Army Air Force, at Ascension Island, which was a secret base. His British liaison officer reported to him that the *Laconia* had been sunk and asked Richardson if he could send help. Two British freighters were in the neighborhood, but they needed air reconnaissance to spot survivors. Richardson dispatched the Liberator, whose captain first thought the submarine was British although it did not answer his recognition signals. Richardson and his staff, however, thought a German U-boat was rescuing German and Italian prisoners of war, who the British liaison officer had told him were on board. Richardson therefore ordered the bombings, he told his interviewer, without knowing British were among the survivors. "But" he added, "even if we had, it would have made no difference. I would have given the order anyway." Richardson thought the safety of the two freighters was his primary responsibility. He said, "It was a simple wartime decision and I have not thought much about it since . . . It was wartime and the submarine had to be destroyed. The major consideration was not to lose two Allied ships." [54]

Submarine war admittedly raised difficult questions. Hitler considered the possibility of ordering the destruction of crews of torpedoed Allied ships supplying both the air war against the Reich and the Russian armies. If ships and their cargoes were sunk, it became increasingly clear, American production could replace them; but crews needed a long period of training and if they could be killed the submarine war would be more effective. Doenitz wrote to Hitler on May 14, 1942, asking for priorities to improve the torpedoes so the ships they struck would sink more rapidly, thus preventing the rescue of crews. He also expressly pointed out to the Fuehrer that it was not possible to attack the crews of merchant vessels once they were in the lifeboats; the only way to prevent them from sailing again was to use more efficient, quicker-acting torpedoes that would not give them a chance to get off the ship; anything else Doenitz refused to consider.

The *Laconia* Order was a harsh one, but worse evidence was to be cited against Doenitz in connection with the charges against the commander of a submarine operating in the Mediterranean in late 1942. The incident that brought Doenitz closest to the gallows concerned the *U-852*, commanded by an inexperienced man, Kapitaenleutnant Heinz Eck. Eck fired on the crew of

* The official British naval historian, Captain S. W. Roskill, wrote on February 1, 1959, in *The Sunday Times*: "In this affair, Doenitz and his crews were doubtless largely in the right."

a ship he had sunk in the Mediterranean, and at his trial he made a half-hearted defense that directly involved Doenitz, pleading that he had acted under orders. His testimony was corroborated by Oberleutnant Peter Josef Heisig, who swore that he had heard Doenitz, in either September or October, 1942, in the course of instructions on how to conduct U-boat warfare, tell officers in training not only that they should make rescue impossible but that priority of attack should be against rescue ships.[55]

Doenitz, according to Heisig, repeated much of what the Fuehrer had said to the visiting Japanese envoy Hiroshi Oshima a little while before, that the United States had enormous construction capacity but that crews were the bottleneck of the Allied supply line. The United States might produce a million tons of shipping a month, but without crews the ships would be useless. Heisig's testimony was corroborated by that of Korvettenkapitaen Karl Heinz Moehle, who had taken part in seventeen missions as commander of a submarine and later had briefed U-boat captains before they left harbor.[56] Doenitz's orders, Moehle testified, were that both ships and their crews should be the object of attack. Moehle not only cited the Laconia Order, but said he had been told by members of the Admiralty staff that a raft a U-boat had sighted in the Bay of Biscay carrying five survivors should have been destroyed. He testified further that orders were given that no events contravening international law were to be written up in the logs. Moehle spoke with considerable authority, for he was the senior officer of the 5th U-boat Flotilla.

His and Heisig's testimony was sharply contradicted not only by Doenitz but by a long list of other submarine officers who had received the Laconia Order and heard Doenitz's verbal instructions. None of them had thought they were being encouraged to shoot at shipwrecked crews. As for the men on the raft in the Bay of Biscay, Doenitz maintained that he had reprimanded the U-boat captain for the opposite reason; he had told him the men should have been taken aboard the submarine for the information they might give and to make sure they would not return to duty.* [57]

A number of the orders Doenitz issued, however, did sound ambiguous. In 1940, as losses of U-boats mounted under the air attack and depth charges of the British defense, he told the submarine crews, "Weather conditions and distance from the coast are not to be taken into account. Pay attention only to your own ship and to the next attack. We must be hard in this war."[58] By 1943 the gloves were off. On October 7 of that year he sent out an order: "A so-called rescue ship is generally attached to every convoy . . . equipped with planes, large motor boats and heavily armed . . . so that they are often called U-boat traps by the commanders." Then came the fateful sentence:

---

* Doenitz could show that in 1943 he had admonished a U-boat captain for not having taken on board survivors from an English ship who were floating on a raft, because he might have gotten important information from them. That would be the only reason for rescuing them.

"In view of the desired destruction of ships' crews their sinking is of great value." [59]

Another charge made against him, that German submarines had deliberately fired on the crews of ships, Doenitz could meet with reasonable explanations. A survivor of the *Noreen Mary* said that the ship had been swept by machine-gun fire from the attacking U-boat, which had also fired on the lifeboats. A witness from the *Antonica*, which had been sunk at night after a surface attack lasting less than twenty minutes, said the *Antonica's* lifeboats too had been fired on. But Doenitz pointed out that shipwrecked crews, including Germans, often had the impression they were being directly fired at when a submarine was attempting to sink a ship by gunfire, and that the accuracy of the testimony was dubious. The witness from the *Noreen Mary* swore he saw a swastika painted on the hull of the U-boat, but Doenitz pointed out that no submarine ever had gone to sea decorated with such a device. As for the *Antonica*, had the submarine commander wanted to kill the crew he would not have broken off the action after the twenty minutes it took to sink the ship.

The case of Kapitaenleutnant Eck, who commanded the *U-852*, was different. Eck sank the Greek tramp steamer *Peleus* in the Mediterranean on the night of March 13/14, 1944. The *Peleus*, a sizable ship of 8,833 tons, was struck by two torpedoes and went down in about three minutes. A dozen or so of the crew of thirty-five managed to get on life rafts, and the *U-852* attacked them with machine guns and hand grenades.

Lieutenant Eck was twenty-nine years old, a volunteer for the submarine service, and this was his first cruise in command of a U-boat. He sailed out of Kiel on January 18, 1944, moved south along the Atlantic coast, and then proceeded to the perilous shoal waters of the Mediterranean. Four sister ships of the *U-852*, all new and commanded by experienced officers, had been sunk in the Mediterranean, and Eck was nervous. The Mediterranean area was known as a graveyard for U-boats, and Eck could see immediately why it had the reputation. The *U-852* had to run submerged after it sighted the *Peleus* because of the danger from the air (U-boats in the Mediterranean usually ran submerged by day and surfaced only by night). His position was in range of Allied land-based aircraft, and two planes were sighted just before his torpedo attack was made. When he surfaced after the torpedoing, Eck ordered the ship's arms to be brought on deck, he said, because submarines were sometimes fired on, after a ship went down. Also, he intended to sink the *Peleus* wreckage because floating debris would show that submarines were operating in the vicinity. He took two survivors on board for interrogation, and after questioning them he put them back on their raft. The submarine then moved away to a distance of about half a mile to get her machine guns ready, as it turned out, and when she slowly sailed back she flashed her signal light to illuminate the targets. Hand grenades were then thrown among the wreckage, which was also machine-gunned. The firing lasted for five hours, and only three men, all of them wounded, survived in the shark-infested waters. The three were picked up on April 20 by a Portuguese ship. One other man lived on the raft for twenty-five days before he died of his wounds. The U-boat itself was later beached in Somaliland by Eck after it had sunk a transport and then had been bombed by a British plane.

Eck's defense was "operational necessity" and the order to take no survivors on board. His crew took refuge in the same plea and in "superior orders" that had come from the captain. Eck thought, he said, that the lives of his crew and the safety of his ship depended on his destroying any traces of wreckage. A plane seeing wreckage would send out an alarm that in short order could result in the spotting and sinking of a U-boat in those shallow waters. Eck therefore told his crew "with a heavy heart" that they must obliterate any signs of the sinking, and to steel their resolve he reminded them of the German women and children at home suffering under the heavy Allied air attacks. His executive officer, Hoffmann, wanted to use the large 3.7cm. gun the submarine carried against the rafts, which were set on hollow pontoons, but the U-boat was too close for such a large weapon to be aimed.

Some difficulties occurred among the crew. Both Hoffmann and the medical officer on board, a man named Weisspfennig, volunteered to man the machine gun, although regulations in the German Navy forbade a medical officer to shoot. The engineer officer Lenz, who fired the gun part of the time, told Eck he was opposed to the whole operation. He took over the machine gun, however, because he believed that the man who ordinarily would have done the job, a nineteen-year-old petty officer named Wolfgang Schwender, had an illegitimate child, and Lenz testified that he thought Schwender unworthy of carrying out this assignment. Schwender therefore shot only one burst at the targets before he was ordered to cease firing. Although Lenz told Eck flatly that he disagreed with his order to fire on the wreckage, the U-boat captain informed him that the shooting had to be carried out. Lenz then took the gun from Schwender and fired, he admitted, at a human shape, because if a survivor had to die, he should be killed by someone like himself rather than by a man like Schwender. Later, his place was taken by Weisspfennig and then Hoffmann. The submarine cruised among the wreckage, firing intermittently; hand grenades were used as well as the machine guns, and the U-boat even tried ramming, but much of the debris, including a buoy marked *Peleus*, remained afloat.

Eck's trial took place while the Nuremberg proceedings were going on, which undoubtedly inhibited his defense, since he had a chance to save his own neck only by placing responsibility on Doenitz. The defense of superior orders was made without much conviction by one of Eck's lawyers, but Eck himself refused to say he had been following Doenitz's instructions. Before his trial he was confronted with Lenz's damning affidavit, which told how the engineer officer had opposed the order to sink the wreckage and related how

Eck had told him to go ahead with the shooting. Eck asked for permission to speak to Lenz to find out whether he had made the statement voluntarily. He was given an hour by the British authorities to make up his mind whether he wanted to issue a statement in rebuttal, but decided against making one except to say, on the subject of superior orders, that he had never been told to shoot at survivors. He did not wish to comment further on the Lenz affidavit. The decision to sink the wreckage, Eck admitted, was his own. He said that he had seen no survivors on the rafts (this must have seemed unlikely to the court since he had put the two men interrogated back on one) and that he had never intended the destruction of any human being. He swore that no survivors were on the rafts when hand grenades were thrown.

The defense testimony was unconvincing. Why should Lenz have disagreed with the order to shoot at the wreckage if it alone was to be destroyed? Eck—half admitting his guilt—said he did not think the survivors could live in any case; they could not be taken on board because of the Admiralty's orders, nor could they be given provisions enough to last until they might get to land. A *Peleus* survivor testified that a voice had cried out in English from the submarine, "Kill them all." But Eck was sure no one had said that. He admitted that he had been depressed after so many hours of shooting and that his crew had been dispirited too, which was why he had addressed them over the loudspeaker and told them why they had to carry out such an assignment. The President of the *Peleus* Court asked him why, if he was concerned only with sinking the wreckage, he had such a heavy heart and why he had made the reference to the Allied bombing of German women and children if the crew were shooting only at rubber rafts. Eck repeated that he had thought the survivors could not live in any case, but he said he regretted the shooting.

Eck's guilt was incontestable although his counsel tried to show that the U-boat commander thought he was obeying the orders handed down to him. The defense cited the case of the British ship *Caroline*, in which an American court in 1840 held a man accused of murder not guilty because he had acted on superior orders of a duly constituted officer of His Majesty's Government. Eck's one possible use of the American court's decision would have been to testify, as did his witness Heisig, that Doenitz's orders had not been clear to him or that they had in fact required that he kill any survivors. This Eck refused to do, although Heisig by his testimony had opened the way for such a defense. Heisig was a close friend of the U-boat's executive officer August Hoffmann; they had discussed the case together and Heisig, convinced that Doenitz in any case would be convicted by the court at Nuremberg, saw a chance to save Hoffmann. In his unsuccessful attempt to rescue his friend, he placed Doenitz in mortal danger.* [60]

* A witness for Doenitz at Nuremberg, Admiral Gerhard Wagner, testified that Heisig had told him while they were in the Nuremberg prison together that he had only wanted to save the lives of the young submarine officers; he had been told the evidence against Doenitz in any event was overwhelming (N XIII, p. 460).

But Eck would go no further than to say he had wanted to destroy the wreckage in accordance with the orders given him, which is probably true; the human lives, Eck thought, had to be sacrificed. One of the defense lawyers, Professor W. Wegner, a German expert on international law who appeared on behalf of all the defendants, based his main defense on a legal doctrine accepted on the Continent: Eck had found himself in a state of extreme emergency, a situation which the law describes as so overwhelming as to leave the perpetrator without a choice if he is to survive. For this argument he also used the case of the *Caroline*, which while in American waters, where insurgents against the Canadian Government were loading guns and ammunition, had been attacked by a loyal Canadian contingent which boarded the ship and then cut it loose to dash itself to pieces over Niagara Falls. Two American lives were lost and a number of Canadians wounded as a result of the attack. An American court in 1840 accepted the plea that the killings had occurred legitimately because of superior orders and the nature of the emergency.

Also testifying for Eck was Kapitaenleutnant Adalbert Schnee, who said he himself had been on sixteen submarine patrols, that he had warned Eck before he sailed that his assignment was a difficult one and that losses in the Mediterranean area had been high. In fact, all the submarines of the type that Eck commanded had been sunk. Schnee testified too that in Eck's place he would have tried to destroy the wreckage. In answer to the court's skeptical question whether in any event oil patches would not have shown that a sinking had occurred, Schnee answered that oil patches could be attributed to the clearing of bilge by observing planes but debris was clear evidence of a sinking. It would not have been better, Schnee testified, for Eck to leave the site of the sinking, because he could have made no more than 150 miles in the course of a night's sailing and could readily have been picked up by Allied search planes. As for the use of machine guns, Schnee said they were the only weapon that could be used under the circumstances because they are effective against flat targets. He pointed out too that both Eck and his crew were under great strain after the two-month voyage from the Atlantic into the Mediterranean, and while floating wreckage is not important in the Atlantic, where the submarine can get away, it is of crucial importance in shallow seas. But the loyal Schnee was forced by the prosecution to admit that Eck must have lost his nerve and that he himself would not have acted as Eck did had he been confronted with the same situation.

Eck was only moderately well defended. One of his counsel, Professor Wegner, was given, as were many of the Germans appearing before Allied courts, to flattering the conquerors—in this case the British, who were conducting the *Peleus* trial. Wegner confided to the court that his heart was broken when the war started and he was now exhausted. He spoke learnedly, in defending Eck's carrying out of superior orders, of the doctrine that the king, the sovereign, can do no wrong, but the Judge Advocate caught him up easily, saying, "If you find any authority justifying the killing of survivors of a sunken ship when they are in the water, will you try to come to it quickly." [61] Wegner could only repeat that he had to stay up all night to prepare the case and told the court that he regretted he had not been able to do better: "I am tired because I had to do this during the night for you." he said. "I was not up to my task, I am sorry to say but I hope I have not taken up your time without being able to help you." [62]

Three of the Germans were sentenced to death—the men immediately responsible for the shootings: Eck, Hoffmann, and Weisspfennig. Lenz was sentenced to life imprisonment, and Schwender, the unworthy one, got fifteen years.[63] But these men had not involved Doenitz directly, and he was aided in his defense by affidavits of former U-boat commanders who were being held in Allied prison camps declaring that they had never been told to attack enemy crews although they had been ordered not to endanger their ships and not to rescue anyone if that would endanger them. One U-boat captain, Hans Witt, said Doenitz had categorically refused to permit attacks on shipwrecked crews—which had been proposed as a reprisal when German survivors reported they had been fired on by British ships.[64] Sixty-seven U-boat commanders at the British prisoner-of-war camp at Featherstone Park declared under oath that Doenitz had never given them either oral or written orders to kill the survivors of ships they had sunk.[65]

The Eck case was the only one during the entire war where a clear case occurred of a U-boat's firing on the survivors of a torpedoed ship, and to this extent the so-called ambiguity of Doenitz's orders cannot be easily sustained. For if he had told the captains of submarines orally or in writing what Heisig, Moehle, and conceivably Eck had understood him to say, many more such cases must have occurred. The evidence, not only from the affidavits of the captured German submarine officers but in the context of what Doenitz had said and written and of the performance of hundreds of submarine commanders and their crews, was in Doenitz's favor. He had certainly tried to prevent his submarines and their crews from being unnecessarily imperiled again, as they had in the *Laconia* rescue, and he had coldly diagnosed the bottleneck of the Allied war effort on the high seas as personnel rather than ships. He wanted to cause as high losses among the enemy forces as he could inflict, to accomplish his aim of reducing the Allied war potential as far as possible. Demanding more efficient torpedoes and refusing to take survivors on U-boats was one thing; killing them, another.

Moreover, the tenor of the orders declaring the rescue of personnel to be undesirable conflicted in no way with the theory and practice of what the Allies did in the course of the war, although the Nuremberg court made it clear that it would hear no evidence of what the Allies had been doing. The President of the Court said the tribunal would not permit a question to be asked about the treatment of German sabotage units. "We are not trying whether any other powers have committed breaches of international law, or of crimes against humanity, or war crimes, but whether these defendants have," he declared when Laternser tried to show what practices on both sides actually were.[66]

The defense urged that the German acts be judged in context—in light of the conduct of the entire war and the actions of the Allies. Admiral Bernhard Rogge, who had commanded the German auxiliary cruiser *Atlantis* in November, 1941, testified that after the sinking of his ship and the supply ship *Python*, no attempt was made by the British to rescue the 414 crewmen. They were eventually picked up by four German U-boats, later joined by four Italian submarines, and brought back 5,000 miles from the West African coast to Germany. The British destroyer *Cossack*, which violated Norwegian neutrality to capture the unarmed German supply ship *Altmark* in Norwegian territorial waters and to release 300 British prisoners of war who were on the ship, fired on the German sailors fleeing across the ice and water of the fjord. Six of them had been killed, three others were severely and five lightly wounded. The British commander of the destroyer was congratulated by the King, and the First Lord of the Admiralty, Winston Churchill, awarded him the Service Cross for heroism. Nor was this the only occasion Germans charged that the British shot at and killed survivors in the water and in lifeboats. The same thing allegedly happened in the sinking of the German minesweeper *Ulm* on September 14, 1942, and at Narvik, where a British commandant defended the killing of German sailors escaping from a ship sunk in the harbor with the statement: "The usages of war permit shooting at crews to prevent their reaching shore and rejoining the enemy's fighting forces." [67]

Few attempts were made by Allied submarines to rescue enemy survivors after their ships were sunk, and many instances occurred where German crews in lifeboats or rafts reported they were fired upon by Allied planes or ships. Doenitz said he knew of no case where an English submarine had rescued German or Italian survivors of a convoy sunk in the Mediterranean, nor had there been any rescues by British submarines of survivors of German ships sunk in Norwegian waters. When Hitler late in the war proposed to Doenitz that the Reich denounce the Geneva Convention in retaliation for the Allied attacks on German cities, Doenitz told him that the disadvantages of such a move would be greater than the advantages. Like Jodl, Doenitz thought it would be better to act in specific instances without giving any advance notice and thus to "save face." [68] Here again what Doenitz meant was not clear; he claimed at Nuremberg he had wanted to prevent German soldiers from surrendering to the Allies—which they were then doing by the thousands in response, he said, to Allied propaganda. It is most likely that he meant what the words say, that in individual instances illegal methods might be used that contravened the Geneva Convention without officially denouncing it. The fierce Allied bombardments of German cities could easily of themselves evoke such statements.

Doenitz's trial defense was sorely burdened with his boundless devotion to the Fuehrer and his fulsome praise of Hitler on both public and private occasions. Even after Hitler's death, Doenitz in broadcasting to the German people and to the armed forces told of imaginary exploits of his hero— exploits, however, which he undoubtedly believed to be true. After, in accord with Hitler's will, he had taken over the Presidency of the tottering Reich and command of its armed forces, he declared over the radio that Hitler's career had been a single life of service to the German people. The Fuehrer had died a hero to the end, devoted to Germany and to Europe and to the whole world of *Kultur* against the Bolshevik tidal wave. He had fallen fighting the enemy, as one of the greatest heroes of German history. In proud honor, Doenitz said, he lowered the flags before him. Doenitz undoubtedly believed all he said. He had always revered Hitler, and at the time the news from the bunker in Berlin was most unclear; Doenitz had been named Hitler's successor in the Fuehrer's last order. Goebbels, named Reich Chancellor, had committed suicide when Doenitz got the news of his own succession as head of state. Hitler might have died as Doenitz thought he had; the Fuehrer had always promised to fight to the last. He had stubbornly remained in Berlin against the pleadings of Jodl and Keitel and of all the others, to die with the city. It would take Doenitz a long time to revise his opinion of his leader.

Over and over again Doenitz made ringing addresses to the German sailors and to the nation, praising everything about Hitler—his peerless leadership, his infallibility. Almost a year after the surrender of the Sixth Army at Stalingrad, on December 17, 1943, he told the commanders of the Navy how deeply he believed in the ideological education of the German soldier, the holy zeal and fanaticism with which the country must fight.[69] Two months later, on February 15, 1944, he addressed another meeting of the same commanders in the same vein. "From the very start the whole officers' corps," he said, "must be so indoctrinated that it feels itself co-responsible with the National Socialist state in its entirety. The officer is the exponent of the state. The idle chatter that the officer is non-political is nonsense." [70]

Doenitz repeatedly declared that he had uncompromisingly accepted the National Socialist ideals and unconditionally given his fealty to the Fuehrer. In addition, he said at Nuremberg—and this was doubtless much more surprising to the court—that he had never received an order from Hitler that was not in accord with international law or that violated in any way the ethics of war. This was doubtless true. Hitler disliked the ocean; it was alien to him. He once told a German naval captain he would be seasick for two weeks if he went to sea. Hitler liked the techniques of the Navy, and its efficiency, but he knew nothing of its mysteries and left them to the experts.[71] In sharp distinction to the land war, Hitler had interfered little with the war at sea.

Doenitz carried his single-minded message to the entire nation. He told the Germans that they must cling to the Fuehrer in fanatical allegiance and love. "German men and women," he asked over the German networks on

March 12, 1944, "what would have become of our country today if the Fuehrer had not united us under National Socialism? Split parties, beset with the spreading poison of Jewry, and vulnerable to it because we lacked the defense of our present uncompromising ideology, we would long since have succumbed under the burden of this war and delivered ourselves up to the enemy who would have mercilessly destroyed us." [72] On July 21, 1944, a day after the attempt on Hitler's life, he spoke again: "Holy anger and measureless wrath fill us today over the criminal attack that was supposed to have cost the life of our beloved Fuehrer." He went on to speak of "the insane little clique of generals . . . with their boundless stupidity that would have led to the extermination of our people, the enslaving of our men . . . and unspeakable misery. The Navy," he said, "remains true to its oath in its unwavering fidelity to the Fuehrer, unconditional in its élan and readiness for battle . . . They will take orders only from me, the Commander in Chief of the Navy, and from its own commanders . . ." [73]

Never in the Fuehrer's lifetime did Doenitz waver in his adoration. He told the Navy on New Year's Day, 1944, "The Fuehrer shows us the way and the goal. We follow him with body and soul in a great German future." [74] On September 15, 1944, he spoke of "the enormous strength the Fuehrer radiates, his unwavering confidence, his far-sighted appraisal of the Italian situation have made it very clear that we are all insignificant in comparison with him . . . Anyone who believes he can do better than the Fuehrer is silly." [75] On March 27, 1945, he told the German people they had to believe unreservedly in their leadership. "Adolf Hitler," he said, "has always been right" even though justification for his decisions sometimes only appeared weeks after they were taken.[76] On April 11, 1945, he declared, "Only the Fuehrer has for years realized with what danger Bolshevism threatens Europe . . . perhaps even this year, Europe will realize that Adolf Hitler is the only statesman of stature in Europe . . . Europe's blindness will one day come to a sudden end and thereby bring Germany psychological help and political possibilities arising therefrom." [77]

Even after the Nuremberg trials Doenitz continued his dogged, one-track defense of Hitler. In a meeting with one of his lawyers, Fregattenkapitaen Meckel, in July, 1946, before the verdicts were announced, Doenitz explained in detail to Meckel how Hitler had been able to keep such a hold on the belief and loyalty of so many of his followers even in the years of reverses. Doenitz compared the Fuehrer to Napoleon, who was also considered a criminal after his death; but the judgment of Napoleon's contemporary detractors, he pointed out, was completely revised forty years later. Doenitz referred to Hitler's uncanny sense for the right decision that, for example, had kept him from accepting the Vice-Chancellorship in Papen's Cabinet, that against the advice of his generals had led to occupation of the Rhineland and to the other great bloodless victories as well as to the triumphs of the war—all of which stamped him for the man he was. England, said Doenitz, was always bound to oppose the strongest power in Europe and if a wicked Hitler hadn't existed, a wicked militarism would have had to be destroyed in his place, along with a too powerful Germany.

Hitler's one mistake, Doenitz thought, was starting the armed conflict in 1939, which, despite the temporary pact with Russia, was really a two-front war from the start. Either Russia or England had to be knocked out if Germany was to win, and Doenitz said he had no doubt whatever that Russia in 1941 was preparing to attack. Here too the Fuehrer had been right in sensing Russian plans for aggression, and German field marshals like Manstein and Rundstedt confirmed Hitler's intuition that the Russians had made vast offensive preparations and that they had been caught off base in the swift and unexpected German attack. The inhumanities of the National Socialist regime, Doenitz thought, were the fault of Himmler's police, but even the terrorist methods were by no means confined to Germany. The police in the Anglo-Saxon countries, too, did not always wear kid gloves. In addition, Doenitz told Meckel, the Gestapo had often been right, as when it had prepared dossiers against men like Schacht and Canaris. And on the favorable side, no corruption paralleling that of World War I besmirched Germany during World War II. No black market flourished, there were no Jewish profiteers, the press and films and art were clean. Corruption existed only in Himmler's realm and in men like Goering. Doenitz thought his idol had remained fit and competent as ever until the very end; Hitler had seen treason all around him and Hitler had been right in this too.[78]

Hitler's military blunders, his senseless defense of every foot of ground in Russia that cost the German armies so much blood, including the lives of generals ordered killed because they were unwilling to sacrifice their troops to Hitler's mania, made no impression on Doenitz. On February 15, 1944, in his address to the higher officers of the Navy, he said he was in complete agreement with the strategy of the Fuehrer—had the Army retreated in Russia, the enemy would now be at the German borders—and he too believed that there should be no unnecessary withdrawals. He said this after spending days at the Fuehrer's headquarters while Hitler was ordering exhausted and battle-worn troops to stand fast without reserves on a front extending across Russia. The desperate importunities of the field commanders and even on occasion of OKW seemed to have made no more impression on him than they did on Hitler.

No alternative existed for the German Army and Navy but to fight hard at all points and to follow Hitler with unquestioning faith, Doenitz told his naval officers. The political contradictions among the Allies were obvious, he said, and if the Allies saw that they could in the near future bring Germany to her knees, their alliance would hold together; but if they saw that Germany would fight to the last, the conflict in their war aims would become apparent. "Stand to the bitter end, stand where you are," he said, echoing the Fuehrer. "This is the terrible need of the moment; be militarily correct and you can change the political situation." The relative strength of the Germans compared to the Russians was 1 to 5 but the losses were 1 to 8. Doenitz took comfort in this, as well as in the exhaustion of the Soviet troops and the German tenacity that was holding off the Allies in Italy as well as in Russia. "England does not want Russia to run Europe, they want the Russians and the Germans to lose as much blood as possible but they also want to end the war as soon as possible." [79]

Doenitz never changed. Two kinds of people existed: those who were German patriots and those who were not. The soldier, he told German naval officers in the autumn of 1944, had to be anti-Marxist and anti-Semitic as well, for during the Weimar Republic the Jews had tried to make a laughing stock of the military virtues of loyalty, involvement in a cause, devotion, willingness to sacrifice. "We must follow the Fuehrer with all our souls," he told them, and at this last stage of the war he still ranged himself against the critics who complained that the High Command should have done this or that differently. "Silly criticism," Doenitz called it, for "one cannot change what has happened." [80] Doenitz, like Hitler, was convinced that the Allied demand for unconditional surrender made it impossible to do anything but fight to the last and hope that the underlying political differences among the Allies came to the surface. "You cannot make yourself defenseless," he told the officers, "and then talk peace, even the smallest weapon in your hands improves your position. Would the Russians," he asked, "after the Germans were defeated have the slightest interest in maintaining German industry? They would," he said, "deport Germans of both sexes who would never see their homes again." [81]

Doenitz many years later defended his policy of having continued the war even when it was hopeless. He saw the map of Germany as it was to be divided among the three powers according to the Morgenthau plan, and he believed this could mean the end of the German nation. He quoted, too, the Russian writer Ilya Ehrenburg, who was importuning the Russian soldiers to "Kill Kill Kill, no one is innocent, living or unborn." Ehrenburg had written: "Break with force the racial arrogance of the German women. Take them as your proper booty. Kill, you brave forward storming Red Army men." [*82] The war, Doenitz was convinced, could not be won after the failure of the submarine offensive in 1943, and he told Hitler so. But he fought on, even in the spring of 1945, and had he not ordered the last resistance, he told his interrogators at Nuremberg, three and a half million soldiers would have gone into Russian captivity. The Russans, even with the best will in the world, which was certainly lacking, could not have taken care of so many

---

* Although the original of this quotation has not been found, German witnesses said it was used as a leaflet distributed in 1944 among Russian troops and printed in Russian frontline newspapers. It was quoted by the former Soviet officer Sabik-Wegulow, in an article, "W Probjedennoj Germaniji" ("In Conquered Germany"), published in 1947. Furthermore, it is not very different from other summons to slaughter that Ehrenburg certainly wrote.

prisoners; even in the West many German soldiers had died because of inadequate care by the Western Allies. Furthermore, Doenitz pointed out, the German troops would not have obeyed the orders to stand where they were and let Soviet troops capture them. In addition, he had to consider the plight of the refugees.* He sent 50,000 of his sailors, with no training in such warfare, to fight on the land, and he also approved Hitler's scorched-earth orders that included destruction of naval installations; for the big thing, Doenitz said as early as 1943, was to save Europe from bolshevism.

In the course of the war Doenitz and Raeder both often repeated that the chief enemy was England, but as far as Doenitz was concerned these were no more than clichés. Every German sailor said that the British were the main enemy because they faced England on every front. No Russian submarines were in the Baltic.† The only place the German and Soviet naval forces met on water was in the Black Sea, but the British were everywhere and were overwhelmingly superior in both world wars in the number of ships they could bring into battle. Aside from this formal sailor talk on behalf of the inferior German Navy, the real enemy was not the British but the Soviet Union, which Doenitz, like the rank and file of the Nazi Party, identified with world Jewry.

Doenitz, once he left behind the well-ordered charts of his Navy and its submarines, was a confused man. He had no compass for politics. Within the area of his competence he was enormously resourceful, and his chief object of devotion was always the German Navy. Upon it he spent his skill and deepest emotions. When Hitler once referred to the feats of the British Navy, Doenitz flared up even to his revered Fuehrer and said coldly that the German Navy was certainly better than the British, that the British were operating after all with a marked superiority of numbers, and that the German sailors were accomplishing everything that could possibly be demanded of them.

Goering was an enemy of both Doenitz and Raeder. The Reichsmarschall, always jealous of his prerogatives, opposed placing reconnaissance, torpedo, and bomber planes under Navy command, although the Luftwaffe could not supply the technical training demanded for identifying ships, laying mines, and attacking with torpedoes from the air. The Navy, its commanders were convinced, had to train its own fliers, who could then be depended on to

---

* The German Navy performed a prodigious task in evacuating soldiers and refugees from the Baltic. More than a million and a half people were rescued from the Russians in warships and passenger ships despite Russian air superiority and the presence of twenty-two Soviet submarines in the evacuation area after the surrender of Finland. A number of German ships were sunk, with very heavy loss of life; 20,000 died in the course of the operations that began in the autumn of 1944 and continued even after the German surrender. Only 0.49 per cent of those transported by the Navy were lost, compared with 15.8 per cent of those who attempted to escape by the land route, where 1,600,000 died (Bidlingmaier, *op. cit.*).

† No Russian submarines operated in the Baltic until near the end of the war when they could use Finnish bases.

send along accurate information on enemy ships and carry out special assign-ments. Once, when Goering—to cover up one of his own innumerable fail-ures—in the presence of the Fuehrer complained of the use the Navy had made of the small and fast surface ships that made hit-and-run raids on English shipping, Doenitz exploded and said to him, "Reichsmarschall, I will tolerate no criticism of the Navy from you, you have more than enough to do with your Luftwaffe." The Fuehrer showed where his sentiments lay by inviting Doenitz to breakfast and taking a cool leave of Goering.

Doenitz had frequent if impersonal connections with the Party hierarchy, especially after he became Commander in Chief. He felt it his duty and privilege not only to be present at the Fuehrer conferences but to spend some time at Hitler's headquarters, and a prefabricated house that had been used by the Fuehrer during the Polish campaign was put at his disposal. Doenitz told a meeting he addressed of Reichsleiters and Gauleiters in Posen that he had been invited to talk by Bormann and of course he would accept such a request from him at any time, because the pillars of the National Socialist State at this critical juncture had to be close to one another.[83]

His personal relations with the Party leaders were never intimate; the only test for Doenitz was their allegiance to Hitler. Having heard the news from Bormann that Himmler was attempting peace negotiations in Sweden and should be regarded as a traitor, Doenitz received Himmler and his guard of six SS men in Ploen—after Hitler's will had made him President—with a cocked revolver on his desk, and brusquely refused to give the Reichsfuehrer SS the place he asked for in the Cabinet. Himmler, desperately clinging to any flimsy shred of respectability he could grasp, assured Doenitz he would gladly be the second man in his government, but the admiral would have none of him. Nor at the end were Doenitz's relations with Bormann and Goebbels any better. In the atmosphere of suspicion and treason that sur-rounded Hitler and his liegemen at the end, Doenitz in fact ordered their arrest if they should appear at his headquarters in Ploen, but by this time Bormann had disappeared and Goebbels had committed suicide. Ribbentrop too wanted a place as Foreign Minister in Doenitz's Cabinet. The British, he said, would always be glad to deal with him. Doenitz, ignoring the naming of Seyss-Inquart as Foreign Minister in Hitler's will, appointed Count Schwerin von Krosigk to the almost imaginary post.

Doenitz never benefited, as did so many (including Raeder) who had won the personal regard of the Fuehrer, from any of the largesse Hitler so generously bestowed on his favorites—of whom Doenitz was certainly one. He never received any of Hitler's princely gifts; no cash except his salary ever was offered him. Perhaps the fact that Hitler had no genuine sympathy for the Navy nor much understanding of its function led him to treat his admir-als on the whole differently from the generals and civil officials whose work he approved of. When Raeder in 1941 got his gift, it was perhaps because he was Commander in Chief of a service for which the Fuehrer still had high hopes.

The testimony that undoubtedly saved Doenitz's life at Nuremberg came from Admiral Nimitz and from the British Admiralty. Both sources admitted that from the beginning of the war they (the United States in the Pacific and the British in the Skagerrak) had ordered their submarines to sink any ship on sight without regard to visit and search.* The lawyers representing Raeder and Doenitz sent a questionnaire to Admiral Nimitz, and in his answers Nimitz affirmed that the entire Pacific Ocean had been declared a theater of operations where American submarines were ordered to attack without warning—an order that went far beyond the German one that at the start of the war limited such attacks to the so-called immediate blockade zone about the British Isles. In the American orders the only exceptions to the unrestricted submarine war were hospital ships and vessels that had been provided with a safe conduct. Furthermore, these orders had gone into effect on the first day of the war, December 7, 1941; they did not arise, as did the German measures, as a result of developments of the war. Nimitz also testified that it was not the practice of American submarines to rescue survivors if such a rescue would be an undue or additional hazard to the submarine, which was limited both by its small passenger-carrying facilities and by the suicidal and homicidal tendences of Japanese who were taken prisoner. It was, Nimitz testified, unsafe to rescue many survivors, although they were frequently given rubber boats and provisions. Almost invariably, Nimitz wrote, any prisoners had to be brought aboard a submarine by force. None of the American practices, he said, was based on reprisals against Japanese submarine warfare. He had thought the unrestricted submarine warfare fully justified by the tactics of the Japanese attack on Pearl Harbor.[84]

German witnesses testifying on behalf of Doenitz told of the strict orders the German Navy was under to follow the customs and usages of war, as well as the Geneva and Hague Conventions.[85] Both Allied and German nationals told of the tolerable conditions prisoners of war lived under in German naval PW camps. A former German naval judge, Fritz Jaeckel, testified to the Navy's strict enforcement of military law against its own personnel. One sailor had been executed for having worked with a French criminal ring that stole property from Jews on the assumption that such activity, since it concerned Jews, was no crime. He was sentenced to death and his accomplice, to twelve years. Another sailor who stole from Russians was also given the death penalty, as was one who committed rape in Greece.[86]

"We are a respectable firm," Doenitz had said at the start of the war, and he considered himself and Raeder the respectable heads of it. At first, as the war ended, it seemed that the Allies had taken the same view of him. Just

---

* The British orders were to sink any German ship by day and any ship by night sailing in the Skagerrak.

after the surrender, when Doenitz first dealt with Allied commanders, he was given the usual military honors accorded an honorable if defeated enemy: the Allied soldiers presented arms, the officers exchanged salutes.* But all this changed when he and Jodl on May 22 were taken on board the houseboat *Patria*, lying near Flensburg, where Doenitz had had his headquarters since May 2.† They had become war criminals. No one presented arms: a group of photographers descended on them, taking their pictures in their new role of accused men who were to stand trial for their lives.

Hitler's successor, the commander of submarines, as well as the last Commander in Chief of the German Navy, had to go before the court to show, if he could, to "the chief enemy England" that he had waged war according to rules that England herself was not always ready to follow. The Russians in the person of one of the Soviet prosecutors, Colonel Pokrovsky, denounced him on a priori grounds. Pokrovsky asked at Nuremberg, "Will you deny, Doenitz, that you were always preaching and always encouraging in every way the murder of defenseless people from among the members of the German Armed Forces for purely political reasons and that you always looked upon such murders as acts of military valor and heroism?" [87] This was vastly exaggerated; at the end of the trial the case against Doenitz came down to the ambiguity of his orders concerning treatment of shipwrecked crews, orders that in their effect were essentially no different from what the Allies were doing. That and his pro-Nazism, his blind devotion to the Fuehrer, his anti-Semitism, the damning fact that he had been named by Hitler as President of the Reich were the charges left against him.

The court found Doenitz guilty of having committed crimes against peace but not of having conspired to commit them. He was also found guilty of war crimes; his plea of tu quoque for German conduct of submarine warfare was accepted, but the court said he was involved in the Commando Order in that he permitted it to stand after he became Commander in Chief; that he had known at least after a conference on December 11, 1944, that concentration-camp prisoners might be used as workers in the navy yards. And it declared rather weakly, "He admits he knew of concentration camps. A man in his position must necessarily have known that citizens of occupied countries in large numbers were confined in concentration camps." [88] This was undoubtedly true, but how was it a crime in the man who commanded the German Navy to have known that such camps existed? Doenitz, however, had known nothing of the extermination camps; until the end of the war

* Winston Churchill had sent a memorandum to the Foreign Office saying: "I neither know nor care about Doenitz. He may be a war criminal . . . the question for us is, has he any power to get the Germans to lay down their arms and hand them over quickly without more loss of life . . . It must of course be remembered that Doenitz is a useful tool that will have to be written off against his war atrocities for being in command of submarines . . ." (Brian Gardner, *The Year that Changed the World* [New York: Coward-McCann, 1964], pp. 172–73).

† Doenitz had moved from Ploen in Holstein when its capture was threatened by the British to makeshift headquarters in Flensburg.

their existence was a carefully guarded secret and the affairs of the Navy were as remote from them as was possible in the Third Reich.

The court merely commented on the ambiguity of Doenitz's orders with regard to shipwrecked crews, but it took a sterner view of his advice to the Fuehrer on the Geneva Convention. Here it thought Doenitz intended to breach the Convention. It found in his proper treatment of prisoners of war a mitigating circumstance. And with regard to one of the main concerns of the tribunal—the waging of aggressive warfare—the judgment in surely one of the most curious statements made on that solemn occasion declared: "It is clear that his U-boats, few in number at the time, were fully prepared to wage war"—a strange finding against a commander of submarines of any nationality. Doenitz was sentenced to ten years, a sentence that took account of his guilt for having submarines under his command ready to shoot, and which is a long time for having headed a respectable firm.

Doenitz had been a good submarine officer, a staunch, salty man of the Navy, and beyond this world he was lost; his political opinions were no more than stale repetitions of what Party orators said: England wanted to destroy Germany; the Jews and bolshevism were working ceaselessly for her destruction; Hitler had cleansed Germany of its poisons; the country had to fight to the last man against the plot to destroy it; and so on. When an inconvenient fact came to light, it was passed off as a misunderstanding. Doenitz seemed proof against learning anything new; the accumulation of testimony on the Nazi barbarities and the insane orders given by the Fuehrer that sacrificed German armies and cities left Doenitz merely with the same opinions he had during the war. Minor figures like Himmler were responsible; the Fuehrer was still beyond criticism—"compared with him we others are worms."

But slowly and subconsciously he did learn; somewhere in his sailor's alphabet of soldierly duties and eternal vows of obedience and duty to be fulfilled, the words and meanings came together in a fashion different than they had before. By the time he wrote his memoirs, ten years after the trial, he knew that the men of July 20 could have been patriots, even that some of them possessed the highest virtues of self-sacrifice and love of country. The evidence finally reached him, too, of the atrocities. But he clung to his prescription, the necessity for having continued the war, the need to hold out. He had fought at sea against formidable odds with the weapons at hand and with as good a conscience as his opponents that he was defending his country. He lacked what another defendant (Keitel) who also stood before the same court called a sense of responsibility to anything non-German, that went beyond what the patriots of the Third Reich believed "right." He was so far removed from political realities that a meeting he attended debated whether the Allies might let him continue as head of state. He took refuge, while he was at Nuremberg, in another tu quoque: the Allied bombing of German civilians, the harsh Allied treatment of Germans, the political differences among them that demonstrated the hollowness of their own claims to moral superiority; he was the narrow and efficient officer who saw the enemy plainly that was pointed out to him and was ready to fight this enemy to the death.

Doenitz had learned his manual on the duty of a naval officer word for word, but his maxims were adapted to an orderly, traditional government, not to a criminal head of state who quoted the same soldierly texts even as he was slaying millions of defenseless people. Doenitz knew only that enemies were all around and had to be fought to the bitter end. He fought well according to the tough if not deliberately inhumane canons of military men of the twentieth century. American and British naval officers wrote to him deploring the verdict. More than one hundred American captains and admirals spontaneously sent him letters praising his conduct of the war and deploring the verdict. They said, usually, that he had done for his country what they had done for theirs; he had fought honorably and well, and they wanted him to know they thought so.

NOTES

1. Erich Raeder, *Mein Leben*, Vol. I (Tuebingen: Fritz Schlichtenmayer Verlag, 1956).

2. *Ibid.*, pp. 231–32.

3. N XXXIV, 017-C, pp. 164–76. *Ibid.*, 156-C, pp. 530–606.

4. N XIII, pp. 627–31. N XIV, pp. 1–6. N XXXIV, 032-C, pp. 205–16. N XXXV, 854-D, pp. 554–68.

5. N XIV, p. 250.

6. NCA, Supp. A, D-877, pp. 997–1013.

7. N XXXIV, 161-C, pp. 647–61. N XXXV, 653-D, pp. 310–14.

8. Walter Baum, "*Marine, Nationalsozialismus und Widerstand*," in *Vierteljahrshefte fuer Zeitgeschichte*, Vol. XI, No. 1, 1963, p. 37.

9. Carl-Axel Gemzell, *Raeder, Hitler und Skandinavien* (Lund: Skanska Centraltryckeriet, 1965, and Frankfurt a.M.: Bernard & Graefe Verlag fuer Wehrwesen), pp. 216–17.

10. N XLI, Raeder-41, pp. 26–29.

11. Churchill, *op. cit.*, Vol. I, pp. 533–47.

12. *Ibid.*, p. 573.

13. Walter Hubatsch, *Weseruebung* (Goettingen: Musterschmidt-Verlag 1960), p. 30.

14. N XLI, Raeder-130, pp. 85–86.

15. *Ibid.*, Raeder-77, pp. 34–37.

16. *Ibid.*, Raeder-41, pp. 26–29.

17. *Ibid.*, Raeder-83, pp. 45–47.

18. *Ibid.*, Raeder-85, pp. 47–48.

19. NCA VI, C-115, pp. 914–15. N XXXIV, 115-C, pp. 342–63.

20. NCA VI, C-66, p. 887.

21. *NCA* II, C-152, p. 862.

22. N XXVI, 498-PS, pp. 100–1.

23. *Ibid.* N XIII, pp. 503–4.

24. N I, p. 317.

25. *TWC*, Vol. XI, pp. 159–64.

26. N V, p. 278. N XXXIV, 176-C, pp. 747–66. N XXXIX, 057-UK, p. 124.

27. N XIII, p. 509. N XXXV, 649-D, pp. 301–3. NCA, Suppl. A, D-919, pp. 1090–97.

28. N XXXIV, 178-C, pp. 770–79. NCA VI, C-178, pp. 1012–14.

29. *Ibid.*, pp. 770–79, 1012–14.

30. NCA II, pp. 863–64.

31. Raeder, *op. cit.*, Vol. I, p. 242; Vol. II, p. 144.

32. N XIV, p. 284.

33. Raeder interrogation of February 26, 1947 (IZG).

34. Karl Doenitz, *10 Jahre und 20 Tage* (Bonn: Athenaeum-Verlag, 1958), p. 59.

35. MA 184 (IZG).

36. N XIII, p. 407.

37. N XXV, 642-D, p. 258.

38. N XIII, p. 412.

39. *Ibid.*, p. 550.

40. *Ibid.*, p. 413.

41. *Ibid.*

42. *Ibid.*

43. *Ibid.*, p. 414.

44. Samuel Eliot Morison, *History of the United States Naval Operations in World War II*, Vol. XIV (Boston: Little, Brown and Company, 1947–59), pp. 290–91.

45. N XIII, p. 420.

46. Doenitz, *op. cit.*, p. 192.

47. Léonce Peillard, *The Laconia Affair*, trans. by Oliver Coburn (New York: G. P. Putnam's Sons, 1963), p. 132.

48. Doenitz, *op. cit.*, p. 256.

49. Peillard, *op. cit.*, p. 183.

50. N XXXV, 630-D, pp. 216–18.

51. *Ibid.*

52. *Ibid.*, 446-D, pp. 118–23. N XL, Doenitz-19, 20, 22, 29, 41, and 53.

53. S. W. Roskill, *White Ensign* (Annapolis: United States Naval Institute, 1960), p. 225.

54. Gerald Kemmett, (London) *Sunday Express*, August 4, 1963.

55. N XXX, p. 160.

56. N XXV, 382-PS, pp. 394–401.

57. N XIII, pp. 423–24. N XL, Doenitz-27, 53, and 67.

58. NCA VII, D-642, p. 124.

59. *Ibid.*, D-663, p. 170.

60. N V, pp. 226–27.

61. John Cameron, ed., *The Peleus Trial* (London, Edinburgh, and Glasgow: William Hodge, 1948), p. 99.

62. *Ibid.*, p. 103.

63. *Ibid.*

64. N XL, Doenitz-41, pp. 66–69.

65. *Ibid.*, Doenitz-53, p. 80.

66. N XIII, p. 521.

67. N XL, Doenitz-39, pp. 61–65.

68. N XXXIV, 158-C, pp. 641–44.

69. NCA VII, 443-D, pp. 54–55.

70. *Ibid.*, 640-D, p. 116.

71. Baum, *op. cit.*, pp. 16–48.

72. N XIII, 2878-PS, p. 392.

73. NCA V, 2878-PS, pp. 541–42.

74. *Ibid.*, 2878-PS.

75. Francis H. Hinsley, *Hitler's Strategy: The Naval Evidence* (Cambridge: Cambridge University Press, 1951), p. 230.

76. MA 127/2, 12957 (IZG).

77. NCA VII, 650-D, pp. 150–51.

78. Baum ZS 1810, Unterredung mit Fregattenkapitaen Meckel (IZG).

79. N XXXV, 640-D, pp. 237–45.

80. Doenitz speech of October 18, 1944 (BDC).

81. *Ibid.*

82. Doenitz, *op. cit.*, p. 431.

83. Baum ZS 1810 (IZG).

84. N XL, Doenitz-100, pp. 108–11.

85. *Ibid.*, Doenitz-48, pp. 69–73.

86. *Ibid.*, Doenitz-49, pp. 74–79.

87. N XIII, p. 399.

88. N I, p. 314.

11

The Proconsuls

HANS FRANK

Hans Frank was Governor General of what was left of Poland, a cut-down piece of territory some two-fifths of its prewar area (the rest of the Polish provinces had been incorporated into the Reich for resettlement by *Volks-deutsche* mainly from Eastern Europe). Frank had only a theoretical background for this post. He had been the chief legal authority of the Party almost from the time he received his law degree in 1926. Because of his youth—he was born in 1900—he had served only one year in the Army during World War I and then had joined a Freikorps formation to help oust the Communist Raeterepublik that ruled Munich for a few bloody days in April, 1919. Anti-Communist, anti-Semitic, an admirer of Spengler and of quasi-socialist doctrines, Frank in 1919 joined the German Workers' Party, which within a few months became the National Socialist German Workers' Party. Later he joined the SA. He took part in the attempted putsch of 1923, in which he had been given the assignment of occupying a bridge crossing the Isar. A number of the burghers of Munich, unimpressed at this early date by the nondescript Brownshirts, commented derisively on Frank and his armed warriors. One man asked him—he was twenty-three years old at the time—if his mother knew he was out with all these deadly weapons. When no enemy appeared at the bridge, Frank returned to the Buergerbraeu Keller, where the high command of the revolution had its headquarters, and joined Hitler and Goering, Hess and Himmler, Ludendorff and their SA followers on the march that was to end in a burst of gunfire when it reached the Feldherrnhalle.

A politically ambitious young lawyer convinced of the just cause and eventual success of the National Socialists, Frank in October, 1927, read in the *Voelkischer Beobachter* of the plight of twelve young SA hooligans who had swaggered into a Berlin restaurant where a number of Jews were eating and had been arrested when they started to break up the place in protest against the presence of the Jews. Frank appeared in court to defend them, and since the Brownshirts were storm troopers one of whose main jobs it was to "win the streets" for the Party, he thereafter was kept busy. One such case quickly followed another—40,000 trials were conducted between 1925 and 1933, Frank wrote in his autobiography.

He was also one of two lawyers for the three young artillery lieutenants Hanns Ludin, Richard Scheringer, and Hans Friedrich Wendt—none older than twenty-four—brought up for trial in Ulm in 1930 on charges of high treason because as Nazi sympathizers they had spread Nazi propaganda in the Army and had allegedly planned to help overthrow the Government.

Frank called Adolf Hitler as a witness for the defendants, and Hitler made the most of the occasion (which was the way he and Frank had planned it) to lecture the court and make headlines in the newspapers on the high patriotism of the Party, its aim to come to power legally, and the selfless motives that had animated the young officers who had joined the ranks of the National Socialists. In the course of the proceedings Hitler also told the court that because of the treason and corruption in Weimar's parliamentary system, when the National Socialists took power—which they would do legally but inevitably—a true German law and comprehension of patriotic duty would take the place of what was passing for justice and citizenship in the degenerate Weimar Republic. He added that when that time came, heads would roll.[1]

Although proof of high treason was lacking, the three lieutenants were clearly guilty of political activity, which was forbidden to soldiers, and were sentenced to a year and a half's imprisonment. One of the three, Scheringer, disillusioned with the Fuehrer, in the course of his imprisonment became converted to communism. Wendt later joined Otto Strasser's dissident group within the National Socialist Party and emigrated at the time Strasser did in 1933. Only Ludin remained a National Socialist after his imprisonment.

Frank declared at Nuremberg that he himself had always believed in a state under law. He said he had reminded the jurists of the Third Reich that the law had to underlie any act of state—even, in some mystical sense, any act of the Fuehrer's. Law applied equally to the regular courts of the Reich and to the police and the special tribunals called People's Courts designed to hand down quick and fierce decisions. The Fuehrer ("that great man," Frank still called him in 1946) had, however, one conspicuous failing: he mistrusted both the law and lawyers, and Frank was unable to persuade him otherwise. Frank in fact struggled for some of the traditional concepts of law against the revolutionary police justice of the Third Reich. After Hitler took power, Frank made innumerable speeches up and down Germany praising the supremacy of the law and making half-veiled references to the outrageous behavior of the Gestapo and the security police when they bypassed the courts and threw prisoners into concentration camps and sometimes killed them without any kind of legal proceeding.

When Frank became Bavarian Minister of Justice before the state ministries were dissolved and he was made Minister Without Portfolio, he immediately had a number of brushes with Heinrich Himmler and the SS. In 1933, after a group of SS men killed a number of Jews in Aschaffenburg, the SS men were arrested. SS authorities claimed their men were not subject to civil authority; Frank questioned the validity of the SS claim, but all he could do was ask the Bavarian Minister-President to discuss the situation with Himmler and Himmler's then-superior, Roehm.* Soon after this, SS guards in Dachau killed three prisoners—two "Aryan" Germans and a Jew— and Himmler again demanded that no charges be brought against them. The Bavarian Minister of the Interior, Adolf Wagner, wrote to Frank asking him to stop any legal proceedings in what was a political act of state, that is, a Party and police matter, which he did.[2] Another case involved a Munich lawyer, a Dr. Strauss, who had died under suspicious circumstances while a prisoner at Dachau. Frank heard that Strauss had been murdered, and he wanted to investigate this case, too, but Himmler refused admission to the concentration camp either to him or to his agents. Hitler backed Himmler, as he had in the other cases—one of the early instances where the power of the Gestapo and SS took precedence over any of the rival government or Party agencies.

Frank had to accept these decisions, as he had to accept many more like them in his years of service to what he rationalized, into a pseudolegal form, as an authoritarian state based on the Fuehrerprinzip, which would be at the same time a state based on law: a Reichsstaat. The inherent contradiction of this rationale never ceased to trouble him during the nine years in which he held high office in the Reich, and he preached a mixed and confused doctrine of the supremacy of the law so long as it did not conflict with the will of the Fuehrer. In all Frank's speeches to legal gatherings on the necessity for nurturing the innate Germanic love of justice, Frank prudently repeated that the law was what brought the Volk happiness and that Hitler's word was law and his will gave the law its legitimacy.

For his services during the years of struggle when the Party was slowly on the rise (he defended Hitler alone in 150 suits), Frank was made the leading jurist of the Reich. He was President of the Academy of German Law, a Reichsleiter of the Party, the founder of the Institute of German Law, and President of the International Chamber of the Law, where Axis jurists could

---

* At this time Roehm, as head of the SA, outranked Himmler; the SS was under him and he had an SS adjutant.

exchange uncritical opinions—all Party organizations designed to keep the practicing lawyers in the Reich aware of their duties under the new legal principles of the National Socialist State. An even greater sign of confidence in his discretion and powers of judicious inquiry was manifested in 1930 when Hitler entrusted to him research into the Fuehrer's own family tree. Disquieting rumors had been spreading that the Fuehrer had Jewish blood, and Hitler was anxious to be able to prove once and for all that the calumny was without foundation.

Frank undertook this delicate task, and he declared in the autobiography written in his cell at Nuremberg that what he had discovered made it appear possible, if not likely, that Hitler's father had been half Jewish. The main facts are clear enough. Hitler's grandmother, a Fraeulein Maria Anna Schicklgruber, worked as a cook for a well-to-do Jewish family named Frankenberger. The Frankenbergers had a son who was nineteen years old at the time Hitler's forty-two-year-old grandmother bore a child out of wedlock, and the Jewish family paid for the support of the child up to the time it was fourteen years old. Frank wrote that the money was given to avoid a public scandal. Apparently, although Frank does not say so, Fraeulein Schicklgruber had threatened to bring a suit against the Frankenbergers. Frank wrote that many letters were subsequently exchanged between them and Hitler's grandmother, which seemed to him to be evidence of a cordial relationship. Nevertheless, both he and Hitler were convinced that the child was actually the offspring of a millworker, Johann Georg Hiedler, a second cousin of Fraeulein Schicklgruber, who five years after the birth of the child married her and legitimatized her son. But Frank, writing in Nuremberg no longer for the benefit of the Fuehrer, was also of the opinion that it was not out of the question that Hitler's father, who later changed his name from Hiedler to Hitler, was half Jewish.

This possibility which Frank wrote down for the benefit of posterity is one of numerous reconstructions of the non-Aryan descent of prominent Nazis that went the rounds of gossip in National Socialist Germany (for example, the proof that Canaris was alleged to have of Heydrich's half-Jewish ancestry was widely believed in the Party). Therefore, the illegitimacy of Hitler's father is certain, but the evidence beyond this is flimsy. What seems most likely is that Hiedler, who legitimatized the young boy Alois who grew up to become Hitler's father, was in fact the father of the child. It is not at all unusual in southern Germany and in Austria for children to be born out of wedlock; one or two are often present at their parents' wedding and no taint attaches to them. The Hitler family was by no means an exception to this widespread custom. Not only was Hitler's father, Alois, born before his parents were married, but he in turn married three times; and while his first wife, Anna Glasl-Hoerer, was still living, his second wife-to-be, Franziska Matzelsberger, bore him a child, Hitler's half-brother, Alois. After his second wife died, he married Hitler's mother, Klara

Poelzl, and she bore her first son, Gustav, five months later.[3] It seems likely that the Frankenbergers, as Frank said, were trying to avoid a public scandal when they agreed to pay for the costs of raising the child, which can only mean that Fraeulein Schicklgruber must have named their young son as the father of her child. This is the core of the mystery: why should the Frankenbergers pay and subsequently keep up a correspondence if they felt they had been railroaded into paying for the baby of their cook by a man other than their son? The matter remains a mystery, but at any rate, in providing for Hitler's family, the Frankenbergers were also contributing to one of the great ironies of history.

After the Germans conquered Poland, Frank became the first civilian administrator of the so-called General Government, that part of Poland that was not annexed to Germany but was designed to be the homeland of the Polish hewers of wood and drawers of water for the Third Reich. Frank was named Governor General on October 26, 1939, with his capital at Cracow, succeeding the military governor. The Army was not reluctant to give up its administrative duties in the occupied territory, where police and SS activities were outside its control and were causing many officers, including the military governor, General Blaskowitz, to protest. Frank held on to his post until the Germans' final retreat in 1945, but his position as the leading Nazi jurist did not last nearly that long. In 1942, as a result of his attacks on arbitrary police authority, Hitler relieved him, ostensibly at Frank's request, of the Party offices he had held. Hitler kept him on in the General Government solely because, as he told Goebbels, Frank had a job that could only be done with force and his successor would not be likely to do much better in administering the province, which was a center of Polish resistance.

A member of the Reichstag from 1930 on, Frank was one of the hundred-odd deputies elected before the big swing to Hitler took place in 1932. His chief role, however, was that of administrator of Nazi doctrines and practices in the East. He was a dedicated anti-Semite, and the Poles, not much higher in his esteem than the Jews, were an inferior race, fit only to serve the Germans, to be "good," to behave themselves and to do as their masters told them without asking any questions.* Himmler reported from his special

---

* At a meeting held in Berlin on September 21, 1939, Heydrich, recapitulating what Hitler and Himmler had said, made a speech at which Adolf Eichmann, among other SS bureau chiefs and Einsatz leaders, was present. Heydrich declared:

About the development of former Poland, the trend of thought is that the former German districts will become German and in addition a foreign-language district will be set up with Cracow as its capital . . . The solution of the Polish problem, as has been repeatedly explained, will be carried out by distinguishing between the stratum of leaders [Polish intelligentsia] and between the lowest stratum, that of the laborers. Of the political leaders in the occupied territories, at the most 3 per cent have remained. These 3 per cent must also be rendered harmless and they will be brought to concentration camps. The operational groups [Einsatzgruppen] will prepare lists of outstanding leaders, and also lists of the middle class of teachers, clergy, nobility, legionnaires, returning officers, etc. These too are to be arrested and to be moved into the remaining area. The care of the souls of the Poles will be placed in the

train on May 28, 1940, that the Fuehrer had read his six-page memorandum on the treatment of the Eastern peoples, had approved, and wanted Frank to read it. Poles, Himmler had written, were to be taught to do simple arithmetic (to count up to 500), to write their names, to learn that it was a divine law to obey the Germans. Those Poles who went to Germany to labor would be leaderless, working people, but they would live better than their fellow countrymen in Poland and under German instruction contribute as simple workers to construction and building of a cultural nature. Polish children of German ancestry might be brought to Germany and trained to live as Germans; these would become part of German society and would change their Polish names to avoid being humiliated by the Germans.[4] Even in death Poles were not allowed to mingle with the Germans; in German-occupied territory Poles were buried in a part of the cemetery that had its own entrances and exits in cases where it could not be entirely segregated from the German burial ground.[5] No Polish intelligentsia was to be permitted to exist in the General Government. Universities and other institutions of higher learning were closed and intellectuals as a class were to be gotten rid of by way of forced labor and the concentration camps, for Hitler regarded them as implacable enemies of Germany and of no use anyway in a country destined to provide pick-and-shovel workers. As attacks on German soldiers and police increased, a "pacification action" was ordered. Thousands of Poles were arrested by the German police and sent to concentration camps, where most of them died. Every professor in the University of Cracow was arrested and sent to a concentration camp inside Germany. Frank declared at Nuremberg that he had succeeded in obtaining the release of some of these men, but he admitted that on the whole he had approved of the action as a means of restoring order and blunting the Resistance movement. Frank disagreed with none of the measures advocated by Himmler and Heydrich; when he resisted them it was never for ideological or humanitarian reasons.

When Frank took office as Governor he issued a series of draconian decrees for both Poles and Jews. He declared German to be the official language of the Government although Polish might also be used. Poles could be sentenced to death for anything they might do directed against either the Reich or German sovereignty or for any act involving the use of force against a German. Any sign of hostility of a Pole toward a German or

---

hands of Catholic priests from the West, but these will not be allowed to speak Polish. The primitive Poles will be included in the labor forces as nomadic laborers and in time they will be evacuated from the German-language area into the foreign-language area . . . Commanders of Einsatz groups . . . must weigh how, on the one hand, to include the primitive Poles within the framework of labor and how, at the same time, to evacuate them. The aim is: The Pole is to remain a seasonal laborer—the eternal nomad. His permanent place of residence must be in the vicinity of Cracow (Eichmann Trial, Session 164, Document 983. Jerusalem, Israel: Eichmann Trial Record, mimeographed, 1961).

German authority was punishable by death. Death was also the penalty for damage to any public installation. Once, when Frank heard that in Prague red posters were being nailed to walls and posts announcing the deaths of Czechs executed as reprisals for acts against the Germans, he said that if he were to do that in Poland there would not be trees enough on which to nail the placards. His job, as he told his aides, was to uproot the former ruling classes in Poland, and he did it with a will.

In addition, as Governor General, Frank had the right to confiscate private property, which he did not only on behalf of the Reich but for himself. When the Americans took an inventory of his house near the Schliersee in southern Germany in 1945, they found a da Vinci portrait of Cecilia Gallerani and a landscape by Rembrandt, both stolen from the Cracow Czartoryski gallery; a codex of Balthazar Bem; ornamental vestments, including one decorated with pearls; a gilded chalice and an ivory chest from the Cracow cathedral; a fourteenth-century Madonna with child from the Cracow National Museum; and portraits by Gerard Dou, Ary de Vois, Terborch, and Pinturicchio, among others.[6] His Governor's palace in Cracow, visitors reported, had the best table in Europe, and during the entire war the choicest wines and foods were served; even at the end, when all Europe including Germany was going hungry, 1,000 eggs a month were consumed at the Governor's table, along with huge quantities of meat and geese and butter. Frau Frank, one German informant said, enjoyed a salary from the Academy of German Law of 750 RM a month, in addition to a free railroad ticket from Berlin to Munich, and both the Army and SS reports stated that she smuggled food and supplies of all kinds across the German-Polish frontier (illegal truckloads protected by the Governor's authority also crossed the border without search), and her railroad car was known as the "smugglers coach."[7]

Many of these reports came from the SS dossier collected on the Franks as a result of the Governor General's continual challenging of the place of the SS and the police apparatuses in Poland which were nominally under his authority but which in fact took their orders from the Reichsfuehrer SS. In speech after speech Frank repeated to his staff that he made the final decisions in Poland, that he held his office by virtue of Adolf Hitler's appointment and disobedience to him was disobedience to the Fuehrer, that only two authorities existed in Poland—the authority of the Wehrmacht, which was limited, and his own, which under the Fuehrer was absolute. But in reality, as Frank slowly learned, his position was very different from what it was in theory. SS Obergruppenfuehrer Friedrich-Wilhelm Krueger, police chief of the General Government, was indeed Staatssekretaer of security under Frank, but although he politely listened to Frank he took his orders from the Reichsfuehrer SS, not from the Governor General. Frank fought a hopeless battle against this division of authority. He told his governors, who had originally been called district leaders but were upgraded in title for reasons of prestige, that they had the full powers granted by him in their districts, but that of course they must cooperate with the police and SS formations which, he said cautiously, were under the governors but were subject to Himmler's directives.*

Himmler, who distrusted everyone and had undercover men everywhere, mistrusted Frank more than most. He had a file prepared on the General Governor, and in it were accounts of the "endless corruption" of the Franks: the lavish dinners they gave, the dealings on the black market with the Poles [8] and with the Jews in the ghetto, to which Frau Frank made frequent visits for loot of all kinds which could be "bought" for fractions of its value. Frank's sister too, as well as relatives of Frau Frank, went back and forth to the ghetto, where furs and jewelry were to be had at prices such highly placed persons could fix for themselves; the Jews called these deals *taxatieren*, which was a prudently disguised way of saying confiscation.† The Jews were starving in their ghetto; children and old people were dying by the hundreds, as can be seen in the terrible moving pictures Goebbels made for propaganda purposes in the Reich. He never dared show them in Germany, these pictures showing the dark rooms and emaciated faces and birdlike legs and arms, the eight- and nine-year-olds dancing jerkily in their rags in the streets to earn a crust of bread from people who had none to give. Thus, while the Governor General with his decrees kept food out of the ghetto, his wife helped to provide the means to bring it in as did one of Frank's retinue, a man named Lorenz Loev, chief of the Central Office of Administration in Warsaw, who was tried by the SS for his dealings in the black market. Loev bought a gold fountain pen in the ghetto as a birthday present for his chief, the Governor General, and he also bought furs. Frank said he had not known of the source of the fountain pen, and as for the furs, the German administrators needed them in the cold northern climate.[9] Everyone dealt in the Polish black market, where currency had little value but one paint brush or a dress would buy a cow, a pair of boots fetched 1,500 zlotys, and one horseshoe nail was worth 3 RM.[10]

Himmler's main drive was for the acquisition of power. The vast number of killings he ordered were final proof for him of his near omnipotence, and like many killers he prided himself on his integrity in lesser matters; he tolerated no chicanery in the SS. Dealings such as those Frank and Lasch indulged in genuinely repelled Himmler, but he could not dislodge Frank from his job, mainly because, as the Fuehrer told Goebbels, Frank had an impossible job anyway and the available replacements would be no better. But the reports continued to pour in; only visitors who brought presents were

* Originally there were four of these governors; another was added after the Germans conquered Galicia.
† The Governor of Radom, Karl Lasch, who owed his appointment to Frank, was denounced by Himmler for his "gigantic corruption." Lasch testified against Frank in hearings conducted by Himmler's SS representatives but was nevertheless turned over to the Gestapo and liquidated.

welcome to the Governor's palace, one SS informer said, and Army reports on the state of the General Government referred to the "unbelievable conduct" of the Franks.* At the end of the war, when Cracow was being evacuated, some of the art treasures Frank had collected were left behind as the Red armies moved swiftly ahead after their halt at the Weichsel (a halt to permit the Germans to put down the Warsaw uprising and to spare themselves having to deal with the troublesome Poles). The German Army reports said that along with the Franks' art treasures were secret documents, a luxurious armored Mercedes, and large quantities of wines and food.[11]

By 1943 Frank had gained in stature. He was a world figure, with his own palace and his private railroad car with the simple identification in bronze letters of "Governor General," for he was the only one with that title in all the Reich and its dependencies. He ruled his satrapy from the ghettos to the Governor's palace with an iron hand—except of course for the police, whose complete obedience continued to elude him.

Frank for five years ran a small but deluxe imitation of the Nazi State. Like the Fuehrer, he had a deputy, a higher SS and police leader, and departments of the interior, justice, education, construction, and propaganda. Aping Hitler, he called himself "a fanatic of administration" with everything so far as he could manage under his control. Frank imitated the forms that Hitler had adopted as much he could: for his conferences he had the same horseshoe-shaped table at the center of which he presided and he imitated the Fuehrer too in having a corps of stenographers take down what he said on these occasions. These imitation "table talks" were the source of the thirty-eight volumes of so-called diary that he turned over to the Allies when he was arrested. The acquisition of booty, he said, is one of the strongest instincts of mankind, and with the Governor's example before them, his aides did their best to enrich not only the Reich with what they took out of Poland but themselves as well. Americans found 10,000 books and large chemical supplies which had been taken from the University of Cracow and brought to Germany, where they were stamped as the property of the Institute for Eastern Research (Institut fuer Ostarbeit), an organization founded in 1940 by Frank to investigate various aspects of occupied Poland.[12]

Altar pieces were taken from churches, food was confiscated from the Polish peasants, and almost everything was stolen from the Jews. Thus, with the supplies that had to be shipped to the Reich, the local requisitions, and the private plunder, shortages of all kinds increased from month to month. Everything edible or wearable rapidly disappeared and market prices skyrocketed by 3,000 and 4,000 per cent.[13]

By 1943 the entire population of the General Government was liable to

---

* Frank grandly had his son taken to Munich in 1942, at least one of his SS critics said, so that the child might have the experience of hearing an air-raid siren, something he had not yet heard in the Bavarian countryside where he lived, and rarer too in that year than it would be later on.

forced labor, and the decrees Frank issued made increasing demands. His first order on October 26, 1939, had placed the population from ages eighteen to sixty at the disposal of the occupation for reconstruction of war-damaged areas, and on December 14 another decree had made young people of both sexes from the ages of fourteen to eighteen subject to labor conscription.[14] Unemployment, as in the case of all the occupied countries, was high (there were two million unemployed in Poland at the end of hostilities), and the occupying power under the Hague Convention, which the Germans had no intention of following, had the obligation to keep the population fed, as well as the right to demand work of them as long as it was not war work. The German decrees, however, immediately established what was in effect slave labor. Jews were paid two zloty (about forty cents) a day. Although Frank said they worked well, he added that this money was not earned but was paid them, as it was the Poles, as an act of charity. The work done in this fashion, the Germans said, paid for the food kitchens that were set up in Cracow and other cities—for the Jews were not yet being exterminated.

By May 13, 1942, all the inhabitants of the General Government regardless of age or sex were liable to compulsory labor of any kind.[15] It was Frank who rounded up for Sauckel the forced laborers sent to Germany, and the two men saw eye to eye on the need for supplying the Reich with Polish labor and for feeding them enough to keep them energetic. In the General Government, pay was considered by the Party theoreticians a kind of alms. Poles had no right to wages. Frank wanted them given pay incentives to get them to work at full speed—part, as he called it, of his "tickling" technique. "The struggle for the achievement of our aims," Frank announced, "will be pursued cold-bloodedly . . . we stop at nothing, and stand dozens of people against the wall." [16] Food rations for the part of the population not working for Germany were to be kept at a minimum, Frank had said at the beginning of the occupation, and these people need not wear leather shoes, wooden shoes would do.[17] He kept repeating in his speeches to his staff, to the Wehrmacht, and to the police that the Poles must be treated "with iron hardness." The Germans would not shrink from draconic measures.[18] Poland would never rise again, he told them. German colonialism in that country would not be like the weak colonialism in Africa: the General Government was to be a work reservoir and nothing more.

In October, 1940, Frank informed a gathering of German soldiers that they could write to their families back in the Reich that there were not so many lice and Jews in Poland any more, although, he added, "of course I could not eliminate all lice and Jews in only one year's time." The figure of the louse occurs more than once in the Governor's writing and speeches. Addressing a meeting of his staff in January, 1940, he said: "My relations with the Poles are like the relations between the ant and the plant louse. When I treat the Poles in a helpful way, when so to speak, I tickle them in a friendly manner, it is to get them to work for me." [19]

Frank, the proconsul, the legalist, was never the sadistic killer that men like Himmler, Heydrich, and Koch were. He wanted the Poles and the Jews to work, and he objected when irreplaceable Jewish artisans were taken from their war work and sent off to the extermination camps, for this damaged the German war effort. The Jews and the Poles had work to do, and the killings gave him no pleasure, although he accepted the basic premises: the Jews eventually had to be gotten rid of; the Poles could continue to exist, but only insofar as they were useful to the Reich.

An estimated 3,474,000 Jews lived in all of Poland when the Germans invaded; about 1,400,000 were in the General Government. Before Frank took over, Heydrich had establishd the first ghetto on the first day of the war, and he planned to ship all the Jews in the rest of the country to the General Government to clear the other Polish provinces for German settlement. The transports—200,000 Poles and Jews in two months—came in to the General Government without Frank's having been previously notified, and he protested about being forced to take care of these large numbers with the limited facilities at his disposal. At this time the Jews were not supposed to remain long in Poland but were to be shipped to Madagascar, as the Foreign Office suggested in 1940, or some other distant area of settlement. The population of the Jews in the General Government went up to 1,600,000, and Frank journeyed to Berlin to protest in person to Goering that he could not take care of such numbers that were merely dumped on him. He won his point, and after March 23, 1940, no further transports were allowed to go to the General Government without Frank's permission. He expected to get rid of the Jews he had quickly; they would go to Madagascar, Frank said, piece by piece, man by man, girl by girl. Lublin would become a decent city again, fit for the German people of the occupation to live in, and Cracow, which Frank said was "crawling with Jews so that a decent person would not step into the street," was soon cleared of Jews as they were sent to the ghettoes established in Warsaw, Lemberg, and Lodz.

The Warsaw ghetto was set up ostensibly to control an epidemic of spotted fever, but other reasons were also given: Jewish black-market activities and price gouging, and then political and moral grounds were also alleged. Both trolley and bus lines had to be rerouted, for the ghettoes were to be cut off completely from the outside world. There were 470,000 Jews in the Warsaw ghetto, and 160,000 in Lodz. Both were administered by a commissar, who in turn dealt with the Jewish Council under a Jewish chairman who held the title of mayor. In this fashion the Jews themselves were made responsible for the administration of the ghetto. In the Warsaw ghetto, 2,400 Jewish policemen kept order, and Germans had only to pass their orders along to the Jewish Council. The Jewish Council provided the labor battalions and supervised the cheap production of the ghetto, where uniforms, ammunition boxes, leather and wooden shoes, brushes, brooms, mattresses, and containers were manufactured and repair work of all kinds might be gotten by the Germans, for the Jews in Poland were skilled artisans, a fact that helped to keep thousands of them alive for some years after the Wannsee Conference decreed their extermination.

On July 31, 1941, Goering signed the message to Heydrich that charged him to bring about the final solution of the Jewish problem (see Goering, Chapt. 3). The Wannsee Conference followed on January 20, 1942, and Frank sent his deputy Buehler to represent him. The Madagascar plan had fallen through. There was no longer any possibility of transporting millions of Jews to a remote French island. Instead they were to be sent to the East, organized into gigantic labor columns which in the course of time with insufficient food and the exhausting work would dwindle to a hard core; after that the exterminations would begin in camps equipped for that purpose. It was in the General Government that the evacuation to the extermination camps began.

In December, 1941, Frank told a meeting of soldiers, "As far as the Jews are concerned, I want to tell you quite frankly that they must be done away with in one way or another." He repeated these phrases to his cabinet meeting in Cracow and added:

> Before I continue, I want to beg you to agree with me on the following formula: We will principally have pity on the German people only, and on nobody else in the entire world . . . This war would be only a partial success if the whole lot of Jewry survived it, while we shed our best blood to save Europe. My attitude toward the Jews will therefore be based solely on the expectation that they must disappear. They must be done away with . . . Gentlemen, I must ask you to rid yourselves of all feeling of pity. We must annihilate the Jews wherever we find them and wherever it is possible . . . The General Government will have to become just as free of the Jews as the Reich.[20]

The SS and SD did the actual clearing of the ghettos with the help of the police forces and auxiliaries. By December, 1942, 85 per cent of the Jews of the General Government had been transported to extermination centers.[21] The rest of the Jews were kept as a labor force in concentration camps, where they worked for the SS industries.

The food situation by 1942 had become catastrophic: a million Jews could no longer be fed, Frank wrote in his diary; the total bread ration was to be canceled for them. Rations would be provided only for the 300,000 Jews who worked for the Germans as craftsmen; the others would get nothing. And the Poles would not do much better. "Before the German people are to experience starvation," he told his aides, "the occupied territories and their people will be exposed to starvation . . . The new demands [from Germany] will be fulfilled exclusively *at the expense of the foreign population* [Frank's italics]. It must be done cold-bloodedly and without pity . . ." The Polish economy, Frank continued, would feel the pinch, as would the transport system. "In view of the worsening living conditions extraordinary hardship will set in for railroad workers and other categories; as the previous quantities of food were already insufficient . . .* The Germans in this area will not feel it." German soldiers returning to the Reich could bring back anything they could carry along. "That we sentence one to two million Jews to die of hunger should be noted only marginally . . ." [22]

In Nuremberg, where he became a convert to Roman Catholicism, he said that the trial had shaken him, that he fully realized the enormity of the crimes that had been committed and in which he himself had participated: "A thousand years shall pass," he told the court in the memorable phrase, "and this guilt of Germany shall not have been erased." But he had been aware of his own responsibility much earlier, as was shown, for example, when he told a gathering of his co-workers on January 25, 1943 (speaking now of Poles not Jews), "We must not be squeamish when we learn that a total of 17,000 have been shot . . . We are now duty bound to hold together . . . we, who are gathered together here figure on Mr. Roosevelt's list of war criminals. I have the honor of being Number One. We have, so to speak, become accomplices in the world historic sense." [23]

He regretted the deportation of Jewish manpower that was still usable—1943 was the peak year of the mass executions in the extermination camps—but the decision for their annihilation had been made in higher quarters. A great building project in the General Government had to be abandoned, and this could have gone forward, Frank pointed out, had the thousands of Jews who were experts at their trades been allowed to remain at work. Whether Frank in coming to this conclusion was more concerned with the production of his General Government or his private war with Himmler is a question. For he waged a continuous war over a period of five years against Himmler's incursions on his territory, and Himmler in turn, so Bach-Zelewski testified at Nuremberg, called Frank a traitor because Frank defended both Polish and Jewish workers against the increasing SS demands for arrests and deportations. But this was scarcely more than a jurisdictional quarrel. When Frank complained of the manner in which his State Secretary and head of the police, Krueger, had carried out Himmler's orders for arrests, what he was emphasizing was that Krueger had acted without consulting him; this was typical, he said, of the way the police behaved, following the orders of the Reichsfuehrer "about which I had no knowledge, in contradiction to the Fuehrer's directives and to which I had not given my consent." Frank's protests about such matters, as well as about the transports of the Jews who were dumped on him, were based not on the brutality of the evacuations or the deaths that occurred en route but on the need for his having to find a place for these Jews, the danger of epidemics which might spread to the rest of the population of the General Government, and the fact that they were ordered by rival authorities without consulting him. All that really interested

* In the spring of 1940 Frank was told the Polish worker was getting only 600–700 calories a day instead of the necessary 2,200 (N XXIX, 2233-PS, p. 395).

Frank was that he be acknowledged the ultimate power in his government as a proconsul following the directives of the distant Fuehrer but sovereign in the state he ruled. He had been, he confessed at Nuremberg, an anti-Semite; the Jews, he believed, were responsible for the war, and they were Germany's implacable enemies. "Think," he said in 1944, when things were going badly for the Reich, "what would have happened if the two million Jews who had once lived in Poland were there now to aid our enemies." Like Speer and Sauckel he was willing to permit them to work while they could and objected to other Reich agencies taking them off and exterminating good technicians; and while they worked he wanted them and the Poles, too, to be fed so they could accomplish their tasks.

Frank had known from the beginning about the planned extermination of the Jews and had approved it. "The Jews," he said, "we will deal with in one way or another"; and the ghettos were, as he knew, only a beginning in the process of "cleansing" Europe of the Jews. His feelings for the Poles fluctuated in a wider arc. With his love for music (he was a gifted pianist) and his desire to make some headway against the bitter Polish resistance to his rule, he established a Chopin museum in Cracow—something the Poles themselves had not been able to do in twenty years, one of his admirers told him—and an orchestra that was permitted to play for the German officials in the Government. He pressed for higher rations for Poles working for the Germans and even went so far in 1944 as to tell the Poles they too might become part of the new Europe.

All Frank was trying to do was to keep a semblance of order in his General Government and in addition get any help he could muster against the Polish underground. To this end he tried to win over the Polish clergy, telling Warsaw Archbishop Jan Sapieha, who complained to him of the killings of Catholic priests in the concentration camps, that this was nothing to what the Russians would do if they invaded Poland. Frank would have liked to enlist a Polish legion at this desperate point in Germany's affairs, but nothing came of this plan or of his attempt to create a Polish committee of advisors to his government, who would in fact have nothing more to do than transmit his orders to the population. The Polish committee would have been the equivalent of the Jewish Councils. Both Himmler and the Fuehrer, however, remained adamant on any question that had to do with altering the planned future of the territory and peoples they had set out to conquer in the East. When they yielded at any point, as when former Soviet General Vlasov finally was able under the SS to send part of his Russian army into action, their moves came so grudgingly and so late as to be of little use. The worse the war went for Germany, the more Frank's friendly feelings for the Poles increased; but his sentiments never went beyond the point he had reached when he declared in a speech to his staff that the Poles might work to help Germany win the war and after that he didn't care if they became mincemeat. Frank's only resistance to acts of violence committed against the Poles and Jews came when he was not consulted about them.

Nevertheless, Frank's was a deeply divided nature. He turned over the damning volumes of his diaries to the Allies at Nuremberg, he acknowledged his own guilt for the atrocities committed, and he always retained at least the dregs of a genuine feeling for what he continued to regard as the majesty of the law. He made speech after speech that seemed designed as much to convince himself as his hearers of the need for a system of law and justice in any state, including the Third Reich, for the independence of the judiciary, for nurturing the inner sense of justice of the people. He said that in the case of the Germans this necessity was especially acute because the German sense of justice was both a tribal and racial inheritance (*urdeutsch*) and a state without justice could not survive. A good part of his rhetoric was directed against Himmler and the erosion of Frank's own authority as Governor of Poland, but through all his speeches on this subject and in his diary too there is a thread of continuity; his belief that the law must preserve its integrity; the accused, if he is a German, must be given a hearing by a competent judge; he must have defense counsel; and he must be charged with a crime that was such before he committed it. What Frank kept saying he wanted—an authoritarian state under law—was a fabulous beast.

At the time of the Roehm putsch, Frank was Minister of Justice in Bavaria. Told of the arrests being made by order of the Fuehrer, he hurried to the prison where the SA leaders were being brought under SS guard and herded into cells in the same fashion many of them in their time had brought prisoners into the SA kangaroo courts, where Jews and other enemies of the State were sometimes killed and sometimes beaten before being sent on to the early versions of the concentration camps. Now themselves accused of a conspiracy to take power, the top brass of the stormtroopers had been arrested. The list of conspirators had been compiled by the Fuehrer himself, and many of the names on it, such as General von Schleicher, Papen's assistants Bose and Jung, and Gregor Strasser, were those of people who had nothing whatever to do with the SA but were merely under suspicion of being dangerous to Hitler. The majority, however, were Brownshirt leaders, and all those brought into the prison of the Ministry of Justice were SA men. The building swarmed with SS men under the command of Sepp Dietrich and Prince Waldeck, but Frank nevertheless visited the cells, including the one Roehm had been thrown into. Frank told Roehm what he told the other prisoners, that he was safe in his charge from any act of violence on the part of the SS because he was in the palace of justice.

Frank's confidence in the writ of his own authority did not last long, for Dietrich and Waldeck told him they had orders to shoot the 110 men whose names appeared on Hitler's list. Frank refused to allow the order to be carried out, and Dietrich telephoned Hitler at the Brown House in Munich.

He first reached Rudolf Hess, the Fuehrer's deputy, and then Hitler came to the telephone and Dietrich handed the receiver to Frank. An irate Fuehrer told Frank that these men were criminals and he, the Reichskanzler, not Frank decided what was to be done with them; the arrested SA men were only in Frank's jail because it was a convenient place to bring them. Then Hitler was gone and Hess was on the telephone again; he told Frank bluntly to carry out the order. Frank's legalistic mind was affronted; some of these prisoners had marched with him and with the Fuehrer at the time of the 1923 uprising and were old Party fighters he had defended in the courts of the Weimar Republic, and they were to be shot down without a trial or any kind of court proceeding by an order given by two SS officers and confirmed over the telephone. He stalled for time, telling Hess that the men had been dragged out of bed without weapons or signs of having plans of any kind, that they gave no impression of preparing an uprising and among them were some of the most decorated officers of World War I.

In 1934, while Hindenburg was still alive, Hitler was not yet the all-powerful ruler he was to become a few years later. According to Frank, the Fuehrer called the Reichspraesident and got Hindenburg's authority to execute the enemies of the State who had planned to rise against him and kill him, but by the time Hitler did this his fury had abated. When next the telephone rang, Frank heard the voice of Hess, who told him to proceed immediately with the executions of the men whose names he would read to him. He thereupon read nineteen names that did not include Roehm's. Frank again tried to ask on what legal grounds these men had been condemned, but this served only to bring a furious Hitler again to the phone. Hitler told him peremptorily to obey orders, that the existence of the Reich was at stake —one of the first times Hitler automatically identified his own fate with that of Germany. When they next met, Hitler said, according to Frank, "You're a fine Minister of Justice, talking about paragraphs when they wanted to kill me." [24] The nineteen were shot and a few hours later the Fuehrer ordered Roehm's execution. Frank's resistance oddly enough did not disturb the relationship between Hitler and his former defense counsel. Hitler hated what he regarded as the small-minded, paragraph-hunting, pettifogging lawyer; his People's Courts, made up of three laymen who were always Party members and two politically dependable, hand-picked judges, were founded after the burning of the Reichstag and the incomprehensible—to Hitler—freeing by the court of four of the defendants, all of them Communists.

Hitler became increasingly impatient of German judges who handed out sentences that seemed to him too light. He read the court decisions carefully and again and again when he thought a jail sentence handed down too mild, he changed it to a death sentence. On April 26, 1942, at the last session of the Reichstag, in which the docile deputies voted him full power over German jurisprudence, he said, "From now on I will interfere and judges who do not know the demands of the hour will be removed from their posts. I will

never rest until every German sees that it is shameful to be a man of law." [25]
As early as 1934, at the time of the Roehm putsch, Hitler had referred to
himself as the highest judge in the Reich when he orderd the arrest and
execution of at least a hundred people. Frank, if he were to remain in the
Fuehrer's good graces, had to take the same view of the law, to declare there
could be no crime without punishment, that the judge's job, as he said, "is
to protect the concrete order of the community, to get rid of wrong-doers;
to avenge conduct disturbing to the community . . . The basis of all sources
of law is the National Socialist philosophy especially as it is expressed in the
Party program and the utterances of our Fuehrer. No judge has the right to
question decisions of the Fuehrer whether they are given in the form of laws
or decrees . . . Legal concepts promulgated before the National Socialist
revolution may not be used if their use would affront the healthy sentiments
of the people." [26]

Frank was never able to solve this dilemma by any process of reasoning.
He worked both sides of the street, talking of law and justice and at the same
time telling the judge, who must be independent and oppose the arbitrary
seizures of life and property by the police, that the law was what Hitler said
it was, for he was Germany and Germany was Hitler. Frank in January,
1936, took his first step in both directions when he told the judges of Germany in a directive that took on a quasi-official character when it was published in the yearbook *German Law*, "The judge is not set up over and above
the citizen of the State but he is a member of the living community of the
German people." [27] The Reich itself, he went on, was but a juridical formulation of the historical will of the Fuehrer. Whether the Fuehrer rules according to a regular constitution or not is not a question of law, he said,
the question of law is only whether the Fuehrer assures the life of the people
in what he does. Why did the State have to have concentration camps, he
asked an audience in the same year, where people could be sent without a
warrant? Only because of the danger of bolshevism, he answered, and since
Germany under Hitler would always be living in a state of emergency threatened by Jews and Bolsheviks the need for the camps continued.

In 1942 when Frank talked on the subject of the law as the foundation
stone of the people's community, he spoke on the same general topic that
seemingly gave him no peace. He told a University of Munich audience on
July 20 that perhaps only he could give the talk because he was an "old
fighter" and a Reichsleiter and thus was in a position to defend judges and
lawyers against the insupportable attacks that were being made on them.
An article in the SS paper *Das Schwarze Korps* had called judges and lawyers
"little cloaca animals," in the quaint Nazi verbiage of true believers aroused
as they thought the Fuehrer wanted them to be. Frank said that since the
Fuehrer had given him the title of Leader of the Chamber of Law of the
Reich (Reichsrechtsamt), it was his duty to protest. At this point the record
of the meeting noted "a storm of applause" from the audience, and Frank

went on to repeat what he had been saying for years—without justice there is no community and for the obtaining of justice an independent judge was needed. The belief in this form of justice was one of the oldest Germanic cultural attributes. It was not possible for a judge to be a danger to the State. The only danger was to those who wanted something other than justice. Even a bad judge gives a defendant the chance to be heard, and without this hearing any action against a defendant is merely an arbitrary police measure. "It may seem," he bleakly told his audience, "as though I am giving you a program for the future . . . that reality speaks another language." And thus, having used up his shots aimed at the realm of Heinrich Himmler, he carefully made sure of his lines of security. "Adolf Hitler lives," he said, "the picture of the Fuehrer is the sun, and we are the fighters in his service and we ask of him: Fuehrer protect the justice of the Reich too." "The German people," Frank added, "had had their ups and downs historically but one thing had always remained luminous . . . the belief in a higher order of existence and the indestructible law of our people." [28] This was all very well on the immediate occasion of a speech given before an audience in a university where students had dared to show signs of resistance to the Party. (It was at the University of Munich that a brother and sister, Hans and Sophie Scholl, prepared their anti-Nazi posters and where a large audience of students openly displayed their antipathy to Party speakers.) Such people could be told that Germany must never be a police state, that power alone does not make a state, and that brutality is not the same as strength; whether they believed him or not, they gladly heard Frank on this subject.

Frank was an easy target for the Reichsfuehrer SS and Bormann and the other direct actionists whom he censured. His own corruption and Hitler's mistrust and dislike of lawyers and legality when it prevented him from doing something he wanted to do left Frank immured in his Polish satrapy. Hitler did not bother to get rid of him there, but he deprived him of his audience of lawyers and students and the balm to his conscience they provided. Frank accepted this decision without demur, as from the beginning he had accepted the many paradoxes of his spirited if theoretical campaign on behalf of the law. His was one of the countless number of schizoid natures of the Reich. Almost everything he did in Poland contradicted his statements on the sanctity of the law, but of course law for Poles was something else than it was for Germans. When the so-called "pacifying action" designed to stop by terror Polish acts of resistance against the German occupiers was underway, Frank said on May 30, 1940, "Any attempt on the part of the legal authorities to intervene in the action, undertaken with the help of the police, should be considered as treason to the State and to German interests." [29] This pacifying action, he said, lay outside the scope of normal legal procedures (the victims were arrested and either executed or sent to concentration camps). Frank said the police and he were cooperating, and whether the action was carried out by the police or by his men made no difference, for the police were under him. The latter part of the statement was a considerable exaggeration, but he succeeded in making clear that there was no competition in this wholesale killing. The problem, he said, was to liquidate the ruling class of Poland and to make sure that it was not replaced.

In Poland Frank's Germanic feeling for the sacredness of law and justice played no role whatever. Neither the lives nor the property of these people had the slightest right to protection if he decided otherwise, and he frequently did. The defense of the law for him, like the sanctity of the word of an SS man for Himmler, was an outward and visible sign of a lost rectitude; it was the same psychological defense that concentration-camp guards made use of when they called themselves soldiers or that the gunmen of the Einsatz squads or commandants of extermination camps used when they spoke of their insupportably hard task. Hoess, the commandant of Auschwitz, thought he was more sensitive than most people—a defect, he declared, that he sought to cover up with an icy exterior. Eichmann said much the same thing; he was so sensitive, he confessed in the course of his hearings in Israel, that he could not bear the sight of blood and so could not have been a doctor. For Frank, self-rescue took the form of his hopeless fight on behalf of the law in an authoritarian state. He actually ran small risks on behalf of his often reiterated ideal, if indeed that ideal ever was much more than a weapon against Himmler. The Fuehrer, as Frank knew, was not likely to forget the old fighters, of which Frank was one; even when they irritated Hitler they rarely fell far from grace unless they conspired against him or questioned his *mana*, something that Frank never did. Nevertheless, in at least one part of Frank's mind some vestiges remained of what his old teachers had told him about the sanctity, stability, and mystique of the law. His posturing was not all a charade; the attempt to save the lives of the SA men, for example, even against the will of the Fuehrer evidenced this. Frank allowed the nineteen to be shot; he had no way of preventing it aside from open revolt, which was unthinkable, and he did manage to save the others. In this instance he had nothing to gain and much to lose.

The division in his soul may also be seen in his conversion to Catholicism and his abject confessions of guilt, which were only occasionally tempered by attacks on the Allies for their treatment of the Germans. Again, in his autobiography, he apostrophized the Polish people, whose ruling classes he had striven to annihilate, wishing them and their country a flourishing and eternal life. Frank knew what his fate would be at Nuremberg; he had known it years before, as was shown when he told his aides about the list of war criminals he headed. Unlike Sauckel, who was surprised that, after all the praise that had been bestowed upon him for his efforts in providing workers for the Reich, he should be suddenly flung into prison and accused of war crimes and crimes against humanity, Frank accepted, now that the Nazi furors had subsided, the point of view of the non-Nazi world and of his accusers. At Nuremberg the ideal of the law for him was vastly overshadowed by reflections on a far higher power and on the eternity to which he had helped to send so many thousands of helpless people. He attacked Hitler, who, he thought, had betrayed the trust and devotion millions of Germans had placed in him; the Fuehrer, the godless one, had deluded them all, although it is not easy to see what Frank learned in Nuremberg about either his leader or what went on under him that he had not known before. The testimony he had heard in the courtroom had shaken him to his roots, he said. But why had it? What could he have heard in Nuremberg that he had not known when he had the power of life and death in the General Government? Perhaps he came blinking back into the light of the ordinary world where he had once studied law and accepted the norms with which he had been brought up and which appeared only wanly and from time to time in his mind when during the long Nazi years at intervals he duly paid them lip service. Hitler had given him a great deal, a province of his own, high life, a chieftainship of the master race, and this had almost but never quite converted him to the same role of exterminator that Himmler had assumed.

ARTUR SEYSS-INQUART

Seyss-Inquart, a Deputy Governor of Frank's in Poland, had also after the *Anschluss* been Chancellor of Austria for four days. With a limp, a bald spot, and thick, heavy-rimmed glasses, he looked at Nuremberg precisely like what he was: a serious-minded, middle-aged attorney. His lawyer opened the defense with the words of the man Seyss-Inquart had helped depose, Kurt Schuschnigg, the Chancellor of Austria before him, "May God protect Austria." It was a feeble gambit—for Seyss, like the Fuehrer, had dreamed and worked most of his life for the *Anschluss* of Austria to Germany. The protection of Austria he gladly would have left to Hitler's Reich and only after that, perhaps, to God.

Seyss-Inquart, like so many of his countrymen, thought the position of Austria after World War I spiritually, economically, and politically hopeless unless Austria became part of the German State. Austria never recovered from the war, after which a half million men (their families brought the total to over a million) out of a population of six million were unemployed in the shrunken remnant of the empire that with its mixture of races and geography had given an economic unity to the Danube area and a prosperity its inhabitants were not to know again until years after the end of World War II. Men who, like Seyss-Inquart, joined the Nazis or one of the other extremist parties working for the *Anschluss* after Hitler came to power were convinced that no other possible means of survival existed for their country, which had twice voted for union with Germany long before their fellow countryman Herr Hitler became Chancellor of the German Reich. When Austrians had a chance to express their preferences, they voted overwhelmingly for the union with Germany. After World War I, the Austrian Provisional National Assembly declared Austria part of the German Republic, a declaration repeated a few months later by the Constitutional National Assembly. Plebiscites held in 1921 in the Tyrol were 98 per cent for *Anschluss*.

Seyss-Inquart was born in 1892 on the frontier of the Slav world in the little town of Iglau in Moravia, which was then a province of the Austro-Hungarian Empire. At the age of fifteen he moved with his family to Vienna, where, after taking his *Abitur*, he studied law at the university. In 1914 he enlisted in the Austro-Hungarian Army; he fought on the Russian and Italian fronts and was wounded and decorated for valor in the presence of the enemy. Seyss received his law degree during a furlough in 1917, and after the war he mildly prospered at his practice. He was a devoted Catholic, but as in the case of thousands of his Austrian co-religionists, his German nationalist sentiments completely dominated his political thinking. He joined one of the many conspiratorial nationalist and racist organizations that sprang up in Austria as in Germany and became a member of the German Brotherhood (die deutsche Gemeinschaft), the stated aim of which was to liberate the German people from Jewish influence. It was a secret organization run on the hierarchical principles that governed all such underground groups of the period, with the lower echelons subject to authority of the higher.

The Brotherhood had suborganizations with different names designed to bring in members who might shy away from the austere tenets of the parent group, but all of these groups had three requirements: the member must be of German blood, must not be a Freemason, and must not be married to a Jewess. Founders were the elite of the Brotherhood; later members were sworn to carry out the orders and assignments given them by those with a low number in the organization. Members' names were not to be mentioned when they joined the society. The members were on the whole a heterogeneous lot, although they included some well-known political figures, including the future Chancellor Engelbert Dollfuss. Dollfuss was a staunch clericalist, but he was also just as staunch an anti-Semite and anti-Social Democrat. He became a bitter opponent of the National Socialists and of the *Anschluss* once Hitler became Chancellor, but in the early days he and men like Seyss-Inquart made common cause based on their anti-Semitism, anti-Freemasonry, and belief in the need for Austria to be part of a Greater Germany.

There were many gatherings such as those of the Brotherhood in the postwar years, in both Austria and Germany as well as other countries of Europe. They were made up of men who had fought in the war and come back to civilian life bewildered by the defeat or, as in France and Italy, by what was regarded as the futility of the victory and the blasted hopes that followed it. In all the countries of Europe little groups, from the Communists and anarchists of the Left to the genuine and proto-Fascists of the Right, met secretly to plan a world nearer to their hearts' desire. The groups were especially numerous in countries where the ex-soldiers of an army that had lost the war found themselves facing a future they could not assess in any way in terms of their own experience of the past. Imperial Austria was gone, and in its place were a rump state, a population now cut off by tariff barriers and the succession states, cut off from the balanced economy the former polyglot empire had provided. Union with Germany was forbidden by the conquerors, who could scarcely have been expected to countenance a German state bigger than the one they had been able to defeat only with the help of an overseas, non-European power.

All through Germany and Austria the protest against the defeat was linked with sentiments that had to do with Germanism, with the feeling that it was the foreign bodies that had killed the empire; the Slavs and the Jews had betrayed the Germans, who had rightfully dominated the cultural, political, and social life of these mixed populations. In the place of the German states had come synthetic constructions like Czechoslovakia, and the whole rickety structure of postwar Europe was held together by a coalition of weakness. The German character of Austria was undeniable, as was the pro-German leaning of its population, even after Hitler became Chancellor.*

Seyss-Inquart's relation to the early Austrian Nazi Party was tenuous. He joined the Styrian Home Guard, which later went over *en bloc* to the National Socialists; the Austro-German Volksbund; and the Fatherland Front, a strongly nationalistic organization, which also amalgamated with the Nazis in later years. In addition, from 1932 on he paid dues of 20 schillings a month to the Nazi Party. Thus, as he assured Himmler after the *Anschluss* when his Party regularity was being questioned, he had from that year considered himself a member of the Party. But Seyss-Inquart had to argue both sides of his own case, for when he was defending his career as a National Socialist at Nuremberg, he made much of the fact that he had put off officially joining the Party as long as possible because he was a Catholic and had deplored their acts of violence. He solemnly assured Himmler, however, that he had never sent a telegram of good wishes to the new Chancellor when Dollfuss took office. Seyss unquestionably subscribed to the main tenets of the Nazis long before he joined them. His belief in a Greater Germany, his anti-Semitism and anti-Freemasonry, his unquestioning acquiescence in the authoritarian form of the parties he did join, as well as his paying dues and the subsequent use the German National Socialist leadership made of

---

* During the trial of Seyss-Inquart, Sumner Welles, who had marked anti-German feelings, could nevertheless be cited by the defense. In his *Time for Decision*, Welles wrote that Chancellor Schuschnigg had admitted that if the Germans invaded Austria, a majority of the country would welcome them, but if the Italians came the country would rise against them as one man. Yet up to a few months before the *Anschluss*, Italy was the chief protector of Austrian sovereignty against Germany, and when the Austrian Chancellor Dollfuss was murdered in a rising of the Nazis in 1934, the Italians promptly mobilized their Alpine divisions and sent them to their positions at the Brenner Pass.

him, evidence the stages of a tentative and then an all-out Party member. He pictured himself at Nuremberg as a nationalist and a believer in the *Anschluss* through natural, evolutionary historical forces. He was actually, as Schuschnigg said of him, a limited, Austrian Nazi; he was cautious, correct, and far removed from the murderers and brawling militant leaders like Captain Leopold, who, while he was nominally head of the Party in Austria, denounced Seyss for lack of fervor and disobedience to Party discipline.* [30]

Seyss was easily persuaded of what he wanted to believe. He testified at Nuremberg that he had heard conditions were good at Auschwitz and that the camp had a hundred-piece orchestra. He said that this information had ended his inquiries into the extermination camp of which he had heard some disquieting rumors. He had sent a member or two of his staff to ask questions, and when they returned with the answers he wanted to hear, that was enough.

In Austria, Schuschnigg regarded Seyss as a moderate, a man with whom he could deal and who could represent him to Hitler and at the same time keep in check the wild men of the Party. This was what Seyss-Inquart the Catholic Austrian Nazi wanted to do. The murder of Dollfuss by the Austrian SS in 1934 had appalled him. It was not only an act of brutality and violence foreign to Seyss-Inquart, it was a tragic deed that did great damage to the goal dearest to his heart—the *Anschluss*. Events, however, were always stronger than Seyss-Inquart's good intentions.†

Schuschnigg never fully trusted Seyss and only reluctantly appointed him to be State Councilor early in 1937, following the meeting with Hitler of July, 1936, designed to reduce tension between the two countries. At this meeting, Schuschnigg had agreed to appoint a National Socialist to his cabinet, and he made a member of the Party, former State Councilor Edmund von Glaise-Horstenau, Minister Without Portfolio. Seyss was elevated to the rank of minister only after the stormy meeting between Schuschnigg and the Fuehrer at Berchtesgaden on February 12, 1938, and his appointment was an express condition of the agreement reached there. The President of Austria, Wilhelm Miklas, took no more kindly to him. At first, when Schuschnigg told him the conditions of the Berchtesgaden agreement, he refused to approve Seyss as Minister of the Interior; only when Schuschnigg said the alternative was his resignation as Chancellor did he yield. Miklas testified at a later trial at Nuremberg that he had never overcome his dislike of Seyss. He struggled against Seyss' influence until he was deposed after his futile effort to keep Austria independent. But, Miklas said, he had been deserted by everyone, by his former foreign allies and by his own countrymen; even Schuschnigg had left him

---

* Leopold, later a lieutenant colonel, was killed in action in Russia.
† Seyss attended the same Jesuit school as Schuschnigg, the Stella Matutina, and served in the Army with Dollfuss.

to take the final steps in relinquishing Austrian sovereignty.

Seyss-Inquart acted out the part that had been written for him when he took his place in the Schuschnigg government in 1937. His first job as State Councilor was to serve as a safety valve for the embittered Nazis, to listen to their complaints and to try to improve their lot. Although Seyss had told both Hitler and Schuschnigg that he would not become a Trojan horse, that is precisely what he became, and his job as Minister of the Interior was to mediate between them, on the one hand to prepare the way for the *Anschluss,* on the other to prevent another putsch of the kind that had killed Dollfuss and greatly damaged, for a time, the pro-German movement in Austria. When Seyss journeyed to Berlin to report to the Fuehrer and when he returned to Vienna to report to Schuschnigg, he had nothing to conceal. He could tell both men to whom he believed he owed his conflicting allegiance what the other said, because the long-range incompatibility of their policies was plain enough and could not possibly be pursued for many months without a final test of strength. Schuschnigg could only hope to yield as little as possible to Hitler and to gain time that would bring foreign support. After becoming Minister of the Interior, Seyss greeted Hitler with outstretched arm and "Heil Hitler," recognizing him in his fashion, he thought, as leader of the Germanic peoples. When he returned to Austria, he greeted Schuschnigg as head of the Austrian State.

Austria no longer had any freedom of action after sanctions were imposed by England and France against Italy at the time of the Ethiopian war. Once Mussolini had to turn to Hitler for support against Italy's former allies, the cause of independent Austria was lost. Nor was the Austrian internal situation propitious. Schuschnigg's was an authoritarian government and, like that of Dollfuss, had to rule without elections (Seyss-Inquart's lawyer at Nuremberg could well ask Miklas how he had held on to the presidency—no election had taken place nor could one take place without immediate danger of civil war). Dollfuss had ruled with much the same methods as Hitler, although he never had the fanatical and widespread support that Hitler had in Germany. Confronted with Communist and Social Democratic opposition on the one side and the Nazis on the other, Dollfuss had declared the Nazi Party illegal in June, 1933. A few months later he put down an uprising of the Social Democratic Party and its armed *Schutzbund* with a ruthlessness that even included the use of artillery against the workers' housing development in Vienna. The casualties included thirty-odd dead and 200 wounded; Dollfuss' moral credit inside and outside Austria could never recover from this act of violence. In February, 1934, the Austrian Socialists organized an attempt on his life, and a few months later, in July, their mortal enemies, the Nazis, killed him.

Although a Catholic, Seyss was against the Austrian brand of clericalism of both Dollfuss and Schuschnigg. Their policy was one of dependence on the Vatican, he thought, instead of on Berlin, and this policy could only result in the perpetuation of an Austria of the post-1918 variety, torn by internal dissension, constantly on the verge of civil war, burdened with chronic economic depression. That this view was shared by thousands of his countrymen—probably by the vast majority—was shown not only by the votes for the *Anschluss* right after the war but by the well-nigh unanimous testimony of witnesses to the ecstatic welcome by the population when the German troops finally marched in. The German invasion was called "the flower war," and it bore far more resemblance to a Mardi Gras than to a military action and occupation such as took place when the Germans marched into Prague. Behind the jubilation lay the bankruptcy of the Austrian regime, and Seyss played no more than a messenger's role in the last fateful events, which were brought on by Schuschnigg himself.

Seyss' appointment as Minister of the Interior was a signal to the Austrian Nazi Party that better times were coming. The Party had been officially outlawed since the murder of Dollfuss, but the members were now allowed to raise their right arms in the Nazi salute and to say "Heil Hitler," provided this was not done in a provocative way. Hundreds of National Socialists were released from prison under the terms of the Berchtesgaden agreement, and Seyss-Inquart joined Glaise-Horstenau as a member of the Government. What constituted provocative or antigovernment behavior was now interpreted by a Nazi Minister of the Interior who was also head of the police and responsible for internal security. Thus, although swastika insignia were not supposed to be worn in public, the Party members bought them in many Austrian towns and then marched through the streets with their colors flying, without interference from the police, who were more likely than not to be pro-Nazi themselves and in any event were under Seyss-Inquart's orders. "The movement was no longer hindered by Seyss' police." [31]

Reacting to the steadily increasing pressure Hitler could place upon him once Italy no longer played the role of protecting power, Schuschnigg made a fatal blunder. He was to know no peace after the meeting with Hitler at Berchtesgaden, where Hitler from the first moment attacked Schuschnigg for sabotaging German-Austrian relations, stormed at him for his anti-Germanism, and worked himself into such a fury that both Schuschnigg and his Undersecretary of Foreign Affairs, Guido Schmidt, thought they would be arrested. Schuschnigg had agreed to the meeting only when Franz von Papen, the German Ambassador, acting apparently in good faith, had told him no unexpected demands would be made of him. The meeting was supposed to deal with points of friction that had appeared since the 1936 agreement, which would be again confirmed, and, Papen told Schuschnigg, such direct conversations would help make Hitler more conciliatory toward Austria. But Papen's optimism was completely unfounded.

Schuschnigg was met at Berchtesgaden by three German generals who, although they said themselves that they did not know why they were present, stood behind, so to speak, every word Hitler uttered. In the course of the stormy session with Hitler, the Austrian Chancellor received the ultimatum he eventually had to accept with only minor changes. In addition to naming Seyss-Inquart and appointing another Nazi, Dr. Hans Fischboeck,* to a high economic post that would smooth the way for union with Germany, Schuschnigg had to agree to reinstate all Nazi officials and officers who had been relieved of their duties and, most important, in Article 6 to declare everyone free to profess the National Socialist creed and to admit National Socialists with equal status to the Fatherland Front. There they would be permitted "to develop legal activities in accordance with Austrian law," although the Nazi Party remained illegal. The Austrian Nazis could well rejoice; it was only a matter of time now. Hitler held all the cards; with a powerful National Socialist movement inside the country, two members of the Party in the Schuschnigg cabinet, and Austria isolated, Hitler had only to maneuver with far less skill than he had needed to become the legal Chancellor of Germany.

Schuschnigg played into Hitler's hands. When the heat became too intense with the rowdy Nazi street demonstrations and the likelihood of another putsch in the offing, he decided to call a plebiscite that would convince the outside world that the National Socialists were a disreputable minority in a country that stood behind its Chancellor and President. The plebiscite was rigged. Only those over twenty-four years of age could vote. The plebiscite was announced on March 9, only four days before the voting would take place; since no voting lists were prepared it was to be held under the control of Schuschnigg's party, the Fatherland Front, which would decide who could vote in improvised booths provided with ballots that, like those in the Reich, made it difficult for "No" votes to be counted. The voting would take place without secrecy, which would make it almost impossible for government officials, for example, to vote "No." Since large numbers of the anti-Schuschnigg forces were not yet twenty-four and because under the Austrian constitution a plebiscite could only be held if it were called for by the President and approved by a Parliament—neither of which had taken place when Schuschnigg announced his decision—the whole process held vast promise of fraud. It could only have been designed to gain a vote of confidence that could never have been obtained through normal voting procedures.

Hitler moved swiftly, and he turned Seyss-Inquart, now the chosen instrument, into the Trojan horse that Seyss had sworn he would never become. On Friday, March 11, 1938, Schuschnigg learned early in the morning that the German-Austrian border had been closed; German customs officials were not at their posts. A little while later Seyss-Inquart appeared in the

* Fischboeck would later serve as Seyss-Inquart's Economic Commissioner in Holland.

Chancellor's office with Glaise-Horstenau, who had just flown in from Berlin, and they demanded that the plebiscite be put off. Nazi sound trucks already were announcing the postponement, and the SA was in the streets. Schuschnigg agreed to the postponement, but it was already too late; Hitler was not going to be content with half measures this time. Characteristically he raised the ante.

At 11:30 in the morning, Seyss-Inquart telephoned Goering to tell him the German demands were accepted, but now there were other demands. Goering said Schuschnigg must resign and Seyss-Inquart take his place as Chancellor. Schuschnigg again sparred for time; but he had no cards to play. He thought of telephoning Mussolini; he even put in the call, but canceled it, for Mussolini would not move. The Austrian Foreign Office reported: "The Italian Government declares it can give no advice under these circumstances in case such advice would be asked for." Schuschnigg could do nothing but resign, and this he did in the afternoon of the 12th, although after seeing Miklas he said he intended to continue in office as ex-Chancellor until his successor was appointed. But the Gestapo was now in the chancellery, and Schuschnigg told Miklas that there was no alternative to the appointment of Seyss-Inquart, who was, after all, a moderate. With Schuschnigg's broadcast to the Austrian people announcing his retirement (made from the same room where Dollfuss had been slain four years earlier), independent Austria came to its end. Seyss made a broadcast, too, as Minister of Security, asking the country to maintain order, and soon afterward Miklas, yielding to overwhelming force, duly appointed him Chancellor.[32]

Goering had prepared a telegram to be signed and sent by Seyss-Inquart that called in the German Army to preserve order in Austria. Since Seyss had become Chancellor in Schuschnigg's place, this telegram would place the seal of legality, so cherished by Hitler after the failure of his 1923 putsch, on the occupation. Seyss denied at Nuremberg that he sent the telegram, and in fact there is no evidence that he did.* Nor did he send the code word ("Agreed") Goering had suggested he use in place of the actual telegram, indicating that the text of the prepared telegram was in force. Seyss did what he had always been prone to do; he went along without compromising himself. In the course of one of the many telephone conversations held the night of the 11th, as the tension mounted and Hitler, Goering, Goebbels, and company eagerly awaited the play-by-play news from Austria, the German Staatssekretaer Wilhelm Keppler, who had just flown in to Vienna from Berlin, told Dietrich, head of the Reich News Bureau, that

---

* The text of the telegram was as follows:

The provisional Austrian government that after the demission of the Schuschnigg regime sees its task as that of restoring peace and order in Austria directs to the German Government its urgent request to assist its task and help it to prevent bloodshed. To this end it asks the German Government to send German troops as soon as possible [NCA V, 2463-PS, p. 207].

Seyss-Inquart had indeed agreed. Keppler had pressed Seyss for action on the telegram and Seyss had wearily said, "Well you know my position— do what you want." [33]

The telegram was merely a cover; whether or not it was sent made no difference. The orders to the troops had been given; they were to march and would in any case have been received joyously by the population. But Seyss held out. The Austrian Nazi to the end, he asked the Fuehrer if Austrian token troops might not march into Germany as a symbol of the togetherness of the countries, and Hitler agreed to the gesture.

The plan that was carried out on March 11 was the same one the Austrian police had captured in a raid on a Nazi headquarters in Vienna in February, 1937—the so-called Tavs plan. Signed by Rudolf Hess, it declared that in view of the international situation the time was ripe for Germany to move. Demonstrations were to be engineered by the National Socialists in Austria, then an ultimatum was to go to the Austrian Government demanding that Nazi Party members enter the Government and government forces withdraw from the frontiers. In case of a refusal, German troops were to march. But if the Austrian Government agreed to accept the ultimatum, the Austrian Nazis were to move into government agencies, the Fatherland Front, and professional organizations on a basis of equality with the other parties. In any event, as Schuschnigg recalled the captured Tavs documents in 1945, the Germans had made their plans for moving into Austria on the same pretext that was used when the real *Anschluss* came, that the Government "is no longer in a position to cope with the unrest in the country. In this case the German Army marches into Austria to restore order.* [34]

President Miklas held on to his office for a few days, and Seyss remained as Chancellor for a space of four days, until Austria was incorporated into the Reich on March 15 and needed no separate chancellery. Seyss-Inquart treated Schuschnigg most courteously, taking him home in his own car after the radio talk to the Austrian people. The SS and the SA were in control of the streets and of the chancellery and, as Schuschnigg was soon to learn (for he was promptly put under house arrest), they had orders to see that he did not escape from the country.

The Council of Ministers met on March 15, 1938, and amended the constitution to make Austria part of the Reich. Under the authoritarian regimes of Dollfuss and Schuschnigg, this too was legal; no plebiscite or legislative act was needed. The Nazis held a plebiscite a month later, on April 20, and the Austrian voters overwhelmingly approved the act of the

---

* Guido Schmidt, the former Austrian Minister of Foreign Affairs, testified at Nuremberg that as he remembered the plan, it included the possibility of shooting the German Ambassador to Austria, Franz von Papen, in order to create an incident that would justify German armed intervention (N XVI, p. 160). A similar plan at the time of the Czech crisis was discussed in Nazi circles; it involved an attempt on the life of the German Minister Ernst Eisenlohr which would be blamed on the Czechs.

Council. Although it was not easy to vote "No," the enthusiasm of the Austrians for their change of citizenship was undeniable.

Seyss-Inquart was introduced a few hours after the Council met as Statthalter (Governor), the chief civic administrator of the country he had delivered to its new rulers. But his actions in the course of the moves and countermoves leading to the *Anschluss* were not contemptible, nor were they different from what either Schuschnigg or Miklas had expected of him. He tried to keep the revolution decorous, and when he hastened to Linz to welcome the Fuehrer, he declared in his speech what everyone knew to be true and what he had been saying for years—that he had been waiting a long time for this moment of unification of the two German peoples and that along with his Austrian compatriots he rejoiced in placing his country's destiny in the hands of the Fuehrer.*

Some weeks later, on April 7, 1938, Seyss returned to the subject and told a Berlin audience gathered at the Sportpalast:

> The National Socialist Party in Austria never tried to hide its inclination for a greater Germany. That Austria would one day return to the Reich was a matter of course for all National Socialists and for true Germans in Austria. I asked the Fuehrer for armed assistance to save Austria from a civil war and from the fate of Spain because I had information that the workers' militia was to act as an armed military force at the Schuschnigg plebiscite.[35]

Here, trying to inflate the part he had played in bringing Austria "*Heim ins Reich*," he asserted the opposite of what he was to say in his own defense at Nuremberg, where he declared that he had not invited the Germans to come in to maintain order in the country. Although he had sent neither the telegram nor the code word, at this high point in the fortunes of Germany he was delighted to keep alive the impression that he had.

In a letter to Goering more than a year later, on July 14, 1939, Seyss wrote in the same vein as he did to Himmler, who was suspicious of the intensity of Seyss' German National Socialist zeal. Seyss explained how indispensable he himself had been to the *Anschluss* and attempted to ward off the attacks of the old fighters who, like Himmler, were never convinced of his unconditional Party loyalty. He wrote to Goering:

> I know I am not of an active fighting nature unless final decisions are at stake. Yet I know that I cling with unconquerable tenacity to the goal in which I believe. That is greater Germany and the Fuehrer. And if some people are already tired out from the struggle, and some have been killed in the fight, I am still around somewhere and ready to go into action . . . I told myself in July, 1934, that we must fight this clerical regime on its own ground in order to let the Fuehrer use whatever method he desires.

---

* Seyss was a good speaker, but of an academic kind that contrasted with the tub thumping of much of the Nazi oratory (Wilfred von Oven, *Mit Goebbels bis zum Ende* [Buenos Aires: Duerer Verlag, 1949]).

I have stuck to this attitude with an iron determination because I and my friends had to fight against the whole political church, Freemasonry, Jewry, in short against everything in Austria. The slightest weakness . . . would have deprived the Fuehrer of the means and tools to carry out his ingenious political solution for Austria . . . I have been fully conscious of the fact that I am following a path which is not comprehensible to the masses and also not to my Party comrades. I followed it calmly and would without hesitation have followed it again because I am satisfied that at one point I could serve the Fuehrer as a tool in his work, even though my former attitude even now gives occasion to very worthy and honorable Party comrades to doubt my trustworthiness. I have never paid attention to such things because I am satisfied with the opinion which the Fuehrer and the men close to him have of me.[36]

Both Goering and Hitler accepted this view of Seyss-Inquart's contribution to the *Anschluss*. But in fact his Party loyalty had not been as whole-hearted as Seyss would have had them believe; it was actually closer to what he later sought to convince the Nuremberg tribunal it had been. Seyss had lived for the *Anschluss* and he wanted to be out in front on the winning side (he immediately appointed as a member of his cabinet a hatchet man, Kaltenbrunner, to his own old post as Minister of the Interior), and from the time the revolt against Schuschnigg was successful, he went along with the strong battalions trying to convince all who would listen that he had never faltered in his sense of National Socialist duty. But he had once complained before the *Anschluss* that as Chancellor he would be forced to appoint Nazis to high posts, and others' doubts of his Party zeal in the years of struggle, which he was never fully able to overcome, were well founded. As he wrote to Goering, he was not of an active fighting nature.

Two years elapsed after the events of 1938 before he took over the job that delivered him to the high court at Nuremberg and earned him his death sentence. In 1939 Hitler toyed with the idea of making Seyss Ambassador to Slovakia after that country became a German satellite, but Seyss' rank as a Reichsminister Without Portfolio seemed too high for such an insignificant post.[37] Nothing he did in Austria, where he served for fourteen months as Reich Governor of Vienna, or later in Poland would have marked him as one of the chief war criminals, although he dutifully placed his rubber stamp on the orders to deport Jews from Vienna and to confiscate their property along with that of the Freemasons and Boy Scouts. Wholesale arrests of Jews and Socialists in Vienna began in the first hours of the *Anschluss* and two weeks later the first deportations to Dachau began. In Poland, when he served under Frank, he issued no orders or proclamations on his own but merely repeated what the other high and low officials were saying. But he did his somewhat routine job efficiently and at the breakfast in the Governor's palace at Cracow, where Frank said farewell to him, each man extravagantly praised the other.

Seyss-Inquart went directly from Poland to the highest administrative post in Holland, where he remained until the end of the war. In Poland he did no more than energetically second the policies of his immediate superior, Hans Frank. In some ways he resembled Frank. Both were lawyers, both were passionately fond of music, both were legalists for whom Hitler had contempt but whom he nevertheless used, and both were convinced of the vast role Germany must play in Middle and Eastern Europe. Seyss was a more cultivated man than Frank, but he shared Frank's anti-Semitism, as well as his attitude toward the Poles. In addition, perhaps because he had been brought up in the neighborhood of a Slavic culture, Seyss felt a mystical attraction for the task he believed destiny had set the German nation in the East. There was indeed work to do in the West, he said, but in the East there was a German mission to be performed and this mission had to do with the need for *Lebensraum*, for acquiring the space occupied by an inferior culture and Germanizing it. Seyss-Inquart did not remain long in Poland (he took over his job as Deputy Governor on October 12, 1939, and he left on May 18, 1940, to become Reichskommissar of Holland), but he impressed those he met, both superiors and underlings, with his devotion to the purposes of the Third Reich. He had time to make an extended inspection trip through the General Government and to repeat at every stop what his chief was saying, that the Poles were to work for the Germans, that no other possibility existed for them, and that the Jews were to be made harmless. But Seyss unlike Frank picked up nothing for himself on his journeys; he served the Reich in Poland as he had in Austria, as a bureaucrat. In Holland, where he held the highest civil authority (as Reichskommissar), he did his best for the Dutch, as he testified at Nuremberg, so long as they collaborated or at least caused no trouble. He was proud of his record; he had confiscated for the armed forces of the Reich, he told his accusers, only 50,000 of the millions of bicycles in Holland; he had refused, he said, to increase the 50-million-marks-a-month charge the Germans were extracting to meet the costs of the occupation (actually the Dutch paid twice as much); and under his rule, he pointed out, 240,000 Dutch had "volunteered" for labor service with the Germans, compared to only 40,000 French under the German military government.* In addition, he told the court, he had tried to increase food rations for Dutch workers, as well as for the rest of their countrymen, and the success of his efforts, he said, appeared in the population statistics, which, despite the desperate food shortages in the last months of the war, went up from 8,845,541 in 1940 to 9,300,000 in 1945. On numerous occasions he succeeded in reducing the number of hostages shot in reprisal for attacks on the German occupation authority (in one instance, from 250 to 50; in another, where a German railroad train had

---

* Not many of these were actually volunteers. Among other measures, Dutch authorities in the autumn of 1940 decreed that any worker who refused to go to Germany would lose his ration coupons.

been blown up and twenty-five persons had been sentenced to die, Seyss got the number down to five). He had nothing against the shootings in principle; he merely wanted none of the trouble that would be sure to arise from wholesale executions or other overly severe measures.

Unlike Frank, whose position as Governor, on paper at least, was unique, Seyss acted as Reichskommissar, the same post that Terboven held in Norway. Under Hitler's decree of May 18, 1940, the Reichskommissar for the Netherlands was directly subordinate to the Fuehrer and represented the supreme civil power of the Government. Seyss had complete legislative power, he could issue decrees, and he could set up courts and bureaus to govern the country. What he had to do basically was to follow instructions issued by the Fuehrer. He operated with four German deputies—Commissioners General—and at the beginning of his rule with an administrative apparatus of Dutch civil servants under eleven Secretaries General, the chief civil officers in the Netherlands, all of whom had held the same posts under the Royal Government. In both Norway and Holland such administrations kept up the fiction of independent countries—in both cases populated by people of Germanic stock—that once rid of their pro-Allied and Jewish influence, might take their place in helping the Third Reich rule Europe.

In Norway Quisling was the leader of the Germanic movement, as well as head of the puppet government. Mussert, his Dutch counterpart, was leader only of the Netherlands National Socialist Party, although he too aspired to head a Dutch government with more than an administrative apparatus.* Neither Quisling nor Mussert had any mass following. Seyss did

---

* Anton Adrian Mussert was a Dutch engineer who founded the Dutch National Socialist Party in 1931. At the age of forty-three he lost his job in the public-works department of the province of Utrecht for his political activities. He was married to an aunt some fourteen years older than he. His apparent desire to submit to authority was transferred, though never quite intact, to the Fuehrer. For Mussert was also a Dutch nationalist and an admirer of both Mussolini's Fascism and the Nazis, and he wanted to be head of a National Socialist Dutch State of a Greater Netherlands which would include Belgian Flanders. He prepared in 1940 an ambitious plan for a League of Germanic Peoples which would include Germany, the Scandinavian countries, and the Netherlands. The League would be led by Hitler, but the component nations were to be independent and have armies of their own. He tried repeatedly to get the Fuehrer's approval of this united front of the Germanic peoples, with Holland at this stage one of its salients under leadership of the Reich. He swore an oath of fealty to Hitler, whom he saw as leader of this Teutonic order, but he resented the idea that Dutchmen should be regarded as Germans and in his three long interviews with the Fuehrer and in many speeches he tried to draw a patriotic line between German imperialism and what he properly suspected to be a plan to incorporate Holland into the Reich as Austria had been. Hitler told him that a union of national states, a Reich of the German nations, was impossible and said that Mussert must be willing to make sacrifices of his national sentiments as the Fuehrer himself had been, despite his Austrian birth. The future, as Hitler saw it, could only be won through the leadership of the Reich. He never stated his object of annexation outright, but he made his purpose clear, and Mussert resisted without, however, coming to a break. Simpleminded and tenacious, Mussert said once that he would either land in the Hague or in Dachau, but he did neither. He came before a Dutch court at the end of the war, was found guilty, and

his best to encourage the pro-German forces under Mussert, but Terboven opposed the similar movement in Norway because he trusted no Norwegians. During the occupation, the SS recruited in both Norway and Holland, from Flemish volunteers as well as from the Walloons of Belgium under the Rexist leader Degrelle, obtaining foreign but "Germanic" legions whose members swore allegiance to Adolf Hitler and would one day, so it was planned, help police the Continent on behalf of an even greater German empire.*

Seyss, according to his SS Police Chief Hanns Albin Rauter, favored making Mussert prime minister of a Dutch government, but Seyss was too convinced of strong Dutch reactions and too doubtful of Mussert's qualifications to try to make him a Quisling.[38] In the early days of the German occupation Seyss would have preferred dealing with a middle-class coalition party, the Nederlandse Unie, than with Mussert's group of National Socialists alone, but Hitler recognized Mussert as the representative of the Dutch people, and parties other than the NSB were forbidden.[39] Although Mussert and Hitler in their meetings gravely discussed the wide range of the common battle against bolshevism, the Fuehrer, too, was disinclined to set up a quasi-independent Dutch government apparatus, for he had other plans for the Netherlands and the Germanic states. Seyss' alleged idea of raising Mussert's status was reported to Himmler by Rauter, but Himmler of course wanted none of it. Both he and Rauter mistrusted Mussert because of his stubborn Dutch nationalism. Rost van Tonningen, an economist who had once worked for the League of Nations, was their candidate to head the Dutch National Socialists.† They thought him both more intelligent and more amenable than Mussert.

Seyss-Inquart's job, as he saw it, was a patriotic one, and he had no ambitions beyond it. He was to keep the Dutch pacified, to use the economy and the people for the benefit of the German war machine, to shift the anti-German sentiment of the country to an understanding and acceptance of its Germanic mission. Seyss, among his offices, was an Obersturmbannfuehrer in the SS (like all high Nazi civil officials he held an honorary rank), and he took this position seriously too. He thought he had a degree of authority in his daily encounters with the SS officials by virtue of his high rank in that organization and his esteem for it, but he never had the

---

was executed (MA 338 [IZG]. Meeting of December 14, 1942. Werner Warmbrunn, *The Dutch Under German Occupation 1940–1945* [Stanford: Stanford University Press, 1963]).

According to postwar estimates the Dutch National Socialist movement probably reached a membership of 88,000, although some sources placed it as high as 100,000. Between 7,000 and 8,000 Dutch National Socialists and 20,000 to 25,000 men from the rest of the population fought in the war on the German side.

* Even Latin elements were eligible, however, for these SS forces: France was represented by the Charlemagne Division, Belgium by "Flandern" as well as "Wallonia."

† Rost van Tonningen, like so many ardent National Socialists, was an outlander. He was born in Surabaja, brought up in Holland, and became one of the most radical members of the Dutch National Socialist Party (Gustav Steinbauer, unpublished manuscript).

bitter conflicts with Himmler that bedeviled Frank. He did, however, have the same battle with the Higher SS and Police Chief Rauter—who was appointed to his Netherlands post without Seyss' knowing about it—as did Frank with Krueger.* Both Rauter and Krueger had orders from Himmler to concern themselves with anything of a political nature occurring in their respective domains that would otherwise have come solely under the civil administrations. In the planned confusion of the Nazi organizations, such concerns had wide ambiance, for Rauter was Seyss' superior in the SS, although in the administrative apparatus he nominally was placed under him, and Rauter in his capacity as Higher SS and Police Chief took his orders directly from Himmler.[40] Seyss lacked Frank's pretensions and flamboyance, and he had no desire to quarrel with Himmler or the SS, for he admired both. He solved his problem by professing that Rauter was obeying his own orders. "I myself have given the Higher SS and Police Leader," he wrote, "all the power which an administrator of courts needs," thus making a claim of authority of the same kind that Frank pretended to. But the source of authority for the SS courts came not from the Reichskommissar but from Himmler, and the best Seyss could do was to maintain the fiction that the system functioned as he said it did, with himself at its head.[41]

Seyss thought the great personages of the Reich incapable of any wrongful act—that is, of any act of injustice against a German. He was a single-minded man who fully identified himself with the cause of a Greater Germany, finding without undue difficulty the soothing explanations he needed to fit the decisions he made or accepted on behalf of his historic mission. Only in the last months of the war, when Hitler's scorched-earth directives (which the Army was inclined to follow) threatened Holland with senseless destruction, did he revolt; for he wished the Dutch no ill and was bewildered by their inability to see how well he and the Germans meant by them. He refused to order the flooding of a number of the polders and agreed with Speer, with whom he talked, that the demolitions must be held to a minimum both in Germany and in the occupied countries.

This is not to say that Seyss was moved mainly by humane sympathies. Far from it. In the General Government he was as harsh as Frank in plotting the tragic roles of the Poles and the Jews. When Sauckel came to him in Holland with the quotas of forced labor to come from the Netherlands, Seyss provided them without reluctance; he would have liked the Dutch to volunteer, but if they did not, then they had to be picked up and sent off to work in Holland, Belgium, France, or the Reich. In Rotterdam and other cities Seyss-Inquart ordered the great razzias in which Dutchmen were rounded up for forced labor, and he never hesitated to use the same hard measures that obtained everywhere in Nazi-occupied Europe to put down any show of resistance. When on February 25-26, 1941, in protest against

---

* Rauter, also, was an Austrian who had been a member of the underground Nazi Party.

the razzias in the Jewish quarter of Amsterdam a general strike was called, Seyss-Inquart imposed a fine of 15,000,000 guldens on Amsterdam, 2,500,000 on Hilversum, and 500,000 on Zaandam.[42] Seyss in any case could not understand why the Dutch refused to take part in the anti-Semitic crusade. With the exception of some people in the rural areas the Dutch had never been anti-Semitic, and Seyss was shocked in May, 1942, when as a demonstration against the Jews' being forced to wear the yellow Star of David, hundreds of people in Amsterdam and elsewhere wore yellow flowers.

Seyss also helped to administer the hostage system. In 1940 he sent 600 prominent Dutchmen as hostages to separate barracks in Buchenwald, where they were given special privileges and lived far better than the other inmates of the camp. In 1941 they were transferred to internment centers in Holland. Another thousand hostages were picked up in 1942. Almost all of them were released by September, 1944, but after that, members of Resistance groups who were caught might simply be shot out of hand.

The Dutch Resistance had a slow but luxuriant growth. Mussert's National Socialists in 1935 mustered some 8 per cent of the total Dutch vote, a number that was reduced to 4 per cent by 1937. With the exception of this group the Dutch people from the start of the invasion were anti-Nazi. The Dutch had no tradition of enmity with Germany, and the sudden assault on them seemed shameless to every Dutchman. An attempt was made by Seyss and the Dutch National Socialists to justify the German attack by Holland's pro-Allied sentiments and the part the Dutch secret service had played in the Venloo incident, in which SD men, masquerading as members of the Resistance against Hitler, had dealt with English agents and then seized them on Dutch territory. The negotiations the English agents had conducted in Holland were held in the presence of representatives of the head of the Dutch secret service, Major General J. W. van Oorschot, whose liaison officer was fatally shot when the Anglo-Dutch party was captured by the Germans. And what seemed to have been an act of terroristic destruction—the bombing of Rotterdam after the city had been surrendered—appeared to be a sign of singular Nazi ferocity. Actually, as Goering testified at Nuremberg, and as later investigations demonstrated, the Dutch willingness to negotiate a surrender had been communicated to the Germans too late to call off the attack on what had up to then been a well-defended city. The radio phones were not operating properly, for the planes' crews had pulled in their trailing antennas once they got over hostile territory, and the flares the Germans placed to signal the pilots not to drop their bombs were recognized by half the bombing group, which turned back. The other half did the bombing.[43]

Numbed with the defeat and uncertain of the future, the country as a whole adopted a wait-and-see attitude, although the first underground newspaper had appeared a day after the occupation began. The Dutch, like the French, were impressed by the correct behavior of the German soldiers and the initial mildness of the rule the occupation under Seyss-Inquart imposed. Some resented the Queen's having taken refuge in England. Seyss' early reports were optimistic; he wrote that there was no sabotage and no need to fear active resistance.[44] But this state of affairs did not last long. The first organized resistance started a few weeks after the end of hostilities, in the summer of 1940. It called itself the Orde Dienst (the Order Service), and it was nationwide by November. The first intention of the Order Service was to set up, when the time came, a transitional government to maintain order after a German collapse, and its main task meanwhile was sending on military information to England. Other Resistance organizations, like the Knokploegen, raided Dutch offices to get hold of ration books for those persons who went underground. Sabotage in the early days of the German occupation was mainly the work of individuals, not of organizations like Knokploegen or Order Service. But as the occupation measures grew more harsh, particularly with the brutal carrying out of anti-Jewish actions and the arrest of Dutch hostages both as a reprisal for the arrest of German nationals in the Dutch East Indies and as a guarantee against acts of sabotage, the Dutch Resistance hardened. With the German attack on Soviet Russia, members of the Communist Party stepped up their part in the Resistance, where hitherto they had played a lone role for their own purely political ends, fomenting small-scale strikes and attacking in their underground papers the Allies, the Dutch Government in London, and the Germans. After June 22, 1941, they were an important part of the active Resistance, as they were throughout occupied Europe and in the Reich itself.* No Communists, however, were among the hostages; Communists were made prisoners, not hostages. The hostages might be treated with comparative courtesy when they were locked up; as members of a Germanic stock they were entitled to special privileges, and they lived for a time in a special section of Buchenwald. It was there, for example, that the noted Dutch historian Pieter Geyl wrote his memorable work on historical writing *Napoleon: For and Against.* But relatively comfortable or not, the prisoners were held for possible slaughter.

From the beginning, the radio broadcasts from London fanned the flame of the Resistance movement. The Dutch Queen spoke, and the BBC after July, 1940, beamed a program, Radio Oranje, as well as its own broadcasts in Dutch. German countermeasures were ineffective; despite threats of heavy penalties it was easy to tune in on the BBC and the risks of discovery were small. In 1943, after the May strike, the SS confiscated all Dutch radios, but SS Police Chief Rauter estimated that one out of five sets was not turned in and many Dutchmen had thriftily surrendered their old sets and kept

---

* Seyss' lawyer, Gustav Steinbauer, recorded that Communists had testified they approved of the shooting of Dutch hostages by the Germans because prominent bourgeois were being done away with and Dutch hostility to the Germans was being strengthened (Steinbauer manuscript).

the good ones. Radio Oranje kept the Dutch in touch with the Free World and with the voices of those the population was convinced would one day deliver them. It helped them endure the Allied bombing attacks; it advised them on strategy (to boycott the Winterhelp collections, to go into hiding when labor drafts threatened); it warned against political assassinations, which Radio Moscow advocated. A two-way service from and to Holland grew up: Dutch Resistance groups sent word on conditions in Holland to London by way of a courier service to Switzerland and Sweden as well as by clandestine radio senders.

A National Organization for Assistance to Divers and a National Action Group to help both Jews and Christians who had "submerged" were soon formed. The great strikes that resulted in Seyss-Inquart's establishing summary courts and the threat of execution or imprisonment of thousands of strikers added both to the need for the operations of the Resistance and to recruiting for its organizations. In 1943, with the threat of an Allied invasion in the offing, the military commander of the Netherlands, General Friedrich Christian Christiansen, issued a decree to reintern the 300,000 Dutch soldiers the Germans had captured and released in 1940. Thousands of these former soldiers went underground, many of them ready to work for the Resistance. Of the Dutch veterans who did report for internment, thousands could do so safely because they already had obtained exemption papers from the Germans allowing them to work in Holland in the interest of the German-dominated war economy. Eight thousand Dutch veterans were sent to the Reich.[45]

The Council of the Resistance was formed in the spring of 1943. Its aim was to unify the various Resistance groups, and while it never accomplished this, it did become a nationwide apparatus with a hard core of organizers and more than 2,000 co-workers who could be called on for specific actions. In addition, a National Committee, consisting mainly of students and professional people, was formed; dozens of clandestine newspapers were published; and sabotage was organized following instructions from London and, in the case of the underground Communist apparatus, from Moscow. The British set up a Special Operations Executive with the job of parachuting men and supplies to the Dutch Resistance and stepping up sabotage. Although the organization was soon infiltrated by German agents, the SOE took part in destructions in 1944 which, with the situation deteriorating everywhere, were blows at both German morale and installations. Dutch saboteurs damaged key sections in industrial plants working for the Germans and in some cases blew up whole plants; they attacked German troop trains; Dutch National Socialists, especially among the police, were assassinated; the chiefs of police in Nijmegen and Utrecht were killed, as were prominent collaborationists, informers, and German agents.

In an early report Seyss wrote that perhaps a third of the population of the Netherlands was ready to collaborate with the Germans, and that percentage is probably not far from accurate. He tried to rule with moderation. He imposed no precensorship of Dutch papers—only severe penalties if they published anything that might be construed as anti-German.[46] He even tolerated a degree of anti-Germanism in his administration. He told the eleven Secretaries General, the permanent heads of the Dutch ministries, that they could resign if they liked (the Queen before going to England had asked them to stay on in their posts), but if they stayed on he expected their full cooperation. He promised Dutch officials that if they came to him with their grievances he would listen and if they chose to retire they would get their full pensions. Thus he succeeded for a time in retaining the chief department heads who would be in a position to keep the wheels of Dutch production rolling, now in the direction of the Reich. Seyss also made adroit use of a mixture of Dutch National Socialists and of German administrators. Rost van Tonningen, Secretary General of the Department of Finance and President of the Netherlands Bank, the rival of Mussert for leadership in the NSB (the National Socialist Movement of the Netherlands), was put in charge of Special Economic Affairs, where he served the cause of the Reich until the end of the war.*

These maneuvers were only partly successful. As the Germans increased their pressure on the Dutch, Seyss had to take measures against those who failed to do what he wanted or who did it in lukewarm fashion. A few months after the occupation began, the Dutch Secretary for Defense, C. Ringeling, objected to Dutch factories' manufacturing arms for the Germans, and he was forced to resign. By 1943 only three of the Secretaries General who had been in office before the war held their jobs. By that time, too, the mayors of all the major cities had been replaced either by Dutch National Socialists or at least by pro-Germans.

The attempt to reorganize Holland according to the ideological principles of the Third Reich was markedly unsuccessful. The devoted civil servants, with their professional habits of duty, worked along, but as the struggle intensified they performed their tasks more and more grudgingly and with a more benevolent eye on industrial sabotage. Seyss founded guilds among the professions where the members were supposed to learn how advantageous it would be to cooperate with the Reich. He started the Kulturkamer, a cultural organization that arranged for concerts and readings of German and Dutch literature. He attempted to reorganize the professions on the authoritarian patterns of the Reich, but the doctors, for one group, immediately resisted his attempt to install the Nazi system of a political medical guild, and they remained among the stoutest and best organized of the anti-German groups in Holland all during the war. Nor did Seyss have much luck with the other professions; a report of one of his assistants said that of 30,000 teachers only 280 were National Socialists.[47] Some of these people went underground, others stayed on in the tricky

* He committed suicide in June, 1945.

world between genuine collaboration and what they thought of as doing their duty to the Dutch people. One of the patriotic Dutchmen who remained on doggedly at his post despite bitter criticism was Hans Max Hirschfeld, Secretary General of Agriculture, Fishing, Commerce, Industry, and Shipping. Seyss made no difficulties about dealing with him, although Hirschfeld's father was a Jew.*

Seyss-Inquart's crimes in Holland were typical of the Nazi Gauleiter's. He participated with conviction in the anti-Jewish measures that, as always, were gradual.† He issued the first of a series of anti-Jewish decrees in Holland in the autumn of 1940, and under them not only Jews as defined in the Nuremberg Laws (full Jews, or Jews with one Christian grandparent, or *Mischlinge* who practiced the Jewish religion) had to register, but people with only one Jewish grandparent. Like Frank, he dealt with the Jewish Council (Joodse Raad) when he had orders either for providing labor or for sending Jews to the transit camps established in Holland, temporary and desperately crowded quarters used before the prisoners were sent to the East. Jews over the age of fifteen had to carry identity cards on which a "J" was stamped. After introducing the Dutch version of the Nuremberg Laws, he decreed the first steps to get rid of the Jews in business and public and professional life. The next step was to send them to the Dutch forced-labor and concentration camps, and by 1942 he was ready to do his share in shipping them off to the gas chambers.[48] In November, 1942, the Jewish fur and textile workers who had been working for the Reich's armament industry were sent to Auschwitz. Amsterdam, which had been the center of the diamond-cutting market of the world, was emptied of its Jews, of whom some 1,200 were sent to the Vught concentration camp, where they were used in war work until 1944 under the supervision of the SS. Then they, too, with their irreplaceable skills developed over centuries, were sent off to Auschwitz.

* Hirschfeld attested both at Nuremberg and in a book published many years later to Seyss' courtesy and his efforts to carry out his orders as humanely as he could (N XVI, pp. 210–16. H. M. Hirschfeld, *Herinneringen uit de Bezettingstijd* [Amsterdam-Elsevier-Brussels: 1960]).

† Seyss-Inquart said at Nuremberg:

I will say quite openly that since the First World War and the postwar period, I was an anti-Semite and went to Holland as such. I need not go into detail about that here. I have said all that in my speeches and would refer you to them. I had the impression, which will be confirmed everywhere, that the Jews, of course, had to be against National Socialist Germany. There was no discussion of the question of guilt as far as I was concerned. As head of an occupied territory I had only to deal with the fact. I had to realize that, particularly from the Jewish circles, I had to reckon with resistance, defeatism, and so on.

I told Generaloberst von Brauchitsch, Commander in Chief of the Army, that in the Netherlands I would remove Jews from leading posts in the economy, the press and the administration. The measures taken by me from May, 1940, to March, 1941, were limited to that. The Jewish officials were dismissed, but they were given pensions. The Jewish firms were registered, and the heads of the firms were dismissed [N XV, p. 666].

He had not, he testified at Nuremberg, objected when Heydrich told him that Jews in Holland would have to be interned but agreed that it was necessary. It was for this reason, he said, that he had ordered the registration of the Jews in March, 1941. Seyss-Inquart added, "And then things went on step by step."

Approximately 140,000 Jews lived in Holland before the war. Perhaps 20,000 of them were in mixed marriages and 20,000 more were *Mischlinge*. They were all cleared out, with the exception of Jews in one of the privileged marriages or of *Mischlinge*. Rauter wrote to Heydrich in September, 1942, that he planned to send the Jewish partners of mixed marriages to the East if they had no *Mischlinge* children.[49] Those Jews and *Mischlinge* who remained had to submit to being sterilized. It was not enough if the partner of the marriage was sterile; the Jew had to be made "racially harmless" and if so he could escape deportation—he could even walk the streets without the Star of David. Seyss-Inquart opposed sterilizing Jewish women; he said the operation was too dangerous. The sterilization, when it was done, was performed by German physicians, but many of the certificates, according to Reitlinger, were fakes sold by the Gestapo to Jews who had money. Dutch doctors in many cases provided Jews with certificates declaring them sterile, so that no operation had to be performed. In 1944, 8,600 Dutch Jews in mixed marriages were at liberty in the Netherlands, and of these 2,256 had a certificate showing they had been sterilized.[50] Of the 140,000 Jews who had been in Holland when the Germans invaded, two-thirds were killed in the extermination camps. They died in Mauthausen and Sobibor, in Auschwitz and Bergen-Belsen. A few of them who had served with the German Army in World War I were sent to Theresienstadt, and some of them survived along with those who had escaped the gas chambers of the extermination camps.*

The steps, as Seyss-Inquart said, came one by one. The Dutch Jews had no chance to escape, as the Danish Jews did by boat across the relatively narrow sea that separated Denmark from Sweden. England was a long way off and on every land side was German-held territory. The first measures Seyss took were designed to get rid of the Jews in official, economic, and professional life of the Netherlands. The Jews of Holland were widely separated economically. Many of them were peddlers or worked at menial labor; a few were counted among the wealthy families of Amsterdam;

---

* Some 110,000 Dutch Jews were sent to Poland and Czechoslovakia, 105,000 of them to extermination camps; 5,000 went to Theresienstadt, of whom 1,300 survived; 2,000 committed suicide. The only Jews left in Holland in the last year of the war were those who were hidden, of whom there were 25,000 in 1942—among them Anne Frank and her family—but of these only 8,000 survived until the end, along with those in the mixed marriages who managed to escape deportation. A total of 5,450 of the deported Jews returned from all the concentration camps, including Theresienstadt (Warmbrunn, *op. cit.*, p. 68. Personal letter to author from Dr. L. de Jong, director, Rijkinstituut voor Oorlogsdocumentatie, Amsterdam).

and there was a thriving middle group. There were 21,000 enterprises in Holland owned or controlled by Jews; most were small businesses, but this number included four big department stores, three banks, and hundreds of wholesale and retail distributors. A firm had to be registered if one member of its board of directors was a Jew and/or if more than one-quarter of its capital was owned by a Jew.[51] These firms were given a chance to "Aryanize" voluntarily, and a carrion-seeking host of German firms came to Holland to buy in. Seyss had to approve the transactions, for the Jewish firms in Holland as in Germany were likely to go for some 10 per cent of their value in the panic of the forced sales. Seyss created a bureau for the examination of such transactions (Wirtschaftpruefstelle). In addition, if the price involved was more than 100,000 gulders, a Generalkommissariat composed of three German bankers had to approve. Prices under these controls went higher, but they never compared onerously with the assets, and the German buyers had ten years in which to pay. About 10,000 of the Jewish-owned firms were liquidated outright; the others were allowed to Aryanize themselves or were acquired by German interests. On January 21, 1941, Seyss-Inquart wrote to Bormann that 400 enterprises worth 60 million RM had been sold to Dutch firms and 340 worth 103 million RM had gone to the Germans. There were 250 firms being held in reserve, to be made available later to German soldiers.[52]

By August, 1941, all Jewish assets were blocked—including valuables, cash, and securities. The Jews of Holland were forced by a decree of Seyss-Inquart of May 21, 1942, to turn over to the designated banking firm, Lippmann, Rosenthal & Co. of Amsterdam, all rights to property, art objects, articles of gold, platinum, and silver, and pearls and precious stones. They were allowed to keep wedding rings and a silver service of four pieces: knife, fork, tablespoon, and teaspoon, as well as their dentures of precious metals.[53] No Jew was allowed to receive more than 250 guldens a month for his personal use. Seyss-Inquart testified at Nuremberg that the Reich in all had confiscated the sum of 400,000,000 guldens from the Jews. But some of the Jews had been able to bribe their way out of the country officially, or unofficially, by way of funds they held in Swiss banks or other sources of foreign exchange. A good many things could be bought in Holland besides the sterilization certificates, and the most important of these were exit permits. Part of the deals made when Jewish enterprises were sold might be the right to migrate; one Dresdener Bank official spoke of "the ransoming of Dutch Jews against the payment of a penance in Swiss francs." [54] By 1942, when the deportations were at hand, the ransom had gone up from 20,000 Swiss francs to 100,000, and even that sum would no longer get an entire family out of the country.

All the anti-Jewish measures taken in Holland, whether they had to do with confiscating small private Jewish property or taking over the great Rosenthal library, which had been given by the owner to the Dutch State, met with Seyss-Inquart's wholehearted approval. He made a speech on March 12, 1941, in Amsterdam after the mass strikes took place, saying that the Germans did not wish to put unnecessary burdens on the Dutch, but the Jews were not Dutch. He added:

> The Jews are the enemy of National Socialism . . . From the time of their emancipation their methods were directed to the annihilation of the folkish and moral worth of the German people and to replace a national and responsible ideology with international nihilism. It was really they who stabbed the Army in the back which broke the resistance of the Germans [in World War I] . . . The Jews are the enemy with whom no armistice or peace can be made . . . We will smite the Jews where we meet them and whoever goes along with them must take the consequences.[55]

It is small wonder that stimulated by Seyss-Inquart's anti-Semitic ardor the Dutch National Socialists some months after the start of the occupation tried to stage a *Kristallnacht* of their own. In February, 1941, they invaded Jewish homes and shops in the Jewish quarter of Amsterdam, and they were resisted by both Jews and Dutchmen. One of the Dutch Nazis was beaten up so badly that he died later. A few days afterward a German security-police patrol attempting to raid an apartment in the southern part of Amsterdam was attacked by Jews with, among other weapons, vials of ammonia; one policeman was slightly wounded. As a reprisal, razzias were held in the Jewish quarter of Amsterdam and 389 young Jews were packed off to concentration camps. It was the razzias that set off the mass sympathy strikes of the Dutch workers: more than 100,000 walked out of armament factories, shipyards stopped work, utilities no longer functioned, traffic stopped. The strike was broken after two days by the threat of the German military commandant to invoke the death penalty for sabotage if the men did not go back to work. The 389 Jews, who were soon followed by 230 more, were sent first to Buchenwald, where 59 died, and then the survivors were shipped to Mauthausen in Austria, where witnesses have described the Sisyphean task given the prisoners, who had to carry great rocks up the 148 steps that led to the top of the quarry and if they slowed down or fell from exhaustion they were beaten. They died under this treatment. Some of them linked hands and threw themselves from the top of the cliff to the stones far below—parachutists, the SS guards called these men. Only one man survived. He had been kept hidden by other inmates in Buchenwald.

Seyss-Inquart had nothing to do directly with sending these men to Mauthausen, but he provided the context in his civil administration, of which the anti-Semitic laws, the secret police, and the so-called security measures were an essential part. He presided over the "Jewish conferences," held with representatives of the security police, the Foreign Office, and the Commissioners General, which decided how the decisions for arrests and deportations arrived at by the RSHA (main office of the Reich Security Service) should be carried out. Whatever warm feelings he may have had for the Dutch as one of the Germanic peoples, they never prevented him from doing what he took to be his stern duty.

In September, 1944, Seyss-Inquart issued a warning to the population reminding them that they were responsible for any damage done German railroad or postal installations in their districts, and he added: "The population of such communities may therefore expect reprisals in the form of seizure of property and the destruction of houses or groups of houses. I advise the communities to arrange for adequate protection of the means of transportation and communication . . . by patrols or other effective means." The actual dirty work was done by the police, as may be seen in an order of December, 1944, following the shooting of two policemen by members of the Resistance. It read: "The Superior SS and Police Chief gives notice . . . that independent of further investigation of the perpetrators, two houses were blasted and 12 Netherlanders were executed at the place of one of the crimes as reprisals." [56]

A decree issued by Seyss on October 1, 1944, ordered all Dutchmen between the ages of seventeen and forty to register for labor service and to appear immediately, equipped for work with warm clothing, stout shoes, blankets, and mess gear. He promised to pay five guldens a day and to take care of relatives left behind. Anyone trying to resist or escape would be shot. The decree was issued on behalf of the Wehrmacht by Seyss as Reichskommissar of the Netherlands. By the end of the year Dutch males up to the age of forty-two had to register.[57] In the late autumn of 1944, as Goebbels proclaimed total war, Seyss-Inquart promptly announced that he had done his part in Holland. An action, he said, had been conducted at Rotterdam on November 9 and 10 with great success; 8,000 soldiers with no mentionable casualties had picked up 54,000 Dutchmen capable of bearing arms against Germany and had sent 14,000 of them to work in the Netherlands; the rest went to the Reich.[58] About 650 of them managed to escape—a small percentage obviously. In a similar action of *Menschenfang* (mantrap) the Wehrmacht complained it lost valuable Dutch workers who were simply arrested and sent off to do any kind of work assigned regardless of their special skills.[59]

The ratio of six hostages shot for every German or Dutch collaborator killed by the Resistance was low; the usual rate was ten and sometimes even fifty to one, depending on what Reich authorities regarded as the heinousness of the crime and what was needed in the way of terror to prevent a recurrence. In 1944 a Dutch helper of the SD was killed and a German wounded, and Berlin ordered fifty hostages killed. Seyss always opposed the execution of such a ratio of hostages, as did the Army, whose Chief of Staff in Holland, General Heinz Helmut von Wuehlisch, protested the excessive numbers the police planned to execute.[60] Rauter's notice of the shootings pointed out that investigations were still in progress and more might be killed when the inquiry reached its end.*

The execution of hostages for such acts of violence was in fact no violation of the Hague Conventions, which merely declared that the occupying power should keep the number down to humane proportions. This, too, Seyss tried to accomplish. For the Dutch reacted violently to the wholesale shootings of people who, far more often than not, were completely innocent. One German report said that even circles friendly to the Germans were becoming hostile as a result of the cold-blooded executions of men the German secret police deemed dangerous: the intelligentsia, Dutch nationalists or Social Democrats, high civil servants, the liberal professions, the leading social and political groups.

Seyss-Inquart had the same impossible task as every other German governor of occupied territory: to keep the country quiet so the German rear would not be menaced, to keep the population working for the German Wehrmacht and civil economy; when acts of sabotage occurred to punish them severely enough so as to deter such activities in the future and yet to restrain the punishment to prevent even greater numbers of the population from joining the ranks of the active Resistance. Seyss-Inquart attempted to meet the dilemma in a number of ways: he tried to cajole the Dutch, to hold out rewards for collaboration, to restrain excessive German demands. He constantly reminded the Dutch they were a Germanic people. He fostered business, professional, and cultural circles of Dutch-German collaboration. He planned a *Reichsschule* for Holland that would bear the name of a seventeenth-century Dutch poet, Marnix van St. Aldegonde, who had been pro-German and a close associate of William the Silent. For the school he hoped to get funds which he calculated would run to about 500,000 RM a year for each branch, and he wanted three branches. In this school Dutchmen would be educated for a genuine and long-range collaboration with the Reich.[61] He intervened with Himmler against the draconian SS punishments; he tried to make the Dutch themselves take on the job of policing their districts by turning over the responsibility for maintaining the peace to local authorities as well as to the Dutch National Socialists and the ardent pro-German collaborators.

In 1943, at the time of the great strikes, he also had to appoint summary courts (Standgerichte) with the power to pronounce sentences ranging from one year to death; for to strike was to commit sabotage. At the same time he exhorted the Dutch to do their share in the war against bolshevism. He even hoped to recruit 300,000 Dutch National Socialists for police work in

---

* In 1945, when Rauter was badly wounded and a number of the men with him were killed as members of the Resistance attacked the car he was riding in, Himmler wanted 500 hostages shot as a reprisal. Seyss told his lawyer he had prevented the shootings; communications with Berlin were uncertain at this date and he was able to circumvent Himmler's orders (Steinbauer manuscript).

the Ukraine, where they would relieve the hard-pressed Germans in their bloody war with the partisans. He wanted the actual job of recruiting the men to be done by Mussert. Although the negotiations with Berlin dragged on for months, time, as well as the Fuehrer's reluctance to see any non-Germans taking part in governing the Eastern territories, worked against the plan. Nothing came of the idea. No one wanted to join a lost war, and everyone but the Germans knew it was lost. Schemes were also afoot to colonize the East with a Dutch population. Rosenberg as Commissioner for Eastern Territories wanted a Dutch settlement on the Baltic, and the Oost-Compagnie was organized in Holland by Dutch Nazis to assist the movement. One Dutch writer thought five million of his countrymen might be settled there; some of the specialists in Berlin thought of three million.

Toward the end of the war the Fuehrer at long last did permit non-Germans to undertake minor occupation duties in the East, for the sorely tried German Army, the police, and the SS units simply could not carry out their assignments. Almost from the start of the Eastern campaign the Army made use of Russian helpers (Hiwis) recruited from among the local population. A decree of April 18, 1944, issued by Goering said that Belgians, Bulgarians, Danes, Estonians, Finns, Frenchmen, Dutchmen, Latvians, Norwegians, Lithuanians, Hungarians and even Croats might now be used in the limited military service of manning antiaircraft guns and similar activities. In addition, the Fuehrer gave permission for the army of the former Soviet General Vlasov, troops recruited from among Russian prisoners of war, to be sent into action. They were to be used only in the West— under Himmler, who was now head of the reserve army as well as of the Waffen SS. Earlier, at the beginning of the Russian campaign, divisions from the Reich's military and ideological allies were used on the Russian front; these included Italian, Spanish, and Rumanian troops, along with the SS divisions recruited in the West from Belgium, Holland, and Norway—a motley gathering of what Nazi propagandists referred to as a United Europe. It was through the hinge in the German lines manned by Rumanian and Italian troops that the initial breakthrough at Stalingrad was made. But the SS formations fought very well, the Dutch among them. The Dutch police, however, were never used, for they were never recruited.* The 300,000 Dutchmen who in 1943 and later would police the East for the Germans were a figment of Seyss-Inquart's imagination.

Seyss did manage to keep a Dutch administrative apparatus functioning and to do remarkably well with it. The Dutch exports to Germany in 1940 were double what they had been in 1938 and went to three times as much in the next years, although by 1944 the total Dutch national product was only half of what it had been in 1939. By January, 1945, the level had gone down to 25 per cent of 1938.[62] The Germans used Dutch police, the num-

---

* Rauter reported to Himmler that 2,000 Dutchmen had volunteered as auxiliary police (Hilfspolizei) as a result of the recruiting appeal (MA 330, 4740).

bers of which Rauter increased in 1940 by taking in men from the demobilized Army; they turned the anachronistic, locally administered forces into a
central state police. In March, 1941, Seyss in response to Rauter's request
proclaimed a police state of siege which made any disobedience to police
orders subject to the death penalty. This authority was used, however, only
once—during the May, 1943, strikes.

Like other Nazi proconsuls operating in foreign territory, Seyss-Inquart
turned to the stick-and-carrot techniques so useful for recalcitrant populations. In May, 1943, he ordered that Dutchmen called up for labor should
no longer receive ration cards and that no unemployment compensation be
given any others fit to work who did not volunteer for labor in the Reich.[63]
Seyss testified at Nuremberg that 530,000 Dutchmen worked for Germany,
of whom less than half were "volunteers." [64] Thousands of these so-called
volunteers only joined under heavy pressure and threats from the Germans
and the Dutch authorities working under them.* On the other hand, Seyss
supplied extra food for Dutch children, and he declared at Nuremberg,
although Dutch historians have been unable to find any evidence to support
his claim, that he tried to improve the living conditions of Dutch workers
in Germany who, he said, objected to being housed in barracks. In any event,
they objected to much more, for they, like the other foreign labor in the
Reich, were subject to the local Party and economic authorities of wherever
they chanced to be, and working and living conditions could be intolerable.†

Before the nonspecialist Dutch Jews were deported, they were sent to
Dutch peat bogs for the manual work the Nazis valued so highly as a means
of punishment and humiliation for the largely middle-class Dutch Jews. If
they were specialized workers, like the diamond cutters from Amsterdam,
they might work for the Army, where they would be kept alive longer than

---

* As early as 1940, Dutch unemployed were refused unemployment compensation if they
would not accept jobs in Germany. By 1942 those who refused to go to the Reich were
taken there by force or put in special camps (Warmbrunn, *op. cit.*, p. 74).

† An order of April 22, 1943, permitted Dutch, Norwegians, and other preferred nationalities, including American and British prisoners of war working for German enterprises,
to walk outside their camps for two hours a week. The racial background of foreign workers
as well as their political sympathies were a constant source of concern and tribulation for
the Reich authorities. Italians, the briefings said, were allies, were brothers-in-arms, part of
the *Kampfgemeinschaft*, and the treatment therefore accorded Italian workers was to take
this into account. The Northern people, the camp authorities were reminded, were racially
closer to the Germans, however, and it was the task of the Reich authorities to win their
allegiance away from the democracies. A *Merkblatt* issued in 1942 said that the racially
assimilable Flemish workers were to be treated like Germans. They could go to German
schools and marry Germans, and when they returned to their homes they would act as
propagandists for the Reich. Still, the non-Germans had to realize that it was the Germans
who were the leaders in the new Europe. But field reports of the Gestapo—one from
Cologne, for example, on January 7, 1943—told how bad conditions in the German work
camps could be; they were so insupportable, in fact, that more and more foreign workers
who had volunteered were fleeing. The reports said the workers refused to accept the conditions under which they worked and lived, and characteristically urged as a solution not an
improvement in their treatment but instead that "the sharpest measures be taken" and
that those workers recaptured be turned over immediately to the Gestapo (BDC, Gestapo
reports).

if they were employed by one of the German industrial firms, for the Army could and did resist the deportation of workers needed for its purposes. But the Army could not compete against the SS in the long run; most of these specialists were brought to the Vught concentration camp, where they worked under Himmler from November, 1942, until their deportation to the East in March, 1944. Some 200 were sent to Bergen-Belsen, where they were kept at specialized work, and a handful survived until the end of the war. The rest, along with the peat cutters, died at Auschwitz.

Dutch workers were used in Holland, Belgium, northern France, and in the Reich in the Krupp firm—which they called a plague firm (*Pest Firma*)—and I. G. Farben and in the blocked plants where Speer could use their talents. Over 92,000 Dutch workers went to Germany in 1940; the next year the number rose to 150,000; by 1942 it was 260,000, and by 1945 it was over 500,000.* Between 400,000 and 500,000 Dutch workers were unemployed in June, 1940, at least half of them as a result of the German occupation, and the first attempts the Germans made to recruit labor were aimed at this group and at the specialists. In Holland, as elsewhere, as volunteers dwindled and German needs for workers grew, conscription and mass arrests were resorted to. A German report to Sauckel from the Reichskommissar's office in Holland, dated June, 1943, stated that the entire class of the years born from 1921 to 1924 had been registered and that 22,986 workers as a result had been sent to Germany. And, the report added, giving credit where credit was due, "Only owing to the hard work of the Germans in Holland was this possible." Dutch university and technological-school students were immediately liable for labor conscription after they had completed their studies.

Holland was squeezed to the pulp. Everything manufactured was produced for the Germans, and in addition the country was plundered. Even Mussert, an SD report said, called what the Germans were doing robbery.[65] German soldiers were allowed to send back in a single package to the Reich 1,000 grams of food or anything else they had gotten hold of, and there was no limit to the number of packages, nor any inspection of them at the border. For two years Seyss' civilian authorities in Holland were also able to ship such packages, but with diminishing goods in the Dutch black market and the mounting shortages in both Germany and Holland, Seyss stopped this so-called "*Schlepp-Erlass*," the "tow decree" as the Germans called it, for civilians.[66] The currency frontier between the two countries was eliminated to make such transactions easier—the mark was as good in Holland as in Germany, and the rate of exchange, set by the Germans, was 1 gulden to 1.33 RM instead of the prewar 1.70.

The black market in the occupied countries was fostered and used by the

---

* Dutch estimates of the number of their workers in Germany are 1940: 92,700; 1941: 151,200; 1942: 263,300; 1943: 382,100; 1944: 388,900. The numbers of unemployed were in April, 1940, 211,000; in May, 1940, 325,000; and in June, 1940, between 400,000 and 500,000 (de Jong, *op. cit.*).

German authorities. A secret report of January 15, 1943, by a German Air Force colonel, J. Veltjens, was sent to a long distribution list, including Goering, as head of the Four-Year Plan, his deputies, the high commands of the Army and Navy, Himmler as RFSS, the Reich Minister of Nutrition, Finance, and Economy, the main office for Reich Security, the military commanders in the occupied territories, and Seyss-Inquart. The purpose of the memorandum was to bring up to date the accounts of the goods being supplied to the Germans by way of the black markets in Serbia and the occupied Western countries and also to make a progress report on the dismantling of Dutch harbor installations and machines from shut-down plants, which were sent to the Reich, and of the results of the so-called "Christmas Action." The latter was designed to provide Christmas presents for the German people, some 300 million RM worth, which were to be collected in Holland between August and December, 1942. The time had been short, Colonel Veltjens wrote, so only 244 million RM worth could be bought up, but still some 2,300 boxcars were filled with cosmetics, toys, and gifts designed mostly for distribution in bomb-damaged areas. Veltjens thought that a good deal of harbor equipment not being sufficiently used in Holland could be shifted to the Reich and thereupon had seized it for use in Oslo and Hamburg. He also arranged for the shipping to the Reich of machinery from Dutch plants that were idle, although he pointed out that such measures met with resistance not only from the plant owners but from the state authorities in the occupied territories. Seyss-Inquart, whose job it was to keep Holland pacified as well as productive, undoubtedly preferred to see such plants remain in Holland, where they could also produce for the Reich if they had manpower and raw materials. The decision, however, was not his.

Veltjens' job as plenipotentiary for special missions eventually brought an end to the black market, but before that happened, he used it for the benefit of the Reich to get the hidden stock, to get hold of the "illegal production." German authorities, Seyss-Inquart among them, had tried first to stop the trading in the black market, but when the difficulties of this task became apparent, the decision was made to use it instead. But since German agencies would bid against one another and the operators in the black market were able as a result to boost prices continually, it became necessary to centralize the buying. To this end the Germans established the Roges Trading Company, a government agency whose job it was to do the buying of raw materials and to arrange for their transportation. Veltjens, as plenipotentiary, set prices and quality standards for the sale to the purchasers in the Reich. He reported that 73,685,162 RM worth of goods, including raw diamonds, metals, leather, furniture, food, and luxury goods, had been bought in Holland since he had taken over. Veltjens wanted, as usual, harsh penalties against any retail dealers who bid up prices when they bought from manufacturers and wholesalers on the black market. It was a canny arrangement, for although the prices were high, they were in large part paid for by the occupied countries. Veltjens calculated that of the purchases in France, amounting to 1,107,792,819 RM, approximately 929,100,000 RM were financed by the French.[67] In this matter, as in the costs of the German occupation, where German accounts said the Dutch supplied all the needs so nothing came out of the Reich budget, the Dutch financed their own destitution. Their contribution came, in all, so later German estimates declared, to more than 12,030 million RM.[68]

Veltjens had five supervisory departments under him (one, for Holland, was in The Hague). In Holland the directive for the operation read: "Instructions for the winding up of stocks of merchandise of uncertain origin." To put his activities in the best possible light when he bought what was needed on the black market, Veltjens worked under what was called a "decree on the clarification of unexplained goods," or alternatively a "general decree." He wrote that among the personnel that would have to be employed if the black market was to be brought under control were spies and *agents provocateurs*, for it was a tricky place even for Germans operating under a general decree.

Dutch plants with half or more of their production going for the benefit of the Reich were to be shipped to Germany. Seyss-Inquart said at Nuremberg that had Germany won the war the Dutch would have had claims against the Reich coming to more than 4,500 million guldens for unpaid deliveries and requisitions.[69] In April, 1942, Seyss called on the Dutch to make a "voluntary" contribution of 50 million guldens a month as their share of the costs of Germany's campaign in the East, and to make it retroactive to July 19, 1941. The "voluntary" contribution alone came to 2,150 million RM. In addition to the occupation costs, the Germans removed more than 3.6 billion guldens' worth of Dutch industrial production and raw materials—a grand total of goods and services estimated at 1938 prices of 11.4 billion guldens.* [70]

The Germans missed nothing. Seyss complained that the Army was taking from their stalls Dutch horses aged from four to fourteen years, but the

* Seyss-Inquart testified at Nuremberg that the Dutch were paying occupation costs of 50 million RM a month (N XV, p. 652). But he understated the amount by half. The Dutch figures were considerably higher and more accurate: they calculated that seven months of occupation in 1940 had cost 477 million guldens; in 1941, 1,124 million; in 1942, 1,181 million; in 1943, 1,328 million; in 1944, 1,757 million; and in the four months of 1945, to 489 million—or a total of 6,356 million guldens. These were the costs in Holland alone; in addition were the considerable sums charged to the Dutch for administration expenses for the occupation incurred in Germany (N XVI, p. 223, 123 RF. N XXXVIII, pp. 523–36).

Holland, one German report of October 10, 1944, pointed out, was the only country in Europe that paid not only for the subsistence of troops and other direct occupation expenses but also for the external costs of occupation. Dutch taxes doubled in the course of the war. The Netherlands paid the occupation costs in gold as long as it lasted and then in Reichsmarks. The German report said that in effect goods could be imported from Holland without payment.

complaint was made not on behalf of the Dutch economy but because the officers requisitioning the horses were not working through him. The numbers of livestock dropped sharply. Poultry went down 90 per cent; 22 per cent of the cattle and two-thirds of the hogs were slaughtered. By the end of 1943 the Germans had taken off 600,000 hogs, 275,000 cattle, and 30,000 tons of preserved meat. The Army and the civil occupation lived off the Netherlands, and its products helped keep up the standard of living in the Reich too.

From the Dutch railways, more than half the locomotives were taken, as well as 28,950 freight cars out of a total of 30,000 and 1,446 passenger cars out of 1,750. Fifty trolley cars were shipped to Hamburg; a million bicycles were confiscated, as were 1.5 million tons of shipping and 600,000 radio sets. Seyss-Inquart himself ordered the confiscation of such items as the microscopes in the University of Utrecht, which were needed by the SS in their hospitals. Current demands from the Germans in January, 1944, were for 703 million RM worth of machinery, of which in the month of January only 61 million RM worth could be delivered.[71] In March, 1943, Seyss-Inquart ordered all the technical equipment, machinery, and blueprints of a plant still operating in Holland to be delivered lock, stock, and barrel to the Brunswick branch of the Hermann Goering Werke. Later, when the demolition orders came, all the machinery and raw materials that could be taken from the doomed Dutch factories were ordered sent to the Reich. "Removal Commandos," that is, groups of technicians working under the "Machine Pool Office," were given the job of finding what machines and supplies could be shipped to Germany and then sending them there. All the gold in the vaults of the Dutch banks had been immediately taken over. After 1944 it was German policy, mainly because of the threat of the invasion and the hostility of the Dutch population, to ship to the Reich entire factories that had been working for Germany.

Everything disappeared from the market except rationed foods. Jewish houses and apartments sometimes looked as if they had been bombed because the Dutch neighbors of the former occupants demolished them to keep their own buildings in repair; the only supplies available were from such empty dwellings.

Whatever Jews, Freemasons, and the proscribed Jehovah's Witnesses or other "international" sects owned was confiscated. Seyss-Inquart declared the Masons in Holland "enemies of the people," a formula used against them in every country where the Nazis could get at them, beginning with Austria. Seyss, on behalf of the State, confiscated the property of the Masonic Order—worth, he estimated, between 8 and 9 million guldens[72]—as he did the possessions of the Dutch royal family, which had gone to England. The palace at Nordeinde, under the decree of confiscation Seyss had proposed to the Fuehrer, was stripped of furniture, silverware, linen, paintings, and tapestries; the wine cellars were gutted and even household utensils were taken off. Some of the stolen goods from the palaces was sent to a convalescent home for German generals. Seyss had wanted to turn over any money obtained from such actions to the Party, but such sums were used in other, divers ways. The Jews, for example, paid for the construction of the concentration camp at Vught, which cost 14 million guldens. Some 400 million guldens, Seyss estimated at Nuremberg, were taken from the Dutch Jews, from whom literally everything of value was stolen. Even wedding rings, which they at first had been allowed to keep, in the end became part of the loot, for they were taken away at the extermination camps. In addition, enormous booty came from confiscation in the form of books, art collections that had been the property of Jews, furniture, and all the personal and collective possessions of the officially declared enemies of the Reich.

The confiscation of paintings and *objets d'art* from the Jews and Masons, the Theosophists, Spiritists, and Esperantists was, in Holland as elsewhere, in the hands of the Einsatzstab Rosenberg, which picked up, the Germans estimated, loot to the value of 30 to 40 million RM.[73] The Rosenberg staff began their operations in the Netherlands as soon as the work could be properly organized—in September, 1940. From the Masons old books, including an invaluable Sanskrit collection, were listed and packed in ninety-six cases and shipped to Germany, where they became part of the rising accumulation of plunder the Reich's emissaries were gathering from all Europe. It is interesting to note in this connection that the Wehrmacht punished plundering with the death penalty, and its harshest penalties were often exacted in the course of the war; even a general who had plundered goods in Yugoslavia was executed. But the rules of the Einsatzstab Rosenberg and of other government agencies were the opposite of this. Millions of dollars worth of loot were collected, including some of the best Dutch paintings, which went to brighten Goering's Karinhall. Holland, with its Rembrandts and its Italian and Spanish masterpieces, was one of the chief sources of Goering's art collection. The Fuehrer, too, was able to get hold of some of the Dutch paintings at what was described as "extraordinarily low prices."[74]

Seyss-Inquart did not personally benefit from the possibilities open to him, but he did what he could to further the activities of Rosenberg and the Reichsmarschall. Aside from the Fuehrer, Goering was Seyss-Inquart's sole superior in administering the Dutch economy, for Holland's production was part of the Four-Year Plan. Seyss testified at Nuremberg that the only use he had made of his advantageous position was when he had bought two or three pictures in Holland and presented them to the art museum in Vienna. At one of his interrogations he said he had paid 800,000 guldens for a Vermeer, using government funds provided for the purpose.* This and a proscribed Van Gogh he sent to the Vienna museum. Here too he wanted nothing for himself; he was merely as a matter of policy ready to lend his

---

* Interrogation of August 31, 1946. The painting was a fake produced by the greatly gifted forger Van Meegeren, who also sold one of his "Vermeers" to Goering.

aid to confiscations of every kind, and these at the end of the war included clothing he ordered taken from the inhabitants of a Dutch town, an act he excused by saying it would have been lost in any case owing to the fighting in the area. But on the whole, Seyss-Inquart wanted things done legally and according to form, with all the receipts duly filed. He said at Nuremberg he had resented the wild pogroms begun against the Jews and Jewish property in Vienna when the threadbare Nazi hoodlums had flung themselves on the booty in the first days of the *Anschluss*. Seyss was still indignant in 1945 at the way the hoodlums had gone about the robbery, and he also said he thought it bad that the Jews received no compensation. But they got no compensation in Holland either; what really disturbed Seyss-Inquart was the untidiness of the action. It seemed to him un-German.

Like Frank, Seyss had to deal with his SS officer, Rauter, whose duty it was to see that the so-called political tasks were taken care of according to Himmler's—not Seyss-Inquart's—notions. And the political assignments, as the SS saw them, included much more than police work. The Final Solution was in the hands of the RFSS, and so were reprisals against sabotage or anything else that might threaten the security of the country. Thus Seyss, too, proclaimed his authority loudly, more explicitly than he could enforce it if Himmler wanted something else. "I will give the orders and they must be carried out strictly by everybody. In the present situation [January, 1943] the refusal to carry out such an order can only be called sabotage. It is equally certain that we must more than ever suppress all resistance against the struggle for life." [75]

In another speech Seyss spoke of the need for annihilating the enemies of Germany. "We remain human because we do not torture our opponents. We must remain hard in annihilating them." [76] These words, cited by the court in its judgment against Seyss-Inquart, had been designed more to impress Himmler and the Fuehrer than to increase the number of executions. Himmler, writing Rauter in October, 1942, said that Seyss-Inquart had agreed that the liquidation of the Jews was now a matter entirely for the police, indicating that Seyss-Inquart had attempted to interpose on behalf of his civil authority. [77] But no records exist of his protesting about anything except details of the treatment, details, for example, such as the overcrowding in the Westerbork camp, where 13,000 Jews had been sent, far more than it could provide for, and where 3,000 had to lie on the floor. Not the exterminations but the manner in which the Jews were handled on their way to them concerned him. He remonstrated with Rauter about this and Rauter reported to Himmler. But in October, 1942, Himmler wrote another of his frequent letters to Rauter and told him triumphantly that Seyss wanted to cooperate more closely than ever before.

If Seyss was a pious Catholic he was a more pious National Socialist. No measures taken against the Church—even the invasions of monasteries and nunneries in Holland in the search for priests and nuns of Jewish origin—

seem to have diminished his enthusiasm for National Socialism. He faithfully repeated the words and views of the Fuehrer and the minor satellites, and he doubtless believed them all.* In June, 1943, when the German losses had become catastrophic on the Eastern front, he told a gathering in Sonthofen that the losses in World War I had been high, too, but one should think of the numbers of people who committed suicide and of those who were never born, and that these latter were higher than the numbers who died in wars. The East, he added to complete the picture, was the horde of Genghis Khan and the Jews. These were speeches that could have been made, and were made, by hundreds of Nazi small fry. But the gap between Seyss and them had never been great.

Seyss-Inquart's qualms easily disappeared when he had no alternatives. He saved what he could of Dutch land from floodings, of buildings from burning, of hostages from executions, but only so much as could be defended before the baleful scrutiny of the Fuehrer. It is true that at the end he told Hitler that Holland should not be defended *à outrance* because of the catastrophe this would bring on the Dutch people and that he had tried to make a pact with the Resistance to the effect that he would take no action against them and would permit the distribution of Allied food to the starv-. ing population if the Resistance ceased its sabotage. Such humanitarian ideas appealed to him, especially when they had to do with the Germanic peoples. But even this came only weeks before the end of the war in April, 1945. His attempt to stop the senseless demolitions came just before then, after he had talked with Speer and they had agreed that nothing more was to be gained by following the orders for destruction, which had become insane. Seyss-Inquart even tried to keep the Army from flooding some of the fields to prevent possible Allied paratroop landings, but this too came in the last weeks, when there no longer seemed much point in being hard.

He undoubtedly had no enmity for the Dutch. If they collaborated he wished them well and wanted them to share in the new order in Europe. He had not ordered the most drastic reprisals; it was General Christiansen, not Seyss-Inquart, who decided on the destructions to be carried out in the village of Putten; it was Berlin that demanded the shooting of so many hostages; in the manhunts he was carrying out orders. One of the witnesses at Nuremberg, F. Wimmer, who had been Seyss-Inquart's Commissioner General for Administration and Justice, testified that the Rosenthal library, consisting of 150,000 volumes, had indeed been moved to the Reich in 150 crates but that this had been done against Seyss-Inquart's instructions; there is no reason to doubt that Seyss would have preferred to keep the library in his domain in Holland. He confiscated everything he thought the Germans needed more than the Dutch, such as woolen goods, which he took from the

* Once, in discussing Americans, he said that the women were all alike, their hair and makeup were the same, and that they represented the decultivation and actually the extinguishing of a true civilization and what was truly racial.

population as early as 1941, when the German Army was having a cold winter in Russia; and by 1943 he was taking off textiles, clothes, underwear, furniture, and household articles as well.[78] But such requisitions could be defended, if not solely on military grounds, as being incited by the ruthlessness of the Allied bombings and the necessity of supplying Germans who had lost their possessions. Moreover, the orders came from Hitler, who wanted the Dutch and the other people in occupied territories as well as the Germans to feel the effect of the air war. Still, houses were blown up not by the Army for military reasons but on Seyss' orders as a reprisal against sabotage, and he could also order that a newspaper that failed to publish an article against the striking Dutch railway workers be destroyed. For Seyss had to be brutal to demonstrate his National Socialist zeal in such emergencies, both to show his mettle as Reichskommissar and to fend off Himmler.

Seyss-Inquart was named by Hitler as Foreign Minister to the Doenitz cabinet, the caretaker regime that ruled for a few days, but Doenitz chose in his place Count Schwerin von Krosigk. Seyss was captured soon after the surrender by the British in Hamburg and tried as a major war criminal. The Nuremberg court found him guilty on three of the four counts against him. He had not planned to wage aggressive warfare, the judgment said, but he had waged it and he had committed war crimes and crimes against humanity. It is difficult to agree that he had waged any kind of war, as the generals and diplomats and propagandists waged it. The *Anschluss*, which the court called "forcible annexation," was far from a war, and Seyss had nothing to do with the decisions to invade Poland, the Low Countries, or Yugoslavia, nor did he plot against any of the intended victims of Hitler's plans. But of the other counts against him, the crimes against humanity and the war crimes, there can be no doubt. Seyss from the time of the Nazi takeover of Austria helped in the expulsion and humiliation and plundering of the Jews, and he was at least a silent partner in the exterminations. Against the Dutch, the judgment said, he had been ruthless in applying terrorism and in annihilating his opponents, and despite the exaggeration in describing what Seyss had actually done in contrast to what he had made small effort to prevent being done, the words "annihilating the opponent" were his own.

NOTES

1. Vogelsang, *op. cit.*, pp. 416–18.
2. D-926, quoted in Hilberg, *op. cit.*, p. 20.
3. August Kubizek, *Young Hitler* (London: Allan Wingate, 1954).
4. "Denkschrift Himmlers ueber die Behandlung der Fremdvoelkischen im Osten (Mai 1940)," in *Vierteljahrshefte fuer Zeitgeschichte*, Vol. V, No. 2, 1957, pp. 196–97.
5. Bernhard Stasiewski, "Die Kirchenpolitik der Nationalsozialisten im

Warthegau 1939–1945," in *Vierteljahrshefte fuer Zeitgeschichte*, Vol. VII, No. 1, 1959, p. 58.

6. 3835-PS (IZG).

7. NCA VI, 3815-PS, p. 751.

8. MA 327 (IZG).

9. *Ibid.*

10. NG 4621 (IZG).

11. NCA VI, 3814-PS, pp. 742–45. *Ibid.*, 3815-PS, pp. 745–52.

12. 3834-PS (IZG).

13. NG 4621 (IZG).

14. NCA VI, 3468-PS, p. 169. NCA, Supp. B, pp. 1393–94.

15. NCA, Supp. B, p. 1394.

16. NCA II, 2233-R-PS, p. 643.

17. EC-1 (IZG).

18. N XXIX, p. 369.

19. *Ibid.*

20. NCA IV, 2233-D-PS, pp. 891–92.

21. NO 5193, Korherr report of April 19, 1943 (IZG).

22. NCA IV, 2233-E-PS, pp. 894–900.

23. *Ibid.*, 2233-AA-PS, p. 917.

24. Hans Frank, *Im Angesicht des Galgens* (Munich: Friedrich Alfred Beck Verlag, 1953), p. 154.

25. Hubert Schorn, *Der Richter im Dritten Reich* (Frankfurt a.M.: Vittorio Klostermann, 1959), p. 11.

26. *Ibid.*, pp. 78–79.

27. *Ibid.*, p. 78.

28. Frank, *op. cit.*

29. N XII, p. 37.

30. NG 3282 (IZG).

31. Wladimir von Hartlieb, *Parole: Das Reich* (Vienna and Leipzig: Adolf Luser Verlag, 1939), p. 499.

32. NCA V, 3254-PS, p. 985.

33. *Ibid.*

34. *Ibid.*, 2994-PS, pp. 703–8.

35. *Voelkischer Beobachter*, April 8, 1938, 3987-PS (IZG).

36. N XXIX, 2219-PS, pp. 331–36.

37. NG 1286 (IZG).

38. MA 328, 1485; MA 328, 1023 (IZG). Hans-Dietrich Loock, "Zur 'Grossgermanischen Politik' des Dritten Reiches," in *Vierteljahrshefte fuer Zeitgeschichte*, Vol. VIII, No. 1, 1960, pp. 37, 64.

39. Loock, *op. cit.*, pp. 37–64.

40. Hans Buchheim, "Die hoeheren SS- und Polizeifuehrer," in *Vierteljahrshefte fuer Zeitgeschichte*, Vol. XI, No. 4, 1963, pp. 362–91.

41. N XVI, p. 208.

42. Hilberg, *op. cit.*, p. 373.

43. David Irving, *The Destruction of Dresden* (London: William Kimber & Co., 1963).

44. N XXVI, 997-PS, p. 424.

45. Personal letter from Dr. L. de Jong, director, Rijksinstituut voor Oorlogs-documentatie, Amsterdam.

46. NCA III, 997-PS, pp. 641–56.

47. MA 328, 1036 (IZG).

48. Reitlinger, *The Final Solution*, pp. 332–35.

49. Hilberg, *op. cit.*, p. 376.

50. *Ibid.*, p. 377.

51. NCA VI, 3333-PS, pp. 58–62.

52. D 60, Rijksinstituut voor Oorlogsdocumentatie, Amsterdam. Hereinafter referred to as Amsterdam.

53. NCA VI, 3336-PS, pp. 64–70.

54. Hilberg, *op. cit.*, p. 370.

55. N XXXII, 3430-PS, pp. 284-89.

56. NCA III, 1163-PS, pp. 819–20.

57. *Ibid.*, 1162-PS, p. 817.

58. NIK 12925 (Amsterdam).

59. NCA V, 3003-PS, pp. 726–27.

60. MA 328, 1016 (IZG).

61. MA 328 (IZG).

62. Werner Warmbrunn, *The Dutch Under German Occupation 1940–1945* (Stanford: Stanford University Press, 1963), pp. 71–72.

63. N XVI, p. 221.

64. N XV, p. 663.

65. MA 328 (IZG).

66. N XVI, pp. 61–62.

67. NCA IV, 1765-PS, pp. 325–43.

68. NCA VII, EC-86, p. 274.

69. N XVI, p. 70.

70. Warmbrunn, *op. cit.*, p. 78.

71. N V, p. 559.

72. RF-1532 (IZG).

73. N V, p. 349.

74. N IX, p. 129. N XVI, p. 73.

75. N XXXII, 3430-PS, pp. 284–89.

76. N V, p. 352.

77. MA 238 (IZG).

78. N VII, p. 102.

12

The War Plant and Forced Labor

ALBERT SPEER

One of the genuinely gifted men to become part of the Nazi war apparatus was the architect Albert Speer. Speer became Minister of Arms and Munitions in 1942, when he was thirty-six years old, after Fritz Todt, builder of the West Wall as well as of more durable structures like the Autobahnen, had been killed in an airplane accident. But Speer was far abler than his predecessor, who was mainly an engineer, an efficient organizer of large-scale construction.* Speer got rid, as far as he could, of the system of coercion; he put full responsibility for the efficiency of a plant into the hands of the local manager; he improvised, exhorted, parceled out authority among bureaucrats and entrepreneurs, and hundreds of his deputies were "honorary co-workers," borrowed from private industry for the duration of the war and paid only a fraction of what they had been getting as managers or technicians. He resisted anyone when production was threatened—Himmler, Bormann, Goebbels, and finally Hitler himself. He took over the job of increasing German armaments in the face of the increasingly devastating bombardments of the industrial centers and did so well that, although the cities of the Reich became rubble and hundreds of thousands of their inhabitants victims of the incendiaries, blockbusters, blasting, and fire storms, German war production went up during the entire period of his ministry until 1945.

It was owing to Speer that the biggest year of German manufacture of

* An article by Alan S. Milward pointed out that many of Speer's organizational reforms had already been introduced by Todt (*Vierteljahrshefte fuer Zeitgeschichte*, Vol. XIV, No. 1, 1966, pp. 40–58).

483

arms was 1944; only ten months before the end of the war, German production of airplanes and munitions reached an all-time high despite the thousands of bombers attacking German cities around the clock, the closing ring of Allied armies, and the blockade. In 1944 seven times as many weapons were produced as in 1942, five and a half times the number of armored vehicles, and six times the amount of ammunitions, but only 30 per cent more workers were employed.[1] Speer made few major miscalculations; he had no part in the decision to put so much material and labor in the costly "V" weapons, expenditures he would have preferred to see devoted to fighter planes so bitterly needed against the Allied bombers. He opposed the diversion of so much labor to the construction of underground factories when other production was vitally needed; nor was it his beltline of factories that failed. The German tanks and planes became sporadically useless after May, 1944, because fuel was lacking following the massed Allied attacks on the synthetic gasoline plants; in these bombings, Speer declared at Nuremberg, 90 per cent of German fuel production was destroyed.

Speer's achievement was of a divided character. He always thought of himself as an artist, and he was certainly a builder and organizer of monumental projects that were intended not only to rescue the Reich from defeat but to help create a resplendent and completely imaginary future Germany in which they would provide a scale of living never before approached in the world; and Speer the builder served with all his talents a nihilistic leader who built only in his own image and who would blow everything up when his luck ran out. In the closing months of the war, when Hitler was at his most deadly in dealing with doubters even when they were old Party comrades—which Speer was not (he had joined the Party only in 1932)—Speer told the Fuehrer bluntly the war was lost. It was the kind of statement that cost the head of many a man who made it to the wrong person, for this was defeatism which immediately became high treason when the Gestapo and the Volksgericht, not to mention the Fuehrer himself, heard of it.

Speer in addition disobeyed the direct and unconditional order of Hitler to blow up not only military strongpoints and plants that could be useful to the Allies, but also those that were the sources of German subsistence then and in the future—the factories and bridges, ships, freight cars, locomotives and railroad installations, power stations, and water supplies of the cities lying in the path of the advancing Allied armies. As one device for salvaging everything he possibly could, he quoted to Bormann—who wanted the German people to be forced to converge in the center of the country where they would fight to the last, leaving only scorched earth behind them—Hitler's assurances that the lost territories would soon be recaptured. Despite the Fuehrer's explicit directives, Speer therefore ordered that factories were to be merely "paralyzed," not destroyed, and moreover this was to be done only at the last moment, keeping production and machinery intact as long as possible, and then with luck the Allies would take the factories over without serious damage.* [2]

Speer salved his patriotic conscience by telling himself that in any event the Allies would gain little or nothing by capturing the factories, since owing to the deficiencies in transport they at best could not use them for at least nine months.[3] In this way he saved the Minette mines in France from destruction, telling Bormann and the other Party fanatics that a German counterattack would soon restore them to the Reich's uses. No one, he wrote to Hitler, had the right to order the destruction of the means of survival of the nation. And when he finally became convinced that Hitler was identifying with his own lost cause the fate of the people he had professed to love so deeply, Speer planned to kill him. Since everyone who visited the Fuehrer was searched after the July 20 attempt on Hitler's life, Speer wanted to put poison-gas grenades in the ventilating system of Hitler's bunker in Berlin, and he was prevented from carrying out his purpose only because the ingenious idea proved to be technically impracticable. Hitler, with his primitive instinct for danger, had ordered a brick chimney four meters high to be built around the vents so they could not be tampered with.[4]

But despite his furious resistance to Hitler's orders for senseless destruction, Speer was one of the very last among the faithful and unfaithful to take his farewell of the Fuehrer; he flew to Berlin to rescue a family friend from the doomed city and at Hitler's request spent the night in the Fuehrer's bunker, only a few days before Hitler committed suicide. In his fashion he remained devoted to the man who had probably wished him as well as Hitler could wish anyone; but Speer would have killed the Fuehrer and the Party leaders with his own hands rather than accept the senseless loss of the machines that would keep the threadbare survivors of the war alive. He intended to kill Himmler, Goebbels, and Bormann, the chief advocates of scorched earth along with Hitler; he organized the automatic pistols and the cars that would ambush them and he planned to drive one of the cars himself. But the plot failed when Speer found no way to get at Hitler and these others at the same time. He came to the same conclusions as the conspirators of July 20, but in terms of his specialty, which had more to do with the efficient manufacture of goods than of ideas.

Some of the people around Hitler, including Speer, thought Speer enjoyed a special freedom with the Fuehrer because he was an architect—a brilliant practitioner of the profession that Hitler had once chosen for himself and to which the Fuehrer gave his full amateur talents when he set out to rebuild the Reich after he became Chancellor. Speer became Hitler's chief architect in 1934, when he was only twenty-nine years old. He was born in Mannheim

---

* "Paralysis" meant partial dismantling, removing essential parts from the machinery, shipping them from the plants, hiding them, but not damaging the machinery which must begin as soon as possible to work again for whatever kind of Germany might survive the war.

on March 19, 1905, the son and grandson of architects. After taking his *Abitur* he studied architecture at Karlsruhe, Munich, and Berlin, where, when Hitler took power, he was an assistant at the Technische Hochschule and practicing his profession at the same time. He deeply impressed the Fuehrer with his new Reichstag, which not only was designed in the heroic style the Fuehrer so doted on, but also was erected in a shorter time than anyone would have thought likely. Speer then, as later, was prodigal with workers and used twice as many as more economical architects might have demanded. Hitler gave him the task of replanning Berlin and along with it the spiritual home of the Party—Nuremberg. Speer told the court that if he had been free to carry out his blueprints, the Reich would have had some of the largest buildings in the world and the whole earthshaking plan would have cost less than two months of war.[5]

Speer thought that if Hitler had permitted himself to have a friend Speer might have been the one chosen because of their common interest. For whatever reason, Speer was able to talk to the Fuehrer in words no one else dared use without incurring any of the penalties inflicted on the generals, for example, who dared to be critical. "Off with their heads" was for doubtful military men and politicians; Speer was neither but he was otherwise everything that Hitler had once dreamed of becoming himself. He told the Fuehrer the task given him was nonpolitical; it had to be carried out by technicians and experts of all descriptions, including the 6,000 "honorary co-workers," many of whom took a dim view of the Party. He recalled this pronouncement to Hitler over and over again when the Party, the Gauleiters, and the SS tried to invade his domain where they thought high treason lurked.

Speer began his rearguard action, his one-man resistance movement, late in the war, after the invasion of Germany had started, but once he began to resist he was ready to go just as far as the men of July 20. Although he never joined them, he was highly enough regarded by the conspirators to be their choice for Minister of Economics in the new regime that would succeed Hitler's, and the Fuehrer not only knew about this but was constantly reminded of it by Bormann and the others who never had believed in Speer's loyalty. In his meetings with Hitler, as well as in the memoranda he sent him, Speer became increasingly defeatist, and in mid-March, 1945, he wrote a long report to the Fuehrer, telling him plainly that German industry would collapse within four to eight weeks with certainty and that the war could not be continued after this breakdown. Speer wrote to Hitler:

> The people in this war have fulfilled their duty and their task under circumstances far worse than in any previous war. It is certainly not due to any failure of theirs if the war is lost. . . . We must do everything to maintain, even if perhaps in a most primitive manner, a basis of existence for the nation to the last. . . . No one may take the position that the fate of the German people is bound to his own. . . . No one has the right to

destroy industrial plants, coal mines, electrical and other power centers, transport facilities, inland waterways and such. Whereas up to now plants have been paralyzed . . . for a period of one to two months so they could be put into use again quickly when they were recaptured, the same standpoint must now prevail even if a reconquest does not seem possible . . . It is of course necessary to destroy bridges over the main rivers as long as it is possible to slow up the enemy advance. But it cannot possibly be the purpose of a war leadership in the homeland to blow up so many bridges that, with the diminished resources in the period after the war, it will take years to rebuild this traffic network. The prepared demolitions of the bridges in Berlin, for example, would have as a result that the city of Berlin could no longer be supplied with food and would make industrial production and the life of the people in this city impossible for years to come. These demolitions would mean the death of Berlin. The demolitions in the Ruhr area of the many railroad bridges over the smaller canals and valleys or of the viaducts would prevent the Ruhr from undertaking the production that is essential to replace the bridges. . . . We have no right at this stage of the war to carry out destructions which would strike at the life of the nation. If the enemy wishes to destroy this nation which has fought with unique bravery then this historic shame will rest solely on him. We have the obligation of leaving to the nation everything possible that in the remote future might be able to insure it a reconstruction.[6]

The memorandum ended without the customary "Heil, mein Fuehrer." *

Speer openly sabotaged Hitler's orders; he had high explosives which were supposed to be used to blow up coal mines hidden from the demolition squads, and he issued machine pistols to factories so their workers could resist any attempts to destroy them. Speer succeeded in saving innumerable plants, dams, and bridges in Germany and the occupied countries, and he operated impartially against the Gauleiters, SS officers, and Army engineer detachments that were determined to carry out orders to blow them up.†

He was tireless in his efforts to prevent demolitions; it was because of his insistence that orders were sent through OKW to preserve intact important railroad lines that would otherwise have been blown up.[7]

It was on March 29 that Speer wrote Hitler a stinging letter summing up their conversation of the day before:

If I write to you again it is because I am not in the position on emotional grounds to share my thoughts with you by word of mouth. First I must tell you how proud and happy I would be if I might continue to work for Germany as your collaborator. To leave my post, even if you ordered me to do so, in this decisive time would seem like desertion to the German people

* The unique freedom with which Speer wrote and talked to Hitler was not one-sided. The Fuehrer told him during one conversation that he knew Goering to be corrupt and a dope addict (N XVI, p. 531).

† Failing to carry out such orders could easily mean death. Hitler, on March 18, 1945, ordered the execution of eight officers for not blowing up a bridge (Ibid., p. 496).

and to my loyal co-workers. Nevertheless I am in duty bound to tell you, without regard to any personal consequences, plainly and unadornedly what my inner feelings are with regard to the situation. I have always told you— as one of the few co-workers—openly and honorably what I think and I shall continue to do so. You distinguished yesterday between the recognition of realities through which one can be convinced that the war no longer may be won and the belief that despite everything it may all come out all right. . . . My belief in a happy turn of fate for us was unbroken up to March 18. . . . I am an artist and as such was given a job that was completely alien and difficult. I have done much for Germany. Without my work the war might have been lost in 1942–43. I mastered the job not as a specialist but with the characteristics proper to an artist: with the belief in his task and in success, with the instinct for what is right, with a sense for generous solutions, with an inner integrity without which no artist can find proper solutions.

I believe in the future of the German people. . . . I was desolate when I saw in the days of victory in 1940 how we in the broadest circles of our leadership lost our bearing. Here was the time when providence demanded of us decorum and inner modesty. Then victory would have been ours. . . . A precious year was lost for armament and development through easy-going ways and laziness and then, as though providence wanted to warn us, bad luck trailed our military accomplishments . . . The frost before Moscow, the fog at Stalingrad and the clear sky over the winter offensive of 1944 [Speer is here talking of the German Ardennes offensive, where the weather played a role, but certainly not a decisive one, in bringing the attack to a halt] . . . When on March 18 I gave you my memorandum I was sure you would approve completely the conclusions I had drawn for the preservation of our people. For you yourself once said that the task of the leadership of a state is to prevent its people at the end of a lost war from coming to an heroic end. Nevertheless you said on that evening, if we have not misunderstood you, clearly and unmistakably: "If the war is lost, the people are lost too. . . . It is not necessary to bother about the fundament that the people will need for its most primitive future existence. On the contrary it would be better to destroy these things. For the people have shown themselves weaker and the future belongs entirely to the stronger peoples of the East. Those who survive the war will in any event be only the inferior ones; the best have fallen." Hearing these words, I was most deeply shaken. . . . Up to then I had believed with all my heart in a good end to this war. I hoped that not only our new weapons and planes but above all the fanatical, growing belief in our future would rouse the people and the leadership to the last sacrifices. I was then myself determined to take a glider and fly against the Russian power stations and through my personal involvement to help out, to change fate and at the same time to set an example.

I can, however, no longer believe in the success of our affairs if in these decisive months at the same time, and according to plan, we destroy the substance of our people. That is so great an injustice against our people that fate could never again mean well by us.

Speer then repeated what he had written on March 15:

> What generations have built up we are not permitted to destroy. If the enemy does so and thus exterminates the German people then the historic guilt is his alone. . . . I can only continue my work with inner probity and with conviction and belief in the future when you, my Fuehrer, acknowledge, as you have before, the necessity for maintaining the substance of our people. . . . Your order of March 19, 1945, takes away the last industrial possibilities and knowledge of it will throw the population into the greatest despair.* . . . I ask you therefore not to complete this act of destruction against your people. Should you be able to make this decision in whatever form then I will again have the faith and the courage to be able to work with the greatest energy. . . ." [8]

And this letter he closed with the words "May God Protect Germany."

Speer did succeed in getting Hitler to modify this insane order. He drew up what became the Fuehrer decree of March 30, which declared that since the destruction order was given to prevent the use of the installations by the enemy, demolitions were only to be carried out under immediate threat of capture and were not to weaken the German ability to fight. Bridges and traffic installations were to be destroyed entirely but supply plants need only be paralyzed. Total destruction of especially important plants was only to be carried out with the approval of Speer; and the Party, State, and Armed Forces were to assist him. This document was a remarkable tribute to Speer's influence on Hitler. In addition, Speer was enabled to issue a directive under his own signature on the same date to accompany the Hitler decree, declaring that his previous orders for paralyzing industrial and supply plants were still in effect. Total destruction of the most important plants and of their essential parts was to be carried out only by order of the Fuehrer transmitted through him, and Speer would name such factories with the counsel of the chairman of the armament committees.[9]

Speer's victory was the more astonishing for its taking place at a time when Hitler suspected high treason on every side, when he was ordering death penalties for his closest former collaborators, and when the hopeless battles of the remnants of the German armies were being fought only to give him a few more weeks of life. At this time, when Hitler was identifying the fate

---

* Hitler's order of March 19 repeated that everything must be done to weaken the enemy and to prevent his farther advance. Every possibility of damaging the striking power of the enemy directly or indirectly must be utilized. Industrial installations should not be paralyzed but destroyed:

It is a mistake to believe that traffic, communications, industrial, and supply centers left undamaged or paralyzed for a short time can be used again when they are recaptured. The enemy in his retreat [this was Hitler's answer to Speer] will leave us scorched earth with no regard for the population. Therefore I order: all military, traffic, information, industrial, and supply centers as well as stocks inside Germany that could be of any use to the enemy . . . are to be destroyed.

The order was to be sent to troop commanders with the greatest possible speed (N XLI, p. 430).

of the German people with his own, Speer succeeded in breaking through the impenetrable barriers of fantasy; he forced the Fuehrer to change his mind. Speer was the only man who succeeded in doing this, and Hitler seemingly bore him no ill will.

A radio speech Speer wanted to make early in April, 1945, was canceled by Goebbels, who thought it defeatist, but on April 16 in Hamburg, Speer made a recording of another speech which he planned to have broadcast when the time came—after Hitler's death. In it he said that further destruction or even "paralyzing" operations were not to be carried out, that they were forbidden in Germany and the occupied territories. No bridges were to be blown up and their demolition charges were to be removed; protection was to be provided for factories, railroads, and communication installations. Anyone who resisted the order was to be dealt with by the Army and the Volkssturm (in which only volunteers were henceforth to serve), if necessary by force of arms. Prisoners of war and foreign workers were to remain in their camps, but if they were already on the road toward their homes they should be sent on their way. Political prisoners and Jews in concentration camps were to be separated from the asocial prisoners and be turned over unharmed to the Allies when the occupying troops appeared. Any Werewolf activity was to stop.[10]

Although this speech was never delivered, all Speer's orders were given in its spirit. He made no secret of his implacable opposition to Himmler, Ley, Bormann, Sauckel, Goebbels, and all the other down-the-line Party men who interfered with his job of supplying Germany with weapons and, while hope remained, of obtaining a stalemate or somehow tolerable conditions for Germany's survival.

A resourceful man of affairs when it came to producing goods with any means at hand, Speer took forced labor for granted, but he wanted a reasonable work week because production slackened off if too much was demanded. He was against a long, twelve-hour day and yet, since the country had come to live under a constant emergency, a seventy-two-hour week was by no means uncommon for concentration-camp workers in the Speer-controlled enterprises. He used concentration-camp workers late in the war as little as possible, the tribunal conceded in its judgment, but not for humane reasons but because he had to deal with Himmler to obtain their services.* At Nuremberg, Speer defended the use of forced foreign labor in Germany, saying he was no international lawyer but he had not thought the practice to be illegal; moreover, he had managed to keep thousands of factory hands at work in their own countries rather than deporting them. He had succeeded in getting

---

* Speer had nothing *per se* against using concentration-camp workers. In 1938 he planned with Himmler to use inmates for manufacturing bricks and stonework under the SS so that concentration camps, too, would be productive (Hans Buchheim, Martin Broszat, Hans-Adolf Jacobsen, Helmut Krausnick, *Anatomie des SS-Staates* [Olten and Freiburg i. Br.: Walter-Verlag, 1965], Vol. II, pp. 92–93).

the factories assigned to him in foreign countries "blocked," so people working in them could not be sent out of the country at the behest of one of the competing Nazi collectors of labor and because the men had more incentive to work in their own country and avoid being deported. He used both the entrepreneur and the factory worker as humanely as he could under the heavy pressures of the constant crises besetting the Reich, but he wanted German women to be forced to work, too, a step that Hitler and Sauckel, with their sentimental image of German womanhood, were most reluctant to take.

Speer's remarkable success in increasing production came from his gift of improvisation and his clear sense of how to organize. He used beltlines and manufactured standardized parts in scattered factories so that if one factory was destroyed, the finished tanks, or whatever, could still be produced. He gave bonuses, threatened punishments, and got rid of as many administrative bureaucrats as he could. The last accomplishment was close to his heart; he was grateful for the fire that destroyed thousands of documents in his ministry, and he used the occasion, he told his co-workers, to drop a long list of officials from their jobs. "We cannot expect occurrences of this kind will continuously bring new vigor to our work," he told his colleagues.[11] He was opposed to large aggregates, preferring a large number of smaller enterprises; huge factories, he thought, produced huge bureaucracies. He ran his vast production empire with a minimum of manpower; he had twenty-one main committees, which were responsible for the finished products of the armament industry, and twelve so-called "rings" to provide for the delivery of raw materials. The committees and rings had the task of streamlining production and deciding on what the factories should concentrate and on how any improvements in manufacture or use of materials might be made. The committees and rings did the planning, working closely with the over-all Planning Commission, and Speer kept emphasizing that their chairmen must keep in close personal touch with the multifarious web of assignments that had to be carried out according to the directives.

The job of the committees, Speer said, was mainly to back up the factory manager. Exchange of information between plants was constant, and secret material, including patents, was made available to all factories, as were any new discoveries. Speer gave the German plants what they always tended to lack: flexibility and a plant-wide morale, a sense of comradeship and of working for the general cause with enthusiasm without regard to salary and social differences. The main incentives for the workers were provided, to be sure, by the war, but they also knew that only in this, in Speer's fashion, could the previous methods of coercion be kept out of the plants. Always lurking in the background was the Party and its hostility to business and industry and anything it did not directly control. Both the committees and the rings were composed of mixed groups from the Wehrmacht and technical experts from industry. The decision on the development of new weapons was in the hands of the chairmen of the committees, who were company officials, engineers, and construction men, and any decision they made could be overruled only by Speer, or by the Wehrmacht, or by Hitler himself. The plant managers had complete authority in their own plants as far as Speer could give it to them and keep them free from Party interference.

His remarkable record was by no means owing to the underground factories of which so much was later to be heard. They provided but a small fraction of German production; at the end of the war only 300,000 square meters of such plants existed, although there were plans for three million square meters more to come. Both Speer and Field Marshal Milch, who was one of the chief men responsible for the production of fighter planes, for which the underground plants were mainly built, and who sat with Speer on the Central Planning Board as well as on the Jaeger Staff,* were against the building of these plants because the idea, they said, had occurred to Goering too late in the war and the time and manpower needed for their building would be better utilized to produce planes in the factories already available.

Speer gladly hired anyone who was able to do the kind of job he needed, and Goebbels, Kaltenbrunner, and Bormann called his ministry a nest of anti-Party sentiment and activity, which it undoubtedly was by their standards in view of the ceaseless attempts of its chief to step up production regardless of the race or political sentiments of his producers and his single-minded efforts to circumvent the destruction orders. Speer was glad to employ Jews or Slavs, Poles, Ukrainians, Czechs, and Russians, all the hated inferior people, if only they could produce. He gratefully put concentration-camp inmates and prisoners of war to work for his enterprises. Foreign workers of all nationalities (volunteers, forced laborers, concentration-camp workers, and prisoners of war) made up 40 per cent of the personnel of the German war factories.[12] More than two and a half million Frenchmen worked for Germany—of the more than one million French prisoners of war, only some 48,000 were unemployed. There were more than a half million Dutchmen and 150,000 Belgians, and workers came by the millions from the East.† [13]

* Milch, when he started the Jaeger Staff in March, 1944, was given the task of deciding on the new models and at the same time raising the production of German fighter planes from 1,000 to 3,000 a month, but he immediately called on Speer and thus the two of them sitting both on the Central Planning Board and the Jaeger Staff almost completely replaced Goering in the economic sphere. Milch was always ready to subordinate himself to Speer, whom he regarded with unstinting admiration.

† A decree issued by the Chief of Staff of OKH on February 6, 1943, declared it was the duty of everyone—male and female—from the ages of fourteen to sixty-five to work in the operational areas of the East. Special rules were to be established for the Jews, and a work period of fifty-four hours per week was to be standard, with overtime, night, and Sunday work a possibility. Regular sickness benefits, however, were to apply. At a later meeting in Rovno on March 10 it was noted that "a million or more workers were to be shipped out within the next four months," largely for agricultural work—the Speer enterprises would get the factory labor from the West. Such was the need for labor that the SD on March 19, 1943, was directed by Sturmbannfuehrer Christensen to relax its most brutal measures in the warfare against the partisans, which resulted in so many of the civilian population joining the bands. The harsh practices Christensen listed were the shooting of the Hungarian Jews, farm workers, and children, and the burning down of villages. He ordered that such measures be curtailed, that "special treatment" be limited. For the time being,

Speer wanted them treated well and paid on scales that compared with the Germans, otherwise they would not work properly. He never hesitated either to make use of the SS or to fight it. He elbowed Himmler out of setting up more concentration-camp factories, bringing these workers as far as he could under his own authority, and he merely agreed to supply Himmler's Waffen SS divisions with more war material in proportion to the concentration-camp workers the Reichsfuehrer SS made available. Speer forbade the Gestapo from making arrests in his factories, and protested against their practice of holding prisoners for months because of some minor defect in their papers when they might otherwise be working. His battle was against whatever they or anyone else did that lost workers for the Reich.[14]

In June, 1944, Speer made use of his close relationship with Hitler to protest to him the stupid misuse of Russian prisoners of war by the SS, pointing out that thousands of them had been shipped to SS factories from plants where they had been usefully employed and that most of them were skilled specialists.* Speer's protest was a direct attack on Himmler, who was extending his empire as far as it would go. The SS had begun to produce goods on its own account with a woodworking plant in Dachau; this was successful enough from Himmler and Pohl's point of view to warrant extending the SS enterprises to other concentration camps—to Oranienburg, Buchenwald, Neuengamme. In addition, concentration-camp labor was supplied on a rental basis to outside factories that needed it. Himmler wanted to keep all concentration-camp labor available for these SS factories alone, but Speer was able to convince the Fuehrer that war production would be damaged by such a wide-scale diversion of Germany's scarce machine tools. Himmler, in his efforts to recruit labor, ordered that 35,000 Eastern workers who had breached their labor contract be sent "by the quickest means" to one of these concentration camps where he could make use of them.† The only ones to

---

Communist Party functionaries, activists, etc., were only to be listed but neither they nor their close relatives were to be arrested. Members of the Comsomols were to be apprehended only if they held leading positions. When villages were burned down the entire population must be put at the disposal of the German authorities, and Christensen added this classical statement on behalf of more humane measures: "As a rule no more children will be shot" (N XXXI, 3012-PS, pp. 481–95).

* Speer testified at Nuremberg that OKW had opposed using prisoners of war, except for Russians and Italian internees, in the armament industries because the Geneva Convention forbade the use of captured military personnel in such work. The prohibition, however, did not apply to the Soviet Union, which had never signed such international agreements. His reasoning again was entirely pragmatic; he explained that the prisoners of war were mainly producing goods that were not specifically military according to the Geneva Convention; he did not regard the work the French prisoners of war were doing as armament production since in modern war almost any product could have a military use. Some 400,000 prisoners of war, he testified, were used directly in the armament industry, but of these from 200,000 to 300,000 were Italian, the rest Russian (N XVI, p. 452).

† The contracts the free workers signed stated that they agreed not to disclose what they had seen in Germany when they returned home; that they were to report any propaganda or espionage immediately to the German management; and that they covenanted to work conscientiously and well and to be punished, if the necessity should arise, under German law (June, 1943, BDC).

be exempt were those in solitary confinement awaiting further interrogation.[15]

Speer stormed against both the attempts of Sauckel to take workers from the protected industries he had set up in the occupied countries and the SS practice of arresting German and foreign workers on some trivial pretext and sending them to concentration camps. Such workers, he said, like the prisoners of war, never came back to the places where they had been employed and their services were lost as they disappeared into the labyrinths of Himmler's domains, for the SS used them in any kind of work. He complained to Hitler that 30,000 to 40,000 workers a month were thus kidnapped out of the economy by Himmler.[16] He told the Fuehrer, too, that the Russians, especially the women workers, if decently treated were usually content with their lot. He wanted humane treatment for the same reasons he wanted coal and oil for his machines, but he loved machines better than people. In one conference he suggested that in order to obtain French specialists who were prisoners of war for German factories the rumor be spread that such men would be freed if they volunteered. The French would have a list of such experts and once the Germans had it on hand they could simply conscript the specialists. There was no great harm in Speer, but he was a machine man, an efficiency expert, and the human beings were essential counters in his task.

His admiration for the order of the machines that he understood so well even led him at the end of the war to try to stop the manufacture of explosives to prevent their being used to blow up the factories Germany would so desperately need after the fighting was over. Once he recognized the war was lost, he threw in his hand; his factories had to play a role in the future; production for its own sake had no meaning for him. Nor did he have any confidence in the miracle weapons, the V-1s and V-2s. He fought against the manufacture of the new and potent gases Tabun and Sarin, which German chemists had succeeded in producing and against which no gas masks were said to be effective.[17] Tabun and Sarin were five times more powerful than the former war gases, and Goebbels and Bormann and a handful of scorched-earth fanatics wanted to use them to stop the Allied advance. Hitler, however, came to agree with the arguments of Speer and the generals that it would be catastrophic for Germany to use poison gases in view of the Allied control of the air and their almost unhindered ability to hit the German cities with bombs—including gas bombs—in retaliation, and Speer was finally able to stop the manufacture of the gases.

With the proclamation by Hitler of total war on July 25, 1944, German men from the ages of sixteen to sixty-five and women from seventeen to fifty had to register for work. At long last Speer's contention that German man and especially woman power was not being adequately employed was acknowledged in the Fuehrer decree. Speer had always wanted the factories manned by German rather than foreign labor, largely because indigenous labor would not increase the demand on the food supplies. But the decree came too late for Speer's purpose; the millions of foreign workers were already in

Germany, and it was precisely at this time that the Allied bombardments of the synthetic oil plants made much of the production useless. German cities had long been under heavy bombardment, and no careful canvass of how many women were working and whether their jobs were indispensable could be made. Whole blocks of houses were disappearing at a time; the task of finding living quarters, lining up for food, and getting to and from work if a woman had a job took strength enough; and the "combing-out" squads sent by the Party only increased anxieties without adding much to the labor force. Many women with children were sent to the country, and sometimes whole schools were evacuated. The working mother stayed at her job. But what she did and how long she worked could not longer be efficiently controlled.

Speer acted on behalf of his own technocracy; he gladly took what labor he could from whatever source; he was gratified by the good performance of concentration-camp workers in his factories, and he would have wanted more of them except for the constant threat of Himmler's interference. He estimated at Nuremberg that not more than 33,000 to 36,000 inmates of these camps were at work in the war factories, although they put in much more time than the others—from seventy-two to even a hundred hours a week. Under some of the camp commanders, Obergruppenfuehrer Pohl told his chief, Heinrich Himmler, there were no limits to the hours of concentration-camp labor. The camp commander alone decided how long the prisoners had to work, but in any event work breaks must be kept to a minimum. "Noon intervals," said Pohl, "only for the taking of meals are forbidden." [18]

Since the concentration-camp laborers Speer had in his factories were for the most part mixed in with other workers, their hours were likely to be limited, and in any event he was against long hours because they were inefficient. But he highly approved of concentration-camp labor for his war industries, as he did prisoners of war, volunteers, and forced laborers. In none of his countless reports, memoranda, or speeches, however, did he write or say anything other than to urge that they be adequately fed and rewarded for their performance. In the environment of hostility and violence in which he operated, he was one of the mildest of the top government officials. His country was, as he saw it, in a life-or-death struggle with its enemies; every German must do his share either at the front or in the factories, and the people in the occupied countries must work too, hopefully in their own plants, where they would do their jobs more efficiently. Speer did not think it his concern to decide the legality of what was being done, but his improvised system was based far more on rewards than on punishments, and the typical Nazi exhortations to be ruthless and to take no account of the suffering of foreigners never appear in anything Speer wrote or said. He conceded in his reports that a small majority of his workers, both German and foreign, needed to be disciplined on occasion, to be sent for a period to special camps or even to concentration camps if they deliberately committed major infractions of the work rules or sabotage. But on the whole he used the carrot rather than

the stick. He had worked closely with the SS when he took over the Organization Todt, which was then operating in the Crimea, where repairs of all kinds
had to be made to roads and bridges and buildings. Speer used Russian
conscript labor under SS guards, but no charges were ever made that he was
responsible for any mistreatment of the workers.[19]

Speer too turned over all his documents to the Allies while he was still free,
in the belief that he had nothing to hide; he had been assigned an important
technical task and had carried it out. Thus the Allies had possession of his
entire correspondence, and the picture that emerged from it was that of a
man for whom nothing was more important than his objectives. He hovered
busily over his employees, writing a sharp letter to Ribbentrop when his co-
workers were slighted at an official function and the Party brass stepped out in
front to take the bows, leaving the Speer contingents who actually did the
work in the background. "You know," he wrote Ribbentrop, "that I personally set little store by such things as table order or the distribution of
awards; I never attend such occasions if it is not absolutely essential." Nevertheless, Speer commented, those who did the work should have a place next
to the chief functionaries at the ceremonies celebrating what they had built.
"You know how I dislike discussions of these matters," he wrote, "but I
cannot tolerate a situation where my closest associates who have volunteered
to work on their own time are pushed to one side."

In the same vein, Speer reprimanded his own co-workers who seemed to
him in any way lax in their departmental loyalties. If under the pressure from
outside agencies colleagues appeared to be in the slightest degree diverted
from the jobs he had assigned them, Speer was immediately on the warpath.
Here again he used his reward-and-punishment formula, telling them that
they could not serve two masters but if they carried out the assignments he
gave them they could call themselves "Deputy Architects of the General
Building Inspector of the German capital." [20] If, however, they did not immediately promise to work for him alone, he pointed out that he had the
power and would use it to abrogate their contracts in whole or in part. When
one of his assistants, unknown to Speer, wrote a strongly unfavorable letter
to Bormann on a man Speer wanted to appoint a ministerial adviser, Speer
demanded that his assistant be sent to a concentration camp and he discharged another member of his staff who was implicated.[21]

Speer had a continual and lively correspondence with the entire Nazi
hierarchy, beginning with Goering, who, always concerned with his prerogatives even when he no longer was capable of carrying out a sizable fraction
of his assignments, complained bitterly of decisions that had been taken in
the economic sphere without consulting him. Since he was head of the Four-
Year Plan, no important step, said the Reichsmarschall, could properly be
taken without consulting him, and Speer replied that he doubtless had
enemies in the Reichsmarschall's entourage who cast a false light on what he
was doing but he had to make decisions to perform his job properly, and he

reminded Goering that a higher authority was over them both, that they too must work patriotically together for the Fuehrer. Goering was evidently appeased, for the main tenor of his correspondence with Speer was friendly after that and he made no further remonstrances. Speer had to deal with everyone in the higher echelons—with the Reichskommissar Terboven in Norway, with Hans Frank in Poland, with Karl Hermann Frank in Czechoslovakia, with the Army and Navy and Air Force, with Gauleiters and Party leaders of all conditions—and as long as they did not interfere with his task he was equally courteous to them all, even the malodorous Heydrich.

But Speer was quick to sense any encroachment on his territory—whether an attempt on Ley's part to undertake a project Speer thought should be under himself [22] or the actions of any of the other muddleheaded Nazi functionaries out to extend their satrapies. One speech of Sauckel's immediately caused him to protest because, Speer said, Sauckel used the occasion as a platform to state his pretensions to controlling what use was made of the labor he recruited. More than once Speer complained to Hitler that he thought Sauckel needed to be kept in line by more powerful weapons than he himself had immediately at hand. One of Speer's collaborators, General of Artillery Wagner, department head in the armaments industry, complained in a letter to Goebbels, a copy of which he sent to Speer, that Sauckel was unwilling to use the Hungarian Jews or permit them to enter his Gau of Thuringia. Speer strongly objected to this, for these concentration-camp workers were industrious and other Gauleiters might follow Sauckel's bad precedent and refuse to admit the Jews into their Gaue, which would badly hurt German production. The presence of the Jews, Speer said, perhaps for the record, was disturbing to him too, but this was an emergency, and since the Jews were in concentration camps they could not offend the sensibility of the German people or damage them in any way.[23]

Of one transport of 509 Eastern workers Sauckel sent, Speer wrote in indignation on January 25, 1944, 161 were children from one month to fourteen years old; forty-nine men and sixty-nine women were in such a physical state as to be incapable of working, and thus 53 per cent of the entire group could not be employed. Some months later he denied Sauckel's request for 7,000 workers to be taken temporarily from the armament factories and to be used in manufacturing sugar, telling Sauckel he certainly must be able to round up workers for a short time without disrupting an essential branch of German industry. He could write a twelve-page letter to the Fuehrer to buttress his position against Sauckel. Sauckel must regard himself as Speer's assistant, Speer told Hitler; Speer himself must decide how workers were to be employed.[24] And he turned down Keitel's request for his key workers as coolly as Sauckel's, for by 1944 he had convinced Hitler that production was as important as the front.[25]

He was equally sharp with Frank, who planned useless projects for the General Government, and told Frank that only if he was certain he could finish a building (a bank that could be used as temporary sleeping quarters for two hundred people) with local labor that could not be used elsewhere might he proceed with the project. Otherwise the labor was needed in the Reich. On other occasions he reprimanded Frank for his extravagant use of materials.[26] Speer made many visits to the front after which he was accustomed to writing long memoranda recommending improvements in weapons and tanks and on one occasion he noted placards in store windows of the Radom district which he considered extravagant. "I must ask you to see to it that the planning and carrying out of all measures is done with the least expense of work and material," he told the Governor, who took no such parsimonious view of his rights and privileges.

Speer was still a youngish man when he undertook the task of providing Germany with its war materials, and he had small patience with either slow-moving bureaucrats or entrepreneurs. He deplored what he called the advanced age of successful German businessmen and wanted the head of any firm who was fifty-five years old or more to have an assistant who was to be no more than forty years old. Youth and decentralization and simplification were three of his primary recipes for improving the German war effort. The simple Panzer fist that replaced the relatively cumbersome antitank weapons and could be shot by one man was his notion of a proper gun. Five million of them were produced in 1944, but Speer was able to point out that more than a million were produced in the month of March, 1945, alone despite all the shortages, the bombardments, and the loss of territory that had shrunk Germany to the size of a small wedge between the Allied armies.[27]

But even Speer's innumerable jobs, his constant speechmaking and journeys to the front, his conferences with Hitler, department heads, generals and admirals did not wholly fill his time. He continued all during the war to plan for grandiose future cities with green belts, sports facilities, and underground railway stations, and where the occupants of apartment houses would not have to leave their immediate neighborhood to shop for everything they needed; he foresaw vast projects where traffic would be rerouted through congested areas like the Ruhr and through cities. On January 10, 1944, he wrote that a million workers would be needed to rebuild German cities after the war. Apartments in huge barracks would be built for young married people; 400,000, maybe 600,000, would be provided in a year, and in addition two and a half million dwellings would be constructed on conventional lines so that the housing crisis would be solved in three years.[28]

Speer asked Goering to use his influence with Terboven in Norway to make sure the cutting of a natural stone available there would continue, despite the demands of the war, so it could be shipped to the Reich. He paid out large sums (150,000 RM for garden figures, 500,000 RM to a sculptor for the monumental and heroic statues he and Hitler so admired) despite his dedication to channeling German resources into war production. For the training of artisans in Germany, Speer wanted 400 RM a year to be given apprentices; to make sure of the interest of the young workers he asked that they invest 100 RM in their training, in return for which they would get from the State 500 RM a semester.[29]

He could overlook everything that marred his ideal picture of a rationally functioning European economy buttressed with vast building projects and integrated industries. Only a few weeks before the end of the war, on April 9, 1945, he said that Germany had built up in the occupied territories a European economy in the real sense. France, Belgium, and Holland had been permitted to manufacture the kinds of goods for which their factories were best equipped and they had even been enabled to rebuild when rebuilding was possible. It was tragic, Speer thought, that this cooperative work was now being broken down, but he was hopeful that the future would restore this European integration. For he saw clearly, as he told the court at Nuremberg, that the future would produce intercontinental rockets capable of destroying cities anywhere on the globe and that the nations of the new and old worlds must collaborate or perish. What he failed to notice was the effect of the Pandora's box of hatred he, with his magic enterprises, had helped to open on the world. "Use the sharpest measures," he told Sauckel, regarding recruiting; in effect, get the workers in any way you need to. Speer was anxious, as he had always been, to comb as many as he could from German sources and he was sure in July, 1944, that 300,000 house workers could be put to work in his factories.[30] But a few months earlier he asked Himmler to provide 400,000 workers from Auschwitz; even 10,000, he said, would be fine.[31] Two months later he appealed again to Himmler; foreign workers were becoming much scarcer; the concentration-camp inmates were sorely needed.

People were counters for him; the Hungarian Jews, whose use, he said, offended his Aryan sensibilities, were nevertheless good workers, and he wanted them brought to Germany, where their talents could be properly employed. He was indifferent to whether the prisoners of war in his factories were French or Russian or Italian; he measured them with his precise, impersonal mind solely by their performance. As the Allied circle drew close around Germany, Speer made careful calculations of how long the Reich could last under the loss of the territory, raw materials, and factories that fell into the hands of the enemy. Thinking of himself always as an artist, he wrote an angry protest in 1944 to the Army because it would not give a painter permission to visit the West Wall; artists, he said, were as necessary as the cameramen who were doing films for the weekly news roundups. When Doenitz, after he became President, asked Speer to become Minister of Economics, Speer declined; at the time he wrote to Foreign Minister Schwerin von Krosigk, who had succeeded Ribbentrop in the admiral's cabinet, that it was as incongruous for an artist to continue to take on such jobs as it had been to employ a champagne salesman as Foreign Minister.

What was Speer's guilt? At Nuremberg he accepted, he said, the common responsibility of German leaders even in an authoritarian system for what had been done and certainly his own for what had gone on in the area of his authority.[32] Speer was self-confident and composed on the witness stand. He refused, in answer to a prosecution demand, to name the people in Hitler's entourage of whom he was critical—this was no time for professional or personal recriminations—and the Russian prosecutor questioning him had no success against his quiet self-assurance. Soviet prosecutors tended to repeat questions which their Western colleagues had already asked and to which adequate answers had already been given by the defendants—whether because the Russians did not follow the trial closely or, which is more likely, because they wanted their own record of their patriotic role in the court proceedings to be clear when they returned to Moscow. The Soviet prosecutor who cross-examined Speer, Raginsky, at one point told Speer that if he did not wish to he need not answer a question truthfully, but the President of the Court intervened to say that Speer had already and properly answered the question. Speer told Raginsky, when asked how he had come to work so closely with the Fuehrer despite his nefarious character, that the Russians too had read *Mein Kampf* and yet had made their pact with Hitler. The dialogue became lively with implications. Raginsky asked him if it was not true that he had given himself without reservations to his war tasks.

> SPEER: "Yes, I believe that was the custom in your State, too."
> RAGINSKY: "I am not asking you about our State. We are now talking about your State . . ."
> SPEER: "Yes. I only wanted to explain this to you, because apparently you do not appreciate why in time of war one should accept the post of Armament Minister. If the need arises that is a matter of course, and I cannot understand why you do not appreciate that and why you want to reproach me for it."
> RAGINSKY: "I understand you perfectly."
> SPEER: "Good." [33]

Speer defended the concerns that employed concentration-camp labor; he pointed out that the firms had no control over the camps, which were run by the SS, and the company officers were not even allowed to inspect them. And to this statement he added with true German entrepreneurial grandeur, "The head of a plant could not bother about conditions in such a camp." [34]

Almost the whole of German production by 1944 was in his hands, including the defense plants for the Army, Navy, and Air Force, as well as those manufacturing consumer goods; only the SS plants were outside his authority. In addition, Speer acted as chairman of the Jaeger Staff, with Field Marshal Milch as co-chairman. This committee of three members with equal powers and votes had infringed, as Hitler intended it should, on the last remnants of Goering's former empire, but the Reichsmarschall by 1944, when the Jaeger committee was established, had to parcel out most of the territory over which he had formerly ruled. Speer, though, until June 20, 1944, when Goering finally turned over the plants to him, had only limited authority over the factories producing for the Luftwaffe, which were manned in part by half-starved Russian workers, because the Reichsmarschall to the end clung to every prerogative as long as he could. Speer tried to improve the Russians' rations, as well as those of the other working prisoners, and he always opposed the barbed wire around the work camps because of its bad effect on morale. From time to time he succeeded in getting supplementary meals for these workers, and after he got those he tried to have consumer goods made available to them, but any such successes were short-lived. The scarcity of food as a result of the bombardments and the subsequent derangement of transport was genuine enough, although there was always enough for the civilian population, and whatever Speer managed to obtain for his workers, the Russians always got less than the others who labored for the Germans except for the Jews.

The final malign effect of the Fuehrerprinzip, Speer said at Nuremberg, was that every order, even if it was criminal or insane, was supposed to be carried out unconditionally, without criticism. But obviously he only became aware of this at the very end of the war; up to the scorched-earth order he was concerned solely with his enormous assignment. Secure in his own sense of the correctness of what he was doing, he visited countless factories and talked with the men, including forced laborers, with no escort such as accompanied other Nazi ministers. A wide cross section of Germans always had confidence in him, from members of the Resistance to Guderian and Jodl, both of whom talked openly to him about Hitler's arbitrary and unreasonable decisions. When they complained to Speer they no longer had much will left to cross Hitler face to face. Speer confessed at Nuremberg that he did not try more than once or twice to approach the Fuehrer directly with criticisms either; the scenes, he said, could be too painful.

German war production, despite Speer's efforts, was always complicated by the incessant battle for power within the State and Party apparatus. Before Speer became Minister of Armaments and instituted his system of self-responsibility for industry, a plant manager faced being sent to a concentration camp if he failed to meet his arbitrarily set norms of production. It had been a coercive system, and Speer tried with success to find a substitute for the rewards and punishments of the competitive, free-enterprise system under the conditions of the war economy. He spent hours talking to meetings of Gauleiters, and the statistics of what he accomplished were so overwhelming that these upholders of the true faith often broke out in loud applause despite their suspicions of him. His speeches were skillfully adapted to the Gauleiters' mentality. Before procurement was coordinated, he told one meeting of Gauleiters at Posen on August 3, 1944, the amount of copper demanded by separate departments was more than the total supply in the world. He gave them astonishing figures on production: in 1941, 75 million shells had been turned out; in 1944, 408 million would be made. Then he gave the figures of fighter-plane production under his Jaeger committee: 3,115 fighter planes and interceptors were constructed despite the Allied bombings in July. He added that new U-boats that had been only sketches in September were being actually put in service in May, with a promise of forty-four a month to come later in the year. These were statistics the most stupid among the Gauleiters could understand. And Speer told them too of the bureaucratic troubles they themselves knew so well, for they often caused them. He related how he had found 180,000 gasoline cans in Breslau lying unused because they had been classified as drinking canteens destined for Rommel's army in Africa and had never been returned to their status as containers for gasoline. He had found trucks immobilized because tires were lacking and had got them on the road within hours; he found other trucks in Army garages—1,000 of them in Vienna—while Panzers could not be shipped to the front for lack of them. Even the Gauleiters were enthusiastic, at least while they were under his spell. But the Party never gave up the battle.[35]

Sauckel, in the chain of command under Speer, tried constantly to expand and strengthen his own organization at Speer's expense. Himmler tried to do the same thing with his SS factories; the Gauleiters under Bormann were always pressing for increased authority over the plant managers and Speer's "honorary co-workers," whom they regarded as well-heeled saboteurs. Goering gave up his authority reluctantly, retreating step by step. On April 22, 1942, he announced that within the framework of the Four-Year Plan, which he directed, the Central Planning Board would be set up with three members, Speer, Milch, and Koerner, as his personal representatives. The board was to have the responsibility of administering the entire economy; allocating raw materials, especially iron, metals, and coal; and deciding on how many workers would be needed for the agreed-on production.* These decisions had to be flexible since the Fuehrer's ideas changed on priorities; one month anti-aircraft defense took first place; another, tanks and bombers or fighters had the highest priorities and materials had to be shifted accordingly. The members of the Central Planning Commission theoretically had equal voices in the decisions—the one important exception to the Fuehrerprinzip, it was pointed out at Nuremberg. A unanimous vote was required for a decision and thus any of the three could cast a veto. The committee was dominated, however, by Speer, to whom both Milch and Koerner were entirely ready to turn over the important decisions on production, and as time went on Goering too had been glad to see Speer take charge after he found his own accumulating failures harder and harder to explain.

Speer and the Central Planning Board continually demanded of Sauckel that he conjure up more thousands of workers, and Sauckel, struggling to carry out his part of the patriotic effort, once promised a million fresh

---

* Paul Koerner was chairman of the board of directors of the Hermann Goering Werke, as well as Staatssekretaer and permanent Deputy of the Commissioner for the Four-Year Plan. His appointment was a face-saving device; Goering would have no voice in the decisions made by the committee.

workers. He was only able to produce 20,000. But this happened toward the end of the war, when all supplies were failing, including manpower and the means for getting it, and up to 1944 he produced his millions of workers. Furthermore Sauckel had increasingly stiff competition in the battle for obtaining manpower, and Speer was one of his chief competitors. For while Speer demanded the vast contingents of new workers, he at the same time made it impossible for Sauckel to get them from the blocked factories where they were concentrated. Speer insisted that Sauckel keep out of these factories. Sauckel, complaining to the Fuehrer that Speer was hoarding in these enterprises labor that was bitterly needed in Germany, demanded the right to investigate Speer's use of manpower; to send his own men into the blocked factories to determine whether, how, and if what they were producing was really essential to the total war effort. Speer was able on the whole to defend his blocked factories successfully, for when it come to a showdown, Hitler knew that Speer was indispensable and that his methods had worked miracles. Sauckel, on the other hand, was ordered to get hold of so and so many millions of workers, and not only Speer was a competitor but Himmler, the Army, which needed workers in the rear areas, and the Luftwaffe, which recruited civilian helpers and before 1944 gathered its own labor for aircraft production. Sauckel had other problems as well: he needed millions of workers for agriculture. Here, too, Speer demanded that those qualified be released for factory work between harvest time and spring. But, as Sauckel resentfully pointed out, many of them never returned for the spring planting but stayed on in Speer's factories.

Speer, the court found, had not been guilty of planning or waging aggressive warfare but he was guilty of war crimes and crimes against humanity. He had known, the court said, that his war factories were using slave labor; he had been present at the conference with Hitler where it was agreed that Sauckel was to bring in foreign labor by force and at the meeting where Sauckel had been told to supply at least four million new workers from foreign countries. Speer had also asked for specific nationalities to be provided—Russians, for example—and his blocked factories too were illegal, although the tribunal conceded that because of them thousands of foreign workers had been enabled to stay in their own countries. The court also noted that Speer had wanted to use as few concentration-camp workers as possible —because, it said, he mistrusted Heinrich Himmler's ambitions. The judgment declared that he had not been directly concerned with the cruelty of the slave-labor system but he had known of it and knew his demands for labor meant that violence would be used in recruiting manpower. He had also complained about malingering, and the court quoted his saying: "There is nothing to be said against the SS and police taking drastic steps and putting those known as slackers in concentration camps." But again, the judgment pointed out, he had insisted on adequate food and working conditions being provided the labor force so that it could work efficiently. And last of all, the tribunal mentioned without comment that he had told Hitler the war was lost and that he had opposed the scorched-earth policy. Then the court sentenced him to twenty years, a sentence, Speer said after his release, he accepted.

FRITZ SAUCKEL

The man who was head of the forced-labor program from March 21, 1942, until the end of the war was the Gauleiter of Thuringia, ex-sailor and factory and construction worker Ernst Friedrich Christoph Sauckel, whose given names were commonly shortened to Fritz. Sauckel had worked for Speer in Weimar before the war and in Berlin when Speer built the new Reichstag, but he owed his demanding post not to his professional training but to his having been an indefatigable and fervent leader of the Party in Thuringia since the early days of the movement. It was Bormann, not Speer, who recommended him to Hitler. A man was needed from whom the Gauleiters would take orders, and the rough and ready Sauckel, who was in every way one of them, seemed to the Fuehrer a good choice for the greatest slave roundup in history, although Speer proposed another Gauleiter named Hanke for the job.

Sauckel carried out his assignment with tireless efficiency as well as with a gross, brutal goodwill as he organized his manhunt for the millions of people to be cajoled or dragooned to work in the factories and on the farms of the Reich. His mandate was far-reaching. The *Reichsgesetzblatt* recorded his power by virtue of a decree signed by Hitler, Lammers, and Keitel on March 21, 1942, to carry out the mobilization of German and foreign workers, including prisoners of war in the Reich and in all the territories occupied by Germany, within the framework of the Four-Year Plan.* [36] Under the decree issued by Goering a few days later, on March 27, Sauckel was accorded the right which had been delegated to the Reichsmarschall by the Fuehrer to issue instructions to "the highest Reich authorities," to the Reich Protector, the Governor General, the military commanders, and the heads of the civil administration. On September 30, Adolf Hitler gave Sauckel the additional authority to appoint commissioners to the civil and military administrations of occupied territories, and these deputies, too, would be entitled to issue directives to military and civil authorities in charge of labor allocation. [37] Sauckel was appointed by the Fuehrer himself and thus his authority was limited only by someone like Speer, who also had direct access to Hitler and thus might be able, when conflicting ambitions met head on, to obtain a decision favorable to his own plans. While Speer appointed technicians, Sauckel named all the Gauleiters to his staff; one of his first decrees, issued

---

* The program was on a far greater scale than that of the "Hindenburg program" of World War I. It was worked out before the war by the High Command of the Armed Forces and the civilian government with the unions.

on April 6, 1942, formally designated them as his commissioners in their respective districts and declared that the chiefs of the highest state and economic offices were to advise them.[38] He had promised the Fuehrer when he took the job to work with "fanatical devotion" and this he did until 1945, when to his genuine surprise he found that the war was lost and the world outside the one he had lived in so long with his Fuehrer and his Party chiefs regarded him as a criminal.

Sauckel was a family man on a heroic scale; he had ten children, two of whom were killed in the course of the war. He was also a man of the people; his wife, he was proud to tell the court, was the daughter of a Social Democrat, and although he had attended a Gymnasium until he was fifteen—obtaining the *Mittlere Reife** [39]—he had been a merchant sailor before World War I. Just after that war started he was captured by the French and he spent almost five years as a prisoner in France, where he was thrown in with a number of other German captives, some of whom later became important in the political and military life of the Third Reich. In the course of the long conversations he had with them he became for the first time concerned with politics.

Sauckel was born in Hassfurt am Main on October 27, 1894. His father was a postman, his mother a seamstress, and it was she whose extra earnings made it possible for the only child to go beyond the Volksschule. He was fifteen years old when he went to sea, and worked on Norwegian and Swedish sailing ships as well as German steamers. Like so many men from the interior of maritime countries who have had a landlocked upbringing, Sauckel never lost his love for the sea or his desire to serve his country as a sailor. Once, in the course of World War II, when his landsman's job seemed too much for him, he stowed away on a submarine and had to be recalled by a wireless order from Doenitz, who pointed out at Nuremberg that Sauckel must have had a strong call to frontline duty; he could have no hope for martial glory by serving on a U-boat.

Sauckel studied engineering for two years after the first war, supporting himself at odd jobs. He officially joined the National Socialists in 1925, but as early as 1921 he was making speeches for the Party, and in 1924 he was one of its chief reorganizers; after the failure of Hitler's putsch had scattered its leadership, he busied himself gathering recruits for it. His Party card had a relatively low number, 1395.[40] In addition to being made Gauleiter of Thuringia in 1927, he served in the Thuringian Landtag from 1927 to 1933, in which year he was appointed Reichsstatthalter of Thuringia and was elected to the Reichstag. With the start of World War II, he was made one of the Reich Defense Commissars, but being a man of considerable energy as well as having been deprived of participating in World War I, he yearned for a more active role. When Sauckel was given the job of Plenipotentiary for

* The *Mittlere Reife* is less than an *Abitur*, which is usually earned by the student at eighteen and which qualifies him for the university.

Labor Allocation, Hitler told him to his delight that now he could be a soldier again, and Sauckel gratefully accepted this view of his task. He told the court at Nuremberg that he regarded himself as a soldier. As in the case of the concentration-camp guards, it was easier not to call a nasty job by its right name; it needed to be dignified. His deputies wore the uniforms of Army officers not only for purposes of identification in the occupied areas but because in Sauckel's and Hitler's view they were conducting a military operation.[41]

Sauckel became the greatest slaver of all time, but he had no notion that he would reach this eminence when he took over the job of providing workers for the booming industries of the Reich that had to be kept going while millions of men were under arms. Sauckel was a simple man; the war had to be fought and won and the armies that would do the job had to be supplied. On October 1, 1938, almost a year before the war started, the Supreme Command of the German Armed Forces had made plans to use forced labor both of prisoners of war and of civilians in the occupied countries.[42] And on May 23, 1939, Hitler, with the Polish campaign only months away, had reaffirmed the policy with regard to civilian labor in a meeting with military leaders, including Goering, Raeder, and Keitel. He had said: "If fate brings us into conflict with the West, the possession of extensive areas in the East will be an advantage. . . . The population of non-German areas will perform no military service and will be available as a source of labor." [43]

The program was well under way before Sauckel took over the job. Thousands of Dutch, Polish, and French workers had already gone to the Reich. In September, 1941, Bormann had sent out a memorandum originating in OKW on the treatment of Russian prisoners of war, saying that those willing to work were to be correctly treated but emphasizing that bolshevism was the deadly enemy of National Socialism and that the smallest sign of opposition should be met by ruthless and energetic measures. To break any resistance, the memorandum said, weapons should be mercilessly used.[44] Reinhard Heydrich, Chief of the Security Police, on February 20, 1942, a month before Sauckel became Plenipotentiary, ordered that no Asiatics be sent to Germany. The Russian prisoners of war who were shipped to the Reich had to be examined first by the SD; they were to be sent in closed transports, to work separately from other nationalities and in their free time, and (this provision included the Russian women working on farms) were not to come in touch with the local population. The conditions for the workers from the Baltic States were to be much the same, but because they were not Communists they did not require the same strict security measures, although they too were to be held in close confinement.[45]

Sauckel took the high purpose of his assignment for granted and as an honor bestowed upon him. Recruiting labor, whether in Poland or any other occupied country, seemed a reasonable if difficult mission to him. Whether the workers came voluntarily or by force, he wanted them to be treated as well as was necessary for them to work efficiently, and he gladly provided them with adequate nourishment, clothing, and housing. He announced his program in a long memorandum on April 20, 1942: "All these people must be fed, housed, and treated in such a way that with the least possible outlay the greatest possible results will be achieved." [46] In the earlier stages of the Russian campaign especially, workers had as added inducements to volunteer to go to Germany not only the promise of food and wages for themselves but increased rations for their families at home. Families could receive, in addition, 120 rubles a month deducted from the pay of the worker.*

Sauckel's recruiting drive started in a relatively humane fashion—or at least with certain humane intentions and instructions from him. From the beginning, however, working and living conditions for thousands of the labor force were subhuman. For one thing, there simply was not enough habitable space available for all these thousands of people; for another, many camp managers either had no interest in how foreign laborers lived or enjoyed mistreating them. The attitude of the SS toward the foreign workers was summed up by Hitler: "What does it matter to us? Look away if it makes you sick." [47] Sauckel either was unaware of much of what went on or ignored it. Since thousands of foreign workers on farms and in factories were moderately well treated, it was possible for him to concentrate his thinking on those.

It was to be taken for granted, Sauckel said, that the Germans would act correctly toward their conquered enemies "even when they are the most terrible and irreconcilable and we will do this too when we expect a useful performance from them." Like Himmler, Sauckel thought of the German as unimaginably chivalrous even when confronted with hard tasks that demanded much of his finer nature and humane sentiments. Foreign workers were supposed to receive the same insurance benefits as did the Germans, and their transport, treatment, and housing in the Reich were intended, by Sauckel at least, to make them content to be there. Sauckel stoutly maintained at Nuremberg—and his own records bore him out—that he had no design of imposing inhuman conditions of labor on his charges, and he had little authority over their living and working conditions once he had delivered them to the German work camps. He, too, struggled against the fixed beliefs

* A main goal of the campaign in the East, it was made clear from the start of the war, was to make Germany blockade proof, to provide the Reich with the food, raw materials, and laboring populations it needed for the war and the years that would follow after Germany became a world power. The Eastern policy, too, was meant to deprive Poland and Russia of not only an industrial, but also a biological, potential; for the Eastern workers were almost always separated from their families, and the sexes were segregated in Germany. The so-called Hay Action (see Schirach, Chapt. 8) was originally intended to send to the Reich Russian children from ten to fourteen years old who could be trained as apprentices, and it was pointed out that not only would they be helpful to the economy but their presence in Germany would also cut down on the future breeding potential of the East.

of thousands of his Party comrades that foreign workers were less important than house animals.[48] And his repeated orders for improving their lot had little relationship to what actually happened.

Like Speer, he wanted no barbed wire around the work camps, and he kept repeating that only well-cared-for workers did their jobs properly. But his own assignment was to round up the millions of workers needed to man the German factories, and the longer the war lasted the more difficult it became. At first in the occupied Russian provinces and the Baltic countries which had been under Soviet occupation, more than in Poland, both men and women were often glad to have a chance to get the higher pay and better rations promised them if they would go to Germany. Sauckel was undoubtedly serious about the promises made to these people, and he told his recruiters that they must not lie and that he wanted the workers to be accorded the treatment they had been led to expect. In France he could make use, in the beginning, of two powerful inducements to volunteers. One was the offer to prisoners of war of immediate release from their camps if they signed a contract to work in a German factory, and the other was to exchange one prisoner of war for every three French civilian volunteers for work in the Reich. The offer to prisoners of war was taken up by many of the French captives—one entire camp, it was said at Nuremberg, "volunteered" for work —but part of the bargain was that they would first be furloughed for two weeks, and of the 8,000 who signed up, 2,000 disappeared after they got back to France.[49]

One thing is certain: Sauckel never for a moment thought of his assignment as conflicting with international law. He wanted to provide the same conditions of pay and work for the Eastern workers as for other foreign labor in German factories. He had been told by Hitler, he said virtuously at Nuremberg, that the use of foreign labor was not contrary to the Hague Convention; but in any event, the Fuehrer had explained, since Russia was not a signatory to the Hague treaty, its provisions would not apply to Soviet citizens. It is, of course, highly unlikely that Sauckel cared much one way or the other about such legal niceties until at Nuremberg they became more important than they had been in the Third Reich. When Sauckel became Plenipotentiary for Labor Allocation, he took over a job that had been largely in Goering's hands as Minister for the Four-Year Plan. A decree of October 26, 1939, issued in accordance with the plans made earlier in 1938 and 1939, had made Poles in the General Government from the ages of eighteen to sixty subject to compulsory labor.[50] Although it provided that payment was to be made "at fair rates" and the welfare of the workers' families was to be safeguarded "as far as possible," Goering had made it plain that these people were to be worked to the uttermost for the benefit of the Reich. "Everything not needed," the Reichsmarschall said, "for the naked life of the country" was to go to Germany; this included factories, too, unless they could be used immediately more easily and more efficiently where they were on behalf of production for Germany.[51] Even eight-year-olds could be conscripted when they seemed either dangerous or a nuisance to the German occupants.[52]

The Governor General of Poland, Hans Frank, wrote to Goering on January 25, 1940, saying that the supply and transportation to Germany of at least one million Poles, male and female, of whom at least 750,000 were to be agricultural workers, must be arranged. He wrote to a receptive minister, for Goering had already pointed out the need for importing a million workers. When Volksdeutsche (people of German descent born in a foreign country) from Rumania were "resettled" in Poland and took over Polish farms, the former owners might either be sent as laborers to Germany or allowed to remain in their villages to work there for the German settlers.[53]

Before Sauckel was appointed to his job, Eastern labor was used mainly in the occupied areas. The Russian campaign, with its insatiable demands for more manpower at the front and for the supplies to feed and equip the Army, caused huge gaps to appear among the ranks of German workers. It was Sauckel's task to fill them, to bring in the essential manpower and womanpower from the occupied West and East by promises or by force. He said once that if more workers had been obtainable in 1942–43 Stalingrad might not have been lost. And he genuinely felt, perhaps because of his undemanding background as a sailor in the pre-World War I merchant ships, that the treatment of the laborers brought to the Reich was excellent, for he wrote to Hitler on March 10, 1943: "I tell you that all the workers of foreign nations are being unexceptionably treated correctly and decently, well taken care of and well clothed. . . . Never before in the history of the world have foreign workers been so well treated." [54] Nevertheless, and this seemed to him in no way inconsistent with the rest of his report, he said too that they were working without a stop ten hours a day and their production varied between 65 per cent and 100 per cent of that of the German workers, "A mighty addition to the reservoir that our enemies do not have." * [55] Sauckel for his part undoubtedly wanted his reservoir to be useful, and he demanded that the undernourished receive medicine and food and good care, for they "must be given the feeling it is to their own interest to work loyally for Germany." [56] All he could do was to make such hopeful speeches; he did not run the camps.

---

* Hours varied greatly. Many work days for foreign labor averaged thirteen hours, and wages paid were purely theoretical since fines, taxes, and other deductions kept them down so the worker rarely received more than a mark or two a week after the deductions. Of a foreign worker's pay, 80 per cent was deducted one way or another, Sauckel said at Nuremberg. A Russian volunteer worker testified that he was given three-quarters of a liter of tea at four in the morning, when his day started, and a quart of nondescript soup fourteen hours later. This together with 240 grams of bread was his daily ration for hard labor (N XXV, 054-PS, pp. 101–11). Eyewitness reports tell of Russian workers catching mice and cooking them after skinning them with bits of glass and metal (TWC, Krupp, IX, p. 1058. N XXXV, D-316, pp. 66–67) and of workers being beaten for stealing a crumb of bread (NCA VII, D-305, pp. 13–14). The judgment in the I. G. Farben case stated that the company had provided extra rations of hot soup at its own expense but the workers were still greatly undernourished (TWC, Farben, VIII, p. 1185).

Sauckel's workers came from all the occupied countries of Europe. He had agreements with the Vichy Government to secure labor from central France; with the military governor of northern France and Belgium; with Seyss-Inquart in Holland; with the administrators and governors of all the satrapies. In theory he was to have the cooperation of the Army. On October 13, 1942, for example, he asked Keitel for assistance in recruiting 500,000 Russian workers before the end of the year and another 500,000 by the end of April 1943.[57] But in practice, Sauckel was still complaining at Nuremberg, this help was rarely forthcoming. Generals said they had more than enough to do with fighting the war. Such help as Sauckel got was sporadic and dependent on local conditions. An operational order of Army Group South, for example, was issued on August 17, 1943, as part of the tactics to slow the Russian advance, "to recruit and transport to the Reich . . . all labor forces [born] during 1926 and 1927." [58] In December of the same year, with the German Army retreating all along the Eastern front, an Army order from the threatened rear area of Belilovka-Berditchev-Zhitomir was issued to evacuate the entire male population from fifteen to sixty-five years old together with the livestock. In the West in October, 1942, the military governor of northern France and Belgium, General Alexander von Falkenhausen, although strongly opposed to the use of forced labor, on Sauckel's order issued a decree for recruiting men from the ages of eighteen to fifty and single women from twenty-one to twenty-five.[59] In November, 1943, General Jodl told an audience of Gauleiters at Munich: "In my opinion the time has come to take steps with remorseless vigor and resolution in Denmark, Holland, France, and Belgium to compel thousands of idle persons to carry out fortification work, which takes precedence over all other tasks. The necessary orders for this have already been given." [60] And in the East, too, the Army similarly recruited masses of workers for repairing roads and bridges, clearing debris, and building fortifications. But it did not often help in rounding up the contingents Sauckel was sending to the Reich.

Sauckel with the Fuehrer's support usually managed to get the formal backing of the High Command. He met with General Warlimont in July, 1944, and as a result OKW prepared an order that when the troops were not engaged in military tasks they were to be made available for Sauckel's purposes. Sauckel declared at Nuremberg that he had accepted this order, with gratitude, but it was never carried out. Sauckel was always disappointed by the lack of cooperation of the field commanders. Army generals more than once protested that Sauckel's methods of recruiting drove men and women to the partisans, and Sauckel complained that the Army regarded his mission as infamous. In Italy, Field Marshal Kesselring said the recruiting drives had a bad effect not only on war production but on the entire Italian theater of war. Kesselring wanted voluntary recruiting or none, and Sauckel protested that in Italy and elsewhere the soldiers instead of helping tried to protect the civilian population from his recruiting squads.[61] Such help as Sauckel got from the Army was largely limited to the convoys of Russian prisoners of war and the actions in the rear areas where the battle against the partisans was being waged. Members of the partisan bands were either shot or sent to labor camps. Partisans, however, were a tough core of resistance, and German security agencies were not eager to have them in the Reich.

Sauckel organized so-called protection squads, mixed groups of local police and his own employees, to get at the workers in the West; sometimes churches or moving-picture theaters were surrounded and hundreds of prisoners corralled at a time. Sauckel denied in Nuremberg that he had actually conscripted in this fashion, saying that the men in the moving-picture theater had completed one job and were suddenly needed for another, which was why they were so summarily sent off. His defense seemed an unlikely one, but Sauckel had written a letter to Heinrich Himmler protesting against such an "action" in Russia; picking up people in this fashion and sending them to Germany, he wrote to the Reichsfuehrer SS on March 29, 1943, damaged everything he was trying to do.[62] However this may be, Sauckel was an old sailor, and he admitted to shanghaiing workers in France by paying agents to get them drunk and to deliver them to the recruiting centers. He once boasted that of all the millions of workers in the Reich not more than 200,000 had come willingly, and while he tried desperately at Nuremberg to explain his words as having been a foolish exaggeration, they were certainly true for his recruiting after 1943 and probably earlier as well.

Every German factory wanted more workers. I. G. Farben, for example, went after concentration-camp labor and got it. One of its officers wrote: "Our new friendship with the SS is proving very profitable." [63] Himmler in turn, as we have seen, corralled workers from industry and sent them to concentration camps, where he could use them as he wished. Speer always needed more workers than he could get for his factories, and he wanted Sauckel to take them not only from foreign countries but from German agriculture and households and hotels, where, he said, guests could serve themselves. Sauckel's department was a turbulent center of conflicting demands. Speer demanded Sauckel's agricultural workers and closed his factories in France to Sauckel's recruiters; at the same time, the Fuehrer ordered Sauckel to get a million workers from France on the basis of estimates of theoretically available manpower that Goering had given him. Since the French police took neither pleasure nor pains in rounding up their compatriots and the German squads were inadequate in numbers, Sauckel's drives in France as in the East produced fewer and fewer workers as time went on.

When the Sixth Army was lost at Stalingrad in 1943, both Speer and Goebbels explained to Sauckel that it could be replaced by a careful combing of the German bureaucracy (Speer in particular was always convinced that the Army had too many support troops and that German manpower was being used inefficiently) but Sauckel said at Nuremberg that there had been no possibility of obtaining the needed numbers of soldiers from his source. Most of the officials and employees working in Germany were over fifty-five and had already been thoroughly screened for military duty. Sauckel struggled desperately with the impossible demands placed upon him for huge numbers of skilled and unskilled labor to be allocated to rival sectors of the economy. Getting even one coal miner, he complained bitterly, meant a selection from among five to seven possible candidates after the workers had been collected.

Sauckel's early assignments in the East as well as in the West had not, with the powers given him, been overly difficult to fulfill, although they were demanding enough. In 1942, for example, he was ordered to produce 20,000 specialized workers from Holland and he did that easily, for the men had to eat and to provide for their families (See Seyss-Inquart, Chapt. 11). In the course of the twelve months between April, 1942, and April, 1943, Sauckel had considerable success; he rounded up 3,638,056 workers of all descriptions for the German economy and, in addition, 1,622,829 prisoners of war.[64] But as the military situation and working conditions deteriorated, the labor supply went down too; the streams of volunteers dried up, and thousands of men and women in the occupied territories disappeared into the underground or joined partisan bands. The "Sauckel actions" in Holland as in the East became sudden raids where 50,000 men were ruthlessly rounded up in one day, as happened in Rotterdam. Dutch factories had to be combed by German commissions for specialists to be sent to the Reich.

Sauckel was told the over-all number of workers that must be provided for a given economic area, and then he would pass along the quotas to the occupied countries under civilian control—to Seyss-Inquart in Holland and to Frank in Poland—for the occupiers to fill with the aid of the deputies he sent them. In Russia he had to deal not only with Rosenberg, who had merely nominal authority, but with actual rulers such as Erich Koch, Gauleiter of the Ukraine, and with the SS and the Army, who wanted to have nothing to do with him except turning over any partisans who had survived. Sauckel was a Gauleiter by profession; he accepted as a matter of course the essentially inferior status of the Eastern or even the Western foreign workers compared with the Germans. On October 3, 1942, in a letter to Rosenberg he demanded "the ruthless application of all measures" in order to get two million Russian workers. A report of October 25, 1942, from Rosenberg's office on the roundup of workers in the East said: " 'Recruiting' methods were used which probably have their precedent only in the blackest periods of the slave trade. A regular manhunt was inaugurated . . . more than 100,000 had to be sent back because of serious illness or other incapacity for work." [65]

A letter from Rosenberg to Sauckel of December 21, 1942, enclosed reports that had come to Rosenberg's attention on the beating of foreign workers as they were being rounded up and transported, and of the burning down of the houses of those who had not reported when called up. "All measures [in the East] are permitted to enable the German administration to carry out their tasks." This was the general directive and Sauckel's motley collection of local police and German agents was not greatly impressed with the necessity for good treatment when Sauckel at the same time demanded that his millions of workers be delivered by any means at hand. Workers were sometimes manacled; they traveled fifty and eighty jammed together in freight cars to the Reich, sometimes going days without food or water; and when they arrived at their destination their living quarters could be subhuman.* They worked in Germany in the clothes they came in and even if they were sick they had to work.[66]

Sauckel told one meeting of Army and Navy officers, Gauleiters, and SS men in April, 1943, that even the Eastern workers who were former Bolsheviks had souls and he intended to care for them; he wanted no besmirching of Germany's fair name or of his own, but the millions had to be recruited or the war would be lost. That was his dilemma—recruiting the millions with a pick-up collection of ruffians both foreign and German whose sole job was to deliver the human goods at any cost. The Germans squads had long been told of the essential inferiority of the people they were sending to the Reich. Sauckel's exhortations to treat them decently had no effect whatever on how his squads behaved. These were Sunday sermons. In a letter he wrote to the Gauleiters on March 14, 1943, he said: "But since we will need foreign labor for many years and the possibility of replacing them is very limited I cannot exploit them on a short-term policy nor can I allow wasting of their working capacity." [67] But the brutal recruiting, the undernourishment, the beatings went on as before because the Gauleiters and their men and the protection squads and the police and the SS had overwhelming numbers to deliver and send to work. They did not doubt that these people were natural enemies of the Reich and were worthy of being fed and kept alive solely for its purposes. Sauckel could preach his gospel, but his men had to bring in the manpower, and Sauckel himself had his motives for such humanitarianism: "Slaves who are underfed, diseased, resentful, despairing, and filled with hate will never yield that maximum of output which they might achieve under normal conditions."

Sauckel could persuade some of his colleagues of the common sense of what he was trying to do. Even Goebbels agreed that only adequately fed prisoners could do a day's work. And as of February 9, 1942, the Poles and the Russian prisoners of war who were working in Germany theoretically

---

* Eyewitnesses tell of Krupp workers being housed in what were described as "dog kennels," in ash bins and baking ovens in one plant (*TWC*, Krupp, IX, p. 1243; *NCA* VII, D-339, pp. 28–29); in barracks unheated in winter, in cellars where they had to sleep in pools of water, of their marching ten and more kilometers to work and then back again to their wretched quarters (Jaeger testimony, *N* XV, pp. 264–83. *N* XXXV, D-258, pp. 55–56. *Ibid.*, D-316, pp. 66–67. *Ibid.*, D-321, pp. 74–75. *NCA* VI, D-272, pp. 1111–12. *TWC*, Krupp, IX, p. 122. *NIK* 9301).

got 2,156 calories a day; heavy workers, 2,615; very heavy workers, 2,909; those who worked long hours and at night, 2,244. By comparison, the normal German consumer got 2,846 calories; the heavy worker, 3,159; and the very heavy worker, 3,839.[68] Reports varied sharply on what the prisoners actually received. Another witness testified that in 1942 German heavy workers got 5,000 calories but Eastern workers only 2,000 in the two meals they received a day.[69] Later, as we have seen, the rations would go far lower than that.

The food given the Eastern workers was vastly inferior to that given other nationalities, and when the Eastern laborer occasionally was given meat, it had been pronounced dangerous by veterinarians since the slaughtered animals were tubercular.* But Sauckel, like Speer, undoubtedly wanted all workers to produce as much as they possibly could without useless distinctions being made among the nationalities of Germany's enemies. And as the war crisis deepened, ideological dogmas weakened. Those who wanted more sensible treatment for the Russians were able to make a little headway against the racial purists; the Army that former General Vlasov recruited was put to some, if limited, use on the Western front, and Sauckel was able to issue a decree on March 25, 1944, that provided for the same wages for the despised Eastern workers as for other foreigners. Nevertheless Sauckel was second to none in his devotion to National Socialist principles; he believed in all the dogmas and he was resolutely administering his slave driving both domestic and foreign in territories where men like Himmler, Ley, Heydrich, and Frank were responsible for the conditions under which foreign laborers worked and whose decrees made far more rigorous distinctions between Eastern and Western workers than anything found in Sauckel's files.

On March 6, 1941, a year before Sauckel became head of the labor allocation, the following rules were issued for Polish workers in the state of Baden by the Minister of Finance and Economy:

> On principle farm workers of Polish nationality no longer have the right to complain; consequently no complaints may be accepted by an official agency. . . . Farm workers of Polish nationality may no longer leave the localities in which they are employed. . . . The use of bicycles or any form of public transportation . . . as well as church going is forbidden. . . . Visits to theaters, cinemas, or other cultural entertainments are strictly prohibited for farm workers of Polish nationality . . . Every employer has the right to give corporal punishment . . . and may not be called to account for this by any official agency.[70]

If a Pole was impudent or did not work properly he was to be reported and his employer would get a replacement. In addition there was to be heavy punishment for the employer if he did not keep the necessary distance between himself and his workers. "Extra rations are strictly pro-

---

* Goering spoke of "special food" for the Russians—"cats, horses etc."—and of providing them, as a rule, with wooden shoes (N III, p. 459).

hibited. . . . All this does not apply to prisoners of war who are under the Wehrmacht which has its own regulations." [71]

The German labor administration in Breslau stamped the picture of a pig on Polish work cards, and, although Sauckel said at Nuremberg he had never seen this device, the general idea was certainly not unfamiliar to him. Poles and Russians were primitive people; the Party never tired of telling how dangerous they were in their inferiority. German farmers were told in the circular just cited that if they had no room for the Polish workers in their homes they could be put in cattle stalls.[72] All kinds of restrictions were imposed on Eastern workers as part of the measures for security for maintaining German racial purity and status as another caste. Women working in German households were allowed outside the home only once a week for three hours; they had to be back by dark or by 8 P.M. in the summer.[73]

Frank and the occupation authorities in Poland, acting on the Fuehrer's and Goering's orders, demanded the ruthless slaughter of cattle; the shipping to the Reich of all machines, raw materials, and workers that might be useful to the German economy; the stripping of Polish agriculture and industry of everything but the bare essentials; the closing of high schools, technical schools, and universities to keep a Polish intelligentsia from emerging. "Poland," Frank reported, "will be handled as a colony, the Poles will be the slaves of the Great German World Empire." [74] Poland was to be turned into a purely agrarian country. Himmler, speaking to his SS officers, said:

> Very frequently a member of the Waffen SS thinks about the deportation of the people here . . . Exactly the same thing happened in Poland in weather 40° below zero, where we had to haul away thousands, tens of thousands, a hundred thousand; where we had to have the toughness—you should hear this and also forget it again—to shoot thousands of leading Poles.[75]

Polish and Russian workers wore on their sleeves an identification patch with an "O" for *Ostarbeiter* (Eastern worker), and they were ordered to be as completely separated as possible from the Germans as though they had some incurable disease that could be communicated by touch or by sight.* [76] Even in the case of "special treatment" there were particular regulations for Eastern workers who tried to escape. They were to be hanged where other prisoners could see what happened to them. The Gestapo enjoined functionaries on February 3, 1943, to see to it that Eastern workers did not use the railroads—if they needed to see one another, exchanges should be arranged so they could work at the same place. In general, the workers were to use the railroads only to go to the hospital or to visit a doctor in a neighboring village; in such cases they must be accompanied by a German.[77]

---

* Only in the summer of 1944 did Himmler give permission to those Eastern workers who were performing well for the Germans to wear a different kind of patch—one with a sunflower on it (BDC).

Eastern women were not supposed to bear children; a Gestapo report of September 4, 1944, said that in Franken the increase in foreign births was becoming dangerous and the only way to deal with the situation was abortions. The father was to be disclosed (presumably for punitive measures) and a form was made available with which the woman could authorize the operation.* [78]

Sauckel objected to none of this. All he wanted was a work force. One of his earliest decrees, on May 7, 1942, declared that accommodations must be models of order and cleanliness and hygiene to convince the workers of German superiority, skill, justice, and integrity. New bed linen, however, since supplies were short, could be ordered by the factories only in exceptional cases and then only for women. But the forced laborers could all save for hypothetical future expenditures even if they had no claim to any free time.[79] A few weeks later he sent a decree to the German plant managers:

> Eastern workers must be treated decently. No unnecessary suffering is to be inflicted aside from what is caused by war shortages and no unnecessary harshness is to be permitted. Complaints are to be carefully investigated . . . It is not necessary to separate families. The workers are to be paid according to the decisions on the Eastern workers . . .[80]

On January 6, 1943 he told 800 of his labor recruiters that the work program should be the best life insurance for the foreign worker.[81]

He told the Gauleiters on October 6, 1942, "Beaten, half-starved and dead Russians do not supply us with coal and are entirely useless for iron and steel production . . . They are an immense burden to our people and a scandal in the eyes of the world." [82] And addressing the Eastern workers themselves he said:

> If you do your duty then the German Reich will be your helper. You will be treated in a way that is consistent with how you conduct yourselves . . . Since your relatives at home receive financial support and you get free meals and lodging you get correspondingly less wages. From these no tax or other deductions are to be paid.[83]

A brochure distributed to Eastern workers told them:

> The Fuehrer of the Great German Reich and his incomparable victorious army have freed you from an insane and criminal bolshevism. That is why you have come to Germany to show your gratitude in a practical form. The Fuehrer of the Great German Reich and the Reichmarschall of the Great German Reich and head of the Four-Year Plan have therefore in their great kindness and humane view of my report on your willingness to work decided to increase your wages. Food may be obtained with this

* Pregnancies of foreign women workers were frequent; of 677 examined in December, 1942, eleven were found to be certainly pregnant and two were likely so (*TWC*, Krupp, IX, p. 895, NIK 9301).

increase; savings are possible, letters will be allowed, as well as papers and radios and films and such. . . . Work well and see to it that your fellow workers do this too. If you tolerate bad elements among you and bad work, you endanger the privileges given you. Remember that the German people have undertaken a heroic and mighty battle for the freedom of mankind. . . . remember you get the same food as the German people and in the same amounts. So big-hearted have their leaders and the German people shown themselves, you must show that you are worthy of them. Be industrious and above all follow orders . . . be courteous and responsive to your superiors.[84]

In the spring of 1943, in an address he was preparing for his co-workers, Sauckel wrote:

> Payment is to be made according to work done. There is to be no grossness or bad manners . . . The foreign worker should feel it is in his deepest interest to work for Germany . . . There should be no arbitrary decisions, no unnecessary harshness, rudeness, or insults when you deal with these workers. This is completely unworthy of the German official and employee . . . Written in a plane over Russian territory, April 20, 1943.[85]

These were Sauckel's directives, and this was his defense at Nuremberg.* But the realities of the work camps and the conditions under which thousands of the forced laborers lived were something else again.

It was, however, the German (not the foreign) accounts of actual conditions that were the most devastating answer to Sauckel's mild directives. Gestapo reports were matter of fact. They were meant merely to give information so steps could be taken for greater security; they had nothing of course to suggest, as had Sauckel, for the welfare of the workers. These reports tell of Russian workers rubbing the leaves of a plant called *Hahnenfuss* (crow foot) on their skins to work up a blister as big as a hazelnut which would then be rubbed with salt and wash powder until it was infected. Others drank salt water to make their feet swell, and some even chopped off their fingers. One man amputated both his hands by placing them on the railroad tracks before an oncoming train; the Gestapo report indignantly declared this to be "work sabotage," and the writer recommended that such people be sent to a concentration camp and on no account allowed to go back to Russia and thus inform their countrymen remaining in Germany how they could get out of their jobs.† [86]

Sauckel was found guilty on two counts: of having committed war crimes and crimes against humanity. Nevertheless, the German policy was not wholly different from that of the Allies after they captured millions of German

---

* Sauckel's directives were often repeated by an agency such as the German Labor Front, which declared too that prisoners were to be treated "sternly but justly."

† The Gestapo also objected to the influence of the émigré Russians on the workers, reporting that they brought to the workers newspapers and propaganda in favor of a greater Russia. These émigrés, said the Gestapo report, were of course against the Communists but they wanted no more than a change of management (August 3, 1942, BDC).

soldiers and occupied the country. The Allies were, however, inflicting punishment as a retaliation for the damage and atrocities that had been committed by the Third Reich, and even the first German directives—before retaliation could be thought of—had gone beyond what had previously been regarded as consonant with military or international law. Requisitions, the German directives stated, could be made not only for the armed forces (which international law countenanced) but for general, domestic needs.[87] German lawyers would later argue before American tribunals (I. G. Farben, Krupp cases) that forced labor too was not a wide departure from what had long been regarded as the traditional obligations of the vanquished to the victor. Germany or any occupying power had the right during the war to make use of local labor; she had the duty in fact to provide the means of livelihood of the population, and it made no substantial difference if such work was done in Germany or in the occupied country provided the workers were decently treated. Furthermore, they argued, it was an impossible incongruity for the population of a defeated France, for example, to live at ease while the Germans were fighting on behalf of Europe against bolshevism. If Germany had the obligation to see that the French were well fed, the French people had the obligation to work.*

In this century forced labor has been a widespread phenomenon both in the domestic affairs of countries like Nazi Germany and Soviet Russia and as an aftermath of war. In 1946 General Clay ordered the registration in the American Zone of Germany of all persons capable of work between the ages of fourteen to sixty-five for men and fifteen to fifty for women. "All persons incapable of work because of illness, disability, etc., must present to the labor office proof of incapacity. The labor office is empowered to direct compulsory labor when necessary."† [88] And as one of the German lawyers in a later trial in Nuremberg (the Flick case) pointed out, the Allies had stated in 1943 their intention of using forced workers outside Germany after the war, and not only did they express the intention but they carried it out. Soviet Russia took from German territory and from among the prisoners of war hundreds of thousands, even millions, of forced laborers (it was in part at least by such labor that Stalingrad was rebuilt and the Soviet rocket program developed). Not only Russia made use of such labor. France was given hundreds of thousands of German prisoners of war

* The President of the Court, expressing in his guarded fashion the traditional view, said in the course of Speer's trial that it made little or no difference where a man was forced to work; the point was that he was coerced. "If they were forced to work there [France] it is just as illegal as if they had been brought to Germany to be forced to work. At least, that is the suggestion that is made by the prosecution" (N XVI, p. 462).

† Under Allied Control Law No. 3 of February 17, 1946, German males from fourteen to sixty-five and women from fifteen to fifty were subject to compulsory labor; the penalty for disobedience was imprisonment and having their ration cards taken away, a penalty that the International Military Tribunal declared inhuman when it was inflicted by the Germans.

captured by the Americans, and their physical condition became so bad that American Army authorities themselves protested. In England and in the United States, too, German prisoners of war were being put to work long after the surrender, and in Russia thousands of them worked until the mid-1950's.

At the time the Flick trial was held in April, 1947,* the Russians were still holding more than two and a half million German prisoners, many of whom were being used at hard labor, and the Soviet Union had deported thousands of German civilians from the east zone of Germany for the same purpose. Members of Parliament and others among the Allied nationals called this practice "utterly wrong," but it nevertheless continued years after the Nuremberg trials were over.

It is undoubtedly true that what Sauckel and his goon squads did was substantially different from the practices of Britain and the United States. The sudden razzias resulting in the ruthless deportation of the people caught in raids, the transporting of workers in chains to the Reich, the setting up of factories in Mauthausen and Buchenwald, where human skeletons worked for some of the most respectable firms in German industry, to say nothing of the scale of the operations and the length of time they lasted, required a National Socialist or similar totalitarian *Weltanschauung*. Nevertheless, ideological convictions had been important on both sides; the Nazis saw the war primarily as one of naked survival with no humanitarian or legal considerations applying to the Russians. The Allies held the Germans responsible for starting and waging an illegal war in an illegal fashion; the German people therefore had the obligation to repair some of the damage they had wantonly caused and to expiate their own crime of using forced labor.

Sauckel, who had promised to carry out Hitler's orders with "fanatical devotion," had done precisely that, and he, no doubt unwillingly, had been the indirect cause of the deaths of thousands of people and the humiliation and suffering of additional hundreds of thousands more. But he had tried to be more "correct" than he could be under the Nazi rules. On April 15, 1942, on behalf of the millions of Russian workers he declared: "The better nourished they are, the better they will perform." [89] As soon as he took office he sought higher wages for these laborers than Goering would concede (Sauckel wanted them to be able to earn half what the German workers received, and what they could not spend in their camps they could keep for savings accounts). Sauckel intended to recruit from 400,000 to 500,000 Russian women workers—volunteers as far as possible—for German household help, but he never succeeded in getting more than a fraction of them. Like Hitler, he was tender on the subject of German womanhood; he was

* One of the main charges against the officers of the Flick concern was that they had used slave labor.

convinced that German women deserved this household help, for he wanted them to be at home.*

Sauckel told his own staff that no promise should be made to foreign workers that could not be kept, but the demands made upon him were not to be met with pious wishes or humane sentiments. The workers had to be brought in and the measures needed to get them became increasingly severe in both the West and the East. In March, 1944, Sauckel wrote to Hitler that the German police were not numerous enough to deal with French workers who failed to appear when they were ordered to do so. A million workers were needed and if the present measures for obtaining them were inadequate, Germany would be forced to call up certain age classes or to conscript all French males as a military requisition.[90]

In that part of France outside the jurisdiction of military government, the arrangements for conscripting labor were made directly with Vichy, with Laval and his colleagues. Sauckel, Speer, and Laval met together in Paris, where Sauckel made the same speech he made in Belgium and the Reich and Holland, stressing that Germany was fighting the battle for European civilization and the least the rest of the Continent could do was to work for the common cause. Germany's enormous sacrifices were being ill requited by French workers who fled to the Maquis and by the police and officials who bore the responsibilities to supply them either lightly or not at all. Laval had to agree reluctantly that the death sentence could be inflicted on French officials who sabotaged the recruiting of labor.[91] But both he and Pétain fought a steady rearguard action against the German demands for more and more French workers to be produced no matter how. Only in July, 1944, did Pétain agree to raise the work week from forty to forty-eight hours inside France. A decree of September 4, 1942, of the Vichy Government required Frenchmen between the ages of eighteen to fifty to register for work if they were not already working more than thirty hours a week. On February 16, 1943, another decree was issued that young men between the ages of twenty-one and twenty-three were to be forced to work.[92] In 1944 French males between sixteen and sixty and women between eighteen and forty-five were declared liable for compulsory labor, and according to an agreement made between Sauckel and Marshal Pétain, women between fifteen and twenty-five were to be employed only where they lived.† [93] Despite

* No German women, Sauckel and Hitler had agreed, ought to be working in a factory in twenty years. Goebbels noted in his war diary on February 16, 1943, that Sauckel had come to see that his weak policy with regard to the use of German female labor had failed, but by the time Sauckel and Hitler were ready to conscript women it was too late. Goebbels said that out of 5,000 women called up in Berlin by Sauckel's bureau, only 200 reported for factory work (ED 83/1, IZG).

† Sauckel wrote to the Fuehrer on January 22, 1944, while he was still negotiating with the French authorities, that Marshal Pétain had agreed to women between the ages of fifteen and twenty-five being forced to work, but only in their own homes, and women from twenty-six to forty-five were to work in France but were not to be sent to Germany. The actual law, however, did not include the work service of girls from fifteen to eighteen.

innumerable evasions and the tacit or active help of many French officials, including police, in aiding escapes, in the course of the war 738,000 French men and women were forced to work for Germany in the blocked French factories and 875,952 worked in factories in Germany, in addition to almost one million prisoners of war.*[94]

Caught as he was between the demands of the war machine and points of view as wide apart as those of Kesselring and Himmler, Sauckel used whatever methods came to hand to get his quotas. The carrot and stick was his rough formula: cajolments, promises of rewards for work well done, but when these failed, clubs, bayonets, and the lashes of his recruiters. As increasing numbers slipped away from the transports, he ordered handcuffs to be used—but Sauckel said that their use should be as unobtrusive as possible. After Stalingrad, the stick had to take the place of the carrot.

He worked on a colossal scale. In July, 1942, when accurate figures were available, 5,124,000 workers from the occupied countries were known to be working in Germany. At the end of the war, when figures became unreliable, there were still some five million there; from seven to ten million in all had been brought to the Reich. Some of them, including prisoners of war, had managed to return home, and thousands had died in transports and in Germany.[95]

From the documents—the orders and speeches and memoranda he wrote at the time—it appears that on the whole Sauckel's defense at Nuremberg was honest. He had wanted his workers treated decently enough both on humanitarian grounds and because they could work better for the Reich and its victory. But the directives he received from the always starving industrial apparatus, from the Central Planning Commission, from Himmler, and from Hitler left him with the sole problem of bringing in millions of workers—and if they could not be recruited one way, obviously others had to be used. The legality or "correctness" of the German conscription of foreign labor and the treatment of the subjugated nations and peoples as the plundered source of supply never troubled Sauckel. His unconditional devotion to the Fuehrer, his aversion to any kind of intellectual effort (he never read a book, he said at Nuremberg), his acceptance of every Nazi dogma left him without a doubt of the justice of all he was told to do. It led him at Nuremberg to say his conscience was clear or at least that it had been at the time he was operating the greatest slave trade in history. Afterward, at Nuremberg, he said he had been appalled at the evidence brought to light at the trial; he bowed his head before the victims, he told his judges. But at the time it simply never occurred to him that what he was doing was not necessary or legal—he only wanted it done as humanely as possible.

* German sources said that in 1942 some 400,000 French had volunteered for work in Germany but that in two "actions" in 1943 after the defection of Italy, only 44,600 Frenchmen had been obtained of the sought-for 900,000 (NCA, Supp. A, 1764-PS, p. 402).

He was found guilty of having committed crimes against humanity and war crimes and was sentenced to be hanged. The death penalty might be considered out of proportion to his responsibility in the light of what the State demanded of him in time of war and of what the later practices of the victorious countries would be. In any event none of the men responsible for the same or similar decisions in the Allied camp was ever tried, although the number of forced laborers they had working for them would reach the millions too. In the case of the English and the Americans, the working prisoners in their hands were well fed and well taken care of; in the case of the Russians and the French, the treatment could be abominable. True, what they did might be defended under the doctrine of tu quoque, but if so, this was a defense the Germans were permitted only once in the Nuremberg trial—in the case of submarine warfare—and everywhere else it was barred.

NOTES

1. N XVI, p. 448.
2. N XLI, Speer-18, teletype to Bormann of September 15, 1944, pp. 417–20.
3. N XVI, p. 486.
4. *Ibid.*, p. 495.
5. *Ibid.*, p. 430.
6. *Ibid.*, p. 497. N XLI, Speer-23, pp. 420–25.
7. N XVI, p. 500.
8. N XLI, Speer-24, pp. 425–29.
9. *Ibid.*, Speer-28, Speer-29, pp. 433–37.
10. *Ibid.*, Speer-30, pp. 437–38.
11. N XVI, p. 435.
12. N III, p. 455.
13. N V, p. 505.
14. N XVI, pp. 471–74, 517–18. N XLI, pp. 408–16.
15. N III, pp. 464–65.
16. N XVI, p. 474.
17. *Ibid.*, p. 527.
18. N III, pp. 461–62.
19. MA 328 (IZG).
20. R 3, Bureau Min. Speer 2/1 (Bundesarchiv Koblenz).
21. *Ibid.*, Speer 6/3.
22. *Ibid.*, Speer 1/11.
23. *Ibid.*, Speer 11/1.
24. *Ibid.*, Speer 6/3.
25. *Ibid.*, Speer 12/2.
26. *Ibid.*, Speer 11/1.
27. *Ibid.*, Speer 6/1.
28. *Ibid.*, Speer 3/1.

29. *Ibid.,* Speer 2/1.
30. *Ibid.,* Speer 5/2, letter to Sauckel of July 14, 1944.
31. *Ibid.,* Speer 11/1.
32. N XVI, p. 586.
33. *Ibid.,* p. 570.
34. *Ibid.,* p. 546.
35. 3967-PS (IZG).
36. N III, p. 454.
37. *Ibid.,* 1903-PS, p. 470.
38. N VIII, pp. 142–43.
39. Sauckel Fragebogen (BDC).
40. MA 135 (IZG).
41. Sauckel interrogation of September 20, 1945 (IZG).
42. N V, p. 391.
43. G. Schmundt, "*Bericht ueber die Besprechung Hitlers am 23. Mai 1939,*" in *Ausgewaehlte Dokumente zur Geschichte des Nationalsozialismus 1933–45* (Bielefeld: Verlag Neue Gesellschaft, 1961).
44. N XXVII, 1519-PS, pp. 273–83.
45. NG 848 (IZG).
46. N XXV, 016-PS, p. 69.
47. *TWC,* Vol. VII, p. 58.
48. NO 3470 (IZG).
49. N XVIII, RF-22, p. 497. NCA, Supp. B, p. 731.
50. *NCA* V, 2613-PS, p. 336.
51. N XXXVI, 410-EC, pp. 482–83.
52. N III, R-103, p. 448.
53. MA 303, 589710 (IZG).
54. 501 VC 103, p. 151 (Nuremberg Staatsarchiv).
55. N XXVII, 1739-PS, p. 594.
56. N XIV, p. 632.
57. NG 1316 (IZG).
58. N III, 3010-PS, p. 421.
59. N XXXVIII, RF-15, pp. 500–3.
60. *NCA* VII, L-172, p. 961.
61. *NCA* VI, 3819-PS, pp. 767–69.
62. MA 316, Himmler files (IZG).
63. *TWC,* Vol. VIII, p. 1051.
64. N III, p. 484.
65. *Ibid.,* p. 422.
66. *NCA* III, 054-PS, pp. 90–99.
67. N V, 633-PS, p. 511.
68. N XV, Sauckel-47, p. 268.
69. N III, affidavit of Dr. Wilhelm Jaeger, p. 442.
70. *Ibid.,* 068-EC, pp. 449-51. N XXXVI, 068-EC, pp. 132–35.
71. *Ibid.*
72. *Ibid.*
73. N XV, p. 163.
74. N XXXVI, 344-EC, p. 329.

75. *NCA* IV, 1918-PS, September 7, 1940, p. 553.
76. *NCA* V, 3040-PS, pp. 744–56.
77. Gestapo reports (BDC).
78. *Ibid.*
79. *NCA* V, 3044-PS, pp. 756–64.
80. *N* XLI, Sauckel-16, pp. 218–19.
81. *Ibid.*, Sauckel-82, pp. 225–28.
82. EC-316 (IZG).
83. *N* XLI, Sauckel-16, p. 222.
84. Foreign Workers, Sauckel Merkblatt No. 1 (BDC).
85. *N* XLI, Sauckel-84, pp. 228–40.
86. Gestapo reports, September 1942 (BDC).
87. *NCA* VII, ECH-10, pp. 630–31.
88. *Manpower* (Office of the Military Governor, January, 1946), pp. 3–5.
89. *N* XXXVI, p. 312.
90. *NCA* VI, 3819-PS, pp. 760–72.
91. *N* V, p. 504.
92. MA 123, 98176 (IZG).
93. *N* V, p. 494.
94. *N* V, p. 505.
95. *N* V, pp. 128–29.

13

The Propagandist

"THIS IS HANS FRITZSCHE"

Nazi propaganda had been a powerful instrument for the schooling of the German people in the doctrines of the new order and for waging the war, but its chief was dead. Goebbels had died in the Fuehrer bunker in Berlin by his own hand; his wife had killed herself together with their six children because a world without the Fuehrer and National Socialism seemed to her as threatening and impossible to live in as the terrible wasteland Goebbels had helped to produce for the Jews. Goebbels and his family were among the last victims of his own fluent oratory and fixed ideas, in which he believed with all the energy of his wiry, misshapen body and twisted mind. With his death the Allies were put to it to find a substitute. Hans Fritzsche, Chief of German broadcasting, made captive in Berlin by the Russians, seemed on the face of it a likely one. He had tried to surrender what was left of Berlin to General Zhukov—he had remained a man of importance until the very end.

His broadcasts, beginning *"Hier spricht Hans Fritzsche,"* were known to every German and to thousands of foreigners, for Fritzsche spoke regularly on the radio network of the Greater Germany. He had been a commentator on political events since Papen was Chancellor in 1932. He was the author of a large number of books and articles, all of them dedicated to convincing the German people that what Hitler decreed expressed their own will and purpose and was the only possible decision. A pleasant-looking man of medium size, with regular features and brown hair—a convincing pitchman— he would have made an excellent television commentator.

525

In the view of some among the Allied prosecutors, the German people were merely the passive instrument on which the skilled Party propagandists had played to produce calculated results. In the view of others—of the French particularly—the German people had been the willing collaborators in their own undoing and had needed no propaganda, only instructions. The Russians, however, looked on propaganda in the same way the National Socialists did, as an essential part of the education and administration of a country. They took it for granted as one of the primary instruments at the disposal of a state. They thought Fritzsche and his collaborators had used it only too well in preparing and waging the war. Hitler had written in *Mein Kampf*: "Propaganda is a truly terrible weapon in the hands of the expert." They regarded Fritzsche as an expert.

The Russians treated Fritzsche relatively well, as they did Raeder, with whom he was flown from Moscow to Berlin. They did not harm him physically, although they subjected him to a hunger cure in the Lubjanka prison, where he was held in solitary confinement. They even gave him books to keep in his cell; he was, however, unable to read them since they took away his glasses. They questioned him closely and then gave him the protocol of his interrogation to sign that put in his mouth exactly the same ready-made phrases other German prisoners who were being held by them were alleged to have used. What they accused him of was essentially no different from what the Western Allies alleged he had done: he had incited the Germans to wage war against other countries and races and to commit war crimes and crimes against humanity. In addition, from the point of view of the Western Allies, Fritzsche had sinned against the truth as well as against the German people and against them. He had vilified the Jews and he had lied to incite the Germans in their criminal acts, sometimes in grotesque fashion, as when he declared in repeated broadcasts that the British themselves had sunk the *Athenia*. Fritzsche had taken a leading part in the criminal Nazi conspiracy and made its successes possible.

The Russian view of his misdeeds was more concentrated. Since neither war nor peace can be waged without propaganda, and Fritzsche was one of the key people in the German propaganda *apparat*, he was clearly guilty of the charges against him and he should now take part, in the Soviet view, in the propaganda case against him and in his own undoing. The Chief Soviet Prosecutor, General Rudenko, following this tactic, offered him an opportunity for giving some of the most telling answers the defendants made in the course of the trial. Rudenko asked Fritzsche how long he had known about the planned attack on Russia. "Five or six hours before," Fritzsche answered. Then the following exchange took place:

> RUDENKO: "You will now be handed document USSR-493. It is your radio speech in connection with the aggression against Poland. . . . Have you acquainted yourself with this document?"
> FRITZSCHE: "Yes, indeed."

RUDENKO: "You do not deny that on 29 August 1939 you made this speech?"

FRITZSCHE: "No, I do not deny that. I should just like to refer to the fact——"

RUDENKO: "Excuse me. Please answer my question first and give your explanations later. This was on 29 August? You do not deny it. I am asking you, did you yourself believe in these explanations of unavoidable war with Poland? Did you yourself believe this at that moment?"

FRITZSCHE: "Whether at that moment I considered a war unavoidable, that I am not in a position to tell you. But I am able to tell you one thing: I did not believe that Germany was to blame. That if this tension should lead to a war——"

RUDENKO: "That is enough."

FRITZSCHE: "I ask to be allowed to add——"

RUDENKO: "But please be brief."

THE PRESIDENT: "General Rudenko, let the man answer."

RUDENKO: "If you please."

FRITZSCHE: "At that time it was a matter of great satisfaction to me that in the weeks that followed I could see from the Soviet press that Soviet Russia and its Government shared the German opinion of the question of war guilt in this case."

RUDENKO: "I believe it is not the time to discuss this now nor did I ask for explanations on this subject. You did not answer my question, but let us pass on to another question." [1]

The Soviet prosecutors in such cases were used to more docile witnesses who either would not bring up such embarrassing matters or could be shouted down if by any chance they tried to. At another point in his cross-examination General Rudenko demanded that Fritzsche admit that the activity of German propaganda was against the church (Nuremberg presented the first spectacle since 1917 of Soviet prosecutors concerning themselves with the heinousness of antireligious policies). The crime, however, was part of the indictment against Fritzsche and his codefendants which read:

> The Nazi conspirators, by promoting beliefs and practices incompatible with Christian teaching, sought to subvert the influence of the churches over the people and in particular over the youth of Germany. They avowed their aim to eliminate the Christian churches in Germany and sought to substitute therefor Nazi institutions and Nazi beliefs, and pursued a program of persecution of priests, clergy and members of monastic orders whom they deemed opposed to their purposes, and confiscated church property.[2]

Fritzsche denied that the official propaganda line had sought to persecute the churches but, he said, it was true of the unofficial Party propaganda. His answer was equivocal. National Socialist leaders and dogmas were basically uncompromisingly antireligious (one of the charges Goering had made to the Fuehrer against Raeder was that he went to church), and Hitler told Goebbels once the war was over he would deal finally with the churches.[3]

Fritzsche was correct insofar as the radio and press did not indulge in a campaign of antireligious polemics, as was the case in Soviet Russia.

Rudenko's cross-examination was in the grandiose manner peculiar to Soviet prosecutors who were used to having their witnesses where they wanted them:

> RUDENKO: "Of course you are aware that in the OKW there was a special section for propaganda which was subordinate directly to defendant Jodl."
>
> FRITZSCHE: "That was known to me, but you are mistaken if you are under the impression that the department was under defendant Jodl. It was under the jurisdiction of General von Wedel——"
>
> RUDENKO: "Very well. I do not wish to deal with this subject any longer." [4]

The Soviet prosecutors often had a bad time at Nuremberg. In the courtroom they paid little attention to what had been asked before by other Allied prosecutors and repeated questions that had already been fully answered by a defendant. They seemed always to be in unfamiliar legal territory; a trial for them was a piece of propaganda, nothing more. The task of the court was to provide a background and to publicize the self-condemnations of the accused. In case after case they returned doggedly to the only formula they knew: get the confession of the accused acknowledged in open court. The President again and again pointed out to the Russians that they were going over ground that had been well covered a short time before. The Russian prosecutors were keyed to Moscow standards and no doubt to the higher Moscow scrutiny of the trial record—their superiors would concern themselves with what they had said, not with the legal points made by the Western Allies.

In one hearing before the trial started, Soviet Colonel Liatscheff, who had interrogated Fritzsche in the Lubjanka prison and then accompanied him to Nuremberg, again examined him. This latter interrogation took place in the presence of representatives of the Western powers and a battery of translators. Liatscheff, according to an account Fritzsche wrote later, had brought with him the full German text of Fritzsche's radio speeches, which the Russians had recorded. The defense was always unable to get a copy of this document, for the Russians flatly denied they had the text when Fritzsche's lawyer asked for it. The defense had to content itself with a partial transcript of Fritzsche's talks made by the British. It is not possible to say whether in fact Liatscheff had all the speeches; he did read from the text of one broadcast made just before the end of the war and accused Fritzsche of having tried to recruit on behalf of the Werewolves, the bands of guerrilla fighters Himmler and Bormann planned to raise. The groups were to be composed mostly of teen-age boys and girls and were to destroy military installations and murder Allied troops when they occupied German territory. Fritzsche denied the accusation, but he added that the Allies could scarcely call the Werewolves criminal when they so highly prized the heroic deeds of the partisans and the Maquis; he had made no attempt to recruit Werewolves but merely made a propaganda case of this double-talk of the Allies. But he had signed in Moscow a statement saying he had called on the population to murder the soldiers and officers of the victorious armies and to commit acts of sabotage.[5]

Colonel Liatscheff had shown him his signature, as General Rudenko would do later in the courtroom, on a protocol of his hearings in Moscow. And in the interrogation room at Nuremberg, Fritzsche wrote later, he could say something that was not permitted him in the courtroom: he said he had told Colonel Liatscheff not only that the protocol was wrong from start to finish and none of the questions had been asked and none of the answers given in the form the colonel had them, but that he had signed so that the three-man tribunal that met twice a month in Moscow and had the right to pronounce death without the accused being heard in his own defense could immediately sentence him to death.* He had been starved and endlessly interrogated; he saw no prospect of a trial and by signing he thought he could get peace even if it was of the grave.[6]

He repeated his charges, although in another context, in the courtroom. General Rudenko again read to him what he had allegedly written in Moscow:

RUDENKO [reading]: " 'During a long time I was one of the leaders of German propaganda . . . I must say that Goebbels valued me as a convinced National Socialist and a capable journalist so that I was considered his confidential aide in the German propaganda machine.' Is that correct?"

FRITZSCHE: "Mr. Prosecutor, that is not correct. I know that I have signed this report but at the very moment I signed it in Moscow I stated: 'You can do what you like with this record . . .' I state that not a single one of the questions contained in this report was put to me in that same form and I go on to declare that not a single one of the answers in that record was given by me in that form and I signed it for reasons which I will explain to you in detail if you want me to."

RUDENKO: "You therefore do not confirm these statements?"

FRITZSCHE: "No, only the signature is true."

RUDENKO: "All right, let us say only the signature is true."

THE PRESIDENT: "One moment. What is it you are saying, Defendant? Are you saying that you did not sign this document or that you did?"

FRITZSCHE: "Mr. President, I signed the document, although its contents did not correspond with my own statements."

THE PRESIDENT: "Why did you do that?"

FRITZSCHE: "I gave that signature after very solitary confinement which lasted for several months; and I wrote that signature because one of my fellow prisoners, with whom I came into contact once, had told me that once every month a court was pronouncing sentences based merely on such

* Fritzsche testified before the court that the tribunal met once a month.

records and without interrogation; and I hoped that in this manner I would at least achieve being sentenced and thus terminate my confinement. So as not to be misunderstood I should like to emphasize that no force was used and that I was treated very humanely, even if my detention was very severe."

RUDENKO: "Very well. Of course, you never thought, Defendant Fritzsche, that after all you had done you would be sent to a sanatorium? It is obvious that you had to land in a prison and a prison is always a prison. This was just an aside, however." [7]

The discrepancies in what Fritzsche, writing after the Nuremberg trial, gave as his reasons for signing the protocols and what he told the court are characteristic. Fritzsche was glib and intelligent and he adapted himself readily to an audience. There is little question that the Russians provided the phrasing of many of his answers; the evidence for this lies in the verbal similarity which the Soviet prosecutors never bothered to disguise that runs through so many of the alleged answers given in their interrogations: "I helped the Fascist war criminals to attack their peace-loving victims" or "I did all I could to further the criminal plans of the Hitlerites," and so on. Such words were put in witnesses' mouths. When the former commander of the Sixth Army, Field Marshal Paulus, came from Russian imprisonment to testify at Nuremberg, he said in open court, speaking of the preparations for the campaign against Russia, "All these measures show that this was a matter of a criminal attack."

Fritzsche allegedly admitted in Moscow that he had prepared aggressions against Austria and Czechoslovakia and that he had tried to get the German people ready for world domination. In connection with the attacks on Belgium, Norway, Holland, and Denmark he said, "I ordered a similar calumnious propaganda . . . and attempted in this way to justify this or that aggressive action on the part of Germany." Admiral Hans Voss, who was held by the Russians, also signed a document saying Fritzsche had preached "that Germans were members of a superior race" and that he had tried to justify "what the German assassins had done in Poland and Russia." [8] Field Marshal Ferdinand Schoerner, also a captive in Moscow, signed a statement in which he allegedly said that Fritzsche's political activity led to "unleashing of the world war against democratic countries. . . . According to the criminal instructions of the Hitler government [he] consciously fed the people with lies." [9]

But Fritzsche was nevertheless putting a gloss on what he had actually written and said; the idea that he had wanted to die in a Soviet prison was a flourish, something perhaps to evoke sympathy from German readers, for he was to have far more difficulty convincing German courts of his innocence than he was the Allies at Nuremberg.

Fritzsche was one of the technicians of the National Socialists, and Goebbels had used him. A clear and persuasive speaker, Fritzsche was a propagandist who, like the Wehrmacht commentator General Kurt Dittmar, made a good impression on the more critical among his listeners, for he avoided as far as he could the extreme claims and unlikely optimism that caused many a German to switch off a broadcast, especially in the later years when the news was all bad. He, too, lost his resonance with sections of his audience. SD reports on his broadcasts in 1943 said mass audiences were no longer impressed by his ironical style; he was more popular among farmers than among city dwellers. But he had not much palatable news to comment on by 1943, and the SD said his style had been better adapted to the victories. They recommended to the Party chancellery that his talks be stopped for a while, but this was not done; Goebbels wanted him at his post.[10]

His full name was August Franz Anton Hans Fritzsche. He was born on April 21, 1900, in Bochum in Westphalia, the son of a post-office official. He attended the humanistic Gymnasia at Halle/Saale, Breslau, and Leipzig and fought in World War I as a private soldier. On his return from the war he studied economics, history, and philosophy at various universities without taking a degree. In 1923 he got a job as editor of the *Preussische Jahrbuecher*, a monthly review of cultural, political, and economic affairs appealing to a conservative middle-class public. After that he held a variety of posts, working successively for the *Weltpolitische Rundschau*, as editor of the *Telegraphen Union*, and then as editor in chief of the Wireless News Service, part of the Hugenberg empire of newspapers and motion pictures.* [11] In the late summer of 1932 he went to the German radio and a year later was made head of the Broadcasting Service. He joined the Party in May, 1933, some months after Hitler took power, but nothing in his broadcasts or writings changed very much from what he had written before. He told his Allied interrogators he had once after World War I thought of becoming a Communist but had fallen under the influence of Moeller van den Bruck and other nationalist, anti-Semitic writers who had turned him in the opposite direction.[12]

Fritzsche needed a hard and fast *Weltanschauung*; once he had that he could make everything plausible to himself and to his audience. He was always an able journalist who had no difficulty explaining to the German people what was going on, in the approved pattern and phraseology; he not only broadcast in the autumn of 1941 that the war against Russia was won, which was the official view of the Fuehrer, but gave his own most lucid reasons for the statement. He attacked the Allied leaders, as directed; he justified the German invasions; he followed the line at every critical point. Only a few times did he refuse to do something that Goebbels wanted done. One such case had to do with Austria. At the time Dollfuss was murdered, Fritzsche refused to transmit the optimistic reports coming

---

* The Hugenberg press had a nationalistic line not far removed from that of the Nazis.

out of Vienna from Theodor Habicht, one of the leading Austrian National Socialists, telling how the revolt was spreading, because he did not trust Habicht. Goebbels fired him for insubordination, but a few days later Fritzsche was reinstated because it turned out his estimate of the situation had been correct. Goebbels would have been in an embarrassing situation had the Habicht reports been transmitted in Germany.

Sober, convincing, literate, Fritzsche was the kind of man the National Socialists needed for a certain portion of their audience. Some people thought his voice sounded like Goebbels' and Goebbels was the chief and most articulate of the Nazi spellbinders aside from the Fuehrer himself. Fritzsche appealed to Germans who were not fanatical Party members and even to those who distrusted the run-of-the-mill expositors. His tactic was closer to that of the Wehrmacht communiqués than to the Party war drummers. Fritzsche said at Nuremberg that he had believed in Hitler's peaceful intentions; in the official reasons given for the attack on Poland, including the faked story of the Polish capture of the German radio stations at Gleiwitz; in what he had been told by the Navy about the impossibility of the *Athenia's* having been sunk by a German submarine, for the Admiralty said none had been in the neighborhood. And he convincingly passed along his own sentiments to the listeners who sat before the sixteen million German radio sets. In fact he was a flexible operator; he had worked for Hugenberg for years, but when Hugenberg lost out in the struggle for power, Fritzsche told his colleagues, "Now we'll hunt the old silver fox." This, at least, was the gossip about him, and it was undoubtedly not far from the truth.

Goebbels needed him and admired his work on the whole, but was sometimes critical. In his diary entry for February 17, 1942, Goebbels wrote:

> I am having some trouble with the press because it doesn't take to my suggestions as I should like. Fritzsche is altogether too much on the side of the press. Why the press ought to howl with joy at being given such material for commentary. Instead the bourgeois papers especially seem to be so tired of using this material that I could burst with anger.[13]

Fritzsche's irony, he thought, was not working on the masses. But he said this, too, late in the war when, as he well knew, no rhetoric could gloss over the bleak facts.[14]

From the beginning of their relationship the two men collaborated at arm's length. Fritzsche declared that he had never belonged to the circle of intimates Goebbels had around him; they met only officially. But it is clear that for many years they regarded one another highly. Fritzsche was working as head of the Wireless News Service in 1932, and when Goebbels took that over in May, 1933, he continued Fritzsche in his job and in addition made him head of the News Service in the Press Section of the Propaganda Ministry, the department that told the German newspapers what to print. Later Goebbels appointed him deputy and then head of the German Press Section, a position Fritzsche kept until 1942, when he left the Press Section and got the resounding title of Plenipotentiary for the Political Organization of the Greater German Radio, at the same time becoming chief of the Radio Division of the Propaganda Ministry.

When Goebbels in May, 1933, asked Fritzsche to stay on as head of the Wireless Service, he attached conditions which were brought to Fritzsche by emissaries, Horst Dressler-Andress, who was head of the Radio Division of the Party, and an assistant, Sadila-Mantau. Goebbels' conditions were three: first, that Fritzsche discharge all Jews; second, that he discharge all employees of the Wireless Service who did not immediately join the Party; and third, that he hire one of the men Goebbels had sent to him, Sadila-Mantau. Two of the conditions Fritzsche turned down; he only accepted the naming of Sadila-Mantau as an assistant. He told Goebbels that the Jews working for the Wireless Service had contracts and were, with the exception of one editor, in minor clerical positions; they must be given time to make other arrangements. Fritzsche told the court at Nuremberg that all the Jews employed by the Wireless Service had soon gotten other jobs in Germany or had emigrated and found jobs (the editor, for example, in Paris). He fired neither them nor the "Aryan" employees who did not want to be Party members; he either kept them on or helped them to find jobs. But his resistance was always circumspect; two secretaries who were Party members soon took the place of two old ones who with his help got other positions in less sensitive enterprises.

Fritzsche thought that Goebbels had taken a liking to him as early as 1928 because of a friendly article on National Socialism Fritzsche had written. But Goebbels objected in 1932 to an article by Fritzsche on the Potempa case, in which Fritzsche criticized Hitler for sending a telegram of sympathy to the five young Nazi hoodlums who had killed a Communist worker and had themselves been sentenced to death. Despite this lapse, Goebbels kept Fritzsche at this post in 1933 because the substance of what he had written was palatable enough even for a fanatic like the Propaganda Minister, who had few replacements of Fritzsche's caliber.

Fritzsche's anti-Semitism was of the stock variety. His broadcasts had a good many unfavorable references to Jews, but he detested Streicher and wanted to have *Der Stuermer* banned, for he thought it harmful to the German cause both inside and outside the Reich. He approached the subject of the Jews in much the same way his former chief Hugenberg did; they were both ardent nationalists who wanted to see a resurgent Germany equipped with a powerful army again, and they disliked the Jews, who were mainly represented in the Left-wing parties that were anti-nationalist and anti-Wehrmacht. It was not much of a step for him to formulate these ideas so that they would be acceptable to Goebbels as head of all German propaganda. Fritzsche maintained the same constant but relatively mild temperature of anti-Semitism throughout the period he served the Third Reich and beyond. In the account of the trial he wrote years after the war may be detected the same points of view that had animated his broadcasts. The Jews were still the enemy but, he said, their enmity was understandable.

Fritzsche had two main jobs in the Third Reich, one with the radio, the other with the press. Under him along with radio news broadcasting were the chief newspaper wire services that went to foreign countries: Transocean, Europapress, Fastservice (Eildienst), and the German News Service (Deutsches Nachrichtenbuero). In December, 1938, he became head of the German Press Section. This meant that he was responsible for some 2,300 daily newspapers, and these together with the Reich's magazines had to be tightly coordinated with the high policies enunciated by Goebbels on behalf of Hitler. Fritzsche was an ideal man for this job as he was for his radio assignment; he had worked for years for privately owned newspapers and not only knew the important writers but also, since he had convinced himself, knew how to persuade them to write in their best style in the new vein.

The National Socialists from the start tolerated no heterodox nonsense in cultural affairs. Every piece of information to be printed or broadcast and any means of communication with the public were carefully supervised. To accomplish this screening, Goebbels had organized the Reich Cultural Chamber under a law of September 22, 1933. The chamber consisted of seven departments: Music, the Plastic Arts, Theater, Writing, Press, Radio, and Film.

Walther Funk, one of the other defendants at Nuremberg, was head of the Press Division, until September, 1937, when he became Economics Minister. He was replaced by a professional journalist, Otto Dietrich, with whom Fritzsche was not to get along as well. They had different notions on how the news should be handled, especially when it began to be unpleasant. But before the war and in its early stages the relationship was tolerable to both. Dietrich was a formidable man, for he had the ear of the Fuehrer and regarded himself, Fritzsche thought, as Hitler's personal press chief. Even Goebbels had to deal gingerly with him. Like all those who got close to the throne, Dietrich was jealous of his prerogatives; he regarded the press as his province and he alone represented it to the Fuehrer. He was able to prevent the appointment Goebbels wanted to make of a press liaison officer at the Fuehrer's headquarters, and Goebbels both feared and mistrusted him. But Dietrich stayed at his job until March, 1945, when Goebbels, at last triumphant, said, "And he thought he could outplay me." [15] Together with a man from the Foreign Office, Dietrich met every day with Goebbels' representatives in the Propaganda Ministry. Out of these meetings he emerged with the daily theme (*Tagesparole*) for the newspapers. Goebbels got a copy of it; Fritzsche was told what it was, usually over the telephone. Fritzsche also attended Goebbels' daily staff conference or was given his directives over the telephone before calling the newspaper men together for their separate briefings. They were told what to emphasize and what to play down and were regularly given a list of subjects and names the Government did not want mentioned in the news.[16]

Between 150 and 250 representatives of the chief German papers were usually present at these briefings conducted by Fritzsche, and a still smaller group of 20 to 25 selected journalists met under Fritzsche's chairmanship for more intimate, behind-the-scenes sessions. The other papers either got ready-to-be-printed handouts from the Press Department or confidential written instructions of much the same kind given orally in the daily briefings. Weekly and monthly periodicals were given a more detailed information service. Thus the entire press, as Fritzsche said at Nuremberg, became a permanent part of the Propaganda Ministry. The *Tagesparole* was read slowly to the assembled group so everyone could write it down accurately, and it was always marked either secret or confidential; any mention of it in the press was forbidden. A breach of the rule would result in the culprit's being brought before a professional court that had the right to oust him. The press, to the last country newspaper, dutifully emphasized the *Tagesparole* in their editorials. The Authoritarian State, the Need for Living Space, the Leadership Principle, the Conspiracy of World Jewry, the Bolshevik Danger, the Plutocratic Democracies, the Soviet Union—all were praised or damned at the same time and according to the same principles.

After Fritzsche took over, the budget of the German Press Section went up ten times what it had been. The papers were told what they could publish, what they couldn't publish but could use as information, and what they were forbidden to publish. Not only were representatives of the Foreign Office present, but after the start of the war the High Command sent officers to provide additional background for the interpretation to be put on the news from the front. The press performed in virtual unison; at the time the Runciman mission was sent to Czechoslovakia it was told to play up the anti-German incidents in that country: the terrorization of the Sudetenlaender by the Czechs and how Slovaks were being kidnapped.[17] For a long period after January, 1934, when Hitler and Pilsudski made their nonaggression pact (*Verstaendigungspakt*), the press could print nothing attacking the Poles. Then in the spring of 1939 the ban was lifted and the anti-Polish campaign began. The press of the Reich could also be used as part of the elaborate camouflage needed to prepare the Russian campaign. Goebbels told the assembled newspaper men a few weeks before the invasion that some among them thought the Reich would attack Russia but the real aim was against England. "Please adapt your work accordingly," he said to them.[18]

The newsmen were also instructed in the shadings of what the Propaganda Ministry considered the true image of the Reich and its leader. Fritzsche told them on April 12, 1941, they could use the sentence which was going the rounds of the highest circles of Hitler idolators only in this fashion: "Adolf Hitler will go into history as one of the greatest military geniuses of all time." Even that phrasing would be damaging enough when the defeats started.

It was on the radio that Fritzsche made the reputation that brought him before the court at Nuremberg. He had spoken over the radio since 1932. First he had a weekly program of both domestic and foreign broadcasts, and with the mounting excitement at the start of the war he spoke every day. The daily broadcasts lasted for only a few months because Fritzsche was a very busy man with his unwieldly Press Section to manage, articles to write, and speeches to give. The talks dwindled to three, then two times, then once a week, and toward the end of the war they came at even greater intervals. Fritzsche was a spellbinder in the Goebbelian mold. He had the same self-assured, alternately biting and euphoric presentation as did Goebbels, and what he said was crystal clear even to a mass audience. Fritzsche's style set him off sharply from most of the press and radio commentary, which was filled with the Party clichés, sentimentalities, and turgid writing to which this generation of revolutionary Germans had become accustomed.

His task was a good deal easier at the start of the war, when the speed and extent of the Wehrmacht victories astonished not only the outside world but the High Command and the German people themselves. Fritzsche could let himself go with the rhetoric and the heavy sarcasm so beloved by Nazi speakers, beginning with Hitler and going down through the ranks of the paragraph writers of the *Voelkischer Beobachter*. After the defeat of France, Fritzsche announced that there was a rumor abroad that British parachutists had landed in Italy. This, said Fritzsche, the Germans found most amusing. The Fuehrer had asked the British to let him know please when they intended to come, at which time he would withdraw the German troops so that the British could land safely. This motif was paralleled by the recurrent playing on the radio and in the movies of the overly optimistic British song "We'll Hang Our Washing on the Siegfried Line."

Fritzsche was all reasonableness in the early part of the war; he could often afford to be because the enemy gave him all openings. The German Navy and Air Force, Fritzsche said, would prevent the delivery of Lend-Lease shipments from the United States to the continent of Europe. Germany in fact was building a new Continent, free of the mutual hatreds which for centuries had been fanned by Britain.

On March 18, 1941, he told the German people:

> America's aid for Britain began with a speech, a speech by President Roosevelt which started off with the sentence that whatever he would have to say would be recorded by history, word for word. Well, it is always a rather dubious matter to want to interfere with the Muse of History or to attempt to guide her pen. It mostly happened that history paid no attention to the words which were whispered in her ear but that she entered the deeds which were achieved into her great book. . . . Roosevelt of course started from the assumption on which his Lend and Lease Bill also rests,

the assumption that the form of life of the young nations with an authoritarian government is nothing but the outcome of the tyranny of a handful of men. Roosevelt also silently assumed that the nations in question, that is to say particularly the German nation, had either been too weak to resist tyranny or that they light-heartedly followed some dictators or others only to destroy the culture of mankind and the achievements of civilization. The great sage of the New World knows of course full well that for instance the Fuehrer of the German people did not seize power as a dictator but that he took over when he had the absolute majority of the German people behind him—strictly according to the rules of the democratic game. A majority which after his advent to power grew until it became a unity . . ."

Fritzsche went on to remind his readers of the *Weltanschauung* that illuminated everything for National Socialists:

> But the crown of all wrongly applied Rooseveltian logic is the sentence: "There never was a race and never will be a race which can serve the rest of mankind as a master." Here, too, we can only applaud Mr. Roosevelt. Precisely because there is no race which can be the master of the rest of mankind, we Germans have taken the liberty of breaking the domination of Jewry and of its capital in Germany, of Jewry which believed itself to have inherited the crown of secret world domination.

And, he added, returning to prosaic political affairs, when Roosevelt talked about political freedom he should make it a point to see the Indian ministers who were being held in British prisons.[19]

When Germany invaded Yugoslavia, Fritzsche said that this action was the result of the British *va banque* policy of risk and lose everything on the turn of a card. Germany had reached the end of her patience with such reckless irresponsibility, and Adolf Hitler had decided to turn over the representation of German interests in Yugoslavia

> to that force which seems solely in a position to protect right and reason —the Wehrmacht. We are full of gratitude to the Fuehrer's farseeing policy which has anticipated all eventualities. It was the fatal mistake of our enemies that they had relied on precisely those émigrés who had failed in Germany, to be their experts on German problems and of course they had been wrongly informed. Germany had never asked the United States or Britain to change their form of government but these powers throw democratic principles overboard when they demand that the Reich change hers. The Germans had had such an unhappy experience with the freedom of the individual that they had decided to put into the hands of the Fuehrer all decisions to conquer and safeguard the freedom of the community.[20]

This was just the kind of thing German audiences loved to hear. It was pitched in the same key as the Fuehrer's oratory; it was beamed to a people who had been fearful of a general European war and its consequences and who had been unexpectedly reprieved by the miraculous swift victories that contrasted so marvelously with the murderous trench warfare of World War I. What Fritzsche said was the easier to swallow because it was washed down by the heady wine of the brilliant conquests.

Fritzsche's broadcasts before the war had also found a quick resonance. It was easy to explain to the German people the reasons for the reoccupation of the Rhineland, for the *Anschluss,* for Munich—as long as no war was involved. As the artificial power complex of Versailles disintegrated, as the Reich became a power again and Hitler won bloodless victory after victory, Fritzsche was not alone in his boundless admiration for the Fuehrer who had restored Germany's position in Europe. He could readily tell enthusiastic audiences of Germans as well as admiring foreigners that the genius of one man had accomplished what all the statesmen and generals of the Wilhelminian Reich and of the Weimar Republic had been powerless to do. Hitler's popularity in Germany was self-propelling. No one in German history had brought to the Reich so much territory and prestige, so many *Volksdeutsche,* as had Hitler in the space of five years, and all without the firing of a shot. The paper tigers of Versailles were torn to shreds; the millions of dead of World War I had not died in vain after all.

With the start of the Russian campaign Fritzsche's task became more difficult. There had not been time to prepare the German public for the attack, which had a bad association for Germans of all ranks. This was the two-front war that had defeated Germany in World War I; many of Hitler's closest advisers had argued against it. But Fritzsche for a time could continue to tell of dazzling victory after victory. In addition, he began to broadcast accounts of atrocities that with the exception of isolated incidents in the Polish campaign had been hitherto lacking in the German reports. He needed now to add fear and hate—much more hate—to his mixture. His broadcasts told of the horrors German soldiers had to confront in Russia. He whipped up his audience with descriptions designed to justify Hitler's brutal orders and the high losses the German Army was beginning to suffer.

As early as July 5, 1941, he said over the radio:

> Even worse than the marks of the mental, economic, and social terror exercised by the Jewish commissars were those of physical terror which the German Army met along the road of its victory. . . . It was only the Fuehrer's decision to strike in time that saved our land from being overrun . . . A few hours before the fall of Lvov, Bolshevist agents, including women, gave vent to their hatred and fury against helpless Ukrainian prisoners. Intoxicated with bloodlust . . . these monsters fell upon their victims with machine guns, pistols, and knives. Nor was murder the worst of the atrocities perpetrated.[21]

The German propaganda company observers had seen these corpses.*

---

* Accompanying the German armies from the start of the war were uniformed cameramen along with reporters and other writers whose job it was to provide the films, photographs, and news stories for the home front.

Fritzsche did not invent them. There had been mass murders of Ukrainians who had been arrested by the NKVD on suspicion of anti-Soviet activity and who could not be evacuated before the Germans occupied the area. But the *Untermenschen* line had to be worked hard now because the German population despite the succession of brilliant victories was still disquieted. The Russian campaign had come as a shock; they had to be shown what horrors the omniscient Fuehrer had spared them and how unavoidable the war was. Fritzsche also pursued the main theme of the Fuehrer and of Streicher, speaking of

> this Jewish united front of the godless and the hypocrites, of the Communists and the fat moneybags, there the extremes touch; they are made of the same dirt. Maisky, the godless Russian Ambassador to London visits Saint Paul's . . . the Jew is master in the art of transformation, he uses economic liberalism that leads from the liberation of Jewish capitalism to the slavery of Jewish bolshevism. . . . Whatever the Moscow Jews invent is taken at its face value in England.[22]

German sentiment like that of all peoples' was fluid. Contrary to what Fritzsche had said in reply to the Roosevelt speech, Hitler had not come to power with a majority of the votes but with 37 per cent of them. And the show of unity was window dressing, as the plots against Hitler would demonstrate. The Fuehrer's popularity undoubtedly went up with the victories on the home front over unemployment, the retrieving of German prestige in the councils of Europe with rearmament and a decisive if primitive diplomacy, and the easy and easily justifiable conquests of Austria, the Sudetenland, and Memel. But the German people were afraid of war. Hitler noted how silent the Berliners had been when he had sent tanks through the city at the time of the Czech crisis, and what he saw disgusted him. Some of the chief propaganda devices fell flat, as both German and foreign observers reported; the *Kristallnacht* and other blatantly anti-Semitic demonstrations, too, had a poor echo among the German public.

What every propagandist has to deal with is the mixture of objective facts and the readiness of readers and hearers to accept loaded interpretations of them. The Russian campaign from the start was difficult to "sell." None other than Hitler had told the Germans of the folly of the leadership facing a two-front war in 1914, and now he willfully did what he had so long denounced. Fritzsche, like countless others, might have been convinced that this was a preventive war, that Hitler had struck just before the 150 Russian divisions mobilized on the German border marched; but the gnawing doubts of the necessity for the attack and of its success would not vanish. The propaganda had to turn now to the theme of a life-or-death struggle, playing up the horrors of the Jewish Bolshevik conspiracy and the kind of war it was waging, for the Fuehrer's orders to the generals to kill commissars in uniform without trial and to ignore the Hague and Geneva Conventions had to be justified. Kill or be killed became the unspoken daily parole behind the parole.

The one hope for keeping German morale at the high pitch it reached with the fall of France and the subsequent victories was the six-week war against Russia that Hitler announced would be his aim when he first talked to his generals about his decision to invade the Soviet Union. So powerful was his wishful thinking that the Fuehrer and the propaganda apparatus announced its fulfillment. On October 9, 1941, Fritzsche broadcast: "With the formations already encircled, [Marshal Semën] Timoshenko has sacrificed . . . the last remaining armies of full fighting strength of the total Soviet front. As the Reich Press Chief emphasized today, the military outcome is no longer doubtful." But this was the last claim of its kind the propaganda authorities would make. The German juggernaut, first slowed down by the autumnal rains and the mud, was caught in the sudden and early freeze of the Russian winter—the coldest in a hundred years. It was also caught in Hitler's decision to turn Guderian's tanks from the center and the attack on Moscow to the south and the great but indecisive victories at Kiev.

By the end of November Fritzsche was emphasizing not the battles but the wire-pulling behind the scenes. In late November he explained to his listeners: "While the clever Jews in Moscow and London always had something new and interesting—amusing combinations, peppery rumors—if they didn't report truthfully, they at least interpreted interestingly." Commenting on the renewal of the Anti-Comintern Pact, he came back to the main theme: ". . . plutocrats, democrats, and Jews started this war . . . The curtain has been blown aside . . . such a breath of wind became evident when the Jewish National Council was stupid enough to send a telegram to Mr. Roosevelt expressing the congratulations of Jewry on the outbreak of the war . . ." [23]

Two weeks after Pearl Harbor, Fritzsche turned again to the cause of all the trouble in the world—the Jew. The Germans had no stomach for war against the United States. In December, 1941, they had trouble enough on their hands with the Soviet forces and the Russian winter. No Japanese victories could compensate for the dread occasioned by the overwhelming coalition now ranged against the Reich and its allies. Fritzsche had hammered before on the theme of the world Jewish conspiracy; when United States forces had landed in Iceland, he had said this was evidence of it. Now he came close to what Streicher was writing in *Der Stuermer*:

> The fate of Jewry in Europe has turned out to be as unpleasant as the Fuehrer predicted it would be in the event of a European war. After the extension of the war instigated by Jews, this unpleasant fate may also spread to the New World, for you can hardly assume that the nations of the New World will pardon the Jews for the misery of which the nations of the Old World did not absolve them.[24]

Now the *Hauptmotiv* of his broadcasts became the fight the brave soldiers of the Allies were making on behalf of the Jews and the Bolsheviks, the alliance of the plutocratic democracies and the Communist hordes, all of them serving the world enemy. Interspersed was the praise of Hitler, which never flagged: "This one man's work and struggle which is at the same time the picture of the entire nation's work and struggle. . . . Truly I felt that destiny itself was speaking with the words of the Fuehrer." [25] These endless eulogies were interspersed with evidence of the threat that now hung over every German, not only from the Soviet Union but from the West as well. Fritzsche quoted Goebbels' editorial in the *Voelkischer Beobachter* of May 28, 1944, with its citations from the *Army Quarterly*: "Germany must be more desolate than the Sahara." And from the *News Chronicle*: "We are for destroying every living being in Germany: man, woman and child, bird and insect. We wouldn't let a blade of grass grow." And from H. G. Wells: "Treat the Germans like a noxious tribe of natives." From Raymond Clapper: "Terror and brutality are the best side of the air war." He quoted what he called an official report of the Church of England made on May 28, 1943: "It is a perverse view of Christianity to expect that civilians shouldn't be killed." He also cited the Archbishop of York, Cyrill Garbett, as having said in his pastoral letter of June 1943, "It is only a small evil to bombard German civilians." [26]

Fritzsche broadcast until the last hours of the war, and until then or very nearby he appears to have believed his own propaganda. When the British and Americans landed at Normandy, he told the German people this was the hour the German Army had been waiting for. The defenses had long been prepared; the German Army was ready to spring the trap. When the Allied bridgehead was won and consolidated, Fritzsche shifted to the acts of banditry committed behind their spearhead as bolshevism followed in their wake.[27] The tone grew increasingly shrill; he quoted the *Israelitisches Wochenblatt fuer die Schweiz*, which had made a survey of Jews in leading positions in the West, and he said that the Jews were ready to remove, by murder if necessary, people inconvenient to their cause. As the destruction of German cities from the Allied bombing attacks became more catastrophic, Fritzsche could only emphasize Allied air losses and the success of German defense; nor could he avoid telling of the major retreats in Russia. He preserved his reputation for candor by saying that it was true the German armies were not willingly giving up so much ground, but he also reminded his listeners how essential the earlier victories had been that now permitted them to wage the war so far from the homeland. Fritzsche was in the same fix as his listeners: they could hope together for more miracle weapons and for dissension among the Allies. Meanwhile Fritzsche could only tell them they had no alternative but to fight. "Hold out to the last," he said, and later the German courts would repeat these words to him that were connected with the senseless slaughter of thousands of soldiers and civilians, including children, drafted into the Army to prolong the war for a few weeks.

In 1942 Fritzsche joined the Sixth Army at Stalingrad for a few months as a member of a propaganda company in Infantry Division 389. He reported directly to General (later Field Marshal) Paulus and was deeply impressed by his resoluteness and qualities of command.* Fritzsche next saw Paulus in Nuremberg, where Paulus was brought by Soviet captors to testify against Keitel and Jodl and the German High Command. Fritzsche was still the expert, glib reporter; what he saw in Paulus was a man merely brainwashed by the Russians, not the commander who had been left with his Army by the Fuehrer to be destroyed because Hitler could not bring himself to admit his strategy had been wrong. Paulus was cross-examined by the German lawyers, who gave him the only opportunity he would have on either side of the Iron Curtain to give some indication of why he was testifying against his brother officers and his own past. Jodl's lawyer, Professor Exner, asked Paulus if he was teaching in the Moscow war college or whether he had another post in Moscow. Paulus answered "No" to both these questions. But that they were asked and that Paulus in answer to the direct examination of General Rudenko used the well-known and worn phrases common to those who had been interrogated often enough by the NKVD gave the courtroom the background. Paulus said in reply to Rudenko's question about the preparations for the attack on the Soviet Union in which he himself had taken part: "All these measures show that this was a matter of a criminal attack." Paulus remembered nothing in answer to Exner's questions of the massing of 155 Russian divisions on the German border, nor under the questioning of the counsel for OKW, Laternser, of the meeting on the Obersalzberg, where Hitler had given his partially convincing version of the Soviet menace.

In his account of the Nuremberg trial Fritzsche made much of these matters in justifying himself. Despite what he told the court and what he later wrote, Hitler had fought no preventive war but had without provocation jumped on the Soviet Union. The Russian Army had been caught flat-footed; for some hours it did not even have orders from Moscow to fire back. In spite of repeated warnings from many sources, including the British, Russian agents in Germany, and the Soviet master spy in Japan, Richard Sorge, Stalin would not budge from his fixed opinion that Hitler would not attack.[28] Russia was almost completely unprepared for the onslaught. Nor did Paulus need to be brainwashed to tell that the Fuehrer's stubborn pride had caused an entire German army to be lost when he refused to let Paulus break out from Stalingrad while there was time. Before the war's end, Paulus undoubtedly was given the full treatment by the NKVD and the propaganda apparatus, for he and many of his chief officers joined the Free Germany Committee and broadcast to the German troops, urging them to end the senseless struggle. But Fritzsche, even at the trial, was clinging

* Fritzsche was flown out of the Stalingrad front to take over his new post as Plenipotentiary for the Political Organization of the Greater German Radio.

to his own brand of propaganda, still thinking of the preventive war and the duplicities of the other side.

Fritzsche in his defense contrasted what he had said during the war with the remark an Allied commentator made on a film being shown in the courtroom at Nuremberg: "Here you see Germans laughing over hanged Yugoslavs." Never, Fritzsche said, had he tried to awaken hatred for a people; he had spoken strongly against governments and systems but he had not preached hatred. He had resisted the line adopted in high quarters that raged against the persons of Roosevelt and Churchill and Stalin and their chief advisers as well as against the systems they represented. He had in fact, he said in answer to the direct examination of his chief counsel, Dr. Fritz, collected anti-German caricatures and anti-German war films from World War I and presented them to audiences of journalists and radio speakers with a commentary of his own. What he had wanted to do was show what the untutored enemy thought of Germans and how unfair and absurd the caricatures were. These themes were very dear to the hearts of German patriots but were far removed from the frothings of the Party propagandists' attacks on the *Untermenschen* and dupes on the opposite side of the line. Fritzsche played heavily on the Allied demand for unconditional surrender, on the super-Versailles that would follow a new lost war, and once he wryly remarked to the court in this connection: "It does not behoove me today to make a comparison with reality." Fritz then asked him if he had not learned from the broadcasts of the Allies that their fight was directed not against the German people but against their leaders. Fritzsche answered, "On the contrary, I did not keep it from them, but repeatedly quoted it. However, I called it 'incredible.' For example, I once used the trick of quoting the wording of a medieval declaration of war in which it had already been said that a war was declared only on the King of France but that one wanted to bring freedom to the French people." He had never used the phrase "master race" and indeed said he had prohibited its use by the German radio and press. He thought that the term had been invented by a man who had been indicted at Nuremberg but who had escaped trial by hanging himself—Dr. Ley—and that it had been enormously, if silently, influential in the thinking of the SS. At any rate, he had not used it.* [29]

Fritzsche idealized himself at Nuremberg. He swore solemnly that he had never lied or committed a single falsification in the case of any serious questions of policy or of the conduct of the war, adding:

> How often I myself became the victim of a falsehood or a lie I cannot say after the revelations of this trial. The same is true, as far as I know, of all my fellow workers, but I do not by any means want to deny that I

---

* Actually the phrase appears for the most part in speeches or writings by Party leaders designed to impress the SS, police, and administrative forces in the East with the importance of their task. Fritzsche was too intelligent to have used it for a mass audience on the radio that was monitored by the Allies.

and my fellow workers selected news and quotations following a certain tendency. It is the curse of propaganda during war that one works only with black and white . . . But to my knowledge it is a mistake to believe that in the Propaganda Ministry thousands of little lies were hatched out. . . . If we had lied on a thousand small things, the enemy would have been able to deal with us more easily than was the case.[30]

What he wanted to do was to win the cooperation of the peoples Germany had invaded, so he was elaborately reasonable in attempting to show them why they ought to enjoy their captivity more than they did. In his somewhat inverted scale of values, the murder of Heydrich was a propaganda success for Germany because it was regarded in Germany, at least, as an outrage. The destruction of Lidice as a retaliation he called "a tremendous success for the Allies." Fritzsche explained to the people of the occupied countries how much Germany was doing for them, how industrial activity in their countries was rising, how supplies of food were being brought in from the Reich; he told them that schools were being opened or reopened and cities supplied despite the sabotage of the obtuse resistance. It was simply not true, he declared at Nuremberg, that the Germans had lived well while the occupied countries starved. The Reich had done what it could and had far-reaching plans for the future of its victims. Fritzsche had wanted a Magna Charta for Europe which would define the basic rights of the European nations. When Fritzsche returned from the front in 1942, Goebbels promised him the charter would be proclaimed. He had dreamed of a united Europe, of a union of the countries of the Continent with Germany on a basis of equality.[31]

When he used harsh words about the Russians, they were against the Soviet system, not against the Russian people. This is what he meant in a speech to which the prosecution referred as evidence of Fritzsche's incitements to hatred. In it he had declared, "In this battle in the East it is not one ideology fighting against another, not one political system against another, but culture, civilization, and human dignity have revolted against devilish principles of an underworld." [32] He talked often about the atrocities committed by the Russians and the horror with which the German soldiers had seen the evidences of them. He told his listeners that Moscow had agreed that the crimes had been committed but attempted to blame them on the Germans. And then in the courtroom at Nuremberg he reaffirmed much of what he had said during the war: ". . . the absolute cleanliness and honesty of the whole German conduct of the war. I still believe today that murder and violence and Sonderkommandos only clung like a foreign body, like a boil, to the morally sound body of the German people and their Armed Forces." [33]

He told the court he had known nothing of the removal of Jews from the occupied countries, although, he admitted, he had heard that certain individuals, both Jews and non-Jews, were being arrested. He also knew that millions of foreign laborers were working for the Reich, but he did not consider them slaves, for he "saw them daily walking about free on the streets of all the cities." He got a good many reports about these workers; all of them said they were treated in exactly the same fashion as Germans. He also got reports that the inferior status decreed for the Eastern workers at the beginning had been remedied, and he even got complaints from Germans that foreign workers were better treated than they. He often talked with these workers and said he had heard no special complaints from them. He never knew that some of them had come to Germany involuntarily; the most damaging reports that reached him said foreign workers had been given extravagant promises when they were recruited, and Fritzsche protested against this practice, for it was damaging to his propaganda. As a man to whom all the sources of information, all foreign broadcasts had been available, he strained the credulity of his listeners by telling the Nuremberg court that he had never heard about the mistreatment of foreign workers in Germany.

As for the charges of anti-Semitism, he said, he was never for "a noisy anti-Semitism"; he was always moderate. Not only had he twice tried to get *Der Stuermer* banned but he never in his thirteen years of broadcasting quoted the paper. He had once been asked to censor it but he had declined to do this; he just wanted to get rid of the paper, for it had only to be literally quoted in the foreign press to be convincing anti-German propaganda. But he wanted to cut down the predominant influence of Jews in German politics, economy, and culture after World War I; he believed Jews ought to be restricted in the professions to their numerical ratio to Germans. After the outbreak of World War II, he set out with enthusiasm to combat the anti-German propaganda of exiles like Emil Ludwig and other writers for the émigré press. He learned only at Nuremberg that something more was at stake in 1939 than Hitler's demand for a road through the Corridor and the city of Danzig, and that the Fuehrer had indeed planned a new partition of Poland and a much more terrible fate for the Jews. "If I had known of these things at the time, then I would have pictured the role of Jewish propaganda before the war quite differently," he said. The "Jewry Department" that kept up a drum fire of anti-Semitic agitation was a branch of the Propaganda Ministry, but Fritzsche never had anything directly to do with it. Still another service of this kind, he said, was maintained by the Party under the title "The National Socialist Correspondence"; this was issued under auspices of the Reich Press Office of the NSDAP, a purely Party production with which Fritzsche also had no connection. His speech about the unpleasant fate of the Jews in Europe that would spread to the New World had not meant, he said at Nuremberg, that he knew of the murders, but merely that he wanted Jews eliminated from politics and economic life. He could not have meant the murders, for they had not yet occurred and the evacuations were not to be carried out for another year or two. The speech, he said, was really concerned with the Pearl Harbor attack then being investigated in the United States, and in this connection he informed his listeners that a Jewish National Council had told President Roosevelt they wanted the United States to enter the war. Fritzsche admitted using the formula of the Jewish-democratic-plutocratic-Bolshevik agitators and talking on the subject of Jewish influence on British policies; but, he said, none of this had to do with the idea of extermination or persecution.

Once, in February or March, 1942, he received a letter from an SS man who commanded a unit that had orders to kill the Jews and the Ukrainian intellectuals in his area. The SS commander had a nervous breakdown as a result of his assignment and wrote to Fritzsche from a hospital. He chose Fritzsche because he said he had confidence in him and because he could not use official channels to make his disclosures. He begged Fritzsche to withhold his name, for he was bound by his oath to silence and breaking it would cost him his life. What did Fritzsche do with this information? He went with it immediately to none other than Reinhard Heydrich and asked him point-blank, "Is your SS there for the purpose of committing mass murders?" Heydrich was indignant that such a question could be asked, but he told Fritzsche that perhaps a man like Gauleiter Koch might be guilty of such a misuse of the SS and said he would investigate. The next day he called Fritzsche and told him Koch had indeed attempted to carry out such an action but had referred to orders from the Fuehrer, and Heydrich was continuing his investigation. Two days later Heydrich called again and told Fritzsche that Hitler had expressly declared he had given no such order, and Heydrich was now starting an investigation of Koch. Heydrich said, "Believe me, Herr Fritzsche, anyone who has the reputation of being cruel does not have to be cruel, he can act humanely." [34] And there the matter ended.

Fritzsche made further investigations on his way to the front to join Paulus' Sixth Army; he asked colleagues connected with the Kiev broadcasting stations what they knew about such matters. He was told that there had been shootings but they had come about as a result of sabotage where blocks of houses had been blown up in Kiev by Soviet time bombs and many German soldiers had lost their lives. Soviet citizens had been shot, but the executions had all followed courts-martial. Fritzsche's further inquiries—he talked with SS officers and with Ukrainians—confirmed these stories. They all said the same thing, that executions had taken place only following due legal proceedings. Fritzsche admitted he had also heard stories of similar German atrocities from the Allied radio stations and had inquired about these at the RSHA, for the alleged brutalities mostly concerned the SS and the Gestapo. Among those who gave him the answers that all was well was Adolf Eichmann. The RSHA people always told Fritzsche the same thing, either that a report was false or that it had a legal basis.

Fritzsche collected both the charges that came up through the foreign press and radio and the answers given him by the RSHA in the archive known as the *Schnelldienst* (Quick Service), designed to provide a repository of background information for broadcasts and articles for the quick refutation of foreign anti-German broadcasts. With the success of Allied propaganda in World War I in mind, Fritzsche kept close track of foreign broadcasts and newspapers. At the start of the war one of his co-workers from the *Schnelldienst* gathered material for an article, "In 8 Weeks of War 107 Lies." At the start of the war against Poland the enemy press accused the Germans of stealing the Black Madonna of Czestochowa, and to counter the story Fritzsche immediately arranged for foreign journalists to visit the spot and see for themselves that the Madonna was in place. He used the same tactics when a British paper, the *News Chronicle*, claimed in 1939 that the Germans had killed 10,000 Czechs in Prague, including the Lord Mayor. He invited German and foreign newsmen to visit Prague to talk with the Lord Mayor and see for themselves that no massacre had taken place.*

Fritzsche said he knew the enemy was making a business of lying, so when he heard the stories of genuine atrocities they seemed to him of a piece with the earlier fabrications. Thus when Goebbels told him the Jews were being shipped from Berlin to camps in the East, he believed him; the idea that they were being taken to extermination camps never occurred to him. When he heard of pogroms during the occupation of Lvov and Kovno, he was told they had been carried out by the local population—but Fritzsche nevertheless was critical of Goebbels, the Gestapo, and the officials of the administration because, he said, "I referred repeatedly to the legal, political and moral necessity of protecting these Jews, who, after all, had been entrusted to our care." [35] Fritzsche also heard of the gassing of Jews in vans, a story broadcast after the Russians recaptured Kharkov, and again he went to seek advice, this time to Goebbels. Goebbels promised to inquire into the matter with Himmler and Hitler, and the next day he called up Fritzsche and said the stories were not true; they were merely an invention of Russian propaganda.

The same thing happened with regard to concentration camps. Fritzsche knew that they existed, but he believed that only enemies of the State were sent to them. He once was told by a journalist who had been sent to Oranienburg that while he had not been tortured, other inmates had been. Again Fritzsche turned to his superiors: to Goebbels and also to Goering, who was then Prussian Prime Minister. An investigation, Fritzsche was told, had been started and as a result the camp commandant was sentenced to death. His further inquiries about the treatment given Pastor Niemoeller and the Austrian Chancellor Schuschnigg all received reassuring answers. He visited a concentration camp only once. In the winter of 1944–1945 he went to the administration building at Oranienburg, where he talked with a

* The story arose from the demonstration of Prague students on the anniversary of Czechoslovakia's independence, during which 1,200 were arrested and nine shot.

number of the prisoners in the presence of guards. The prisoners told him they were well enough treated; they complained only that they had been unjustly arrested. The officials at the camp assured him the internees were treated not only humanely but well.

Summing up his sentiments at Nuremberg, Fritzsche said that he now realized he had been wrong in his estimate of Hitler and the cause which he had served; he knew now that the Fuehrer had wanted to exterminate the German people, and his own last act on May 2, 1945, had been to broadcast the story of Hitler's suicide so as to prevent any legend about him from starting. During his months in prison Fritzsche learned of the tortures undergone by prisoners of the Gestapo from a fellow prisoner who had been in their hands. Further, he learned that the idea of a preventive war by Hitler had not much validity. Another prisoner, General Niedermeier, who shared a cell with the interpreter who had been present, told him that Molotov in 1941 had put forth no new demands when he visited Berlin but had merely wanted Germany to carry out what had been agreed upon. The last point Fritzsche wanted to make had to do with the murder of five million Jews. He had heard and seen the evidence of these killings in Nuremberg and, he said, it had convinced and shaken him.

The court accepted, or three-quarters of it did, what Fritzsche told them; propaganda was a new weapon, no international codes existed to define its excesses as they did for land and naval warfare, and Fritzsche's performance was not substantially different from that of the Allied propagandists—he was merely on the other side.* When he asserted that he had never consciously lied in important matters, this was certainly news for the assembled Allied and German listeners, but there is no doubt that Fritzsche believed what he said. His account of the trial, written after it was over, and his testimony before the German courts were elaborations on the theme not only of his own essential integrity but of that of the German people and of a number of his fellow defendants in the great trial. In the pages of his reminiscences of the trial he lukewarmly defended Ribbentrop, who, he thought, did himself needless harm in his testimony, and Sauckel, who had the welfare of foreign workers at heart; even Kaltenbrunner got a good word when Fritzsche praised the objective quality of the reports that came from one of his offices.

Fritzsche was accustomed to making a case. His entire training was for putting the best possible face on events both pleasant and unpleasant; the habit was ingrained, or perhaps better said, the man who could learn the habit was born to be the most persuasive of propagandists—the man who believes in what he is selling. He readily deceived himself. When he needed to believe that Hitler had forestalled a Russian attack by his invasion, he believed it; when the Allies won and he was placed on trial, he needed to

---

* The Russian judges dissented, as they did in the cases of Schacht and Papen. Fritzsche was guilty—that is why he had been brought to trial.

be convinced of the nefariousness of the designs of the Fuehrer, and he swung over to the prevailing postwar view of both Allies and Germans. Still, he played it safe; everything had to be understood in context. The Russian divisions had been massed on the German frontier, but General Niedermeier knew that Molotov had made no unfriendly demands. Both stories were right.

He was an echo chamber; even when he wrote the book about the trial he was appealing to a different postwar audience than the one he had been addressing in the Palace of Justice. He was addressing Germans, and while it was necessary to admit the monstrous crimes committed in the name of the German people, it was important to explain how the Allies too were guilty and how many mitigating circumstances there had been for the defendants in the dock. He had always been able to trim his opinions. Once the Nazis were in power and Fritzsche had joined them, Hugenberg, for whom he had worked in amity and seeming agreement for many years, overnight became the fox who had to be hunted. When Fritzsche had doubts about what was happening to the Jews, he turned to official channels, to the executioners, to find out if the stories were true. He asked Heydrich, he asked Goebbels and Eichmann and Himmler. When he wanted to check further, he talked to other German officials or to Ukrainians who would scarcely dare tell a German of his eminence anything unfavorable to the Reich. He visited Oranienberg but only got as far as the administration building, where again he questioned officials and prisoners with their guards present. It is obvious that he was not interested in getting at the facts but at the palatable facts. He wanted to be able to refute what he heard from the Allied broadcasts, not to confirm it.

Although he said he had made no call to arms to the Werewolves, he came close to it; he had broadcast on April 17, 1945:

> Let no one be surprised to find the civilian population, wearing civilian clothes, still continuing the fight in the regions already occupied and even after occupation has taken place. We shall call this phenomenon "Werewolf" since it will have arisen without any preliminary planning and without a definite organization, out of the very instinct of life.[36]

This was not a call to arms except for those who wanted to fight; it was of a piece with his clarion "Hold out to the last," and he could not have continued to broadcast without saying these things. He kept his job and said his brave words until the end; then he made a new case for himself before a different and more critical audience.

The German courts took a much sterner view of his transgressions than did the high court at Nuremberg. Under the denazification laws he was sentenced by the Spruchkammer at Nuremberg to nine years at hard labor as a major offender. He lost his rights to a pension and to vote; he could never hold public office again or be a newspaperman or broadcaster. After he was freed he could work only as a common laborer. In addition, he was to pay the costs of the trial. This was all standard procedure for those found guilty under the denazification laws. The verdict of the great trial at Nuremberg was quoted by Fritzsche and his lawyer, but this time he was being tried by people who had heard his broadcasts, who had lived under the regime he served, and who were unimpressed by disclaimers of responsibility, dedicated devotion to the truth, and the unfortunate deception he had suffered by believing what he was told. The transcript of the Nuremberg trial was introduced as evidence in his German trial, as was the text of his broadcasts, a document that had been lacking except for cut versions of some of the talks supplied by the British. But Fritzsche's defense was not proof against the charge that he had been one of the wheels of the National Socialist Government in peace and war and had served the aims of the Hitler state as best he could.

The German police wanted to arrest him right after he was freed at Nuremberg. But his lawyer, Dr. Fritz, waved the decision of the Nuremberg Court at his would-be jailers and Fritzsche was not taken into custody until February 4, 1947. He told the German court that he welcomed the opportunity to state his case, that he wanted the trial, so he surrendered himself to the Spruchkammer at Nuremberg, which had a reputation for being severe. This court, with the full texts of his broadcasts before it, could refute some of the testimony Fritzsche had given at the great trial. He had said, for example, that the Jews had started this war and now they had to pay for it; far from keeping away from the vitriolic personal attacks he had said at the trial he had avoided, he had called Roosevelt "crazy" and "a criminal phantast," and Churchill "satanic," and the court pointed out that only when Goebbels told him that the war was irretrievably lost, when Russians were fighting in the streets of Berlin and grenades bursting in the radio station where he was broadcasting, had he finally accepted Germany's defeat —perhaps another example of his ability to believe whatever was necessary.

He also, testimony showed, was directly responsible for the execution of a man, a Johannes Wild, who had written him anonymous letters protesting his broadcasts and enclosing crude drawings of Hitler's great-grandfather depicted as an orangutan wearing a helmet; Wild had called the Fuehrer "a bloodthirsty crook." Fritzsche turned the material over to the security police; the man was traced, tried, and executed. Fritzsche sought to plead in extenuation that he had not called in the Gestapo, but this could not have mattered much to Herr Wild. The prosecution at his Spruchkammer trial (all of whom, including the judges, were long-time enemies of the Nazi regime) accused him of having approved of the Party's taking over the unions and of having seen their leaders arrested and many of them killed, and it said Fritzsche had known about these events as well as any man in Germany. He had strengthened anti-Semitism, the German court found, had given the German people false information, and had urged them on to battle long after the war was lost.

He was pardoned on August 9, 1950, and freed on September 29, 1950. The President of the Spruchkammer, Sachs, said the sentence of nine years seemed disproportionately hard in the climate of 1950. Sachs visited Fritzsche in jail and the prison authorities too had occasion to observe him. They all said they saw no sign of repentance. He was still self-confident and brash; he felt superior to the prison discipline and saw no reason to accept criticism.[37] He was still playing the role of the fanatic of justice. This was the opinion of the director of the prison, and Sachs said he could only agree with it. But Fritzsche was freed nonetheless in time to live a couple of years with his second wife (he had been divorced after the initial trial). He died of cancer on September 27, 1953, in a hospital in Cologne, convinced he had done all in his power to serve his country.

NOTES

1. N XVII, p. 218.

2. N I, p. 33.

3. Joseph Goebbels, *War Diary* (unpublished), entry for June 3, 1942, p. 53 (IZG).

4. N XVII, p. 197.

5. Interrogation of September 12, 1945 (Amtsgericht).

6. Hildegard Springer, *Es sprach Hans Fritzsche* (Stuttgart: Thiele Verlag, 1949). Hildegard Springer, *Das Schwert auf der Waage* (Heidelberg: Kurt Vowinckel Verlag, 1953).

7. N XVII, pp. 203–4.

8. Interrogation of September 14, 1945 (Amtsgericht).

9. N XVII, p. 216.

10. SD reports: Kassel, April 27, 1943; Wuerzburg, May 31, 1943 (Amtsgericht).

11. NCA V, p. 993.

12. *Ibid.*

13. Louis P. Lochner, *The Goebbels Diaries 1942–1943* (Garden City: Doubleday & Company, Inc., 1948).

14. Wilfred von Oven, *Mit Goebbels bis zum Ende* (Buenos Aires: Durer, 1949), p. 138.

15. *Ibid.*

16. Dietrich, *op. cit.* N XXXII, 3469-PS, pp. 305–28. NG 4351 (IZG).

17. NG 3633 (IZG).

18. N XVII, p. 252.

19. N XXXII, 3064-PS, pp. 32–34.

20. Fritzsche Spruchkammer, broadcast of May 8, 1941 (Amtsgericht).

21. Fritzsche Spruchkammer (Amtsgericht).

22. N XXXII, 3064-PS, pp. 30–39.

23. Fritzsche Spruchkammer, Fritzsche broadcasts (Amtsgericht).

24. N XXXII, p. 38.

25. Fritzsche Spruchkammer, broadcast of October 4, 1941 (Amtsgericht).

26. *Ibid.*, broadcast of May 28–29, 1944. N XXVII, 1676-PS, pp. 436–37.

27. Fritzsche Spruchkammer, broadcast of September 9, 1944 (Amtsgericht).

28. Viktor Maevskii, "*Tovarishch Richard Sorge,*" in *Pravda,* September 4, 1964; *The New York Times,* September 5, 1964.

29. N XVII, pp. 148–50.

30. *Ibid.*, pp. 154-55.

31. *Ibid.*, p. 159.

32. *Ibid.*, p. 161.

33. *Ibid.*, p. 162.

34. *Ibid.*, p. 172.

35. *Ibid.*, p. 177.

36. N I, USSR-496, p. 353.

37. Fritzsche Spruchkammer, August 9, 1950 (Amtsgericht).

14

The Organizations

Along with the men of flesh and blood who sat in the prisoners' dock, six organizations were accused of being criminal—that is, the prosecution asked the tribunal to declare it a crime for an individual to have belonged to them. These were the Reichskabinett, the Leadership Corps of the Party, the SS and SD (including the Criminal Police, the Security Police, and the RSHA), the SA, the Gestapo, and the General Staff and High Command. Such a declaration would simplify thousands of pending trials; even though the prosecution declared that an accused person would be entitled to a hearing before a court and thus given the opportunity to show he had joined one of the proscribed groups involuntarily, it would be *prima facie* a criminal offense to have been a member. The organizations presented a major issue in the view of the prosecution. Mr. Justice Jackson stated, "It would be a greater catastrophe to acquit these organizations than it would be to acquit the entire twenty-two individual defendants in the box." [1]

The precedents for declaring an organization criminal were such laws as the British India Act of 1836 (if it were proved a man was a member of the Thugs he might be given a life sentence at hard labor), the American laws against the Ku Klux Klan, and the California Act against criminal syndicalism of 1919. Another American precedent was the law of June 28, 1940, declaring it unlawful for anyone to organize or knowingly join any society, group, or assembly formed to overthrow the Government by force. [2]

Soviet Russia had laws prohibiting "criminal gangs" that were directed against "banditry." Rudenko said that under Soviet law a person might be considered a member of such an organization even if he did not formally belong to it. French law prohibited membership in subversive organizations; and in German law too, both in the Weimar period and earlier, it had been a crime to belong to a secret organization that was antigovernment. In 1923, for example, the National Socialist Party, the Communist Party, and the German People's Freedom Party were declared illegal.

What the prosecution was getting at was clear and plausible enough. It seemed to the Allies that while crimes had been committed by individuals they had nevertheless had to act together; and on the basis of the evidence accumulated before and during the trial, some of the groups these individuals belonged to were not much different from a band of thugs in India or anywhere else sworn to kill or despoil their victims. Had the SA not marched through the streets of Germany beating up and sometimes murdering their enemies, yelling their slogans in front of Jewish shops, holding their kangaroo courts after the Party took power? The guilt of the SS, the SD, and the Gestapo too seemed patent enough. These had been no ordinary organizations; the SS had run the concentration camps; the SD controlled the intelligence service within Germany and much of the extermination apparatus outside the country; the Gestapo was the very symbol of a terroristic police force. The Party had administered much of the daily life of the population through the political leaders—from the Gauleiter, the Kreisleiter, and such eminences who supervised the economic and political life of their districts down to the Blockwart who saw to it that flags were displayed on patriotic occasions and noted who failed to hang one out or to subscribe to the *Voelkischer Beobachter*. The Reichskabinett had in theory for a time helped govern the country, as they voted unanimously in favor of the Fuehrer's decisions and paved the way for his assuming sole power (see Papen, Chapt. 5).

Spearheading all the criminal organizations, in the opinion of many observers both in and outside the courtroom, was the German General Staff. An American Assistant Prosecutor, Brigadier General Telford Taylor, summed up this view at Nuremberg:

> These characteristics of the German military leaders are deep and permanent. . . . Their philosophy is so perverse that they regard a lost war, and a defeated and prostrate Germany, as a glorious opportunity to start again on the same terrible cycle. . . . We are at grips here with something big and evil and durable; something that was not born in 1933, or even 1921 . . . The tree which bore this fruit [human skins being used as lampshades in concentration camps] is German militarism. . . . The first steps toward the revival of German militarism have been taken right here in this courtroom.[3]

Such views were widespread. Sumner Welles wrote:

> The authority to which the German people have so often and so disastrously responded was not in reality the German emperor of yesterday or the Hitler of today, but the German General Staff . . . the real master of the German race, namely German militarism, personified in and channeled through the German General Staff . . . It is this living, continuing

destructive force that must be extirpated if the German people are ever to make a constructive contribution to the stability of Europe and if any organized, international society is to be able to safeguard the security of free peoples . . . The German General Staff is convinced that over a period of years it can gain a controlling influence in labor unions, in chambers of commerce and through these channels, an indirect influence in the press.[4]

Each of the organizations in theory was represented by at least one of the defendants at the trial. The General Staff and High Command had five representatives: Goering, Keitel, Jodl, Doenitz, and Raeder. The Leadership Corps brought Sauckel and Streicher; the Cabinet, Goering, Neurath, Ribbentrop, Papen, and Schacht; the SS and SD, Kaltenbrunner; the SA had a number of honorary members among the defendants; and the Gestapo was represented, although inadequately, by Hermann Goering, who had founded it but had been replaced by Himmler in 1936.

The organizations were sometimes ably, sometimes windily, defended, in the latter cases with many citations from antiquity and from Goethe. They were assigned counsel mainly from among the lawyers who were taking part in the defense of individuals. Egon Kubuschok, who was Papen's lawyer, was one of three attorneys given the job of representing the Reichskabinett; Robert Servatius, who defended Sauckel, appeared for the Leadership Corps; Hans Laternser, who was co-counsel for Seyss-Inquart, and Franz Exner, who represented Jodl, appeared for the General Staff and High Command. The unpromising job of defending the Gestapo went to an able lawyer, Rudolf Merkel.

The German lawyers were faced here as they were in their other defense assignments with a task of formidable proportions. They needed to get affidavits from thousands of members of the accused organizations, almost all of whom were in prisoner-of-war camps. Although the court did its best to provide transportation for the lawyers and access to the camps, it was no easy matter to get around; in the case of prisoners in the Russian zone it was sometimes impossible. But the German lawyers succeeded in obtaining over 300,000 affidavits.[5] Three thousand documents were submitted and 200 witnesses heard before commissions or before the tribunal.* More documents than these were sent out from the prisoner-of-war camps. One of the lawyers told the court that he had been unable to get the affidavits prepared in one of the camps because the camp commander said this would contravene his orders to keep the prisoners from communicating with the outside world. Nor could many witnesses be brought from the prisoner-of-war camps in the Russian zone. The orders of the commanders of those camps came not from the International Military Tribunal but from points east.

One of the objections the Germans made to the indictment of the organi-

---

* These figures include the much smaller number of affidavits and witnesses submitted on behalf of the twenty-two defendants.

zations was the collective guilt it implied. More than four and a half million men had been in the SA, hundreds of thousands more had been in the SS, some 600,000 to 700,000 in the Leadership Corps. A quarter to half of the German population would be involved in the indictments, Kubuschok pointed out, and under the Allied Control Council Law No. 10, if the organizations were found guilty, the mere fact of anyone's having belonged to one of them would leave him open to the penalties, including death, prescribed in that document.* The whole concept, it seemed, either was a regression to medieval notions † or represented a wholesale judgment of the kind that the Western powers themselves were condemning.

Of chief importance among the tribulations of the defense counsel for most of the organizations was the character of their witnesses. Some of them were hopelessly bewildered by finding themselves in an anti-Nazi world. One man, a pastor, testifying on behalf of the SA before a commission appointed to take evidence, declared that he was unable to say that the SA had been anti-Semitic.[6] Witnesses for the SS spoke of its belief in God, of its high moral principles,[7] of Himmler's exhortations that held the SS to strict ethical duties such as, said one witness, former SS judge Guenther Reinecke, the upholding of the sanctity of private property and consideration for the religious conviction of others. Now we know, he said, that Himmler had another face which he hid from the rank and file. But at the time, Reinecke and his comrades had thought only of the moral commandments that were higher than the law itself.[8] Another SS judge told how well prisoners were fed at such camps as Buchenwald, Auschwitz, and Dachau and how it was forbidden for guards to strike them.[9] In all the quotations from Himmler's Sunday sermons on the word of an SS man's being more important than any signed contract it was not easy to recognize the SS that subsidized the ghastly medical experiments at Dachau or the divisions that conducted the massacres at Oradour and in the East, where eyewitnesses told of Russian women and children shut up in barns which were then set on fire.[10]

The SD too had its hapless defenders: one man told of how it had organized meetings in Germany where everyone who came could speak his mind openly and where it was even possible to talk of dissolving the Party.[11] Another solemnly swore that the SD had never had orders to liquidate the Jews.[12]

* Control Council Law No. 10 was promulgated by all four powers on December 20, 1945, to establish "a uniform legal basis . . . for the prosecution of war criminals and other similar offenders, other than those dealt with by the International Military Tribunal." Membership in categories of criminal groups or organizations as specified by the International Military Tribunal was also a crime. The occupying powers in the four zones were to arrest anyone suspected of having committed any of these crimes and to bring them to trial.

† In the Middle Ages the inhabitants of a German town were all considered guilty if a peace breaker took refuge among them and they did not surrender him; they could be slaughtered to the last man, woman, and child (Gerhard Rauschenbach, Der Nuerenberger Prozess gegen die Organisationen [Bonn: Ludwig Roehrscheid Verlag, 1954], p. 18).

The political leaders too, although some of them admitted they had reported on their constituents' Party loyalty, described themselves as humane
fellows who protected Allied flyers from the angry populace, who played no
part in the persecution of the Jews and had known nothing of the atrocities
in the concentration camps but on the contrary had helped out the families
of inmates.[13] One of them who saw the crematory ovens in Auschwitz
thought them "very hygienic." [14] Asocial people and delinquents were in the
concentration camps, one man said, and he had thoroughly approved of the
Gestapo and SS because, from what he knew, they had only useful, patriotic
functions.[15]

The counsel for the SA made their case on the large numbers who had been
forced to join the organization and on its rapid loss of importance after the
Roehm purge. One of the SA lawyers, Georg Boehm, pointed out that under
the German Civil Service Law, adopted in 1937, every young German official
had had to belong to a Party formation and if his physical condition permitted to either the SA or the SS. There was no escaping membership in the
SA for any student in a university or technical school; they came under the
jurisdiction of the local *Stuerme* and only after they had joined were they
enrolled in the National Socialist Students' League.[16] The SA lawyers further
pointed out that among the four and a half million members of the organization, perhaps 2 per cent had committed the atrocities and contributed to
the disorders charged in the indictment—in other words, the SA was a mass
organization which thousands of Germans had in one way or another been
forced to join.

Egon Kubuschok, appearing for the Reichskabinett, told the tribunal that
this was a wholly legal group established under German law which moreover provided for criminal proceedings only against individuals. Furthermore,
the Cabinet had taken little part in law or decision making; it had not been
consulted when the Nuremberg Laws were issued or at the time of the
occupation of the Rhineland, about which the Ministers were told only
after the event. The Commander in Chief of the Wehrmacht could only
attend meetings when the Fuehrer specifically invited him, and a Minister
like Schirach could appear only when some question involving his Hitlerjugend was to come up and the Fuehrer wanted to hear his views. Meetings
became less and less frequent as Hitler tired of any discussions. The Cabinet
Ministers prepared drafts of recommendations to be submitted to Hitler.
These they talked over first with their departments, but there was no discussion of them in the Cabinet meetings. Every political decision was made by
the Fuehrer himself; the bills to be enacted were circulated among the
Ministers beforehand, but Hitler alone determined what was to become law.
The Fuehrer, referring to the Cabinet, had said he wanted no club of de-
featists discussing his plans, and in many Ministries a subordinate might be
entrusted with secret information furnished by the Reich Chancellery that

was not meant to be given the Minister. Remaining a member was an empty honor.

Counsel for the SS, SD, and Gestapo did what they could with bad cases. They limited themselves to arguing against the notion of collective guilt (one of them said that had been the reason given for the reprisal murder of the inhabitants of Lidice) and to pointing out that many of the members of the organizations had not been involved in the atrocities and that one of these bodies was often mistaken for the other since the SS, the Criminal Police, the Security Police, and the SD all wore similar uniforms during the war and could only be distinguished by the relatively small identifying badges. It was a weak defense and was made without conviction on the part of the lawyers.

The most eloquent and telling defense was presented by Hans Laternser on behalf of the General Staff and the High Command. The President of the Court, who was sharp with a number of the German lawyers who complained about the trouble they were having with the Russians or in getting copies of documents they needed, took occasion to compliment Laternser as he delivered his carefully prepared, scholarly presentation. Laternser point by point refuted the testimony of the witnesses appearing against the General Staff, some of whom, like the SS Generals Schellenberg and Ohlendorf, wanted to strengthen whatever case they had by placing as much blame as possible for the atrocities on the Army. The Army had done its military job, Laternser maintained, and no more. In the days when Russian soldiers were being taken prisoner in large numbers, commanding generals had ordered their troops to share rations with the Soviet prisoners of war. Plundering was forbidden in Russia, as well as in the West, and death sentences were carried out against soldiers found guilty of rape or mistreating the population.

The Commissar Order had been disobeyed in the only way it could be, by being ignored and circumvented.* Field Marshal von Brauchitsch issued his Maintenance of Discipline Order on May 24, 1941, almost a month before the start of the attack on the Soviet Union. It was expressly designed, Brauchitsch testified, to mitigate the effects of Hitler's Commissar Order, which had deeply disturbed all the generals present, including Brauchitsch, when the Fuehrer on March 30 had announced his intention to issue it.[17] The Brauchitsch order, which was distributed to 340 commands (the same number that got the Commissar Order), told the commanders that movement

* The order for "the Use of Court Martials in the Barbarossa Area" (*Erlass ueber die Ausuebung der Kriegsgerichtbarkeit im Gebiet "Barbarossa"*), permitting the German troops to take extreme measures against the civilian population without recourse to military courts and without necessarily being subject to prosecution for any such action even if it had been a military crime, was issued on May 13, 1941. The Commissar Order was issued on June 6 as a supplement to the order of May 13 (Buchheim, *et al., op. cit.,* Vol. II, pp. 176–77, 225. Szymon Datner, *Crimes Against POW's* [Warsaw: Zachodnia Agencja Prasowa, 1964]).

and combat were the real task of the troops and they should not conduct mopping-up operations. Under all circumstances excesses of individual members of the Army were to be prevented lest the troops become unmanageable.[18] The Brauchitsch order was vague—had it been anything else Hitler would have countermanded it.

Issuing vague supplemental orders was the same method the Army used during the Polish campaign to weaken Hitler's orders that soldiers not be punished for any offenses against Jews. The Army supplement to the directives provided for the usual court-martial proceedings in the event that a soldier had won any personal advantage or had enriched himself by any act he had undertaken against Jews.[19]

Witnesses testified that the Commissar Order was withdrawn in 1942, when General Kurt Zeitzler finally succeeded in making clear to the Fuehrer how damaging it was to the German cause—the commissars naturally urged the troops to fight to the last. No subsequent evidence has come to light, however, to show that Hitler ever formally withdrew the order, although General Zeitzler told General Adolf Heusinger in 1944 that he had succeeded after a long struggle in getting Hitler to rescind it.[20] What seems to have happened was that Hitler made use of a halfway measure instead of canceling the order. The official diary of the Historical Section of OKW for May 6, 1942, read: "The Fuehrer gives instructions that in order to increase the readiness to desert or to capitulate of Soviet Russian troops who have been surrounded, authorization is given temporarily and as an experiment for a guarantee to be given in such cases that the lives of commanders, commissars, and politruks will be spared." [21] That was the *de facto* end of the Kommissarbefehl. But up to that time it had been only sporadically carried out. In the first months of the war, field commanders, when reports were demanded on how many commissars were executed, often faked the figures by using those for commissars who had been killed in battle. Such reports stop in 1942. The Army also resisted the Commando Order on such a scale that Hitler had to threaten punishment if it was not carried out. This latter order was in another category, for here one of Laternser's witnesses said what other Army and Navy witnesses also testified, that he had thought it a legal reprisal.

The Army had played no part, Laternser maintained, in the extermination of the Jews. The Einsatz squads were directly under the orders of Himmler and were assigned to the rear areas behind the fighting front.* The authority of the Army field commander was limited to the zone of combat which was defined as the front and a rear area of about ten kilometers (roughly as far as enemy artillery could reach).[22] Beyond this distance the political authority

---

* Keitel's directive of March 13 read:
  In the zone of operations of the Army the Reichsfuehrer SS receives special tasks in preparation for political administration, by the direction of the Fuehrer, tasks which result from the final encounter of two political systems. Within the framework of these tasks the Reichsfuehrer acts independently and on his own responsibility" (N XXVI, 447-PS, p. 54).

took over.* Most of the generals said they had known nothing of the liquidations; the Army was responsible only for supplying the rations and the gasoline of the Einsatz formations that were presumably organizing the rear territory for the coming civilian administration and also spearheading the endless campaign behind the lines of the fighting troops against the partisans. Field commanders took action when they heard rumors of the Einsatz squads' executions. Field Marshal von Kleist, for example, called the Higher SS and the Police Leaders to him as soon as he heard such a report and told them he would permit no excesses in the area of his command; the Einsatz leaders assured him that none were taking place and that they had orders forbidding any unduly harsh measures. Field Marshal von Manstein testified at his trial that he had ordered an investigation and was told by his officers that the rumors were not true.†

Laternser produced witnesses or their affidavits to show that wounded Russian soldiers were treated exactly like the Germans, and when infantile paralysis broke out in a prisoner-of-war camp, the German Army had sent a plane to the Reich for serum. As for the treatment of prisoners of war from the armies of the Western Allies, Laternser produced letters of thanks received by German camp commanders from former captive British soldiers. Laternser countered the charges that the German Army had willfully destroyed churches and historical monuments in the Soviet Union by bringing out testimony to the contrary, that those that had not already been turned into museums and workshops by the Soviet authorities had been preserved. The Tolstoy museum at Yasnia Polyana, as one example, was not damaged during the fighting and German occupation. Such destruction as did occur, such as the great damage caused at Leningrad by the German bombardment, he characterized as having been done under "military necessity." On the high seas, too, Laternser said, the Germans had followed the customs and usages of war. The *Scharnhorst* and the *Gneisenau* had rescued survivors of a British auxiliary cruiser, the *Rawalpindi*, despite the fact that the ship had sent out a call for help as she was being attacked and a converging British force might well have cut off the return voyage of the German ships.

---

* The Army made an agreement with the Gestapo and SS in late April, 1941, when the operations of the police units behind the front lines were being planned before the start of the Russian campaign. General Wagner, representing Field Marshal von Brauchitsch, met with Heinrich Mueller, chief of the Gestapo, Reinhard Heydrich, and Walter Schellenberg of the SS to arrange for the division of responsibility. The Army was to feed and billet the police units that would be used behind the front under Himmler's command, but the Army generals had complete authority in the combat zone (Leeb, Case XII, p. 2123 [Goettingen]).

† The evidence in the Manstein case is very contradictory. SS generals said he had welcomed their cooperation and while, as Laternser showed, they may have exaggerated Manstein's favorable attitude, he had certainly issued orders of which they could wholly approve. On November 20, 1941, he addressed himself to his troops, insisting "that the Jewish Bolshevik system be wiped out once and for all . . . The German soldier therefore not only has the task of destroying this system . . . he is the avenger of all the cruelties committed against him and the German people" (N XXXIV, 4064-PS, p. 130).

Laternser tried to show, and the American *Army and Navy Journal* agreed with him in an article published in December, 1945,* that the indictment of the German High Command was an indictment not of the German Army only but also of the military profession as such. Generals, Laternser said, do not prepare for aggressive warfare, they prepare for war; that is their job. Furthermore, the indictment declared that there was a group or organization where there was none. In Hitler's time no general staff for all the armed forces existed as had been the case in World War I. The Navy had no general or admiralty staff of any kind. The Oberkommando des Heeres, the High Command of the Army, had consisted, to be sure, of a Chief of Staff and other staff officers, but it was a purely technical organization, and between 1935 and 1938 General Beck, who was chief of OKH, was received by Adolf Hitler only twice. The only thing voluntary about belonging to the High Command, OKW, or to the Army General Staff, OKH, was the act of joining the Reichswehr; after that an officer was promoted or assigned to a post by his superiors. And far from lusting after war, as the prosecution alleged was characteristic of the Prussian and German generals, Laternser pointed out how clearly eminent German generals had spoken against war.

Helmut von Moltke had called war "the last means of the safeguarding the existence, independence, and honor of a state," and had added:

> It is to be hoped that this last means will be applied ever more infrequently with our progressing culture. Who would wish to deny that every war, even a victorious one, constitutes a misfortune for one's own nation, because no territorial aggrandizement, no war reparations amounting to billions can replace the loss of life and offset the grief of mourning families.[23]

The ideal of the German General Staff officer, as stated before World War I by Alfred von Schlieffen, was the precise opposite of that of the Nazis: "To be rather than to appear"—to keep away from every form of publicity, to do the job assigned quietly and modestly.† Laternser also quoted Mackensen, who in World War I had given the orders that led to the breakthrough at Gorlice. Mackensen said on the day the German forces attacked:

> Today my expectations center around a murderous battle . . . It is expected of me that I should win a great success, but decisive and great successes in war are mostly achieved at the cost of considerable losses. How many death sentences does my order of attack involve? It is this thought that weighs heavily on me whenever I give an order; but I am myself acting under order, driven by unavoidable necessity. How many of the strong and healthy boys who marched past me yesterday and are today

* Mr. Justice Jackson called the article appearing in the *Army and Navy Journal* nonsense when it said he had sought to discredit the profession of arms (*The New York Times*, December 5, 1945).

† Schlieffen also said: "Even a victorious war is a national disaster" (*TWC*, Leeb, X, p. 160).

on their way to the front lines will lie dead on the battlefield within a few days . . . Many of the radiant pairs of eyes into which I was able to look will soon be closed forever . . . That is the reverse side of a military leader's job.[24]

The High Command of the Armed Forces, OKW, Laternser said, was no more than Hitler's operations staff; it had no power to issue orders except as Hitler directed. Its power and authority from the beginning were resisted by OKH as well as by the Luftwaffe and Navy; only the Fuehrer held the reins.[25] The 129 officers the prosecution indicted under the name of General Staff and High Command were neither a group nor an organization; they were the separate "holders of the highest ranks in the German Armed Forces" perhaps, but they had to be sought out one by one. They had no common denominator other than high rank. They belonged to different agencies and neither before nor during the war did they ever meet together. The Schlieffen Society, also declared by the prosecution to be a conspiratorial association of General Staff officers, met once a year to listen to a lecture and a report. Its purpose was "to cultivate the spirit of comradeship between former General Staff officers and those on active service," nothing more. When from time to time Hitler met with the commanders in chief of Army groups, the meetings always were concerned with purely military questions. The commanders had no organized contact with one another.

Hitler, said Laternser, had attacked the generals as an obsolete class that had failed "as early as 1914," and only nine generals and admirals had held on to their posts during the entire war. None of them had been in Hitler's confidence, and Manstein, who had been told nothing of the Fuehrer's plans, had to prepare the orders for the march into the Rhineland only the day before it occurred. At the time of the *Anschluss*, the Army had been given no advance notice of the march into Austria and had no plans for one. General Beck wrote a memorandum when war seemed likely between Germany and Czechoslovakia saying that Germany could not fight both France and Britain and opposing Hitler's plans for a showdown. The campaign against Poland came as a surprise to the Army.* After the campaign was over, the High Command opposed Hitler's plan to invade the Low Countries and France, and although the Army believed that the war against Russia was a preventive action, it opposed becoming involved in a two-front war.[26]

Of seventeen field marshals, ten were relieved of their commands by the Fuehrer in the course of the war, three were killed in the rising of July 20, 1944, two were killed in action, one was taken prisoner, and only one remained throughout the war without being subject to discipline. Of thirty-six generals, twenty-six were removed from their posts, of whom three were

---

* In Hitler's view the Polish campaign was not a war but a "special employment" of the Wehrmacht; he therefore wanted no preliminary steps taken to disturb the life of the country. The Army mobilized in stages (Walter Warlimont, *Inside Hitler's Headquarters 1939–45* [New York: Frederick A. Praeger, Inc., 1964], p. 26).

executed and two were dishonorably discharged; seven were killed in action and only three remained in service throughout the war without disciplinary action.[27] This was the group or organization, as Laternser described it, that the prosecution regarded as the longest lived and most sinister among the organizations, that was even now planning new wars as it took every defeat as an impulse for fresh conquests.

The tribunal was influenced only in part by the prosecution's arguments. The court held that the General Staff and High Command were not a group or organization and therefore with some reluctance found them not guilty but made plain that its finding was based on this consideration and on the relatively small number of men involved who could be brought to trial separately, not on what the German generals had done during the war. For, it said, the high German military leaders were responsible in large measure for the misery and suffering of millions. It added:

> They have been a disgrace to the honorable profession of arms. Without their military guidance the aggressive ambitions of Hitler and his fellow-Nazis would have been academic and sterile. Although they were not a group . . . they were certainly a ruthless military caste. The contemporary German militarism flourished briefly with its recent ally, National Socialism, as well as or better than it had in the generations of the past. Many of these men have made a mockery of the soldier's oath of obedience to military orders. When it suits their defense they say they had to obey; when confronted with Hitler's brutal crimes, which are shown to have been within their general knowledge, they say they disobeyed. The truth is that they actively participated in all these crimes, or sat silent and acquiescent, witnessing the commission of crimes on a scale larger and more shocking than the world has ever had the misfortune to know. This must be said. Where the facts warrant it, these men should be brought to trial so that those among them who are guilty of these crimes should not escape punishment.[28]

Thus the General Staff and High Command were judged not guilty, as were the Reich Cabinet, which, the court said, had not been an organization after 1937, and the SA, which had been reduced in significance after the purge of 1934. The other organizations, the SS (including the General SS, the Deathhead Units, the Waffen SS, and the police forces), Gestapo, SD, and Leadership Corps, were all found guilty. The Leadership Corps was declared guilty only in its upper echelons of Gauleiter, Kreisleiter, and Ortsgruppenleiter, and the verdict included the Amtsleiter only when they were heads of staffs of the higher departments. The court took pains to point out that guilt was always personal, that mass punishments might not be inflicted, and that punishments might never be greater than those provided for in the denazification laws of the four zones. The British zone did away with the death penalty for belonging to an organization and provided for imprisonment not to exceed ten years.[29]

The evidence that has come to light since the tribunal handed down its decision does not seem to cast doubt on its verdicts on the part of any of the organizations—the Gestapo, SD, Leadership Corps, and SS have fared no better in the judgment of historians since the trial. It is true that many of the SS men were drafted and some members of the Hitler Youth were shanghaied into the Blackshirt formations, but the component organizations on the whole played the roles during the war that the tribunal found them guilty of, and the efforts of the former members of the Waffen SS to rehabilitate their organization as nothing more than an elite fighting unit of the German forces have had no success among either German or other historians.

The court's observations on the German General Staff and High Command have fared differently. As early as 1950, when at the time of the Korean war it began to seem desirable to the Western Allies to include German military units among the forces of the Free World, strong revisionist tendencies developed among Germany's former enemies as far as the Army was concerned. General Dwight Eisenhower, at the request of President Truman, journeyed to the Bundesrepublik when the reluctant Germans were debating whether or not to reintroduce conscription to tell the German people that its Army had never by its conduct during World War II lost its honor. His was only one of the first of such official statements that were to be often repeated by men who had fought against the Third Reich. Much of the writing on the German Army published since the war has been influenced by the East-West struggle. Soviet, German East-Zone, and other writers behind the Iron Curtain have repeated not only that the German High Command of World War II was guilty of the crimes charged but that members of the High Command were now eagerly welcomed in the Bundeswehr, where they were preparing new aggressions and new war crimes and crimes against humanity. But the record is more complicated than either the new-found friends or the old enemies proclaim. The subsequent trials of the German generals held by the American Military Tribunal at Nuremberg, as well as those before other Allied and German courts, together with the study of documents that have come to light bear out Laternser's case only in part.*

The generals in the first place were a mixed group. On the whole they were strongly anti-Communist and in varying degrees anti-Semitic.† Before World War I no Jew could serve as an officer in the Prussian Army and, although some 2,000 Jews were commissioned in the course of the war and 35,000 were decorated for bravery, many high-ranking officers remained implacably anti-

---

* The later Nuremberg trials, including Case No. 7, against Field Marshal Wilhelm List, General Lothar Rendulic, and ten others, and Case No. 12, against Field Marshals Leeb, Kuechler, and twelve others, although called military were held before American civilian judges.

† General Westphal declared, "the Army was not friendly to Jews but was not anti-Semitically inclined," meaning, one gathers, that it did not favor active measures against Jews (Karl Demeter, *Das deutsche Offizierkorps in Gesellschaft und Staat 1650–1945* [Frankfurt a.M.: Bernard & Graef Verlag fuer Wehrwesen, 1962], p. 204).

Semitic. Fritsch, who lost his office because of Hitler and the machinations of the SS, and who said before the Polish campaign he would serve with his regiment "only as a target because I cannot stay at home," shared with Hitler only one sentiment—antagonism toward the Jews.[30] Anti-Semitism was one of the strongest bonds between Ludendorff and the Nazis.* Army frontline newspapers ran the same kind of attacks on the Jews as did the Party press.[31] Army commanders like Field Marshal von Rundstedt were careful to point out that dealing with Communist and Jewish elements among the civilian population of the Soviet Union was a matter for the SD and that soldiers were not to take part in any atrocities committed by the Ukrainian population or to photograph them. But that was all; the excesses were bad for discipline, otherwise they were no affair of the Army.[32]

Keitel obediently issued directives in the same language that Himmler might have used. Some of the generals like Field Marshal Walter von Reichenau, who commanded Army Group South on the Russian front, and General Hermann Reinecke, who commanded the prisoner-of-war camps during the Russian campaign and was one of the judges at the trial of the generals after the July 20 attempt on Hitler's life, were not easily distinguishable from the high command of the SS in their hatred of Jews and Communists, and the orders they issued were made in the letter and spirit of the Fuehrer's most vindictive directives.† Others, like Manstein, were caught in a one-sided conflict between their years of schooling in honorable warfare and

* Bach-Zelewski, who became chief of the antipartisan units and a general in the SS, first joined the Army in 1914. He had been forced, he testified at Nuremberg, to resign in 1924, when two of his sisters married Jews. Bach-Zelewski was not one of the most reliable witnesses, but this part of his statement could be true, although what he was trying to explain to the court was the background to his SS career. He said he had joined the National Socialists because he feared anti-Semitism might again ruin his career (NCA VI, 3712-PS, p. 425).

† Reichenau's directive of October 10, 1941, read:
　　The most essential aim of war against the Jewish-Bolshevistic system is a complete destruction of their means of power and the elimination of Asiatic influence from the European culture. . . . The soldier in the Eastern Territories is not merely a fighter . . . but also a bearer of ruthless national ideology and the avenger of bestialities which have been inflicted upon German and racially related nations. Therefore, the soldier must have full understanding for the necessity of a severe but just revenge on subhuman Jewry (N IV, p. 459).
The order of September 8, 1941, sent out by General Reinecke, read:
　　Bolshevism is the mortal enemy of National Socialist Germany. For the first time the German soldier faces an enemy not trained merely as a soldier but with Bolshevik political schooling, which is so pernicious to the people. For this reason the Russian soldier loses all claim to treatment as an honorable soldier according to the Geneva convention.
The order then went on to say that rifle butts and similar weapons were to be used against Russian prisoners of war at the slightest sign of resistance, active or passive; they were to be fired on immediately without calling on them to halt or firing a warning shot if they attempted to escape. "As a rule the use of arms against Soviet prisoners of war is legal." Russian prisoners were to be chosen by the Germans to act as a kind of police and they were to be armed with clubs and whips which were expressly forbidden the Germans as beneath their status (N XXVII, 1519-PS, pp. 273–83).

an ideology to which they in large part subscribed. Thus Manstein testified at Nuremberg and at his own later trial that he had ordered the death sentence for a German soldier who had committed rape in Russia and the court-martial of a soldier he had seen beat a Russian prisoner and that never in his command had the Commissar Order been carried out, but he was also the man who had written that the goal of the war was "the extermination of the Jewish Bolshevik system." [33] General Halder, who was no friend of National Socialism but a member of the Resistance, nevertheless could calmly write in his war diary two and a half months before the start of the Russian campaign: "Destruction of Bolshevik Commissars and the Communist Intelligentsia. The new states must be socialist states and without their own intelligentsia. A new intelligentsia must be prevented from arising. A primitive socialist intelligentsia is enough here." * [34]

General (later Field Marshal) Georg von Kuechler, commanding the Eighteenth Army in Russia, testified that he had never had the Commissar Order in his hands, but the prosecution could show in his trial that if that was true he had nevertheless taken lethal measures against people other than commissars. He had ordered the execution of anyone who could not plausibly explain his presence in the area under Kuechler's authority, he had used Soviet prisoners of war to clear minefields, and he had issued orders that made it easy for his soldiers to tolerate such crimes and worse ones. On July 22, 1940, he told his troops, "I ask further that any soldier, especially officers, refrain from criticisms of the racial struggle which is being carried out, in for example the treatment of the Polish minority, the Jews and church matters. The racial struggle which has raged in the East for centuries requires for its final racial solution decisive measures carried out in an energetic manner." [35] And yet Kuechler only a few months before, during the Polish campaign, had ordered courts-martial over Himmler's protests for those who had committed atrocities in the area of the Third Army, then under his command. Kuechler apparently had first gotten used to atrocities and then had come to approve them. [36]

In the autumn of 1941, when the High Command discussed executions of feebleminded patients in Russian asylums, General Halder noted that such killings were necessary. [37] This seems to have been the position of the generals at the front, who were mainly concerned with keeping the rear area free of trouble. [38] In December, 1941, 230 to 240 women patients in the Soviet hospital at Makarjewo were liquidated, and the reports of such executions in the course of the usual Army routine would have gone to Leeb and Kuechler, among others.† The reason given for the killings at Makarjewo was the

---

* Halder was quoting the Fuehrer when he wrote these lines, but he gives no sign that he did not accept them.

† The Eighteenth Army report said that the commander in chief (Kuechler) assented to the solution of the problem of the asylum, but Kuechler denied at his trial that he had ever heard of the executions at Makarjewo (*TWC*, Leeb, X, pp. 1200, 1202).

danger of infection to the troops since no medicines were available for these women and diseases like spotted fever were a constant menace.[39]

General Roettiger, commanding the Fourth Army, said in an interrogation on December 8, 1945, that the troops in the East were told "from the highest authority . . . to use the harshest methods." Under these circumstances it is not surprising that Army reports complain that for many German soldiers fighting the partisans "it is second nature to go around beating the civilian population with a club." [40]

Commissars and *politruks* were certainly shot, but officer after officer testified that the Commissar Order had never been carried out and figures they cited on the whole substantiate their denials.[41] Field Marshal Wilhelm von Leeb pointed out during his trial that between 2,000 and 2,500 commissars and *politruks* must have been assigned to the 200,000–220,000 Russian troops who had been captured within a short period at the start of the war, and yet only 96 were reported executed in accordance with the Fuehrer order and some of those had certainly been killed in action.*[42] Nevertheless the men of Panzer Group 3, for example, were told that they were not to spare the bearers of the enemy ideology but to kill them.†[43] Leeb's figures seem far too low; some have concluded that several hundred commissars were executed in the early months of the campaign.[44]

* Leeb was one of the generals who did not hesitate to take issue with Hitler. He energetically opposed on October 11, 1939, an attack on the Low Countries and France—it was another thing, he wrote, to defend Germany against attack, and the Army was prepared to do this (Hans-Adolf Jacobsen, ed., *Dokumente zur Vorgeschichte des Westfeldzuges 1939–1940* [Goettingen: Musterschmidt-Verlag, 1956], pp. 79–85). In a memorandum of October 31, 1939, addressed to Brauchitsch he urged that an autonomous Czechoslovakia be reconstituted, together with an independent Poland, and that, if possible, peace be made with the Western powers. If Hitler did not agree, Leeb urged that the generals commanding the three army groups resign in a body (Gert Buchheit, *Soldatentum und Rebellion* [Rastatt/Baden: Grot'sche Verlagbuchhandlung, 1961], p. 241. Jacobsen, *op. cit.*, pp. 85–86).

† Before the war started, commissars were believed to be the most fanatical political soldiers in the Soviet Army. After the fighting was underway their role was confirmed in interrogations and by instructions captured from the Russians by German units. One such read:

> . . . The patriotic war is the most justified of all wars . . . officers and soldiers must never forget that the great Stalin stands at the head of our forces no matter how difficult the situation at the front. The whole Slavic world unites for the destruction of fascism . . . The war commissar is the eye and ear of bolshevism and of the Soviet Union . . . the moral leader of his unit . . . the military leader of his unit next to the commander. It is his job to see that all comrades and political workers give a courageous example to the troops . . . He is an example of bravery and courage in battle—the bravest soldier in his unit. Death or victory are the laws for Communists and Comsomols at the front. The commissar and the commander are fully responsible . . . any attempt to go over to the enemy is to be met at once by shooting. The task of the commissars and political workers is to educate their men in the spirit of hate . . .

The commissars were to give daily political instructions to their troops and to organize partisan operations in German occupied territory (NO 4784 [IZG]).

Field Marshal Kuechler wrote on October 26, 1941: "Nothing particular to report. Sixteen commissars shot." * Army reports gave advice to the individual commanders that commissars who had torn off their insignia could be discovered because the part of their uniform under these badges was of a different color.[45] Another bit of advice said they might be recognized by their gold teeth since only commissars would be likely to afford them.[46]

The preachments of the ideological struggle took effect. An OKH directive for the treatment of Russian prisoners of war declared that the Geneva Convention was not valid for the Soviet Union and that the regulations for treating Russian prisoners were entirely different from those for Western prisoners. Military service for the Soviet Union was not to be considered military duty and because of the murders committed by the Russians "it is characterized in its totality as a crime." Hence the validity of international legal standards, said Canaris in protesting against this OKH statement, was denied in the war against bolshevism. This, he added, "would lead to arbitrary mistreatment and murder." [47]

Canaris did not understate the matter. Of the 5,700,000 Russian prisoners of war only two million survived.† These included the contingents aiding the Germans: the Vlasov army and the Armenian, Caucasian, and Muhammadan formations.[48] Prisoners died on the roads as they marched, for example from Kiev, where 600,000 had been captured, as much as a thousand kilometers to their prison camp.[49] A critical Army report had said it was stupid to shoot those who could go no farther, in the middle of a village.[50] They died of undernourishment and of disease, because the mass of prisoners was so great the Germans could not take care of them and because they were in bad physical condition when they surrendered. But they also died because of criminal orders and because large numbers were shot for breaches of discipline or as reprisals for the shootings of Germans by partisans. But Soviet prisoners of war also worked for the Germans.‡ These were the ones mainly who survived; for Reinecke made it clear that only those who worked were to be fed. On the other hand, thousands of Russians, including prisoners of war, voluntarily retreated with the German armies when the tide turned

---

* These are routine reports; others read: "In the course of the afternoon 30–40 prisoners of war were taken away . . . suspected of being commissars," and "80 partisans, 13 commissars, 3 women were shot" (NOKW 2264, 2186, 1538, 2179. See also NOKW 2062, 1220, 1536, 2771, 3353). Also NOKW 3318, 7/8/41, demanding "a report on the number of commissars killed up-to-date and further reports every two weeks." Also NOKW 2239: "Leave political commissars alone; they will be taken care of later by special commandos."

† Some 473,000 were executed according to official German figures (Alexander Dallin, *German Rule in Russia 1941–1945* [London: The Macmillan Company, 1957], pp. 407, 427).

‡ The Russians pointed out at Nuremberg that Soviet prisoners were paid half the wages of prisoners of war from the Western Allies working for the Germans—10 to 60 pfennigs a day instead of .20 to 1.20 RM (N XXXIX, 427-USSR, pp. 515–16).

and the Soviet armies took the offensive. Thousands more joined the German Army as Hiwis (*Hilfswillige*), helpers manning antiaircraft guns and performing noncombatant jobs. Treatment depended on the local commander, and the evidence is clear that thousands of Russian prisoners of war fared as well as the circumstances permitted.

The Army in waging war against the partisans as well as against the regular Soviet Army used, as its orders demanded, "the harshest methods." The bitter partisan war had little place for any of the amenities of warfare in the West. Partisan warfare, which was fought in the roads and forests and villages of the rear areas, was usually conducted with mixed units of Police, SD, and Wehrmacht under the command of a Higher SS and Police officer. In cases where Wehrmacht units outnumbered the others, an Army commander might be in charge.[51] German forces had captured partisan manuals of instruction telling the units that any means were justified against the invaders, and the evidence the Army saw before them made it plain enough that the instructions were being followed. Partisans had missions to infiltrate the German lines and to use women agents to put poison in the Germans' food. German soldiers found the bodies of comrades with eyes gouged out and of others who had been crucified, and they reacted with fire and sword. Villages from which the partisans operated were burned down, the male inhabitants slaughtered, the women sent to work. The decision as to the extent of the reprisals was made not by a military court or by higher authority but by the troop leader of the action. No holds were barred in the East on either side.[52]

Jodl, discussing with Hitler how to fight the war against the partisans, said that the SS had more experience in these matters than the Army. Hitler replied, "They do have the greater experience. But just listen to what is said about the SS because they have that experience. It is always said that they are brutal." To this Jodl said, "That's not true at all. They do it very skillfully; they do everything with sugarplums and the whip, as it's done everywhere else in the world." [53]

In June, 1941, Panzer Group 3 was instructed that if the Tilsit-Insterburg railroad line was damaged all the village inhabitants who lived along it were to be shot. If any doubt existed in the mind of the commander, suspicions would have to suffice.[54] A forty-five-page report of the commander of the Army police of Heeresgruppe Nord was made on July 31, 1942, to Kuechler and Manstein, describing measures that had been taken against the partisans. It said Gypsies were a real danger; if only some of those under suspicion were dealt with, the remainder would still be enemies of the Wehrmacht and therefore they must all be ruthlessly exterminated. This was in accord with National Socialist racial doctrines, but Gypsies were considered generally unreliable and likely to be used as spies.[55] As an ethnic group they were marked for liquidation—not some Gypsies helping the partisans; Gypsies as such.[56] The disregard of soldierly tradition was not limited to the war against the partisans; Reichenau ordered that every man, woman, and child trying to escape from Leningrad was to be fired on.

Some of the Higher Police and SD commanders reporting back to Himmler told of their good relationship with the Army. One such report of November 3, 1941, called it "excellent," but added that only the Jewish problem was a block and that Army commanders had objected to the transfer to the SD of 362 Jewish prisoners of war. "Unfortunately," said the writer, "the Einsatz has to suffer more or less hidden reproaches for their steadfast attitude on the Jewish problem," and he complained further that one camp commander had forbidden the Einsatz units to enter the transit camp. A new order from Reichenau directed the Army to cooperate.[57] SS Lieutenant General Walter Schellenberg of the SD declared his relations with the Army to be good; with General Erich Hoepner, they were "close, almost heartfelt." [58] Another Major General of Police and of the Waffen SS, Ernst Rode, said at Nuremberg that the fact that Jews were turned over to the SD was proof that the executions had the Army's approval.[59]

Like the Commissar Order, the Commando Order (see Keitel, Chapt. 9, and Raeder, Chapt. 10) aroused strong reactions when it was distributed (Rommel burned his copy as soon as he got it), but here, too, councils were divided as to whether it was justified or not. Kesselring testified that it had been carried out only once in the area under his command, by General Anton Dostler; although Commandos often landed behind his lines, they were otherwise always treated as ordinary prisoners of war.* [60] Other Commandos were shot, however, and many of the officers of the Army and Navy who carried out the order thought it justified.

Some generals refused to order their troops to round up labor in occupied countries, saying they had more pressing duties. But others, particularly as the situation worsened, took another view, and the Wehrmacht in one operation provided 2,000 troops to comb an area for workers. In all the Eastern territory the population was required to construct roads and defenses, and in some cases the civil population had to work an eleven-hour day.[61] Requisitions were ruthless. A counterintelligence (Abwehr) report protested the Army's taking the last hen and the last cow from the Russian peasants.[62]

The Army played mainly a passive part in the roundups and shootings of the Jews in the East. On the whole, troop commanders shared the views of the SS, although they did not like the way the Einsatz operated. Commenting on the campaign against the partisans, an Army Field Police report pointed out that Jews often denied their racial origins and a physical inspection might be necessary—obviously to determine whether they were to be separated after their capture from the other prisoners and delivered to the

---

* General Dostler ordered the shooting without trial of fifteen American Commandos who had landed in Italy on a sabotage mission, although they were wearing uniforms and had no civilian clothes. Dostler was tried and executed.

SD.* Jews were not to be kept in prisoner-of-war camps. While Army commanders repeatedly protested the brutal treatment of the Jews and sometimes took steps to protect them when they were working for the Wehrmacht, the Army officers in such cases were usually powerless against the SS and the orders coming from the Fuehrer or from his appointed specialists in solving the Jewish problem. In addition, some of their own commanders, like Reichenau, told the troops of the necessity for "the severe but just retribution against the Jewish subhuman elements." [63]

General Hans Roettiger, who had been Chief of Staff of the Fourth Army, testified at Nuremberg that the SD units in the front areas where he served caused great disturbances among the civil population and Field Marshal Guenther von Kluge was forced to order them to withdraw. Their wild killing of Jews and others, Kluge said, so aroused the population that they threatened the security of the Army. But such an order as Kluge issued was not long lived; other SD units soon were reassigned on orders from Berlin. Then, too, as the SS General Rode pointed out, had the field marshals felt as strongly as they later said they had about the operations of the SD, they could have made a united protest which would have resulted in a change of missions and methods. But the Army needed the antipartisan units, and although individual commanders ordered that the war against the partisans be waged no more severely than necessary, it often seemed essential to annihilate an enemy that himself used the most atrocious methods of fighting.[64]

When individual commanders objected to the brutalities, not much could be done aside from undertaking isolated acts of resistance or making formal protests. General Blaskowitz in October, 1939, after the end of the Polish campaign, wrote a memorandum to Field Marshal Walther von Brauchitsch denouncing the atrocities of the SS and the police formations in Poland, and although Jodl said at Nuremberg that he had heard of the document he had never read it, for it never got to OKW. Brauchitsch did nothing about it; Hitler was merely irritated by it. Some months later, on February 6, 1940, Blaskowitz told his officers that the SS and Police had killed 10,000 Poles and Jews and the Wehrmacht was powerless to intervene. Blaskowitz said the formations responsible should be sent from the area, for among other things the atrocities were having a bad effect on the morale of the troops, who oscillated in their reactions between revulsion and hate for the German authorities who were responsible. He said the Army, too, had executed Poles

* The Army also had orders to turn over any Jews or Gypsies among its prisoners of war or corps of military helpers to the SD (Leeb, Case XII, 2938, NOKW 2535 [Goettingen]. E. H. Stone, ed., *Trial of Nikolaus von Falkenhorst* [London, Edinburgh, and Glasgow: William Hodge & Co., Ltd., 1949], Vol. VI, pp. 16, 105, 133, 270).

A report of the Field Police to the Eleventh Army stated that four Jews were still living in the area of Sargil and the SD had been notified; and another report from the MPs of the same army told of the executions of twenty-five Jews and Communists (Leeb, Case XII, 712a, NOKW 1285 [Goettingen]).

but only for acts of sabotage or because they had forbidden weapons and the population understood the necessity for such security measures. But what was going on under the SS and Police rule was something entirely different, and such measures could never conquer the Poles. On the contrary, what was going on was dangerous for military security.[65]

Blaskowitz was not an exception; a report of the Army command at Posen in November, 1939, objected to the SS interference with the administration of the area, the senseless executions, the plundering, and the grave excesses.[66] General Wilhelm Ulex, protesting the SS brutalities in a memorandum of February 2, 1940, spoke of the "incomprehensible lack of human and moral sensibilities so that one can really speak of a bestializing [Vertierung]." Ulex said the only way out of this unworthy situation that besmirched the honor of the entire German people was to break up all the police formations and their higher leaders.[67] The German Army in its campaigns in the West and in Poland had the strictest orders to follow international law, and even its enemies acknowledged that on the whole it had. Men like Blaskowitz were deeply affronted when they saw such atrocities committed in the name of their country, and they took what measures they could—short of resigning—to have them stopped.

But as German lawyers were to point out later, the crucial fact in the assessing of responsibility for taking part in a crime is whether it might have been prevented, and here the military commanders for the most part were powerless. They might circumvent the Commissar Order but they had no power of discipline or punishment over SS and Einsatz squads. The records are filled with protests of the generals, but on the other hand they are blank regarding further action. When Field Marshal Rommel wanted to take measures against the SS Das Reich Division for the massacre at Oradour, he was told by Hitler that he had nothing to do with the matter.[68] When the SS Adolf Hitler Division shot Jews, the Army commander wanted to take disciplinary action against them, but the division had moved out, the Army report said, and he could do nothing further.[69] Colonel Friedrich Jaeger, who commanded the island of Corfu, spoke of his abhorrence for the deportation of Jews that the Army was carrying out. On the other hand, General Ulrich Kleemann, who commanded the German forces at Rhodes, ordered the evacuation of Jews from the island to be ruthlessly pursued by the troops "with National Socialist zeal." Because of the lack of sufficient ships to transport the refugees, they seem to have been deliberately drowned.[70]

Jodl, who disliked the Commissar Order when he first heard of it, merely wondered if it might not be justified as a reprisal—although this was some months before the campaign against Russia had started. But Field Marshal Kesselring, for example, could not prevent the killings of 335 Italian hostages in the Ardeatine Caves, which were carried out on Hitler's orders by the SD.[71] Nor could the Army command in northern Greece prevent the killing at Klissura in May, 1944, of nine babies under one year old, 29 children of the ages of one to five, and 30 old people between sixty and ninety, after German soldiers had been fired on by partisans from the village and two killed. An SS officer had ordered Klissura to be "combed through," and he later claimed that the killings had occurred as his SS regiment recaptured the town. But witnesses testified that most of the killings had been deliberate, and while a number of Army officers protested when they learned of the massacre, the higher echelons preferred to accept the story of the SS commander.[72] The authority for such actions came from the Fuehrer himself. The Army knew of the wholesale killings. Soldiers witnessed them by chance and reported on them; slaughter on the scale of the massacres in the East could not be hidden.

Documents submitted at the later trials of the generals in Nuremberg showed clearly that Ist Army Corps had known what the Einsatz squads were doing and that Jews and Gypsies were being "specially treated"—the euphemism for executed.[73] A staff officer of Heeresgruppe Mitte officially reported in December, 1941, that the facts of the atrocities were widely known and that the shooting of Jews, prisoners, and commissars was rejected almost generally in the officer corps.[74] A member of the German Foreign Office also testified to the widespread rumors of the mass executions that followed the capture of Kiev, and he said that of course the High Command had been aware of them.[75] General Lahousen, one of the chief witnesses at the first Nuremberg trial, told the Allies that he had known of the executions of Russian prisoners of war.[76] Army orders had to be couched in the terms of the Fuehrer's directives. The enemy was to see his land and houses destroyed as far as they could be of use to him "for a long time," Hitler's directive read, and the Army orders followed it: "The enemy must have only useless land that cannot be lived on." Stone houses were to be blown up, the others burned; railroads, dams, and anything that could help the enemy were to be destroyed.[77]

General Reinecke declared that bolshevism was the mortal enemy of National Socialism and anyone showing any friendliness to Russian prisoners of war should be punished.[78] Reichenau, in his order of October 10, 1941, told his troops to use draconic measures and added:

> the feeding of the natives and of prisoners of war who are not working for the Armed Forces from Army kitchens is a . . . misunderstood humanitarian act, as is the giving of cigarettes and bread. . . . When retreating, the Soviets have often set buildings on fire. The troops should be interested in extinguishing fires only as far as it is necessary to secure sufficient numbers of billets. Otherwise, the disappearance of symbols of the former Bolshevistic rule, even in the form of buildings, is part of the struggle of destruction. Neither historic nor artistic considerations are of any importance in the Eastern Territories.[79]

Almost the same words were used by Manstein in addressing his troops in November, 1941.[80] An order of August 7, 1941, to the XXX Army Corps told the troops they were not harsh enough in their attitude toward Russian prisoners of war, taking into consideration their "inhuman brutality." [81]

Orders of a completely opposite kind were also issued: General Hans Reinhardt, commanding the XLIst Army Panzer Corps, had his propaganda company prepare a statement on the "Political Task of the German Soldier in Russia Under Total War," in which he told his troops the Germans were making no war against peoples. On the contrary, Reinhardt said, the Russians must be won to the German side so they could be used against bolshevism. He added that the Russian was honorable in his character, truth-loving, loyal, and accustomed to suffer; that he bore with hard measures but he wanted justice; that he was not for bolshevism but was a patriotic Russian. The Germans should not be lenient with bolshevism but the good Russian was no enemy. Reinhardt's words came somewhat late in the war (in May, 1943), but commanders like him undoubtedly helped to account for the thousands of Russians who willingly retreated with the German armies.* [82]

The mixed story of the behavior of the German High Command was of strict discipline, the following of the military conventions in conducting the war in the West,† but of a very different kind of war in the East, where before the start of the Russian campaign Fuehrer directives demanded that the Army fight without paying any attention to the rules of war. As German lawyers in later trials were to observe, however, neither in World War II nor in the subsequent minor wars have war crimes and crimes against humanity been confined to Germans. The inherent contradictions in the waging of modern war, with its impersonal weapons of mass destruction, and in the demand for absolute obedience on the one hand and for preserving some kind of human decency on the other have never been solved either by the German or by any other army in this time. One German lawyer recounted the following incidents: in the wake of World War II when a Dutch unit, operating against native troops, was ordered to burn down a village in Indonesia and they refused, the men were given heavy penalties by their

---

* Reinhardt also used Brauchitsch's order on discipline to countermand the Commissar Order, which, he said flatly, would not be carried out in his corps. His immediate superior, General Hoepner, agreed with him, as did Generals Hoch and Ullersperger, Field Marshal von Kluge, and many others. (Leeb, Case XII, 2981, and 3335, session of March 27, 1948 [Goettingen]. Also *TWC*, Leeb, XI).

Reinhardt also ordered the execution of three German soldiers who had tossed a grenade into a bunker instead of bringing out the partisans who were hidden there as prisoners of war (Leeb, Case XII, 3478 [Goettingen]).

† "The people, their property, public installations, and the economy are to be spared, monuments as far as possible are to be protected." Troop commanders were to act ruthlessly against German soldiers' plundering and to assure the nourishment of the civil population and the continuing of economic life. Soldiers were to pay in cash at local prices for purchases up to 500 RM; for anything costing more special receipt forms were issued. Taking any goods without payment was forbidden and was punished as plundering (*N* XXX, 2329-PS, pp. 211–19).

superiors for insubordination. An English patrol, operating in Burma, killed between twenty and thirty unarmed Japanese prisoners because to leave them unharmed where they were would have betrayed the whereabouts of the British troops. The German lawyer pointed out the inconsistency between these men going unpunished and the case of the German submarine commander Eck, who tried to kill the survivors of the ship he had sunk for the same reason—that they would betray the presence of his U-boat in the shallow Mediterranean waters (see Doenitz, Chapt. 10)—and who was subsequently sentenced to death by an Allied court.[83]

Any crimes the German Army may have committed were matched by those of the Russian armies and by the partisans fighting on behalf of their countries and of the Soviet Union. A German lawyer who had studied the record estimated that the partisans committed several thousand crimes a day, without telling how he arrived at this figure, and that one of their own guerrilla leaders boasted that they had accounted for the deaths of more than 500,000 German soldiers. The Western Allies themselves were capable of a kind of warfare that was not foreseen in the Hague Conventions, such as the orders given the British soldiers in the *Handbook of Irregular Warfare*. One of the few international conventions that had a general observance was the one against the killing of prisoners of war, but here again the records show that not only the German soldiers in the Soviet Union failed to follow it. Even during the American Civil War, General Sherman ordered the execution of sixty-four Confederate prisoners of war after twenty-seven of his own soldiers had been found killed with signs pinned to them saying, "death to the plunderers." [84]

As for the killing of hostages, it is an old and deplorable practice, but it is one of the few ways of preventing the killing of one's own troops by partisans or other staunch patriots on the home front. During the Russo-Turkish war (1877–1878), the Russian commander in Thessaly had the inhabitants of houses from which shots had come hanged at their doorsteps. And after the close of World War II, the French commander at Stuttgart threatened to kill Germans at the rate of twenty-five to one, a figure that was upped to two hundred to one by the Americans in the Harz region of Germany. At Reutlingen the French shot four German hostages for the killing of a French soldier. In September, 1944, forty German prisoners of war were shot by the French because a Russian battalion in German service had allegedly committed atrocities, and on the same day forty more Germans were executed apparently for the same reason. Eight German prisoners were shot by an American detachment in the spring of 1945 after an American had been killed by someone shooting from a house. General Rudolf Lehmann, Judge Advocate General with OKW, told Admiral Canaris, head of German counterintelligence, that about 10,000 German prisoners of war had been executed by the Allies and that the Germans had to take reprisals. Canaris pointed out that this was illegal under international law, but Lehmann said some kind of reprisal had to be undertaken, and when Canaris was given the facts, he agreed.[85]

The tribunal's denunciation of the High Command went too far; it did not apply to many honorable officers who were typical of the old General Staff however well it fitted many of the others who shared the racial or political views of Adolf Hitler. What they all had done was to serve a criminal regime with much the same devotion, courage, and skill they would have given an emperor or president in the tradition of a legitimate, normal government. They had given countenance to illegal orders, as they had to the murder of Schleicher and the humiliation of Fritsch. Many of them had refused to carry out such orders and many of the best had joined the Resistance when they had to make the terrible decision of conscience as to whether they would rise in time of war against a head of state who they saw was destroying Germany or to fight on only against the foreign enemy. When they had acted against Hitler they had acted alone; no gleam of hope came from outside Germany, no German government in exile existed, and the Allies would hear of nothing but unconditional surrender. All that was left them was their own consciences. Some of those who had fought on hopelessly until the end of the war were as opposed to Hitler as those who plotted against him, but they saw their duty otherwise.[86]

The landmarks, outside the individual conscience for those who resisted as well as those who fought on, had disappeared. Superior orders were supposed to come from a head of state who thought and lived and made his decisions in terms of the tradition and military code that had nourished them all. But Hitler was *sui generis*, a nihilist, a demonic revolutionary, a primitive destructive force, a man with no code but his own purposes, and the Army had no instructions in its handbooks or in its codes on how to obey and serve that kind of head of state. The High Command was a long way from the conspiratorial group of the prosecution's imaginings, but step by step it also moved a long way from the values of the officer corps of Moltke, Schlieffen, and Hindenburg.

The generals were caught in a monumental dilemma. Patriotism, duty, and honor became, like everything else in the Third Reich, what Hitler said they were, and how could they serve Germany against its enemies when its chief enemy might be the head of state they had sworn to obey? Some of them, like Jodl, who had disliked or been skeptical of Hitler, came to revere him for his genius; others remained dubious; still others wavered between belief and mistrust; and some in the end, convinced of his perfidy, tried to kill him. But they all, if one can speak of such disparate men as a group, were caught in a tragedy that was not of their making. Their job was to defend the Reich against its external foes, and they had no ready weapons against its head of state and their commander in chief. Step by step they yielded ground to him and to the Party; its swastika appeared on their helmets and its preachments in their barracks and in many of their heads, and at the end those who remained adopted its salute and shared with it the destruction of the country they all placed above life itself.

NOTES

1. *NCA*, Supp. A, p. 291.
2. *History of UNWCC*, p. 303.
3. *N* XXII, pp. 294–96.
4. Sumner Welles, *The Time for Decision* (New York: Harper & Row, Publishers, Incorporated, 1944), pp. 338–46.
5. *N* XXII, pp. 175, 239.
6. Theophil Burgstaller testimony, Commission Protocol June 13, 1946 (IZG).
7. Fritz Schwaben testimony, Commission Protocol July 1, 1946, pp. 1928 ff. (IZG).
8. Guenther Reinecke testimony, Commission Protocols July 5–6, 1946, pp. 2657 ff. (IZG).
9. *N* XX, Georg Konrad Morgen testimony, pp. 487–515. *N* XLII, SS-65, SS-67, Georg Konrad Morgen affidavits, pp. 551–65.
10. *SS im Einsatz* (Berlin: Kongress-Verlag, 1957), pp. 293–382, 551–54.
11. Hans Roessner testimony, Commission Protocol, pp. 2620 ff. (IZG).
12. Hans Ehlich testimony, Commission Protocol July 4, 1946 (IZG).
13. Bruno Biedemann testimony, Commission Protocol June 27, 1946, p. 2025 (IZG).
14. Albert Hoffmann testimony, Commission Protocol July 3, 1946, pp. 2366 ff. (IZG).
15. Eduard Kuehl testimony, Commission Protocol June 28, 1946, pp. 2260 ff. (IZG).
16. *N* XXI, pp. 408–10.
17. Szymon Datner, *Crimes Against POW's* (Warsaw: Zachodnia Agencja Prasowa, 1964), p. 71.
18. *TWC*, Vol. XI, pp. 518-19. *N* XX, p. 582. NOKW 3357 (IZG).
19. Judge Advocate General Erich Lattmann testimony of December 8, 1947, 4257 Interrogation Summary (IZG).
20. Adolf Heusinger, *Befehl im Widerstreit* (Tuebingen; Rainer Wunderlich Verlag Hermann Leins, 1957), p. 295.
21. Walter Warlimont, *Inside Hitler's Headquarters 1939–45* (New York: Frederick A. Praeger, Inc., 1964), pp. 169–70.
22. *N* XXII, p. 75.
23. *Ibid.*, p. 58.
24. *Ibid.*, pp. 58–59.
25. Warlimont, *op. cit.*
26. *N* XXII, p. 84.
27. *Ibid.*, p. 86.
28. *Ibid.*, pp. 522–23.

29. *History of UNWCC*, p. 321.

30. Letters to Baronin von Schutzbar of December 11, 1938, and August 7, 1939, cited in John W. Wheeler-Bennett, *The Nemesis of Power* (London: The Macmillan Company, Ltd., 1954), pp. 379–81.

31. Léon Poliakov and Joseph Wulf, *Das Dritte Reich und seine Diener* (Berlin-Grunewald: Arani Verlags-GmbH., 1956), pp. 398–416.

32. Document CXLVIII-32, cited in *ibid.*, p. 459.

33. NCA, Supp. A, 4064-PS, p. 827.

34. Halder, *op. cit.*, entry of March 30, 1941, Vol. II, p. 337.

35. *TWC*, Vol. X, p. 41. Leeb, Case XII, 2715 (Goettingen).

36. Gert Buchheit, *Soldatentum und Rebellion* (Rastatt/Baden: Grot'sche Verlagsbuchhandlung, 1961), p. 208.

37. Halder, *op. cit.*, entry of September 26, 1941, Vol. III, p. 252.

38. *TWC*, Vol. X, pp. 1205–7.

39. NOKW 2268 (IZG).

40. NCA VI, 3713-PS, p. 429. NOKW 2535, p. 38 (Goettingen). OKH, 48-page report of July 31, 1942 (IZG).

41. General Nehring's affidavit, OKW 324 (IZG). General Dessloch's affidavit, OKW 501 (IZG).

42. *TWC*, Vol. X, p. 1098.

43. *Ibid.*, p. 1133.

44. Datner, *op. cit.*, p. 78.

45. NOKW 2239 (IZG).

46. NI 1600, September 16, 1943 (IZG).

47. *TWC*, Leeb, XI, September 15, 1941, p. 3.

48. Buchheim, *et al.*, *op. cit.*, Vol. II, p. 197.

49. Juergen Thorwald, *Wen sie verderben wollen* (Stuttgart: Steingrueben-Verlag, 1952).

50. 501 V C 103, p. 138 (Nuremberg Staatsarchiv).

51. NCA VI, 3717-PS, Heusinger testimony, p. 434.

52. John A. Armstrong, ed., *Soviet Partisans in World War II* (Madison: University of Wisconsin Press, 1964). Leeb, Case XII, 3795 (Goettingen).

53. Felix Gilbert, *Hitler Directs His War* (New York: Oxford University Press, 1951), p. 8.

54. NOKW 2672 (IZG).

55. *Cf.* Hans-Joachim Doering, "Die Motive der Zigeuner-Deportation vom Mai 1940," in *Vierteljahrshefte fuer Zeitgeschichte*, Vol. VII, No. 4, 1959, pp. 419–28.

56. NOKW 2535, p. 39 (Goettingen).

57. NO 3157 (IZG).

58. N XXXII, 3710-PS, p. 471.

59. *Ibid.*, 3716-PS, pp. 482–83.

60. Kesselring hearing, July 3, 1946 (IZG).

61. *TWC*, April 24, 1944, Leeb, XI, p. 282.

62. 501 V C 103, p. 138 (Nuremberg Staatsarchiv).

63. N XXXV, 411-D, order of October 10, 1941, p. 85.

64. NCA VI, 3713-PS, 3714-PS, 3715-PS, 3716-PS, pp. 429–33.

65. Blaskowitz interrogation of October 29, 1945 (NA). Jacobsen and Jochmann, eds., *op. cit.*, February 6, 1940.

66. N XXXV, 419-D, p. 87.

67. Document CXXXVI-15, cited in Poliakov and Wulf, *op. cit.*, p. 518.

68. Desmond Young, *Rommel—The Desert Fox* (New York: Harper & Row, Publishers, Incorporated, 1950), p. 207.

69. Leeb, Case XII, 3137 (Goettingen).

70. Buchheit, *op. cit.*, p. 291. Poliakov and Wulf, *op. cit.*, pp. 355–61.

71. Hans Laternser, *Verteidigung deutscher Soldaten* (Bonn: Girardet, 1950).

72. NOKW 469 (IZG).

73. NOKW 2977 (IZG). Leeb, Case XII, 2943 (Goettingen).

74. Buchheim, *et al.*, *op. cit.*, Vol. II, p. 376.

75. Braeutigam interrogation of May 5, 1948 (NA).

76. Lahousen interrogation of September 24, 1945 (NA).

77. TWC, Leeb, XI, p. 310. NOKW 1300. 501 V C 103, p. 185 (Nuremberg Staatsarchiv).

78. N XXVII, 1519-PS, pp. 275–76.

79. N XXXV, 411-D, pp. 81–86.

80. N XXXIV, 4064-PS, pp. 129–32.

81. TWC, Leeb, XI, pp. 67–69. NOKW 1906.

82. Leeb, Case XII, 3497 (Goettingen).

83. August von Knieriem, *The Nuremberg Trials* (Chicago: Henry Regnery Company, 1959), p. 254.

84. *Ibid.*, pp. 368, 385.

85. Leeb, Case XII, 8291 (Goettingen).

86. Frido von Senger und Etterlin, *Krieg in Europa* (Cologne and Berlin: Kiepenheuer & Witsch, 1960).

15

Two Decades Later

The trial has left many questions unanswered. Was the Nazi period, as some Germans say, an aberration of a basically humane and enlightened society, or was it the final expression of the *furor teutonicus* always latent in the German character? Were the twenty-two defendants tried involved in crimes specifically related to German traits or were they, like the accused before conventional tribunals, guilty or innocent of specific criminal acts that might occur in any country? Is there, or was there as some writers have alleged, a paranoid Germany, or a Germany dominated by a father image that made it easier for these men than for Frenchmen, Englishmen, or Americans to say, "Fuehrer, command; we follow," whatever the consequences to themselves or to their country? Was the Hitler dictatorship a purely German phenomenon? Could it have occurred in the forms we have witnessed anywhere else in the world? Could it have been prevented had the opposition been more resolute, or, given the German character and the external situation, was it inevitable—did there have to be either Hitler or someone like him?

To ask such questions is essentially to ask whether there is a fixed German character; it is not very different from asking whether the eternal Jew exists, or perfidious Albion, or the spiritless serfs of a Russian state whether under the Czars or the Secretaries of the Communist Party. And it is evident that what passes for national character changes; the volatile Elizabethan Englishman bore little resemblance to the slow-paced, phlegmatic, inscrutable Britisher of the nineteenth century; Washington's Farewell Address was written for a different audience of Americans from the one that met in San Francisco for the founding of the UN in 1945. The saber-rattling France of the Bourbons and Napoleons could be contrasted a hundred years ago with the peace-loving, *gemuetliche* Germans, who preferred beer steins to muskets and a variety of provincial courts and customs to domination by a centralized Reich.

Every society has in it at all times negative, criminal, sadistic, asocial forces. What holds them in check more than law and police is the consensus of the society—a general belief that despite everything wrong and stupid and muddleheaded in its politics, the state is a going concern that will somehow make its way into the future. The German State between 1870 and 1914 had such a consensus. But the German society after World War I was sick; it was psychologically bled white. Like so many American Southerners after the Civil War, millions of Germans were unable to digest a defeat that was made the more incomprehensible by a war-guilt clause in the Treaty of Versailles that neither the German people nor many future historians would regard as just, by the measures codifying international "morality" that applied only to Germans, by an inflation that wiped out their savings, by reparations, by unending political disorder and an economy that soon appeared to produce more unemployment than goods. A Hitler who before 1914 was the inmate of a flop house in Vienna was after the war listened to in a society of the disinherited. A man like Goering no longer had a place, no longer had any purpose unless it might be to redress the wrongs inflicted by the Treaty of Versailles. The Streichers exist everywhere—and in a sick society they can flourish.

The generals and the admirals, like the generals and the admirals of every country, had the job of protecting their people with the forces at hand, and in the case of post-World War I Germany this seemed impossible without violating the treaty that was the cornerstone of a rickety structure of legality dominated by a France that the German armies had twice defeated in the space of less than half a century. These military men were Germans and nothing they did as a group seems very different from what the generals and admirals of any nationality would have been likely to do under the same circumstances.

As for the diplomats, only one—Ribbentrop—was in his absurd fashion a man of the revolution. He got along well with his Canadian, English, and French friends before and after World War I and with Jews before he joined Hitler; not very intelligent but ingratiating and ambitious, he would have done well selling his wares in any conventional society. Neurath, the respectable if uninspired functionary of the Foreign Office; Papen, the pleasant, well-bred opportunist who nevertheless spoke up at Marburg—such men are in the foreign service of every country, dealing for and with administrations of which they disapprove and keeping their jobs as long as they can.

The Schachts and the Funks can only be bracketed by their offices. Schacht talked the same language as the financiers of England and the United States and would have been at home in any foreign bank or chancellery, while Funk owed his eminence solely to the revolution. In the Funks we perceive the officials of the borderland territory that leads over to the purely National Socialist, to the German phenomenon. Funk was never more than a second-class financier who accepted gold teeth because they, too, passed for security in the banks of the Third Reich.

The Rosenbergs, Kaltenbrunners, Seyss-Inquarts were all fellow travelers of the anti-Communist revolution, of a counterrevolution that took hold in Germany although it started in Italy. They were international in their aptitudes and to some degree in their backgrounds. Rosenberg, the Balt who may have fought in the Russian Army of World War I, was an ideologue not without resemblances to Houston Stewart Chamberlain, Count Gobineau, and Henry Ford. Kaltenbrunner was, like Seyss-Inquart, an Austrian lawyer, but there the resemblance between the two ceases. For Seyss, like Frick and to some degree like Frank, was a circumspect man of law dominated by a fanatical ideology, while Kaltenbrunner was a man of the secret police, another international type that is at home in the MVDs and the security forces of every totalitarian state.

As for Speer and Fritzsche, they, too, might have operated in any society that offered them the chances for the exercise of their talents. Fritzsche, the plausible pitchman, needed mass media—newspapers and the radio—to persuade his audience; Speer needed the efficient, hard-working German artisan to attain his most dramatic results—otherwise he could be the technician, the organizer, the rationalizer of a work force anywhere.

Hess and Schirach, both risen to exalted positions as a result of the National Socialist revolution, were undoubtedly typical products of its doctrines, but they might have fitted into the pattern of any ideological movement, one the dour, devoted logic-proof apostle of the superiority of the Northern races and of the wisdom of the Fuehrer; the other the eternal boy scout, eager, idealistic when it came to Germans, sentimental, full of bad poetry and easy solutions—his kind, too, is international, and when the Schirachs are not part of youth movements, they may lead church pageants or amateur theatricals or take part in marches with uplifting slogans.

Every country has its special brand of cruelty, of brutality. There are many ways to kill and to justify killings. The British and Americans, for example, have preferred to use long-range methods of extermination, with their bombings of civilian centers and the hunger blockade that was kept in force after the armistice of World War I until the German Government signed the treaty that every German would regard as infamous. The orders given the British Commandos in World War II were as illegal and brutal as the Commissar Order; and it is not easy to see the German Army issuing a similar order, or the SS either, because their own gangster tactics had to be masked with elaborate moral imperatives that talked a good deal about honor.

The Government of Soviet Russia has also been the executioner of millions of its people, including officers of its pre-World War II Army, not to mention the Polish officers who died in the Katyn forest. Few individuals in the Soviet Army raised a finger against the dictator Stalin; the equivalent of the German resistance to Hitler, so far as we know, never existed in the Soviet Union. The class enemy in Russia has been as ruthlessly exterminated as were the Jews in the Third Reich. The Polish officers, like victims of the Warsaw uprising, were killed because they, too, were regarded as class and ethnic enemies.

What marked the German slaughter was its cool, impersonal, organizational efficiency, the methodical lists of executions, the Gestapo and SD operations, the complicated State and Party bureaucracy that listed, sorted, catalogued, and kept such accurate files that almost nothing was lost from the plunder. Pogroms, racial murders, lynchings have usually been spontaneous local reactions toward people believed to be inferior. In the Third Reich they were the result of a well-considered, duly codified, and paragraphed public policy. When all the tu quoques are taken into consideration, it still seems that the crimes of the Nazi regime supported for some twelve years by the sacrifices and *Treue* of huge sections of the population were a phenomenon not to be matched elsewhere in the civilized world.

While few of the defendants and still fewer, proportionally, of the German people took a direct part in the killings and only a small fraction of the population knew about them, the German people all knew that Hitler was telling the truth when he said that in the event of war he would not like to be a Jew in the Third Reich. The Resistance, too, it may be added, was characteristically German; its idealism, its willingness to sacrifice, its careful planning, its obvious blunders, its selflessness—this was no junta aspiring to jobs and power.

The single-minded pursuit on the part of men like Eichmann, Bormann, Heydrich, and Kaltenbrunner of their goal of getting rid of Jews was evidence of their fanaticism; and fanatics, while not limited to Germans or Austrians, have an easier time attaining their goals when they have the apparatus of a devoted, well-trained bureaucracy at their disposal. It was above all the crime of mass murder that was being tried at Nuremberg, and the persons believed to be implicated in it were not only the men in the dock but millions of their countrymen outside the walls of the Palace of Justice.

Nothing like these beltline mass murders had ever occurred in the entire history of man's inhumanity, and the smoke of the crematories covered the entire proceedings from the start of the trial to its end and beyond. The other charges might have been dealt with in a purely judicial fashion had it not been for the mass slaughter of these defenseless people.

We have seen what role the individual defendants played in the exterminations, but no matter what the degree of individual guilt or innocence, these murders dominated the trial of the twenty-two and the attitudes of the prosecution, of the defense, of the judges, and of the German people toward the trial and toward themselves. The defendants were deliberately selected to represent what the Allies regarded as the high command of the Nazi Party and State. But it was widely believed that their guilt was not entirely unlike that of the individual German in the cross section of the population that served in the armed forces, the bureaucracy, the police, the party formations, the factories, and on the farms. It might be conceded that millions of people knew nothing of the exterminations. It was certain, however, that they all knew a great deal about the persecutions and that they nevertheless took arms against the world to keep these men in power. The trial therefore was the trial of the Germans.

Probably no army in history fought better than the German Army in World War II, and certainly none fought in a worse cause. From Norway to the Caucasus, from the North Atlantic to the deserts of Africa, the German troops battled with a courage and skill and fortitude that could be the envy of any military commander. But they fought, although they did not know it, for nothing at all, for a nonworld, a diabolic and antihuman system that in the end, following the orders of the Fuehrer, would grind them down as sadistically as it would the Jews and the Bolsheviks. The German people had shown themselves the weaker, said Hitler; what remained of them was not worthy to survive.

It is not easy to think of, let us say, Italians, or British, or Americans fighting as desperately in such a cause, but to thousands of Germans it was not such a cause any more than chattel slavery was the cause for which the Confederate soldier fought in the American Civil War. The doctrines of racism were undoubtedly widely accepted among the German people, although we have only the records of what they were taught, not what they believed, but it should be borne in mind that racism, too, is no German monopoly. The responses of sizable sections of the United States and of South Africa to the problem of race are not totally different from those of the Third Reich. Even in the United States thousands of Americans of Japanese ancestry with the approval of the Supreme Court could be put into well-run concentration camps during World War II for no crime other than that of being Japanese. And the hostility of millions of whites to Negroes, as such, is of long standing in thousands of non-Germanic communities in many countries. Abundant evidence, too, lies before us in our time that the hostility can be proof against reason and the standards of morality that are otherwise firmly rooted in the society and that it can erupt into slaughter.

So perhaps we may say this: something not unlike the National Socialist phenomenon exists potentially in many non-Germanic areas; it is kept in check when the society is functioning, when it pursues its normal, unthreatened courses. The fanaticism, even of a final solution, lurks in the background, latent, ready to strike, to spread, to impress its image of the pure society whenever it can gain enough converts, and those may come when people see no other way to turn. Papen, Neurath, Jodl, Raeder,

Schacht in the course of time and for varying periods came to accept National Socialism, although not until the alternatives seemed exhausted, not until Hitler succeeded with his legerdemain in winning internal and external victories that the parties of reason and goodwill had failed to win. For it should be remembered that only two contemporary political systems have presented a blueprint for rationalizing the technological society with its recurrent economic crises and tidal waves of unemployment: communism and its mirror image, fascism—National Socialism. To millions of their adherents and to many observers who never adopted all their principles, communism or National Socialism, particularly in times of depression and crises, has seemed to have the answers lacking in the traditional societies they replaced, and it was not only the defendants at Nuremberg who believed that a leader of genius had at long last come up with the hitherto missing answers.

Hitler's rise might have been prevented—we have seen the attempts at resistance—had there been more resolution and more knowledge of the consequences of his revolution on the part not only of Germans but also of the statesmen in foreign countries who made it impossible for the republican government of the Weimar period to remake a viable and self-respecting Germany to take its equal place among the nations of the Continent. It was, for example, the Munich agreement, paradoxically the first serious attempt of the victorious powers to remedy the inferior treatment accorded Germans in the post-World War I world, that at a critical time kept Hitler in power. Beck and the other generals tried to prevent a war against the seemingly overwhelming coalition that would be ranged against Germany in 1938; the conspiracy was defeated by the Allies' readiness to concede to Hitler what they never had been willing to grudge in any important measure to his democratic predecessors.

When the Hitler in ourselves, as Max Picard once called it, is recognized, National Socialism remains, in its massive form, a Germanic phenomenon. Similar movements in other countries no more compare with its wholesale, protracted assault on the Western tradition than they could with the disciplined phalanxes of the German Army and the German work force still struggling at the end toward no goal at all. It seems impossible that a Speer, in the face of the bombings, the shortages, the hopelessness of the strategic situation, could for all his talent have organized the workers of Italy or France or the United States or England to produce what he was able to achieve in the dying days of the Third Reich. Perhaps he might have been able to accomplish something of the kind in the Soviet Union or in Japan, where the habits of obedience and lack of criticism of authority are not dissimilar to those in Germany. For this is something which, if not specifically Germanic, nevertheless clearly divided German habits of thought from, for example, the American cynicism—the Bronx cheer, the ineradicable suspicion that any leader is likely to have clay in both his feet and his head.

This quality of respect for the *Obrigkeit* has changed in the West Germany of post-World War II. If after the war Adenauer seemed to have become another father figure for Germans, he never evoked, wanted, or could have had the kind of sycophantic hero worship accorded many of his historic predecessors. Nor has anyone else on the political scene during the twenty years since the end of World War II seemed capable of inspiring among Germans anything more than the limited confidence Americans or British accord their politicians. The Nazi period seems truly to have been an aberration in German history, a grotesque summation of a German national character that had never before had a Hitler as head of state; and the aberration is not likely to occur again, not in the East or in the West or in any combination of the two. No radical rightist party in the Bundesrepublik has been able to build up any kind of mass following or even to stay long on the ballot under the constitutional requirement that it poll at least 5 per cent of the total vote. The swastikas that have appeared on Jewish synagogues in West Germany have been the handiwork of a few young hoodlums, and any sign of anti-Semitism or of any revival of National Socialism is immediately and unanimously denounced by the entire German press as well as by public opinion. A few journals of insignificant circulation continue to justify the Nazi period, but both among the German youth and among their elders the papers have no influence and the number of readers to which they appeal, while showing sporadic signs of growth, remains a lunatic fringe.* The Nazi period was a time when the criminal psychopaths took over, and no one knows better than the German people what its costs came to.

A trial had to take place for political and for psychological reasons; what the Nazis had done was no matter of lurid propaganda like the stories of the priests used as bell clappers to stir emotions in World War I. Shocking crimes had been committed, war crimes and murder on a huge scale; the question was how their perpetrators were to be dealt with so that victors and those of the vanquished capable of reeducation would see at long last that justice was being done.

Admittedly, the question became more complicated when the attempt was made to create new law, to try acts of violence that have been crimes for millennia along with acts that had never before been considered crimes, and to try them before a court composed only of the victorious powers. For many, the trial was faulted from the beginning. State and federal judges, including

---

* In 1959 the total membership of the radical right was 56,200; in 1964 it was 22,500. Its chief representative, the Deutsche Reichspartei, polled in 1949 1.8 per cent of the German vote; in 1953, 1.1 per cent; and 1961, 0.8 per cent. Only in the local elections of the Rhineland-Palatinate did the party have a temporary success when in 1959 it polled 5.1 per cent of the vote and elected one representative. He was, however, defeated in 1963. The vote in 1966 of between 7 and 8 per cent in Hesse and Bavaria for the National Democratic party is the highest right radical parties have attained. Its members are a mixed group and have included even anti-Nazis as well as neo-Nazis.

the Chief Justice of the United States Supreme Court, were dubious of its morality and its dicta, as were jurists and politicians in the United States, England, France, and Germany.* Others saw in it the hope of the world, the milestone of a new era, the tablets of a new international code made possible by indicting the worst of crimes—the waging of aggressive war. So confident were they of the long-range validity of the court's findings and the vitality of the UN that many of them as late as 1950 no longer felt it necessary to codify rules of war. War itself was outlawed; how could rules be established for an illegal thing? † ¹

Secretary Stimson, in the January, 1947, issue of *Foreign Affairs*, wrote:

> We have now seen again . . . what has been proved in 1917—that peace is indivisible . . . The man who makes aggressive war at all makes it against all mankind. This is an exact, not a rhetorical description of the crime of aggressive war . . . There was somewhere in our distant past a first case of

* Chief Justice Stone, speaking of the power of the victors over the vanquished, wrote: "It would not disturb me greatly if that power were openly and frankly used to punish the German leaders for being a bad lot, but it disturbs me some to have it dressed up in the habiliments of the common law and the constitutional safeguards to those charged with crime" (Alpheus T. Mason, "Extra-Judicial Work for Judges: The Views of Chief Justice Stone," *Harvard Law Review*, Vol. LXVII, No. 2, December, 1953).

Senator Taft said much the same thing: "My objection to the Nuremberg trials is that while clothed with the forms of justice they were in fact an instrument of government policy determined months before at Yalta and Teheran," and he, too, objected to their *post facto* law (Jeschek, *op. cit.*, p. 15. *The New York Times*, October 6, 1946).

Judge Radhabinode Pal, a member of the Calcutta High Court and of the International Military Tribunal for the Far East, wrote, "The so-called trial held according to the definition of crime now given by the victors obliterates the centuries of civilization which stretch between us and the summary slaying of the defeated in a war. A trial with law thus prescribed will only be a sham employment of legal process for the satisfaction of a thirst for revenge" (M. P. A. Hankey, *Politics, Trials and Errors* [Chicago: Henry Regnery Company, 1950], p. 26).

Protests against the trials were also made by among others, the secretary of the American Association of International Law, Pitman B. Potter (letter to *The New York Times*, June 2, 1946), and Federal Judge Charles E. Wyzanski, Jr. (*Cf.* also Maugham, *op. cit.*; and Montgomery Belgion, *Victor's Justice* [Chicago: Henry Regnery Company, 1949]).

On the other side, Walter Lippmann compared Nuremberg with the Magna Charta, habeas corpus, and the Bill of Rights: "A development in human justice which our descendants may well consider the event of modern times" (*The New York Times*, June 8, 1946.).

† The principle that war is a crime has been discussed and approved in declarations in the United Nations, but there the matter rests. On December 11, 1946, the General Assembly of the UN voted unanimously that it

affirms the principles of international law recognized by the Charter of the Nuremberg Tribunal and the judgment of the Tribunal;

Directs the Committee on the codification of international law . . . to treat as a matter of primary importance for the formulation, in the context of a general codification of offenses against the peace and security of mankind, or of an international criminal code, of the principles recognized in the charter of the Nuremberg Tribunal and in the judgment of the Tribunal. (*History of the United Nations War Crimes Commission* [London: H. M. Stationery Office 1948], p. 260).

murder . . . The charge of aggressive war is unsound therefore only if the community of nations did not believe in 1939 that aggressive war was an offense. Merely to make such a suggestion, however, is to discard it . . .

That only eight of the twenty-two defendants had been found guilty of conspiracy seemed surprising to him and he added that the atomic bomb had been used by the United States to save lives not only of our troops but of the enemy as well.[2]

In 1948 the members of the International Law Committee of the UN were given the task of carrying out the December, 1946, vote of the Assembly to formulate the findings of Nuremberg, and in 1950 they produced seven principles which the committee emphasized were merely formulations and were not to be taken as an attempt to evaluate the Nuremberg principles in the light of international law. The General Assembly agreed. Subsequent attempts to define such offenses have been no more concrete. On January 21, 1951, the Genocide Convention came into effect. This convention for the prevention and punishment of mass murders had been unanimously adopted by the General Assembly on December 9, 1948, but it was a statement of principle only. The detection and punishment of any malefactor is left for the signatory powers to arrange. And neither in the 1956 report of the Special Committee on the Question of Defining Aggression nor in any subsequent attempt to deal with the matter has the United Nations succeeded in coming up with a definition of aggression.[3]

Despite many euphoric views, like those of Mr. Stimson, the existence of armed conflicts following World War II was unmistakable whether they were called limited wars or police actions. Behind the forms of hostilities was the specter of another war different from any of these and from any in the past, a war served by computers and waged by missiles that would attack entire populations. As one international lawyer observed: "One must ask oneself whether the revolution in the nature of war by the new weapons will not mean only the disappearance of the laws of war but in its consequence a rapid fall of the whole law of nations." [4]

A committee of the International Red Cross in 1951 found that many of the provisions of the Hague Conventions were no longer applicable, and a committee of the American Society of International Law in 1952 declared the laws of war to be in "a chaotic state." [5] Three of the prisoner-of-war conventions adopted in Geneva in 1949 came to be questioned within a year, for, as the Korean war showed, prisoners of war in ideological conflicts may have uses for the belligerent nations long after active hostilities have ceased for the captives. Chinese Communist and North Korean soldiers, after being made prisoners, staged riots in their detention camps. Captured American soldiers were put under physical and psychological "reeducation processes" to make them denounce their own country and its allegedly inhuman methods of warfare. Nor is it easy under conditions of modern warfare to find a protecting power satisfactory to both sides to oversee the treatment of prisoners of war. Communist countries question the impartiality of the Red Cross, which they regard as a tool of the West.[6]

Since February, 1956, the United States has been bound by four multilateral treaties drawn up in 1949. Their provisions are incorporated in the *American Army Field Manual* of 1956, which provides that hostages may not be taken; reprisals may be taken only against enemy soldiers who have not yet been made prisoners; partisans and members of the Resistance are accorded a legal status if they can be readily identified, carry arms openly, and conduct their operations in accordance with the laws and customs of war; medical supplies and essential food for children may not be subject to blockade; only the civilian population over eighteen may be forced to work and then only within the occupied territory on essential tasks for the occupying power, on public utilities, or in other work on behalf of the population. Civilians may not be sent outside their own country except for their own security or for imperative military reasons. Prisoners of war may not be killed because a danger exists that they may be freed by their own troops or because they hinder the movements of the forces that captured them. Taxes are to be levied against the enemy population to pay for the costs of occupation only—the occupying power is not to tax to enrich itself.

In these laws of warfare no attempt was made to ban new weapons; the bombardment of undefended places is prohibited, but if a city or town is surrounded by detached defense positions or has soldiers in it or passing through it, it is not considered undefended. In other words, in practice little or no distinction is made between combatants and noncombatants in conducting bombing operations.[7] Nevertheless, on the whole, these are humanitarian conventions that, if followed, would ameliorate the lot of both civilian populations and prisoners of war.

In addition, with the problem of superior orders in mind, both the American and the British military manuals declare that a soldier is obliged to obey lawful orders only.[8] The West German Constitution or Basic Law declares in Article 25 that international law is part of German Federal Law. No order is to be carried out in the Army of the Bundesrepublik if it would lead to the committing of a crime or a transgression. In the Soviet Union a soldier has the right to complain to his superiors if he receives an order he deems unlawful; he incurs no responsibility for an unlawful order issued by an officer; the responsibility is that of the officer alone unless the order is clearly criminal, in which case both the soldier and the officer are responsible.

As for the resort to war, the two worlds—Communist and non-Communist —remain divided. For the Communists any war of "national liberation" is a "just war," as is any war in which a Communist country is engaged.[*] The aggressor is identified well ahead of time and the war criminals are its heads of state and government. So far the Western powers have succeeded in using the counterformulas of Nuremberg only in isolated cases. During the Korean war and the fortuitous absence of the Soviet Union from the Security Council, members of the United Nations sent troops to aid the American and South Korean forces; but the troops fought under an American commander and not as an army representing a supranational organization bent on subduing an illegal attack. In general, major conflicts remain nonjusticiable. The recurrent flare-ups over Berlin, the Cuban crisis, and the fighting in Vietnam are in a different category from border disputes between India and Pakistan, Arab-Israeli incidents, and civil war in the Congo. The difference lies in how deeply the major powers, especially the Soviet Union and the United States, are involved.

In major conflicts, it is obviously true that to be successfully indicted an aggressor or a war criminal one must first lose the war. No victor is likely to call himself by such names or to submit to an international court (nor does one exist) where he would be answerable to such charges—the aggressors must be members of the defeated nation. This holds true for the commission of war crimes and crimes against humanity; such crimes can only be committed by members of the losing side. Who other than the victor is to judge them? Since the end of the various trials of the Germans and Japanese, no one has been haled before an international tribunal for any of the delicts punished at Nuremberg, although in the last twenty years the world has not been lacking in armed conflicts and atrocities. The trials that have taken place have been held under the auspices of powers that have held prisoners and could enforce their own notions of guilt and innocence. In these latter years it would be difficult to find many cases in which accused enemies were found not guilty.

As for the basic crime, the German Federal Republic declares in its constitution that preparations for aggressive war are illegal and are to be punished. There the matter rests, as it does in the UN. In its legal statutes the Bundesrepublik has made no provision for punishing whoever might be plotting aggression. In place of the legally undefinable word, a committee on international and foreign law of the Philadelphia Bar Association has

---

[*] Lenin called World War I an imperialist war on both sides. "It is unavoidable," he wrote, "that imperialism must often create national wars" (*Imperialism as the Highest Stage of Capitalism*, 1916, Collected Works [Moscow, 1946], p. 850). In November, 1949, Soviet Foreign Minister Vyshinsky told the United Nations that war was inevitable in capitalist, imperialist countries but "the power of the solidarity of the peace loving countries is capable . . . of rescuing the world from this terrible catastrophe" (Jeschek, *op. cit.*, p. 227). Despite the post-Stalin doctrine of peaceful coexistence, the same denunciations have recurred in every case where the United States, whether in Cuba or Africa or Asia, has opposed Soviet policy (*cf.* Reinhart Maurach, *Die Kriegsverbrecherprozesse gegen deutsche Gefangene in der Sowjetunion* [Hamburg: Arbeitsgemeinschaft vom Roten Kreuz in Deutschland, 1950]).

suggested that the term "aggressor" be abandoned and an effort made to define as a crime against the people of the world the attempt to do bodily harm to those individuals outside areas governed by the accused.[9] In short, no international instrument, whether court or police power, exists that may be said to carry out the doctrines of the Nuremberg tribunal and their reaffirmation by the United Nations. The UN Charter provides that only states may be parties before the International Court of Justice.

The German lawyers at Nuremberg held the same view, and they still do. No individual, they said, could commit a crime against international law, which is binding upon states. An individual could only commit a crime under municipal law for which statutes and penalties and means of enforcement exist, and it was the municipal law of his own country that could be invoked against him if he refused to serve in its armed forces because he thought his government an aggressor.[10] In addition, one of the points repeatedly made by the German defense lawyers at the trial seems to be substantiated by the Declaration of Human Rights adopted by the General Assembly of the United Nations on December 10, 1948. It reads: "No one shall be held guilty of any penal offense on account of any act or omission which did not constitute a penal offense, under national or international law, at the time when it was committed. Nor shall a heavier penalty be imposed than the one that was applicable at the time the penal offense was committed." Whatever else may be said of the Kellogg-Briand Pact, which the German defendants were accused of having violated, there was nothing in it, or in any national legislation or other treaty, that made its violation the penal offense of an individual. Yet aggression remains with us. The word is still part of the language of statesmen, publicists, and commentators. Public opinion, which is an essential underpinning for modern war, even of the limited variety we have seen practiced in the past twenty years, still makes use of the concept of aggressor and still demands that the enemy be so stigmatized. And in an era when one bomb carries three times more destructive power than all the explosives used during World War II, more than forensic debate is involved.

By 1949 Mr. Justice Jackson himself had come to express some doubts of what had been accomplished at Nuremberg.[11] But the general revulsion to war all over the globe was such that governments had to justify an armed conflict as a war of defense, a war against imperialism or injustice—never as a war for *Lebensraum* or glory. Thus Nuremberg was attempting to say something that was universally felt, was trying to reify, to codify, to make plain in some sense that war for millions of people had another meaning from what it had in past centuries. War had become very different from the kind of conflict Vattel described in the eighteenth century: "At the present day war is carried on by the regular armies; the people, the peasantry, the townsfolk have nothing to fear from the sword of the enemy." [12]

The tribunal was doubtless not the best forum to establish the rules for a new order. The victors judging the vanquished, accusing them of crimes which in some cases had been participated in by one of the countries represented on the bench and which in others (the Katyn murders) had been committed by it, did not have the moral or judicial stature to command the long-term respect of jurists and public opinion throughout the world. At its best, in the person especially of the President of the Court, the tribunal could demonstrate a remarkable fairness and a fine show of legal forms, but in the treatment of the defendants and their counsel it was often evident that a long, bitter war had just ended between the countries represented by the prosecution and the judges and the country represented by the defeated. A few months after the end of a war it was humanly impossible to hold trials that would be convincing in their manifest justice to the vanquished as well as to the victors and to later generations.

And yet what in an imperfect world was to be done? To have added neutrals to the bench would have strengthened the authority of the court, although it might not have affected the verdicts substantially. Everyone knew by 1945 of the mass murders and the war crimes committed by the National Socialist Government. Less was known of the crimes committed by the Allies. But in what never-never land could the men who fought against Hitler's tyranny and his gas chambers be held to account for the manner in which they had won the war? The bombing of Dresden, to take an example, was undoubtedly an atrocity—but before what court would Winston Churchill be tried for having permitted the attack? Hiroshima, it may be well argued, too, was an atrocity, and if not Hiroshima, then certainly the bomb thrown over Nagasaki when Japan and all the rest of the world knew that the United States had the atomic weapon and the means of using it. In the cases of both Dresden and these Japanese cities the attacks occurred when the war was won. Could Messrs. Truman and Stimson be haled before any court for these acts? And if they should have been, before what court? And what precedents or principles might have allowed the victors to punish their own leaders, despite the crimes of the enemy?

In a world of mixed human affairs where a rough justice is done that is better than lynching or being shot out of hand, Nuremberg may be defended as a political event if not as a court. For one thing, it brought documents and witnesses to light that succeeded in convincing some of the defendants that they had been serving a criminal regime far worse than anything they had ever known or expected to know. It caused Hans Frank to say that a thousand years would pass and the guilt of Germany would not be erased, and this was done by submitting evidence—not by the rhetorical flights of the premature one-worlders but by the testimony of witnesses and the accumulation of thousands of documents that made a legal case against many of the defendants. Some of the sentences, as we have seen, seem too severe, and in the case of the men who were executed they were irreversible. Nor were the long years spent in Spandau to be restored to those who were given disproportionate jail sentences. And yet unfair as these sentences, too, may have been, they still compare favorably with those meted out to innocent people by the regime these men served, to be sure some of them blindly, and served well.

It is out of such records that the estate not only of Germans but of other peoples as well may be reevaluated. The lot of a man under a dictatorship demands both more and less of him than in the free world—less if he goes along and accepts his assignments of duty and obedience; more, far more, if he resists and thereby risks everything to let his conscience speak. Not many of the men whose careers we have reviewed resisted. The generals remained generals carrying out their orders; the functionaries did their jobs, some of them with a passion beyond the call of duty, some of them reluctantly when they disagreed. It is interesting to speculate on whether their successors of any nationality may act differently. During the late Algerian war, where atrocities were by no means lacking, a number of high French officers resigned rather than carry out their orders. This was perhaps some reflex of the Nuremberg trials, of revulsion from the criminal behavior of hitherto honorable men which has been codified in military manuals.*

At least it may be said that the full evidence of what the leaders of the National Socialist State spoke and did and thought lies before us. Not much of importance remains unrevealed about the nature of Nazism. In a certain sense the trial succeeded in doing what judicial proceedings are supposed to do: it convinced even the guilty that the verdict against them was just. So millions of Germans felt after the war, Nazis and non-Nazis alike. But in some of the individual cases of the Nuremberg trial this was manifestly not so. After trials where German generals were sentenced to death, sentences were commuted to imprisonment and they were soon freed. It is difficult to avoid the uneasy notion that a man like General Jodl was executed because he came before the tribunal of the first trial instead of before a later court or preceding the executive clemency that marked the years after 1946.

One red thread runs through the trial and binds in a curious way both the victors and the vanquished. It is the power exerted by an ideology. The power was manifested in those on the German side who accepted the fixed ideas of their society, in their Russian opposite members who could coolly accuse the Germans of a crime they knew the defendants had not committed (the Katyn massacre), in the American and British who could swallow almost any legal nostrum as long as it made them see a postwar

---

* The French officers resigned in a democratic state; to resign or resist in a totalitarian state is something else again. In the case of Germany, Hitler would rather have shot one of his generals than allow him to resign for moral reasons, and to join the Resistance was not only to risk one's own life and endanger the lives of one's family but to act alone or at best with a handful of trusted friends. The rest of the world—except for the Russians, who had pragmatic uses for it—had no interest in the German Resistance; nothing it did or offered found any echo among the Western Allies.

society of their imagining. Small things were rescued at Nuremberg (although they meant in some cases the difference between life and death), such as the unspoken principle that no one be convicted of the same crime the Allies conceded their side had committed; that no one be hanged for the crime of having waged or plotted to wage war. For the deeper answers we must look to history and its meaning for ourselves.

NOTES

1. Joseph L. Kunz, "The Chaotic State of the Laws of War and the Urgent Necessity for their Revision," in *American Journal of International Law*, January, 1951.

2. Henry L. Stimson, "The Nuremberg Trial, Landmark in Law," in *Foreign Affairs*, Vol. XXV, January, 1947, pp. 179–89.

3. "Genocide: A Commentary on the Convention," in *Yale Law Journal*, Vol. LVIII, 1949, pp. 1142–57. Eric Gabus, *La criminalité de la guerre*, Dissertation, Université de Genève (Geneva: Editions Générales, 1953).

4. Max Huber, quoted in Joseph L. Kunz, "The Laws of War," in *American Journal of International Law*, April, 1956, p. 337.

5. *Proceedings American Society of International Law*, Vol. XLVI, 1952.

6. Joseph B. Kelley, "A Legal Analysis of the Changes in War," in *Military Law Review*, July, 1961.

7. William F. Fratcher, "The New Law of Land Warfare," in *Missouri Law Review*, April, 1957. *The Law of Land Warfare. Department of the Army Field Manual FM 27-10* (Washington: US Government Printing Office, 1956).

8. Guenter Lewy, "Superior Orders, Nuclear Warfare and the Dictates of Consc ence," in *The American Political Science Review*, March, 1961, pp. 3–23.

9. John R. McConnell, "Can Law Impede Aggressive War?" in *American Bar Association Journal*, February, 1964.

10. Herbert Kraus, "The Nuremberg Trial of the Major War Criminals: Reflections After Seventeen Years," in *De Paul Law Review*, Vol. XIII, No. 2, 1964, pp. 233–47. Carl Haensel, "The Nuremberg Trial Revisited," in *ibid*., pp. 248–59. Otto Kranzbuehler, "Nuremberg Eighteen Years Afterwards," in *De Paul Law Review*, Vol. XIV, No. 2, 1965, pp. 333–47. Otto Pannenbecker, "The Nuremberg War-Crimes Trial," in *ibid*., pp. 348–58.

11. "Nuremberg in Retrospect," in *Canadian Bar Review*, Vol. XXVII, August–September, 1949.

12. Kelley, *op. cit.*

Bibliography

Bibliography

Abshagen, Karl Heinz. *Canaris.* Stuttgart: Union Verlag, 1959.

Akten zur deutschen auswaertigen Politik 1918–1945. Ser. D, 1937–1945. Vols. I–VII, Baden-Baden: Imprimerie Nationale, 1950–1964. Vols. VIII–X, Baden-Baden/Frankfurt a.M.: K. Keppler Verlag K.G. Vol. XI, Teil 1 and 2, Bonn: Gebr. Hermes K.G.

American Army and Navy Journal (now called *The Journal of the Armed Forces*), December, 1945.

Andics, Hellmut. *Der Staat den keiner wollte.* Vienna: Herder Verlag, 1962.

Archiv, Peter, ed. *Spiegelbild einer Verschwoerung: Die Kaltenbrunner-Berichte an Bormann und Hitler ueber das Attentat vom 20. Juli 1944.* Stuttgart: Seewald Verlag, 1961.

Arentz, Wilhelm, trans. "Die Vernehmung von Generalfeldmarschall Keitel durch die Sowjets." *Wehrwissenschaftliche Rundschau,* 1961.

———. "Die Vernehmung von Generaloberst Jodl durch die Sowjets." *Wehrwissenschaftliche Rundschau,* 1961.

Armstrong, John A., ed. *Soviet Partisans in World War II.* Madison: University of Wisconsin Press, 1964.

Assmann, Kurt. *Deutsche Schicksalsjahre.* Wiesbaden: Brockhaus Verlag, 1951.

———. "Der deutsche U-Bootskrieg und die Nuernberger Rechtssprechung." *Marine Rundschau,* January, 1953.

———. "Grossadmiral Dr. hc. Raeder und der Zweite Weltkrieg." *Marine Rundschau,* 1961.

Auerbach, Hellmuth. "Die Einheit Dirlewanger." *Vierteljahrshefte fuer Zeitgeschichte,* Vol. X, No. 3, 1962.

"Ausgewaehlte Briefe von Generalmajor Helmuth Stieff." *Vierteljahrshefte fuer Zeitgeschichte,* Vol. II, No. 3, 1954.

Ausgewaehlte Reden des Fuehrers. Munich: Zentralverlag der NSDAP, Franz Eher Nachf., 1938.

Baeumler, Alfred. *Alfred Rosenberg und der Mythus des 20. Jahrhunderts.* Munich: Hoheneichen-Verlag, 1943.

Ball-Kaduri, Kurt Jakob. *Das Leben der Juden in Deutschland im Jahre 1933.* Frankfurt a.M.: Europaeische Verlagsanstalt, 1963.

Bardèche, Maurice. *Die Politik der Zerstoerung.* Goettingen: Plesse Verlag, 1950.
Basic Field Manual FM 27–10. Rules of Land Warfare. Washington: US Government Printing Office, 1940.
Bauer, Elvira. *Ein Bilderbuch fuer Gross und Klein.* Nuremberg: Stuermer-Verlag, 1936.
Bauer, Fritz. *Die Kriegsverbrecher vor Gericht.* Zurich and New York: Europa Verlag, 1945.
Baum, Walter. "Marine, nationalsozialismus und Widerstand." *Vierteljahrshefte fuer Zeitgeschichte,* Vol. XI, No. 1, 1963.
———. "Die Reichsreform im Dritten Reich." *Vierteljahrshefte fuer Zeitgeschichte,* Vol. III, No. 1, 1955.
Beck, Earl R. *Verdict on Schacht.* Tallahassee: Florida State University Press, 1955.
Becker, Howard. *German Youth: Bound or Free.* New York: Oxford University Press, 1961.
Becker, Josef. "Zentrum und Ermaechtigungsgesetz 1934." *Vierteljahrshefte fuer Zeitgeschichte,* Vol. IX, No. 2, 1961.
Bein, Alexander. "Der moderne Antisemitismus und seine Bedeutung fuer die Judenfrage." *Vierteljahrshefte fuer Zeitgeschichte,* Vol. VI, No. 4, 1958.
Belgion, Montgomery. *Victor's Justice.* Chicago: Henry Regnery Company, 1949.
Bell, George K. A., "Die Oekumene und die innerdeutsche Opposition." *Vierteljahrshefte fuer Zeitgeschichte,* Vol. V, No. 4, 1957.
Bennecke, Heinrich. *Hitler und die SA.* Munich: Guenter Olzog Verlag, 1962.
Benton, Wilbourn E., and George Grimm, eds. *Nuremberg: German Views of the War Trial.* Dallas: Southern Methodist University Press, 1955.
Benze, Rudolf. *Erziehung im grossdeutschen Reich.* Frankfurt a.M.: Moritz Diesterweg Verlag, 1943.
Bernadotte, Count Folke. *The Curtain Falls.* New York: Alfred A. Knopf, Inc., 1945.
Berndoff, H. R. *General zwischen Ost und West.* Hamburg: Hoffmann und Campe Verlag, n.d.
Bertrand, Henri. *Le docteur Schacht.* Paris: Gallimard, 1939.
Bertraux, Pierre. *La Vie Quotidienne en Allemagne.* Paris: Hachette, 1962.
Bewley, Charles. *Hermann Goering.* Goettingen: Goettinger-Verlagsanstalt, 1956.
———. *Hermann Goering and the Third Reich.* New York: Devin-Adair, 1962.
Bidlingmaier, Ingrid. *Entstehung und Raeumung der Ostsee-Brueckenkoepfe 1945.* Neckargemuend: Scharnhorst Buchkameradschaft, 1962.
Billung, R. *Die Geschichte einer Bewegung.* Munich: Funck Verlag, 1931.
Blumentritt, Guenther. *Von Rundstedt, the Soldier and the Man.* Trans. Cuthbert Reavely. London: Odhams Press, 1952.
Boberach, Heinz, ed. *Meldungen aus dem Reich.* Neuwied and Berlin: Hermann Luchterhand Verlag, 1965.
Boersenzeitung, January 15, 1934.
Boissier, Pierre. *Voelkerrecht und Militaerbefehl.* Stuttgart: K. F. Koehler Verlag, 1953.
Boldt, Gerhard. *Die letzten Tage der Reichskanzlei.* Hamburg: Rowohlt Verlag, 1947.
Bonnet, Georges. *Fin d'une Europe.* Geneva: Les Editions du Cheval Ailé, 1948.
Bor, Peter. *Gespraeche mit Halder.* Wiesbaden: Limes Verlag, 1950.

Borchard, Edwin, and William Potter Lage. *Neutrality for the United States.* New Haven: Yale University Press, 1937.

Bormann, Martin. *Le Testament Politique de Hitler.* Notes Recueillies par Martin Bormann. Paris: Librairie Arthème Fayard, 1959.

Boveri, Margaret. *Der Diplomat vor Gericht.* Berlin and Hannover: Minerva Verlag, 1948.

Bracher, Karl Dietrich. "Das Anfangsstadium der Hitlerschen Aussenpolitik." *Vierteljahrshefte fuer Zeitgeschichte,* Vol. V, No. 1, 1957.

————. *Die Aufloesung der Weimarer Republik.* Stuttgart: Ring-Verlag, 1955.

————. "Stufen totalitaerer Gleichschaltung: Die Befestigung der nationalsozialistischen Herrschaft 1933–34." *Vierteljahrshefte fuer Zeitgeschichte,* Vol. IV, No. 1, 1956.

Bracher, Karl Dietrich, Wolfgang Sauer, and Gerhard Schulz. *Die nationalsozialistische Machtergreifung.* Cologne: Westdeutscher Verlag, 1962.

The British Handbook of Irregular Warfare. Quoted in *Trials of War Criminals before the Nuremberg Military Tribunals under Control Council Law No. 10, October 1946–April 1949.* Washington: US Government Printing Office, 1946–1949, Vol. XI.

British Manual of Military Law. London: Command of the Army Council, 1929.

Bross, Werner. *Gespraeche mit Hermann Goering.* Flensburg and Hamburg: Christian Wolff Verlag, 1950.

Broszat, Martin. "Zum Streit um den Reichstagsbrand." *Vierteljahrshefte fuer Zeitgeschichte,* Vol. VIII, No. 3, 1960.

————. "Zur Perversion der Strafjustiz im Dritten Reich." *Vierteljahrshefte fuer Zeitgeschichte,* Vol. VI, No. 4, 1958.

Bruegel, J. W. "Das Schicksal der Strafbestimmungen des Versailler Vertrages." *Vierteljahrshefte fuer Zeitgeschichte,* Vol. VI, No. 3, 1958.

Brungs, Colonel Bernard J. "The Status of Biolgical Warfare in International Law." *Military Law Review,* April, 1964.

Buchheim, Hans. *Glaubenskrise im Dritten Reich.* Stuttgart: Deutsche Verlag-Anstalt, 1953.

————. "Die hoeheren SS- und Polizeifuehrer." *Vierteljahrshefte fuer Zeitgeschichte,* Vol. XI, No. 4, 1963.

————. "Die SS in der Verfassung des Dritten Reiches." *Vierteljahrshefte fuer Zeitgeschichte,* Vol. III, No. 2, 1955.

Buchheim, Hans, et al. *Anatomie des SS-Staates.* 2 vols. Olten and Freiburg i. Br.: Walter-Verlag, 1965.

Buchheit, Gert. *Soldatentum und Rebellion.* Rastatt/Baden: Grote'sche Verlagsbuchhandlung, 1961.

Buckreis, Adam. *Politik des 20. Jahrhunderts.* 3 vols. (1901–1939). Nuremberg: Panorama-Verlag, n.d.

The Bulletin. Bonn: Press and Information Office of the German Federal Government, January 7, 1964; March 16, 1965.

Bullock, Alan. *Hitler—A Study in Tyranny.* New York: Harper & Row, Publishers, Incorporated, 1952.

Burckhardt, Carl J. *Meine Danziger Mission 1937–1939.* Munich: Deutscher Taschenbuch Verlag, 1962.

598　　　　　　　　　　　　BIBLIOGRAPHY

Bussche, Freiherr von dem. *Frankfurter Allgemeine Zeitung*, February 5, 1952.

Butler, Ewan, and Gordon Young. *Marshal Without Glory*. London: Hodder & Stoughton, Ltd., 1951.

Cameron, John, ed. *The Peleus Trial: Trial of Heinz Eck, August Hoffmann, Walter Weisspfennig, Hans Richard Lenz, and Wolfgang Schwender*. In *War Crimes Trials*, ed. Sir David Maxwell-Fyfe. London, Edinburgh, and Glasgow: William Hodge, 1948.

Carsten, Francis L. *Reichswehr und Politik 1918–1933*. Cologne and Berlin: Keipenheuer & Witsch, 1964.

Castell, Clementine zu, ed. *Glaube und Schoenheit. Ein Bildbuch von den 17–21 jaehrigen Maedeln*. Munich: Zentralverlag der NSDAP, Franz Eher Nachf., n.d.

Castellan, Georges. *Le Réarmament clandestin du Reich*. Paris: Plon, 1954.

Churchill, Sir Winston S. *The Second World War*. 6 vols. Boston: Houghton Mifflin Company, 1948–1953.

Ciano, Count Galeazzo. *Ciano's Hidden Diary 1937–1938*. Trans. Andreas Mayor. New York: E. P. Dutton & Co., Inc., 1953.

Conrad, Walter. *Der Kampf um die Kanzleien*. Berlin: Toepelmann, 1957.

Coulondre, Robert. *De Stalin à Hitler. Souvenirs de deux ambassades 1936–39*. Paris: Hachette, 1950.

Craig, Gordon A., and Felix Gilbert, eds. *The Diplomats 1919–1939*. Princeton: Princeton University Press, 1953.

Czech-Jochberg, Erich. *Adolf Hitler und sein Stab*. Oldenburg i. O.: Gerhard Stalling Verlag, 1933.

Czechoslovakia Fights Back. Washington: American Council on Public Affairs, 1943.

Dahlerus, Birger. *Der letzte Versuch*. Munich: Nymphenburger Verlagshandlung, 1948.

Dallin, Alexander. *Deutsche Herrschaft in Russland 1941–1945*. Duesseldorf: Droste-Verlag, 1958.

———. *German Rule in Russia 1941–1945*. London: The Macmillan Company, Ltd., 1957.

Daniel, J. *Le Problème du châtiment des crimes de guerre d'après les enseignements de la deuxième guerre mondiale*. Cairo: R. Schindler, 1946.

Datner, Szymon. *Crimes Against POW's*. Warsaw: Zachodnia Agencja Prasowa, 1964.

Davignon, Jacques. *Berlin 1936–40. Souvenirs d'une mission*. Paris: Editions Universitaires, 1951.

Degrelle, Léon. *Die verlorene Legion*. Stuttgart: Veritas Verlag, 1955.

Deist, Wilhelm. "Schleicher und die deutsche Abruestungspolitik im Juni/Juli 1932." *Vierteljahrshefte fuer Zeitgeschichte*, Vol. VII, No. 2, 1959.

Demeter, Karl. *Das deutsche Offizierkorps in Gesellschaft und Staat 1650–1945*. Frankfurt a.M.: Bernard & Graefe Verlag fuer Wehrwesen, 1962.

"Denkschrift Himmlers ueber die Behandlung der Fremdvoelkischen im Osten (Mai 1940)." *Vierteljahrshefte fuer Zeitgeschichte*, Vol. V, No. 2, 1957.

Deuerlein, Ernst. "Dokumentation. Hitlers Eintritt in die Politik und die Reichswehr." *Vierteljahrshefte fuer Zeitgeschichte*, Vol. VII, No. 2, 1959.

Deutsche Allgemeine Zeitung, October 19, 1944.

Dietrich, Otto. *Mit Hitler in die Macht*. Munich: Zentralverlag der NSDAP, Franz Eher Nachf., 1938.

———. *12 Jahre mit Hitler*. Munich: Isar Verlag, 1955.

Dissmann, Willi, and Max Wegner, eds. *Jungen und Maedel im Krieg*. Berlin and Leipzig: Franz Schneider Verlag, 1941.

Documents on German Foreign Policy, 1918–1945. Ser. D, 1937–1945, 11 vols. Washington: US Government Printing Office.

Documents on United States Foreign Relations 1943–44. Washington: US Government Printing Office.

Dodd, Thomas J. "The Nuremberg Trials." *Journal of Criminal Law and Criminology*, Vol. XXXVII, January, 1947.

Dodd, William E. *Ambassador Dodd's Diary, 1933–1938*. New York: Harcourt, Brace & World, Inc., 1941.

Doenitz, Karl. *10 Jahre und 20 Tage*. Bonn: Athenaeum-Verlag, 1958.

Doering, Hans-Joachim. "Die Motive der Zigeuner-Deportation vom Mai 1940." *Vierteljahrshefte fuer Zeitgeschichte*, Vol. VII, No. 4, 1959.

Dokumente und Materialien aus der Vorgeschichte des Zweiten Weltkrieges aus dem Archiv des Deutschen Auswaertigen Amtes 1937–38. Berlin: Ministerium fuer Auswaertige Angelegenheiten der UdSSR, n.d.

Donnedieu de Babres, Henri. *Le Procès de Nuremberg*. Paris: Editions Domat-Montchrestien, 1947.

Dos Passos, John. "Der Autokoenig. Zum Bilde von Henry Ford." *Sueddeutsche Zeitung*, May 5/6, 1962.

"Dr. Wilhelm Frick." *Nationalsozialistische Monatshefte*, August 4, 1930.

Dunbar, N. C. H. "Act of State in the Law of War," *Juridical Review*, December, 1963.

Dutch, Oswald. *The Errant Diplomat*. London: Edward Arnold, 1940.

Earle, George H. "FDR's Tragic Mistake." *Confidential*, August 25, 1958.

Edmunds, Palmer D. "Impressions of the Athens Conference on World Peace Through Law." *Illinois Bar Journal*, November, 1964.

Ehard, Hans. "The Nuremberg Trial Against the Major War Criminals and International Law." *American Journal of International Law*, Vol. XLIII, April, 1949.

Eichmann Trial. Mimeographed trial record. Jerusalem, 1961.

Epstein, Fritz T. "War-Time Activities of the SS-Ahnenerbe." In *On the Track of Tyranny*, ed. Max Beloff. London: Wiener Library, 1960.

Die Erhebung der oesterreichischen Nationalsozialisten im Juli 1934 (Akten der Historischen Kommission des Reichsfuehrers SS). Vienna: Europa Verlag, 1965.

Eschenburg, Theodor. "Zur Ermordung des Generals von Schleicher." *Vierteljahrshefte fuer Zeitgeschichte*, Vol. I, No. 1, 1953.

———. "Franz von Papen." *Vierteljahrshefte fuer Zeitgeschichte*, Vol. I, No. 2, 1953.

Europaeische Revue. March 29, 1939.

Eyck, Erich. *Geschichte der Weimarer Republik*. 2 vols. Erlenbach-Zurich and Stuttgart: Eugen Rentsch Verlag, 1956.

―――. "Papen als Historiker." *Deutsche Rundschau*, 1952.

Fabricius, Hans. *Reichsinnenminister Dr. Frick: der revolutionaere Staatsmann*. Berlin: Deutsche Kulturwacht, 1939.

Faschismus—Getto—Massenmord. Frankfurt a.M.: Roederberg-Verlag, 1960.

Foertsch, Hermann. *Schuld und Verhaengnis*. Stuttgart: Deutsche Verlags-Anstalt, 1951.

Foreign Relations of the United States. The Conference of Berlin (the Potsdam Conference) 1945. 2 vols. Washington: US Government Printing Office, 1960.

François-Poncet, André. *Souvenirs d'une Ambassade à Berlin Septembre 1931– Octobre 1938*. Paris: Ernest Flammarion, 1946.

Frank, Hans. "Diary." 38 vols., unpublished. Washington: National Archives.

―――. *Friedrich Nietzsche*. Krakau: Burg Verlag, 1944.

―――. *Im Angesicht des Galgens*. Munich: Friedrich Alfred Beck Verlag, 1953.

―――. *Neues Deutsches Recht*. Munich: Zentralverlag der NSDAP, Franz Eher Nachf., 1936.

―――. *Die Technik des Staates*. Berlin, Leipzig, and Vienna: Der Rechtsverlag, 1942.

Franz-Willing, Georg. *Die Hitlerbewegung*. Hamburg: R. v. Decker's Verlag G. Schenck, 1962.

Fratcher, William F. "The New Law of Land Warfare." *Missouri Law Review*, April, 1957.

Freund, Michael, ed. *Geschichte des Zweiten Weltkrieges in Dokumenten*. 3 vols. Freiburg: Herder Verlag, 1953.

Frick, Wilhelm. "Ein Volk—ein Reich." *Paedagogisches Magazin*, 1934.

―――. *Freiheit und Bindung der Selbstverwaltung*. Munich: Franz Eher Verlag, 1937.

―――. *Germany Speaks*. London: Butterworth & Co., Ltd., 1938.

―――. "Kampfziel der deutschen Schule." *Paedagogisches Magazin*, 1933.

―――. *Die Nationalsozialisten im Reichstag 1924–1928*. Munich: Franz Eher Verlag, 1928.

―――. *Die Rassengesetzgebung des Dritten Reiches*. Munich: Franz Eher Verlag, 1934.

―――. "Student im Volk." *Paedagogisches Magazin*, 1934.

Frick, Wilhelm, and Arthur Guett. *Nordisches Gedankengut im Dritten Reich*. Munich: J. F. Lehmanns Verlag, 1936.

Friedman, Philip. *Auschwitz*. Buenos Aires: Sociedad Hebraica Argentina, 1952.

Fritzsche, Hans. *Krieg den Kriegshetzern*. Berlin: Brunner-Verlag Willi Bischoff, 1940.

―――. *Zeugen gegen England*. Duesseldorf: Voelkischer Verlag, 1941.

"Fuehrer Conferences on Matters Dealing with the German Navy." Mimeographed. Washington: Office of Naval Intelligence, US Department of the Navy.

Funk, Walther. *Grundsaetze der deutschen Aussenhandelspolitik und das Problem der internationalen Verschuldung*. Berlin: Junker und Duennhaupt Verlag, 1938.

———. *Das wirtschaftliche Gesicht des neuen Europa.* Pamphlet. Berlin, January 15, 1942.

———. *Wirtschaftsordnung gegen Waehrungsmechanismus.* Pamphlet. Koenigsberg, 1944.

———. *Wirtschaftsordnung im neuen Europa.* Vienna: Suedost-Echo Verlagsgesellschaft, 1941.

Gabus, Eric. *La Criminalité de la guerre.* Dissertation, Université de Genève. Geneva: Editions Générales, 1953.

Gardner, Brian. *The Year that Changed the World.* New York: Coward-McCann, Inc., 1964.

Gardner, Richard N., "The Development of the Peace Keeping Capacity of the UN." *Annual Proceedings of the American Society of International Law,* April 25–27, 1963.

Der gelbe Fleck. Mit einem Vorwort von Leon Feuchtwanger. Paris: Edition du Carrefour, 1936.

Gemzell, Carl-Axel. *Raeder, Hitler und Skandinavien.* Lund: Skanska Centraltryckeriet, 1965, and Frankfurt a.M.: Bernard & Graefe Verlag fuer Wehrwesen.

"Genocide." *Yale Law Journal,* Vol. LVIII, 1949, pp. 1142–57.

Gentz, Erwin. *Das Landjahr.* Eberswalde: Verlagsgesellschaft R. Mueller, 1936.

Germania, February 6, 1938.

Gibson, Hugh, ed. *The Ciano Diaries 1939–1943.* Garden City: Doubleday & Company, Inc., 1946.

Gilbert, Felix. *Hitler Directs His War.* New York: Oxford University Press, 1951.

Gilbert, G. M. *Nuremberg Diary.* New York: Farrar, Straus & Young, Inc., 1947.

Gisevius, Hans B. *Bis zum bitteren Ende.* Zurich: Fretz & Wasmuth Verlag, 1946.

Glennon, A. N. "The Weapon that Came Too Late." *U.S. Naval Institute Proceedings,* March, 1961.

Glueck, Sheldon. *The Nuremberg Trial and Aggressive War.* New York: Alfred A. Knopf, Inc., 1946.

———. *War Criminals: Their Prosecution and Punishment.* New York: Alfred A. Knopf, Inc., 1944.

Goebbels, Joseph. *Vom Kaiserhof zur Reichskanzlei.* Munich: Zentralverlag der NSDAP, Franz Eher Nachf., 1934.

———. "War Diary." Unpublished. Munich: Institut fuer Zeitgeschichte.

Goering, Hermann. *Aufbau einer Nation.* Berlin: E. S. Mittler & Sohn, 1934.

Goerlitz, Walter. *Der deutsche Generalstab.* Frankfurt a.M.: Verlag der Frankfurter Hefte, 1950.

———. *Keitel—Verbrecher oder Offizier?* Goettingen: Musterschmidt-Verlag, 1961.

Gostner, Erwin. *1000 Tage im KZ.* Innsbruck: Wagner'sche Universitaets-Buchdruckerei, 1945.

Greenspan, Morris. *The Modern Law of Land Warfare.* Berkeley: University of California Press, 1959.

Greiner, Helmuth. *Die Oberste Wehrmachtfuehrung 1939–1943.* Wiesbaden: Limes Verlag, 1951.

Grewe, Wilhelm, and O. Kuester. *Nuernberg als Rechtsfrage: Eine Diskussion.* Stuttgart: Ernst Klett Verlag, 1947.

Griessdorff, Harry. *Unsere Weltanschauung.* Berlin: Nordland Verlag, 1941.

Gritzbach, Erich. *Hermann Goering: Werk und Mensch*. Munich: Zentralverlag der NSDAP, Franz Eher Nachf., 1939.

Gros, Otto. *850 Worte Mythus des 20. Jahrhunderts*. Munich: Hoheneichen Verlag, 1938.

Gunther, John. *Inside Europe*. New York: Harper & Row, Publishers, Incorporated, 1940.

Haensel, Carl. "The Nuremberg Trial Revisited." *De Paul Law Review*, Vol. XIII, No. 2, Spring–Summer 1964.

———. *Das Organisationsverbrechen*. Munich and Berlin: Biederstein Verlag, 1947.

Hagemeyer, Hans L., ed. *Einsamkeit und Gemeinschaft*. Stuttgart: Spemann Verlag, 1939.

Hagen, Hans W., *Zwischen Eid und Befehl*. Munich: Tuermer Verlag, 1959.

Hager, Gustav. *Fuehrer im neuen Deutschland*. Berlin: Verlag fuer soziale Ethik und Kunstpflege, n.d.

Halder, Franz. *Kriegstagebuch*. 3 vols. Stuttgart: W. Kohlhammer Verlag, 1962–1964.

Hammerstein, Christian Freiherr von. *Mein Leben*. Private printing, 1962.

Hammerstein, Kunrat Freiherr von. "Schleicher, Hammerstein und die Machtuebernahme." *Frankfurter Hefte*, No. 11, 1956.

Hankey, M. P. A. *Politics, Trials and Errors*. Chicago: Henry Regnery Company, 1950.

Harris, Whitney R. *Tyranny on Trial: The Evidence at Nuremberg*. Dallas: Southern Methodist University Press, 1954.

Hart, S. Th. *Alfred Rosenberg*. Munich: J. S. Lehmanns Verlag, 1933.

Hart, W. E. *Hitler's Generals*. London: Cresset Press, 1944.

Hartlieb, Wladimir von. *Parole: Das Reich*. Vienna and Leipzig: Adolf Luser Verlag, 1939.

Hartmann, Martha. *Maedel, Sonne, Zelte*. Berlin: Junge Generation Verlag, n.d.

Hassell, Ulrich von. *Vom anderen Deutschland*. Zurich and Freiburg i. Br.: Atlantis Verlag, 1946.

Hedin, Sven. *Ohne Auftrag in Berlin*. Buenos Aires: Duerer Verlag, 1949.

Heiber, Helmut. *Adolf Hitler*. Berlin: Colloquium Verlag, 1960.

———. "Aus den Akten des Gauleiters Kube." *Vierteljahrshefte fuer Zeitgeschichte*, Vol. IV, No. 1, 1956.

———. "Der Fall Gruenspan." *Vierteljahrshefte fuer Zeitgeschichte*, Vol. V, No. 2, 1957.

———, ed. *Hitlers Lagebesprechungen*. Stuttgart: Deutsche Verlags-Anstalt, 1962.

———. "Zur Justiz im Dritten Reich: Der Fall Elias." *Vierteljahrshefte fuer Zeitgeschichte*, Vol. V, No. 3, 1955.

Heiden, Konrad. *Hitler*. 2 vols. Zurich: Europa Verlag, 1936–1937.

Heinrichsbauer, A. *Schwerindustrie und Politik*. Essen-Kettwig: West Verlag, 1949.

Heinze, Kurt, and Karl Schilling, eds. *Die Rechtsprechung der Nuernberger Militaertribunale*. Bonn: Girardet Verlag, 1952.

Helwig, Werner. *Die Blaue Blume des Wandervogels*. Guetersloh: Sigbert Mohn Verlag, 1960.

Henkys, Reinhard. *Die nationalsozialistischen Gewaltverbrechen.* Stuttgart: Kreuz-Verlag, 1964.

Hermelink, Heinrich, ed. *Kirche im Kampf.* Tuebingen and Stuttgart: Rainer Wunderlich Verlag Hermann Leins, 1950.

Herriot, Edouard. *Jadis.* Vol. II. Paris: Ernest Flammarion, 1952.

Herzog, Robert. *Besatzungsverwaltung in den besetzten Ostgebieten, Abteilung Jugend.* Tuebingen: Institut fuer Besatzungsfragen, 1960.

Hess, Ilse. *England—Nuernberg—Spandau: Ein Schicksal in Briefen.* Leoni am Starnberger See: Druffel-Verlag, 1952.

———. *Gefangener des Friedens. Neue Briefe aus Spandau.* Leoni am Starnberger See: Druffel-Verlag, 1955.

Heusinger, Adolf. *Befehl im Widerstreit.* Tuebingen and Stuttgart: Rainer Wunderlich Verlag Hermann Leins, 1957.

Hilberg, Raul. *The Destruction of the European Jews.* Chicago: Quadrangle Books, 1961.

"Himmler Rede." *Sammelheft ausgewaehlter Vortraege und Reden.* Munich: Zentralverlag der NSDAP, Franz Eher Nachf., 1939.

Hinsley, Francis H. *Hitler's Strategy: The Naval Evidence.* Cambridge: Cambridge University Press, 1951.

Hirschfeld, H. M. *Herinneringen uit de Bezettingstijd.* Amsterdam: Elsevier, 1960.

History of the United Nations War Crimes Commission. Compiled by the United Nations War Crimes Commission. London: H. M. Stationery Office, 1948.

Hitler, Adolf. *Mein Kampf.* Munich: Zentralverlag der NSDAP, Franz Eher Nachf., 1941.

Hoehn, Reinhard. *Die Armee als Erziehungsschule der Nation. Das Ende einer Idee.* Bad Harzburg: Verlag fuer Wissenschaft, Wirtschaft und Technik, 1963.

Hoeing, Trude, ed. *Jungmaedelleben. Ein Jahrbuch fuer 8–14 jaehrige Maedel.* Leipzig: Verlag Schmidt & Springer, n.d.

Hoess, Rudolf. *Kommandant in Auschwitz.* Stuttgart: Deutsche Verlags-Anstalt, 1958.

Hofer, Walther. *Die Entfesselung des Zweiten Weltkrieges.* Frankfurt a.M.: S. Fischer Verlag, 1964.

Hoffmann, Heinrich. *Hitler Was My Friend.* London: Burke Publishing Company, Ltd., 1955.

Hohlfeld, Johannes, ed. *Dokumente der deutschen Politik und Geschichte von 1848 bis zur Gegenwart.* Vol. IV. Berlin: Dokumenten-Verlag Dr. Herbert Wendler & Co., n.d.

Horkenbach, Cuno. *Das Deutsche Reich von 1918 bis heute.* Berlin: Verlag fuer Presse, Wirtschaft und Politik, 1930.

Hossbach, Friedrich. *Zwischen Wehrmacht und Hitler 1934–1938.* Wolfenbuettel and Hannover: Wolfenbuetteler Verlagsanstalt, 1949.

Hubatsch, Walther. *Weseruebung.* Goettingen: Musterschmidt-Verlag, 1960.

Hull, Cordell. *The Memoirs of Cordell Hull.* 2 vols. New York: The Macmillan Company, 1948.

Irving, David. *The Destruction of Dresden.* London: William Kimber & Co., 1963.

Jackson, Robert H. *The Nuremberg Case.* New York: Alfred A. Knopf, Inc., 1947.

————. "Nuremberg in Retrospect." *Canadian Bar Review*, Vol. XXVII, August–September, 1949.

————. *Report* (Department of State Publication 2420). Washington: US Government Printing Office, 1945.

————. *Report to the International Conference on Military Trials, London, 1945* (Department of State Publication 3080). Washington: US Government Printing Office, 1949.

Jacobsen, Hans-Adolf, ed. *Dokumente zum Westfeldzug 1940*. Goettingen: Musterschmidt-Verlag, 1960.

————, ed. *Dokumente zur Vorgeschichte des Westfeldzuges 1939–1940*. Goettingen: Musterschmit-Verlag, 1956.

————. *Fall Gelb*. Wiesbaden: Franz Steiner Verlag, 1957.

————. *1939–1945. Der Zweite Weltkrieg in Chronik und Dokumenten*. Darmstadt: Wehr und Wissen Verlag, 1961.

Jacobsen, Hans-Adolf, and Werner Jochmann, eds. *Ausgewaehlte Dokumente zur Geschichte des Nationalsozialismus 1933–1945*. Bielefeld: Verlag Neue Gesellschaft, 1961.

Jaspers, Gotthard. "Ueber die Ursachen des Zweiten Weltkrieges. Zu den Buechern von A. J. P. Taylor und David L. Hoggan." *Vierteljahrshefte fuer Zeitgeschichte*, Vol. X, No. 3, 1962.

Jaspers, Karl. "The Significance of the Nuremberg Trials for Germany and the World." *Notre Dame Lawyer*, Vol. XXII, January, 1947.

Jeschek, Hans-Heinrich. *Die Verantwortlichkeit der Staatsorgane nach Voelkerstrafrecht*. Bonn: Ludwig Roehrscheid Verlag, 1952.

Jonca, Karol, and Alfred Konieczny, eds. *Festung Breslau*. Warsaw: Pañstwowe Wydawnictwo Naukowe, 1962.

Joos, Joseph. *So sah ich sie*. Augsburg: Winfried Werk, 1958.

Judenfragen, February 10, 1944.

Judgment of the International Tribunal for the Far East. Tokyo, November, 1948.

Juedische Selbstbekenntnisse. Leipzig: Hammer Verlag, 1929.

Kamenetski, Ihor. *Hitler's Occupation of Ukraine*. Milwaukee: Marquette University Press, 1956.

Kastner-Bericht ueber Eichmanns Menschenhandel in Ungarn. Munich: Kindler Verlag, 1961.

Keenen, J. B., and B. F. Brown. *Crimes Against International Law*. Washington: Public Affairs Press, 1950.

Keesing's Contemporary Archives. Vol. V. London, 1943–1946.

Kelley, Douglas M. *22 Cells in Nuremberg*. New York: Greenberg: Publisher, Inc., 1947.

Kelley, Joseph B. "A Legal Analysis of the Changes in War." *Military Law Review*, July, 1961.

Kelsen, Hans. *Law and Peace in International Relations*. Cambridge: Harvard University Press, 1942.

————. *Peace Through Law*. Chapel Hill: University of North Carolina Press, 1944.

Kemmet, Gerald. *Sunday Express*, London, August 4, 1963.

Kempner, Robert M. W. *Eichmann und Komplizen*. Zurich, Stuttgart, and Vienna: Europa Verlag, 1961.

Kersten, Felix. *Totenkopf und Treue.* Hamburg: Robert Moehlich Verlag, 1952.

Kesselring, Albert. *Soldat bis zum letzten Tag.* Bonn: Athenaeum-Verlag, 1953.

Kintner, Earl W., ed. *Hadamar Trial of Alfons Klein, Adolf Wallman, et al.* London: William Hodge, 1948.

Kirkpatrick, Ivone. *The Inner Circle. Memoirs.* London: The Macmillan Company, Ltd., 1959.

Klee, Karl, ed. *Dokumente zum Unternehmen "Seeloewe."* Goettingen: Musterschmidt-Verlag, 1959.

Klein, Fritz. "Neue Dokumente zur Rolle Schachts bei der Vorbereitung der Hitlerdiktatur." *Zeitschrift fuer Geschichtswissenschaft,* Vol. V, No. 4, 1957.

Kloenne, Arno. "Die deutsche Russland- und Besatzungspolitik 1941–45." *Stimmen der Zeit,* 1955–1956.

———. *Gegen den Strom.* Hannover and Frankfurt a.M.: Norddeutsche Verlagsanstalt O. Goedel, 1957.

———. *Hitlerjugend.* Hannover and Frankfurt a.M.: Norddeutsche Verlagsanstalt O. Goedel, 1955.

Klose, Werner. *Generation im Gleichschritt.* Oldenburg and Hamburg: Gerhard Stalling Verlag, 1964.

Kluke, Paul. "Der Fall Potempa." *Vierteljahrshefte fuer Zeitgeschichte,* Vol. V, No. 3, 1957.

Knieriem, August von. *The Nuremberg Trials.* Chicago: Henry Regnery Company, 1959.

Knoll, Karl. *Die Gesellung der deutschen Jugend in der Gegenwart.* Dissertation. Munich, 1962.

Koessler, Maximilian. "American War Crimes Trials in Europe." *Georgetown Law Journal,* November, 1950.

Kogon, Eugen. *Der SS Staat.* Frankfurt a.M.: Europaeische Verlagsanstalt, 1946.

Koller, Karl. *Der letzte Monat.* Mannheim: Wohlgemuth Verlag, 1949.

Komitee der Antifaschistischen Widerstandskaempfer in der Deutschen Demokratischen Republik, ed. *SS im Einsatz.* Berlin: Kongress-Verlag, 1957.

Konzentrationslager Buchenwald. Vol. I. Weimar: Thueringer Volksverlag, 1949.

Kordt, Erich. *Nicht aus den Akten.* Stuttgart: Union Deutsche Verlagsgesellschaft, 1950.

———. *Wahn und Wirklichkeit.* Stuttgart: Union Deutsche Verlagsgesellschaft, 1948.

Krannhals, Hanns von. *Der Warschauer Aufstand 1944.* Frankfurt a.M.: Bernard & Graefe Verlag fuer Wehrwesen, 1962.

Kranzbuehler, Otto. "Nuremberg Eighteen Years Afterwards." *De Paul Law Review,* Vol. XIV, No. 2, Spring–Summer 1965.

———. *Rueckblick auf Nuernberg.* Hamburg: Zeit Verlag E. Schmidt, 1949.

Kraus, Herbert. "The Nuremberg Trial of the Major War Criminals: Reflections after Seventeen Years." *De Paul Law Review,* Vol. XIII, No. 2, Spring–Summer 1964.

Kraus, Otto, and Erich Kulka. *Die Todesfabrik.* Berlin: Kongress Verlag, 1958.

Krebs, Albert. *Tendenzen und Gestalten der NSDAP.* Stuttgart: Deutsche Verlags-Anstalt, 1959.

Kroch, Hugo. *Rosenberg und die Bibel.* Leipzig: Theodor Fritsch, 1935.

Kubizek, August. *Young Hitler*. London: Allan Wingate, Ltd., 1954.

Kunz, Josef L. "The Chaotic State of the Laws of War and the Urgent Necessity for their Revision." *American Journal of International Law*, January, 1951.

————. "The Laws of War." *American Journal of International Law*, April, 1956.

Lang, Serge, and Ernst von Schenck, eds. *Portraet eines Menschheitsverbrechers. Nach den hinterlassenen Memoiren des ehemaligen Reichsministers Alfred Rosenberg*. St. Gallen: Zollikofer, 1947.

Langbein, Hermann. *Wir haben es getan*. Vienna: Europa Verlag, 1964.

Lange, Eitel. *Der Reichsmarschall im Kriege*. Stuttgart: Curt E. Schwab, 1950.

Langer, W. L., and E. S. Gleason. *The Undeclared War, 1940–41*. New York: Harper & Row, Publishers, Incorporated, 1953.

Laqueur, Walter Z. *Die deutsche Jugendbewegung*. Cologne: Verlag Wissenschaft und Politik, 1962.

Laternser, Hans. *Verteidigung deutscher Soldaten*. Bonn: Girardet Verlag, 1950.

The Law of Land Warfare. Department of the Army Field Manual FM 27–10. Washington: US Government Printing Office, 1956.

Lawrence, Lord Justice (Lord Oaksey). "The Nuremberg Trial." *International Affairs*, Vol. XXIII, April, 1947.

Leasor, James. *The Uninvited Envoy*. New York: McGraw-Hill Book Company, 1962.

Leber, Annedore, and Freya Graefin von Moltke. *Fuer und Wider*. Berlin: Mosaik-Verlag, 1961.

Leibholz, Gerhard. " 'Aggression' als zeitgeschichtliches Problem." *Vierteljahrshefte fuer Zeitgeschichte*, Vol. VI, No. 2, 1958.

Leur, Salvatore S. I. *Crimini di guerra e delitti contro l'umanità*. Rome: Edizioni La Civiltà Cattolica, 1948.

Lewy, Guenter. "Superior Orders, Nuclear Warfare, and the Dictates of Conscience: The Dilemma of Military Obedience in the Atomic Age." *The American Political Science Review*, March, 1961.

Leyen, Ferdinand Prinz von der. *Rueckblick zum Mauerwald*. Munich: Bidderstein, 1965.

L'Huillier, F. "Joachim von Ribbentrop." *Revue d'Histoire de la Deuxième Guerre Mondiale*. Paris: Presses Universitaires de France, 1957.

Liddell Hart, B. H. *The German Generals Talk*. New York: William Morrow and Company, Inc., 1948.

Life, May 28, 1945.

Lippe, Viktor von der. *Nuernberger Tagebuchnotizen November 1945 bis Oktober 1946*. Frankfurt a.M.: Fritz Knapp, 1951.

Lochner, Louis P. *The Goebbels Diaries 1942–1943*. Garden City: Doubleday & Company, Inc., 1948.

————. *Tycoons and Tyrant*. Chicago: Henry Regnery Company, 1954.

Loock, Hans-Dietrich. "Zur 'Grossgermanischen Politik' des Dritten Reiches." *Vierteljahrshefte fuer Zeitgeschichte*, Vol. VIII, No. 1, 1960.

Lossberg, Bernhard von. *Im Wehrmachtfuehrungsstab*. Hamburg: H. N. Noelke Verlag, 1949.

Luedde-Neurath, Walter. *Regierung Doenitz. Die letzten Tage des Dritten Reiches*. Goettingen: Musterschmidt-Verlag, 1953.

Maevskii, Viktor. "Tovarishch Richard Sorge," in *Pravda*, September 4, 1964. *The New York Times*, September 5, 1964.

Manstein, Erich von. *Aus einem Soldatenleben: 1887–1939*. Bonn: Athenaeum-Verlag, 1958.

———. *Verlorene Siege*. Bonn: Athenaeum-Verlag, 1959.

Manvell, Roger, and Heinrich Fraenkel. *Doctor Goebbels: His Life and Death*. New York: Simon and Schuster, Inc., 1960.

———. *Hermann Goering*. London: William Heinemann, Ltd., 1962.

Marsalek, Hans. *Mauthausen mahnt*. Vienna: Mauthausen-Komitee des Bundesverbandes der oesterreichischen KZler, Haeftlinge und politisch Verfolgten, Selbstverlag, 1950.

Maschke, Hermann M. *Das Krupp-Urteil*. Goettingen: Musterschmidt-Verlag, 1951.

Maschmann, Melita. *Fazit*. Stuttgart: Deutsche Verlags-Anstalt, 1963.

Mason, Alpheus T. "Extra-Judicial Work for Judges: The Views of Chief Justice Stone." *Harvard Law Review*, Vol. LXVII, No. 2, December, 1953.

Matthias, Erich. "Hindenburg zwischen den Fronten 1932." *Vierteljahrshefte fuer Zeitgeschichte*, Vol. VIII, No. 1, 1960.

———. "Die Sitzung der Reichstagsfraktion des Zentrums am 23. Maerz 1933." *Vierteljahrshefte fuer Zeitgeschichte*, Vol. IV, No. 3, 1956.

Mau, Hermann. "Die 'Zweite Revolution'—Der 30. Juni 1934." *Vierteljahrshefte fuer Zeitgeschichte*, Vol. I, No. 2, 1953.

Maugham, Viscount. *UNO and War Crimes*. London: John Murray, Publishers, Ltd., 1951.

Maurach, Reinhart. *Die Kriegsverbrecherprozesse gegen deutsche Gefangene in der Sowjetunion*. Hamburg, 1950.

McConnell, John R. "Can Law Impede Aggressive War?" *American Bar Association Journal*, February, 1964.

Meissner, Otto. *Staatssekretaer unter Ebert, Hindenburg und Hitler*. Hamburg: Hoffmann and Campe, 1950.

Meissner, Otto, and Harry Wilde. *Die Machtergreifung*. Stuttgart: J. G. Cotta'sche Buchhandlung, 1958.

Die Memoiren des Stabchefs Roehm. Saarbruecken: Uranus-Verlag, 1934.

Merker, Manfred. *Die deutsche Politik gegenueber dem Spanischen Buergerkrieg*. Bonn: Ludwig Roehrscheid Verlag, 1961.

Merle, Marcel. *Le Procès de Nuremberg et le châtiment des criminels de guerre*. Paris: Editions A. Pedone, 1949.

Meyer-Abich, Friedrich, ed. *Die Masken fallen*. Hamburg: Morawe & Scheffelt Verlag, 1949.

Meyrowitz, Henri. *La répression par les tribunaux allemands des crimes contre l'humanité*. Paris: Pichor et Durand-Auzias, 1960.

Militaerstrafgesetzbuch in der Fassung vom 10. Oktober 1940—mit Einfuehrungsgesetz und Kriegsstrafrechtsordnung. Berlin: Walter de Gruyter Verlag, 1943.

Milward, Alan S. "Fritz Todt als Minister fuer Bewaffnung und Munition." *Vierteljahrshefte fuer Zeitgeschichte*, Vol. XIV, No. 1, 1966.

Moeller, Kurt Detlev. *Das letzte Kapitel*. Hamburg: Hoffmann and Campe Verlag, 1947.

Mommsen, Hans. "Der nationalsozialistische Polizeistaat und die Judenverfolgung vor 1938." *Vierteljahrshefte fuer Zeitgeschichte*, Vol. X, No. 1, 1962.

Morison, Samuel Eliot. *History of the United States Naval Operations in World War II.* Vols. I and XIV. Boston: Little, Brown, and Company, 1947–1959.

Morsey, Rudolf. "Hitler als Braunschweiger Regierungsrat." *Vierteljahrshefte fuer Zeitgeschichte*, Vol. VIII, No. 4, 1960.

———. "Hitlers Verhandlungen mit der Zentrumsfuehrung am 31. Januar 1933." *Vierteljahrshefte fuer Zeitgeschichte*, Vol. IX, No. 2, 1961.

Mosley, Sir Oswald. *The Facts.* London: Euphorian Distribution, 1957.

Munske, Hilde, ed. *Maedel im Dritten Reich.* Berlin: Freiheitsverlag, 1935.

Murawski, Erich. *Der deutsche Wehrmachtbericht 1939–1945.* Boppard: Harald Boldt Verlag, 1962.

Namier, Lewis. *In the Nazi Era.* London: The Macmillan Company, Ltd., 1952.

Nazi Conspiracy and Aggression, 8 vols. and Supp. A and B. Washington: Office of the US Chief of Counsel for Prosecution of Axis Criminality, 1946.

Neinast, Major William H. "United States Use of Biological Warfare." *Military Law Review*, April, 1964.

Nelte, Otto. *Das Nuernberger Urteil und die Schuld der Generale.* Pamphlet. Hannover: Verlag Das Andere Deutschland, 1947.

Neuhaeusler, Johannes. *Kreuz und Hakenkreuz,* 2 vols. Munich: Verlag der katholischen Kirche Bayerns, 1946.

Neumann, Peter. *The Black March.* Trans. Constantine Fitzgibbon. New York: Bantam Books, Inc., 1960.

News Chronicle (London), January, 1938.

The New York Times, December 5, 1945; June 2, June 8, October 6, October 16, 1946.

Niemoeller, Wilhelm. *Die evangelische Kirche im Dritten Reich.* Bielefeld: Ludwig Bechauf Verlag, 1956.

"Der Oberste Befehlshaber. Ein Nuernberger Gespraech mit Generaloberst Jodl" (by an anonymous German defense lawyer). *Nation Europa*, May, 1960.

O'Brien, William V. "Some Problems of the Law of War in Limited Nuclear Warfare." *Military Law Review*, October, 1961.

Occupation of Japan (Department of State Publication 2671). Washington: US Government Printing Office.

Oervik, Nils. "Das englisch-norwegische Handelsabkommen und die alliierten Interventionsplaene im russisch-finnischen Krieg." *Vierteljahrshefte fuer Zeitgeschichte*, Vol. IV, No. 4, 1956.

Oestreich, Paul. *Walther Funk, ein Leben fuer die Wirtschaft.* Munich: Zentralverlag der NSDAP, Franz Eher Nachf., 1940.

Oppenheimer, L. *International Law* (8th ed.). Ed. H. Lauterpacht. London, New York, Toronto: Longmans, Green & Co., Ltd., 1954.

Orlow, Dietrich. "Die Adolf-Hitler-Schulen." *Vierteljahrshefte fuer Zeitgeschichte*, Vol. XIII, No. 3, 1965.

Oven, Wilfred von. *Mit Goebbels bis zum Ende.* Buenos Aires: Duerer Verlag, 1949.

Paetel, Karl O. "Die deutsche Jugendbewegung als politisches Phaenomen." *Politische Studien*, July, 1957.

———. "Geschichte und Soziologie der SS." *Vierteljahrshefte fuer Zeitgeschichte*, Vol. II, No. 1, 1954.

———. *Jugendbewegung und Politik*. Bad Godesberg: Voggenreiter Verlag, 1961.

Paget, R. T. *Manstein: His Campaigns and His Trial*. London: William Collins Sons & Co., Ltd., 1951.

Pal, R. P. *International Military Tribunal for the Far East, Dissenting Judgment*. Calcutta: Sanyal, 1953.

Pannenbecker, Otto. "The Nuremberg War-Crimes Trial." *De Paul Law Review*, Vol. XIV, No. 2, Spring–Summer 1965.

Papen, Franz von. *Einige Bemerkungen zum Buch "Reichswehr, Staat und NSDAP" von Dr. Thilo Vogelsang*. Private printing, n.d.

———. *Europa was nun?* Goettingen: Goettinger Verlagsanstalt, 1954.

———. *Der Wahrheit eine Gasse*. Munich: Paul List Verlag, 1952.

Franz von Papen—Wegbereiter des Nationalsozialismus. Pamphlet. Bielefeld: Freie Presse, n.d.

Parker, John J. "The Nuremberg Trial." *Journal of the American Judicature Society*, Vol. XXX, December, 1946.

Der Parteitag der Ehre. Munich: Zentralverlag der NSDAP, Franz Eher Nachf., 1936.

Peillard, Léonce. *The Laconia Affair*. Trans. Oliver Coburn. New York: G. P. Putnam's Sons, 1963.

Pfundtner, Hans. *Dr. Wilhelm Frick und sein Ministerium*. Munich: Zentralverlag der NSDAP, Franz Eher Nachf., 1937.

Philippes, Ramond, ed. *Trial of Joseph Kramer and Forty-four Others (The Belsen Trial)*. London, Edinburgh, Glasgow: William Hodge, 1949.

Picker, Henry. *Hitler's Table Talk*. Trans. Norman Cameron and R. H. Stevens. London: Wiedenfeld and Nicolson, 1953.

———. *Hitlers Tischgespraeche im Fuehrerhauptquartier 1941–42*. Bonn: Athenaeum-Verlag, 1951.

Der Pimpf, September, 1940.

Pohle, Heinz. *Der Rundfunk als Instrument der Politik*. Hamburg: Hans Bredow Institut, 1955.

Poliakov, Léon, and Josef Wulf. *Das Dritte Reich und seine Denker*. Berlin-Grunewald: Arani, 1959.

———. *Das Dritte Reich und seine Diener*. Berlin-Grunewald: Arani, 1956.

Polnische Dokumente zur Vorgeschichte des Krieges. Munich: Zentralverlag der NSDAP, Franz Eher Nachf., 1940.

Pompe, C. A. *Aggressive War an International Crime*. The Hague: Martinus Nijhoff, 1953.

Priepke, Manfred. *Die evangelische Jugend im Dritten Reich 1933–1936*. Hannover and Frankfurt a.M.: Norddeutsche Verlagsanstalt O. Goedel, 1960.

Proceedings American Society of International Law. Vol. XLVI, 1952.

Pross, Harry. *Vor und nach Hitler*. Olten and Freiburg i. Br.: Walter-Verlag, 1962.

Punishment for War Crimes. The Interallied Documents Signed at St. James' Palace, London, 13 January 1942, and Relative Documents. London: H. M. Stationery Office, July, 1942.

Puttkamer, Karl Jesko von. *Die unheimliche See.* Vienna and Munich: Karl Kuehne Verlag, 1952.

Raabe, Felix. *Die buendische Jugend.* Stuttgart: Brentano Verlag, 1961.

Rabenau, Friedrich von. *Seeckt: Aus seinem Leben 1918–1936.* Leipzig: Hase & Koehler Verlag, 1940.

Raeder, Erich. *Mein Leben.* 2 vols. Tuebingen: Fritz Schlichtenmayer Verlag, 1956–1957.

Rank, Richard. "Modern War and the Validity of Treaties." *Cornell Law Quarterly,* Spring–Summer 1953.

Raschhofer, Hermann. *Der Fall Oberlaender.* Tuebingen: Fritz Schlichtenmayer Verlag, 1962.

Rauschenbach, Gerhard. *Der Nuernberger Prozess gegen die Organisationen.* Bonn: Ludwig Roehrscheid Verlag, 1954.

"Die Rede Himmlers vor den Gauleitern am 3. August 1944." *Vierteljahrshefte fuer Zeitgeschichte,* Vol. I, No. 4, 1953.

Rees, J. R., ed. *The Case of Rudolf Hess: A Problem in Diagnosis and Forensic Psychiatry.* London and Toronto: William Heinemann, Ltd., 1947.

Reichsjugendfuehrer, ed. *HJ im Dienst.* Berlin: Bernard & Graefe Verlag, 1940.

———. *Jahrbuch des BDM-Werkes Glaube und Schoenheit 1943.* Munich: Zentralverlag der NSDAP, Franz Eher Nachf.

———. *Das Jugendwohnheim.* Stubenrauch Verlagsbuchhandlung, 1943.

———. *Kriminalitaet und Gefaehrdung der Jugend.* Berlin, 1941.

Reid, Thorburn, and James F. Sams. "Conference on World Peace Through Law Held at Tokyo and Lagos." *American Bar Association Journal,* July, 1962.

Reitlinger, Gerald. *The Final Solution.* London: Vallentine, Mitchell & Co., 1953.

———. *The SS: Alibi of a Nation.* London: William Heinemann, Ltd., 1957.

———. "The Truth About Hitler's 'Commissar Order.' " *Commentary,* July, 1959.

Rendulic, Lothar. *Gekaempft, gesiegt, geschlagen.* Heidelberg: Verlag Welsermuehl, 1952.

Reuter, Franz. *Schacht.* Stuttgart: Deutsche Verlags-Anstalt, 1937.

Ribbentrop, Joachim von. *Zwischen London und Moskau.* Leoni am Starnberger See: Druffel-Verlag, 1953.

Riess, Curt. *Joseph Goebbels, A Biography.* Garden City: Doubleday & Company, Inc., 1948.

Rintelen, Captain von. *The Dark Invader.* London: Lovat Dickson, 1933.

Ritter, Gerhard. *Das deutsche Problem.* Munich: R. Oldenbourg Verlag, 1962.

Ritthaler, Anton. "Eine Etappe auf Hitlers Weg zur ungeteilten Macht." *Vierteljahrshefte fuer Zeitgeschichte,* Vol. VIII, No. 2, 1960.

Roberts, Stephen H. *The House that Hitler Built.* New York: Harper & Row, Publishers, Incorporated, 1938.

Roh, Franz. *Entartete Kunst.* Hannover: Fackeltraeger-Verlag Schmidt-Kuester, 1962.

Rosenberg, Alfred. *Letzte Aufzeichnungen.* Goettingen: Plesse Verlag, 1955.

———. *Der Mythus des 20. Jahrhunderts.* Munich: Hoheneichen-Verlag, 1930.

———. *Die Protokolle der Weisen von Zion und die juedische Weltpolitik.* Munich: Hoheneichen-Verlag, 1923.

———. *Sammelheft ausgewaehlter Vortraege und Reden fuer die Schulung in nationalpolitischer Zielsetzung.* Berlin Zentralverlag der NSDAP, 1939.

———. *Die Spur der Juden im Wandel der Zeiten.* Munich: Volksverlag, 1920.

———. *Der staatsfeindliche Zionismus.* Munich: Zentralverlag der NSDAP, Franz Eher Nachf., 1938.

———. *Unmoral im Talmud.* Munich: Volksverlag, 1920.

Roskill, S. W. *The War at Sea* 1939–1945. London: H. M. Stationery Office, 1956.

———. *White Ensign. The British Navy at War* 1939–1945. Annapolis: US Naval Institute, 1960.

Ross, Hans. "Die 'Praeventivkriegsplaene' Pilsudskis von 1933." *Vierteljahrshefte fuer Zeitgeschichte,* Vol. III, No. 4, 1955.

Sadila-Mantau, Hans Heinz, ed. *Deutsche Fuehrer. Deutsches Schicksal.* Berlin: Riegler, 1933.

———. *Unsere Reichsregierung.* Berlin: C. A. Weller, 1936.

Sand, Trude. *Zickezacke Landjahr Heil!* Stuttgart: Union Deutsche Verlagsgesellschaft, 1938.

Sasse, Heinz Guenther. "Das Problem des diplomatischen Nachwuchses im Dritten Reich." *Forschungen zu Staat und Verfassung.* Berlin: Duncker & Humblot, n.d.

Satterfield, John C. "The San Jose Conference on World Peace Through Law." *American Bar Association Journal,* October, 1961.

Sautter, Reinhold. *Hitlerjugend.* Munich: Carl Roehrig Verlag, 1942.

Schacht, Hjalmar. *Abrechnung mit Hitler.* Hamburg and Stuttgart: Rowohlt Verlag, 1948.

———. *Das Ende der Reparationen.* Oldenburg: Gerhard Stalling Verlag, 1931.

———. *Kleine Bekenntnisse.* Private printing, 1949.

———. *76 Jahre meines Lebens.* Bad Woerishofen: Kindler & Schiermeyer Verlag, 1953.

Schaefer, Werner. *Konzentrationslager Oranienburg.* Berlin: Buch- und Tiefdruck Gesellschaft, 1934.

Schaumburg-Lippe, Friedrich Christian Prinz zu. *Zwischen Krone und Kerker.* Wiesbaden: Limes Verlag, 1952.

Schellenberg, Walter. *Memoiren.* Cologne: Verlag fuer Politik und Wissenschaft, 1956.

Schierer, Herbert. *Das Zeitschriftenwesen der Jugendbewegung.* Dissertation. Berlin-Charlottenburg: Lorentz, 1938.

Schirach, Baldur von. *Die Feier der Neuen Front.* Munich: Volksverlag, n.d.

———. *Die Hitlerjugend—Idee und Gestalt.* Berlin, 1934.

———. *Rede zur Eroeffnung der Mozartwoche.* Weimar: Gesellschaft der Bibliophilen, 1943.

———. *Revolution der Erziehung. Reden aus den Jahren des Aufbaus.* Munich: Zentralverlag der NSDAP, Franz Eher Nachf., 1938.

———. *Das Wiener Kulturprogramm.* Rede im Wiener Burgtheater, April 6, 1941. Vienna: Franz Eher Verlag Zweigniederlassung.

———. *Wille und Macht.* Rede, July 1, 1938. Munich: Zentralverlag der NSDAP, Franz Eher Nachf., 1938.

Schirach, Max von. *Geschichte der Familie von Schirach*. Berlin: Walter de Gruyter Verlag, 1939.

Schlabrendorff, Fabian von. *Offiziere gegen Hitler*. Zurich: Europa Verlag, 1946.

Schmidt, Paul. *Statist auf diplomatischer Buehne 1923–1945*. Bonn: Athenaeum Verlag, 1949.

Schmidt-Pauli, Edgar von. *Hitlers Kampf um die Macht*. Berlin: Georg Strilke Verlag, 1933.

———. *Die Maenner um Hitler*. Berlin: Verlag fuer Kulturpolitik, 1932.

Schmundt, G. "Bericht ueber die Besprechung Hitlers am 23. Mai 1939." In *Ausgewaehlte Dokumente zur Geschichte des Nationalsozialismus 1933–45*, ed. Hans-Adolf Jacobsen and Werner Jochmann. Bielefeld: Verlag Neue Gesellschaft, 1961.

Schnabel, Reimund. *Macht ohne Moral*. Frankfurt a.M.: Roederbergverlag, 1957.

Schneider, Hans. "Das Ermaechtigungsgesetz vom 24. Maerz 1933." *Vierteljahrshefte fuer Zeitgeschichte*, Vol. I, No. 3, 1953.

Schneider, Peter. "Rechtssicherheit und richterliche Unabhaengigkeit aus der Sicht des SD." *Vierteljahrshefte fuer Zeitgeschichte*, Vol. IV, No. 4, 1956.

Schorn, Hubert. *Der Richter im Dritten Reich*. Frankfurt a.M.: Vittorio Klostermann Verlag, 1959.

Schroeter, Heinz. *Stalingrad*. Trans. Constantine Fitzgibbon. New York: Ballantine Books, Inc., 1958.

Schuetze, H. A. *Die Repressalie unter besonderer Beruecksichtigung der Kriegsverbrecherprozesse*. Bonn: Ludwig Roehrscheid Verlag, 1950.

Schulthess' Europaeischer Geschichtskalender. Vols. LXXIII and LXXV. Munich: C. H. Beck'sche Verlagsbuchhandlung, 1932, 1935.

Schulz, Joachim. *Die letzten 30 Tage*. Stuttgart: Steingrueben-Verlag, 1951.

Schuschnigg, Kurt von. *Austrian Requiem*. New York: G. P. Putnam's Sons, 1946.

———. *Ein Requiem in Rot-Weiss-Rot*. Zurich: Amstutz, Herdeg & Co., 1946.

Schwarz, Paul. *This Man Ribbentrop. His Life and Times*. New York: Julian Meissner, 1943.

Schweitzer, Arthur. *Big Business in the Third Reich*. Bloomington: Indiana University Press, 1964.

———. "Business Policy in a Dictatorship." *The Business History Review*, Vol. XXXVIII, No. 4, 1964.

Schwerdtfeger-Zypress, Gertrud. *Das ist der weibliche Arbeitsdienst*. Berlin: Junge Generation Verlag, 1940.

Schwerin von Krosigk, Count Lutz. *Es geschah in Deutschland*. Tuebingen and Stuttgart: Rainer Wunderlich Verlag Hermann Leins, 1952.

Seabury, Paul. "Ribbentrop and the German Foreign Office." *Political Science Quarterly*, December, 1951.

———. *The Wilhelmstrasse*. Berkeley: University of California Press, 1954.

Senger und Etterlin, Frido von. *Krieg in Europa*. Cologne and Berlin: Kiepenheuer & Witsch, 1960.

Seraphim, Hans-Guenter. *Das politische Tagebuch Alfred Rosenbergs 1934–35 und 1939–40*. Goettingen: Musterschmidt-Verlag, 1956.

Seraphim, Hans-Guenter, and Andreas Hillgruber. "Hitlers Entschluss zum Angriff auf Russland." *Vierteljahrshefte fuer Zeitgeschichte*, Vol. II, No. 3, 1954.

Seyss-Inquart, Artur. *Idee und Gestalt des Reiches*. No publisher, no date.

Siegert, Karl. *Repressalie, Requisition und hoeherer Befehl*. Goettingen: Goettinger Verlagsanstalt, 1953.

Simpson, Amos E. "The Struggle for the Control of the German Economy 1936–37." *Journal of Modern History*, 1959.

Skorzeny, Otto. *Geheimkommando Skorzeny*. Hamburg: Hansa Verlag Josef Toth, 1950.

Snyder, Orville C. "It's Not Law. The War Guilt Trials." *Kentucky Law Journal*, November, 1949.

Sohn, Louis B. "U. N. Charter Revision and the Rule of Law: A Program for Peace." *Northwestern Law Review*, January–February, 1956.

Soldaten-Zeitung (Munich), May 16 and 25, 1962.

Sontheimer, Kurt. *Antidemokratisches Denken in der Weimarer Republik*. Munich: Nymphenburger Verlagshandlung, 1962.

Speer, Albert, ed. *Neue deutsche Baukunst*. Berlin: Volk und Reich Verlag, 1940.

Speidel, Hans. *Invasion 1944*. Tuebingen: Rainer Wunderlich Verlag Hermann Leins, 1949.

Springer, Hildegard. *Es sprach Hans Fritzsche*. Stuttgart: Thiele Verlag, 1949.

———. *Das Schwert auf der Waage*. Heidelberg: Kurt Vowinckel Verlag, 1953.

Stahn, R. O., and Filippo Bojano, eds. *Wir haben's gewagt!* Stuttgart and Berlin: J. G. Cotta'sche Buchhandlung, 1934.

Stasiewski, Bernhard. "Die Kirchenpolitik der Nationalsozialisten im Warthegau 1939–1945." *Vierteljahrshefte fuer Zeitgeschichte*, Vol. VII, No. 1, 1959.

Stein, George H. *The Waffen SS*. Ithaca: Cornell University Press, 1966.

Steinbauer, Gustav. *Ich war Verteidiger in Nuernberg*. Klagenfurt: Eduard Kaiser Verlag, 1950.

Stevens, E. H., ed. *Trial of Nikolaus von Falkenhorst*. London, Edinburgh, and Glasgow: William Hodge & Co., 1949.

Stimson, Henry L. "The Nuremberg Trial, Landmark in Law." *Foreign Affairs*, Vol. XXV, January, 1947.

Stodte, Hermann. *Die Wegbereiter des Nationalsozialismus*. Luebeck: Rahtgens, 1936.

Stoecker, Jakob. *Maenner des deutschen Schicksals*. Berlin: Oswald Arnold Verlag, 1949.

Stolper, Gustav. *Deutsche Wirtschaft 1870–1940*. Stuttgart: Franz-Mittelbach Verlag, 1950.

Strasser, Otto. *Hitler und ich*. Buenos Aires: Editorial Trenkelbach, 1940.

Strauss, Walter. "Das Reichsministerium des Innern und die Judengesetzgebung." *Vierteljahrshefte fuer Zeitgeschichte*, Vol. IX, No. 3, 1961.

Streicher, Julius. *Kampf dem Weltfeind. Reden aus der Kampfzeit*. Gesammelt und bearbeitet von Dr. Heinz Preiss. Nuremberg: Stuermer-Verlag, 1938.

Stroop Bericht. Es gibt keinen juedischen Wohnbezirk in Warschau mehr. Neuwied: Hermann Luchterhand Verlag, 1960.

Stubbe, Walter. "In Memoriam: Albrecht Haushofer." *Vierteljahrshefte fuer Zeitgeschichte*, Vol. VIII, No. 3, 1960.

Studnitz, Hans-Georg von. *Als Berlin brannte*. Stuttgart: W. Kohlhammer Verlag, 1963.

Der Stuermer, January 19, 1927.

Sunday Times, February 1, 1959.

Der Tag von Potsdam. Munich: Der Jugendverlag, 1933.

"Tatsachen sprechen fuer den Sieg." Die Reden der Reichsminister Speer und Dr. Goebbels im Berliner Sportpalast am 5. Juni 1943.

Taylor, Telford. *Final Report to the Secretary of the Army on the Nuremberg War Crimes Trials under Control Council Law No. 10*. Washington: US Government Printing Office, 1949.

———. *Sword and Swastika*. New York: Simon and Schuster, Inc., 1952.

Thorwald, Juergen. *Das Ende an der Elbe*. Stuttgart: Steingrueben-Verlag, 1950.

———. *Die grosse Flucht*. Stuttgart: Steingrueben-Verlag, 1949.

———, ed. *Ernst Heinkel. Stuemisches Leben*. Stuttgart: Mundus Verlag, 1953.

———. *Wen sie verderben wollen*. Stuttgart: Steingrueben-Verlag, 1952.

Thursfield, H. G., ed. *Brassey's Naval Annual 1948*. New York: The Macmillan Company.

Thyssen, Fritz. *I Paid Hitler*. New York: Farrar & Rinehart, Inc., 1941.

Tiburtius, J. "Hitlers letzte Tage." *Der Bund*, February 17, 1953.

Tobias, Fritz. *Der Reichstagsbrand: Legende und Wirklichkeit*. Rastatt/Baden: Grote'sche Verlagsbuchhandlung, 1962.

Tondel, Lyman, Jr. "The European Conference on World Peace Through the Rule of Law." *American Bar Association Journal*, December, 1962.

Trainin, A. N. *Hitlerite Responsibility under Criminal Law*. Ed. A. Y. Vishinsky. Trans. Andrew Rothstein. London: Hutchinson & Co., Ltd., 1945.

———. *La Responsibilité pénale des Hitlériens*. Paris: La Presse Française et Etrangère, 1945.

Treue, Wilhelm. "Zum nationalsozialistischen Kunstraub in Frankreich." *Vierteljahrshefte fuer Zeitgeschichte*, Vol. XIII, No. 3, 1965.

Trevor-Roper, H. R. *The Bormann Letters: The private correspondence between Martin Bormann and his wife from January 1943 to April 1945*. London: Weidenfeld & Nicolson, 1954.

———. *The Last Days of Hitler*. New York: The Macmillan Company, 1947.

———. "Martin Bormann." *Der Monat*, May, 1954.

Trial of the Major War Criminals before the International Military Tribunal, Nuremberg, 14 November 1945–10 October 1946. 42 vols. Nuremberg, 1947–1949. (Official text in the English language.)

Trials of War Criminals before the Nuremberg Military Tribunals under Control Council Law No. 10, October 1946–April 1949. 15 vols. Washington: US Government Printing Office, 1946–1949.

United States House of Representatives: Select Committee on the Katyn Forest Massacre. Hearings: 82nd Congress 1st and 2nd sessions 1951–52. Washington: US Government Printing Office, 1952.

Utermann, Wilhelm, ed. *Jungen—Eure Welt*. Munich: Zentralverlag der NSDAP, Franz Eher Nachf., 1941.

Vanwelkenhuyzen, Jean. "Die Niederlande und der 'Alarm' im Januar 1940." *Vierteljahrshefte fuer Zeitgeschichte*, Vol. VIII, No. 1, 1960.

Veale, F. J. P. *Advance to Barbarism.* Appleton, Wis.: C. C. Nelson Publishing Co., 1953.

Vigrabs, Georg. "Die Stellungnahme der Westmaechte und Deutschlands zu den baltischen Staaten im Fruehling und Sommer 1939." *Vierteljahrshefte fuer Zeitgeschichte,* Vol. VII, No. 3, 1959.

Voelkischer Beobachter, April 8, 1938; March 29, 1941; May 28, 1944.

Vogelsang, Carl Walther. *Dieter lernt fliegen.* Eisenberg/Thueringen, and Leipzig: Dege Verlag, 1943.

Vogelsang, Thilo. "Zur Politik Schleichers gegenueber der NSDAP 1932." *Vierteljahrshefte fuer Zeitgeschichte,* Vol. VI, No. 1, 1958.

———. *Reichswehr, Staat und NSDAP.* Stuttgart: Deutsche Verlags-Anstalt, 1962.

Voggenreiter, Heinrich, ed. *Taschenbuch fuer den deutschen Jugendfuehrer.* Potsdam: Ludwig Voggenreiter Verlag, n.d.

Wagenfuehr, Horst, ed. *Gefolgschaft.* Hamburg: Hanseatische Verlagsanstalt, 1935.

Warlimont, Walter. *Inside Hitler's Headquarters 1939–45.* New York: Frederick A. Praeger, Inc., 1964.

Warmbrunn, Werner. *The Dutch Under German Occupation 1940–1945.* Stanford: Stanford University Press, 1963.

Watt, D. C. "Die bayerischen Bemuehungen um Ausweisung Hitlers, 1924." *Vierteljahrshefte fuer Zeitgeschichte,* Vol. VI, No. 3, 1958.

Weinberg, Gerhard L. "Der deutsche Entschluss zum Angriff auf die Sowjetunion." *Vierteljahrshefte fuer Zeitgeschichte,* Vol. I, No. 4, 1953.

———. *Germany and the Soviet Union 1939–1941.* Leiden: Brill, 1954.

———. "Schachts Besuch in den USA im Jahre 1933." *Vierteljahrshefte fuer Zeitgeschichte,* Vol. XI, No. 2, 1963.

Weizsaecker, Ernst von. *Erinnerungen.* Munich: Paul List Verlag, 1950.

Welles, Sumner. *The Time for Decision.* New York: Harper & Row, Publishers, Incorporated, 1944.

Wendt, Hans. *Hitler regiert.* Berlin: E. S. Mittler & Sohn, 1933.

Wer Ist's? Berlin: Degener Verlag, 1935.

Westphal, Siegfried. *Heer in Fesseln.* Bonn: Athenaeum-Verlag, 1952.

Wheeler-Bennett, John W. *The Nemesis of Power.* London: The Macmillan Company, Ltd., 1961.

Wichert, Erwin. *Dramatische Tage in Hitlers Reich.* Stuttgart, 1952.

Wilmowsky, Tilo Freiherr von. *Warum wurde Krupp verurteilt?* Duesseldorf and Vienna: Econ-Verlag, 1962.

Woodward, E. L., and Rohan Butler, eds. *Documents on British Foreign Policy 1919–39,* 2nd series, Vol. V, 1933. London: H. M. Stationery Office, 1956.

Wright, Quincy. "The Outlawing of War and the Law of War." *American Journal of International Law,* July, 1953.

———. "The Prevention of Aggression." *American Journal of International Law,* July, 1956.

Wucher, Albert. *Die Fahne hoch.* Munich: Sueddeutscher Verlag, 1963.

Wulf, Josef. *Die bildenden Kuenste im Dritten Reich.* Guetersloh: Sigbert Mohn Verlag, 1963.

———. *Das Dritte Reich und seine Vollstrecker.* Berlin-Grunewald: Arani, 1961.

————. *Martin Bormann—Hitlers Schatten.* Guetersloh: Sigbert Mohn Verlag, 1962.

Young, Desmond. *Rommel: The Desert Fox.* New York: Harper & Row, Publishers, Incorporated, 1950.

Zawodny, J. K. *Death in the Forest.* Notre Dame: University of Notre Dame Press, 1962.

Zeller, Eberhard. *Geist der Freiheit: Der 20. Juli.* Munich: Gotthold Mueller Verlag, 1963.

Zoller, Albert. *Hitler privat.* Duesseldorf: Droste Verlag, 1949.

Index

Index

Adam, Gen. Wilhelm, 198, 330
Adenauer, Konrad, 586
Admiral Hipper (ship), 387
Adolf Hitler Division, 572
Adolf Hitler schools, 298, 299
Adolf Hitler *Spende*, 103
Aggressive war, 1, 29, 357; as crime, 4, 12–15, 19; concept of, 10–15; trial of individuals for, 12–13; Russian position on, 13; concept re war of liberation, 13; Germany indicted for waging, 23; relation to international law, 360–61, 587–91
Ahrens, Col. Friedrich, 73
Alabama (ship), 385n
Albania, 15
Albert, Dr. Heinrich, 178
Albrecht, Ralph G., 21n
Alderman, Sidney S., 21n
Alfieri, Dino, 154, 160, 162
Allied Control Council, 14n, 18, 29, 83, 556
Allied Supreme Council, 4
Allies: military occupation of Germany, 4; terror bombing of cities, 33, 60, 83–84, 364; air supremacy, 62; attacks on Rumanian oilfields, 94n; invasion of Normandy, 95; submarine warfare policy, 421
Altmark (ship), 376, 377, 414
Alvensleben, Werner von, 183
Amen, Col. John Harlan, 21n, 323
American Society of International Law, 588

Anders, Gen. Wladyslaw, 72–74
Annamite (ship), 405
Anschluss. See Austria
Anti-Comintern Pact, 540
Anti-Jewish World League, 47
Anti-Semitism: Streicher's, 40–57 *passim*; history of, 40–42; in USA, 41; in *Der Stuermer*, 44–45; attempts to combat, 49; in England, 51; decrees issued by Bormann, 104; in Czechoslovakia, 171–72; in German youth movement, 284, 286, 291–92. *See also* Concentration camps; Deportations; Einsatz commandos; Exterminations; Forced labor; Ghettos; Jews; Nuremberg Laws
Anti-Stuermer (newspaper), 49
Antonica (ship), 409
Ardeatine Caves, 572
Argentina, 28
Army. *See* German Army
Army and Navy Journal, 561
Army Quarterly, 541
Aschaffenburg camp, 429
Ashcan. *See* International Military Tribunal
Assmann, Adm. Kurt, 380
Association of Jewish War Veterans, 55
Astel, Kurt, 54–55
Athenia (ship), 381, 526, 532
Atlantis (ship), 414
Attlee, Clement, 26, 119
Attolico, Bernardo, 159
Auschwitz camp, 8–9, 101, 174, 317, 320, 445, 449, 465, 466, 473, 499, 556, 557

About the Author

Photo by Gloria Hamilton

Eugene Davidson is the author of numerous books on the Nazi regime, including *The Making of Adolf Hitler* and *The Unmaking of Adolf Hitler* (both available from the University of Missouri Press). Davidson, who lives in Santa Barbara, California, is President Emeritus of the Conference on European Problems and former President of the Foundation for Foreign Affairs.